C0-AVO-009

Nag Hammadi and Manichaean Studies

Editors

Einar Thomassen *&* Johannes van Oort

VOLUME 63

The *Panarion* of Epiphanius of Salamis

Book I (Sects 1-46)

Second Edition, Revised and Expanded

Translated by

Frank Williams

BRILL

LEIDEN • BOSTON
2009

This book is printed on acid-free paper.

Library of Congress Cataloging-in-Publication-Data

Epiphanius, Saint, Bishop of Constantia in Cyprus, ca. 310–403.
[Panarion. Book 1. English]
The panarion of Epiphanius of Salamis. Book I (Sects 1-46) / translated by Frank Williams.
p. cm. — (Nag Hammadi and Manichaean studies ; v. 63)
Includes bibliographical references and index.
ISBN 978-90-04-17017-9 (hardback : alk. paper) 1. Heresies, Christian—Early works to 1800. 2. Gnosticism—Early works to 1800. I. Williams, Frank. II. Title. III. Series.

BR65.E653P36413 2008
273'.4—dc22

2008031553

ISSN 0929-2470
ISBN 978 90 04 17017 9

PRINTED IN THE NETHERLANDS

For Charlotte

CONTENTS

(Most sections of the work are titled as in the manuscript. Modern titles are noted with an asterisk.)

ACKNOWLEDGMENT

I need to thank Professor Christoph Markschies for his kindness in furnishing me in advance of publication with a copy of the *Wortregister* to Holl's *Panarion*. I must also thank Herr Friedrich-Christian Collatz, our Series editor Stephen Emmel, and Ivo Romein and Ellen Girmscheid of Brill for their understanding and support, and my daughter Marge for her important technical help.

INTRODUCTION

This translation of Book I of Epiphanius' *Panarion* was originally published in 1987 and was reprinted with a few changes in 1997. Demand for it has been sufficient to warrant a second edition, which is offered here. The opportunity has been taken to review and revise the translation, edit and expand the notes and index and add indices of references. Together with its companion volume, *The Panarion of Epiphanius of Salamis, Books II and III, De Fide* (1994) this is the only current version in a modern language of the *Panarion* in its entirety.[1]

Several works of significance have appeared since 1983. Aline Pourkier's important *L'héresiologie chez Épiphane de Salamine* (1988) carries further the study of the *Panarion*'s sources which was begun in the nineteenth century by Richard Lipsius, and also analyzes Epiphanius' ways of dealing with his data. Pourkier tests Lipsius' conclusions on ten Sects, seven of them from Book I. In the course of her study she translates extensively from the *Panarion* and from Epiphanius' predecessors Irenaeus and "Pseudo-Tertullian" and his younger contemporary, Filaster of Brescia.

Philip Amidon's *The Panarion of St. Epiphanius of Salamis, Selected Passages* (1990) could be termed a modern epitome of the *Panarion*. It renders those passages which describe sects but omits Epiphanius' refutations. Amidon's rendition amounts in all to about two fifths of the work.

Jon Dechow's *Dogma and Mysticism in Early Christianity, Epiphanius of Cyprus and the Legacy of Origen* appeared in book form in 1998 although it had previously been available on microfilm. Dechow translates excerpts from Epiphanius only incidentally but provides a penetrating study of his life, the anti-Origenist aspect of this thought, and the Origenist controversies of his last years.

Finally, of extreme importance to students of Epiphanius is the 2006 publication of Holl's *Wortregister* to the *Panarion* through the good offices of Friedrich-Christian Collatz, Christoph Markschies and other scholars. Awaited for nearly a century, this invaluable tool also includes grammatical and subject indices, and besides facilitating the study of the *Panarion* should make practicable the revision of Holl's critical text.

---

[1] A nineteenth century Russian version exists but is rare, and long out of print.

The present work has been compared with all of these and is indebted to them all.

Text

We render Karl Holl's critical text of the *Panarion*'s Book I. The first 33 Sects are from Holl's *Ancoratus, Panarion Book I* which was issued, with Sachapparat and textual notes, in 1913. The rest are from Holl's second volume, republished in 1980 by Jürgen Dummer. The 1980 volume includes an appendix in which Dummer assembled suggestions which various scholars had made for the improvement of Holl's text. We translate these in the body of our work, marking them with an asterisk and providing a short appendix which gives the Greek alternatives.

The revision of Holl's text has often been mooted, but the lack of the *Wortregister* has stood in its way. The enterprise ought now to be practicable. However, to revise this enormous text must be a long drawn out affair requiring the cooperation of many scholars.

Holl published the principles of his treatment of the *Panarion*'s text in 1910. He concluded that the eleven extant manuscripts, none of them complete, all descend from a single poorly copied archetype, and that the text has been contaminated by atticizing scribes. In the preface to his 1913 edition he complained that modern editors' dislike of Epiphanius had influenced their view of his text, that on the one hand they had emended without reference to his distinctive style and vocabulary, but on the other had allowed absurdities to stand because Epiphanius was thought to be "konfus."

In fact, within his parameters Epiphanius is a particularly clear thinker. His Greek has its peculiarities but he sets forth his aims and methods clearly at the outset, carries them through consistently, seldom digresses and returns to his point when he does, and provides the reader with every help he can. The difficulties of the text are the results either of scribal error or of Epiphanius' language.

Holl's is a carefully edited critical text. He sometimes emends, but more often restores a word or phrase, occasionally a longer unit. His restorations clear up many difficulties and usually appear to be the most logical choice. Now and then the text gives a good sense without restoration and the *Panarion*, partly written but mostly dictated and that under pressure of time, may not have been as smooth as Holl supposed. Nonetheless there can be little doubt that Holl has given us a fair approximation of what Epiphanius wrote.

Epiphanius' Life and Writings

Our chief sources of information about Epiphanius are his own works and correspondence, references in the writings of his friend Jerome, in Palladius' *Dialogue on the Life of John Chrysostom*, and in Basil of Caesarea, Theophilus of Alexandria, and the histories of Socrates and Sozomen. The short biographical notice prefaced to ancient editions of Epiphanius' *Ancoratus* is of doubtful value, as is the legendary life ostensibly by the monks John and Polybius.

Early in the fourth century C.E., perhaps between 310 and 320, Epiphanius was born in Palestine at Besanduc, a village in the environs of the city of Eleutheropolis, near Gaza. It has been suggested that his parents were Jewish converts to Christianity. In favor of this are the facts that he was bilingual in Greek and Syriac and knew a good deal about Jewish Christian sects; against it, that his attitude toward Jews was antagonistic and his knowledge of their customs meager.

That Epiphanius' family sent him to Egypt in young manhood suggests that they were well to do. If his *Letter to Theodosius*[2] is authentic they had brought him up "in the faith of the fathers of Nicaea," and Sozomen says that he received his early education from monks (*Hist.* 6.32). An important influence on him was his friend and mentor Hilarion, who is credited with bringing the monastic life to Palestine and who in his turn had been taught by Anthony of Egypt.

Epiphanius' childhood background helps us understand him. Indoctrinated in childhood with Nicene Christianity, he was under monastic influence in his early years. His education, Christian and scriptural rather than classical, would have reinforced his childhood training. The homoousian version of Christianity was crucial to his identity from the first. It is no wonder that any rival approach appeared to him as a threat—Epiphanius would have termed it a "poisonous snake"—to be repelled at all costs.

Epiphanius' destination in Egypt would have been the school of a rhetor in the great city of Alexandria. Here he had the disturbing encounter with a sexually oriented group whom he identifies as Gnostics and describes in the *Panarion*'s Sect 26. Although we cannot know this, this episode, dangerous to his chastity and described by him, even years later, in an emotional manner,

[2] Cited in Nicephorus *Adversus Epiphanium* XIV, 61, Pitra, *Spicilegium Solesmense*, p. 340,8-10. See Holl, "Schriften."

might have been a turning point. At the least it helps explain his detestation of anything gnostic, and his conviction that all Gnostics were immoral.

His literary style, or lack of it, shows that he did not complete his rhetorical training. Instead he joined an Egyptian monastic community, where he remained for some years. Unfortunately we do not know which one. Given his avid reading it must have emphasized knowledge as well as praxis. On the other hand, his virulent anti-Origenism almost guarantees that it took the anti-Origenist side of the controversy then raging among the monks of Egypt.

Returning to Palestine, probably nearer to the age of 30 than to the 20 the preface to the *Ancoratus* mentions, Epiphanius founded a monastery near Eleutheropolis and served as its abbot. His friendship with Hilarion, whose monastery was also near Gaza, continued. Jerome tells us (*Vita Hilarionis* 1) that when Hilarion died Epiphanius circulated a short work in his praise.

Of his years as an abbot we know only his efforts to foster and defend what he regarded as Christian orthodoxy. *Panarion* 40,1,6, his only personal reminiscence of his abbacy, shows him exposing and banishing a Gnostic monk. When in 359 the bishop of Eleutheropolis, Eutychius, signed the evasive creed of the Council of Seleuceia (*Panarion* 73,25,1-26,8) and attempted to enforce the homoeousion on his diocese, Epiphanius was uncooperative. It was during this period that he visited the homoousian bishop Eusebius of Vercelli, in exile at Tiberias, and there met the converted Jew Josephus of Tiberias who told him the colorful story he relates at *Panarion* 30,4,1-12,9.

According to Jerome (*Contra Joannem* 4, PL 23,358D) Epiphanius was instrumental in persuading Eutychius to change his mind. It has been suggested, however, that it was the discomfort of the relations between homoousian abbot and homoeousian bishop which prompted Epiphanius' move to Cyprus—a move which led to his election to the see of Salamis in 366.[3]

The clergy of Cyprus, restive under the patriarchate of Antioch and inclined to look to Alexandria for guidance, would have welcomed a homoousian of wide reputation, a friend of Athanasius and an ascetic. The *Panarion* shows so much interest in the monastic life that we must visualize Epiphanius, once a bishop, as continuing his own austerity. (He did not require abstinence from meat and wine, however, and was suspicious of

[3] A conflict with Eutychius, however, is by no means the only possible reason for Epiphanius' move. For various alternatives see Dechow, *Dogma and Mysticism*.

leaders who enforced this requirement.) Jerome's *Vita Paulae* tells us that he fostered the monastic movement, and that his fame attracted novices from all over the world. He allowed a degree of autonomy to the other bishops of his far flung province. *Ancoratus* 102-107 shows us that he was missionary-minded, eager to convince pagans of their error and bring them into the fold. And though we have no information about his episcopal administration, the *Panarion*'s clear organization and meticulous attention to detail suggest administrative capacity. It may have been Epiphanius who began the construction of the great basilica, the ruins of which still stand near Famagusta.

Epiphanius' prestige was great; Jerome refers to him as Papa Epiphanius, and others may have done the same. The abbots Acacius and Paul, whose letter he publishes at the beginning of the *Panarion*, write, "For not we alone, but all who hear of you, confess that the Savior has raised you up as a new herald, a new John, to proclaim what ought to be observed by those who resolve on this (monastic) course" (*Letter of Acacius and Paul* 1,6). At a time when the Arianizing emperor Constantius did not hesitate to exile an Athanasius, the Arian emperor Valens left Epiphanius in peace (Jerome, *Contra Joannem* 1.4, PL 23,358-359). To interfere with him would presumably have risked an uproar.

Epiphanius was respected not only for his piety and rectitude but for his learning. Churches far from Cyprus consulted him on doctrinal issues. The *Ancoratus*, of which we treat below, is his reply to inquiries from the church at Syedra in Pamphilia. The *Letter to Arabia* concerning Mary's perpetual virginity (*Panarion* 78), is another example of his responses to queries. At some time he gathered a collection of extracts from Marcion's canon which could be used to refute Marcion's thesis; he publishes these, together with his comments on them, in the long *Panarion* 42. "Even in extreme old age," Jerome tells us at *De Viris Illustribus* 114, Epiphanius continued to publish short works.

His earliest surviving datable work is a fragment of a *Letter to Eusebius, Marcellus, Bibianus and Carpus*, preserved on pages 218 and 219 of Codex Ambrosianus 515. This was written somewhere between the years 367 and 373. It defends the Antiochean dating of Easter, used by the church on Cyprus, on the Sunday after Nisan 14, rather than on the Sunday after the spring equinox, the Alexandrian observance.[4] It includes a chronology of Christ's last week on earth which resembles one found in the *Apostolic*

[4] See Holl, *Bruchstück.*

Constitutions, and to which there may be an allusion at Nag Hammadi's *Apocryphon of James* 5,9-14.

Arguably Epiphanius' best work is the *Ancoratus*, written in 374. The "barque" of the church of Syedra, says the introductory correspondence, cannot enter harbor because of contrary winds of wrong doctrine, particularly concerning the Holy Spirit. Epiphanius shows how a man can become "anchored" (*Letter of Palladius* 1,3; *Ancoratus* 119,16). Besides the Holy Spirit the work discusses the Trinity and Christ's incarnation and resurrection, attacks the doctrines of Origen, and includes a polemic against Greek religion. At 12,7-13,8 we find the outline of what was to become the *Panarion*, showing that Epiphanius already had this work in mind. This was begun, in fact, in 374 or 375 and can be considered a sequel to the *Ancoratus*. We discuss it below.

During this same period, about 376, Epiphanius attempted to resolve a scandalous schism in the important church of Antioch; he tells the story at *Panarion* 77,20,3-24,2.[5] The Christian community there was divided into four factions, headed respectively by the Arian Euzoeus and three representatives of homoousian Christianity, Melitius, Vitalius and Paulinus. Melitius had the allegiance of the majority but was in exile.[6] Vitalius had been consecrated by Apollinarius of Laodicea, a respected bishop whose Christology was, however, suspect. The third, Paulinus, had the support of Damasus of Rome; he was a disciple of the former bishop of Antioch, Eustathius, staunch homoousian and participant in the Council of Nicaea who, however, had been exiled on a charge of Sabellianism. Unknown to Epiphanius the situation was further complicated by Vitalius' teaching, learned from Apollinarius, that Christ's mind (νοῦς) was not human but only divine.

Epiphanius had already encountered distorted forms of this doctrine, brought to Cyprus about 370 by young disciples of Apollinarius. *Panarion* 77,2,1-6 describes some of their ideas and speaks of the calling of a synod to condemn persons of this kind. On his visit to Antioch Epiphanius discovered Vitalius' adherence to the same doctrine, in a milder form but one which he still found shocking. Thus he could not enter into communion with Vitalius. Nor, for reasons we do not know, did he consider communion with Melitius. On the strength of Paulinus' written confession of faith Epiphanius, and the Cypriote church with him, recognized him as the lawful bishop of Antioch.

5 Dechow's *Dogma and Mysticism* gives a full account of this complex episode.

6 *Panarion* 73,28,1-34,2. Nautin, however, doubts that Melitius was ever exiled.

This unfortunately left Paulinus' and Vitalius' congregations at odds with each other. Epiphanius attempted to gain support for Paulinus from the influential Basil of Caesarea, but to no avail. Apollinarius in the meantime rejected both Epiphanius and Paulinus and consecrated new bishops. The results of Epiphanius' measures at Antioch show both the extent of his influence and the limitations of it. On the one hand, no one appears to have resented his intervention in a see not his own; but on the other, his word was by no means always taken as law.

Whether Epiphanius attended the First Council of Constantinople in 381 is very doubtful. During the winter following, however, in 382, he traveled to Rome with Paulinus and Jerome to attend a synod called by Damasus to discuss the relations between the western and eastern churches. If Epiphanius hoped that Damasus would affirm his earlier support of Paulinus he was disappointed; Damasus now suspected him of Sabellianism. During this time, however, Epiphanius boarded with the wealthy widow Paula and was instrumental in persuading her to abandon the luxurious life of a Roman aristocrat for the cloister. She journeyed east with Jerome as her chaplain and founded a convent at Bethlehem (Jerome, *Vita Paulae* 20). A few years later, perhaps in 385, we find Epiphanius visiting her on her sickbed and laboring, unsuccessfully, to convince her that drinking wine when ill is proper (Jerome, *Vita Paulae* 20).

Seven years later, in 392, Epiphanius published his *De Mensuris et Ponderibus*, a manual of information for students of scripture In 393 we find him on another visit to Palestine, traveling to Bethel to share a service with the bishop of Jerusalem, John. In a village church he found a curtain painted with the image of Christ or a saint, tore it down at once, and advised the parishioners to use it as a burial shroud for the poor. His *Letter to John* (Epiphanius/Jerome *Epistle* 51) relates the incident and includes Epiphanius' promise to replace the curtain. It also, rather lamely, explains Epiphanius' ordination to the priesthood of Jerome's brother Paulinian—an uncanonical one since, although it took place at Epiphanius' monastery near Eleutheropolis, Paulinian was to serve at Bethlehem, in John's diocese. Most importantly, however, this *Letter* addressed to the convinced Origenist, John, is an anti-Origenist tract and was circulated as such.

Epiphanius' war on Origenism and Origenists dominates what we know of his last years. This had nothing to do with Origen himself, who was long dead. Epiphanius admired Origen's *Hexapla* and appreciated some of his writings (cf. *Panarion* 64,3,5-7 and 5,5-6), but considered his doctrine gnostic and the source of Arianism. Important among his objections, published as early as the *Ancoratus* and repeated in the *Panarion*, were Origen's allegedly subordinationist view of the Trinity, his doctrine of the preexistence, fall and restoration of all souls including Christ's and Satan's, and his denial—or so Epiphanius saw it—of the resurrection of the body.

From 393 until 397 Epiphanius fought against Origenism in Jerusalem and Palestine. His opponents were John of Jerusalem and Rufinus, almoner to the abbess Melania on the Mount of Olives and translator into Latin of Origen's περὶ ἀρχῶν. His chief ally was Jerome. A monk named Atarbius, it is thought at Epiphanius' instigation, made the rounds of Jerusalem's monasteries demanding that monks who were suspected of favoring Origen sign a formal denunciation of his teachings. Jerome signed. Rufinus, predictably, refused to see Atarbius.

Either the festival of the Encaenia or the Holy Week of 397 saw an ugly incident at Jerusalem. Invited to preach in the morning, Epiphanius delivered a denunciation of Origen which was plainly aimed at John. John retorted in the afternoon with a sermon against anthropomorphism, a view which some monks certainly held and with which Origenists often stigmatized their accusers. A few days later John published a confession of faith. Epiphanius could find no fault with it but, still unsatisfied, wrote in 394 his *Letter to John.* This was circularized among the bishops and monks of Palestine, accompanied by another letter which urged them to break communion with John. Instead of replying John wrote an apologia to Theophilus, Athanasius' successor as patriarch of Alexandria. This in turn called forth Jerome's *Contra Joannem* which stated his own version of the case against Origen. Jerome also wrote a *Contra Rufinum*, although he and Rufinus made peace in 397.

Next followed the crisis of the Origenist controversy in Egypt. Under heavy pressure from anti-Origenist monks, Theophilus abandoned his previous tolerance of Origenism and proceeded against the Origenist monks of Nitria, 40 miles from Alexandria. Early in 400 he convened a synod which condemned the reading or possession of Origen's works. This was followed by a decree of exile for the Nitrian Origenists, accompanied by the wrecking of their cells and the burning of their books. Theophilus wrote for support to the churches of Palestine and Cyprus, and in particular urged Epiphanius to convene a similar synod on Cyprus. This he did, and jubilantly announced the result in a letter to Jerome (Epiphanius/Jerome *Epistle* 91).

Meanwhile the exiles from Nitria had made their way to various Christian and monastic centers. Led by Isidore and the distinguished Tall Brothers (Ammonius, Dioscurus, Eusebius and Euthymius) about 80 came to Constantinople and appealed for help to the patriarch, John Chrysostom.

Whatever his own attitude toward Origen, Chrysostom showed sympathy for the exiles and wrote to Theophilus urging their reinstatement. Epiphanius was then moved to set out on what proved to be his last journey, a voyage to Constantinople for the defense of Christian orthodoxy and the unmasking of John's supposed Origenism.

Arriving in the spring of 402 or 403, Epiphanius declined Chrysostom's offer of hospitality and communion. He, however, held his own service outside the city and, uncanonically, ordained a deacon. Socrates (*History* 6.10.12-14) and Sozomen (*History* 8.14-15) give differing accounts of the subsequent events. According to the later Sozomen Epiphanius had an encounter with Ammonius which convinced him of his own injustice. Socrates, however, says that while on his way to a public appearance in the Cathedral of the Holy Apostles Epiphanius was confronted by Chrysostom's archdeacon Serapion, who accused him of uncanonical behavior and warned him of the danger of a riot. Whatever the truth of the matter, Epiphanius left Constantinople without taking any public action. He died at sea on his way home to Cyprus. His refusal to communicate with John was used as ammunition by John's opponents at the Synod of the Oak in 404.

Nautin has written: "Il est assurément dommage pour le mémoire d'Épiphane, que sa dernière intervention dans l'histoire de l'Église ait été celle-là." Epiphanius' savage harassment of anyone who appeared to approve of Origen is indeed difficult to stomach. In his defense it may be urged that he was Palestinian, and had also lived for many years in Egypt. Was he not defending hearth and home against what he saw as a dangerous virus? As to his support of the rather unsavory Theophilus, Riggi has reminded us of his reverence for the see of Alexandria. Our heresiologist would have been unlikely to suspect the motives of a successor to Athanasius.

Epiphanius' writings against images appear to date from the same decade as the *Letter to John*. This concern makes itself apparent already in the *Panarion* where, at 27,6,9-10, he attacks Christian image-making. Three writings against Christian images can be partially reconstructed from conciliar *acta* and other sources.[7] These are called a *Treatise against Those Who, by Idolatrous Custom, Are Accustomed to Make Images Representative of Christ, the Mother of God*

[7] John of Damascus, *De Imaginibus Oratio* I.25; *Acts of the Council of 754*, Mansi XIII 292D; *Acts of the Council of 787*, Mansi XIII 293D; Nicephorus *Apologia Minor* PL 100 837B; *Adversus Eusebium*, Pitra *Spicilegium Solesmense* IV 292-294; Theodore Studita *Antirrhetum* II PG 99 388A; 484A/B; *Epistula* 36 *Ad Naucratem* PG 99 1213D.

and the Martyrs and further, of Angels and Prophets; a *Letter to Theodosius*; and a *Testament to the Citizens* (of Salamis).

Another of Epiphanius' works, *De Gemmis*, also comes from the last decade of the fourth century. Preserved only in a Latin epitome, it discusses the symbolism of the stones in the high priest's breastplate. It was written for Diodore of Tarsus and witnesses, both to the close attention with which Epiphanius read scripture and to the fact that during this period of his life he was engaged in other pursuits than an obsessive opposition to Origen. In fact we do not have all of his writings; Jerome's notice at *Vir. Ill.* 114 implies that there were a large number. To their contents we have no clue, but Quasten's criticism of the smallness of his *oeuvre* seems unjustified.

The Panarion

Epiphanius' major effort is very long, and was divided by its author, first into three Books and then into seven Sections. Holl's edition, with notes and apparatus, occupies about 1500 pages. It was begun in 374 or 375 (*Panarion* Proem II 2,3) and produced in great haste, in less than three years. Book I, translated here, extends through Sect 46 and comprises somewhat more than a third of the whole.

The *Panarion* is an heresiology: that is, it is a work which describes bodies, systems and views which the author regards as subversive of true religion and presents his arguments against them. The genre is found in the Christian, the Muslim and some oriental traditions, and is alive today. In Epiphanius' time it was well established; his Book I is deeply indebted to Hippolytus and Irenaeus, both of whom had Justin Martyr for a predecessor. Epiphanius in his turn served as a source for Theodoret and others.

Unusually for an ancient author, Epiphanius titled his own work. At the very outset he explains this title and its meaning and lays out the plan and purpose of his book:

> (Proem I 1,1-2)...I am writing you a preface to give the gist of my <treatise> against sects. Since I shall be telling you the names of the sects and exposing their unlawful deeds like poisons and toxic substances, matching the antidotes with them at the same time—cures for those who are already bitten, and preventatives for those who will have this misfortune—I am drafting this Preface here for the scholarly, to explain the "Panarion", or chest of remedies for the victims of wild beasts' bites. It is a work in three Volumes and contains eighty Sects, which answer symbolically to wild animals or snakes.

Epiphanius' intent then is to convert and to protect. His means of doing so is to identify wrong doctrines so that his fellow Christians can keep away from them, and to convince of the truth those who have stumbled into these doctrines. He has been called an "heresy hunter" but the term scarcely expresses what he meant to do. It has also been pointed out that he was following conventions which by his time had been fixed. While this is so, his vehemence makes it plain that he was not merely falling in with some established pattern; he meant every word of what he wrote.

In his second Proem he explains what he means by "antidotes":

> (Proem II 2,3) "And to correspond with these (serpents and beasts) I shall give as many arguments, like antidotes, as I can in short compass—one or two at most—to counteract their poison and, after the Lord, to save anyone who cares <to be>, when he has willingly or inadvertently fallen into these snakelike teachings of the sects."

These quotations will show that Epiphanius is writing, not simply of heretical ideas as such but of heretical ideas in the context of the sects which hold and teach them. As he most often uses it the term αἵρεσις refers to the party or faction—the "sect"—which holds a particular error. Typical of this usage is Epiphanius' description of the followers of Simon Magus:

> (21,1,1) "Simon Magus's makes the first αἵρεσις to begin in the time since Christ. It is made up of persons who do not rightly or lawfully <believe> in Christ's name, but who do their dreadful deeds in keeping with the false corruption that is in them."

Epiphanius does occasionally use αἵρεσις to mean "heresy" as at 21,5,6 where we read, "For who can fail to realize that this sort of αἵρεσις is a myth..." Nonetheless "sect"—which we prefer to "faction" because of its ecclesiastical connotation—is what he usually means by the word. Further, he terms the individual chapters of the *Panarion* "Sects"; when this is his meaning we capitalize.

The *Panarion* opens with two Proems, the first consisting of Epiphanius' own tables of contents, the second a formal Introduction which explains the work more fully. The whole concludes with a "brief and accurate description of the catholic faith and apostolic church," usually called *De Fide*.

Epiphanius sets his Sects in an historical framework. They begin, not after Christ as we might expect, but with Adam, and extend through the author's own lifetime. His total of 80 sects comes from Song of Songs 6:8-9: "There are threescore queens, and fourscore concubines, and virgins without number. My dove, my undefiled, is but one." The 80 concubines are groups which bear Christ's name but lack his faith, as a concubine uses her master's name but is not his wife. The one dove is the catholic church. The virgins without number are various "philosophies" which are in no way related to Christ—or to anything important (*Panarion* 35,3,5 and *De Fide* 6,9). The 60 queens are the generations from Adam until Christ, with their number rounded off (*De Fide* 4,1-5,4). This last exegesis is labored but, given Epiphanius' historical approach, not inappropriate.

Epiphanius felt his procedure to be justified because of Colossians 3:11, "...there is neither Hellene nor Jew...barbarian, Scythian...but Christ is all and in all." Barbarism, Scythianism, Hellenism and Judaism, to which Epiphanius adds Samaritanism, are the first sects and the "mothers" of the rest. To these five Epiphanius adds four badly misreported Greek philosophies, four Samaritan groups, and seven types of Judaism, making a total of 20 before Christ. Next follows his attractive account of "Christ's sojourn here, and true advent in the flesh in person," a short description of Christ's ministry and of the planting of the church, which we call *De Incarnatione*. Then, in what the author believes to be the order of their succession, follow the 60 sects which have arisen after Christ. The *Panarion* may fairly be called an historical encyclopedia of sectarianism.

Preceding each Section of the work is an Anacephalaeosis, or "summary."[8] These are not authentic. Epiphanius makes no mention of them in the body of his work, though he does speak of the Proems and of his concluding essay. The Anacephalaeoses are so worded as to suggest that they are meant to be read as a whole. III, for example, ends "this will summarize the three Sections of Volume I, which includes 46 Sects," although this summary begins only with Sect 34. The Anacephalaeoses sometimes disagree, in small details or even in order, with the material of the *Panarion*. They are an epitome of the work which originally circulated independently but at an early date was edited into it. Augustine used them, presumably in Latin translation, as the basis of his *Contra Omnes Haereses*; whether he ever saw the *Panarion* itself is highly doubtful.

In discussing a sect Epiphanius, consciously or unconsciously, falls into a sort of four part form.[9] First comes a brief introduction giving the sect's name—to Epiphanius a very important matter—relating it to the sects which our author believes preceded it, and furnishing biographical details

[8] Amidon calls it an "abstract."

[9] Pourkier believes that Epiphanius' form was influenced by that of Hippolytus' *Syntagma*, a document which will be discussed below.

concerning its founder. Then follows a concise description of the sect's beliefs and practices. The third part, the refutation, is normally the longest. The usual close is a few lines which compare the group under discussion to some noxious animal, most often a poisonous snake. However, this form is not always strictly adhered to; description and refutation are often mixed together.

In the later portions of the *Panarion* where Epiphanius is discussing his contemporaries and persons of the recent past, what he says about the succession of various groups or the influence of one leader upon another comes from his own knowledge. In Book I, where the leaders of whom he speaks are well in the past, he is dependent upon his sources for this sort of information. He knows, for example, that Simon Magus is the father of all the sects since Christ's coming because Irenaeus says so. From Irenaeus, again, he learns that a number of sects which called themselves Gnostics arose, all at once, from Valentinus. That Lucian was Marcion's disciple, and Apelles Lucian's, he learns from Hippolytus. When his sources give him no specific guidance of this kind he is more cautious:

> (29,1,1) After these (Cerinthians) come Nazoraeans, who originated at the same time or even before, or in conjunction with them or after them. In any case they were their contemporaries. I cannot say more precisely who succeeded whom.

In other words, Epiphanius has little or no independent information about the genesis of the various sects. Nor are the names that he and his predecessors apply to the sects to be relied on. These are really labels, meant to identify and classify some group of whom Christians must beware. Epiphanius himself says that the terms Alogi (51,3,1-2) and Antidicomarians (Proem I 4,1) are his own coinage. Rarely are such names the ones the group in question gave themselves, though "Gnostic" may be an exception. Equally rarely do they represent organized bodies—though, again, there were Marcionite and Valentinian churches. The *Panarion* contains much material of historical value, but Epiphanius' names for the sects and his reports of their successions are not the best areas in which to look for it.

For the content of his refutations of sects Epiphanius takes inspiration where he finds it. He often draws on other authors. Thus his arguments against the Noetians (Sect 57) are adapted from a document which is called *Zwei Predigten Hippolyts* by Schwarz and *Contra Noetum* by Holl, but which is thought by Pourkier and others to be a fragment of Hippolytus' lost *Syntagma*. Apart from this we cannot be certain how much refutatory material Epiphanius found in Hippolytus, but a number of his logical arguments against Gnosticism are inspired by Irenaeus' *Haereses*, especially his Book II. Our footnotes occasionally refer the reader to such passages.

However, Epiphanius does not use the work of earlier heresiologists in a wooden or mechanical manner. He often quotes from them at length, but as often adapts or expands on their points in his own fashion. They served as stimuli to his thinking.[10]

We can be the most certain that we are hearing Epiphanius' own voice when, as he does time after time, he quotes scripture to prove a point. He was proficient in biblical exegesis as his age understood the discipline, and his scriptural refutations can be pithy and forceful. A good example of his manner is his censure of the Nasaraeans' refusal to eat meat:

> (18,2,4-3,1)...not only are the events recorded in scripture famous to this day, but even the sites of the wonders are preserved. First there is the spot where Abraham offered the ram to God, called Mount Zion to this day. Moreover, the site of the oak of Mamre, where the calf was served to the angels. But if Abraham served a meat-dish to angels, he would not fail to share some of it himself. Moreover, the tradition of the lamb <which> was slaughtered in Egypt is still famous among the Egyptians

and our author goes on to discuss an Egyptian folk custom of which we learn only from him. Similarly revelatory of his controversial ability are his anti-Marcionite arguments at 42,11,15f, based on excerpts from Marcion's canon of scripture.

Epiphanius strove for brevity, and achieved it more often than the *Panarion*'s length would suggest. Sometimes his subject runs away with him, as in Sect 30 where he first relates the long story Josephus of Tiberias told him (30,4,1-12,10) and later discourses against Ebionite doctrines at considerable length. More often when a Sect is lengthy it is because Epiphanius has quoted source material. Thus Sect 31 reproduces in full an otherwise unknown Valentinian document (31,5,1-6,10) and then an extensive passage from Irenaeus (31,9,1-32,8). 33,3,1-7,10 quotes the whole of the *Epistle of Ptolemy to Flora*, our only text of this work. Such quotations form an important part of the *Panarion*'s usefulness.

---

[10] Cf. Pourkier's discussion of this subject in *L'héresiologie*.

The Sources of the Panarion

As plainly as he lays out his purpose and format, Epiphanius sets forth his sources of information at Proem II 2,4:

> Some of the things <about> sects and schisms which I shall be telling the reader, I owe to my fondness for study. Certain things I learned from hearsay, though I came into contact with some through my ears and eyes. I am confident that I can give an account, from accurate report, of the origins and teachings of some sects, and part of what goes on among the others. Of these latter, I know one from the works of ancient authors, another by listening to learned men who confirmed my notion precisely.

The *Panarion* then is based on information gained both from others and at firsthand, and on literary research. Of Epiphanius' search for informants we find an echo at Basil *Epistle* 258, in which Basil answers his inquiry about Magusaeans, a group Epiphanius decided to classify as a "philosophy" (*De Fide* 13,1). When he speaks of personal experience he is thinking chiefly of the "Gnostics" of Sect 26, but he knew a great deal at firsthand about the Archontics of Sect 40 and something about the Sethians of Sect 39. Besides he often had lively interchanges with persons of other persuasions and the *Panarion* contains reminiscences of these.

However, the majority of his information is documentary. Of the many sources of the long *Panarion* we list only those which underlie Book I; Epiphanius often assists the reader by naming them. He speaks of "Clement (of Alexandria), Irenaeus, Hippolytus and many more" (28,33,3); of Eusebius (29,4,1), the *Book of Jubilees* (39,6,1), the *Travels of Peter* (30,15,1), the *Ascents of James* (30,10,6), a Clementine treatise addressed to "elders and virgins" (30,2,6), a *Gospel according to the Hebrews* (30,13,1-8), the *Book of Elkasai* (19,2,1-4,9) and the *Apostolic Constitutions* (45,4,5).

At 27,6,4 Epiphanius quotes Clement of Rome without remembering that his source is the *First Epistle*. Works which he uses without giving their names are Eusebius' *Chronicle* and *Praeparatio Evangelica* and Hippolytus' *Chronicle*. In addition to the long quotations from Gnostic works which we have mentioned, he gives shorter ones from some others. These will be discussed below.

Of all of these sources the two most important are the lost *Syntagma* of Hippolytus and the *Contra Omnes Haereses* of Irenaeus. The former supplies much of the framework of Book I and of Sects 48, 50, 54-55 and 57 of

Book II. We know of it from the catalogue of the library of Photius, ninth century patriarch of Constantinople, where it is called a βιβλαρίδιον:

> There was read: a βιβλαρίδιον of Hippolytus. Hippolytus was a disciple of Irenaeus. It was the syntagma against αἱρέσεις which begins with the Dositheans and continues until Noetus and the Noetians. He says that Irenaeus refuted them in his preaching with arguments which he, Hippolytus, says that he has summarized in the book he has composed.

A series of sects or heresies which seems to correspond with this is found in the *Panarion* and in two other documents: the *Diversarum Haereseon Liber* of Epiphanius' younger contemporary, Filaster of Brescia; and the spurious thirtieth chapter of Tertullian's *Praescriptio Haereticorum*, commonly referred to as Pseudo-Tertullian. This latter, the earliest of the three, is thought to be a third century epitome of the *Syntagma*. It mentions 29 sects or heresies, although for the Noetus with whom the *Syntagma* was said to end it has substituted the third century monarchian Praxeas. With some variations, and sometimes with other groups interspersed between Pseudo-Tertullian's 29, Epiphanius and Filaster contain substantially the same list in substantially the same order; further, the three documents between them share many items of information. The *Syntagma* then appears to be the common source of all three, and from them some of its content may be reconstructed.

The *Panarion*'s dependence upon the *Syntagma* was proposed by Lipsius in 1865 and elaborated by Hilgenfeld in 1884, and in our time has been tested by Pourkier. Objections can be offered to the idea, but it accounts for the data in so many cases that it must be taken as preferred.[11]

As important as Hippolytus to Epiphanius is Irenaeus whom he calls "successor of the apostles," "elder beloved of God," "holy." Epiphanius has read at least three of his Books, probably his entire work, and often quotes him—never Hippolytus—at length. He introduces Irenaean material in Sect after Sect, and when discussing the Valentinians and their relatives depends upon him entirely. This is the case with Sects 22, 23, 27, 31 and 34-36.

None of these sources are Latin and nothing in the *Panarion* is taken from Books V-VIII of Hippolytus' (or Josephus') *Refutatio*.[12] Whether this

[11] For a full presentation of the arguments see Pourkier, *L'hérésiologie*. Despite much evidence to the contrary, it is possible that, as well as the *Syntagma*, Filaster knew at least something about the *Panarion* and on occasion used it as a source. See the notes to Sect 42.

[12] For convenience we refer to this as a work of Hippolytus. Pourkier, following Nautin,

is because Epiphanius did not know the work, or simply because he was uninterested in philosophy, is a "judgment call." When the *Panarion* seems to include Hippolytean material, this is usually from the *Syntagma* or Irenaeus, sources which are utilized by Epiphanius, and apparently in some books of the *Refutatio*. Ideas or doctrines similar to those mentioned by Epiphanius of course appear now and then in the *Refutatio*; we refer to them in our footnotes.

Finally, an extremely important source of Book I and of all the Books of the *Panarion*, is holy scripture. Where its testimony is available Epiphanius prefers it to all others.

The Panarion *and Gnostic Literature*

Sect 26 is rich in references to Gnostic literature. We find a short passage from a *Gospel of Eve* at 26,3,1, one from a *Questions of Mary* at 26,8,1 and one from a *Gospel of Philip* (not identical with Nag Hammadi's) at 26,13,2. At 26,2,5 Epiphanius names a *Gospel of Perfection* but cites nothing from it. At 26,8,1 he refers to *Apocalypses of Adam* which may or may not include the one we know from Nag Hammadi, and to "books about Ialdabaoth" and "books in the name of Seth." This last is of interest since both NHC VII,2 and VII,5 have Seth's name in their titles. *Panarion* 39,5,1 also speaks of books "in the name of Seth"—in this case, seven of them—and 40,7,4 of books "in the name of Seth and his seven sons."

There are likewise several mentions of books called *Allogeneis*, or Strangers. These are found at 39,5,1, 40,2,1 and 40,7,5. Again, we have found works which bear this title. NHC XI,3 is called *Allogenes*; the fourth tractate in the Codex Tchacos, *The Book of Allogenes*. The Codex Tchacos, also, has recently shown us that there was indeed a *Gospel of Judas*, which Epiphanius read of in Irenaeus and mentions at 38,1,5.

The discoveries at Nag Hammadi, and now of the Codex Tchacos, have enlarged our understanding of Gnosticism and its relationship with the great church. We can now see the data from the viewpoints both of persons who loved Gnosticism and persons who hated it. Epiphanius knows the teachings of the Gnostics only superficiallly. He does not appreciate their seriousness, or the delicate allegory, exegetical ingenuity and imaginative beauty of some of their writings. He says repeatedly that Gnostics mean

takes the author of this work to have been one Josephus. For the arguments see Nautin, *Hippolyte et Josipe*.

merely to glorify themselves and cause trouble and that they are all immoral or, if chaste, hypocritically so. In reporting their doctrines he sometimes commits gaffes. He confuses the roles of the exalted aeon Barbelo and the fallen Sophia, identifies the Demiurge with an entity he calls Deficiency, and believes inaccurately that the Gnostic Christ is no more than a wraith or phantasm. Nor is he correct in asserting that Gnostic resurrection is merely a "resurrection of the soul," although some Nag Hammadi passages might give this impression.

Nonetheless he and his fellow heresiologists provide a fairly good index of the characteristic ideas, exegeses and mythologumena, the most important personae, and the most typical expressions of Gnostic literature. Nag Hammadi and our other Gnostic discoveries on the one hand, and the heresiologists on the other, are witnesses confirmatory of each other, and should both be read by the student of the period. It is difficult to read either the *Panarion* or the Nag Hammadi tractates without being reminded of some passage in the other. We have documented a number of parallels in our footnotes; others will find more.

Epiphanius as a Writer

The poorness of the *Panarion*'s style must not lead us to suppose that Epiphanius was an uneducated lout. This important Christian leader who was on friendly terms with Athanasius, conferred with Damasus, corresponded with Basil, and was in contact with dignitaries of the first rank, had been exposed to good written and spoken Greek. The excerpts from others' writings which he includes in the *Panarion* are enough to show us this.

Though he came nowhere near matching the great Christian rhetoricians of his century, Epiphanius, when he took pains, could write an acceptable ecclesiastical style. His *Letter to Arabia*, found in Sect 78, compares in quality with Athanasius' *Letter to Epictetus of Corinth* of Sect 77. It follows the outline proper for an epideictic oration and is couched in simple but effective sentences. Much of the *Ancoratus*, in form an epistolary reply to letters from three well educated correspondents, is in smooth Greek. Its opening, though turgid, is flowery enough for any rhetorician.

Proem II of the *Panarion* likewise exhibits the elements which were expected in a preface: the deprecation of the author's competence, the explanation of the work's subject and of its intent. That Epiphanius did not complete his rhetorical training does not mean that he learned nothing from it.

For the *Panarion*'s awkwardness there are other reasons than Epiphanius' lack of a classical education. One is his attitude toward Greek culture. He distrusted Greek education, and the art of rhetoric with it: "I do not care for the art of rhetoric, but for my readers' benefit" he says at 31,35,1. Moreover, he is concerned that his work be accessible to simple monks, "the little ones in the cloisters," of whom Acacius and Paul speak. At Proem II 2,5 he states that he intends to write "not with eloquence of language or any polished phrases, but with plain speech in a plain dialect, but with accuracy of the facts my speech conveys." This may explain the avid reading of his work "by the simple *pro verbis*," as Jerome remarks. "The simple" could understand what he wrote.

Most importantly the huge *Panarion*, begun and finished within three years, is for the most part oral Greek. It was chiefly dictated, we may suppose in haste, and taken down just as Epiphanius delivered it. His stenographer and scribe, the deacons Anatolius and Hypatius, sign their names at the end of *De Fide*. Presumably Epiphanius had notes before him, or copies of some of his sources, but much of his composition is plainly *ad lib*. Thus at 30,13,2 he suddenly interrupts his discussion of Matthew's gospel in Hebrew to bark out, "And they call this thing 'Hebrew'!" His assistants must have grinned.

Epiphanius' sentences show more coordination than subordination and will often simply run on until they finish a story. A short example—which we break into more than one sentence—is found at 30,18,3, where Epiphanius tries in one breath to tell the reader all he knows of Ebionite customs. When in a hurry he may cover his ground with a long string of genitive absolute phrases. Not often but in a few instances a sentence will not quite construe throughout; this is due, one assumes, to the speaker's haste. An Epiphanian sentence can be a tangle as in his invective against Valentinians and Gnostics at 31,1,1-2. Sometimes, as at 29,3,7-9, one can be no more than several elements set side by side, scarcely deserving the name of "sentence." All this evidences oral composition and probably lack of time for revision—the busy bishop would have had little time for that.

This oral delivery can be effective. There are passages of lively argument, like the discussions of the Demiurge and "matter" at 36,4,5f or of the origin of evil at 24,6,1-3. Epiphanius' imaginary "dialogues" with heretics long dead are vivid and amusing. Sometimes we find a well arranged extemporaneous sermon, as when Epiphanius pillaries the Ophites in Sect 37. Sometimes he almost achieves the level of diatribe:

> (21,5,1) But this doctrine is refuted by the truth itself. If Simon is the supreme power of God and the tart he has with him is the Holy Spirit,

> as he says himself, then he should give the name of the power—or else say why a title has been found for the woman, but none at all for himself! (2) And how does it happen that Simon went the way of all flesh one day at Rome when his turn came—when the wretch fell down and died in the middle of the city of Rome?
>
> 5,3 <And> why did Peter declare that Simon has no part or share in the heritage of true religion? (4) And how can the world not belong to a good God, when all the good have been chosen from it?
>
> 5,5 And how can the power which spoke in the Law and the prophets be "lefthand," when it has heralded Christ's coming <from the> good God in advance and forbids all wrongdoing? (6) And how can there not be one Godhead and the same Spirit, of the New Testament and of the Old, since the Lord has said, "I am not come to destroy the Law, but to fulfill"? And to show that the Law was delivered by himself and proclaimed through Moses, while the grace of the Gospel has been preached by himself and his advent in the flesh, he told the Jews, "Had ye believed Moses, ye would have believed me also, for he wrote of me."

A strength of Epiphanius is his ability to tell a story. What he says at 40,4-7 of the Gnostic Peter is a short example, the colorful narrative of Josephus at 30,4-12 a long one. The brief anecdotes he relates here and there in the course of his arguments are always interesting.

Opposed to this, however, are long stretches of dull prose, recurring theological formulas always in the same words, repetitious sentences resulting from a combination of sources and, as mentioned, some passages which are nothing but a tangle. The most accurate description which can be given of the *Panarion*'s style is "uneven."

Many idioms in the *Panarion* are distinctive and, again, suggestive of oral Greek. There are periphrastic constructions with such verbs as σχεῖν, λαμβάνειν, ἀναδέχεσθαι, ποιεῖν. We find wordy noun locutions where another writer might have preferred a simple preposition: ἐν τῇ περὶ... περιτομῆς σχέσει for "in relation to circumcision"; even, if the text is in order, καθ' ἑκάστην ὑπόθεσιν λέξεως for "concerning each expression." μαχόμενοι θᾶτερον εἰς θᾶτερον πρός... means simply "inconsistent with"; τὸ πᾶν μέρος means "all of."

Words are not always used in the obvious senses which one would expect. μυθολόγημα, μυθολογία and μῦθος are synonyms, for example, and the two former are never found in the *Ancoratus*, a more formal treatise than the *Panarion*. πυργοποιία means, not the "building of the tower" but simply the "tower (of Babel)," so that the "Scythians" κτίζουσι τὴν πυργοποιίαν. σχέσις, which often carries its common meaning of "relation," may also mean "kind, type" or even "occurrence." ὑπόθεσις, employed in several senses by Epiphanius, can also mean "kind, type." ὑπόνοια sometimes means "speculation." μοχθηρίαι are "bad arguments." A patristic dictionary will often document an unusual shade of meaning of some word with an example from Epiphanius—and that from the *Panarion* rather than from the *Ancoratus*.

While we do not know the reason for Epiphanius' distinctive vocabulary, a plausible explanation is that it is colloquial—not a demotic but an everyday Greek which some educated persons employed in discussing serious subjects. A study of the *Panarion*'s vocabulary by a Greek philologist might prove fruitful. As characterizations of the *Panarion*'s style, Holl's erhobenes Koine and the ungeschickt or Geschwätz of others seem equally wide of the mark. "Colloquial Koine" would answer best.

Epiphanius the Controversialist

Of all the church fathers, Epiphanius is the most generally disliked. It would be easy to assemble, from the writings of patrologists and historians of religion, a bill of particulars against him. He is a heresy hunter, a name caller and "nasty." His judgments are uncritical. His theology is shallow and his manner of holding it intransigent. Above all he vehemently opposed the teachings of the great commentator Origen, the first Christian systematic theologian and as a thinker far superior to Epiphanius.

As to the last charge, Origen had many opponents; Epiphanius only commanded the widest audience. Further, he admired some of Origen's achievements; his attack on him was not that of an obscurantist on an intellectual but that of a doctrinal purist on a teacher whom many considered heretical.

As to the epithet, "nasty," name calling was characteristic of controversial writings in the fourth century, though it must be admitted that Epiphanius carried it to extremes. He in fact apologizes for this in his first Proem. The terms of abuse he uses, he says, are his way of distancing himself from doctrines he abhors. Gnostics, whom he particularly abhorred, tend to be the objects of his least pleasant epithets; with others he can be a little more polite.

To the charge of uncritical judgment, an advocate of Epiphanius must allow him to plead guilty. Though he was a serious researcher he believed the testimony he wanted to believe. When he had direct contact with his opponents, it was with the intent of convincing rather than of listening to them. He who is without this sin must cast the first stone.

As a theologian Epiphanius in no sense matches, say, the Cappadocian Fathers or even Athanasius. He can, however, be underrated. Though in the *Panarion* he again and again repeats the same doctrinal formulas, his discussion of the Holy Spirit's divinity shows careful thought. Epiphanius was not at home in philosophy and his quasi-philosophical arguments are generally inspired by others. He is, however, very proficient in scripture, and in the *Ancoratus* and elsewhere uses his proficiency to good effect.

Intransigence is characteristic of religious thought in most ages, and was certainly so in that of Epiphanius. His was the time of the bitter Arian controversy and his work was a product of it. In any case all sides in the fourth century held in common the premise that God's absolute truth was available, conveyed by an infallible scripture, and that to deny it was sinful and imperiled one's salvation. A century before Epiphanius Origen had written:

> I am of the opinion that it is indeed evil for one to err in his manner of life, but far worse to go astray in doctrines and not think in accordance with the most true rule of the scriptures. Since we are to be punished (for indulging) in moral sins, how much more when we sin because of false doctrines? For if a life of good morals sufficed men for salvation, why is it that many philosophers among the gentiles who live continently, and many among the heretics, can by no means be saved, as if the falseness of their doctrine obscured and sullied their manner of life?[13]

Gnostic writings themselves often exhibit the intransigence of their day; the *Gospel of Judas* furnishes us with an example.

Though Epiphanius devoted great effort to his battle against heresy this was by no means his sole interest. We have already noted that his *De Mensuris* and *De Gemmis* date from precisely the period in which he was most occupied with the Origenist controversy. Passages in the *Ancoratus* show us that he was a missionary; his continued connection with his monastery at Eleutheropolis, that he was a pastor. That his message was positive, not negative, can be seen in the opening chapters of the *Ancoratus*, where he

[13] Origen, Commentariorum in Matthaeum Series 33, (Klostermann p. 33). Author's translation.

promises his correspondents "neither to refuse nor to postpone" his answer concerning

> (Anc. 1,3) the teachings of the divine, sacred scripture with regard to the salvation which is among us, the firm foundation of our faith concerning Father, Son and Holy Spirit and all the rest of the salvation in Christ—I mean concerning the resurrection of the dead and the advent in the flesh of the Only-begotten, concerning both the old and the new covenants and, in general, the other supports of complete salvation.

To these imperatives Epiphanius devoted his life. His controversial writings are intended to teach them and to defend them from attacks which he considered perverse and dangerous.

As we have tried to show, the student of Nag Hammadi and other Gnostic literature needs Epiphanius and his fellow heresiologists in order to see the full picture of what was at stake. Beyond this, a church historian or historian of religion has several reasons for consulting this writer. As is well known he preserves documents which are not available elsewhere and is an important witness to the Greek text of Irenaeus and the events of the fourth century, in which he was a participant.

For another reason the historian needs to know something of him. His is the fourth century voice of what in our day we would call "fundamentalism." Nautin has said of him, Épiphane sera resté jusqu'à son dernier souffle un moine égyptien. Persons and schools of Epiphanius' kind have always had great influence, not only throughout Christian history but throughout that of all the great religions. To understand the past, and therefore the present, it is as necessary to know them as it is to know the great creative thinkers.

Footnotes

This volume's footnotes refer chiefly, either to patristic or to Gnostic literature. The former are intended to show both Epiphanius' sources and the places where the same information may be found in his contemporaries or near contemporaries; the latter, the manner in which he and Gnostic sources agree or disagree with each other.

The patristic notes are based on Holl's Sachapparat, though they usually refer to editions more recent that those used by Holl. We use Holl selectively, limiting our notes to the matters which seem most directly relevant; for further information Holl must be consulted. Our contribution, the Gnostic notes, are references to passages in Nag Hammadi, the Berlin Gnostic Codex, the Codex Tchacos and the Askew and Bruce codices. They aim at completeness, but omissions will of course be found.

Occasionally we cite an interesting parallel from Manichean or Mandean literature, but the comparison of these with the Christian heresiologists must be made by specialists in these fields. Unfortunately, lack of space prevents our including many quotations in our notes; we must refer the readers to the patristic or Gnostic texts themselves. We provide indices of references. We hope that this book will prove to be a useful aid in historical study and scholarship.

Frank Williams
Las Cruces, NM, USA
March 24, 2007

EDITIONS AND WORKS CONSULTED

Adriaen, Mark, *S. Hieronymi presbyteri commentariorum in Esaiam Libri I-XI, CC* 73, Turnholt, 1963

——, *Commentarii in Prophetas Minores, CC* 76, 1969

Aland, Barbara, "Gnosis" in Aland, Barbara ed., *Festschrift für Hans Jonas*, Göttingen, 1977, pp. 209-215

Allberry, C. R. C., *A Manichean Psalm Book*, Stuttgart, 1938

Amidon, Philip, *The Panarion of St. Epiphanius of Salamis, Selected Passages*, Oxford, 1990

Attridge, Harold W., ed., *Nag Hammadi Codex I, Texts and Translations*, Leiden, 1985

Bauer, Adolf and Helm, Rudolf, *Hippolytus Werke: Die Chronik, GCS*, Berlin, 1955

Benko, S., "The Libertine Gnostic Sect of the Phibionites according to Epiphanius" in VC 21 (1967), pp. 103-119

Biddle, M., "The First Epistle of Clement on Virginity" in Roberts, Alexander and Donaldson, James edd., *The Ante-Nicene Fathers* VIII, Grand Rapids, 1951, pp. 55-60

Böhlig, Alexander and Wisse, Frederik, *Nag Hammadi Codex III,2 and IV,2, The Gospel of the Egyptians*, Grand Rapids, 1975

Borret, Marcel, *Origene contre Celse, livres I et II, SC* 132; *livres V et VI, SC* 132, 147, Paris, 1967, 1969

Canellis, A. *Altercatio Luciferiani et Orthodoxi, CC* 79B, Turnholt, 2000

Charlesworth, James H., ed., *The Old Testament Pseudepigrapha* II, New York, 1985

Cohen, Martin Samuel, *Shi'ur Qomah, Texts and Recensions*, Tübingen, 1983

Crouzel, Henri and Simonetti, Manlio, *Origene, traité des princips, SC*, Paris, 1978, 1980

Dechow, Jon, *Dogma and Mysticism in Early Christianity, Epiphanius of Cyprus and the Legacy of Origen*, Macon, GA, 1998

Dekkers, E., Tertullian, *Apologetum, CC* I, p. 85f

Dietrich, Albrecht, *Abraxas*, Teubner, 1891

Dummer, Jürgen, "Die Angaben über das gnostische Literatur bei Epiphanius Panarion" in *Koptische Studien in der DDR*, Halle, 1965, pp. 191-219

Emmel, Stephen, ed., *Nag Hammadi Codex II,5, The Dialogue of the Savior*, Leiden, 1984

Fraenkel, P., "Histoire sainte et hérésie chez Sainte Épiphane de Salamine, d'après le Tome I du *Panarion*", in *Revue de théologie et de philosophie* 12 (1962), pp. 175-191

Freedman, Simon M., *Midrash Rabbah* I, London, 1983

Gardner, Iain, *The Kephalaia of the Teacher*, Leiden, 1995

Grant, Robert M., *Theophilus of Antioch ad Autolycum*, Oxford, 1970

Gressmann, Hugo, rev. Laminski, Adolf, *Eusebius Werke, Die Theophanie, GCS*, Leipzig, 1904,

Guillaumont, Antoine, *Le 'Kephalaia Gnostica' d'Evagre le Pontique, et l'histoire de l'origenisme chez les grecs et chez les syriens*, Paris, 1962

Havelaar, Henriette W., *The Coptic Apocalypse of Peter (Nag Hammadi-Codex VI,3)*, Berlin, 1999

Helm, Rudolf, *Die Chronik des Hieronymos, GCS*, Berlin, 1956

Hennecke, Edgar and Schneemelcher, William, *New Testament Apocrypha*, Louisville, 1991

Hilgenfeld, A, *Die Ketzergeschichte des Urchristentums* 1885, repr. Hildesheim, 1963

Holl, Karl, *Ancoratus. Panarion (haereses 1-33)*, Leipzig, 1915

——, rev. Dummer, Jürgen, *Epiphanius II: Panarion (haereses 34-46), GCS*, Berlin, 1980

——, rev. Dummer, Jürgen, *Epiphanius III: Panarion (haereses 65-80). De Fide, GCS*, Berlin, 1985

——, rev. Collatz, Friedrich-Christian et al., *Register zu den Bänden I-III (Ancoratus, Panarion 1-80, De Fide), GCS*, Berlin, 2006

——, *Die handschriftliche Überlieferung des Epiphanios (Ancoratus und Panarion)*, Leipzig, 1910

——, "Die Schriften des Epiphanius gegen die Bilderverehrung," in *Gesämmelte Aufsätze zur Kirchengeschichte* II, Tübingen, 1928, pp. 351-398

James, Montague Rhodes, *The Apocryphal New Testament*, Oxford, 1960

Janssens, Yvonne, *La Prôtennoia trimorphe, NHC XIII,1*, Quebec, 1978

Kaisers, Ursula Ulrike, *Die Hypostase der Archonten (Nag-Hammadi-Codex II,4)*, Berlin, 2006

Karst, Josef, *Die Chronik aus dem Armenischen übersetzt mit kritischem Commentar*, Leipzig, 1911

Kasser, Rodolphe, Meyer, Marvin, Wurst, Gregor, *The Gospel of Judas*, Washington, 2006

Kennedy, George A., *Greek Rhetoric under the Christian Emperors*, Princeton, 1983

Kirchner, Dankwart, *Epistula Jacobi Apocrypha, die zweite Schrift aus Nag Hammadi Codex I,2*, Berlin, 1989

Klijn, Albertus Frederik Johannes and Rinnick G. J., *Patristic Evidence for Jewish-Christian Sects*, Leiden, 1973

Klostermann, Erich, rev. Treu, Ursula, *Originis Matthäuserklärung, Die lateinische Übersetzung der Commentatorium Series, GCS*, Berlin, 1976

——, rev. Nautin, Pierre, *Jeremiahomilien, Klagelieder Kommentar, Erklärung der Samuel und Königsbücher, GCS* 3, Berlin, 1983

Kroymann, Aemilian, Tertullian, Adversus Valentianos, *CC* 1, Turnholt, 1954, p. 441f

——, Adversus Marcionem, *CC* 1, p. 437f

——, Adversus Valentianos, *CC* 2, Turnholt, 1954, p. 751f

——, Adversus Omnes Haereses *CC* 2, p. 1339f

Layton, Bentley, ed., *Nag Hammadi Codex II,2-7 together with XIII,2*, Leiden, 1989

Lidzbarski, Mark, *Ginza, der Schatz, oder das Grosse Buch der Mandäer*, Leipzig, 1925

——, *Das Johannesbuch der Mandäer*, Berlin, 1966

Lipsius, Richard Adelbert, *Zur Quellengeschichte des Epiphanius*, Wien, 1865

MacDermot, Violet, *Pistis Sophia: Text Established by Carl Schmidt, Translation and Notes by Violet MacDermot*, Leiden, 1978

——, *The Books of Jeu and the Untitled Text in the Bruce Codex*, Leiden, 1978

Marcovich, Miroslav, *Hipppolytus Refutatio Omnium Haeresium, PT*, Berlin, 1986

——, *Justini Martyris Apologiae, PT* 38, Leipzig, 1994

——, *Justini Martyris dialogus cum Tryphone, PT 47*, Berlin, 1997

Marcus, Ralph, *Josephus, Jewish Antiquities, Books XII-XIV*, Cambridge, 1961

Metzger, Marcel, *Les constitutions apostoliques, SC* 320, 336, 339, Paris, 1985

Montsoulas, E., "Der Begriff 'Häresis' bei Epiphanius von Salamis," in *Studia Patristica* VII (TU 92), Berlin, 1966

Morard, Francoise, *L'Apocalypse d'Adam*, Quebec, 1985

Moreschini, C., *Hieronymi Presbyteris Dialogus contra Pelagianos, CC* 80, Turnholt, 1990

Nautin, Pierre, "Sainte Epiphane de Salamine," in DHGE 15, Paris, 1965, pp. 175-191

——, *Hippolyte et Josipe*, Paris, 1947

Nock, A. D. And Festugière, A.-J., *Corpus Hermeticum vol. I*, Paris, 1972

——, *Vol. II, XIII-XVIII and Asclepius*, Paris, 1973

Parrott, Douglas M., ed., *Nag Hammadi Codices V,2-5 and VI, with Papyrus Berolinensis 8502,1 and 4*, Leiden, 1979

Pearson, Birger A., ed., *Nag Hammadi Codex VII*, Leiden, 1996

——, *Nag Hammadi Codices IX and X*, Leiden, 1981

Porter, Stanley E, ed., *Handbook of Classical Rhetoric in the Hellenistic Period*, Leiden, 2002

Pourkier, Aline, *L'hérésiologie chez Epiphane de Salamine*, Paris, 1988

Quasten, Johannes, "Epiphanius of Salamis" in *Patrology* III, Utrecht, 1986, pp. 384-396

Raspanti, Giacomo, *S. Hieronymi Presbyteris in Epistulam Pauli Apostoli ad Galatos, CC* 77A, Turnholt, 2006

Rehm, Bernard, *Die Pseudoklementinen in Rufinus Übersetzung, GCS*, Berlin, 1965

Richardson, Ernest Cushing, *Hieronymus, Liber de Viris Illustribus, TU 14*, Berlin, 1896

Riggi, Carlo, "Il termine haeresis di Epifanio di Salamina" in *Salesianum* 29 (1967) pp. 3-37

——, "La Figura di Epifanio nel IV secolo" in *Salesianum* 93, pp. 86-107

Robinson, James M., ed., *The Nag Hammadi Library in English*, San Francisco, 1988

Rousseau, Adelin and Doutreleau, Louis, *Irénée contre les hérésies, livre I, SC* 264, Paris, 1979; *livre III, SC* 211, 1974

Siegert, Folker, *Nag-Hammadi-Register*, Tübingen, 1982

Schenke, Hans-Martin, *Der Gott, "Mensch" in der Gnosis*, Göttingen, 1962

——, "Die Relevanz der Kirchenväter für der Erschliessung der Nag-Hammadi Texte," in Irmscher and Treu, *Das Korpus der griechischen-christlichen Schriftsteller, Historie, Gegenwart, Zukunft*, Berlin, 1977

Schneemelcher, Wilhelm, "Epiphanius" in *RAC* 909-927

Scholem, Gershom, *Jewish Gnosticism, Merkavah Mysticism, and Talmudic Tradition*, New York, 1965

Schwarz, Eduard, "Zwei Predigten Hippolyts," in *Sitzungssberichte der Bayrischen Akademie der Wissenschaft*, No. 3, München, 1936, pp. 32-38

Swartz, Michael D., *Mystical Prayer in Ancient Judaism: an Analysis of Ma'aseh Merkavah*

Stählin, Otto, rev. Frichtel, Ludwig, *Clemens Alexandrinus, GCS*, Berlin, 1960

——, *Stromata Books VII und VIII, Excerpta ex Theodoto, GCS*, Berlin, 1970

Strecker, Georg, *Das Judenchristentum in den Pseudo-Klementinen*, Berlin, 1981

Tardieu, Michel, "Les Gnostiques," in *Tel Quel* 88, 1981

Thackeray, Henry St. John, *Josephus, Jewish War, Books I-III*, Cambridge, 1951

Unger, Dominic J., rev. Dillon, John J., *St. Irenaeus of Lyons against the Heresies*, New York, 1992

Van der Vliet, Jacques, "Judas and the Stars" in *Journal of Juristic Papyrology* 36 (2006), pp. 137-152

Waldstein, Michael and Wisse, Frederik, *The Apocryphon of John*, Leiden, 1995

Waszink, J. H., Tertullian, De Anima, *CC* 2, p. 781f

Winkelmann, Friedhelm, *Eusebius, die Kirchengeschichte, GCS*, Berlin, 1999

Wisse, Frederick, "The Nag Hammadi Library and the Heresiologists" in VC 1972, pp. 205-233

Williams, Frank, *The Panarion of Epiphanius of Salamis, Book I, Sects 1-46*, Leiden, 1987, repr. 1997

——, *The Panarion of Epiphanius of Salamis, Books II and II, De Fide*, Leiden, 1994

ABBREVIATIONS

Adam. Rect. Fid.	Adamantius, *De Recta Fide*
Allog.	*Allogenes*
Apoc. Adam	*Apocalypse of Adam*
1 Apoc. Jas.	*First Apocalypse of James*
2 Apoc. Jas.	*Second Apocalypse of James*
Apoc. Paul	*Apocalypse of Paul*
Apoc. Pet.	*Apocalypse of Peter*
Apocry. Jas.	*Apocryphon of James*
Apocry. Jn.	*Apocryphon of John*
Asc.	*Asclepius*
Aug.	Augustine
Auth. Teach.	*Authoritative Teaching*
BG	Codex Berlinensis 8502
CC	*Corpus Christianorum*
CG	Cairo Gnostic documents
CD	*Covenant of Damascus*
1 Clem	*First Epistle of Clement*
Clem. Alex. Strom.	Clement of Alexandria, *Stromateis*
Exc. Theod.	*Excerpta ex Theodoto*
Clem. Hom.	Pseudo-Clementine *Homilies*
Recog.	*Recognitions*
Cod. Tch.	Codex Tchacos
Const. Ap.	*Apostolic Constitutions*
Corp. Herm.	*Corpus Hermeticum*
Did.	*Didache*
DHGE	*Dictionaire de Géographie et Histoire Ecclésiastique*
Dia. Sav.	*Dialogue of the Savior*
Ep.	*Epistle*
Epist. Apost.	*Epistula Apostolorum*
Ep. Pet. ad Jac.	Pseudo-Clementine *Epistula Petri ad Jacobum*
Eug.	*Eugnostos*
Eus.	Eusebius
Chron.	*Chronicon*
H. E.	*Historia Ecclesiastica*
In Isa.	*Commentarium in Isaiam*
Praep. Ev.	*Praeparatio Evangelica*
Exeg. Soul	*Exegesis on the Soul*
Fil.	Filaster of Brescia
GCS	*Die griechischen-christlichen Schriftsteller der ersten drei Jahrhunderte*
GT	*Gospel of Thomas*
Gos. Egyp.	*Gospel of the Egyptians*
Gos. Jud.	Codex Tchacos *Gospel of Judas*
Gos. Phil.	*Gospel of Philip*
Gos. Tr.	*Gospel of Truth*
Gr. Pow.	*The Concept of our Great Power*
Gr. Seth	*The Second Treatise of the Great Seth*
H-S	Hennecke-Schneemelcher, *New Testament Apocrypha and Pseudepigrapha*

Hipp.	Hippolytus
Chron.	*Chronicle*
Refut.	*Refutatio Omnium Haeresium*
Synt.	*Syntagma*
Hyps.	*Hypsiphrone*
Inc.	*De Incarnatione*
Iren	Irenaeus, *Refutatio Omnium Haeresium*
Jer.	Jerome
Adv. Jov.	*Adversus Jovinianum*
Chron.	*Chronicle*
C. Pelag.	*Contra Pelagianos*
In Gal.	*Commentarium in Galatas*
Vir. Ill.	*De Viris Illustribus*
Vit. Paul.	*Vita Paulae*
Jub.	*Book of Jubilees*
Justin	Justin Martyr
Apol.	*Apology*
Dial.	*Dialogus cum Tryphone*
Let. Pet.	*Letter of Peter to Philip*
Man. Hom.	*Manichaean Homilies*
Man. Keph.	*Manichean Kephalaia*
Man. Ps.	*Manichean Psalms*
Mars.	*Marsanes*
Melch.	*Melchizedek*
Method. Conviv.	Methodius,*Convivium*
Nat. Arc.	*The Nature of the Archons*
NHC	Nag Hammadi codices
Or. Wld.	*The Origin of the World*
Orig.	Origen
Cels.	*Contra Celsum*
Com. in Matt. Ser.	*Commentariorum in Matthaeum Series*
Hom. in Sam. Frgt.	*Homilia in Samuelem Fragmentum*
In Gen. Hom.	*Commentarium in Genesim Homilia*
In Matt.	*Commentarium in Matthaeum*
Princ.	*De Principiis*
Pan.	*Panarion*
Para. Shem	*Paraphrase of Shem*
PS	*Pistis Sophia*
PsT	"Pseudo-Tertullian"
PT	*Patristic Texts*
1 Q apGen	*Genesis Apocryphon*, Qumran Cave 1
1 Q Serek	Serek scroll, Qumran Cave 1
1 Q W	War scroll, Qumran Cave 1
RAC	*Realenzyklopädie des antiken Christentums*
Test. Tr.	*Testimony of the Truth*
Tert.	Tertullian
Adv. Lucif.	*Adversus Luciferanios*
Adv. Marc.	*Adversus Marcionem*
Adv. Val.	*Adversus Valentianos*
Carn. Chr.	*De Carne Christi*
Praescr.	*Praecriptio Haereticorum*
Res. Mort.	*De Resurrectione Mortuorum*
Treat. Res.	*Treatise on the Resurrection*
VC	*Vigiliae Christianae*
Val. Exp.	*Valentinian Exposition*
Zost.	*Zostrianus*

LETTER OF ACACIUS AND PAUL

A letter written in the ninety-second year of the Diocletian era, the twelfth of the reign of Valentinian and Valens and the eighth of Gratian,[1] to Epiphanius of Eleutheropolis in Palestine, <some time> abbot in the country about Eleutheropolis, now bishop of the city of Constantia in the province of Cyprus, from the presbyters Acacius and Paul, archimandrites, that is, abbots in Chalcis and Beroea in Coelesyria. <They requested that he> write a complete heresiology and not only they, but many <others> as well, urged and practically compelled him to take up the task.

Greetings in the Lord from the archimandrites, Acacius, presbyter, and Paul, presbyter, to the most godly Father, the bishop Epiphanius, our master and most highly honored in every way.

1,1 A glimpse of your Reverence would suffice us, Father, by filling us with spiritual speech and implanting as much affection in us as has arisen in those who enjoy your acquaintance. (2) But by its heralding of the fragrance of the sweet odor of his words and deeds, fame, which runs before a disciple of the Savior, presses one to take one's fill of his words and thought. We ought to have come in person to partake of the grace which God has given to you, as to the apostles.

1,3 But since the journey is prohibited by bodily infirmity and distress, we are unable to come ourselves, fall prostrate at your feet, and hear and learn the sacred, spiritual words as they issue from your lips. (4) (For we are confident that if we came and heard them, were we worthy, we would be set upon the way of life we have undertaken—provided that we are fit to attain its goal.)

1,5 Since infirmity has overtaken us, therefore, we beseech your Reverence in all your greatness not to grudge sharing with us the gifts you have truly been given by the Savior. (6) For not we alone, but all who hear of you, confess that the Savior has raised you up in this generation as a new apostle and herald, a new John, to proclaim the things that ought to be observed by those who have undertaken this course.

1,7 As Marcellus, a brother to us both, is pressed by your fame in its greatness and drawn by affection for your Reverence, and since he is a

[1] 376 A.D.

member of our community, we have employed his services, although he is a recent catechumen, for the making of such a long journey, and have committed to him the venture, in all its daring, of us sinners towards you, the Savior's disciple. (8) And our request is that you give us, for our instruction, some of the words you have spoken to certain brethren. For you, the righteous, this can be no burden but for us sinners it will be rejoicing in the Lord when we partake of them; for the load of our transgressions is lightened when we are filled with your spiritual uttterances. (9) We have heard names assigned to the sects by your Honor, and are asking your Reverence to tell us explicitly the heresy held by each of these cults. For <not> everyone's gift is the same.

1,10 We likewise ask you, the righteous, to pray to the Lord for all who long for you and are awaiting the gift from you. (11) We are in fasting and prayer that the brother of us all may be received gladly by your Honor and obtain the gift of your bestowing, and so offer the accustomed prayers to Father, Son and Holy Spirit.

1,12 All the brethren hope to be established by your prayer on their behalf. Since yours is a God-given grace of apostles we urge you to share it ungrudgingly. (13) All the little ones in the cloisters are praying the greater that they may enjoy a spiritual gift from your Reverence. May you remain well in the Lord, and happy in Christ and the Holy Spirit <as you administer> the throne that has been granted you and your God-given gift, till you receive the crown that awaits you.

PROEM I

Epiphanius' reply to the presbyters Acacius and Paul, concerning their letter to him about his writing an heresiology. (Proem I)

Greetings in the Lord from Epiphanius to his highly esteemed brothers and fellow-presbyters, Masters Acacius and Paul!

1,1 By drawing up a preface or opening statement as a sort of title, authors of old would give a glimpse, by means of the hint, of the entire work that followed. In the same style, beloved, I too am writing a preface for you, to give a brief summary of my <treatise> against sects. (2) Since I am going to tell you the names of the sects and expose their unlawful deeds like poisons and toxic substances, and at the same time match the antidotes with them as cures for those already bitten and preventatives for those who will have this misfortune, I am drafting this Preface for the scholarly to explain the "Panarion," or chest of remedies for those whom savage beasts have bitten. It is composed in three Books containing eighty Sects, symbolically represented by wild beasts or snakes.

1,3 But "one after the eighty" is at once the foundation, teaching and saving treatment of the truth and Christ's holy bride, the church. It has always been but was revealed in the course of time, through Christ's incarnation, in the midst of these sects. (4) I have made mention it in connection with the preaching of Christ and again, after all the iniquities of these sects, given a concise, clear account of it in accordance with the apostles' teaching, for the refreshment of those who by reading have labored their way through the sects.

2,1 Please, all you scholarly readers of the Preface, the Sects that follow it, and the Defense of the Truth and Exposition of the Truth and the Faith of the Holy Catholic Church: pardon me—who am only human and am trying my best, with hard labor and God-given zeal, to defend the true religion,—(2) if I <attempt> too much in my desire to make the best defense in my power, in the all-holy, all-august Name itself. For God allows me this, though I am investigating matters too difficult for me, since what I say is for the truth's sake, and my work is for the sake of true religion.

2,3 And I further beg your <pardon> if you should find—though it is certainly not my way to mock or ridicule people—but if, from zeal against the sects and for the readers' dissuasion, I may speak in anger or call certain persons "frauds," or "tramps" or "wretches." (4) The very necessity for the words of the controversy is putting me in such a sweat, for the readers' dissuasion and to show that these persons' practices, rites and doctrines are the furthest thing from my mind, and thus prove my independence of them with the words and the bitterness of my opposition, and turn people away from them precisely by the words that appear too harsh.

3,1 And here are the contents of the entire work in its three Volumes, Volumes One, Two, and Three—which three Volumes I have divided into seven Sections with a certain number of Sects and Schisms in each section, making eighty in all. Their names and the occasions of them, are these: (2) The first, Barbarism. The second, Scythianism. The third, Hellenism. The fourth, Judaism. The fifth, Samaritanism. (3) Derived from these are the following. Before Christ's incarnation, but after Barbarism and the Scythian superstition, the sects which sprang from Hellenism are these: The sixth, Pythagoreans or Peripatetics, a sect which was separated (from Hellenism) by Aristotle. The seventh, Platonists. The eighth, Stoics. The ninth, Epicureans.

3,4 Then the Samaritan sect, an offshoot of Judaism, and its four peoples: The tenth, Gorothenes. The eleventh, Sebuaeans. The twelfth, Essenes. The thirteenth, Dositheans.

3,5 Then the afore-mentioned Judaism itself, which derived its character from Abraham, was amplified through the Law given to Moses, and inherited its name, "Judaism," from Judah the son of Jacob or Israel, through David, the king from the tribe of Judah. (6) And derived from Judaism itself are the following seven sects: The fourteenth, Scribes. The fifteenth, Pharisees. The sixteenth, Sadducees. The seventeenth, Hemerobaptists. The eighteenth, Ossaeans. The nineteenth, Nasaraeans. The twentieth, Herodians.

4,1 From these sects, and later on in the course of time, appeared the saving dispensation of our Lord Jesus Christ—that is to say, his incarnation, preaching of the Gospel, and proclamation of a kingdom. This alone is the fount of salvation, and the faith in the truth of the catholic, apostolic, and orthodox church.

4,2 From this the following sects, which have Christ's name only but not his faith, have been broken away and split off: (3) The first, Simonians. The second, Menandrians. The third, Satornilians. The fourth, Basilideans. The fifth, Nicolaitans. The sixth, Gnostics, who are also known as Stratiotics and are the same as the Phibionites, but some call them Secundians, others, Socratists, others, Zacchaeans, and by some they are called Coddians, Borborites, and Barbelists. The seventh, Carpocratians. The eighth, Cerinthians, also called Merinthians. The ninth, Nazoraeans. The tenth,

Ebionites. The eleventh, Valentinians. The twelfth, Secundians, with whom Epiphanes and Isidore are associated. The thirteenth, Ptolemaeans.

4,4 The fourteenth, Marcosians. The fifteenth, Colorbasians. The sixteenth, Heracleonites. The seventeeth, Ophites. The eighteenth, Cainites. The nineteenth, Sethians. The twentieth, Archontics. The twenty-first, Cerdonians. The twenty-second, Marcionites. The twenty-third, Lucianists. The twenty-fourth, Apelleans. The fwenty-fifth, Severians. The twenty-sixth, Tatianists.

4,5 The twenty-seventh, Encratites. The twenty-eighth, Phrygians, also known as Montanists and Tascodrugians. But again, these Tascodrugians are differentiated as a group in themselves. The twenty-ninth, Pepuzians, also known as Priscillianists and Quintillianists, with whom Artotyrites are associated. The thirtieth, Quartodecimans, who observe one day of the year as the Paschal festival. The thirty-first, Alogi, who do not accept the Gospel and Revelation of John. The thirty-second, Adamians. The thirty-third, Sampsaeans, also known as Elkasaites. The thirty-fourth, Theodotianists. The thirty-fifth, Melchizedekians. The thirty-sixth, Bardesianists. The thirty-seventh, Noetianists. The thirty-eighth, Valesians. The thirty-ninth, Catharists, also known as Navatians. The fortieth, Angelics. The forty-first, Apostolics, also known as Apotactics. The forty-second, Sabellians. The forty-third, Origenists who are also known as the immoral Origenists. The forty-fourth, Origenists who are also known as Followers of Adamantius.

4,6 The forty-fifth, Disciples of Paul of Samosata. The forty-sixth, Manichaeans, also known as Acuanites. The forty-seventh, Hierakites. The forty-eighth, Melitians, who are an Egyptian schism. The forty-ninth, Arians, also known as Ariomanites.

4,7 The fiftieth, The Audian schism. The fifty-first, Photinians. The fifty-second, Marcellians. The fifty-third, Semi-Arians. The fifty-fourth, Pneumatomachi, also called Macedonians and Disciples of Eleusius, who blaspheme the Holy Spirit of God. The fifty-fifth, Aërians. The fifty-sixth, Aetians, also called Anhomoeans, with whom Eunomius, or rather, "Anomus," is associated.

4,8 The fifty-seventh, Dimoirites, who do not confess Christ's incarnation in the full sense, also called Apollinarians. The fifty-eighth, those who say that St. Mary, the ever-virgin, had intercourse with Joseph after giving birth to the Savior. Such people I have called "Antidicomarians." The fifty-ninth, those who offer a loaf in the name of the Virgin Mary, who are called Collyridians. The sixtieth, Massalians, with whom the Martyrians, who are of pagan origin,and the Euphemites and Satanists, are associated.

5,1 Now I go back to the beginning again, divide these sects by volume and indicate, in this one of my summaries, how many of the eighty sects are contained in the first Volume, and so on through the second and the third, and also, for each of the seven Sections which have been arranged in the three Volumes, how many Sects are to be found in it. Thus:

5,2 In the first Volume there are three Sections and forty-six Sects, including <their mothers and the original> names for them, I mean Barbarism, Scythianism, Hellenism, Judaism and Samaritanism. In the second Volume there are two Sections and twenty-three Sects. And in the third Volume there are two Sections and eleven Sects.

5,3 In the first Section of the first Volume there are twenty Sects, as follows: Barbarism, Scythianism, Hellenism and Judaism. Varieties of Hellenes: Pythagoreans or Peripatetics, Platonists, Stoics, Epicureans. The Samaritan sect, which is derived from Judaism. Four Samaritan peoples, as follows: Gorothenes, Sebuaeans, Essenes, Dositheans. Seven Jewish sects as follows: Scribes, Pharisees, Sadducees, Hemerobaptists, Ossaeans, Nasaraeans, Herodians.

5,4 There are likewise thirteen Sects in the second Section of the first Volume, as follows: Simonians; Menandrians; Satornilians; Basilideans; Nicolaitans; Gnostics, also called Stratiotics and Phibionites, but Secundians by some, Socratists by others, Zacchaeans, Coddians, Borborites and Barbelists by others; Carpocratians; Cerinthians, also called Merinthians; Nazoraeans; Ebionites; Valentinians; Secundians, with whom Epiphanes and Isidore are associated; Ptolemaeans.

5,5 In the third Section of this first Volume there are thirteen Sects as follows: Marcosians; Colorbasians; Heracleonites; Ophites; Cainites; Sethians; Archontics; Cerdonians; Marcionites; Lucianists; Apelleans; Severians; Tatianists. This is the summary of the first Volume with its three Sections.

5,6 There are two Sections in the second Volume. And in the first Section of the second Volume—the fourth in numerical order from the beginning—there are eighteen Sects as follows: Encratites; Phrygians, also known as Montanists and Tascodrugians. But the Tascodrugians are differentiated from the (two) preceding. Pepuzians, <also known as Priscillianists> and Quintillianists, with whom Artotyrites are associated. Quartodecimans, who observe one day in the year as the Paschal fesstival; Alogi, who do not accept the Gospel and Revelation of John; Adamians; Sampsaeans, also known as Elkasaites: Theodotianists; Melchizedekians; Bardesianists; Noetians; Valesians; Catharists; Angelics; Apostolics, also known as Apotactics, with whom the so-called Saccophori are associated; Sabellians; the immoral Origenists; the Origenists who follow Adamantius.

5,7 In the second Section of this second Volume which, counting as before, is the fifth, there are five Sects, as follows: Disciples of Paul of Samosata; Manichaeans, also known as Acuanites; Hierakites; Melitians, an Egyptian schism; Arians. And this is the summary of the second Volume, with its <two> Sections.

5,8 Similarly, there are also two Sections in the third Volume. In the first Section of the third Volume, the sixth according to the previous enumeration, there are seven Sects, as follows: Audians, a schism; Photinians; Marcellians; Semi-Arians; Pneumatomachi, who blaspheme the Holy Spirit of God; Aërians; Disciples of Aetius the Anhomoean, with whom Eunomius, also known as Anomus, is associated.

5,9 In the second Section of this Volume Three, seventh as we have enumerated the Sections—which is a seventh Section and the last in the work—there are four Sects as follows: Dimoirites, who do not confess Christ's incarnation in the full sense, also known as Apollinarians. Those who say that St. Mary, the ever-virgin, had intercourse with Joseph after giving birth to the Savior—I have called them "Antidicomarians." Those who offer a loaf in the name of Mary, and are called Collyridians. Massalians. And the brief defense of the orthodox faith and the truth, "The Holy, Catholic and Apostolic Church."

This is the summary and superscription of the entire Treatise Against Eighty Sects, and one (further treatise), the Defense of the only Truth, that is "The Catholic and Orthodox Church." It is arranged in three Volumes below and divided into seven Sections.

ANACEPHALAEOSIS I

The following are contained in the first Section of the first Volume of the Refutation of the Sects <which includes twenty Sects > as follows:

First, the mothers and original names of all the sects, from which five mothers the others sprang. And these are the first four:

1,1 < 1.> The first is Barbarism, a sect which is underived and lasted from Adam's time for ten generations until Noah. (2) It has been called Barbarism because the people of that time had no leader or common consensus. Everyone was in agreement with himself instead and served as a law for himself, according to the inclination of his own will.

2,1 <2.> A second is Scythianism, from the time of Noah, and afterwards until the building of the tower and Babylon, and for a few years after the time of the tower, that is until Peleg and Reu. (2) Since they bordered on the latitude of Europe these people were assimilated to Scythia and its peoples from the time of Terah, the ancestor of the Thracians, and afterwards.

3,1 <3.> A third is Hellenism, which began from the time of Serug,[1] through idolatry and people's adoption, each in accordance with some superstition, of a more civilized way of life, and of customs and laws.

3,2 However, when idols began to be set up, the various breeds of men made gods of <the leaders> they <were> then adopting, originally by painting pictures to portray the autocrats or sorcerers they had honored of old, or persons who had done something in the world that appeared memorable, <and excelled> in courage and strength of body. (3) But then, from the time of Terah[2] the father of Abraham, they also introduced the imposture of idolatry by means of statuary. They honored their ancestors, and those who had died before them, with images, first by making them with the potter's art and then by representing them through every craft—builders by carving stone, silversmiths and goldsmiths by crafting them with their media, and so with woodcarvers and the rest. (4) (The Egyptians, together with the Babylonians, Phrygians and Phoenicians, were the first to introduce this religion of image manufacture and mystery[3] rites. The greater part of

[1] Jub. 11.1-4
[2] Jub. 11.16; 12.2
[3] Jub. 11.16; 12.2

these were brought to the Hellenes from Cecrops'[4] time and onwards.) (5) Afterwards, and much later, they designated Cronus, Rhea, Zeus, Apollo and the rest as gods.

3,6 Hellenes are named for Hellen, who was one of the settlers of Hellas and gives the country his name. But as others tell it, it is named for the olive[5] that sprouted at Athens. (7) Actually the Ionians were the first of the Hellenes <and were named for> Iovan, one of the men who built the tower at the time when people's languages were divided. Thus they are all called Meropes as well, because of the "divided"[6] speech. (8) But afterwards, at a later period, Hellenism was made into sects—I mean the sects of Pythagoreans, Stoics, Platonists, Epicureans and the rest.

3,9 But the character of true religion[7] existed as did the natural law, and was practiced apart from these peoples, marking itself off amid Barbarism, Scythianism and Hellenism from the foundation of the world and onwards until it was combined with the true religion of Abraham.

<4.> And next after these came Judaism which received its character through circumcision from the time of Abraham and was expanded during the lifetime of Moses the seventh from Abraham, by the Law which was given by God through him, and which got its final name, "Judaism," from Judah the fourth son of Jacob surnamed Israel, through David, the first of this Judah's tribe to reign as king.

For it was plainly of these four sects that the apostle said as a reproof, "In Christ Jesus there is neither Barbarian, Scythian, Hellene nor Jew, but a new creation."[8]

Varieties of Hellenes:

5,1 <5.> Pythagoreans, or Peripatetics. Pythagoras taught the doctrines of the monad, providence, the prohibitions of sacrifice to the supposed gods and the eating of meat, and abstention from wine. (2) As well, he distinguished between what is above the moon, which he called immortal, and what is below it, which he called mortal. He taught the transmigrations of souls from body to body, even of beasts and insects, as well as the keeping of a five-year period of silence. Lastly he pronounced himself divine.

---

[4] Cecrops is mentioned at Eus. Praep. Ev. 10.9; Eus. Chron. (Karst p. 159); Jer. Chron. (Helm 21,24).

[5] ἐλαία

[6] μεμερισμένη

[7] θεοσεβεία. Or simply: piety. See 2,7. The author of the Anacephalaeosis is trying to emphasize, more strongly than does Epiph, that there is something distinctively heretical even about the four earliest sects which existed in the world without competition.

[8] Col 3:11

6,1 6. Platonists taught the doctrines of God; matter and form; that the world is generate and perishable, while the soul is ingenerate, immortal and divine; that the soul has three parts, the rational, the emotional and the appetitive; (2) that wives are common to all and that no one has one spouse of his own, but that anyone who wishes may have intercourse with any women who are willing; likewise the transmigrations of souls into various bodies, even those of insects; but at the same time, also, the origin of many gods from the one.

7,1 7. Stoics, who held that the universe is a body and believed that this visible world is God; and some declared that it has received its nature from the substance of fire. (2) They also define God as "mind," and like a soul of the whole existent vault of heaven and earth. And the universe is a body, as I said, and the luminaries are his eyes. The flesh of all things perishes, and the soul is transferred from body to body.

8,1 8. Epicureans supposed that indivisible and simple bodies, homogeneous and infinite in number, are the first principle of all things. And they held that pleasure is the consummation of happiness, and that neither God nor providence orders affairs.

9,1 9. Samaritanism and the Samaritans who derive from it, which is derived from Judaism. The occasion for it came at the time of Nebuchadnezzar and the captivity of the Jews, before the establishment of sects among the Greeks and the rise of their doctrines, but after there was a Greek religion, and midway through the period of Judaism. (2) Samaritans were immigrants from Assyria to Judaea and had received only Moses' Pentateuch, since the king had sent it to them from Babylon by a priest named Ezra. (3) All their opinions are the same as the Jews', except that they abominate gentiles and will not even touch any, and except that they deny the resurrection of the dead and the other prophecies, the ones subsequent to Moses.

Four Samaritan peoples:

10,1 10. Gorothenes, who celebrate the festivals at different times of year than the Sebuaeans.

11,1 11. Sebuaeans, who differ from the Gorothenes for the same reason, the festivals.

12,1 12. Essenes, who are not opposed to either party and celebrate without distinction with anyone they happen to be with

13,1 13. Dositheans, who follow the same customs as the Samaritans—circumcision, the Sabbath and the rest—and use the Pentateuch; but, going beyond the others, they abstain from meat and live a life of constant fasting. (2) And some are celibate as well, while others practice continence. And they believe in the resurrection of the dead, an idea which is foreign to Samaritans.

Seven Jewish sects:

14,1 14. Scribes, who were persons learned in the Law and persons who repeated the traditions of their elders. Because of their extra would-be religion they observed customs which they had not learned through the Law but had formulated for themselves, observances of the ordinance of the legislation.

15,1 15. Pharisees, meaning "persons set apart," whose lives were most exemplary and who were, if you please, more highly regarded than the others. They believed in the resurrection of the dead as the Scribes did, and agreed as to the existence of angels and the Holy Spirit. And they had a superior way of life: continence for a time, and celibacy; fasting twice a week; and cleansings of vessels, platters and goblets, (as was the case with the Scribes); (2) tithes; first-fruits; constant prayer, and the would-be religious styles of dress with their shawls, their robes or rather tunics, the width of the "phylacteries," or borders of purple material, fringes, and tassels on the corners of the shawl. Things of this sort were signs of their periods of continence. And they also introduced the ideas of destiny and fate.

16,1 16. Sadducees, meaning "most righteous," who were descended from the Samaritans and from a priest named Zadok as well. They denied the resurrection of the dead and did not recognize the existence of angels or spirits. In all other respects they were Jews.

17,1 17. Hemerobaptists. These were Jews in all respects, but claimed that no one can attain eternal life unless he is baptized every day.

18,1 18. Ossenes, meaning "boldest."[9] They were observers of the Law's provisions but also made use of other scriptures after the Law, though they rejected most of the later prophets.

19,1 19. Nasaraeans, meaning "rebels," who forbid the eating of any meat and do not partake of living things at all. They have the holy names of patriarchs which are in the Pentateuch, up through Moses and Joshua the son of Nun, and they believe in them—(2) I mean Abraham, Isaac, Jacob, and the earliest ones, and Moses himself, and Aaron, and Joshua. But they hold that the scriptures of the Pentateuch are not Moses' scriptures, and maintain that they have others besides these.

20,1 20. Herodians, who were Jews in all respects, but thought that Herod was Christ, and awarded the honor and name of Christ to him.

This is the first Section, containing refutations of all of these twenty sects. The subject of Christ's advent is in it as well, and the confession of the truth.

---

[9] Or: the most headstrong

The Heresiology of Epiphanius, Bishop, Entitled "Panarion," or "Medicine Chest" (Proem II)[1]

1,1 As I begin my account and discussion of faith and unbelief, of correct views and divergent views, I am going to start by mentioning the world's creation and what followed it[2]—though I am not beginning by my own power or with my own reasoning but as God, the Lord of all, the Merciful, has vouchsafed to reveal the knowledge of everything to his prophets and through them, as far as human nature allows, to us.

1,2 And I feel quite anxious at the outset, as soon as I begin to consider the subject. Indeed I am extremely frightened at undertaking a task of no small difficulty, and I call on the holy God himself, on his only-begotten Son Jesus Christ, and on his Holy Spirit, to give light to my poor mind, for its illumination with the knowledge of these things.

1,3 For the Greek authors, poets and chroniclers would invoke a Muse when they undertook some work of mythology. A Muse, not God—their wisdom was devilish, "earthly, and not descended from above,"[3] as scripture says. (4) I, however, am calling upon the holy Lord of all to come to the aid of my poverty and inspire me with his Holy Spirit, so that I may include nothing spurious in my treatment of the subject. (5) And having made this very petition—for "according to the measure of faith and in proportion,"[4] I know my inadequacy—I beseech him to grant it.

2,1 To a person reading a work on any question the aim <of the treatise> ought to be <clear>—the discoveries which training enables my small mind to grasp lie in the temporal realm, and I certainly do not promise <to impart the knowledge> of everything in the world. (2) There are things which cannot be uttered, and things which can. There are things untold, beyond counting, inaccessible so far as man is concerned, and known only to the Lord of all. (3) But we are dealing with variance of opinions and kinds of knowledge, with faith in God and unbelief, with sects, and with heretical human opinion which misguided persons have been sowing in the world from man's formation on earth till our own day, the eleventh year of the reigns of Valentinian and Valens and the seventh of Gratian's.[5]

---

[1] Epiph considers his account of the four "mothers" of the sects to be part of this Proem, as he shows by his wording of 2,13. For convenience we title 1,1-3,9 Proem II.

[2] At 1,1 below. Epiph's account begins with Adam.

[3] Jas 3:15

[4] Cf. Rom 12:6.

[5] 375 C.E.

2,4 Some of the things <about> sects and schisms which I shall be telling the reader, I owe to my fondness for study. Certain things I learned from hearsay, though I happened on some with my own ears and eyes. I am confident that I can give an account, from accurate report, of the origins and teachings of some sects, and part of the what goes on among the others. Of these latter, I know one from the works of ancient authors, another by listening to learned men who confirmed my notion precisely.

2,5 I did not gather all this reflection together on my own initiative, or by spending further time on subjects which go beyond my limited intelligence. In fact <I have also written> this work[6]—which, by God's will, I have consented to compose—<at the request> of scholarly persons who urged my weakness on at various times and in various ways, and practically forced me to get at it. Such a request your Honors made in writing, my most esteemed brothers and scholarly fellow presbyters, Acacius and Paul, in a letter of recommendation. (6) Now since, not without God's help, I have given the fullest consideration to the number of the requests, and from extreme love for the servants of God have consented to take the step, I shall begin—not with eloquence of language or any polished phrases, but with plain speech in a plain dialect,[7] but with accuracy of the facts my speech conveys.

3,1 The author Nicander too gave an account of the nature of beasts and reptiles. And other authors <described> the qualities of roots and plants—Dioscurides the Wood-Cutter, Pamphilus, King Mithridates, Callisthenes, Philo, Iolaus of Bithynia, Heraclidas of Tarentum, Cratenus the Root-Collector, Andrew, Bassus the Tulian, Niceratus, Petronius, Niger, Diodotus, and certain others. (2) In the same way I, in trying to reveal the roots and beliefs of the sects, am not <describing them> in order to harm those who care to read (my description). (3) Those authors made a diligent effort, not to point evil out, but to frighten people and ensure their safety, so that they would recognize the dreadful, dangerous beasts and be safe and escape them by God's power, by taking care not to engage with such deadly creatures if they encountered them, and were menaced by their breath or bite, or by the sight of them. And <at the same time>, from the same concern, the same authors prescribed remedies made from roots and plants, to counteract the evil of these serpents.

[6] In addition to the Ancoratus

[7] In other words, Epiph intends to write without rhetorical ornamentation, and in the Koine. Cf. what he says about "languages" at 42,12,1 elenchi 13 and 21.

3,4 Thus, dearest, my work too <has been compiled> as a defense against them and for your <safety>, to reveal the appearance of the dreadful serpents and beasts, and their poisons and deadly bites. (5) And to correspond with these I shall give as many arguments, like antidotes, as I can in short compass—one or two at most—to counteract their poison and, after the Lord, cure anyone who wants <to be cured>, if he has fallen, willingly or inadvertently, into these snake-like teachings of the sects.

1.
<*Barbarism*>

1,1 For at the beginning Adam was brought to life on the sixth day, after being formed from earth and infused with (God's breath). He was not begun on the fifth day, as some think, and finished on the sixth; the idea of those who say this is a mistaken one. He was unspoiled and innocent of evil and had no other name, for he had no additional name of an opinion, a belief, or a distinctive way of life. He was simply called "Adam," which means "man." (2) A wife like himself was formed for him out of himself—out of the same body, <by> the same infusion of breath. Adam had male and female children, and after 930 years of life he died.

1,3 The child of Adam was Seth, the son of Seth was Enosh, and his descendants were Cainan, Mahalaleel and Jared. And the tradition which I have learned says that wickedness first appeared in the world at this point.[1] It had also appeared at the beginning through Adam's disobedience, and then through Cain's fratricide. But now, in the lifetime of Jared and afterward, came sorcery, witchcraft, licentiousness, adultery and injustice. (4) <However> there was no divergent opinion, no changed belief; there was one language, and one stock which had been planted on earth at that time. (5) This Jared had a son named Enoch, who "pleased God and was not; for god took him away" and he "did not see death."[2] Enoch was the father of Methuselah, Methuselah of Lamech, and Lamech of Noah

1,6 God's righteous judgment brought a flood on the world and wiped all humanity out, and all other <living things>. But by his decree he preserved Noah in the ark, since he had pleased God and found favor—Noah himself; his three sons, Shem, Ham and Japheth; Noah's own wife; and his three sons' wives. (7) So eight human beings were preserved from the water

[1] Perhaps cf. Jub. 4.15, which says that the Watchers came to earth in the days of Jared.
[2] Gen 5:24; Heb 11:5

of the flood in the ark of those days. And some of every kind of animal and living thing, cattle and everything else on earth, were preserved—pairs in some cases, sevens in others—to renew the existence of every kind of thing in the world. (8) And thus a tenth generation had passed making 2262 years.[3] And the flood came to an end, and Noah and his household served as a surviving stock in the world.

1,9 But there was no difference of opinion yet, no people that was at all different, no name for a sect, and no idolatry either. Since everyone followed his own opinion, however, the name, "Barbarism," was given to the era then, during the ten generations. (For there was not one law. Everyone served as a law to himself and conformed to his own opinion. Hence the apostle's usage, not only of "Barbarism" but of the other terms as well; for he says, "In Christ Jesus there is neither Barbarian, Scythian, Hellene nor Jew.")[4]

2.
<*Scythianism*>

2,1 After the flood, since Noah's ark had come to rest in the highlands of Ararat between Armenia and Cardyaei on the mountain called Lubar,[1] the first human settlement following the flood was made there. And there the prophet Noah planted a vineyard and became the original settler of the site. (2) His children—there is no indication that he had more—had children and children's children down to a fifth generation, 659 years in all, omitting Shem. But I shall list the descendants of the one son in succession. Shem, then, was the father of Arphachshad; Arphachshad, of Kenah; Kenah, of Shelah. Shelah was the father of Eber, the pious and godfearing. Eber was the father of Peleg.[2]

2,3 And there was nothing on earth, no sect, no opinion clashing with another one, but only "men" were spoken of, "of one speech and one language."[3] There were only ungodliness and godliness, the natural law and the natural error of each individual's will, not learned from teaching or writings. There was no Judaism, no Hellenism, no other sect at all. But in

---

[3] Cf. Jer. Ep. (Epiph/John of Jerusalem) 51.6.7.
[4] Col 3:11; Gal 3:28

[1] Jub. 5.28; 7.1; 17, and 10.15. In this last, Lubar is said to be Noah's burial place.
[2] Gen 11:10-17
[3] Gen 11:1

a sense there was the faith which is now native to God's present day holy catholic church, a faith which was in existence from the beginning and was revealed again later. (4) Anyone who is willing <to make an> impartial <investigation can> see, from the very object of it, <that> the holy catholic church is the beginning of everything. Adam, <the> man who was formed at the first, was not formed with a body circumcised, but uncircumcised. He was no idolater, and he knew the Father as God, and the Son and Holy Spirit, for he was a prophet.

2,5 Without circumcision he was no Jew and since he did not worship carved images or anything else, he was no idolater. For Adam <was> a prophet, and knew that the Father had said, "Let us make man,"[4] to the Son. What was he, then, since he was neither circumcised nor an idolater—except that he exhibited the character of Christianity? (6) And we must take this to be the case of Abel, Seth, Enosh, Enoch, Methuselah, Noah and Eber, down to Abraham.

2,7 Godliness and ungodliness, faith and unbelief, were operative then—a faith which exhibited the image of Christianity and an unbelief which exhibited the character of ungodliness and transgression, contrary to the natural law, until the time I have just mentioned.

2,8 In the fifth generation after the flood, now when humanity was multiplying from Noah's three sons, through the succession of children's children and their children a total of 72 founding fathers and chieftains had arisen in the world. (9) And in going on and advancing from Mt. Lubar and the borders of Armenia, that is, from the land of Ararat, they arrived at the plain of Shinar where, we suppose, they chose to <settle>. Shinar is now in Persia but anciently it belonged to the Assyrians.

2,10 Consulting together there they took counsel with each other to build a tower and a city. Because they had migrated to Asia from the region next to Europe they were all called Scythians in the parlance of the time.

2,11 They laid the foundations of the tower and built Babylon. And God was not pleased with their foolish work, for he confounded their languages and divided them from one to 72, to correspond with the number of the men who were then alive. Thus they have been called Meropes because of the divided speech.[5] A blast of wind blew the tower over.

---

[4] Gen 1:26
[5] μεμερισμένοι

2,12 And so they were divided right and left over the whole earth, some returning to the place from which they had set out and some going to the east ahead of them, but others reached Libya. (13) Thus, if anyone wanted to determine the precise facts about these people he could find, in the case of each country, how each received his allotment. Thus Mistrem was allotted Egypt, Cush Ethiopia, Put Axumis, Ragman and Sabteka and <Dedan, also called Judad>, the region bordering on Garama. But not to go on too long in the composition of this preface here, I shall return to the subject and again take up the order in succession.

3.
<*Hellenism*>

3,1 And then, during the time between Eber, and Peleg and the building of the tower and the first city after the flood—which was founded in its actual building—came the beginning of the taking of counsel, and of autocracy. (2) For Nimrod[1] the son of Cush the Ethiopian, the father of Asshur, ruled as a king. His kingdom arose in Orech, Arphal and Chalana, and he also founded Tiras, Tubal and Laban in Assyria. The Greeks say that this is the Zoroaster who went on further to the east and became the original settler of Bactria

3,3 The world's transgressions were spread abroad from there, for Nimrod was the originator of wrong doctrine, astrology and magic—which is what some say of Zoroaster.[2] But in actual fact this was the time of Nimrod the giant; the two, Nimrod and Zoroaster, are far apart in time.

3,4 Peleg was the father of Reu, and Reu was the father of Serug, which means "provocation"; and, as I have been taught, idolatry and Hellenism began among men with him.[3] It was not with carved images yet, or with reliefs in stone, wood or silver-plated substances, or ones made <of> gold or any other material, that the human reason invented evil for itself and, with its freedom, reason and intellect, invented transgression instead of goodness, but only with paintings and portraits.

3,5 Nahor was born as a son to Serug and became the father of Terah. The making of images with clay and pottery began at this point, with the

[1] "Zoroaster the magus" is ruler of Bactria at Jer. Chron. 20,13 (Helm).

[2] For Nimrod as a magician, identified with Zoroaster, cf. Clem. Hom. 9.4-5.

[3] Idolatry begins with Serug at Jub. 11.1-6, but Jub. 11.14-17 and 12.1-8; 12-14 ascribe it to Terah.

art of this Terah. And with him the world arrived at its twentieth generation, comprising 3332 years.

3,6 And of the earlier men no one died before his father;[4] fathers died before their children and left their sons to succeed them. (Never mind Abel—he did not die a natural death.) (7) But since Terah had set up a rival to God by making one with his own pottery he was rightly repaid with the like of what he had done and was provoked to jealousy himself, through his own son. (8) Hence sacred scripture remarked with astonishment, "And Haran died before the eyes of his father, Terah, in the land of his nativity."[5]

3,9 A kind of succession of Scythianism, and the name for it, remained in being until his time, but there was no such thing as a sect yet, no device other than simply a "<first> fornication, thinking on idols."[6] And after that people made gods of wretched despots, or sorcerers who had deceived the world, by honoring their tombs. (10) And much later they made Cronus, and Zeus, Rhea, Hera and the rest of them into gods, and then they made one by worshiping Acinaces—and the Scythian Sauromatians made gods by worshiping Odrysus and the ancestor of the Thracians, from whom the Phrygian people are derived. This is why Thracians are named for the person called Thera, who was born during the building of the tower.

3,11 When error had its beginning history had arrived at the point I have indicated. <Hellenism began with the Egyptians, Babylonians and Phrygians>, and then made a hash of <men's> ways. After that historians and chroniclers borrowed from the imposture of the Egyptians' heathen mythology <and conveyed it to the other nations>, and this was how sorcery and witchcraft were invented. (12) These things were brought to the Greeks from the time of Cecrops. And at this time Ninus and Semiramis, Abraham's contemporaries, were living in Assyria, and it was the sixteenth Egyptian dynasty. But the only kings then were the kings of Sicyon,[7] the kingdom founded by Europs.

---

[4] Cf. Clem. Recog. 1.31.3 where, however, the crime for which Terah is punished is incest.

[5] Gen 11:28

[6] Cf. Wisd Sol 14:12.

[7] This chronological information comes from Eus. Chron. 42a,28 (Helm); cf. Jer. Chron. 16,2-17 (Helm).

4.
<*Judaism*>

1,1 And God chose Abraham who—again, characteristically of the holy catholic church—was faithful in uncircumcision, and was perfection itself in godliness, a prophet in knowledge, and in life, conformed to the Gospel. (2) For he had lived at home to honor his father <but>, like Peter, Andrew, James and John, he bade farewell to his family when he was called by God's bidding, in obedience to the One who was calling him.

1,3 And to avoid prolonging the account again, I am going to summarize. On reaching the age of 99 this patriarch was given the commandment of circumcision by God, and the character of Judaism originated from this, after Hellenism. And it was the twenty-first generation, 3431 years, <after> the foundation of the world. (4) For from the flood till the tower and Serug there was Scythianism, and there was Hellenism from Serug till Abraham—and until now. But there was no name of a sect derived from Abraham, other than simply the name of his godly self; and so those who were derived from Abraham were called Abramians.

1,5 For Abraham had eight sons, but Isaac was the sole heir. This was both because, as his father wished, he was living as an adherent of the true religion, and because he had been given to his father by God's promise. (6) Before him Abraham had Ishmael by the maidservant Hagar, and Khetura bore him six children. These were dispersed over the land called Arabia Felix—Zimram, Jokshan, Ishbak, Shuah, Medan and Midian. And the "son of the bondmaid"[1]—as I said, his name was Ishmael—also took up residence in <the wilderness> and founded the city called Paran in the wilderness. He had twelve children altogether; these were the ancestors of the tribes of the Hagarenes, or Ishmaelites, though today they are called Saracens.

1,8 Isaac had two sons, Esau and Jacob, and then the nation of the godly were called both Abramians and Isaacites. When Esau had gone off to Idumaea, the territory lying to the southeast of Canaan, he became the original settler of Mount Seir, and in his turn founded Edom, known as Rekem and Petra. (9) He had sons who were also called the "princes of Edom,"[2] and they ruled, each in turn, in Idumaea. The fifth in succession from him, leaving Abraham out of this number but counting from Isaac,

[1] Gal 4:30
[2] Cf. Exod 15:15.

was Job. (10) For Isaac was the father of Esau, Esau of Raguel, Raguel of Zara, and Zara of Job, who was called Jobab earlier, but was later named Job, shortly before the trial that came upon him. Circumcision was the custom (of all these persons).

1,11 By his father's and mother's advice Jacob fled from his brother Esau because of Esau's anger, to Padan in Mesopotamia beyond Souba in Mesopotamia. From there he took four wives in all of his own kin, and they bore him twelve children, also called "the patriarchs." (12) During his return to Canaan, to his father, Isaac, and his mother, Rebecca, he had a vision from God near the sources of the Jordan—the stream is called the Jabbok—perhaps where he had seen hosts of angels. (13) "And lo," we are told, "(there appeared) a man"—by which the scripture meant an angel—"at even, and wrestled with him until the breaking of the day."[3] As a blessing he gave Jacob a title of honor, "Israel." (14) When he left there Jacob named the place, "Sight of God." <Now> since the One who told him, "Thy name shall be called no more Jacob, but Israel shall it be called,"[4] <had named him Israel>, and had distinguished him by saying, "Thou hast had power with God, and with men thou shalt be mighty,"[5] they have been called Israelites from that time on.

2,1 Israel too went down to Egypt after Joseph's descent—he too, with his whole household of sons and grandsons, the wives we have spoken of and others, 70 souls in all. (2) The people of Israel lived in Egypt for five generations. For Jacob was the father of Levi and Judah and the other ten patriarchs; Levi was the father of Kohath; Judah of Pharez. Kohath was the father of Amram; Amram was the father of Moses. Pharez was the father of Esrom; Esrom was the father of Aram; Aram was the father of Aminadab, and Aminadab was the father of Nahshon.

2,3 During the lifetime of Moses and Nahshon, in the fifth generation reckoned from Levi, Israel departed miraculously from Egypt through the Red Sea, and encamped in the wilderness of Sinai. (4) And when God directed his servant Moses to make a count of men between 20 and 50 who could draw a sword and bear arms, he found as many as 628,500.

2,5 Inachus[6] was well known among the Greeks at that period. His daughter was Io, also called Atthis, for whom the present day Attica[7] is

---

[3] Cf. Gen 32:30.
[4] Gen 32:28
[5] Gen 32:28
[6] Clem. Alex. Strom. 1.102.4; Eus. Praep. Ev. 10.10; Jer. Chron. 7,20
[7] Jer. Chron. 44,1

named. Bosporus,[8] for whom the city of Bosporus on the Black Sea is named, was her son as well. The Egyptians call her Isis,[9] and also worship her as a goddess. Also with the same name as his is a river called Inachus.

2,6 It was then that the Greeks' mysteries and rites began. They had unfortunately been invented previously among the Egyptians, Phrygians, Phoenicians and Babylonians, but they were brought to the Greeks from Egypt by Cadmus,[10] and by Inachus himself—who had previously been named Apis, and had built Memphis.[11] They also originated with Orpheus and certain others (7) and were formed into heresies later, during the lifetimes of Epicurus, Zeno the Stoic, Pythagoras and Plato. These were in vogue from this time until the period of the Macedonians and Xerxes, king of Persia, after the first fall of Jerusalem and the captivity under Nebuchadnezzar and Darius, and the time of Alexander of Macedon's contemporaries. (8) For Plato was noted at that period, and his predecessors, Pythagoras and the later Epicurus. From this, as I said, the Greek writings got their impetus and reached their established form, and the philosophers' celebrated sects afterwards. These agree among themselves in error and produce a concordant science of idolatry, impiety and godlessness, but within the same error they clash with each other.

5.

Against Stoics. <Sect> three from Hellenism, but five of the series

1,1 And the Stoic notion of deity is as follows. They claim that God is mind, or the mind of the whole visible vault—I mean of heaven, earth and the rest—like a soul in a body. (2) But they also divide the one Godhead into many individual beings: sun, moon and stars, soul, air and the others. (3) And <they teach> the reincarnations of souls and their transmigrations from body to body, with <souls> being removed <from> bodies, entering others in turn and being born once more—along with much deceit of theirs they cap it all with this impiety. And they think that the soul is a part of God, and immortal.

1,4 Zeno was the founder of their Stoa, and there is much confused chatter about him. Some have said that he was <the son> of one Clean-

[8] Jer. Chron. 42,15
[9] Jer. Chron. 27,14
[10] Jer. Chron. 46,23
[11] Jer. Chron. 32,9

thes of Tyre. But others claim that he was a Citean, a Cypriote islander, and that he lived at Rome for a while but later advocated his doctrine at Athens, at the so-called Stoa. Some, however, say that there are two Zenos, Zeno of Elis and the one I have been speaking of. Both taught the same doctrine anyhow, even though there might be two of them. (5) He too, then, like the other sects, claims that matter is contemporaneous with God, and that there is a fate and fortune by which all things are directed and influenced.

1,6 Now then, I am going to <administer> a remedy for Zeno's condition, so far as this brief discussion of mine can do it. For rather than overloading the contents of the treatise, <I need only> give <the main points>. However, skimming the surface so as not to digress, I shall say to Zeno:

2,1 Where did you get the teaching of your doctrine, Mister? Or which Holy Spirit has spoken to you from heaven about your imposture? For you are obliged to say that two things, matter and God, are contemporary with each other. Your assertion will fall flat and prove untenable. (2) For you admit that someone whom you also call "almighty" is the creator, and you divide him into a plurality of gods. But what can he be the creator of, if matter is his contemporary? A matter which did not originate from any cause and is not subject to one must be its own master for itself. (3) And if the creator took his material from it and acquired it as a loan, this argues his weakness and must be a contribution which, due to his bankruptcy, has been made to a person who has not provided for the subsistence of his handiwork from his own resources, but from someone else's.

2,4 And there is a great deal wrong with your spurious notion of the transmigration of souls, you would-be sage with your promise of knowledge to humanity! For if the soul is part of God and immortal and yet you associate wretched bodies with its fashioning—not just <human> bodies, I suppose, but bodies of four-legged beasts and things that crawl and disgusting bugs—you associate them with the fashioning of the soul, which you say it has from God! And what could be worse?

3,1 You bring in fate besides, as though it is the cause of what happens to human and other beings. But your mythology is going to be refuted by one succinct argument. If wisdom, understanding, rationality and irrationality and everything else is brought about by fate, then forget about laws! Fate is in control of the adulterers and the others. Rather than the man, who acts under necessity, the stars which have imposed the necessity should pay the penalty.

3,2 Indeed I shall say some more about this, in another different way. No more diatribes! No more sophists, rhetoricians and grammarians, no more doctors and the other professions, and the countless manual trades! If it is fate that equips the educated and intelligent, no one should learn from a teacher. Let the thread-spinning Fates <weave> the knowledge by nature, as your imposture with its boastful oratory says.

6.
Platonists, Sect four from Hellenism, but six of the series

1,1 So much for Zeno and the Stoics. Although Plato tended in the same direction too <by his adherence to> reincarnation, the transmigration of souls, polytheism and the other idolatries and superstitions, he probably did not entirely agree with Zeno and the Stoics about matter. (2) For he himself knows God, and that all that is has been caused by the God who is.[1] But there is a first cause and a second and a third. And the first cause is God, but the second has been caused by God, <together with> certain powers. Through it and the powers matter has come into being.

1,3 For Plato makes the following claim: "Heaven came into being with time, and will thus be destroyed with it as well."[2] This is a revision of his own previous statements about matter. For at one time he too said that matter is contemporaneous with God.[3]

7.
Pythagoraeans, Sect five from Hellenism, but seven of the series

1,1 Pythagoras and the Peripatetics characterized God as one before Plato, but still adhered to other philosophies, and to the principles <of the philosophers I have been discussing>. Like them, Pythagoras and his followers in their turn proclaim the wicked, extremely impious doctrine of the immortalizations and transmigrations of souls and the dissolution of bodies.

1,2 Pythagoras finally died in Media. He says that God is a body, meaning heaven, and that the sun and the moon, the other stars, and the planets of heaven are God's eyes and his other features, as in a man.

---

[1] Plato Ep. 2, 312E
[2] Plato Timaeus, 37B
[3] Cf. Hipp. Refut. 1.19.6.

8.

Epicureans, Sect six from Hellenism, but eight of the series

1,1 Next after them, Epicurus introduced the world to the doctrine that there is no providence. He said that all things arise from atoms and revert back to atoms. All things, even the world, exist by chance, since nature is constantly generating, being used up again, and once more renewed out of itself—but it never ceases to be, since it arises out of itself and is worn down into itself.

1,2 Originally the entire universe was like an egg and the spirit was then coiled snakewise round the egg, and bound nature tightly like a wreath or girdle. (3) At one time it wanted to squeeze the entire matter, or nature, of all things more forcibly, and so divided all that existed into the two hemispheres and then, as the result of this, the atoms were separated. (4) For the light, finer parts of all nature—light, aether and the finest parts of the spirit—floated up on top. But the parts which were heaviest and like dregs have sunk downwards. This means earth—that is, anything dry—and the moist substance of the waters. (5) The whole moves of itself and by its own momentum with the revolution of the pole and stars, as though all things were still being driven by the snakelike spirit.[4]

I have spoken of these things if only in part, and in the same way these four sects ought to be refuted. <But this has been foregone> for the sake of shortness in reading.

(Judaism, continued)

2,1 And then as I have said already,[1] poets, prose authors, historians, astronomers, and the ones who introduced the other kinds of error made men's opinion giddy and confused by accustoming their minds to any number of bad cases and arguments. And this "first mistake" and misfortune of doctrine, "the invention of idols",[2] came into being.

2,2 Everything was divided into Hellenism and Judaism. However, it was not called Judaism yet, but until <five> persons had been born in succession it had the ancestral name of the true religion through Israel. (3) For Nahshon, who was born in the wilderness as head of the tribe of

---

[4] Cf. Ascl. 17.

[1] At 3,11

[2] Cf. Wisd Sol 14:12.

Judah, was the father of Salmon. Salmon was the father of Boaz; Boaz, of Obed; Obed of Jesse—while the godly were still being called Israelites. Jesse was the father of King David, the first of the tribe of Judah to reign as king. From him there then arose the successive kings of his line, one after another, with son succeeding father.

2,4 The actual first king in Israel before David himself, was Saul the son of Kish, of the tribe of Benjamin. <But he was rejected>, and no son succeeded him; his kingship passed to David and through David, the first, to the tribe of Judah. (5) For as a first child, Reuben was born to Jacob himself; as a second, Simeon; as a third, Levi, and as a fourth, Judah, and thus they are called Jews because of the tribe of Judah, with the name of the godly people changed in this way. Hence they were called (both) Israelites and Jews.

3,1 The four breeds on earth followed each other in succession until this time, with these four divisions distinguished from the earliest times until this one which I have mentioned here, and beyond. (2) That is: from Adam until Noah, Barbarism. From Noah until the tower, and until Serug two generations after the tower, the Scythian superstition. After that, from the tower, Serug and <Terah> until Abraham, Hellenism. From Abraham on, the true religion which is associated with this same Abraham—Judaism, (named) for his lineal descendant Judah. (3) God's Spirit-inspired, holy apostle Paul bears me out in this with some such words as, "In Christ Jesus there is neither barbarian, Scythian, Hellene nor Jew but a new creation."[3] (For at first, when creation had been made, it was new and had not been given any different name.) (4) And again, Paul says in agreement with this in another passage: "I am debtor both to the Hellenes and to the barbarians; both to the wise and to the unwise"[4] (meaning the Jews by "wise" but the Scythians by "unwise". And he says, "I am debtor," <meaning that "salvation is of the Jews.">)[5]

3,5 And so the entire nation of Israel were called Jews from the time of David. And all Israel continued to be called by their ancestral name of "Israelites," and to have the additional designation, "Jews," from the time of David, of his son Solomon, and of Solomon's son—I mean Rehoboam, who ruled in Jerusalem after Solomon.

---

[3] Col 3:11; Gal 6:15

[4] Rom 1:14

[5] John 4:22. Epiph gives these explanations to harmonize his two quotations, since Paul has mentioned only "Hellenes and Barbarians."

3,6 But to keep from getting side-tracked, bypassing the topic of the Jews' religion, and failing to touch on the subject of their beliefs, I shall give a few examples of them. For the facts about the Jews are, as we might say, perfectly plain to everyone. Hence I shall certainly not take the trouble to deal with this subject in great detail, but I must still give a few examples here.

4,1 Now Jews, who are Abraham's lineal descendants and the heirs of his true religion, have Abraham's circumcision, which he received by God's command at the age of ninety-nine, for the reason I have given earlier. It was so that his descendants would not repudiate the name of God on becoming strangers in a foreign land, but would bear a mark on their bodies instead to remind and convict them, and keep them true to their father's religion. (2) And Abraham's son, Isaac, was circumcised on the eighth day as God's commandment had directed. It is acknowledged that circumcision was by God's ordinance then, but then it had been ordained as a type. I shall prove this of it later, as we go on in order.

4,3 So Abraham's own children in succession—I mean beginning with himself, and Isaac and Jacob next, and Jacob's children after him—continued to be circumcised and adhere to the true religion in the land of Canaan (called Judaea and Philistia then, though its name is now Palestine) and in Egypt as well. (4) For Jacob, or Israel, went down to Egypt with his eleven children in the hundred and thirtieth year of his life. (Joseph, his other son, was already in Egypt reigning as king, though he had been sold by his brothers from envy. God's provision, which serves the righteous well, had turned their plot against this Joseph into a wonder.)

4,5 So Jacob went down to Egypt as I said, and his sons, wives and grandchildren, to the number of 75 persons—as the first book of Moses' Pentateuch, which clearly explains all this, tells us. (6) And they remained there for five generations—as I have said often enough, but must now repeat. For Jacob's posterity were the generations which are reckoned through Levi, the ancestor of the priests; and the ones which are reckoned through Judah, from whom in time came David, the first king. (7) And Levi was the father of Kohath and the others; Kohath was the father of Amram; Amram was the father of Moses, and of Aaron the high priest. Moses brought the children of Israel out of Egypt by the power of God, as the second book in the legislation says.

5,1 Still, it is obviously impossible to say distinctly what the regimen of the children of Israel was until this time, other than simply that they had the true religion and circumcision. (Though scripture does say, "The children of Israel multiplied in the land of Egypt and became abundant."[6] It must surely have been due to laxity that the period of their sojourn and intercourse (with gentiles) produced this "abundance.") (2) But it had not yet been indicated with full clarity what they should eat, what they should forbid, or the other things they were commanded to observe by the Law's injunction. (3) However, when they were departing from Egypt, in the second year of their exodus they were vouchsafed God's legislation at the hands of Moses himself.

5,4 The legislation God gave them taught them like a pedagogue—indeed the Law was like a pedagogue in giving its precepts physically,[7] but with a spiritual hope. It taught them circumcision; Sabbath observance; the tithing of all their produce and of any human or animal offspring which was born among them; the presentation of firstfruits both on the fiftieth and on the thirtieth days; and to know God alone and serve him. (5) His Name, then, <was> proclaimed under its aspect of Monarchy, but the Trinity was always proclaimed in the Monarchy and was believed in by the foremost of them, that is the prophets and nazirites.[8] In the wilderness Israel offered sacrifices and various kinds of worship to the all-sovereign God in the service of the holy tabernacle, which Moses had constructed from patterns God had shown him.

5,6 These same Jews received prophetic oracles too, concerning the Christ to come. He was called "prophet," though he was God; and "angel," though he was the son of God, but would become man and be reckoned with his brethren. So say all the sacred scriptures, especially Deuteronomy the fifth book in the legislation, and <the ones> that follow it.

6,1 By the time of the captives' return from Babylon these Jews had gotten the following books and prophets, and the following books of the prophets: (2) 1. Genesis. 2. Exodus. 3. Leviticus. 4. Numbers. 5. Deuteronomy. 6. The Book of Joshua the son of Nun. 7. The Book of the Judges. 8. Ruth. 9. Job. 10. The Psalter. 11. The Proverbs of Solomon. 12. Ecclesiastes. 13. The Song of Songs. 14. The First Book of Kingdoms. 15. The Second Book of Kingdoms. 16. The Third Book of Kingdoms. 17. The Fourth Book of Kingdoms. 18. The First Book of Chronicles. 19. The Second Book of Chronicles. 20. The Book of the Twelve Prophets. 21. The Prophet Isaiah. 22. The Prophet Jeremiah, with the Lamentations

[6] Exod 1:7
[7] The pedagogue was authorized to beat his charges.
[8] ἡγιασμένοις

and the Epistles of Jeremiah and Baruch. 23. The Prophet Ezekiel. 24. The Prophet Daniel. 25. I Ezra. 26. II Ezra. 27. Esther. (3) These are the 27 books given the Jews by God. They are counted as 22, however, like the letters of their Hebrew alphabet, because ten books are doubled and reckoned as five. But I have explained this clearly elsewhere. (4) And they have two more books of disputed canonicity, the Wisdom of Sirach and the Wisdom of Solomon, apart from certain other apocrypha.

6,5 All these sacred books taught Judaism and Law's observances until the coming of our Lord Jesus Christ. (6) And the Jews would have been all right under the Law's tutelage if they had accepted the Christ whom their pedagogue, I mean the Law, foretold and prophesied to them so as to learn, not of the Law's destruction but of its fulfillment, by accepting Christ's divinity and incarnation. For the types were in the Law, but the truth is in the Gospel.

6,7 The Law provides for physical circumcision. This served for a time until the great circumcision, baptism, which cuts us off from our sins and has sealed us in God's name. (8) The Law had a sabbath to keep us for the great Sabbath, the rest of Christ, so that in Christ we might enjoy a Sabbath-rest from sins. (9) And in the Law a lamb, a dumb animal, was sacrificed to guide us to the great, heavenly Lamb, slain for us and "for the whole world."[9] (10) And the Law ensured tithing, to keep us from overlooking the "iota," the ten, the initial letter of the name of Jesus.

7,1 Now since the Jews were guided by the type and did not reach the fulfillment which is proclaimed by the Law, by the prophets and others, and by every book (in scripture), they were put off the estate. And the gentiles came on, since Jews can no longer be saved unless they return to the grace of the Gospel. For every ordinance has been violated by them as each text says, in every scripture. (2) But briefly, with one text, I shall state the inevitability and unalterability of the declaration against them. Their sentence is plain to see as Scripture says, "Whatsoever soul will not hearken unto that prophet shall be cut off from his tribe, and from Israel, and from under the heavens."[10] (3) In other words the Lord is to give a final, saving confirmation of the truths he has imparted mystically through the Law, and a person who does not listen to him, and refuses to, cannot be saved even though he keeps the Law. For the Law cannot perfect the man, since the ordinances in it have been written physically and their real fulfillment is in Christ.

[9] John 2:2
[10] Deut 18:19; Exod 12:15; 19

7,4 So much for Judaism—I did mention a few points, so as not to omit all the facts about them, but to give them in part. For the subject of the Jews, and the refutation of them, is known beforehand, as we might say, to everyone. (5) I also explained their origin, how they had their beginning. At first <the> godly people were named <Abramians> after the patriarch Abraham's godly self because they were his descendants, but Israelites after his grandson, I mean Jacob or Israel. (6) But all the twelve tribes were called both Jews and Israelites from the time of David, the king from the tribe of Judah, and until David's son Solomon, and Rehoboam, who was Solomon's son but David's grandson.

7,7 And because of God's chastisement and Rehoboam's unworthiness, the twelve tribes were divided, and became two and a half with Judah—that is, with Rehoboam—and nine and a half with Jeroboam. (8) The nine and a half were called both Israelites and Israel, and were ruled by Jeroboam, the son of Nebat, in Samaria. But the two and a half at Jerusalem were called Jews, and were ruled by Solomon's son, Jeroboam. (9) And in turn there was a succession of kings. Rehoboam was the father of Abijah; Abijah, of Asa; Asa, of Jehoshaphat; Jehoshaphat, of Jehoram; Jehoram, of Ahaziah; Ahaziah, of Joash; Joash, of Amaziah, Amaziah, of Azariah or Uzziah; Azariah or Uzziah, of Jotham; Jotham, of Ahaz; Ahaz, of Hezekiah. At the time of Hezekiah and Ahaz, tribes from Israel were taken as captives to the mountains of Media. (10) After this, Hezekiah became the father of Manasseh. Manasseh was the father of Amon; Amon, of Josiah. Josiah was the father of Jeconiah, or Shallum, also called Amasiah. This Jeconiah was the father of the Jeconiah who is known as Zedekiah and Jehoiakim.

8,1 And no reader need have any doubt about him. Rather, he should admire the full discussion which has helpfully been set down here for good people who, for the sake of useful learning, would like to understand the precise sense of scripture. Simultaneously with the help they must feel relieved at once, at having regained the wording which, because of an ambiguity, certain ignorant persons have removed from the text with the intent of improving it.

8,2 For St. Matthew enumerated the generations (of Christ's genealogy) in three divisions,[11] and said that there were fourteen generations from Abraham tilll David, fourteen from David till the captivity, and fourteen from the captivity until Christ. The first two counts are plain to be seen with no lack of an item, for they include the times previous to Jeconiah. (3) But

[11] Matt 1:1-17

we see that the third count no longer has the total of fourteen generations found in a succession of names, but the total of thirteen.[12] This is because certain persons found a Jeconiah next to another Jeconiah, and thought that the item had been duplicated. (4) It was not a duplication however, but a distinct item. The son had been named "Jeconiah the son of Jeconiah" for his father. By removing the one name as though for scholarship's sake, certain persons ignorantly made the promise (which is implied in the text) come short of its purpose with regard to the total of the fourteen names, and destroyed the regularity of the arrangement.

8,5 So the Babylonian captivity began then, from the time of Jeconiah. During this time of the captivity, the elders approached Nebuchadnezzar in Babylon and begged that some of his own subjects be sent to Israel as settlers, to keep the country from becoming an uninhabited wasteland. (6) He accepted their appeal—he did not put them off—and sent four groups of his own people, called the Cuthaeans, Cudaeans, Seppharuraeans and Anagogavaeans. They then migrated to Samaria with their idols and settled it, choosing this land because of its richness and very great fertility.

8,7 But in time, because they kept being mauled by the wild beasts—lions, leopards, bears and the other predators—they sent to Babylon, asking with extreme astonishment what sort of life <the> former settlers had lived to be able to withstand the rapine and violence of the beasts. (8) The king sent for the elders and asked how they had conducted themselves <when> they held Judaea, and how they had escaped the rapine of the beasts, since there were so many onslaughts and maimings by animals in that country.

8,9 They told him of God's legislation and wisely pointed out to him the conclusion a reasonable judgment must draw, by saying that no nation could settle there unless it kept the Law of the God of heaven, given through Moses. For God is the protector of the land, and will not have the sins of idolatry and the rest committed in it by gentile nations.

8,10 The king paid attention, was convinced by his informants' entirely true explanation, and demanded a copy of the Law. They gave him one without demur, and with the Law also sent from Babylon Ezra, a priest, as a teacher of the Law, to teach the Law of Moses to the Assyrians who had settled in Samaria—the Cuthaeans and <the> others. (11) This happened in about the thirtieth year of the captivity of Israel and Jerusalem.

So Ezra and his successors taught the nation in Samaria; and those who had received the Law through Ezra, who came from Babylon, were called

[12] Cf. Matt 1:12-17.

Samaritans. Another forty years went by and the captivity was revoked, and Israel returned from Babylon.

9,1 It is an amazing coincidence that, to correspond with the four nations, four sects have also arisen in that very nation—I mean first, the sect of Essenes; second, of Gorothenes; third, of Sebuaeans; and fourth, of Dositheans. Here I can begin my treatment of the subject of sectarianism,[13] and shall briefly explain how it <arose>. (2) How else but <in the same way in which> tribes arose from the proliferation of the different languages, various nations emerged to correspond with each tribe and clan, every nation chose its own king to head it, and the result was the outbreak of wars, and conflicts between clashing nations. For each used force to get its own way and, from the insatiable greed which is common to us all, to appropriate its neighbors' property. (3) So too at this time we have been discussing. Since there had been a change in Israel's one religion, and the scripture of the Law <had been transferred> to other nations—I mean to Assyrians, the ancestors of the colonist Samaritans—the division of Israel's opinion also resulted. (4) And then error arose, and discord began to sow seed from the one true religion in many counterfeit beliefs, as each individual thought best, and thought that he was proficient in the letter (of scripture) and could expound it to suit himself.

9.

Against Samaritans,[1] *Sect seven from Hellenism, but nine of the series*

1,1 The Samaritans are the first of the sects which were founded on sacred scripture after those Greek heresies—which were <invented> by men by crack-brained thinking, with their own reason without sacred scripture. (2) The whole nation, then, were called the nation of Samaritans.

1,2 "Samaritans" means "watchmen"—because of their being stationed in the land as watchmen, or because of their being observers of the commandment in accordance with the Law of Moses. (3) Also, the mountain where they settled was named Somoron—and Somer too for one of the ancients, Somoron the son of Somer was his name. (4) Somoron was a son of one of the Perizzites and Girgashites who inhabited the land at that time.

[13] Epiph is about to conclude his Proem. Cf. his wording of 2,13 with that of 9,4.

[1] Fil. 7 gives a description of the Samaritans which is not unlike that of Epiph, but is plainly from a different source.

They were descendants of Canaan,[2] who had seized this land, the one that is now called Judaea or Samaria. It belonged to the sons of Shem and was not their own,[3] since Canaan himself was the son of Ham, Shem's uncle (sic). (5) And thus they are called Samaritans for various reasons—Somer, Somoron, their guardianship of the land, and their observance of the precepts of the Law.

2,1 The first difference between them and Jews is that they were given no text of the prophets after Moses but only the Pentateuch,[4] which was given to Israel's descendants through Moses, at the close of their departure from Egypt. (By "Pentateuch" I mean Genesis, Exodus, Leviticus, Numbers and Deuteronomy; in Hebrew their names are B'reshith, Elleh sh'moth, Vayyiqra, Vayidabber and Elleh ha d'varim.) (2) There are intimations of the resurrection of the dead in these five books, but it is certainly not proclaimed plainly. There also hints in them of God's only-begotten Son, of the Holy Spirit, and of opposition to idolatry, but as the most obvious doctrine in them the subject of <the> Monarchy is introduced, and in the Monarchy the Trinity is proclaimed spiritually.

2,3 Those who had received the Law were eager to abandon idolatry and learn to know the one God, but had no interest in more precise information. Since they had gone wrong and not clearly understood the whole of the faith and the precise nature of our salvation, they knew nothing about the resurrection of the dead and do not believe in it.[5] And they do not recognize the Holy Spirit, for they did not know about him.

2,4 And yet this sect, which denies the resurrection of the dead but rejects idolatry, (is) idolatrous in itself with knowing it, because the idols of the four nations are hidden in the mountain they libelously call Gerizim. (5) Whoever cares to make an accurate investigation of Mount Gerizim, should be told that the two mountains, Gerizim and Ebal, are near Jericho—across the Jordan east of Jericho, as Deuteronomy and the Book of Joshua the son of Nun tell us.[6] (6) They are unwitting idolaters then, because, from wherever they are, they face the mountain for prayer, <thinking> it sacred, if you please! For scripture cannot be telling a lie when it says, "They continued even to this day keeping the Law and worshiping their idols,"[7] as we learn in the Fourth Book of Kingdoms.

[2] Fil. 7.1 makes Samoreus the son of Canaan.
[3] Jub. 10.27-34
[4] Cf. Fil. 7.1.
[5] Cf. Fil. 7.2.
[6] Cf. Deut 11:29-30.
[7] Cf. 4 Kms 17:32-34.

3,1 But they are refuted in every way with regard to the resurrection of the dead. First from Abel, since his blood conversed with the Lord after he died. But blood is not soul; the soul is in the blood. And God did not say, "The soul crieth unto me," but, "The blood crieth unto me,"[8] proving that there is hope for a resurrection of bodies.

3,2 Moreover Enoch was translated so as not to see death, and was nowhere to be found. Sarah too, made fruitful again at the implantation of seed, after her womb was dead and her menstrual flow dried up; conceiving a child by promise in her old age, because of the hope of the resurrection.

3,3 And this is not all. When Jacob too was <seeing to> his own bones, he was giving orders about them as of things that were not going to perish. And not only he but Joseph too, when he gave his orders in his turn, gave indication of the form of the resurrection.[9] (4) And this is not all. Moreover Aaron's rod, which budded when it was dry, bore fruit again in hope of life, showing that our dead bodies will arise, and pointing to resurrection. And Moses' wooden rod similarly gave token of resurrection, since it was brought to life by God's will and became a serpent.

3,5 Moreover, in blessing Reuben Moses says, "Let Reuben live, and let him not die,"[10] though he <means> someone who has died long ago. This is to show that there is life after death, but a sentence of second death, for damnation. So he gives him two blessings by saying, "Let him live," at the resurrection, and "Let him not die," at the judgment—not meaning death by departing the body, but death by damnation.

3,6 These few points will suffice against the Samaritans. But they have some other customs too, perfectly stupid ones. They wash with urine when they return from a foreign land, <as though> they had been contaminated, if you please! Whenever they touch someone else, who is a gentile, they immerse themselves in water with their clothes on.[11] For they think it is pollution to take hold of one person, or touch another,[12] if he is of another persuasion. But they have a bad case of insanity.

4,1 But pay attention, friend, and you will know what an easy thing their foolishness is to refute. They abhor a dead body on sight since they

---

[8] Gen 4:10

[9] I.e., resurrection is bodily.

[10] Deut 33:6

[11] Cf. Hipp. Refut. 9.15.3-6.

[12] A similar attitude toward outsiders sometimes appears in the Qumran documents; see 1Q S 5,14-20 (Wise et al. p. 132); CD 12,6-11 (op. cit. p. 70); 13,12-15 (op. cit. p. 71).

are dead in their works themselves. For not one but many testimonies witness that a corpse is not unclean, but that the Law was speaking symbolically. (2) For no "two or three witnesses," but 620,000 bear me out in this, the ones which were counted in the wilderness, <and buried the people that lusted in the wilderness>. And as many others and more, and many more still—the ones which followed Joseph's burial urn. It was carried with them for forty years during the entire period of the sojourn, and it was not abhorred and did not pollute.

4,3 The Law was telling the truth in saying, "He that toucheth the corpse remaineth unclean until even, and shall wash himself with water and be purified."[13] But it was saying this symbolically of the death of our Lord Jesus Christ from his suffering in the flesh. (4) This can be demonstrated from the word, "the," the so-called definite article. Wherever the article appears, it is confirmatory of someone who has been specified and is easily recognizable because of the article. But without the article we must understand the word indeterminately, of anyone. (5) If we say "king," for example, we mean the name but have not shown clearly which king is specified; we speak both of a "king" of Persians, and a "king" of Medes and Elamites. But if we say "the king" with the addition of the article, what we mean is beyond doubt. The king in question, someone called king, someone known to be king, or the ruler of this or that kingdom is implied by the article.

4,6 And if we say "god" without the article, we have spoken either of any heathen god, or of the actual God. But if we say "the God," it is clear that because of the article we mean the actual God, who is the true God and is known to be. And so with "man" and "the man."

4,7 And if the Law were saying, "If ye touch *a* corpse," the sentence[14] would be pronounced against everyone, and the word in question would simply apply <to> every dead body. But since it says, "If one touch *the* corpse," it is referring to one particular corpse—I mean to the Lord, as I have already explained. (8) The Law was saying this symbolically, of those who would lay hands on Christ and consign him to a cross, since they had need of purification till their sun should set, and another light dawn on them through the baptism of water, the "laver of regeneration."[15] (9) Peter bears me out here in speaking to the Israelites at Jerusalem who asked

[13] Cf. Lev 11:24-25.
[14] I.e., the sentence, "You must go into temporary exile."
[15] Titus 3:5

him, "Men and brethren, what shall we do?"[16] because he had said "this Jesus whom ye have crucified," to them. And when they were pricked to the heart he said, "Repent, men and brethren, and let every one of you be baptized in the name of our Lord Jesus Christ, and your sins will be forgiven, and ye shall receive the gift of the Holy Spirit."[17]

4,10 So the law is not speaking of a corpse—or, even though the Law speaks of a corpse, it is speaking of a particular one. <For of an unspecified corpse> it gives a different decree, since it says, "If a corpse pass by, shut your doors and windows, lest the house be defiled"—as though it were saying, with reference to the hearing of a sin, "If you hear a sound of sin, or (see) a sight of transgression, shut your eye to lust, your mouth to evil-speaking, and your ear to wicked rumor, lest the whole house"—that is, the soul and the body—"be killed." (11) This is why the prophet too says, "Death is come up through the windows,"[18] and surely does not mean our actual windows—otherwise we could shut our windows and never die. But the bodily senses—sight, hearing and so on—are our windows through which death enters us if we sin with them.

4,12 Joseph buried Israel, then, and was not rendered unclean, even though he had fallen on his face and kissed him after his death. And scripture does not say that he washed for purification. (13) The tradition I have been taught says that the angels buried the body of the sainted Moses,[19] and they did not wash; and neither were the angels profaned by the saint's body. (5,1) And again, I am afraid of dragging out the solution of our problem.[20] Bby one argument, or a second, a wise man will be given skill in the Lord against the opposition.

5,2 And even though I shall need to speak briefly of the Spirit I do not mind. For example, the Lord expressly says to Moses, "Bring up unto me seventy elders into the mount, and I shall take of the Spirit that is upon thee, and will pour it out upon them, and they shall lend thee aid."[21]

5,3 And to inform us about the Son, <the> Father says, "Let us make man in our image and after our likeness."[22] "Let us make," does not mean one person (alone), and neither does, "The Lord rained upon Sodom and Gomorrah fire and brimstone *from the Lord* out of heaven."[23]

---

[16] Acts 2:37
[17] Acts 2:36
[18] Jerem 9:20
[19] Cf. Evodius/Aug. Ep. 158.6.
[20] The problem posed at 4,1
[21] Num 11:16-17
[22] Gen 1:26
[23] Gen 19:24

5,4 And <there is no point in arguing with Samaritans> about prophets. Since they were given <only> the Pentateuch at first and no further scriptures, they conformed only to the Pentateuch alone and not the rest. Hence today, even if someone speaks of the others to them—I mean David, Isaiah and the prophets after them—Samaritans do not receive them. They are prevented from that by the tradition they have, which has been brought on to them from their own ancestors.

5,5 And let this conclude my sketch of the Samaritans. I have deliberately given it in brief, for fear of stringing out the content of my treatise.

10.
Against Essenes, Sect one after Samaritans,[24] *but ten of the series*

1,1 The Samaritans were divided into four sects. These agreed <on> circumcision, the Sabbath and the <other provisions> of the Law. But each of the three differed from its fellows—with the sole exception of the Dositheans, in unimportant ways and to a limited extent.

1,2 The Essenes continued their original practice and never went beyond it. After them, the Gorothenes disagreed over a certain small point for a dispute has arisen between them, I mean between the Sebuaeans, Essenes and Gorothenes. (3) The nature of the dispute is this. The Law directed the Jews to gather at Jerusalem from all quarters—often, <and> at three times of the year, the Feast of Unleavened Bread, Pentecost and Tabernacles. (4) There were Jews living here and there within the boundaries of both Judaea and Samaria, and they naturally used to cross Samaria on their way to Jerusalem. (5) Since (Jews and Samaritans) would meet at one season, (each) with their gathering for the festival, clashes would result. Besides, when Ezra was building Jerusalem after the return from Babylon, and the Samaritans asked if they could contribute aid to the Jews and take part in the building, and were refused by Ezra himself, and by Nehemiah

[24] The tradition which surprisingly locates the Essenes in Samaria might find some justification in Josephus' remark that they were widely dispersed, see Jos. Bel. 2.8.4. See also Wise's Introduction in *The Dead Sea Scrolls: A New Translation*. At Eus. H. E. 4.22.7 Essenes are called a Jewish sect. Fil. 9, which makes the Essenes Jewish rather than Samaritan, gives a description of them which is not dissimilar to that of Josephus.

11.

Against Sebuaeans, Sect two from Samaritans, but eleven of the series

1,1 then in rage and anger the Sebuaeans changed the dates of these festivals, first because of their anger at Ezra, but secondly for the reason I have mentioned, the one which provoked them to battle because of the people crossing their land. (2) They put the new moon of the Feast of Unleavened Bread after the new year, which falls in the autumn—that is, after the month of Tishri, which is called August by the Romans but Mesori by the Egyptians, Gorpiaeus by the Macedonians, and Apellaeus by the Greeks. (3) They begin the new year at that point and celebrate the Days of Unleavened Bread immediately, but they celebrate Pentecost in the fall, and observe their Feast of Tabernacles at the time when the Days of Unleavened Bread and Passover are being kept among the Jews.

12.

Against Gorothenes,[25] *Sect three from Samaritans but twelve of the series*

1,1 But the Gorothenes and the others were not convinced by the Sebuaeans. When Essenes are in the neighborhood of the others they do the same as they;[26] only the Gorothenes and Dositheans have the quarrel with the Sebuaeans. (2) And they, I mean the Gorothenes and Dositheans, keep the Festivals of Unleavened Bread, Passover, Pentecost and Tabernacles, and their one set fast day, when the Jews observe them. The others though (i.e., the Sebuaeans) do not keep them then, but in in their own way in the months I have mentioned.

13.

Against Dositheans,[27] *Sect four from Samaritans, but thirteen of the series*

1,1 Now Dositheans differ from these (others) in many ways. They acknowledge the resurrection and have ascetic disciplines. They abstain

[25] Gorothenes are mentioned at Eus. H. E. 4.22.5 where they are said to have been founded by a Gorothaeus.

[26] This seems most unlikely, especially given the strictness as to the dates of festivals in the Qumran community. See, e.g., 1Q S 1,14-15 (Wise et al. p. 140) and Qumran's calendrical texts in general (op. cit. p. 317f.).

[27] Dositheans are mentioned or discussed at Eus. H. E. 4.22.5; PsT 1.1; Fil. 4; Orig. In

from meat; moreover some abstain from matrimony <after having lived in that state>, while others are even virgins. (2) They likewise have the customs of circumcision, the Sabbath, and not touching one person or another out of loathing for all humanity. It is said that they keep fasts and have a rigorous discipline.

1,3 Dositheus' reason for holding these views was the following. Coming from the Jews, he joined forces with the Samaritan peoples.[28] He was foremost in their legal education and mishnahs,[29] and was ambitious for the highest rank, and because he failed to achieve it and was not considered of any account among the Jews, he defected to the Samaritans and founded this sect.

1,4 From an excess of would-be wisdom he retired to a cave somewhere. It is said that he persisted in futile, hypocritical fasting, and so died from lack of bread and water—willingly, if you please! After a while people came to visit him, and found his body reeking with decay and breeding worms, and a cloud of flies swarming on it.[30] By ending his own life in this futile way he became the cause of their sect, and his imitators are named Dositheans, or Dosithenes, after him.

2,1 And as far as I have learned, these are the differences between these four sects; they will be refuted by what I have said about them. (2) But I shall return to the successive infiltrations (into our ranks), both linking the victims of imposture with each other, and giving the case against them by exposing their vile practices and briefly refuting the poisonous bite of these vicious, deadly serpents.

This concludes the four Samaritan sects. Judaism remains to be dealt with. Judaism was divided into seven sects.[31]

Joh 13.27; Princ. 4.3.2, and Comm Ser. In Matt 33 (Klostermann p. 59) where Dositheus' Sabbath regulations are ridiculed. See also Clem. Rec. 1.54.2-5; Hom 2.24; Const. Ap. 6.8.1; Jer. Vit. Paul. 13.

[28] Eus. and the Pseudo-Clementines make Dositheus Jewish, while PsT and Fil. say he is Samaritan. Epiph might be attempting to reconcile the two traditions.

[29] δευτερώσεις

[30] Or. In Joh. 13.27 notes that the Samaritans believed that Dositheus had not died. The above appears intended to refute this.

[31] Eus. H. E. 4.22.5, quoting Hegesippus, also counts seven: Essenes, Galileans, Hemerobaptists, Masbotheans, Samaritans, Sadducees, Pharisees.

The Seven Sects of Judaism

1,1 Again, after these Samaritan sects and <the> Greek ones I spoke of earlier, a total of seven arose in Judaea and Jerusalem among the Jews,[1] before Christ's incarnation.

14.
Against Sadducees, Sect one from Judaism, but fourteen of the series

2,1 First are the Sadducees, who were an offshoot of Dositheus.[2] These give themselves the name of "Sadducees," and the title is derived from "righteousness," if you please; "zedek" means "righteousness." (But anciently there was also a priest named Zadok.)[3]

2,2 However, these did not abide by their master's teaching. They rejected the resurrection of the dead[4] and held an opinion like the Samaritans'. But they do not admit the existence of angels, though Samaritans do not deny this. And they do not know the Holy Spirit,[5] for they have not been deemed worthy of him. All their observances are just like the Samaritans'. (3) But they were Jews, not Samaritans; for they offered sacrifice in Jerusalem, and cooperated with Jews in everything else.

3,1 But they too will be demolished by the Lord's trustworthy saying, which they brought on themselves through his solution to their problem, when they came to him and said, "Can there be a resurrection of the dead?"

And "There were seven brothers,"[6] they said, "and the first married a wife and died childless. And the second took her—Moses commands a man to perform the levirate for his brother's wife if he has died childless, and marry her for his brother's sake, to beget offspring in the name of the deceased. So the first took her, and the second," they said, "and died, and so with all seven. But at the resurrection of the dead whose wife will she be, since all seven knew her?"

---

[1] For other lists of Jewish sects see Justin Dial. 80.4; Eus. H. E. 4.22.7; in NHC, Tri. Trac.112,18-22 accuses the Jews of spawning sects.

[2] Sadducees are traced to Dositheus at Clem. Recog. 1.54.4; PsT 1.1. Hipp. Refut. 9.29 links them with Samaria. Christian sources refer to them as a "sect" at Eus. H. E. 4.22.7; Justin Dial. 80.4; Const. Ap. 6.6.2.

[3] Cf. Ezek 40:46; 43:19; 44:15; 48:11; Matt 1:14. Priests at Qumran are regularly "sons of Zadok."

[4] Cf. Matt 22:23 and see PsT 1.1.

[5] Cf. Acts 23:8.

[6] Cf. Mark 12:18-27 parr.

3,2 But the Lord replied, "Ye do err, not knowing the scriptures nor the power of God. In the resurrection of the dead they neither marry nor are given in marriage, but are equal unto the angels. But that the dead will be raised Moses will teach you, as God declared to him and said, 'I am the God of Abraham, and the God of Isaac, and the God of Jacob.' But he is a God of the living, not of the dead."[7] And he "put them to silence." For they are easily cured and cannot hold out even for an instant against the truth.

15.
Against Scribes, <Sect> two from Judaism, but fifteen of the series

1,1 After these Sadducees came the Scribes—part way through their time or even exactly contemporary with them. Scribes were persons who repeated the Law as though they were teaching it as a sort of grammar. They observed the other Jewish customs but introduced a kind of extra, quibbling teaching, if you please. (2) They did not live just by the Law but in addition observed the "washing of pots, cups, platters"[8] and the other vessels of table service as though they were bent on the pure and holy, if you please—"washing their hands thoroughly," and also thoroughly cleansing themselves, in natural water and baths, of certain types of pollution. (3) And they had certain "fringes" as signs of their way of life, to vaunt their boast of it and win the praise of the onlookers. And it was their custom to put "phylacteries"—that is, broad borders of purple cloth—on their clothes.

1,4 One would think—since this too is in the Gospel—that it might be speaking of amulets, since some people used to call their amulets "phylacteries." (5) But the expression has nothing whatever to do with this. Scribes used to wear dresses or shawls, and robes or tunics[9] made of broad strips of cloth and made "purple woven"[10] with purple fabric, and precise speakers used to change the names of the purple strips to "phylacteries." Thus the Lord has called them "phylacteries" as they did. (6) But the sequel too, "and the craspeda of their outer garments," explains the meaning of the

[7] Matt 22:34

[8] Mark 7:4

[9] Cf. Ep. Aristeas 158; Justin Dial. 46.

[10] This is a folk etymology. Epiph derives φυλακτήριον from ἁλουργοῦφεῖς, "purple woven," by a rearrangement of its letters. For κοκκινὸν ῥᾶμμα and φυλακτήρια see Justin Dial. 46.4-5.

term; <it says> "the craspeda" to mean fringes, and "the phylacteries" to mean the purple strips. <For it says,> "Ye make broad the phylacteries and enlarge the craspeda, of your outer garments."[11]

1,7 Each Scribe had certain tassels at the four corners of his cloak, tied right to the thread, during the time when he was keeping continence or practicing celibacy. For each Scribe would set and designate a time of chastity or continence, and they had these tassels principally to give public notice of their undertaking, so that no one would lay a hand on the supposedly sanctified.

2,1 Scribes had four "repetitions."[12] One <was in circulation> in the name of the prophet Moses,[13] a second in that of their teacher called Aqiba or Bar Aqiba, another in the name Addan or Annan, also called Judas, and another in the name of the sons of Hasmonaeus. (2) Whatever customs they derive from these four traditions under the impression that they are wisdom—they are unwisdom mostly—are boasted of and praised, and celebrated and acclaimed as the teaching to be given first place.

16.

Against Pharisees,[14] *<Sect> three from Judaism, but sixteen of the series*

1,1 Another sect, that of the Pharisees, follows next after these two. They had the same ideas as they, I mean as the Scribes—whose name means "teachers of the Law," for the Lawyers were associated with them as well. (2) But again, the Pharisees also thought differently, since they had more regulations. For some of them, when they were practicing asceticism and had marked off a ten- or eight-year period or, similarly, a four-year period of chastity or continence, would quite often, along with constant prayer, enter upon the following ordeal—to avoid an accident or wet dream, if you please! (3) In order to live as much as possible without sleep, they would make their beds on benches only a span wide and stretch out on these at evening so that, if one went to sleep and fell on the floor, he could get up

---

[11] Mark 23:5

[12] δευτερώσεις. This would render "mishnahs," but whether Epiph understood the term in that form is uncertain.

[13] In the Mishnah, some anonymous regulations are designated *halakhah d'Mosheh mi-Sinai.*

[14] Pharisees are termed a "sectarians" at PsT 1.1; Hipp. Refut. 9.28; Eus. H. E. 4.22.7; Clem. Rec. 1.54.6; Justin Dial. 80.4; Const. Ap. 6.6.3.

again for prayer. (4) Others would gather pebbles and scatter them under their bedclothes, so that they would be pricked and not fall fast asleep, but be forced to keep themselves awake. Others would even use thorns as a mattress, for the same reason.

1,5 They fasted twice a week, on the second and fifth days.[15] They paid the tithe, gave the firstfruits—those of the thirtieth and those of the fiftieth days—and rendered the sacrifices and prayers without fail. (6) They went out in the Scribes' style of dress which we have been speaking of, with the shawl, the other fashions, and women's cloaks, and they walked in wide boots, and with wide tongues on their sandals. (7) But they were called "Pharisees" because they were separated from the others by the extra voluntary ceremonies they believed in;[16] "pharesh" is Hebrew for "separation."

2,1 They acknowledged the resurrection of the dead and believed in angels and a Spirit,[17] but like the others they knew nothing of the Son of God. (2) Moreover fate[18] and astrology meant a great deal to them. To begin with, they have other names in Hebrew for the Greek names that are taken from the astrology of the misguided. (3) For example, Helius is Chammah and Shemesh. Selene is Jareach, or Ha-l'banah, and hence is also called Mene—the "month" is called "the mene" and the moon is called "mene," as it also is in Greek because of the month.

Ares is Kokhabh Okbol; Hermes is Kokhabh Chochmah; Zeus, Kokhabh Ba'al; Aphrodite, Zerva or Lilith; Cronus is Kokhabh Shabb'tai. (They have other terms for him too, but I cannot give the names of these things exactly.)

2,4 Moreover, here again are their Hebrew names for what the misguided futilely regard as planets, though <the Greeks, who> wrongfully misled the world into impiety, call them the signs of the zodiac: Tela', Sor, T'omin, Zar'tan, Ari, Bethulah, Moznaim, 'Akrabh, Qesheth, G'di, Dalli, Daggim. (5) Following the Greeks to no purpose, they, I mean the Pharisees, translated the same terms into Hebrew as follows. Aries is what

[15] Cf. Luke 18:12; Matt 23:23. For the "second" and "fifth days" see Did.8.1; Const. Ap. 7.23.1.

[16] Cf. PsT 1.1; Clem Hom. 11.28.4; Orig. In Matt 23:23.

[17] Cf. Acts 23:8.

[18] According to Josephus, Pharisees believe that "some things, but not all, are the work of fate," Ant. 13.5.9. For Christian references to a Pharisaic belief in fate see Hipp. Refut. 9.28.5; Const. Ap.6.6.3.

they call Tela'; Taurus is Sor; Gemini, T'omim; Cancer, Zar'tan; Leo, Ari; Virgo, Bethulah; Libra, Moznaim; Scorpio, Akrabh; Sagittarius, Qesheth; Capricorn, G'di; Aquarius, Dalli; Pisces, Daggim.[19]

3,1 I have not put these things down in order to confuse the reader, or to endorse the vulgar chatter of those who introduced the confused, crazy nonsense of astrology to the world. The truth convicts this of incoherence and error. (2) In other treatises I have said a great deal in refutation of those who believe in fortune and fate; furthermore, I have written briefly against them in the preface to this work. But lest it be thought that I make vexatious attacks on people rather than finding out the exact truth from (their own) traditions and publishing it, I have mentioned these things even by name.

3,3 But (all this) is their ultimate embarrassment, and for people who acknowledge the resurrection and believe in a just judgment it is uncommon silliness. (4) How can there be (both) judgment and fate? It must be one or the other of the two. Either there is such a thing as fate, and then there is no judgment, since the (human) agent does not act of himself but of necessity, under fate's control. (5) Or else there is a judgment which really looms ahead, there are laws which serve as judges, and evildoers who stand trial—with law acknowledged to be just, and God's judgment absolutely trustworthy. Then fate means nothing, and there is no proof whatever of its existence.

4,1 The determination that, according to the difference between them, one person must be punished for his sins while another is commended for his good behavior, is made because of their ability to sin or not sin. (2) This <can be proved> concisely with one saying, <the> truth uttered by the prophet Isaiah in the person of the Lord, "If ye be willing and hearken to me, ye shall eat the good of the land; but if ye are not willing and do not hearken to me, a sword shall devour you. (3) For the mouth of the Lord hath spoken it."[20] Thus it is plain and clear to everyone, and not open to doubt, that the God <who> said in his own person, "If ye be willing and if ye are not willing," has granted free agency, so that whether he does right or pursues an evil course is up to the man.

4,4 Thus the notion of those who believe in fate is mistaken, most of all the Pharisees. What the Savior told them, not with just one saying but frequently, must be said of them even many times more often: "Woe unto

[19] For examples of the zodiac as a synagogue floor decoration with the signs named in Hebrew, see Goodenough vols. 1; 9.

[20] Isa 1:19-20

you, Scribes and Pharisees, hypocrites! For ye have abandoned the weightier matters of the Law, judgment and mercy, and pay tithes of dill and mint and rue. And ye make clean the outside of the cup and of the trencher, but their interior is full of uncleanness and excess."[21]

"And ye hold as binding an oath by that which lieth upon the altar, but deem void the oath by the altar itself. And ye say that to swear by heaven is nothing, but if one swear by that which is above heaven, this is demanded of him. Doth not the altar bear that which lieth upon it, and is not heaven the throne of him that sitteth upon it?[22]

"Ye say, if a man shall say to his father and mother, It is Corban, that is to say, a gift, by which thou mightest be profited by me, he shall no longer honor his father, and ye have made the commandment of God of none effect through the tradition of your elders.[23] (7) And ye compass sea and land to make one proselyte, and when he is made ye make him twofold more the child of hell than yourselves."[24]

4,8 What more than the sacred sayings could one cite in opposition to them? Indeed, I prefer to rest content with the Savior's wise, true statements, which the Pharisees could not face even for an instant.

17.

Against Hemerobaptists,[25] *Sect four from Judaism, but seventeen of the series*

1,1 A sect of Hemerobaptists, as they are called, accompanies these. It is no different from the others, but has the same ideas as the Scribes and Pharisees. However, it certainly does not resemble the Sadducees in the denial of resurrection of the dead, although it does in the unbelief which is found in the others.

But this sect had acquired this additional characteristic, of being baptized every day in spring, fall, winter and summer, so that they got the name of Hemerobaptists. (3) For this sect alleged that there is no life for a man unless he is baptized daily with water, and washed and purified from every fault.

---

[21] Cf. Matt 23:25.

[22] Cf. Matt 23:181-22.

[23] Mark 7:11; 9

[24] Matt 23:15

[25] Hemerobaptists are mentioned at Eus. H. E. 4.22.7; Const. Ap. 6.6.5; Justin Dial. 80.4. Clem. Hom. 11.23.1 uses the term of John the Baptist. Josephus attributes the custom of daily bathing to the Essenes (Jos. Bel. 2.8.1). The term translates the Hebrew טובלי יום, which in itself means persons who have incurred uncleanness on a particular day and bathed to remove it, and must "remain unclean until evening."

2,1 But this sect too I can refute with one argument, since the words[26] are expressions of unbelief on their part rather than of faith. If they are baptized every day their conscience is convincing them that the hope they had yesterday is dead, the faith and the purification. (2) For if they were satisfied with one baptism they would have confidence in this as in something living and forever immortal. But they must think it has been nullified since they bathed today, not to cleanse the body or get rid of dirt, but because of sins. Again, by taking another bath the next day, they have made it plain that the previous baptism of yesterday is dead. For unless yesterday's had died they would not need another the next day for the purification of sins.

2,3 And if they do not simply avoid sin, supposing that the water will cleanse them as they keep sinning every day, their supposition is of no use and their deed is undone and come too late. (4) Neither Ocean nor all the rivers and seas, the perennial streams and brooks and all the water in the world, can wash away sin, for this is not reasonable and is not by God's ordinance. Repentance cleanses, and the one baptism, through the pronouncing of the Name in the mysteries.

2,5 But I shall pass this sect by as well. I believe that I have given sufficient indication of the concise remedy for their lunacy, as it has been set down here for the benefit of the readers.

18.

Against Nasaraeans,[27] *Sect five from Judaism but eighteen of the series*

1,1 Next I shall undertake the describe the sect after the Hemerobaptists, called the sect of the Nasaraeans. They are Jews by nationality, from Gileaditis, Bashanitis and the Transjordan as I have been told, but descendants of Israel himself. This sect practices Judaism in all respects and have scarcely any beliefs beyond the ones that I have mentioned. (2) It too had been given circumcision, and it kept the same Sabbath and observed the same festivals, and certainly did not inculcate fate or astrology.

[26] I.e., the words ἡμέρα and βαπτίζειν.

[27] This group has some traits in common with the Mandaeans, whose usual name for themselves is "Nazoraeans", and who reject the Pentateuch. Lidzbarski explains the term, Nazoraean, as "Vertreter eines Berufes, besonders eines bestimmtes Lehrtätigkeit", *Ginza* pp. ix-x. However, the two groups are certainly not the same. Fil. 8 spells the name of the group "Nazoraeans"; his very uncomplimentary description of it has nothing in common with that of Epiph.

1,3 It also recognized as fathers the persons in the Pentateuch from Adam to Moses who were illustrious for the excellence of their piety—I mean Adam, Seth, Enoch, Methuselah, Noah, Abraham, Isaac, Jacob, Levi and Aaron, Moses and Joshua the son of Nun. However, it would not accept the Pentateuch itself. It acknowledged Moses and believed that he had received legislation—not this legislation though, they said, but some other.[28] (4) And so, though they were Jews who kept all the Jewish observances, they would not offer sacrifice or eat meat;[29] in their eyes it was unlawful to eat meat or make sacrifices with it. They claimed that these books are forgeries[30] and that none of these customs were instituted by the fathers. (5) This was the difference between the Nasaraeans and the others; and their refutation is to be seen not in one place but in many.

2,1 First, <in> their acknowledgment of the fathers and patriarchs, and Moses. Since no other writing speaks of them, how do they know the fathers' names and excellence if not from the Pentateuchal writings themselves? (2) And how is it possible that there is truth and falsehood in the same place, and that scripture partly tells the truth but partly lies, (3) when the Savior says, "Either make the tree good and his fruits good; or else make the tree corrupt and his fruits corrupt. For a good tree cannot bring forth evil fruit, neither can a corrupt tree bring forth good fruit?"[31]

2,4 Hence their idea and the teaching they inculcate is futile, and there are many grounds for its refutation. Thus not only are the events recorded in scripture famous to this day, but even the sites of the wonders are preserved. (5) First there is the spot where Abraham offered the ram to God, called Mount Zion to this day. Moreover, the site of the oak of Mamre, where the calf was served to the angels. But if Abraham served a meat-dish to angels, he would not fail to share some of it himself.

3,1 Moreover, the tradition of the lamb <which> was slaughtered in Egypt is still famous among the Egyptians, even the idolaters. (2) At the time when the Passover was instituted there—this is the beginning of spring, at the first equinox—all the Egyptians take red lead, though without knowing why, and smear their lambs with it. And they also smear the trees, the

[28] Jews are said to falsify the Law and the works of Abraham at the Mandaean *Ginza* 43,21-23.

[29] Animal sacrifices are, in effect, termed obsolete in the NHC tractate Gos. Phil. 54,34-55,1; they are also deprecated at Gos. Phil. 62,35-63,4 and Melch. 6,28-7,1.

[30] Lidzbarski translates the term with which Mandaeans reject the Torah as a Buch des Frevels, *Johannesbuch* 192,15-193,2.

[31] Matt 12:33 and 7:18

fig-trees and the rest, and spread the report that fire once burned up the world on this day. But the fiery-red appearance of the blood is a protection against a calamity of such a magnitude and such nature.

3,3 But where can I not find evidence of the rite?[32] Thus even today the remains of Noah's ark are still shown in Cardyaei.[33] (4) And if one were to make a search and discover them—it stands to reason—he would surely also find the ruins of the altar at the foot of the mountain. That was where Noah stayed after leaving the ark; and when he had offered some of the clean beasts, and their fat, to the Lord God, he was told, "Behold, I have given thee all things even as herbs of the field. Slay and eat!"[34]

3,5 But once more, I shall also pass by the sect's strangeness and foolishness. I am content with the few words I have said, inserted here with my limited ability to oppose the error of the sect we have been discussing.

19.
Against Ossaeans,[35] *Sect six from Judaism, but nineteen of the series*

1,1 After this sect in turn, comes another one which is closely connected with them, the one called the sect of the Ossaeans. These are Jews like the others, hypocritical in their behavior and horrid in their way of thinking. (2) I have been told that they originally came from Nabataea, Ituraea, Moabitis and Arielis, the lands beyond the basin of what sacred scripture calls the "Salt Sea." This is the one which is called the "Dead Sea." (3) And from the translation of the name, this "People of the Ossaeans" means "sturdy people."

1,4 The man called Elxai[36] joined them later, in the reign of the emperor Trajan[37] after the Savior's incarnation, and he was a false prophet. He wrote a book,[38] supposedly by prophecy or as though by inspired wisdom. They also say that there was another person, Iexaeus, Elxai's brother.

1,5 Elxai was deluded by nature and a deliberate fraud. Originally he was a Jew with Jewish beliefs, but he did not live by the Law. He introduced

---

32 Or: of the series (of instances of meat-eating)

33 Hipp. Refut. 10.30.7; Theoph. Ad Autol. 3.19.16-17 (Grant p. 124)

34 Gen 9:3 and Acts 10:13

35 This Sect is comparable with Hippolytus' Elchasaites, Hipp. Refut. 9.13.1-17.3, but Epiphanius' sources are not the same as Hippolytus'and are more ample.

36 Cf. Hipp. Refut. 9.13.1.

37 For this date see Hipp. Refut. 9.13.4.

38 Hipp. Refut. 9.13.1. At Eus. H. E. 6.38 the book is said to have fallen from heaven.

one thing after another and formed his own sect, (6) and designated salt, water, earth, bread, heaven, aether, and wind as objects for them to swear by as worship. But again, at some time he designated seven other witnesses—I mean the sky, water, "holy spirits" <as> he says, the angels of prayer, the olive, salt, and the earth.[39] (7) He has no use for celibacy, detests continence and insists on matrimony. And as though <by> revelation, if you please, he introduced some further figments of his imagination. (8) But he taught hypocrisy, by saying that even though <one> should happen to worship idols in time of persecution, it is not a sin—just so long as he does not worship them in his conscience and, whatever confession he may make with his mouth, he does not make it in his heart.

1,9 In addition the fraud ventured to produce a witness. He said that a Phineas, a priest of the stock of Levi, Aaron, and the ancient Phineas, escaped death in Babylon during the captivity by bowing down to the image of Artemis at Susa in the reign of King Darius. Thus all the things he teaches are false and futile.

2,1 <As has been said> earlier, Elxai was connected with the sect I have mentioned, the one called the Ossaean. Even today there are still remnants of it in Nabataea, which is also called Peraea near Moabitis; this people is now known as the Sampsaean. They imagine that they are calling Elxai a power revealed,[40] if you please, since "el" means "power" but "xai" is "hidden." (2) But the whole of the insolence of the custom[41] was exposed in our own time, and incurred serious disgrace in the eyes of those who were capable of perceiving the truth and being certain of it. (<For the sect> still <survived> even <in our time>, during the reigns of Constantius and the current emperors.) (3) For until Constantius' time a Marthus and a Marthana, two sisters descended from Elxai himself, were worshiped as goddesses in the Ossaean territory—because they were descended from this Elxai, if you please! Yet Marthus has recently died, (though Marthana is still alive)! (4) The deluded sectarians in that country would take even the sisters' spittle away with them, and the other dirt from their bodies, supposedly as a protection against diseases. They surely didn't

[39] The second of these two lists is found at Hipp. Refut. 9.15.2;5. A similar but shorter list, found in the Pseudo-Clementines at Ep. Pet. Jas. 4.1, is heaven, earth, water, air.

[40] ἀποκεκαλυμμένην. The Hebrew כסה means "hide." Is the meaning "a hidden power (which has now been revealed to the elect)"? Amidon, and Klijn and Rinnick, render "hidden power," perhaps from context taking the participle to mean "hidden away"?

[41] I.e., of giving Elxai a divine title. Since one of his "divine" descendants has died, he cannot have been divine.

work! But something that has gone astray is always proud and ready to be fooled—evil is a blind thing, and error a stupid one.

3,1 And how long shall I spend my time in speaking of all this charlatan's lies against the truth—(2) first, by teaching the denial of God and hypocrisy, with his claim that one can participate in the abominable sacrifices of idolatry, deceive the ones who hear him, and deny his own faith with his lips and not incur sin? It follows that their condition is incurable and cannot be corrected. (3) For if the mouth that confesses the truth is already prepared to lie, who can trust them not to have a deceived heart? The divine Word declares this expressly when he teaches in the Holy Spirit, "With the heart man believeth unto righteousness, and with the mouth confession is made unto salvation?"[42]

3,4 In turn, moreover, he supposedly confesses Christ by name when he says "Christ is the great king."[43] But from the deceitful, false composition of the book of his foolishness, I am not quite sure whether he taught this of our Lord Jesus Christ. For he does not specify this either but simply says "Christ," as though—from what I can gather—he means someone else, or is awaiting someone else. (5) For he forbids prayer facing east. He claims that one should not face this direction, but should face Jerusalem from all quarters. Some must face Jerusalem from east to west, some from west to east, some from north to south and south to north, so that Jerusalem is faced from every direction. (6) And notice the craziness of the fraud! He bans burnt offerings and sacrifices, as something foreign to God and never offered to him on the authority of the fathers and Law, and yet he says we must pray towards Jerusalem, where the altar and sacrifices were—<this man who> rejects the Jewish custom of eating meat and the rest, and the altar, and fire as something foreign to God! (7) In the following words he claims that water is fortunate while fire is hostile: "Children, go not unto the sight of fire, since ye are deceived; for such a thing is deceit. Thou seest it as very nigh," he says, "and yet it is afar off. Go not unto the sight of it, but go rather unto the sound of water." And he has lots of tall tales.

4,1 Then he describes Christ as a kind of power, and even gives his dimensions—his length of 24 schoena, or 96 miles, and his width of twenty-four miles, or six schoena, and similar prodigies about his thickness and feet, and the other stories. (2) And the Holy Spirit—a feminine one at that—is like Christ too, and stands like an image, above a cloud and

[42] Rom. 10:10
[43] Cf. Hipp. Refut. 9.15.1.

in between two mountains.[44] And I am going to skip the rest, so as not to trick the readers' hearing into mythology.

4,3 Later in the book he practices a deception with certain words and empty phrases by saying, "Let none seek the interpretation but let him say these things only in prayer." These too he has taken from the Hebrew, if you please—as I understand them in part—though Elxai's imaginings are worthless. He claims to say, "Abhar anid moibh nochile daasim ane daasim nochile moibh anid abhar selam." This can be interpreted as follows: (4) "Let the humiliation <which> is from my fathers pass, (the humiliation) of their condemnation, degradation and toil, by degradation in condemnation through my fathers. (Let it pass) from bygone humiliation by an apostleship of perfection."[45] (5) But all this applies to Elxai; his power and imposture have come to nothing.

If anyone cares to hear one word painfully rendered by one word, I do not mind doing even this. For the full satisfaction of those who want to hear them exactly, I shall give his very words, and their translations opposite them, thus: (6) "Abhar": Let it pass away. "Anid": "humiliation." "Moibh": "which is from my fathers." "Nochile": "of their condemnation." "Daasim": "and of their degradation." "Ane": "and of their toil." "Daasim": "by degradation." "Nochile": "in condemnation." "Moibh": "through my fathers." "Anid": "from humiliation." "Abhar": "bygone." "Selam": "in apostleship of perfection."

5,1 This, then, is the sect of those Ossenes, which lives the Jewish life in Sabbath observance, circumcision, and the keeping of the whole Law. Only by renouncing the books <of Moses> does it cause a schism—as the Nasaraeans do—since it differs from the other six of these seven sects. (2) <One text> will be enough to expose its foreignness to God, since the Lord plainly says, "The priests in the temple profane the Sabbath."[46] (3) But what can this profanation of the Sabbath be except that no one did work on the Sabbath, but the priests broke it in the temple by offering sacrifice, and profaned it for the sake of the continual sacrifice of animals?

---

[44] The Jewish document of the sixth century C.E., the Shiʿur Qomah, gives "the dimensions of the Creator" (Cohen p. 221 ff.) in parasangs. See also in Swartz, *Maʿashe Merkavah.* While this might be culturally related to the material in Elxai, there is no obvious literary dependence.

[45] Epiph has misread this as Hebrew, presumably from a Greek transliteration, and given a forced translation. Holl, following M. A. Levy, suggested that the words were an Aramaic formula, אנא מסעד עליכון ביום דינא רבא, "I am your help in the day of the great judgment," written as a palindrome. σελάμ might mean "finish" or even "peace."

[46] Matt. 12:5

5,4 And I shall pass this sect by as well. For again, Elxai is associated with the Ebionites after Christ, as well as with the Nazoraeans, who came later. (5) And four sects have made use of him because they were bewitched by his imposture: Of those <that came> after him, <the> Ebionites <and> Nazoraeans; of those before his time and during it the Ossaeans, and the Nasaraeans whom I mentioned earlier.

5,6 This is the <sixth> sect of the seven in Jerusalem. They persisted until the coming of Christ, and after Christ's incarnation until the capture of Jerusalem by the Emperor Titus, Domitian's brother but Vespasian's son, in the second year of his father Vespasian's reign. (7) And after Jerusalem's fall this, and the other sects which enjoyed a brief period of celebrity—I mean the Sadducees, Scribes, Pharisees, Hemerobaptists, Ossaeans, Nasaraeans and Herodians—lingered on until, at its time and season, each was dispersed and dissolved.

6,1 Any sensible person has only to prepare his own remedy, from their lunacy itself and the words of the proclamation of the deadly poison, despising their vulgar teaching and chatter. (2) Especially as the Lord says at once, in the Law and in the Gospel, "Thou shalt have none other gods,"[47] and, "Thou shalt not swear by the name of any other god."[48] And again he says in the Gospel, "Swear not, neither by heaven, nor by earth, neither any other oath. But let your Yea be Yea, and your Nay, Nay; whatsoever is more that these cometh of the evil one."[49] (3) It is my opinion that the Lord was making a prediction about this because certain persons would command us to swear by other names—in the first place, because it is wrong to swear, by the Lord himself or anything else; swearing is <of> the evil one. (4) Hence it was the evil one who spoke in Elxai—the one who compelled him not only to swear by God, but also by salt, water, <bread>, aether, wind, earth, and heaven. Anyone willing to be cured need only take an antidote, in passing as it were, through the two arguments in opposition to Elxai's imposture.

6,5 Next, passing by Elxai's nonsense and the deceitfulness of this sect, I shall compose the rebuttal of the seventh sect which was current among the Jews of that period. And it is this:

[47] Exod 20:3
[48] Cf. Exod 23:13.
[49] Jas 5:12 and Matt 5:37

20.
Against Herodians.[50] *Sect seven from Judaism, but twenty of the series*

1,1 And again, after this sect and the others there was a seventh, called the sect of Herodians. These had nothing different but <were> altogether Jews, good for nothing and hypocrites. They believed, however, that Herod was Christ, thought that the Christ awaited in all scriptures of the Law and prophets was Herod himself, [51](2) and were proud of Herod because they were deceived about him. This was because, (besides holding the vain opinion in order to gratify the reigning king), they were won to it by the wording of the text, "There shall not fail a leader from Judah, nor a ruler out of his loins, till he come for whom it is prepared"[52]—or, "for whom are the things prepared," as the other copies say.

1,3 [53]This was because Herod was the son of an Antipater of Ashkelon, a temple slave of the idol of Apollo. This Antipater's father was named Herod, and he too was the son of an Antipater.

Antipater was taken prisoner by Idumaeans and fathered Herod during his stay in Idumaea. (4) Since his father was poor and could not ransom his son—I mean Antipater—he remained there for a long time as a slave. But later, with his young son Herod, he was ransomed by public subscription and returned home. This is why some call him an Idumaean, though others know he was from Ashkelon.

1,5 Afterwards he made friends with Demetrius,[54] was appointed governor of Judaea, and became acquainted with the Emperor Augustus. Because of his governorship he became a proselyte, was circumcised himself, and circumcised his son, Herod. The rule of the Jews was allotted to Herod and he was king in Judaea as a tributary ruler, under the Emperor Augustus.

1,6 Since this person of gentile extraction was reigning as king, while the crown had come down in succession from Judah and David but the rulers and patriarchs of the tribe of Judah <had come to an end> and the crown had passed over to a gentile, the mistaken belief that he was Christ

---

[50] Herodians are mentioned at PsT 1.1; Fil. 28; Jer. Adv. Lucif. 23; Eus. H. E. 1.6.2-4. This last is probably Epiph's source, though he does not have it before him but is working from memory. On the subject of Epiph's faulty memory of Eusebius, see Pourkier, *L'hérésiologie.*

[51] Cf. PsT 1.1; Fil. 28.

[52] Gen 49:10. For the application of this see Eus. H. E. 1.6.2.

[53] For the following story see Eus. H. E. 1.6.2-4; 1.7.11.

[54] Eus. H. E. 1.6.7 mentions Hyrcanus rather than Demetrius, and says that Herod is appointed governor by the Senate and Augustus after Hyrcanus is taken prisoner by the Parthians.

seemed persuasive to the opinion of the deluded—(7) in consequence of the wording of the text I have quoted, "There shall not fail a ruler from Judah till he come for whom it is prepared."[55] It was as though they were obliged to take it <in the sense of> "It was 'prepared' for this ruler. The rulers from Judah have 'failed,' and this one is not descended from Judah—indeed, is not a descendant of Israel at all. <The> role of Christ was 'prepared' for someone like this."

2,1 But what follows refutes them because it says, "He is the expectation of the nations, and in him shall the peoples hope."[56] Which of the nations "hoped" in Herod? Which "expectation of the nations" awaits Herod? How did they think "He slept as a lion, and as a lion's cub; who shall raise him up?" applied? (2) Where did Herod "wash his garment in blood," or "his covering in the blood of the cluster,"[57] as our Lord Jesus Christ did by spattering his body with his own blood, and his covering with the blood of the cluster? (3) No, "Consider what I say, for the Lord will give thee understanding in all things."[58] For the purification of the whole of the Lord's people he came to cleanse their teeth of men's teaching with his own blood since these had been stained in the blood of fat and unlawful sacrifice. (4) And why should I say the multitudes of things (that suggest themselves)? There are many, and the time I have for the rebuttal of these sects does not permit me to prolong the discussion.

3,1 At all events, these were the seven sects in Israel, in Jerusalem and Judaea, and the four I mentioned in "Samaritans" in Samaria. But most of them have been eliminated. There are no Scribes any longer, no Pharisees, Sadducees, Hemerobaptists or Herodians. (2) There are only a handful of Nasarenes, perhaps one or two, above the Upper Thebaid and beyond Arabia; and the remnant of Ossaeans, no longer practicing Judaism but joined with the Sampsites, who in their turn <live> in the <territory> beyond the Dead Sea. Now, however, they have been united with the sect of the Ebionites. (3) And as a result they have lapsed from Judaism—as though a snake's tail or body had been cut off and a snake with two heads and no tail had sprouted from it, grown on and attached to a body chopped in half.

---

[55] Gen. 49:10.
[56] Gen 49:10b
[57] Gen 49:11
[58] 2 Tim 2:2

3,4 So much for my discussion of the four Samaritan and the seven Jewish sects, none of which exist any longer except just three Samaritan ones, I mean <those of the> Gorothenes, Dositheans and Sebuaeans, but no Essenes at all—as though they have been buried in darkness. And there are no more sects among the Jews except those of the Ossaeans, and a few isolated Nasaraeans. But Ossaeans have abandoned Judaism for the sect of the Sampsaeans, who are no longer either Jews or Christians. That will do for these.

Christ's sojourn here, and the presence of his advent and truth in the flesh, which is the one and only Faith of God (De Incarnatione)

1,1 Right on their heels came the arrival in the flesh of our Lord Jesus Christ, which overtook these seven sects at Jerusalem; his power extinguished and scattered them. But then, after his sojourn, all of the later sects arose. I mean they arose after Mary had been given the good tidings at Nazareth by Gabriel and in a word, after the Lord's entire sojourn in the flesh—or in other words, after his ascension.

1,2 For God was pleased that, for man's salvation, his own Son should descend and be conceived in a virgin womb although he was the Word from heaven, begotten in the bosom of the Father, not in time and without beginning but come in the last days; the divine Word truly begotten of God the Father, of one essence with the Father and in no way different from the Father, but immutable and unalterable, impassible and entirely without suffering, though he shared the suffering of our race.

1,3 He came down from heaven and was conceived, not of man's seed but by the Holy Spirit. He had truly received a body from Mary, for he had fashioned his own flesh from the holy Virgin's womb, had taken the human soul and mind and everything human apart from sin, and by his own Godhead united it with himself. (4) He was born in Bethlehem, circumcised in the cavern, presented in Jerusalem, embraced by Simeon, confessed in her turn by Anna the daughter of Phanuel, the prophetess, and taken off to Nazareth.

The following year he came to appear before the Lord in Jerusalem (5) and arrived at Bethlehem borne in his mother's arms, because of (her) kindred (there). Once more he was taken back to Nazareth, and after a second year came to Jerusalem and Bethlehem, borne by his own mother as before. And in Bethlehem he came to a house with his own mother and Joseph, who was an old man but was Mary's companion. And there, in the second year of his life, he was visited by the magi, was worshiped, received gifts, (6) and was taken to Egypt the same night because an angel had warned Joseph. He came back again from Egypt two years later, since Herod had died and Archelaus had succeeded him.

2,1 The Savior was born at Bethlehem of Judaea in the thirty-third year of Herod,[1] the forty-second of the Emperor Augustus. He went down into Egypt in the thirty-fifth year of Herod and returned from Egypt after Herod's death. (2) And so in the thirty-seventh year of that same reign of Herod, when Herod died after a reign of 37 years, the child was four years old.

2,3 Archelaus ruled for nine years. When Joseph left Egypt with Mary and the child at the beginning of his reign, hearing that Archelaus was king he went back to the Galilee and at this time settled in Nazareth. (4) Archelaus had a son, Herod the Younger,[2] and this Herod succeeded him as king in the ninth year of the reign of his father Archelaus; and the years of Christ's incarnation numbered thirteen.

2,5 In the eighteenth year of Herod surnamed Agrippa Jesus began his preaching and at that time received the baptism of John and preached an "acceptable year" opposed by no one—Jews, Greeks, Samaritans or anyone else. (6) Then he preached a second year, in the face of opposition; and this Herod had reigned for nineteen years while it was the Savior's thirty-second.

2,7 But in the twentieth year of Herod called the tetrarch came the saving passion and impassibility; the tasting of death, even of the death of a cross, of One who truly suffered and yet remained impassible in his divine nature. ("Forasmuch as Christ hath suffered in the flesh for us"[3] says the sacred scripture, and again, "being put to death in the flesh, but quickened by the Spirit,"[4] and what follows.) (8) He was crucified and buried, descended to the underworld in Godhead and soul, led captivity captive, and rose again the third day with his sacred body itself, having united the body to his Godhead—a body no longer subject to dissolution, no longer suffering, no longer under death's dominion (as the apostle says, "Death hath no more dominion over him?)[5] (3,1) truly the body itself, the

[1] Cf. Jer. Chron. 160,1-5 (Helm).

[2] Epiph identifies Herod the Younger with Herod Agrippa, and makes him the son of Archelaus.

[3] 1 Pet 4:1

[4] 1 Pet 3:18

[5] Rom 6:9

flesh itself, the soul itself, the whole humanity itself. He had quickened, not something other than his actual body but his actual body, and united it with one unity, one Godhead: the fleshly imperishable, the bodily spiritual, the gross ethereal, the mortal immortal and never having seen corruption. For the soul had not been left in hell, (2) its instrument not severed from it on sin's account, its mind not defiled by change. He had taken all the characteristics of man and preserved them all entire, since <the> Godhead had bestowed them on the true Manhood for its proper needs. By these I mean the needs <that arise> from a body, soul and human mind, and confirm the fullness of <the true humanity>—(confirm it,) that is, by hunger and thirst, weeping and discouragement, tears and sleep, weariness and repose. (3) For these are no form of sin but a token of truest humanity, since the Godhead truly dwells with the Manhood, the Godhead not undergoing human vicissitudes but consenting to what is proper, and to what is free from sin and forbidden change.

3,4 He arose, moreover, and entered where doors were shut to prove that his solid body was ethereal—though it was his very body itself, with flesh and bones. For after his entry he exhibited his hands and feet, his pierced side, his bones, sinews and the rest, so that the sight they saw was not an illusion, for he was giving the promise of our faith and hope since he had fulfilled all of it himself.[6]

3,5 And he broke bread with them not in appearance in reality, and taught them in his instruction to proclaim the kingdom of heaven in truth, (at the same time) indicating the supreme, crowning <mystery>[7] to his disciples by saying, "Make disciples of the nations"—that is, convert the nations from wickedness to truth, from sects to a single unity—(6) "baptizing them in the name of Father, Son and Holy Spirit."[8] (Baptizing them, that is), by the royal naming of the Trinity, the sacred, kingly seal to show, by the word, "name,"[9] that there has been no alteration of the one Unity.[10] (7) For since he commands the candidates <to be sealed> "in the *name* of Father..." the praise of God is assured. Since he commands this "in the *name* of...Son," the (divine) surname[11] is no less assured. Since he

[6] I.e., exhibiting what the resurrection body will be. Having risen himself, he is qualified to do so.

[7] The sacrament of baptism

[8] Matt 29:19

[9] I.e., the one word ὄνομα in the singular is applied to each of the Persons, meaning that the reference is to only one God.

[10] Because the noun is singular. More than one "name" would imply alteration.

[11] υἱός is here treated as the ἐπίκλησις, or surname, of πατήρ.

commands it "in the *name* of ... Holy Spirit," the bond, neither cut nor severed, bears the seal of the one Godhead.

4,1 And he was taken up to heaven in his body itself and his soul and mind, conjoining them as one unity and perfecting them as a spiritual, divine entity. He sat down at the Father's right hand after sending messengers into all the world: (2) Simon Peter, his brother Andrew, and James and John the sons of Zebedee, whom he had chosen at the outset—Philip and Bartholomew, Matthew, Thomas and Judas and Thaddeus, Simon the Zealot. For though Judas Iscariot had originally belonged to the twelve, he turned traitor and was stricken from the sacred roll of the apostles.

4,3 And he sent seventy-two others as well to preach, among whom were the seven who were put in charge of the widows, Stephen, Philip, Prochorus, Nicanor, Timon, Parmenas and Nicolaus—(4) but before them was Matthias, who was included among the apostles in place of Judas. After these seven, and Matthias who preceded them, he sent Mark and Luke, Justus, Barnabas and Apelles, Rufus, Niger and <the> rest of the seventy-two. (5) After them all, and along with them, he chose the holy apostle Paul with his own voice from heaven to be at once apostle and herald of the gentiles and the one to complete the apostolic doctrine. (6) It was Paul who found St. Luke, one of the seventy-two who had been scattered, brought him to repentance, and <made him> his own follower, both a co-worker in the Gospel and an apostle. And in this way all of the work of preaching the Gospel has been done, down to this time.

4,7 So much for my discussion of the twenty Sects, and the sequel to them which I have given as briefly as I could: the bringing of the light of the Gospel into the world by Christ and his disciples. (8) Similarly, it would be possible to gather and cite oracles and prophecies from the Law and Psalms, observe the passages and the proofs in the other scriptures, and understand precisely how Christ's incarnation and evangelical teaching are not spurious, but are true, were announced beforehand by the Old Testament, and are open to no doubt. But not to make the work of composition too long a job, I shall rest content with this.

4,9 Moving on now, I am similarly going to describe the opinions which sprouted up in the world later for a wrong reason. I have already given a fairly good enumeration of the eleven that originated with the Jews and Samaritans and the nine that originated with the Greeks, the barbarians and the others before the Lord's advent and until his time.

ANACEPHALAEOSIS II

Here in turn are the contents of this second Section of Volume One. It includes thirteen Sects as follows:

21,1 21. Simonians, the sect founded by Simon the magician from the Samaritan village of Gitthon, who lived during the time of the apostle Peter. He was Samaritan in origin and adopted Christ's name only. (2) He taught that an unnatural act, sexual congress for the pollution of women, is a matter of moral indifference. He rejected the resurrection of bodies, and claimed that the world is not God's. (3) He gave his disciples an image of himself in the form of Zeus to worship, and one <in the> form of Athena of the whore named Helen who accompanied him. He said that he was the Father to Samaritans, but Christ to Jews.

22,1 22. Menandrians, who originated from this Simon through a Menander, but were somewhat different from the Simonians. Menander said that the world was made by angels.

23,1 23. Satornilians, who lent support to the Simonians' pornography throughout Syria, but preached differently from the Simonians in order to create a further sensation. Their founder was Satornilus. (2) He too, like Menander, said that the world was made by angels—but only by seven—against the wishes of the Father on high.

24,1 24. Basilideans, votaries of the same obscenity, derived from Basilides who, together with Satornilus, was trained by the Simonians and Menandrians. He held similar views but was somewhat different. (2) He said that there are 365 heavens, and gave angelic names for them. Thus the year too has the same number of days, and the name, Abrasax, has the same numerical value and totals 365. And he says that this is the holy name.

25,1 25. Nicolaitans, founded by the Nicolaus who was placed placed in charge of the widows by the apostles. From envy of his own wife he taught his disciples, along with the others, to perform the obscene act, (2) and taught them about Kaulakau, Prunicus, and other outlandish names.

26,1 26. Gnostics are the successors of these sects, but insanely perform the obscene action more than all of them. In Egypt they are called Stratiotics and Phibionites; in Upper Egypt, Secundians; in other places, Socratists, and Zacchaeans in others. (2) But others call them Coddians, others, Borborites. They boast of Barbelo, who is also known as Barbero.

27,1 27. Carpocratians, founded by one Carpocrates, a native of Asia, who taught his followers to perform every obscenity and every sinful practice.

And unless one progresses through all of them, he said, and fulfills the will of all the demons and angels, he cannot mount to the highest heaven or get by the principalities and authorities.

27,2 He said that Jesus had received an intellectual soul, knew what is on high and made it known here; and that if one does things like the things that Jesus did, he is like Jesus. (3) Like the sects from Simon on, Carpocrates repudiated the Law together with the resurrection of the dead. (4) Marcellina at Rome was a follower of his. He secretly made images of Jesus, Paul, Homer and Pythagoras, burned incense to them and worshiped them.

28. Cerinthians, also known as Merinthians. These are a type of Jew derived from Cerinthus and Merinthus, and boast of circumcision, but say that the world was made by angels and that Jesus was named Christ as an advancements.

29. Nazoraeans, who confess that Christ Jesus is Son of God, but all of whose customs are in accordance with the Law.

30,1 30. Ebionites are very like these Cerinthians and the Nazoraeans; and the sect of the Sampsaeans and Elkasaites was associated with them to a degree.

30,2 They say that Christ was created in heaven, also the Holy Spirit. But Christ lodged in Adam at first, and from time to time takes Adam himself off and puts him on again—for this is what they say he did at the time of his advent in the flesh.

30,3 Although they are Jews they have Gospels, abhor the eating of flesh, take water for God, and, as I said, hold that Christ clothed himself with a man at the time of his advent in the flesh. (4) They immerse themselves in water regularly, summer and winter for supposed purification, like the Samaritans.

31,1 31. Valentinians, who deny the resurrection of the flesh and, although they read the Old Testament and prophets, accept (only) such things as can be interpreted allegorically to sound like their own sect. (2) They accept and introduce some other tales as well and give names of thirty aeons, which are male and female and were begotten all together by the Father of all, and which they hold to be both gods and aeons. (3) Christ has brought a body from heaven, and passed through Mary as though through a conduit.

32,1 32. Secundians, with whom Epiphanes and Isidore are associated, also believe in the same pairs of aeons; for their ideas are like Valentinus', though to a certain extent they teach different things. (2) In addition, they teach the performance of the obscene act. They too repudiate the flesh.

33 33. Ptolemaeans, also disciples of Valentinus, with whom Flora is associated. They say the same things about the pairs of aeons as the Valentinus and the Secundians do, but they too are different to some extent.

This, in turn, is the summary of the thirteen Sects of the second Section of Volume One.

21.

Against Simonians,[1] *first after the only Faith of Christ, but twenty-one of the series*

1,1 Simon Magus's makes the first sect to arise in the time between Christ and ourselves. It is made up of people who do not rightly or lawfully <believe> in Christ's name, but perform their dreadful activities in keeping with the false corruption that is in them.

1,2 Simon was a sorcerer, and came from Gitthon,[2] the city in Samaria—though it is a village now. He deluded the Samaritan people by deceiving and catching them with his feats of magic, (3) and said that he was the supreme power of God and had come down from on high.[3] To the Samaritans he called himself the Father; but to Jews he said he was the Son,[4] though he had suffered without suffering, but suffered only in appearance.[5]

1,4 Simon made up to the apostles and, together with many he too, like the others, was baptized by Philip. All except Simon waited for the arrival of the chief apostles, and received the Holy Spirit through the laying on of their hands. (Philip, being a deacon, did not have the faculty of the laying on of hands in order to give the Holy Spirit through it.) (5) Now since

---

[1] Epiph's main source for this Sect is Hipp. Synt., the content of which is also reflected by PsT 1.2 and Fil. 29.1. He also makes use of Irenaeus. The account of Simon found at Eus. H. E. 2.12.3-15.1 is based on Justin and Irenaeus and some version of the debate between Simon and Peter. Hippol. Refut. 6.7; 19.1-20.2 may come in large part from Irenaeus; Tert. De Anima 34 surely does.

The oldest accounts of Simon are found at Justin Apol. 26.2-3; 56.1-2 and Dial. 120.6. Clem. Recog. 2.5-15 gives a fundamentally different version of his biography; Const. Ap. 6.7-9 draws on some version of this latter account. See also Orig. Cels. 5.62. There may be NHC allusions or references to the Simonians at Apoc. Pet. 74,28-34 and Test. Tr. 58,2-4.

[2] Justin Apol. 26.2; Hipp. Refut. 6.7.1; Clem. Recog. 2.7.1; Hom. 2.22; Fil. 29.1; Const. Ap. 6.7.

[3] Acts 8:9; Justin Apol. 26.2; Hipp. Refut. 6.7.1; Iren. 1.23.1; PsT 1.2; Fil.29.1.4.

[4] Iren. 1.23.3; Hipp. Refut. 6.19.6; Fil. 29.2; Tert. De Anima 34. Hippolytus and Irenaeus both say Simon claims to have appeared to gentiles as the Holy Spirit; Epiph omits this, probably because he believes Simon called Helen the Holy Spirit, see 21,2,3-4.

[5] Iren 1.23.1; Hipp. Refut. 6.19.6; Fil. 29.3

Simon's heart was not right or his reason either, but he was addicted to a sordid covetousness and avarice and was certainly not ready to abandon his evil practice, he offered money to Peter the apostle, to give him the faculty of conveying the Holy Spirit through the laying on of hands. For he had counted on spending a little money, and amassing a huge fortune and more in return for a small investment, by giving the Holy Spirit to others.[6]

2,1 Since his mind was deranged and deluded by the devilish deceit in magic, and he was always ready to display the barbarous deeds of his own wickedness and demon's wickedness through his magic arts,[7] he came out in the open and, under the appearance of Christ's name, induced death in his converts by slipping a poison into the dignity of Christ's name—as though he were mixing hellebore with honey—for those whom he had trapped in his baneful error.

2,2 Since the tramp was naturally lecherous, and was encouraged by the respect that had been shown to his professions, he trumped up a phony allegory for his dupes. He had gotten hold of a female vagabond from Tyre named Helen, and he took her without letting his relationship with her be known.[8] (3) And while privately having an unnatural relationship with his paramour, the charlatan was teaching his disciples stories[9] for their amusement and calling himself the supreme power of God, if you please! And he had the nerve to call the whore who was his partner the Holy Spirit, and said that he had come down on her account.[10] (4) He said, "I was transformed in each heaven in accordance with the appearance of the inhabitants of each, so as to pass my angelic powers[11] by unnoticed and descend to Ennoia[12]—to this woman, likewise called Prunicus and Holy

[6] Acts 8:12-19; Iren. 1.23.1; PsT 1.2; Tert. De Anima 34

[7] Cf. Hipp. Refut. 6.7.1 τὰ μὲν παίξας πολλοὺς κατὰ τὴν Θρασυμύδους τέχνην...τὰ δὲ διὰ δαιμόνων κακουργήσας; Iren. 1.23.1; Fil. 29.1; Tert. De Anima 34; Clem. Rec. 2.7.

[8] Justin Apol. 26.3; Iren. 1.23.2; Hipp. Refut. 6.19.3-4; Tert. De Anima 34.2; Orig. Cels. 5.62

[9] Cf. Hipp. Refut. 6.19.4 ἐρασθεὶς τοῦ γυναίου...τοὺς μαθητὰς αἰδούμενος τοῦτον τὸν μῦθον ἔπλασεν

[10] Just. Apol. 26.3; Iren. 1.23.3; Hipp. Refut. 6.19.4; Fil. 29.7; Tert. De Anima 34.3; PsT 1.2. At Tri. Prot. 40,8-18 the Protennoia descends for the sake of the conquered Sophia.

[11] The redeemer changes form or becomes invisible during his descent at Hippol. Refut. 6.19.6; Iren. 1.23.3; 30,12; Epist. Apost. 13; Gos. Phil. 57,28-58,2; Gr. Seth 56,21-32; Zost. 4,29-30; Tri. Prot. 49,15-23; PS 1.7 (MacDermot p. 12). The direct quotes which Epiph gives in this Sect are his own dramatization of his sources.

[12] In NHC Ennoia is often the first emanation of the invisible God and a synonym for Barbelo. See Apocry. Jn. BG 8502,2 where, among other things, she is "the power who is before the All...the perfect πρόνοια of the All...the image of the invisible One, the perfect power, Barbelo (at II,1 4,36 "the glory of Barbelo)...the first thought, his image." Cf. Zost. 82,23-83,24; Norea 27,11. At II,1 30,11-31,4 she descends three times into the prison of the body. Her descent is elaborately worked out in NHC XIII,1, where she is the

Spirit,[13] through whom I created the angels.[14] But the angels created the world and men. But this woman is the ancient Helen on whose account the Trojans and Greeks went to war."[15]

2,5 Simon told a fairy tale about this, and said that the power kept transforming her appearance on her way down from on high,[16] and that the poets had spoken of this in allegories. For these angels went to war over the power from on high—they call her Prunicus, but she is called Barbero or Barbelo[17] by other sects—because she displayed her beauty <and> drove them wild, and was sent for this purpose, to despoil the archons who had made this world. She has suffered no harm, but she brought them to the point of slaughtering each other from the lust for her that she aroused in them.[18] (6) And detaining her so that she should not go back up,[19] they all had relations with her[20] in each of her womanly and female bodies—for she kept migrating[21] from female bodies into various bodies of human beings, cattle and the rest—so that, by the deeds they were doing in killing and being killed, they would cause their own diminution through the shedding of blood. Then, by gathering the power[22] again, she would be able to ascend to heaven once more.

Trimorphic Protennoia (First Ennoia); see Tri. Prot. 36,4-9; 40,12-18; 40,29-41,1; 41,20-24; 32-25; 42,17-18; 47,11-13; 17-22; 47,12-22 and Turner's Introduction in Hedrick, *Nag Hammadi Codices XI, XII, and XIII.* "Hypsiphrone" descends at Hyps. 70,14-17, the NHC tractate of this name.

[13] The Holy Spirit is equated with Prunicus at Iren. 1.29.4. Here Epiph has equated both the Holy Spirit and Prunicus with Simon's Ennoia.

[14] Iren. 1.23.2; Hipp. Refut. 6.19.3; PsT 1.2; Fil. 29.4. At Gos. Phil. 63,30 "Barren Wisdom" is the "mother of the angels."

[15] Iren. 1.23.3; Hipp. Ref. 6.19.2; Tert. De Anima 3.4-5

[16] The female revealer disguises herself at Apocry. Jn. 30,11-13;3 49,15-23.

[17] Barbelo appears in seven NHC tractates, mostly Sethian, and in Gos. Jud. She is regularly the first emanation of the highest God and is often called his first Thought as at Apocry. Jn. II,1 4,27; 5,4-6; Allog. 53,27-28; Tri. Prot. 38,8-9. She is an "aeon" (Zost. 14,27 et al.; Allog. 53,22-28 et al; Gos. Jud. 35,17-18. She is as it were the source of the other aeons, see Apocry. Jn. II,1 5,4-6: This is the first Thought, his image, she became the womb of everything, for she is prior to them all.

In this sense, "Simon's" "through whom I created the angels" is not inappropriate. However, Barbelo does not descend, suffer or weep; Epiph confuses her role with that of Sophia.

[18] Hipp. Refut. 6.19.2; cf. Manichaean Keph. 35,15-17; 80,25-29. There may be allusions to the idea at Thunder 18,23-25 or Apoc. Pet. 74,27-34.

[19] Iren. 1.23.2; Fil. 29.7; Orig. Wld. 116,15-18; PS 1.30 (MacDermot pp. 43-45. At Apocry. Jn. II,1 30,12-21 Pronoia enters the "prison," but has to hide "because of their wickedness."

[20] Hipp. Refut. 6.19.2; Orig. Wld. 116,15-20; Exeg. Soul 127,25-128,1

[21] Iren. 1.23.2; Hippol. Refut. 6.19.2; Tert. De Anima 34.6. At Tri. Prot. 45,21-27 the Protennoia hides herself in everyone and transforms their forms into other forms.

[22] Cf. Apocry Jn. II,1 19,15-31, "And when the mother wanted to retrieve the power

3,1 "This woman was then, she who by her unseen powers has made replicas of herself[23] in Greek and Trojan times and immemorially, before the world and after. (2) She is the one who is with me now, and for her sake I am come down. But she herself awaited my arrival; for this is Ennoia, she whom Homer calls Helen.[24] And this is why Homer is obliged to describe her as standing on a tower, signaling her plot against the Phrygians to the Greeks with a lamp.[25] But with its brightness, as I said, he indicated the display of the light from on high."

3,3 Thus again, the charlatan said that the wooden horse, the device in Homer which Greeks believe was made as a ruse, is the ignorance of the gentiles.[26] And "as the Phrygians, in drawing it, unwittingly invited their own destruction, so the gentiles—the persons who are outside of my knowledge—draw destruction on themselves through ignorance."

3,4 In turn, what is more, the impostor would say that this same woman whom he called Ennoia was Athena, using the words of the holy apostle Paul if you please, and turning the truth into his falsehood—the words, "Put on the breastplate of faith and the helmet of salvation, the greaves, the sword and the shield."[27] In the style of Philistion's mimes the cheat now turned all these things, which the apostle had said with reference to firm reason, the faithfulness of chaste behavior, and the power of divine, heavenly discourse, into a mere joke. "What else?"he said. "Paul was describing all these things symbolically, as types of Athena."[28] (5) Thus again he would say, meaning, as I said, that woman with him whom he had taken from Tyre, the namesake of the ancient Helen, calling her by all these names—Ennoia, Athena, Helen and the rest—"For her sake I am come down. For this is that which is written in the Gospel, the sheep that was lost.[29]

---

which she had given to the Chief Ruler, she petitioned the Mother-Father of the All..." etc. Yaltabaoth is then persuaded to blow the power into Adam.

[23] This seems to be Epiph's own interpretation of Ennoia's transmigrations.

[24] Iren. 1.23.2; Hippol. Refut. 6.19.1-3; Fil. 29.5-7; Tert. De Anima 34.5

[25] Hipp. Refut. 6.19.1. An analogous though considerably different story about "Luna" is found at Clem. Recog. 2.12.4.

[26] Hippol. Refut. 6.19.1; Fil. 29.8. For the Trojan horse see Vergil Aeneid 6.515-519.

[27] Cf. Eph. 6:14-17.

[28] This may be Epiph's own conjecture, based on the image of Athena which he mentions at 21,3,6.

[29] Matt 18:12 parr.; Iren. 1.23.2; Hippol. Refut. 6.19.2; Tert. De Anima 34.4. This is the "allegory" referred to above.

3,6 Furthermore, he has given his followers an image, supposed to be one of himself, and they worship this in the form of Zeus. He has likewise given them another, an image of Helen in the form of Athena, and his dupes worship (both of) these.[30]

4,1 He instituted mysteries consisting of dirt[31] and, to put it politely, the fluids that flow from bodies—men's through the seminal emission and women's through the regular menses, which are gathered as mysteries by a most indecent method of collection. (2) And he said that these are mysteries of life <and> the fullest knowledge. But for anyone to whom God has given understanding, knowledge is above all a matter of regarding these things as abomination instead, and death rather than life.

4,3 This man offers certain names of principalities and authorities too, and he says that there are various heavens, describes powers to go with each firmament and heaven, and gives outlandish names for them.[32] He says that one cannot be saved unless he learns this catechism and how to offer sacrifices of this kind to the Father of all, through these principalities and authorities. (4) This world has been defectively[33] constructed by wicked principalities and authorities, he says. But he teaches that there is a decay and destruction of flesh, and a purification only of souls—and of these (only) if they are established in their initiation through his erroneous "knowledge". And thus the <imposture> of the <so-called> Gnostics begins.[34]

4,5 He claimed that the Law is not God's[35] but the law of the lefthand power, and that prophets are not from a good God either, but from one power or another. And he specifies a power for each as he chooses—the Law belongs to one, David to another, Isaiah to another, Ezekiel to still another, and he attributes each particular prophet to one principality.[36] But

[30] Iren. 1.23.4.; Hipp. Refut. 6.20.9

[31] Epiph means the practice he describes at 26,4,5-5,1 in connection with the "Gnostics". Since he believes that all heresy stems from Simon and, in any case, Irenaeus and probably Hippolytus accuse Simonians of immorality, Epiph feels justified in making this assumption.

[32] Tert. Praescr. 33

[33] ἐν ἐλαττώματι, which seems here to mean no more than "faultily." See n. 9 p. 170.

[34] That is, Simon is the author of Gnosticism. Cf. Iren. 1.23.2 ex quo universae haereses substiterunt; Hippol. Refut. 6.20.4 which makes Simon Valentinus' resource.

[35] This idea is attributed to Simon at Clem Hom. 3.2.2.

[36] Iren. 1.23.3 and especially 1.30.11; Hippol. Refut. 6.19.7. At PS 3.135 (MacDermot p. 351) it is the archons of the aeons who speak to the prophets.

all of these are from the power on the left[37] and outside of the Pleroma;[38] and whoever believes the Old Testament is subject to death.

5,1 But this doctrine is refuted by the truth itself. If Simon is the supreme power of God and the tart he has with him is the Holy Spirit, as he says himself, then he should give the name of the power—or else say why a title has been found for the woman, but none at all for himself! (2) And how does it happen that Simon went the way of all flesh one day at Rome when his turn came—when the wretch fell down and died in the middle of the city of Rome?[39]

5,3 <And> why did Peter declare that Simon has no part or share in the heritage of true religion? (4) And how can the world not belong to a good God, when all the good have been chosen from it?

5,5 And how can the power which spoke in the Law and the prophets be "lefthand", when it has heralded Christ's coming <from the> good God in advance and forbids all wrongdoing? (6) And how can there not be one Godhead and the same Spirit, of the New Testament and of the Old, since the Lord has said, "I am not come to destroy the Law, but to fulfill"?[40] And to show that the Law was delivered by himself and proclaimed through Moses, while the grace of the Gospel has been preached by himself and his advent in the flesh, he told the Jews, "Had ye believed Moses, ye would have believed me also, for he wrote of me."[41]

5,7 And many other arguments <can be found> in opposition to the charlatan's drivel. How can unnatural acts be lifegiving, unless perhaps it is the will of demons, when the Lord himself in the Gospel speaks in reply to those who told him, "If the case of the man and wife be so, it is not good to marry," and he said to them, "All men cannot receive this, for there be eunuchs which have made themselves eunuchs for the kingdom of heaven's sake,"[42]—and proved that true abstention from marriage is

---

[37] In NHC good and evil, or the realms of spirit and matter, are very commonly characterized as "right" and "left": See Gos. Tr. 31,36-32,14; Tri. Trac. 98,12-20; 104, 9-11; 106,2-5; 18-21; Gos. Phil. 53,14-15; Nat. Arc. 95,35-96,3; Test. Tr. 43,10-12; Val Exp. 38,27-33. See also PS 4.139;140 (MacDermot pp. 361-363); U 19 (MacDermot p. 261). At Gos. Phil. 60,26-32 both "right" and "left" are said to have their proper places.

[38] PS 3.135 (MacDermot p. 351) makes it clear that no prophet has yet entered the light, though they will in the future.

[39] At Fil. 29.9 Simon is said to die at Rome percussus ab angelo. For his fall see Const. Ap. 6.9.3-4; Acts of Peter 32 (H-S II p. 313). At Hippol. Refut. 6.23.3 his disciples are said to have buried him alive at Gittha in the vain expectation of his resurrection.

[40] Matt 5:17

[41] John 5:46

[42] Matt 19:10

the gift of the kingdom of heaven? (8) And again, of the lawful wedlock which Simon himself shamefully corrupts to make provision for his own lust, he says elsewhere, "Those whom God hath joined together, let not man put asunder."[43]

6,1 Again, why does the swindler refute himself by overlooking his own nonsense, as though he does not know what he has previously said? After saying that the angels were created by himself through his Ennoia, he said in turn that he was transformed at each heaven so as to escape their notice during his descent. In other words he was evading them from fear; and why is the driveler afraid of the angels he made himself?

6,2 And how can it not be perfectly easy for the wise to expose his secret sowing of error when the scripture says, "In the beginning *God* created the heaven and the earth?"[44] And in agreement with this statement the Lord in the Gospel as though speaking to his own God and Father, says, "Father, Lord of heaven and the earth."[45] (3) Now if the maker of heaven and earth is God the Father of our Lord Jesus Christ, there is nothing to any of the humbug Simon's assertions—that the world was produced defectively by angels, and all the other random things the impostor insanely told the world and deceived certain persons, the people he duped.

7,1 And these things which I have said briefly about his sect will suffice my readers as an occasion of truth and healing, and for the refutation of those who are trying to harm the ignorant with such beastly filth. (2) Having crushed his poison fangs sufficiently I shall pass them by and go on in turn to the refutation of another sect. For there is inconstancy and uncertainty in him, since he is an impostor but has assumed the appearance of the name of Christ—like the snake-like filth of the aborted issue which is hatched from the infertile eggs of asps and other vipers. (3) As the prophet says, "They have broken the eggs of asps, and he who would eat of their eggs hath found an egg infertile, and in it a basilisk."[46]

But beloved, now that, as I have said, by Christ's power we have struck Simon with the words of the truth and done for his corruption, let us go on to the rest.

[43] Matt 19:6
[44] Gen 1:1
[45] Matt 11:25 par.
[46] Isa 59:5

22.

Against Menander[1]

Sect two from Christ's Advent, but twenty-two of the series

1,1 One Menander follows next after this sect. He was Samaritan[2] and was Simon's pupil at one time. He likewise said that the world is the creation of angels,[3] and he said that he himself had been sent from on high as a power of God.[4] (2) To perpetrate worse trickery than his predecessor for men's deception, he said that he had been sent "for salvation"[5]—supposedly to gather certain persons into his own mystery,[6] so that they would not be ruled over by the angels, pincipalities and authorities who have made the world. (3) He wove everything together like his own teacher and never desisted from his reliance on on spells and the other magic arts.

2,1 But he has incurred the same defeat that his teacher has and will be overthrown by the same refutation of the words of the truth. For <he has died> and his sect has mostly gone out of existence. (2) I shall pass it by, proceed with my instruction and go on to another. Indeed, the ancients tell the story that of the many asps that were collected in a single earthen jar and buried in the foundations of the four corners of each temple of the idols that was erected in Egypt, the one that was stronger than the others would set upon them and eat them. (3) But when it was left by itself and could get no food it would bend round and eat <the whole> of its body, from its tail up to a certain part. And so it remained, no longer whole but half of a snake. (4) Hence they called it an "aspidogorgon," showing us that, though there was such a thing long ago, now it no longer exists; it has been wiped out. In the same way, while this entirely defunct sect has been opposed by myself, it has been wiped out by the power of Christ. Let us pass it by too, beloved, and go on to the rest.

---

[1] The probable source of this Sect is Hipp. Synt., assuming that this is echoed by PsT 1.3 and Fil. 30. Epiph also draws on Iren. 1.23.5. For other references see Justin Apol. 26.4; Hipp. Refut. 7.4; Tert De Anima 50. Eus. H. E. 4.7.3-4, which depends upon Justin, mentions Menander as the source of Saturninus' doctrines.

[2] Iren. 1.23.5; Justin Apol. 26.4

[3] Iren. 1.23.5; Hippol. Refut. 7.4

[4] Iren. 1.23.5; Tert. De Anima 50.2

[5] Iren. 1.23.5: missus sit... salvatorem pro salute hominum negans habere posse quemquam salutem, nisi in nomine suo bapizatus fuisset; cf. PsT 1.3; Tert. De Anima 50.2.

[6] I.e., his baptism. See the references in n. 5.

23.
Against Satornilus,[1] *number three from The Lord's Advent but twenty-three of the series*

1,1 A Satornilus arose after him taking his own cue from those people, I mean from Menander and his predecessors. Satornilus lived near Syria—that is, near Antioch by Daphne—and brought lots of the theory and practice of deceit into the world.

1,2 For these two, Basilides and Satornilus, were fellow students. Basilides went to Egypt, and preached the dark recesses of the depth of his imposture there. But Satornilus spent his life in the place I have just mentioned,[2] and like Menander declared that the world was made by angels.

1,3 He said that there is one unknowable Father, and that he has made powers, principalities and authorities.[3] But the angels are at odds with[4] the power on high, and a certain seven of them have made the world and everything in it.[5] The world, however, has been parceled out by lot to each of the angels.[6]

1,4 These angels met and deliberated, and created the man together, in the form of the luminous image that had peeped down from on high—for, not being able to detain it when it peeped down because it withdrew suddenly, they wanted to make a reproduction of it.[7] (5) And the man was fashioned by them, for no other reason but this one. For since this light had somehow stimulated these angels when it peeped down from on high, from longing for the likeness on high they undertook to fashion the man.

---

[1] The outline of this Sect comes from Hipp. Synt, as a reading of PsT 1.4 suggests. Much material from Iren. 1.24 has been inserted. Hipp. Refut. 7.28.3 might come from Iren. Fil. 31 may be drawn either from Hipp. Synt or from Epiph, or from both. See also Eus. H. E. 4.22.5 (from Hegesippus); Justin Dial. 35.6; Tert. De Anima 23.1; Const. Apost. 6.8.1.

[2] Basilides and Saturninus, or Satornilus, are also paired at Iren. 1.24.1; Hipp. Refut. 7.28.1; Eus. H. E. 4.7.3.

[3] The wording to this point is closest to that of Iren. 1.24.1; cf. Hipp. Refut. 7,28.1-2. PsT 1.4. and Fil. 31.1 only imply the idea.

[4] διεστάναι. That Epiph means "disagree, be at variance" is suggested by the content of 2,2; 4,1-2. PsT, however, has longe distanter ab hoc (deo). Amidon: The angels parted from the upper power.

[5] So worded at Iren. 1.24.1. Cf. Hipp. Refut. 7.28.2. "Made the world" without "and everything in it" is found at PsT 1.4; Fil. 31.1; cf. Acts of Paul 8.1.15 (H-S II p. 254).

[6] An angelic "prince" is in charge of every nation at Dan 10:13; 18-20. Cf. Gos. Egyp. III,2 58,3-5: And (Sakla) said to the [great angels] "Go and let each of you reign over his world."

[7] For the withdrawal of the light see Tri. Trac. 79,10-13; Nat. Arc. 94,29-39; Orig. Wld. 103,29-32; Zost. 27,12.

(6) For since they had fallen in love with the light from on high,[8] and were held spellbound with desire for it and enjoyment of it when it appeared and (then) disappeared from them—being in love with it and yet unable to sate themselves with its loveliness, because of the immediate withdrawal of this light—this charlatan represents the angels in his skit as having said, "Let us make man in the image and after the likeness."[9]

1,7 To lend plausibility to his imposture he has excised the word, "our" which was used in Genesis by the holy God, <but> retained "in the image," as though, if you please, some persons were making an image of someone else, and <showing this by> saying, "Let us make a man in *an* image and after *a* likeness."

1,8 But once the man was made, he says, they could not finish him because of their weakness. He lay quivering, flat on the ground like a worm with no legs, unable to stand up or do anything else, until the power on high peeped down, had compassion because of its own image and semblance, and out of pity sent a spark of its power, raised the man up with this, and so brought him to life;[10] Satornilus claims, if you please, that the spark is the human soul.[11]

1,9 And thus the spark is sure to be preserved, but the whole of the man must perish. What has come down from on high will sooner or later be received back on high, but what is from below, everything the angels have fashioned, is left here for them.[12]

1,10 The charlatan claims that Christ himself has come only in the form and semblance of man, and has done everything in appearance—being born, living a human life, being visible, suffering.[13]

---

[8] The desire for the image in the waters is erotic at Nat. Arc. 87,11-14; Corp. Herm. 1.14, and Fil. 31.2, who might be drawing on Epiph for this point.

[9] Cf. Gen 1:26. This exegesis of Gen 1:26, which makes use of the plural "Let *us* make man", is a common one in Gnostic and similar sources. In NHC see Apocry. Jn. II,1 14,.24-15,6; Nat. Arc. 87,11-88.3; Or. Wld. 100,21-22; 103,29-32; Gr. Pow. 38,5-9. *Ginza* 174,1-6 has a similar story, and cf. Corp. Herm. 1.14.

The word, "our" is also omitted at Iren. 1.24.1; Hipp. Refut. 7.28.2, PsT 1.4; Gos. Jud. 52,14-17; Let. Pet. 136,7-10; Cod. Tch. Let. Pet. 4,14-17; Irenaeus 1.30.6 (Ophites). Fil. 31.3 inserts it. Apocry. Jn. II,1 15,2-3 reads: 'Come, let us create a man according to the image *of God* and according to *our* likeness.'

[10] Iren. 1.24.1; 1.30.6; Hipp. Refut. 7.28.3; Fil. 31.4. Comparable exegeses of Gen 1:27 appear at Gos. Tr. 30,16-32; Apocry. Jn. II,1 19,10-33; Nat. Arc. 88,3-17; Or. Wld. 115,3-116,8.

[11] The spark is important at Para. Shem 31,22-23; 46,13-15. Only Epiph explicitly identifies this spark as the soul.

[12] Iren. 1.24.1. Cf. Hipp. Refut. 7.28.4; Fil. 31.5; Auth. Teach 32,16-23.

[13] Hipp. Refut. 7.28.4; Iren. 1.24.2; PsT 1.3; Fil. 31. Teachings which might be termed docetic or quasi-docetic are found at 1 Apoc. Jas. 30,2-6; 31,14-22; 2 Apoc. Jas. 57,10-19; Cod. Tch. James 16,15-21; 18,6-11; Acts of John 87-97 (H-S II pp. 179-185).

2,1 From him "knowledge," as it is falsely called, begins again to add to the depth of its wickedness. It found its origin and occasion in Simon, but (now) it is augmented with other, further nonsense, whose refutation I shall give later. (2) For Satornilus claims when speaking of the angels that the God of the Jews is one of them too, and that he and they are at odds with the power on high. But the Savior has been sent from the Father against the power's wishes, for the destruction of the God of the Jews and the salvation of those who trust in <him>.[14] And they, the members of this sect, are the ones who have the spark of the Father on high.

2,3 For Satornilus claims that two men were fashioned at the first, one good and one evil. Descended from these are two breeds of men in the world, the good and the evil. (4) But since the demons were assisting the evil, for this reason the Savior came, as I said, in the last days, to the aid of the good men and for the destruction of the evil and the demons.[15]

2,5 This tramp also says that marriage and procreation are of Satan, so that the majority of them abstain from meat, to attract certain persons to their deceit, if you please, with this pretended asceticism.[16] (6) Again, the charlatan claims that some of the prophecies were delivered by the angels who made the world, but some by Satan. For Satan too is an angel, he claims, who acts in opposition to the angels who made the world, but especially to the God of the Jews.[17]

3,1 But whenever the oaf makes these claims he himself will surely be shown to be confessing one God, and tracing all things to one monarchy. For if the angels have made <the man>, but angels in turn have as the cause of their being the power on high, then they are not the causes of the fashioning of the man. This must be the power on high which made the angels by whom the fashioning of the man was done.[18] (2) For the tool is not the cause of the products it makes, but the person who, with the tool, performs the operation by which the product is made. As scripture says, "Shall the axe boast itself without him who wieldeth it?"[19] and so on. (3) Thus we see that the sword is not the cause of the murder, but the person who undertook the murder with the sword. And the mold cannot make the vessels itself, but the one who made the mold and the vessels can.[20]

---

[14] Iren. 1.24.2. cf. Hipp. Refut. 7.28.5; A polemic against the OT God and his teachings is found at Test. Truth 47,14-50,11.

[15] Iren. 1.24.2; Hipp. Refut. 7.28.6.

[16] Iren. 1.24.2; cf. Hipp. Refut. 7.28.7.

[17] Iren. 1.24.2; cf. Hipp. Refut. 7.28.7.

[18] This argument, which Epiph uses in several connections, is found at Iren. 2.2.3.

[19] Isa 10:15

[20] Irenaeus at 2.2.3 uses the illustrations of a battle, a saw and an axe.

3,4[21] Hence the angels are not the cause, but the angels' maker is the cause, even though it did <not> order them to make a man. (5) It may be that Satornilus is accusing the power on high of ignorance, and unawareness of the things that were going to be done against its will. Or else <he is saying> that it was with its consent, for a useful purpose, that the angels prepared the man, even though it did not order them to finish the project—that is, the model of the man, as we learn from Satornilus' mythological construct.

4,1 Or why not reply to the myth-maker with the question, "Did the power on high know what they would do?"

"Yes," he says.

"Very well, if it knew, then it, not they, made the man,. And if it knew but didn't want it done, and they still undertook the project themselves against its wishes, why didn't it stop them? (2) But if it had no way of stopping them, this is its first fault. It created the angels it has made to its own disadvantage, in opposition to itself and for its own provocation; and in the second place, it could have stopped them but didn't, and instead lent its assistance to the evil work that was done by the angels.

4,3 "But if it didn't assist in the work, and couldn't stop it even though it wanted to, there is a great deal of weakness in this power that wanted to prevent the work but couldn't. And the band of the angels that the power made must be more powerful than the power, even though it is the cause of the angels it made." In every respect, then, the sect's thesis is caught out, and incurs (a verdict of) untenability, not of truth.

4,4 "But if it knew, and yet it had to make these angels who <would> do something wrong against its will, it will find itself with one more fault." To hear Satornilus tell it, nothing in the power on high will turn out right.

4,5 But let's go on questioning him. "Hey you, tell us, since you squinted through a window—my way of making fun of your nonsense—and took a peek at the way the angels were created, and then saw <how they went about> making the clay figure of the man, and spied on the supreme power's industry! Did the angels know what they were going to create, or were they unaware of it? But if they were unaware of it, was anyone forcing them to finish the thing <they had done> in ignorance?"

"No," he says, "they were not unaware. They knew what they were going to do."

[21] 3.4-4,7 are the expansion of an argument which is stated at Iren. 2.5.3-4.

4,6 "Well, did the power on high know that they would undertake this, or was it unaware?"

"It was not unaware."

"Then did it, or didn't it, make them for the purpose of doing this?"

"No," he says, "it just made them, but they undertook to fashion a model against the wishes of the power on high."

4,7 "Then, you supreme fool, according to what you say the angels knew but it was unaware. And the preparation of men must be their origin, and the angels who are the causes of this are privy to it, but the power that made the angels is in ignorance! (8) But this would be foolish and absurd—that the work is more perfect than the workman, and the workman weaker than the angels he made, since they are the causes of the origin of man. Hence for every reason you must admit that <one has to> trace the universe to the same creator, the One, and to the one monarchy."

5,1 For in fact God the Father made man, and all things, of his own good pleasure—not the angels, nor has anything been made with the counsel of the angels. For in saying, "Let us make man," God said, "in *our* image," not merely "in *an* image."[22] (2) He was inviting his Word and Only-begotten into his act of creation as co-creator—as is the opinion, based on truth, of the faithful, and as is the exact truth. In many other works on the subject I have confessed, distinctly and at length, that the Father invited the Son, through whom he made all other things as well, to join him in making the man. (3) And I would say that he invited not only the Son, but the Holy Spirit as well: "By the Word of the Lord were the heavens established, and all the host of them by the Spirit of his mouth."[23] (4) Willingly or even unwillingly—I mean Satornilus, the founder of this sect—he will be forced for every reason to confess that God is one, God and Lord, creator and maker of all that is, along with man.

5,5 And he will be exposed as a slanderer for every reason, both in what he says about prophets, and his cheap accusation of lawful wedlock. Our Lord Jesus Christ himself makes an express pronouncement in the Gospel and says, in agreement with the prophet, "Lo here am I, that speak in the prophets"—and again, "My Father worketh hitherto, I too am at work".[24] (6) But to show which work his Father and he are doing, he declared it by saying to those who asked him if one may divorce a wife for every cause, "How is it written? When God made man, he made them male and female," and again, later in the passage, "For this cause shall a man leave his father

[22] Gen 1:26
[23] Ps. 32:6
[24] John 5:17

and his mother and cleave unto his wife, and they twain shall become one flesh"; and he added immediately, "That which *God* hath joined together, let not man put asunder.[25] Thus Savior teaches in every way that the God of all is the maker of men, and is his Father.

5,7 And as to marriage's not being of Satan, but of God, in the first place the Lord says, "That which God hath joined together, let not man put asunder."[26] Then the holy apostle: "Marriage is honorable and the bed undefiled."[27] And he gives a similar commandment to the true widows, and says through Timothy, "Younger widows refuse; for after they have waxed wanton against Christ, they will marry." And later, "Let them marry, bear children, guide the house"[28]—making a law which may not be transgressed, since it is from God and has been solemnly granted to men.

6,1 And there are any number of things to say about the unfounded suspicions he has raised against God's prophecies, as though they are not from God. As the Only-begotten himself says <when> he makes his proclamation that the world is his, first, "Our father Abraham desired to see my day, and he saw it, and was glad."[29] And again he says, "Had ye believed Moses, ye would have believed me, for he wrote of me."[30]

6,2 And who is there, of sound mind and with God-given understanding, who can fail to show the cheat Satornilus up—knowing that, when the Savior was revealed in glory in support of the truth, he showed his glory in no other way than between Elijah and Moses, who themselves appeared with him in their own glory?

6,3 But there are any number of other things like these, said by the Lord himself and throughout the New Testament, which unite the Law, the prophets and the whole Old Testament with the New—since they are both Testaments of one God, as he says, "They shall come and recline on the bosoms of Abraham, Isaac and Jacob in the kingdom of heaven, and shall find rest from the east and west,"[31] and so on. (4) And again, the prophecy concerning him which is given as David's, "The Lord said unto my Lord, sit thou on my right hand."[32] And again, the words he himself says to the Pharisees, "Did ye never read, the stone which the builders

---

[25] Matt 19:6
[26] Matt 19:6
[27] Heb 13:4
[28] 1 Tim 5:11;14
[29] John 8:56
[30] John 5:46
[31] Matt 8:11
[32] Ps. 109:1

rejected?"[33] (5) And Luke affirms that the Savior himself appeared on the road to Nathanael and Cleopas after his resurrection from the dead, and admonished them from the psalms and the prophets that "Thus it behooved Christ to suffer and to rise from the dead the third day."[34] And there is no discrepancy whatever between Christ's incarnation and the oracles of the prophets.

7,1 But this will do for Satornilus' sect—not to waste time by becoming involved in his foolish disputations and the refutations of them. (2) Next, moving on from this one, I shall describe the sect of Basilides, Satornilus' fellow-student and companion in error. For these men share <the same material> as though they had borrowed their poison from each other, as in the familiar proverb of "an asp borrowing poison from a viper." For they each belong to the other's school and council, though each stands by himself as founder of his own sect. And they borrowed the wickedness from each other, but were the authors of the discrepancy between them.

7,3 So whether, like a viper, Satornilus got his venom from the ancients and has imparted it to Basilides, or whether Basilides imparted it to Satornilus, let us leave their poison behind us, deadly as it is, and coming from such serpents as these, (but) weakened and deprived of its strength with the Lord's teaching as with an antidote. Let us, however, call on God, beloved, and go on to the next.

24.
Against Basilides[1] *Number four, but twenty-four of the series*

1,1 Basilides then, as I have already explained, made his way to Egypt and spent some time there, then went to Prosopitis and Athribitis, and moreover, to the environs, or "nome," of Saites and Alexandria.[2] (2) For

[33] Matt. 21:42
[34] Luke 24:26

[1] The primary source of this Sect is Hipp. Synt., cf. PsT 1.5. However, Epiph also uses Irenaeus (1.24.3-7) and mentions him by name at 8,1. Fil. 32 may depend either upon Hipp. Synt. or upon Epiph.

The very long account of Basilides at Hipp. Refut. 7.23.7 is from a source unrelated to the ones mentioned, and contradicts them at some points. Eus. H. E. 4.7.3-7 describes Basilides from a source he identifies as Agrippa Castor. Clem. Strom. 7.17.106 says that Basilides claimed to have been taught by Paul's interpreter Glaucias. For a mention of "Basilideans" see Justin Dial. 35.6. The NHC tractate Test. Tr., as reconstructed by Giverson and Pearson mentions Basilides pejoratively at 57,6-8.

[2] Iren. 1.24.2: Alexandrii; Fil. 32.2 simply says Aegyptum.

the Egyptians call the neighborhood or environs of each city a "nome." You may find even this of use to you, scholarly reader, for love of learning and clarity's sake, as a pious confirmation and explanation of the points in sacred scripture that baffle some because of their inexperience. (3) Whenever you find a mention of "nomes" of Egyptian cities in the holy prophet Isaiah—such as the "nomes" of Tanis or Memphis, or the "nome" of Bubastis—it means the area around one city or another. And there, for love of learning's sake, you have the translation.

1,4 So this tramp spent his entire life in these places, the ones where his sect, which flourishes even today after having taken occasion from his teaching, appeared. (5) And he began to preach much more material than the charlatan who was his fellow-student, and was left in Syria—for the sake of seeming to to deceive his audience more completely, if you please, by telling them more than he had,[3] and of gratifying and gathering more of a crowd than his colleague, Satornilus. (6) Now then, to fob some of his fairy stories off on us he begins them as follows—though <to tell> the truth, he does not begin these shocking, deadly things from a notion of his own but by taking his cue from Satornilus, and from Simon whom we have already mentioned. He, though, wants to handle them differently, and give his mythology at greater length.

1,7[4] There was one Ingenerate, he says, who alone is the Father of all. From him Mind has been emitted, from Mind Reason, from Reason Prudence, from Prudence Power and Wisdom,[5] and from Power and Wisdom, principalities, authorities and angels. (8) From these powers and angels a highest first heaven has come, and other angels have come from them. And the angels who come from them have made a second heaven, and made angels themselves in their turn. (9) And the angels who come from them have made a third heaven. And so, by producing another heaven and other angels in turn, the angels of each heaven have brought the number of heavens to 365,[6] from the highest to this one above us.

---

[3] Cf. Iren. 1.24.3, Basilides, ut altius aliquid et verisimilius invenisse videtur, in immensum extendit sententiam doctrinae suae.

[4] With the paragraph which follows cf. PsT 1.5; Iren. 1.24.3; Fil. 32.2-3.

[5] These emanations are roughly paralleled by the archons Ogdoas and Hebomas and their sons, at Hipp. Refut. 7.23.1-24.7. However, no angels follow these, and at Refut. 7.22-23 Basilides is said to deny the idea of emanation as such.

[6] Forms of this teaching are found in NHC at Apocry. Jn. II,1 11,23-25; Eug. 84,1-85,4; Val. Exp. 30,29-38, and at Gos. Jud. 49,9-50,2. Cf. Hipp. Refut. 6.53.5; U 3 (MacDermot p. 230); 6 (p. 236); 9 (p. 240); 10 (p. 245); PS 3.132 (MacDermot p. 342).

2,1 For fools this might serve as a temptation to believe his crazy nonsense, but for the wise it is easy to refute his speech and his way of perverting his own opinion into extreme, unbounded mischief. (2) As though thunderstruck by some poetic frenzy, the pathetic excuse for a man assigns names to every archon in the heavens and, to the ruin of his dupes' souls, publishes them to win credence from the weak-minded through the names he makes up. What is more, the cheat never flagged in his devotion to conjuror's devices and mumbo-jumbo.[7]

2,3 He says that this creation was produced later by the angels of our heaven and the power in it. One of these angels he calls God and distinguishes him by saying that he alone is the God of the Jews—though he made him one of the number of the angels whose names he coined for us as though he were composing a mime.[8] By him the man was fashioned.[9]

2,4 The angels, including himself, have parceled the world out by lot to the multitude of the angels; but this God of the Jews has drawn the Jewish people.[10] And to insult this same almighty Lord who alone, and no other, is the true God—for we confess that it is he who is the Father of our Lord Jesus Christ—Basilides, as I have shown, denies him and represents him as one of his so-called angels.

2,5 The Jews have fallen to his lot, and he defends them. But he is the most self-willed of all the angels, and he led the children of Israel out of Egypt by the self-will of his own arm,[11] since he was more reckless and self-willed than the others. (6) Hence this God of theirs has plotted—because of his willfulness, the charlatan blasphemously says—to subject all the other nations to the stock of Israel, and has launched wars for this purpose.

2,6 Altogether pathetic himself though he is, he does not hesitate to give free rein to his tongue, speak up, and say many other things against the holy God. (7) He says it is for this reason that the other nations made war on this one and inflicted many evils on it, because of the other angels' jealousy. Provoked, since they felt despised by the God of the Jews—they

---

[7] Irenaeus accuses Basilideans of employing magic at 1.24.5.

[8] Iren. 1.24.5; Fil. 32.4. At PsT 1.5 this angel is called novissimum.

[9] Cf. Iren. 1.24.4; PsT 1.5.

[10] PsT 1.5: huic sortito obtigisse semen Abrahae. Cf. Iren. 1.24.4; Fil. 32.4.

[11] Iren. 1.24.4; PsT 1.5; Fil. 32.5-6. αὐθαδείᾳ is a play on βραχίονι ὑψηλῷ at Exod 6:6. Neither Iren. nor PsT reports the term αὐθάδης, Fil. may have taken it from Epiph. In NHC this term, or αὐθάδεια, appears in connection with the wicked archon at Apocry. Jn. II,1 13,26-28; Let. Pet. 135,16-22; 136,5. Cf. PS 1.29 (MacDermot p. 42); 1.30 (MacDermot p. 44).

stirred their own nations up against the nation of Israel, which was under his command.[12] And this is why wars and disorders constantly broke out against them.

3,1 This is the fraud's specious argument. He too, likewise, believes that Christ was manifest (only) in appearance. He says that since he "appears," he is an "appearance"; but he is not man and has not taken flesh.[13]

3,2 This second mimologue[14] mounts another dramatic piece for us in his account of the cross of Christ; for he claims that not Jesus, but Simon of Cyrene, has suffered. For when the Lord was marched out of Jerusalem, as the Gospel passage says, one Simon of Cyrene was compelled to bear the cross. (3) From this he finds his trickery's <opportunity> for composing his dramatic piece and says: Jesus changed Simon into his own form while he was bearing the cross, and changed himself into Simon, and delivered Simon to crucifixion in his place. (4) During Simon's crucifixion Jesus stood opposite him unseen, laughing[15] at the persons who were crucifying Simon. But he himself flew off to the heavenly realms after delivering Simon to crucifixion, and returned to heaven without suffering. (5) It was Simon himself who was crucified, not Jesus. Jesus, Basilides says, passed through all the powers on his flight to heaven, till he was restored to his own Father.[16] (6) For he is the Father's Son of whom we have spoken, sent to men's aid because of the disorder that the Father saw both in men and in angels.[17] And he is our salvation, he says, who came and revealed this truth to us alone.

---

[12] At Tri. Trac. 100,3-4 in NHC, each archon has his own γένος and ἄξια though Israel is not mentioned. The archons and their nations war on Israel at Iren. 1.24.4; PsT 1.5; Fil. 32.

[13] PsT 1.5; Fil. 32.6. Iren. 1.24.6 says that Christ "appeared" (apparuisse), and also identifies him with Nous.

[14] The "first" μιμόλογος is Satornilus. There is no covert allusion here to CG VII,3, The Second Logos of the Great Seth; on the subject see also Pourkier. When Epiph makes humorous allusions, he typically lays heavy emphasis upon them rather than inserting them in passing.

[15] Cf. Apoc. Pet. 81,7-21; 82,4-16.

[16] Iren. 1.24.4; PsT 1.5; Fil. 32.6. In NHC, Gr. Seth 55,15-56,11 has been but should probably not be interpreted as the same story. Various quasi-docetic views of the crucifixion appear in NHC at 1 Apoc. Jas. 31,14-22; perhaps Apoc. Adam 77,9-18; Apoc. Pet. 81,6-83,15; perhaps Let. Pet. 139,15-25 and Cod. Tch. Let. Pet. 8,1-5. See also Acts of John 97-99; 101; 102 (H-S II pp. 184-186). The reality of the crucifixion is insisted on at Melch. 5,7-8. At Hipp. Refut. 7.26.13 Basilides himself is said to teach that it is real.

[17] Iren. 1.24.4... Patrem, videntem perditionem ipsorum... Irenaeus goes on to say that Christ came to free humanity from the power of those who made the world. At NHC's Tri. Trac. At 80,4-19 and 83,34-84,24 the creatures of the Demiurge quarrel.

3,7 Such are the recitals of the tramp's mythology. And at this point, moreover—since the uncleanness which began with Simon is making strides—Basilides gives his disciples permission to perform the whole of every kind of badness and licentiousness, and gives his converts full instruction in the promiscuous intercourse of an evil kind between men and women.[18] (8) Of them and their kind the apostle says, "The wrath and righteous judgment of God is revealed against those who hold the truth in unrighteousness."[19] For many fall into the heresy for this reason of self-indulgence, since through these unnatural acts they find a way of doing their pleasure with impunity.

4,1 Again, he gives a permissive sort of teaching by alleging that there is no need to be a martyr.[20] There will be no reward for a martyr, since he is not bearing witness to man's creator; he is testifying for the crucified, Simon. (2) Now, how can he have a reward when he dies for Simon, the one who was crucified, while avowing that he is doing this for a Christ whom he knows nothing about, dying for someone he does not know he is dying for? One must deny then, and not die rashly.[21]

5,1 But this man will be apprehended as heading a host of devils against souls by teaching them the denial of God, since the Lord himself says, "Whosoever denieth me before men, him will I deny before my Father which is in heaven."[22] (2) But the tramp says, "We are the 'men.'[23] The others are all swine and dogs. And this is why he said, 'Cast not thy pearls before swine, neither give that which is holy unto dogs.' "[24] (3) For Basilides hides his own wickedness from people with sense, but discloses it to his own coterie and the ones he has duped. Because it is indeed a "shame even to speak"[25] of the things they say and do, he says that one must confess the truth "before 'men'—for we are the 'men', but the others are swine and dogs," as I said.

---

[18] Epiph deduces this from the universae libidinis of Iren. 1.24.5; cf. Fil. 32.7. Basilideans are accused of immorality at Clem. Alex. Strom. 3.1.

[19] Rom 1:18

[20] Iren. 1.24.4; Fil. 32.7-8; Eus. H. E. 4.7.7; Orig. Com. in Matt. 24:7-8 Ser. 38 (Klostermann p. 73). In NHC martyrdom is deprecated at Test. Tr. 33,24-34 and perhaps at Gr. Seth 49,26-27, but is strongly recommended at Apocry. Jas. 5,9-6,20.

[21] Clem. Strom. 4.1.81.1f quotes Basilides as teaching that the martyr's death is really a punishment for previous sins.

[22] Matt. 10:33

[23] Cf. Gos. Phil. 80,23-81,4. Pourkier suggests that the quotation is in fact an inference drawn by Epiph himself.

[24] Matt 7:6

[25] Eph. 5:12

5,4 Basilides claims that <they may> not reveal anything at all to anyone about the Father, and about his own mystery, but <must> keep it secret within themselves[26] and reveal it to one out of thousands and two out of ten thousands.[27] He cautions his disciples by saying, "Know all men yourself, but let no man know you."[28] (5) When questioned, he and his followers claim that they are no longer Jews and have not yet become Christians, but that they always deny, keep the faith secret within themselves, and tell it to no one—anticipating his own shame because of the unspeakable nature of his obscenity and bad doctrine.

6,1 The beginning of his wicked pretense had its cause in searching for the origin of evil[29] and saying what it was. But what every person is like will be shown by his business. Hence these people who love evil and not good are merchants of evil, as the scripture said: "They that seek mischief, it shall come unto them."[30] (2) There never was such a thing as "evil," there has never been a "root of evil," and "evil" is not a thing. At one time evil did not exist, but in anyone who does it, it exists as something that has been imported into him, by reason (of his doing it). In one who does not do it it does not exist, as explained above. (3) For after he has made all things the Lord says, "Behold, all things are very good,"[31] proving that evil is not primordial, and did not exist at the beginning before it was begun by men. Through us it comes into being, and through us it does not. (4) Therefore, since everyone has the ability not to do evil and the ability to do it, evil exists when he does it but is non-existent when he does not. So what becomes of the "root of evil," or the substance of wickedness?

7,1 Basilides has arrived at a point of great folly by claining that the power <on high> emitted Mind, that Mind emitted Reason, Reason emitted Prudence, Prudence emitted Power and Wisdom, and that authorities, powers and angels spring from Power and Wisdom. (2) Yet (over and above that) he says that the power and first principle above these is Abrasax,[32]

[26] Iren. 1.24.6. Similar directions appear in NHC at Apocry. Jn. II,1 31,29-37; 1 Apoc. Jas. 36,13-16 and Cod. Tch. James 23,10-16. Cf. Corp. Herm. 13.116; Ascl. 32 (Nock-Festugière p. 341) and, in the Qumran material at 1QS 9,16-18 (Wise et al., p. 139).

[27] Iren. 1.24.6 unum a mille et due a myriadibus. Versions of this saying are found in NHC at GT 23, and in other literature at PS 3.134 (MacDermot p. 350).

[28] Iren. 1.24.6

[29] Contrast Apoc. Peter 77,23-32: Others... will set up their error and their law against these pure thoughts of mine... thinking that good and evil are from one (source).

[30] Prov 11:27

[31] Gen 1:31

[32] At Iren. 1.24.7 Abrasax is princeps of the 365 heavens, and at Hipp. Refut. 7.26.6 τὸν μέγαν ἄρχοντα αὐτῶν. PsT 1.5 makes Abrasax simply the Basilidean name for God: hunc esse dicit summum deum. At NHC Gosp. Egyp. III,2 52,26

because the sum of the letters of Abrasax is 365—so that from this he tries to establish the evidence for his myth of the 365 heavens. (3) He even maps out the locations of these heavens with great care, by his practice of dividing and combining them like the mathematicians.[33] For he and his subordinates have taken their futile speculations and applied them to their own type (of speculation), for the sake of their own delusive, false teaching.

7,4 And they would like to give proof of these things from figures that are similar to them—since "Abrasax" makes 365, as I said—and prove, if you please, that this is why a year has 365 days per cycle.[34] (5) But his silly argument is a failure; a year, in fact, consists of 365 days and three hours. (6) Then, he says, man also has 365 members for this reason, so that he can assign one member to each of the powers.[35] His contrived, spurious teaching fails in this as well; there are 364 members in a man.

8,1 But the blessed Irenaeus, the successor of the apostles, has gone into detail about him and given a marvelous refutation of his stupidity. (2) Now too there will be a refutation for the nonsense of this Basilides, who has come down from on high after taking a good look at what is up there—or rather, who has fallen down, wide of the mark of the truth. (3) For if this heaven has been made by its angels, and they by the higher ones and the higher ones by ones higher still, then the power on high, also called Abrasax, will have to be the one which has made everything, and the cause of all that is. And nothing can have been made apart from it (4) since they declare it to be the cause and first archetype, and their so-called "deficiency"[36] of this world can have been produced by nothing other than the first principle and cause of the things that came later.

8,5 But we need to ask him, "Why take us to such a bunch, Mister, and not rather to the first principle—that is, to the one God, the Almighty?"—since by all accounts he either means this or, on his premises, ought to confess the one Cause of all as Master.

Abrasax is the minister of the great light Eleleth; he is Eleleth's eternal life at 53,91 and one of the four lights at 65,1; he is an angelic or aeonic being at Apoc. Adam 75,17-27; 78,9-11; Zost. 47,11. The name is common on Graeco-Roman amulets, see Preisendanz *Papyri Graeci Magici* 3, and can be given to Hermes, the creator, See the material in Dietrich, *Abraxas*.

[33] Iren. 1.24.7

[34] Iren. 1.24.3; Hipp. Refut. 8.26.6; Jer. In Amos 3:10 (Adriaen p. 451)

[35] At NHC's Apocry. Jn. II,1 19,2-3 it is said that the 365 "angels" who have just been mentioned create, or rule over the members of the body; at PS 3.132 (MacDermot p. 342) 365 "leitourgoi" fulfill this function.

[36] See p. 170 n. 9.

8,6 "And moreover, you composer of this work of fiction, give us an answer on the subject of Christ! If Simon of Cyrene was crucified, then our salvation has not been secured by Jesus but by Simon, and the world can no longer hope to be saved through Jesus Christ, who did not suffer for us. For Simon cannot save us either; he is a man and nothing but. (7) And at the same time you are also accusing God's only-begotten Son of false prosecution, if the good God delivered someone else by force to be murdered in his place. (8) And for the rest, something like this must be a dream or rather, must be a work of malignity and trickery—that <the> Lord concealed himself by some trickery or other and delivered someone else in his place. And your foolish chatter amounts to a false prosecution of the truth, a prosecution that cannot succeed but stands convicted by the truth itself of introducing fiction without proof."

9,1 For the truth altogether refutes this heresiarch in the Old and New Testaments. Anyone can see that Christ went to his passion freely, and that he took flesh and became man among us by his own will and his Father's, with the Holy Spirit's consent. This though he was perfect God from the first, (2) begotten of the Father without beginning and not in time. But in the last days he consented to enter a Virgin's womb, formed flesh for himself, was truly born and assuredly made man, to suffer for us in the flesh itself, and give his life for his own sheep. (3) And so he refutes these people by saying, "Behold, we go up to Jerusalem, and the Son of Man shall be delivered up and put to death, and the third day he shall rise again."[37] And to the sons of Zebedee he said, "Are ye able to drink the cup that I shall drink of'?[38]—(4) as the apostle Peter also says, "being put to death in the flesh but quickened by the Spirit,"[39] and again, "who suffered for us in the flesh."[40] (5) And again, John says, "Whoso denieth that Christ is come in the flesh, the same is Antichrist."[41] And St. Paul says, "having tasted of death, even the death of the cross"[42]—as Moses also foretold, "Ye shall see your life hanging on a tree."[43] (6) And Simon is not our life, but the Lord who suffered for us to put an end to our sufferings; and who, by dying in the flesh, has become the death of death to break the sting of death, descending to the underworld to shatter the unbreakable bars. And having done this he led the host of captive souls to the heavens, and emptied Hades.

[37] Matt 20:18-19
[38] Matt 20:22
[39] 1 Pet 3:18
[40] 1 Pet 4:1
[41] Cf. 1 John 4:2-3.
[42] Phil 28
[43] Cf. Deut 28:66

10,1 Christ was not responsible for Simon's death, he surrendered himself! What do you mean, you craziest man in the world? If he didn't want to be crucified, couldn't he have said so frankly and gone away from them? Would the <Son> of God, the divine Word, lay a treacherous snare and hand someone else over to death by crucifixion in his place—the One who said, "I am the truth?" For he says, "I am the truth and the life."[44] The life would not engineer a death for someone else, nor would the truth conceal what it was truly doing and misrepresent it. Truth cannot be truth if it practices imposture and conceals its own act, but works through an artifice which is the opposite of it.

10,4 And to say it all in a word so as not to prolong the discussion, "Woe to the world because of offenses" and "them that work iniquity!"[45] How many have turned out to be darkness for themselves, and darkness for the others after them who trust in their darkness! But to the wise the truth will be made clear, but the business of Basilides and his kind be exposed as a work of imposture.

10,5 And so much for this sect, and this myth; I shall go on from here to another heresy. (6) For who can fail to realize that this sort of heresy is a myth and, like a horned asp, lies buried in sand, but pokes up into the air with its horn, and inflicts death on those who happen upon it? (7) However, "The Lord hath broken the horn of sinners, and the horn of the righteous alone"—which means trust in truth—"shall be exalted."[46] (8) Therefore, since we have broken Basilides too with the doctrine of the truth, let us go on to the sects following, calling as our help on God to whom be glory, honor and worship, forever and ever. Amen.

25.

Against Nicolaitans,[1] *number five, but twenty-five of the series*

1,1 Nicolaus was one of the seven deacons chosen by the apostles, together with the saint and first martyr Stephen, and Prochorus, Parmenas and the

[44] John 14:6
[45] Matt 18:7 and 7:23
[46] Ps 74:11

[1] This Sect's points of contact with PsT 1.6 and Fil. 33 suggest that one of its sources is Hipp. Synt. However, Epiph supplies many details from Irenaeus' reports of Gnostic teachings, in the conviction that Nicolaus is the father of the Gnostics (cf. Hipp. Refut. 7.36.3 Γνωστικῶν <μὲν> δὴ διαφοραὶ <αἱ> γνῶμαι…πολλῆς δὲ αὐτοῖς συστάσεως αἴτιος γεγένηται Νικόλαος…and cf. Fil. 33.2). Iren. 1.26.3 and Hipp. Refut. 7.26.2-3 are based on Acts and Revelation. Fil. 33 is dependent upon Hipp. Synt. but might also draw on Epiph.

others. (2) He was from Antioch and became a proselyte. But after that he received the message of the proclamation of Christ, joined the disciples himself, and <was> at first ranked among the foremost. He was thus included among the ones who were chosen at the time to care for the widows.[2] (3) Later, however, the devil slipped into him and deceived his heart with the same imposture of the ancients whom we have been discussing, so that he was more severely wounded than the ones before him.

1,4 Though he had a beautiful wife he had refrained from intercourse with her, as though in emulation of those whom he saw devoting themselves to God.[3] He persevered for a while but could not bear to control his incontinence till the end. Instead, desiring to return like a dog to its vomit, he kept looking for poor excuses and inventing them in defense of his own intemperate passion. (<Being ashamed and repenting> would have done him more good!) Then, failing of his purpose, he simply began having sex with his wife. (5) But because he was ashamed of his defeat and suspected that he had been found out, he ventured to say, "Unless one copulates every day, he has no part in eternal life."[4] (1,6) For he had shifted from one pretense to another.

Seeing that his wife was unusually beautiful and yet bore herself with modesty, he envied her. And, supposing that everyone was as lascivious as he, he began by constantly being offensive to his wife and making certain slanderous charges against her in speeches.[5] And at length he degraded himself not only to normal sexual activity but to a blasphemous opinion, the harm of perverse teaching, and the deceit of the covert introduction of wickedness.

2,1 And from this source the <founders> of what is falsely termed '"Knowledge" began their evil sprouting in the world[6]—I mean the people

---

This Sect also incorporates Epiph's interpretation of the story of Nicolaus' fall as told at Clem. Alex. Strom. 3.4.25.5-26.3/Eus. H. E. 3.24.2-4. Epiph agrees with the other heresiologists in considering Nicolaus the main source of Gnostic immorality, as Rev 2:14-15 would have suggested to them.

[2] Acts 6:1-6. The same passage is used at Iren. 1.26.3; PsT 1.6; Fil. 33.1.

[3] At Clem. Alex. Strom. 3.4.25.5-26.3/Eus. H. E. 3.29.2 this story is intended to display Nicolaus' chastity. Epiph has interpreted it in accordance with his convictions about Nicolaus and the Nicolaitans. With "as though from envy" etc., cf. Clement's πρὸς τῶν ἀποστόλων ὀνειδισθὲν ζηλοτυπίαν.

[4] Epiph interprets the quotation made at Clem. Alex. Strom. 3.4.26.6/Eus. H. E. 3.29.2 παραχρήσασθαι τῇ σαρκὶ δεῖ, as "one must misuse the flesh." Clement, however, meant "deny, discipline" the flesh, and interprets Nicolaus' act as intended to teach εγ̓κράτεια.

[5] Clem. Strom. 3.4.26.6/Eus. H. E. 3.29.2: εἰς μέσον ἀγαγὼν τὴν γυναῖκα γῆμαι τῷ βουλμένῳ ἐπέτρεψεν.

[6] See Hipp. Refut. 7.36.3; Fil 33.1.

who are called Gnostics and Phibionites, the so-called disciples of Epiphanes, the Stratiotics, Levitics, Borborites and the rest. For each of these, in attracting his own sect with his own passions, invented countless ways of doing evil.

2,2 For some of them glorify a Barbelo[7] who they claim is on high in an eighth heaven,[8] and say she has been emitted by the Father. For some of them say she is the mother of Ialdabaoth,[9] others, of Sabaoth.[10] (3) But her son has ruled the seventh heaven with a sort of insolence, and tyrannically. To the ones below him he says, "I am the first and I am the last, and there is none other God beside me."[11] (4) But Barbelo has heard what he says, and weeps.[12] And she keeps appearing in some beautiful form to the archons and stealing the seed which is generated by their climax and ejaculation—supposedly to recover her power[13] which has been sown in various of them.

2,5 And so, on such a basis as this, he covertly brought his smutty mystery to the world. And as I said, some of the others too, with much turpitude, taught the practice—it is not right to say how they did it—of promiscuity with women and unnatural acts of intolerable perversity as the most holy apostle somewhere says, "It is a shame even to speak of the things that are done of them in secret."[14] (3,1) But if anyone would like to

---

[7] For Barbelo see Iren. 1.29.1; Fil. 33.2. In the Sethian tractates of NHC, Barbelo is regularly God's first emanation, the aeon of thought, and the source (sometimes the "mother") of the other aeons. See especially Apocry. Jn. II,1 4,26-5,11; in other tractates, Gos. Egyp. (III,2)42,11-12; 61.25-62,1; 69,3; Stel. Seth 121,20-25; Zost. 14,3-6; 53,10; 62,21; 119,23; 129,11; Melch. 5,27; 16,25-26; Mars. 4,11-12; 8,28-29; Allog. 51,12-17; 53,21-28; 59;1-9; Tri. Prot. 38,7-10; also, Gos. Judas 35,18.

[8] For the Mother in the eighth heaven, see Iren. 1.30.4.

[9] Iren. 1.30.5; Fil 33.3. In NHC the ignorant or wicked creator/ruler of the material universe is often named Ialdabaoth. See Apocry. Jn. 10,19;11,16; 35; 14;15; 19,23; 23,35-37; 24,12; Nat. Arc.95,5-13; 96,3-5; Orig. Wld. 100,1-26; 102,11-23; 103,1; SJC BG,3 119,14-15; Tri. Prot. 39,26-28. Cf. also Gos. Jud. 51,15. Ialdabaoth may originally have been a Jewish euphemism for JHVH Sabaoth; note that in the Hebrew alphabet, ד is one place removed from ה.

[10] At Iren. 1.30.5 Sabaoth is the son of Iao. In the Sethian documents of NHC he is the son or creature of Ialdabaoth, never of Barbelo. For Sabaoth see Apocry. Jn. 9,25-10,19; Nat. Arc. 95,5-25; Or. Wld. 103,32-104,10;106,19-26; 113,12; 114,15-17; Gos. Egyp. 58,14-15.

[11] Iren. 1.30.6. This interpretation of Isa 44:6 or 45:5 is common in NHC and Gnostic literature. In NHC see Apocry. Jn. II,1 11,18-22; Nat. Arc. 86,27-32; 94,19-23; Or. World 103,1-13; Gos. Egyp. III,2 58,23-59,1; 2 Apoc. Jas 56,23-57,1; Tri. Prot. 43,31-44,2, and for comparable ideas: Tri. Trac. 79,12-19; 84,3-6; 100,36-101,5; SJC 106,24-107,11; 1 Apoc. Jas. 35,13-17; Para. Shem 2.15-17.

[12] Sophia weeps at the results of her activity at Apocry. Jn. II,1 13,30-14,1.

[13] See p. 65 n. 18.

[14] Eph 5:12

see the Holy Spirit's rebuttal in the case of Nicolaus' sect, he must learn it from the Revelation of St. John. John writes in the Lord's name to one of the churches—that is, to the bishop appointed there with the power of the holy angel at the altar—and says, "One good thing thou hast, that thou hatest the deeds of the Nicolaitans, which I also hate."[15]

3,2 But others honor one "Prunicus"[16] and like these, when they consummate their own passions with this kind of disgusting behavior, they say in mythological language of this interpretation of their disgusting behavior, "We are gathering the power of Prunicus from our bodies, and through their emissions." That is, <they suppose they are gathering> the power of semen and menses. (3) A little later, whenever I undertake to speak of them by themselves, I shall describe them in detail—not to sully the ears of the listeners or readers, but to arouse enmity against these persons in the wise, and prevent the doing of their evil deeds. I shall not be accusing the guilty parties falsely, but truthfully making public the things that go on among them.

3,4 Others glorify the Ialdabaoth we spoke of and claim, as I said, that he is Barbelo's eldest son. And they say he is to be honored because he has revealed many things. (5) And so they fabricate certain books in Ialdabaoth's name and make up any number of outlandish names for archons—<as> they say—and authorities, which oppose the human soul in every heaven.[17] And in a word, the plot which is hatched against mankind by their imposture is a serious one.

3,6 Others likewise glorify Kaulakau,[18] giving this name to an archon, and do their best to impress the innocent with the frightfulness of this artificial name's barbarity. But to those who are experienced and have received grace from God about every name and subject of God's true knowledge, how can the <un>warranted teachings of their myth and imposture not be refutable at once?

---

[15] Rev. 2:6. Cf. PsT 1.6.

[16] For Prunicus see Iren. 1.29.4, and also 1.30.3; 7; 9; 11-12, where she plays the role of the fallen Sophia. In 7 and 9 she is the benefactress of Adam and Eve; in 11-12 she assists Elizabeth and Mary and is united with the Christ who descends from heaven. In Origen's discussion of the Ophites at Cels. 6.34.1 she is "a virgin and living soul"; at 6.35.2 a "kind of wisdom." For Prunicus in NHC, see Apocry. Jn. BG2: 51,4; Thunder 13,18; 19; Gr. Seth 50, 25-28. Macrae at Thunder 13,18 and Bullard and Gibbons at Gr. Seth 50,28 translate Prunicus as "whore."

[17] This is reported of Basilides at Iren. 1.24.5.

[18] Cf. Fil. 33.3. This is the Basilidean name for Christ at Iren. 1.24.6; at Hipp. Refut. 5.8.4 it is the Ophites' heavenly Adamas.

4,1 For if they say, "Prunicus," this is just a belch of lustfulness and incontinence. Anything called "prunicus" suggests a thing named for copulation, and the enterprise of seduction. (2) For there is a Greek expression which is used of men who deflower slave women, "He seduced so-and-so." And the Greek swindlers who compose erotica also record the word in myths by saying that beauty is "seductive."

4,3 Furthermore, how can any knowledgeable person not laugh at Kaulakau? To plant their imposture in the simple by means of something imaginary, they turn the good Hebrew words, correctly rendered in Greek, <still> clear to those who read Hebrew, and containing nothing obscure, into images, shapes, real principles, practically statuary, for the sowing of their shameful art with its fictitious basis. (4) "Kaulakau," is in Isaiah, and is an expression in the twelfth vision, where he says, "Await tribulation upon tribulation, hope upon hope, a little more a little more."[19] (5) I am going to give the Hebrew words themselves here in full, word for word as they are written. "Tsav l'tsav, tsav l'tsav," means "tribulation upon tribulation." "Qav l'qav, qav l'qav" means "hope upon hope." "Z'eir sham, z'eir sham" means, "Await a little more a little more."

4,6 Where does this leave their mythology? How did they conceive their fantasy? How did the world get these tares? Who forced men to draw destruction upon themselves? (7) For if they knowingly changed the terms into an illusion, they are obviously responsible for their own ruin. But if they ignorantly said things that they did not know, there is nothing more pathetic than they. For these things are really foolish, <as> anyone with God-inspired understanding can see. (8) For the sake of their lustfulness they have destroyed, and are destroying, both themselves and whomever they can convince.

4,9 For there is a spirit of imposture which, like breath in a flute, sets every fool in motion against the truth with its various movements. Indeed, the flute itself is a replica of the serpent through which the evil one spoke and deceived Eve. (10) For the flute was prepared to deceive mankind, on its model and in imitation of it. And see what the flutist himself represents as he plays his flute; he throws his head back as he plays and bends it forward, he leans right and leans left like the serpent. (11) For the devil makes these gestures too, to display blasphemy of the heavenly host and to destroy earth's creatures utterly while at the same time getting the world into his toils, wreaking havoc right and left on those who trust the imposture, and are charmed by it as by the notes of an instrument.

[19] Isa 28:10

5,1[20] Certain others of them make up some new names, and say that there were Darkness, Depth and Water, and that the Spirit in between them formed their boundary.[21] But Darkness was angry and enraged at Spirit, and this Darkness sprang up, embraced it,[22] they say, and sired something called "Womb."[23] After Womb was born it conceived by Spirit itself. (2) A certain four aeons were emitted from Womb,[24] but fourteen others from the four, and this was the origin of "right" and "left,"[25] darkness and light. (3) But later, after all these, a certain ignoble aeon was emitted. It had intercourse with the Womb we mentioned above, and by this ignoble aeon and Womb gods, angels, demons and seven spirits were produced. (4) But it is easy to detect the cheap mime of their imposture. They have given it away by saying first that there is one "Father," and later designating many gods—to prove that error itself arms its falsehoods against itself and destroys itself, while the truth always proves <consistent> at every point.

6,1 Well, what should I say to you, Nicolaus? Which arguments shall I use? Where have you come from, you, to bring us an ignoble aeon, a root of wickedness, a fertile Womb, and a whole lot of gods and demons? (2) When the apostle says, "Though there be so-called gods,"[26] he is implying that there are no such things. By the words, "so-called," he showed that they are gods in name only—not existent in actuality, but in the opinion of certain people. (3) "But to us," he says, obviously meaning, "to us who are acquainted with the knowledge of the truth," "there is one God."[27] And he did not say, "so-called god," but actual "God." And if there is one God for us, there cannot be many gods.

6,4 And the Lord in the Gospel says, "that they might know thee, the only true God,"[28] to refute the notion of those who talk mythology and believe in polytheism. For our God is one—Father, Son and Holy Spirit, three subsistences, one Lordship, one Godhead, one Praise—and not many gods.

---

[20] Versions of this paragraph appear at PsT 1.6 and Fil. 33.4-5.

[21] This is an interpretation of Gen 1:1. Cf. NHC's Dia. Sav. 127,22-128,1; Para. Shem 1,25-28. With the entire paragraph cf. PsT 1.6.

[22] Cf. Para. Shem 4,27-30.

[23] Cf. At Iren. 1.31.2 we find Hysteran fabricatorem caeli et terrae vocant. 3,30-4,26 gives an account of the origin of Womb. In NHC an hypostatized Womb is not common outside of Para. Shem but see perhaps Int. Know. 3,26-32.

[24] Cf. Para. Shem 5,6-27.

[25] "Light and darkness, life and death, right and left" Gos. Phil. 53,14-15; "My remaining garments, those on the right and those on the left" Para. Shem 39,12-14

[26] 1 Cor 8:5

[27] 1 Cor 8:6

[28] John 17:2

6,5 And on your terms, Nicolaus, where is the application of the Savior's saying, "There are some eunuchs which were made eunuchs of men, and there are some which were eunuchs from birth, and there be eunuchs which have made themselves eunuchs for the kingdom of heaven's sake?"[29] (6) If there are eunuchs for the kingdom of heaven's sake, why have you deceived yourself and those who trust you, by holding God's truth in unrighteousness with your copulation and unnatural vice, and teaching <licentiousness>?

6,7 And where do you see the application of, "Concerning virgins I have no commandment of the Lord; but I give my judgment, as one that hath attained mercy, that it is good so to be"?[30] And again, "The virgin careth for the things of the Lord, how she may please the Lord, that she may be holy in body and in spirit."[31] (8) And how much there is to say about purity, continence and celibacy—for the whole filth of uncleanness is brazenly spelled out by yourself! But with these two or three texts <which I put before> the reader in refutation of the absurd sect, my purpose is served here.

7,1 But next I shall go on and describe the sect which is closely associated with Nicolaus, like a wood overgrown with grass, a thicket of thorns tangled together in every direction, or a heap of dead trees and scrub in a field, ready for burning—because of <its union> with this sect of the wretched Nicolaus. (2) <For> as bodies contract infection from other bodies through inoculation, a malignant itch, or leprosy, so the so-called <Gnostics> are partly united with <the Nicolaitans>, since they took their cues from Nicolaus himself and his predecessors—I mean Simon and the others. They are called "knowledgeable," but they are[32] known all too well for the wickedness and obscenity in the transactions of their unclean trade.

7,3 For with the reed that was placed in Christ's hand we have truly struck and destroyed this man as well, who practiced continence for a short while and then abandoned it—like the creature called the newt, which comes from the water to land and returns to the water again. Let us move on to the sects which follow.

---

[29] John 17:3
[30] Cf. 1 Cor 7:25-26.
[31] Cf. 1 Cor 7:32; 34.
[32] Epiph plays on Γνώστικοι and κατάγνωστοι

26.

Against Gnostics, or Borborites,[1] *Number six, but twenty-six of the series*

1,1 In turn these Gnostics have sprouted up in the world, deluded people who have grown from Nicolaus like fruit from a dunghill,[2] in a different way—something that is plain and observable to anyone by the touchstone of truth, not only to believers I should say, but perhaps to unbelievers too. For how can speaking of a "Womb" and dirt and the rest not appear ridiculous to everyone, "Greeks and barbarians, wise and unwise?"[3] (2) It is a great misfortune, and one might say the worst of hardships, that these despicable, erring founders of the sects come at us and assault us like a swarm of insects, infecting us with diseases, smelly eruptions, and sores through their error with its mythology.

1,3 These people, who are yoked in tandem with this Nicolaus and have been hatched by him in their turn like scorpions from an infertile snake's egg or <basilisks> from asps, introduce some further nonsensical names to us and forge nonsensical books. They call one Noria,[4] and interweave falsehood and truth by changing the mythological rigmarole and fiction of the Greeks from the Greek superstition's real meaning. (4) For they say that this Noria is Noah's wife.[5] But they call her Noria in order to create an illusion for their dupes by making their own alteration, with foreign names, of the things the Greeks recited in Greek, so that they too will translate Pyrrha's name by calling her Noria. (5) Now since "*nura*" means "fire" in Syriac, not ancient Hebrew—the ancient Hebrew for "fire" is "esh"—it follows that they are making an ignorant, naive use of this name.[6]

---

[1] The organization of this material is Epiphanius' own. He has certainly drawn on Hipp. Synt. and on Gnostic works (see 17,8). He mentions at least eight of these by name, (see 1,3; 2,5;6; 8,1 and 11,12) though he may not have read all of them. However, he quotes from a Questions of Mary, a Gospel of Philip, and a Birth of Mary and is especially dependent upon the first (see Tardieu, and also Dummer, "Angaben"). He also reports his own experience in Egypt, with a group which called themselves Gnostics, see 17,4-18,4. His placement of the "Gnostics" here, in association with the Nicolaitans might be due to his reading of Irenaeus, see n. 2 below.

[2] Cf. Iren. 1.28.2 Alii autem rursus a Basilide et Carpocrate occasiones accipientes, indifferentes coitus et multas nuptias induxerunt et neglegentiam ipsorum quae sunt idolothyta ad manducandum, non valde haec curare dicentes Deum. Cf. Pourkier p. 103.

[3] Rom 1:14

[4] CG IX,2 is entitled The Thought of Norea. Or. Wld. 102,10-22 refers to a first Book of Noraia, and 102,24-25 to a first Account of Oraia.

[5] Cf. Fil. 33.2. Norea or Orea is Seth's sister and, as it were, represents the ideal Gnostic at Nat. Arc. 91,34-92,3; 92,19-93,13. She is Seth's sister and wife at Iren. 1.30.9. In the Mandaean *Ginza* she is Noah's wife at 46,4-5, Dinanukht's at 211,36; 39.

[6] Epiph apparently connects Norea with nura, fire, because of the burning of the ark, see below at 1,8.

(6) Noah's wife was neither the Greeks' Pyrrha nor the Gnostics' mythical Noria, but Barthenos.[7] (And indeed, the Greeks say that Deucalion's wife was called Pyrrha.)

1,7 Then these people who are presenting us with Philistion's mimes all over again give a reason why Noria was not allowed to join Noah in the ark, though she often wanted to. The archon who made the world,[8] they say, wanted to destroy her in the flood with all the rest. (8) But they say that she sat down in the ark and burned it[9] a first and a second time, and a third. And this is why the building of Noah's own ark took many years[10]—it was burned many times by Noria.

1,9 For Noah was obedient to the archon,[11] they say, but Noria revealed the powers on high and Barbelo[12] the scion of the powers, who was the archon's opponent as the other powers are. And she let it be known that what has been stolen from the Mother on high by the archon who made the world, and by the other gods, demons and angels with him, must be gathered from the power in bodies, through the male and female emissions. (2,1) It is just my miserable luck to be telling you of all the blindness of their ignorance. For it would take me a great deal of time if I should wish go into detail here in the treatise I am writing about them and describe one by one the outrageous teachings of their falsely termed "knowledge".

2,2 Others of them, who in their turn are differently afflicted, and blind their own eyes and (so) are blinded, introduce a Barkabbas[13] as another prophet—one worthy of just that name! (3) "Qabba" means "fornication" in Syriac but "murder" in Hebrew—and again, it can be translated as "a quarter of a measure." And to persons who know this name in their own languages, something like this is deserving of jeering and laughter—or rather, of indignation. (4) But to persuade us to have congress with bodies that perish and lose our heavenly hope, they present us with a shameful narrative by this wonderful "prophet"; and in turn, they are not above reciting the amatory exploits of Aphrodite's whoredom in so many words.

---

[7] See Jub. 4.28. In the Genesis Apocryphon of the Qumran literature at 1QapGn col. 3 ll. 3; 8;12 (Wise et al. p. 76) Barthenos is Lamech's wife.

[8] See 21,2,5 p. 65.

[9] This story is found at Nat. Arc. 92,14-17.

[10] The building of the ark requires 100 years at Apocalypse of Paul 50 (H-R II p. 740); 300 at *Ginza* 409,4-5; 120 at Genesis Rabbah 30.7.

[11] At Apoc. Adam 69,1-75,14 Noah and his sons are represented as the servants of "god the almighty" = Sakla, rather than of the real God.

[12] See p. 65 n. 17.

[13] Cf. Fil. 33.6. At Eus. H. E. 4.7.7 Basilides is said to regard Barkabbas and Bar Koph as prophets.

2,5 Others of them in their turn introduce a fictitious work of pornography, a fabrication they have named by claiming that it is a "Gospel of Perfection." And truly, this is not a gospel of perfection but a dirge for it; all the perfection of death is contained in such devil's sowing.

2,6 Others are not ashamed to speak of a "Gospel of Eve." For they sow <their stunted> crop in her name because, supposedly, she obtained the food of knowledge by revelation from the serpent which spoke to her[14] And as, in his inconstant state of mind, the utterances of a man who is drunk and babbling at random cannot be alike, but some are made with laughter but others tearfully, the deceivers' sowing has come up to correspond with every sort of evil.

3,1 They begin with foolish visions and proof texts in what they claim is a Gospel. For they make this allegation: "I stood upon a lofty mountain, and saw a man who was tall, and another, little of stature.[15] And I heard as it were the sound of thunder and drew nigh to hear, and he spake with me and said, I am thou and thou art I, and wheresoever thou art, there am I;[16] and I am sown in all things. And from wheresoever thou wilt thou gatherest me, but in gathering me, thou gatherest thyself."[17] (2) What a devil's sowing! How has he managed to divert the minds of mankind and distract them from the telling of the truth to things that are foolish and untenable? A person with good sense hardly needs to formulate these people's refutation from scripture, illustrations or anything else. The acting out of the foolish words of adulterers and the putting of them into practice is plain for sound reason to see and detect.

3,3 Now in telling these stories and others like them, those who have yoked themselves to Nicolaus' sect for the sake of "knowledge" have lost the truth and not merely perverted their converts' minds, but have also enslaved their bodies and souls to fornication and promiscuity. They foul their supposed assembly itself with the dirt of promiscuous fornication and eat and handle both human flesh and uncleanness. (4) I would not dare to utter the whole of this if I were not somehow compelled to from the excess of the feeling of grief within me over the futile things they do—appalled

[14] See p. 265 n. 4. Cf. Nat. Arc. 89,31-90,11; Or. Wld. 118,24-119,18. On the subject see Pagels.

[15] Two spirits, a little one and a big one, appear at Dia. Sav. 136,17-23.

[16] Variations of this formula appear at GT 108; PS 2.96 (MacDermot pp. 231; 232; 233; Acts of John 100 (H-S II p. 185) Corp. Herm. 5:11; Hipp. Refut. 5.9. And see Marcus' speech to his female partner at Iren. 1.13.3.

[17] For comparable "gathering" see Tri. Trac. 66,24-25; Thunder 16,18-19; Man. Keph. 228,1-12; Man. Ps. at Allberry I p. 175,19.

as I am at the mass and depth of evils into which he enemy of mankind, the devil, leads those who trust him, so as to pollute the minds, hearts, hands, mouths, bodies and souls of the persons he has trapped in such deep darkness.

3,5 And I am afraid that I may be revealing the whole of this potent poison, like the face of some serpent's basilisk, to the harm of the readers rather than to their correction. Truly it pollutes the ears—the blasphemous assembly of great audacity, the gathering and the interpretation of its dirt, the mucky (βορβορώδης) perversity of the scummy obscenity. (6) Thus some actually call them "Borborians." But others call them Koddians—"*qodda*" means "dish" or "bowl" in Syriac—because no one can eat with them. Food is served to them separately in their defilement, and no one can eat even bread with them because of the pollution. (7) And so, regarding them as outcastes, their fellow immigrants have named them Koddians. But in Egypt the same people are known as Stratiotics and Phibionites, as I said in part earlier. But some call them Zacchaeans, others, Barbelites.

3,8 In any case, neither will I be able to pass them by; I am forced to speak out. <For> since the sacred Moses too writes by the Holy Spirit's inspiration, "Whoso seeth a murder and proclaimeth it not, let such a one be accursed,"[18] I cannot pass this great murder by, and this terrible murderous behavior, without making a full disclosure of it. (9) For perhaps, if I reveal this pitfall, like the "pit of destruction,"[19] to the wise, I shall arouse fear and horror in them, so that they will not only avoid this crooked serpent and basilisk that is in the pit, but stone it too, so that it will not even dare to approach anyone. And so much for the few things I have said about them up till now, as a partial account.

4,1 But I shall get right down to the worst part of the deadly description of them—for they vary in their wicked teaching of what they please—which is, first of all, that they hold their wives in common.[20] (2) And if a guest who is of their persuasion arrives, they have a sign that men give women and women give men, a tickling of the palm as they clasp hands in supposed greeting, to show that the visitor is of their religion.

4,3 And once they recognize each other from this they start feasting right away—and they set the table with lavish provisions for eating meat and drinking wine even if they are poor. But then, after a drinking bout and, let

[18] The source of this is unclear. Tardieu suggests Lev 5:1.

[19] Cf. Ps. 54:24

[20] Cf. Gos. Judas 38,16-19: (Some "priests") sacrifice their own children, others their wives, "in praise and humility with each other".

us say, stuffing their overstuffed veins,[21] they get hot for each other next. (4) And the husband will move away from his wife and tell her—speaking to his own wife!—"Get up, perform the Agape[22] with the brother." And when the wretched couple has made love—and I am truly ashamed to mention the vile things they do, for as the holy apostle says, "It is a shame even to speak" of what goes on among them. Still, I should not be ashamed to say what they are not ashamed to do, to arouse horror by every means in those who hear what obscenities they are prepared to perform. (5) For after having made love with the passion of fornication in addition, to lift their blasphemy up to heaven, the woman and man receive the man's emission on their own hands. And they stand with their eyes raised heavenward but the filth on their hands and pray, if you please—(6) the ones they call Stratiotics and Gnostics—and offer that stuff on their hands to the true Father of all,[23] and say, "We offer thee this gift, the body of Christ." (7) And then they eat it[24] partaking of their own dirt, and say, "This is the body of Christ; and this is the Pascha, because of which our bodies suffer and are compelled to acknowledge the passion of Christ."

4,8 And so with the woman's emission when she happens to be having her period—they likewise take the unclean menstrual blood they gather from her, and eat it in common. And "This," they say, "is the blood of Christ." (5,1) And so, when they read, "I saw a tree bearing twelve manner of fruits every year, and he said unto me, "This is the tree of life," in apocryphal writings,[25] they interpret this allegorically of the menstrual flux.

5,2 But although they have sex with each other they renounce procreation.[26] It is for enjoyment, not procreation, that they eagerly pursue seduction, since the devil is mocking people like these, and making fun of the creature fashioned by God. (3) They come to climax but absorb the seeds of their dirt, not by implanting them for procreation, but by eating the dirty stuff themselves.

5,4 But even though one of them should accidentally implant the seed of his natural emission prematurely and the woman becomes pregnant,

---

[21] ὡς ἔπος εἰπεῖν τὰς φλέβας τοῦ κόπου ἐμπλήσαντες Or: practically stuffing the boy's (κόρου) veins. Epiph could be recalling some experience of his own.

[22] So Benko. Tardieu renders simply fais l'amour.

[23] Rather than to the gnostic god

[24] The practice is mentioned, and sharply condemned at PS 4.147 (MacDermot p. 381) and 2 Jeu 43 (MacDermot p. 100). Christians are accused of it by Mandaeans at *Ginza* 229,20-22.

[25] Cf. Rev 22:1-2. Epiph might have mistaken the source of the quotation, or indeed seen it so worded in some apocryphon.

[26] See the polemic against procreation at Test. Tr. 30,2-17.

listen to a more dreadful thing that such people venture to do. (5) They extract the fetus at the stage which is appropriate for their enterprise, take this aborted infant, and cut it up in a trough with a pestle. And they mix honey, pepper, and certain other perfumes and spices with it to keep from getting sick, and then all the revellers in this <herd> of swine and dogs assemble, and each eats a piece of the child with his fingers.[27] (6) And now, after this cannibalism, they pray to God and say, "We were not mocked by the archon of lust, but have gathered the brother's blunder up!" And this, if you please, is their idea of the "perfect Passover."

5,7 And they are prepared to do any number of other dreadful things. Again, whenever they feel excitement within them they soil their own hands with their own ejaculated dirt, get up, and pray stark naked with their hands defiled. The idea is that they <can> obtain freedom of access to God by a practice of this kind.

5,8 Man and woman, they pamper their bodies night and day, anointing themselves, bathing, feasting, spending their time in whoring and drunkenness. And they curse anyone who fasts[28] and say, "Fasting is wrong; fasting belongs to this archon who made the world. We must take nourishment to make our bodies strong, and able to render their fruit in its season."

6,1 They use both the Old and the New Testaments, but renounce the Speaker in the Old Testament.[29] And whenever they find a text the sense of which can be against them, they say that this has been said by the spirit of the world. (2) But if a statement can be represented as resembling their lust—not as the text is, but as their deluded minds take it—they twist it to fit their lust and claim that it has been spoken by the Spirit of truth. (3) And this, they claim, is what the Lord said of John, "What went ye out into the wilderness for to see? A reed shaken with the wind?"[30] John was not perfect, they say; he was inspired by many spirits, like a reed stirring in every wind. (4) And when the spirit of the archon came he would preach Judaism; but when the Holy Spirit came he would speak of Christ. And this is the meaning of "He that is least in the Kingdom"[31] <and so on>. "He said this of us," they say, "because the least of us is greater than he."

7,1 Such persons are silenced at once by the truth itself. For from the context of each saying the truth will be plainly shown and the trustworthiness

---

[27] Mandaeans accuse Christians of this at *Ginza* 136,12-13.

[28] Fasting is condemned for other reasons. at GT 14; 104 and at Gos. Judas 40,12-13. The Mandaean *Ginza* 136,12-13; 34-39 condemns the Christian practice of fasting.

[29] The "God of the Law" as such is condemned at Test. Tr. 45,23-48,26.

[30] Matt 11:7

[31] Matt 11:11

of the text demonstrated. (2) If John had worn soft clothing and lived in kings' houses the saying would fit him exactly and be in direct refutation of him. But if <it says>, "What went ye out for to see? A man clothed in soft raiment?"[32] and John was not such a man, then the saying's accusation cannot apply to John, who did not wear soft clothing. The reference is to those who expected to find John like that, and who were often hypocritically flattered by persons who lived indoors, in kings' houses. (3) For they thought that they could go out and get praises and congratulations from John as well, for the transgressions they committed every day. (4) But when they did not they were reprovingly told by the Savior, "What did you expect to find? A man borne hither and yon with you by your passions, like people in soft clothing? No! John is no reed shaken by men's opinions, like a reed swayed by the authority of every wind."

7,5 Since the Savior did say, "Among them that are born of woman there is none greater than John,"[33] as a safeguard for us, lest any think that John was greater than even the Savior himself—who was also born of woman, of the ever-virgin Mary through the Holy Spirit—he said that he who is "less" than John, meaning in the length of his incarnate life, is greater in the kingdom of heaven. (6) For since the Savior was born six months after the birth of John, it is plain that he <appeared younger than he>—though he was older than John, for he was always, and is. But to whom is this not plain? So all the things they say are worthless fabrication, good things turned into bad.

8,1 And they too have lots of books. They publish certain "Questions of Mary"; but others offer many books about the Ialdabaoth we spoke of, and in the name of Seth.[34] They call others "Apocalypses of Adam[35] and have ventured to compose other Gospels in the names of the disciples, and are not ashamed to say that our Savior and Lord himself, Jesus Christ, revealed this obscenity. (2) For in the so-called "Greater Questions of Mary"—there are also "Lesser" ones forged by them—they claim that he reveals it to her after taking her aside on the mountain, praying, producing a woman from his side, beginning to have sex with her, and then partaking of his emission, if you please, to show that "Thus we must do, that we may live." (3) And when Mary was alarmed and fell to the ground, he raised her up and said to her, "O thou of little faith, wherefore didst thou doubt?"[36]

---

[32] Matt 11:8

[33] Matt 11:11

[34] Cf. The titles of CG VII,2, The Second Treatise of the Great Seth, and CG VII,5, The Three Steles of Seth.

[35] Cf. The title of CG V,5, The Apocalypse of Adam.

[36] Matt 14:31

8,4 And they say that this is the meaning of the saying in the Gospel, "If I have told you earthly things and ye believe not, how shall ye believe the heavenly things?"[37] and so of, "When ye see the Son of Man ascending up where he was before"[38]—in other words, when you see the emission being partaken of where it came from. (5) And when Christ said, "Except ye eat my flesh and drink my blood,"[39] and the disciples were disturbed and replied, "Who can hear this?"[40] they say his saying was about the dirt. (6) And this is why they were disturbed and fell away; they were not entirely stable yet, they say.

8,7 And when David says, "He shall be like a tree planted by the outgoings of water that will bring forth its fruit in due season,"[41] they say he is speaking of the man's dirt. "By the outgoing of water," and, "that will bring forth his fruit," means the emission at climax. And "Its leaf shall not fall off" means, "We do not allow it to fall to the ground, but eat it ourselves."

9,1 And so as not to do more harm than good by making their prooftexts public, I am going to omit most of them—otherwise I would cite all their wicked sayings and go through them here. (2) When it says that Rahab put a scarlet thread in her window, this was not scarlet thread, they tell us, but the female organs. And the scarlet thread means the menstrual blood, and "Drink water from your cisterns"[42] refers to the same.

9,3 They say that the flesh must perish and cannot be raised, and this belongs to the archon. (4) But the power in the menses and organs is soul, they say, "which we gather and eat. And whatever we eat—meat, vegetables, bread or anything else—we are doing creatures a favor by gathering the soul[43] from them all and taking it to the heavens with us." Hence they eat meat of all kinds and say that this is "to show mercy to our race." (5) And they claim that the same soul has been implanted in animals, insects, fish, snakes, men—and in vegetation, trees, and the fruits of the soil.[44]

---

[37] Cf. John 3:12.
[38] John 6:62
[39] John 6:53
[40] John 6:60
[41] Ps. 1:3
[42] Prov. 5:15
[43] This idea is fundamental to Manichaean practice: see, e.g., Man. Keph. 191,16-17; 212,10-22; 236,7-27. And see Iren. 1.30.14: consummationem autem futuram, quando tota humectatio spiritus luminis collegatur.
[44] A comparable idea is found at PS 25 (MacDermot pp. 34-35) Man. Keph. 124,3-6; 210,24-25; Man. Hom. 27,11-16; Corp. Herm. 10.7.

9,6 Those of them who are called Phibionites offer their shameful sacrifices of fornication, which I have already mentioned here, in 365[45] names which they have invented themselves as names of supposed archons, making fools of their female partners and saying, "Have sex with me, so that I may offer you to the archon." (7) And at each act of intercourse they pronounce an outlandish name[46] of one of their fictitious archons, and pray, if you please, by saying, "I offer this to thee, So-and-so, that thou mayest offer it to So-and-so." But at another act he supposes again that he is likewise offering it to another archon, so that he too may offer it to the other. (8) And until he mounts, or rather, sinks, through 365 falls of copulation, he calls on some name at each, and does the same sort of thing. Then he starts back down through the same acts, performing the same obscenities and making fools of his female victims. (9) Now when he reaches a mass as great as that of a total number of 730 falls—I mean the falls of unnatural unions and the names they have made up—then finally a man of this sort has the hardihood to say, "I am Christ, for I have descended from on high through the names of the 365 archons!"

10,1 They say that these are the names of the archons they consider the greatest, although they say there are many.[47] In the first heaven is the archon Iao. In the second, they say, is Saklas,[48] the archon of fornication. In the third, they say, is the archon Seth and in the fourth, they say, is Davides. (2) For they suppose that there is a fourth heaven, and a third—and a fifth, another heaven, in which they say is Eloaeus, also called Adonaeus. Some of them say that Ialdabaoth is in the sixth heaven, some say Elilaeus. (3) But they suppose that there is another, seventh heaven, and say that Sabaoth is in that. But others disagree, and say that Ialdabaoth is in the seventh.

10,4 But in the eighth heaven they put the so-called Barbelo;[49] and the "Father and Lord of all," the same Self-begetter;[50] and another Christ, a

---

[45] See n. 78 p. 6.

[46] For the powers "each in its own name" see Clem. Strom. 3.4.29.2, and cf. Iren. 1.31.2.

[47] Comparable lists are found at Iren. 1.30.5; Orig Cels. 6,31; Apocry. Jn. II,1 11,19-12,33.

[48] In NHC Saklas ("Fool") is an alternate name for Ialdabaoth at Nat. Arc. 95,5-8. At Gos. Egyp. 56,16-19 he is the "begetting spirit of the earth";at Apoc. Ad. 74,7-30 "the god of the aeons"; at Apocry. Jn. 16,32, a demon. At Gos. Judas 51 Yaltabaoth and Saklas are among the twelve angels who rule over the abyss.

[49] At Or. Wld. 121,28-35 Sophia Zoe lives in the "first heaven." At Eug. 89,9 the heavens are made for the glory of Immortal Man and Sophia his consort.

[50] αὐτογενής. The "divine Autogenes" or the like is found in five NHC tractates, most often in Apocry. Jn., Gos. Egyp. and Zost. At Apocry. Jn. II,1 7,19-20; 8,23; 9,1-2 the divine Autogenes is "the Christ" or "Christ."

self-engendered one,[51] and our Christ,[52] who descended and revealed this knowledge to men, who they say is also called Jesus. (5) But he is not "born of Mary" but "revealed through Mary." And he has not taken flesh but is only appearance.

10,6 Some say Sabaoth has the face of an ass;[53] others, the face of a pig.[54] This, they say, is why is why he forbade the Jews to eat pork. He is the maker of heaven, earth, the heavens after him, and his own angels. (7) In departing this world the soul makes its way through these archons, but no <one> can get through them unless he is in full possession of this "knowledge"—or rather, this contemptibility—and escapes the archons and authorities because he is "filled."[55]

10,8 The archon who holds this world captive is shaped like a dragon.[56] He swallows[57] souls that are not in the know, and returns them to the world through his phallus, here <to be implanted> in pigs and other animals, and brought up again through them.

10,9 But, say they, if one becomes privy to this knowledge and gathers himself from the world through the menses and the emission of lust, he is detained here no longer; he gets up above these archons. (10) They say that he passes Sabaoth by and—with impudent blasphemy—that he treads on his head. And thus he mounts above him to the height, where the Mother of the living, Barbero or Barbelo, is, and so the soul is saved.

10,11 The wretches also say that Sabaoth has hair like a woman's.[58] They think that the term, Sabaoth, is some archon, not realizing that where scripture says, "Thus saith Lord Sabaoth" it has not given anyone's

---

[51] αὐτολόχευτον. "The divine Autogenes, Christ," is found at Apocry. Jn. II.1 9,2 and III,1 13,6; 11,8-9; "the great Logos, the Autogenes" at Gos. Egyp. III,2 50,18-19; "the great self-begotten living Word" at Gos. Egyp. IV,2 60,1-2; 65,5-6; 66,17-18. The expression, "Self-begotten Christ" as such does not occur in NHC but see the preceding note.

[52] See Or. Wld. 105, 25-29,...another being, called Jesus Christ, who resembles the savior above in the eighth heaven and who sits at his right upon a revered throne...

[53] An ass-faced archon is mentioned, e.g., at Apocry Jn. 11, 27-28; the fragment of Jeu at MacDermot, *Books of Jeu*, p. 141; Orig. Cels. 6.30.

[54] A pig-faced archon is mentioned at 2 Jeu 43 (MacDermot *Books of Jeu*, p. 101).

[55] "Filled" is a term of approbation common in the religious literature of the early Christian centuries. See, among many other examples, 1 Cor 4:8; Eph 3:19; Col 2:10 and in NHC Apocry. Jas. 2,29-35; 3,34-37.

[56] For the dragon-shaped archon see, e.g., Apocry. Jn. II,1 11,30-32; Man. Keph. 33,33; 77,33; Man. Ps. 57,18 (Allberry II p. 208).

[57] See PS 3.126 (MacDermot pp. 317-319) and cf. 1.26-27 (MacDermot pp. 36-38); in Mandaean literature *Ginza* 433,36; *Johannesbuch* 191,4-5; in NHC perhaps Dia. Sav. 122.19.

[58] Cf. The long-haired temptress archon Paraplex is found at PS 4.139 (MacDermot p. 359).

name, but a term of praise for the Godhead. (12) Translated from Hebrew, "Sabaoth" means "Lord of hosts." Wherever "Sabaoth" occurs in the Old Testament, it suggests a host; hence Aquila everywhere renders "Adonai Sabaoth" as "Lord of armies." (13) But since these people are frantic against their Master in every way they go looking for the one who does not exist, and have lost the one who does. Or rather, they have lost themselves.

11,1 <They do> any number of other <things> and it is a misfortune to speak of their mad behavior in them. Some of them do not have to do with women, if you please, but pollute themselves with their own hands, receive their own dirt on their hands, and then eat it. (2) For this they cite a slanderously interpreted text, "These hands sufficed, not only for me, but also for them that were with me"—and again, "Working with your hands, that ye may have to give also to them that need."[59] (3) And I believe that the Holy Spirit was moved to anger over these persons in the apostle Jude, I mean in the General Epistle written by Jude. ("Jude" is our Jude, the brother of James, and called the Lord's brother.) For the Holy Spirit taught, with Jude's voice, that they are debauched and debauch like cattle, as he says, "Insofar as they know not, they are guilty of ignorance, and insofar as they know they are debauched, even as brute beasts."[60] (4) For they dispose of their corruption like dogs and pigs. Dogs and pigs, and other animals as well, are polluted in this way and eat their bodies' discharge.

11,5 For in fact they really do "defile the flesh while dreaming, despise dominion, and speak evil of dignities. But Michael the archangel, when contending with the devil he disputed about the body of Moses, brought not a railing accusation, but said, The Lord rebuke thee. (6) But these speak evil of things which they naturally know not."[61] For they blaspheme the holiest of holy things, bestowed on us with sanctification, by turning them into dirt.

11,7 And these are the things they have ventured to say against the apostles, as the blessed Paul also says, "So that some dare <blasphemously to report> of us that we say, Let us do evil that good may come upon us; whose damnation is just."[62] (8) And how many other texts I could cite against the blasphemers! For these persons who debauch themselves with their own hands—and not just they, but the ones who consort with women too—finally get their fill of promiscuous relations with women and grow

---

[59] Eph. 4:28
[60] Jude 10
[61] Jude 8-10
[62] Rom 3:8

ardent for each other, men for men, "receiving in themselves the recompense of their error"[63] as the scripture says. For once they are completely ruined they congratulate each other on having received the highest rank.[64]

11,9 Moreover they deceive the womenfolk who put their trust in them, "laden with sins and led away with divers lusts,"[65] and tell their female dupes, "So-and-so is a virgin"—one who has been debauched for so many years, and is being debauched every day! For they never have their fill of copulation, but in their circles the more indecent a man is, the more praiseworthy they consider him. (10) They say that virgins are women who have never gone on to the point of being inseminated in normal marital relations of the customary kind. They have sex all the time and commit fornication, but before the pleasure of their union is consummated they push their villainous seducer away and take the dirt we spoke of for food—(11) comparably to Shelah's perversity with Tamar. <They boast of virginity>, but instead of virginity have adopted this technique of being seduced without accepting the union of seduction, and the seminal discharge.[66]

11,12 They blaspheme not only Abraham, Moses, Elijah and the whole choir of prophets, but the God who chose them as well.[67] (12,1) Indeed, they have ventured countless other forgeries. They say that one book is a "Birth of Mary," and they palm some horrid, baneful things off in it and say that they get them from it. (2) On its authority they say that Zacharias was killed in the temple because he had seen a vision, and when he wanted to reveal the vision his mouth was stopped from fright. For at the hour of incense, while he was burning it, he saw a man standing there, they say, with the form of an ass.[68] (3) And when he had come out and wanted to say "Woe to you, whom are you worshiping?" the person he had seen inside in the temple stopped his mouth so that he could not speak. But when his mouth was opened so that he could speak, then he revealed it to them and they killed him. And that, they say, is how Zacharias died. (4) This, they say, is why the priest was ordered to wear bells by the lawgiver himself.[69] Whenever he went in to officiate, the object of his worship

---

[63] Rom 1:27

[64] Hipp. Refut. 6.19.5 says, of Simonians, μακαρίζουσιν ἑαυτοὺς ἐπὶ τῇ ξένῃ μίξει, ταύτην εἶναι λέγοντες τὴν τέλειαν ἀγάπην.

[65] 2 Tim 3:6

[66] Epiph makes the same accusation in Sect 63, against the group he calls "The first type of Origenist, who are shamefully behaved as well."

[67] Cf. Iren. I.30.10-11.

[68] Cf. Tacitus Historiae 4; Tert. Apol. 16.1-5, and see n. 43 above.

[69] Cf. Exod 28:33-34.

would hear them jangle and hide, so that no one would spy the imaginary face of his form.

12,5 But all their silliness is an easy business to refute, and chock-full of absurdity. If the object of their service were visible at all, he could not be hidden. But if he could be hidden at all he could not be visible. (6) And again, we must put it to them differently: If he was visible, then he was a body and could not be a spirit. But if he was spirit, he could not be counted among the things that are visible. And since he was not something visible, how could he provide for the reduction of his size at the jangling of bells? For since he was by nature invisible, he would not be seen unless he wished to be. (7) But even though he was seen, he would not have appeared of necessity because his nature required him to appear; he must have appeared as a favor—not manifesting his appearance inadvertently, fearfully and with unease if there was no sound of bells. And thus their false, spurious statement has failed from every standpoint.

12,8 And there are many other foolish things that they say. <For they say Zacharias was killed—and they are right>—although Zacharias was surely not killed immediately. Indeed he was still alive after John's birth, and prophesied the Lord's advent, and his birth in the flesh of the holy Virgin Mary, through the Holy Spirit. (9) As he says, "And thou, child, shalt be called the prophet of the highest; for thou shalt go before the face of the Lord to prepare his ways.[70]...To turn the hearts of the fathers unto the children, and the disobedient to wisdom," and so on. And how much else is there to say about their lying and their pollution?

13,1 The ones they call "Levites" do not have to do with women, but with each other. And these are their supposedly distinguished and praiseworthy persons! And then they make fun of those who practice asceticism, chastity and celibacy, as having taken the trouble for nothing.

13,2 They cite a fictitious Gospel in the name of the holy disciple, Philip,[71] as follows. "The Lord hath shown me what my soul must say on its ascent to heaven, and how it must answer each of the powers on high.[72] 'I have recognized myself,' it saith, 'and gathered myself from every quarter, and have sown no children for the archon. But I have pulled up his roots,

[70] Luke 1:17

[71] The quotation which follows is not found in the NHC Gospel of Philip.

[72] The soul makes such a speech at Iren. 1.21.5; Orig. Cels. 6.31; and in NHC at Apoc. Paul 23,1-28; 1 Apoc. Jas 33,2-36,1, and see Cod. Tch. James 19,26-22,20. There may be a reference to it at Apocry. Jas. 8,35-36. See also Gos. Mary BG 8502,1 15,1-17,7. At PS 3.112 (MacDermot pp. 286-291) the soul escapes the archons by repeating mysteries to them; a speech for it to make is found on p. 289.

and gathered my scattered members, and I know who thou art. For I,' it saith, 'am of the ones on high.'" And so, they say, it is set free. (3) But if it turns out to have fathered a son, it is detained below until it can take its own children up and restore them to itself.

13,4 And their silly fictions are of such a character that they even dare to blaspheme the holy Elijah, and say that when he was taken up he was cast back down into the world. (5) For they say that one she-demon came and caught hold of him[73] and said to him, "Whither goest thou? For I have children of thee, and thou canst not ascend and leave thy children here." And he replied, they say, "Whence hast thou children of me, seeing I lived in purity?" And she answered, "Yea, for when oft, in dreaming dreams, thou wert voided of bodies in thine emission, it was I that received the seeds of thee and bare thee sons."[74]

13,6 How silly the people are who say this sort of thing! How can a demon, an invisible spirit with no body, receive anything <from> bodies? But if she does receive something from bodies and become pregnant, she cannot be a spirit, but must be a body. And being a body, how can she be invisible and a spirit?

13,7 And their drivel is simply outrageous. They like to cite the text which tells against them, if you please, the one from Epistle of Jude, in their own favor instead—where he says, "And they that dream defile the flesh, despise dominion and speak evil of dignities."[75] But the blessed Jude, the Lord's brother, did not say this of bodily dreamers. He goes right on to show that he means dreamers <in mind>, who utter their words as though they were dreaming and not in the waking state of the alertness of their reasoning powers. (8) (Even of the teachers at Jerusalem in fact, Isaiah says, "They are all dumb dogs, they cannot bark, dreaming on their couches,"[76] and so on.) And here in the Epistle of Jude, Jude shows (that this is what he means) by saying, "speaking of that they know not."[77] And he proved that he did not mean dreaming while asleep, but was saying of their fictitious bombast and nonsense that it was spoken in their sleep, not with a sound mind.

---

[73] Gershom Scholem suggested that this is a parody of a Jewish story in which the prophet Elijah vanquishes the demoness Lilith. See Scholem, *Jewish Gnosticism* pp. 73-74.

[74] This folk belief is attested at the Mandaean *Ginza* 50,8-11. At Corp. Herm. 9.3 it is used as an image of the mind and its ideas.

[75] Jude 8

[76] Isa 56:10

[77] Cf. Jude 10.

14,1 It is truly a misfortune for me to tell all this; only God can close this stinking pit. And I shall go on from here, praying the all-sovereign God that no one has been trapped in the mud, and that his mind has not absorbed any of the reeking filth. (2) For in the first place the apostle Paul grubs up the entire root of their wickedness with his injunction about younger widows: "Younger widows refuse, for after they have waxed wanton against Christ they will marry; having damnation, because they have cast off their first faith...But let them marry, bear children, guide the house."[78] (3) But if the apostle says to bear children, but they decline procreation, it is the enterprise of a serpent and of false doctrine. Because they are mastered by the pleasure of fornication they invent excuses for their uncleanness, so that their licentiousness may appear to fulfill (Paul's commandment).

14,4 Really these things should neither be said nor considered worth mentioning in treatises, but buried like a foul corpse exuding a pestilent vapor, to protect people from injury even through their sense of hearing. (5) And if a sect of this kind had passed away and no longer existed, it would be better to bury it and say nothing about it at all. But since it does exist and has practitioners, and I have been urged by your Honors to speak of all the sects, I have been forced to describe parts of it, in order, in all frankness, not to pass them over but describe them, for the protection of the hearers—but for the banishment of the practitioners. (6) For where can I not find proof of their murders and monstrous deeds, and of the devil's rites which have been given the nuts by the inspiration of that same devil?

15,1 They are proved wrong at once in what they imagine and allege about the tree in the First Psalm of which it is said that it will "bring forth his fruit in due season, and his leaf shall not fall." For before that it says, "His delight is in the Law of the Lord, and in his Law will he exercise himself day and night."[79] But these people deny the Law and the prophets. (2) And if they deny the Lord's Law, together with the Law they are also slandering the One who spoke in the Law. They are wrong as to the meaning of the truth and have lost it, and they neither believe in judgment nor acknowledge resurrection.

15,3 They reap the fruit of the things they do in the body to glut themselves with pleasure through being driven insane by the devil's pleasures and lusts.[80] Of this they are altogether and everywhere convicted by

---

[78] 1 Tim 5:11; 14

[79] Ps. 1:3; 2

[80] I.e., their devil-inspired madness is reflected in their inability to interpret scripture correctly.

the speech of the truth. (4) John says, "If there come any unto you, and bring not this doctrine."[81] Which doctrine? "If any confess not that Christ is come in the flesh, this is an antichrist. Even now there are many antichrists"[82]—meaning that those who do not acknowledge that Christ has come in the flesh are antichrists.

15,5 Moreover the Savior himself says, "They which shall be accounted worthy of the kingdom of heaven neither marry nor are given in marriage, but are equal unto the angels."[83] (6) And not only that, but to show (his) manifest chastity[84] and the holiness which is achieved through the solitary life, he tells Mary, "Touch me not, for I am not yet ascended to my Father"[85]—proving that chastity has no congress with bodies and no sexual relations.

15,7 Furthermore in another passage the Holy Spirit says prophetically, both for the ancients and for <the> generations to come, "Blessed is the barren that is undefiled, which hath not known the bed sinfully; and the eunuch which with his hand hath wrought no iniquity"[86]—ruling out the indecencies with the hands which are sanctioned by their myth.

16,1 And how much else there is to say! In one passage the apostle says, "He that is unmarried, and the virgin, careth for the things of the Lord, how he may please the Lord"[87]—and he says this to show (his) true chastity, at the Holy Spirit's solemn bidding. But he then says of the lawfully married, "Marriage is honorable, and the bed undefiled; but whoremongers and adulterers God will judge."[88] (2) Furthermore he cries out against them in his letter to the Romans, and exposes the obscenities of those who commit the misdeeds by saying, "For even their women did change the natural use into that which is against nature"—and of the males, "men with men working that which is unseemly."[89] (3) Moreover in the Epistle to Timothy he says of them, "In the last days perilous times shall come, for men shall be lovers of pleasure";[90] and again, "forbidding to marry, having their consciences seared with an hot iron."[91] (4) For they forbid chaste wedlock

---

81 2 John 10
82 2 John 1:7; 1 John 2:18
83 Luke 20:35-36
84 See 16,1 below
85 John 20:7
86 Wisd Sol 3:13-14
87 1 Cor 7:32; 34
88 Heb 13:4
89 Rom 1:27
90 2 Tim 3:1;2;4
91 1 Tim 4:2-3

and procreation, but are seared in their consciences since they have sex and pollute themselves, and yet hinder procreation.

16,5 Indeed it is already shown by the prophet, even from the first, that the very thing they call a sacrifice, filthy thing that it is, is snake's flesh and not, heaven forbid, the Lord's—for he says, "Thou brakest the head of the dragon, and gavest him to be meat for the peoples of Ethiopia."[92] (6) For their loathsome worship is truly snake's food, and those who celebrate this rite of Zeus—a daemon now but once a sorcerer, (7) whom some people futilely take for a god—are Ethiopians made black by sin.

For all the sects have gathered imposture for themselves from the Greek mythology, and altered it by making it mean something else which is worse. (8) The poets introduce Zeus as having swallowed Wisdom, his own daughter. But no one could swallow a baby—and to poke fun at the disgusting activities of the Greek gods St. Clement said that Zeus could not have swallowed the baby if he swallowed Wisdom, but <the myth of Zeus appears> to mean its own child.[93]

17,1 But what else should I say? Or how shall I shake off this filthy burden since I am both willing and unwilling to speak—compelled to, lest I appear to be concealing any of the facts, and yet afraid that by revealing their horrid activities I may soil or wound those who are given to pleasures and lusts, or incite them to take too much interest in this? (2) In any case may I, and all the <body>[94] of the holy catholic church, and all the readers of this book, remain unharmed by such a suggestion of the devil and his mischief! (3) For if I were to start <in> again on the other things they say and do—which are like these and as numerous, and still more grave and <worse>—and if, for a curative drug, I should also wish to match a remedy, like an antidote, with each thing they say, I would make a heavy task of composing this treatise.

17,4 For I happened on this sect myself, beloved, and was actually taught these things in person, out of the mouths of people who really undertook them. Not only did women under this delusion offer me this line of talk, and divulge this sort of thing to me. With impudent boldness moreover, they even tried to seduce me themselves—like that murderous, villainous Egyptian wife of the chief cook—because they wanted me in my youth.

[92] Ps 73:13-14

[93] Cf. Ps.-Clem Hom. 4.16.2.

[94] Text: ἐλπίς Holl: σύστασις

(5) But he who stood by the holy Joseph then, stood by me as well. And when, in my unworthiness and inadequacy, I had called on the One who rescued Joseph then, and was shown mercy and escaped their murderous hands, I too could sing a hymn to God the all-holy and say, "Let us sing to the Lord for he is gloriously magnified; horse and rider hath he thrown into the sea."[95]

17,6 For it was not by a power like that of Joseph's righteousness but by my groaning to God, that I was pitied and rescued. For when I was reproached by the baneful women themselves, I laughed at the way persons of their kind were whispering to each other, jokingly if you please, "We can't save the kid; we've left him in the hands of the archon to perish!" (7) (For whichever is prettier flaunts herself as bait, so that they claim to "save"—instead of destroying—the victims of their deceit through her. And then the plain one gets blamed by the more attractive ones, and they say, "I'm an elect vessel and can save the suckers[96] but you couldn't!")

17,8 Now the women who taught this dirty myth were very lovely in their outward appearance but in their wicked minds they had all the devil's ugliness. But the merciful God rescued me from their wickedness, so that after reading their books, understanding their real intent and not being carried away with it, and after escaping without taking the bait, (9) I lost no time reporting them to the bishops who were there, and finding out which ones were hidden in the church. <Thus> they were expelled from the city, about 80 persons, and the city was cleared of their tare-like, thorny growth.

18,1 Perhaps someone, if he remembers my promise I made earlier, may even commend me. I indicated before that I have encountered some of the sects, though I know some from documentary sources, and some from the instruction and testimony of trustworthy men who were able to tell me the truth. So here too, in all frankness, I have not avoided the subject, but have shown what this one of the sects which came my way is like. (2) And I could speak plainly of it because of things which I did not do—heaven forbid!—but which <I knew> by learning them in exact detail from persons who were trying to convert me to this and did not succeed. They lost their hope of my destruction instead, and did not attain the goal of the plot that they and the devil in them were attempting against my poor soul (3) so that,

---

95 Exod 15:1

96 ἀπατώμενοι persons to be deceived. For "dupes," meaning those who are already members of a sect, Epiph normally says ἠπατημένοι.

with the most holy David, I may say that "Their blows were weapons of babes,"[97] and so on, and, "Their travail shall return upon their own head, and their wickedness shall fall upon their own pate."[98]

18,4 As I encountered and escaped them, read, understood and despised, and passed them by, so, reader, I urge you in your turn to read, despise <their pernicious doctrine> and pass by, so that you will not fall into the depravity of these wicked serpents. (5) But if you should ever happen on any of this school of snake-like persons, may you pick the wood the Lord has made ready for us right up, the wood on which our Lord Christ was nailed. <And> may you hurl it at the serpent's head at once, and say, "Christ has been crucified for us, leaving us an example'[99] of salvation. (6) For he would not have been crucified if he had not had flesh. But since he had flesh and was crucified, he has crucified our sins. I am held fast by faith in the truth, not carried off by the serpent's false imposture and the seductive whisper of his teaching."

19,1 Now, beloved, having passed this sect by I am going to tread the other rough tracks next—not to walk on them but to teach, from a safe distance, such as are willing to recognize the roughest spots and flee by the narrow, arduous path that leads to eternal life, and leave the road which is broad and roomy, and yet thorny, full of stumbling-blocks, miry, and choked with licentiousness and fornication. (2) The like of this fornication and licentiousness may be seen in the extremely dreadful snake the ancients called the pangless viper."[100]

19,3 For the nature of such a viper is similar to the wickedness of these people. In performing their filthy act either with men or with women they forbear insemination, rendering impossible the procreation God has given his creatures—as the apostle says, "receiving in themselves the recompense of their error which was meet,"[101] and so on. (4) So, we are told, when the pangless viper grew amorous, female for male and male for female, they would twine together, and the male would thrust his head into the female's gaping jaws. And she, in the throes of passion, would bite off the male's head and so swallow the poison that dripped from its mouth, and conceive a pair of snakes of the same kind within her, a male and a female. (5) When this pair had come to maturity in her belly and had no way of being born,

---

97 Ps 63:8
98 Ps. 63:8
99 1 Pet 2:21
100 ἀπειρώδινος ἔχιδνα
101 Rom 1:27

they would tear their mother's side and be born like that, so that both their father and their mother perished. This is why they called it the pangless viper; it has no experience of the pangs of birth. (6) It is more dreadful and fearsome than all the snakes, since it carries out its own extermination within itself and receives its dirt by mouth; and this crack-brained sect is like it. And now that we have beaten its head, body and offspring here with the wood of life, let us go on to examine the others calling, as our help, on God, to whom be honor and might forever and ever. Amen.

27.

Against Carpocratians[1] *Number seven, but number twenty-seven of the series*

1,1 Carpocrates makes another, for he founded his own unlawful school of his falsely named opinion, and his character is the worst of all. (2) (For the sect of what is falsely termed "Knowledge," which called its members Gnostics, arose from all of these—Simon and Menander, Satornilus, Basilides and Nicolaus, Carpocrates himself, and further, because of Valentinus. I have already given a description of one branch of it—the "Knowledgeable," though in their behavior they are despicable.)

2,1 Carpocrates says in his turn that there is one first principle on high, and just like the others he wants to introduce a Father of all, unknowable and unnameable. But he says that the world, and everything in the world, has been made by the angels, who are far inferior to the unknowable Father.[2] For he says that they rebelled against the power on high, and therefore have made the world.

2,2[3] And he says that Jesus our Lord was begotten of Joseph, just as all men were generated from a man's seed and a woman.[4] He is like all men but is different in his life—in prudence, virtue and a life of righteousness.[5]

[1] This Sect reads like an expansion of Iren. 1.25.1-6, although the repetitiousness of the sentences in 2,2-7 suggests a combination of this source with Hipp. Synt. Hipp. Refut. 7.32 reads like a condensation of Irenaeus. Justin Dial. 35.6 and Orig. Cels. 5.62 mention Carpocratians/Harpocratians. Eus. H. E. 4.7.9-11 and Tert. De Anima 23.2; 35.1-2 are dependent on Irenaeus. The brief PsT 3.1 and Fil 35 agree more closely with each other than with Irenaeus or Hipp. Refut. and may represent Hipp. Synt.

[2] Iren. 1.25.1; PsT 3.1; Fil. 35.1.

[3] Cf. PsT 3.1; Fil. 35.2. However, the material from this point through 3,11 is taken almost word for word from Iren. 1.25.1-2. Cf. also Hipp. Refut. 7.32.1-3.

[4] See also PsT 3.1; Fil. 35.2. And perhaps cf. Melch. 5,2-3: they will say of him that he is unbegotten though he has been begotten.

[5] See also PsT 3.1; Fil. 35.3.

(3) Because he received a more vigorous soul than other men's, and he remembered what it had seen on high when it was on the unknowable Father's carousel,[6] powers were sent to his soul by the Father (4) so that it would be able to recall what it had seen, and gain the power to escape the angels who made the world by progressing through all the acts in the world and all the deeds that men can do, even strange, unlawful works done in secret (5)—and so this same soul of Jesus, once freed by all he acts, could ascend to the same unknowable Father who had sent it the powers from above in order that it could win through to him on high by progressing through all the acts and being released.

2,6 And what is more, the souls like his <which> embrace the same experiences as his can be freed in the same way and soar aloft to the unknowable Father, by performing all the acts, and similarly being quit of them all and then released.

2,7 Though it had been reared in Jewish customs Jesus' soul despised them[7] and for that reason received powers by which it could <put> the passions <to rest>[8] which accrue to man as punishments, and rise above the world's creators. (8) But not only Jesus' soul itself has this capacity; the soul as well that can progress through <all> the acts will rise above these angels who made the world. It too will <soar aloft>—like Jesus' soul, as I said—if it receives powers and does the same sort of thing.

2,9 Hence these victims of this fraud's deception have become so extremely arrogant that they consider themselves superior even to Jesus. (10) Some of them say that they are not superior to Jesus, but are to Peter, Andrew, Paul and the other apostles, because of the superiority of their knowledge and their greater progress in the achievement of various ends. Others of them, though, claim they are no different from our Lord Jesus Christ.[9] (11) For their souls are from the same carousel,[10] similarly to Jesus' soul have shown contempt for everything, <and will go to the same place>. <In fact>, they say, all souls have been vouchsafed the same power that Jesus' soul has. And thus, they say, they too progress through all activity, as Jesus' soul has of course gone through it. Again, if indeed one can despise more thoroughly than Jesus, he will be better than he.[11]

---

[6] For the carousel see Plato *Phaedrus* 347B-D, 348.

[7] Cf. Test. Tr. 29,26-27: the defilement of the Law is manifest.

[8] Holl: καταργῆσαι; Text: πρᾶξαι

[9] Cf. Tert. De Anima 23.

[10] Cf. Apocry. Jas. 10,34-38; Gos. Tr. 41,3-7; Nat. Arc. 96,19-22; GT 49; 50; Man. Keph. 63,14-15; the Mandaean *Ginza* 176,38-177,2 and *passim*.

[11] For equality with or superiority to Jesus, cf. Apocry. Jas. 4,32-5,3; 5,13; 6, 9-21. The Apocry. Jas passages, however, probably refer to martyrdom.

3,1[12] The members of this unlawful school put all sorts of horrid, pernicious deeds into practice. They have thought up magic devices and invented various incantations—love charms and spells—for every purpose. What is more, they summon familiar spirits too, in order to <gain> great power over everyone with the aid of much magic <so that>, they say, each of them can be master of anyone he wishes, and in any activity he may venture to undertake. (2) They deceive themselves in this way in order, if you please, to convince their blinded minds that the <souls> which have undertaken such things, have prevailed through acts of this sort, and have despised the angels who made the world and the things that are in the world, can escape the jurisdiction of these angelic fabricators—I don't care to say, "creators"—to embrace the freedom on high and attain the flight aloft.[13]

3,3[14] But they have been prepared by Satan, and put forward as a reproach and stumbling-block for God's church. For they have adopted the name of "Christian," though Satan has arranged this so that the heathen will be scandalized by them and reject the benefit of God's holy church and its real message, because of their wickedness and their intolerable evil deeds—(4) so that the heathen, observing the continual behavior of the evildoers themselves and supposing that the members of God's holy church are of the same kind, will refuse the hearing of God's real teaching, as I said, or even, seeing certain (of us) <behave in this profane way>, blaspheme us all alike. (5) And so, wherever they see such people, most of the heathen will not come near us for conversation or an exchange of views, or to listen to sacred discourse, and will not give us a hearing, since they are frightened by the unholy deeds of the wicked people.

4,1[15] These people spend all their time in dissipation, and in doing everything possible for their bodily comfort, and they never come near us, except perhaps to catch wavering souls with their wrong teaching. They resemble us only in proudly giving themselves a name—in order, through that name, to obtain the cover for their own wickedness.

4,2 But in the words of scripture, "Their damnation is just,"[16] as the holy apostle Paul said. Because of their evil deeds the due return will be awarded them. (3) By recklessly giving their minds to frenzy they have surrendered themselves to the sensations of countless pleasures. For they say that such

[12] With the following paragraph cf. Iren. 1.25.3 and Hipp. Refut. 7.32.5.
[13] Cf. Corp. Herm I.32.
[14] With the next paragraph cf. Iren. 1.25.2-3.
[15] See Iren. 1.25.3.
[16] Rom 3:8

things as men consider evil are not evil but good by nature[17]—nothing is evil by nature—but are regarded as evil by men. (4) And if one does all these things in this one incarnation the soul will not be embodied again to be cast down once more. By performing every action in one round it will escape, freed and with no more debt of activity in the world.

4,5 Again, I am afraid to say what sort of actions, or I might uncover a trench like a hidden sewer, and some might think that I am causing the blast of foul odor. Still, since I am constrained by the truth to disclose what goes on among the deluded, I am going to make myself speak—with some delicacy and yet without overstepping the bounds of the truth. (6) The plain fact is that these people perform every unspeakable, unlawful thing, which is not right even to say, and every kind of homosexual union and carnal intercourse with women, with every member of the body[18]—(7) and that they perform magic, sorcery and idolatry and say that this is the discharge of their obligations in the body, so that they will not be charged any more or required to do anything else, and for this reason the soul will not be turned back after its departure and go on to another incarnation and transmigration.

5,1[19] Their literature is such that the intelligent reader will be astounded and shocked, and doubt that human beings can do such things—not only civilized people like ourselves, but even those who <live with> wild beasts and bestial, brutish men, and all but venture to behave like dogs and swine. (2) For they say they absolutely must make every use of these things, or their souls may depart shy some work, and so be returned to bodies, to do all over again what they have not done. (3) And this, they say, is what Jesus in the Gospel meant by the parable, "Agree with thine adversary whiles thou art in the way with him, and do thy diligence to be quit of him, lest at any time the adversary deliver thee to the judge, and the judge deliver thee to the officer, and the officer cast thee into prison. Verily I say unto thee, thou shalt by no means come out thence till thou hast paid the uttermost farthing."[20]

5,4 But they make up a story to explain this parable and says that the "adversary" in it is one of the angels who have made the world and has

---

[17] The distinction between conventional "good" and "evil" is deprecated at Gos. Phil. 53,14-20; 66,9,13.

[18] Epiph may have deduced this from Iren. 1.25.4:...uti et omnia quecumque sunt irreligiosa et impia in potestate habere et operari si dicant.

[19] With 5,1-3 cf. Iren. 1.25.4.

[20] Matt 5:25-26. For Gnostic uses of this verse see Test. Tr. 30,15-17; PS 3.113 (MacDermot, pp. 294-296).

been appointed for this very purpose—to bring the souls to the judge when they quit their bodies here and are put on trial there. And if they have not done every act they are given by the archon to the "officer." (5) The officer is an angel whose service to the judge who made the world is to bring the souls back and bottle them up in different bodies.[21] And they identify the "adversary," whom I said the Lord has mentioned in the Gospel, as one of the angels who made the world, with the name of "Devil."[22]

5,6[23] For they say that the "prison" is the body, and would have it that the "uttermost farthing"is reembodiment. <Now> (the soul) <must> accomplish its "last act" in every incarnation, and not be left behind any more to do some wicked thing. For they say, as I have indicated, that when it has progressed through them all, performed them one by one and been liberated, it must ascend to the Unknowable One on high, passing the world's makers and maker by. (7) Again, they say that after they have done them all, even if in one incarnation, souls must then be freed and go to the heights afterwards. But if they do not do them in one, they work gradually through the performance of every unlawful deed in each incarnation, and are then freed.[24] (8) Again, they say, "We deign to tell this to those who are worthy,[25] that they may do the things that seem to be evil although they are not evil by nature, so that they may learn this and be freed." (9) And this school of Carpocrates marks the right ear-lobes of the persons they deceive with a burning iron,[26] or by using a razor or needle.

6,1 I heard at some time of a Marcellina[27] who was deceived by them, who corrupted many people in the time of Anicetus, Bishop of Rome, the successor of Pius and the bishops before him. (2)[28] For the bishops at Rome were, first, Peter and Paul, the apostles themselves and also bishops—then Linus, then Cletus, then Clement, a contemporary of Peter and Paul whom Paul mentions in the Epistle to the Romans. And no one need wonder why others before him succeeded the apostles in the episcopate, even though he was contemporary with Peter and Paul—for he too is the apostles' contemporary. (4) I am not quite clear as to whether he received the episcopal

[21] A NHC example of punishment by reincarnation is found at Apoc. Paul 21,19-21.

[22] I.e.: accuser

[23] With 6-7 cf. Hipp. Refut. 7.32.7; Iren. 1.25.4.

[24] Cf. Hipp. Refut. 7.32.7.

[25] Iren. 1.25.5: Jesum dicentes... illos expostulasse, ut dignis et adsentientibus seorsum haec traderent.

[26] Cf. Iren. 1.25.6; Hipp. Refut. 7.32.8.

[27] Iren. 1.25.6

[28] Cf. Iren. 3.3.3; Eus. H. E. 5.6.1-2.

appointment from Peter while they were still alive, and he declined and would not exercise the office—for in one of his Epistles he says, giving this counsel to someone, "I withdraw, I depart, let the people of God be tranquil,"[29] (I have found this in certain historical works)—or whether he was appointed by the bishop Cletus after the apostles' death.

6,5 But even so, others could have been made bishop while the apostles, I mean Peter and Paul, were still alive, since they often journeyed abroad for the proclamation of Christ, but Rome could not be without a bishop. (6) Paul even reached Spain, and Peter often visited Pontus and Bithynia. But after Clement had been appointed and declined, if this is what happened—I suspect this but cannot say it for certain—he could have been compelled to hold the episcopate in his turn, after the deaths of Linus and Cletus who were bishops for twelve years each after the death of Saints Peter and Paul in the twelfth year of Nero.)

6,7 In any case, the succession of the bishops at Rome runs in this order: Peter and Paul, Linus and Cletus, Clement, Evaristus, Alexander, Xystus, Telesphorus, Hyginus, Pius, and Anicetus, whom I mentioned above, on the list.[30] And no one need be surprised at my listing each of the items so exactly; precise information is always given in this way. (8) In Anicetus' time then, as I said, the Marcellina I have spoken of appeared at Rome spewing forth the corruption of Carpocrates' teaching, and corrupted and destroyed many there. And that made a beginning of the so-called Gnostics.

6,9[31] They have images painted with colors—some, moreover, have images made of gold, silver and other material—which they say are portraits of Jesus, and made by Pontius Pilate! That is, the portraits of the actual Jesus while he was dwelling among men! (10) They possess images like these in secret, and of certain philosophers besides—Pythagoras, Plato, Aristotle, and the rest—and they also place other portraits of Jesus with these philosophers. And after setting them up they worship them and celebrate heathen mysteries. For once they have erected these images, they go on to follow the customs of the heathen. But what are <the> customs of the heathen but sacrifices and the rest? (11) They say that salvation is of the soul only, and not of bodies.

7,1 And so we are bound to refute these people with all our might; no one should despise argumentation, most of all against cheats! But someone might say, "Aren't these things that are easy to spot, and foolish through

---

[29] 1 Clem. 54.1

[30] 6,1 gives a sort of list. Pourkier renders: en tête de la liste.

[31] Cf. Iren. 1.25.6.

and through?" Yes, but even foolish things have a way of convincing the foolish and subverting the wise, if no mind trained in the truth is there. Now since Carpocrates too has fallen into the magic of Simon and the rest, I am also going to refute him with the same arguments.

7,2 For if the unknowable, unnameable power was the cause of other angels, either there is ignorance in it—that is, in the Father of all—if he did not know what the angels he was making would do, not realizing that they would rebel and create things he did not want created. Or else he made them knowing that they were going to make things, but something he did not want got made by them—and by knowledge and consent he must be the maker of the things they have dared to make. (3) Now if, as I said, he knew what they would make but didn't want them to, why would he make the makers, to do what he didn't want done?

7,4 But if he has made the angels himself so that they would make what they have, then he wanted it made—that is why he prepared the angelic makers beforehand. And if he prepared them beforehand to create, but forbids what they created, this would be blatant false prosecution. (5) If, however, he consented to their creating, but chooses to repossess their creation—meaning men and souls—against their wishes, this will be just plain greed and nothing else—if the men the angels <made> are seized by the One on high, against the angels' wishes. Furthermore it must be weakness since, not being able to create for himself, he seizes his creatures' creations.

7,6 And for the rest it's a yarn and nonsense—with the ones below able to rise above the ones in the middle, and the ones in the middle being punished for being the causes of the ones below—and the ones below, I mean the souls of the ones in this creation, being brought safely past the ones in the middle to the One above, and set free. And the One above, who cannot create, must be adjudged feeble, but his creatures must be adjudged <powerful>, since they could make the things he did not want made, or wanted to make but couldn't.

7,7 For what he desires cannot be bad for him or be produced by beings which are bad. If it were bad, it should perish. But if any part of the work is preserved, the work cannot be bad—even if (only) part of it is going to be preserved. Nor can its makers be bad, <the ones who> executed the part that is going to be preserved. (8) And if the soul does come from angels, and receives power from on high after being brought into being, then all the more will angels attain salvation—since the soul they produced is saved although it comes from bad beings! And if it is saved, then neither the soul itself which was made by the angels, nor the angels whose product the soul is, can be bad. (8,1) But anyone in his right mind must know that this whole cheap piece of work is a product of insanity.

8,2 But these people will be shamed again, from their other words as well. For if Jesus is not the offspring of a virgin, Mary, but of Joseph's seed and the same Mary, and yet Jesus is saved, then the persons whose offspring he is will also be saved. And if Mary and Joseph are of the demiurge, then they have said that the demiurge is <also> the creator <of Jesus>; and the maker of Mary and Joseph, by whose agency Jesus has come from the unknowable Father on high, cannot be defective.[32] (3) But if Jesus too is the product of the angels, and the demiurge is one of the angels, then they will surely all fall foul of the same sort of absurdity that the angels have. And there can be no proof of their dramatic piece, which is full of poison, and crammed with every kind of virulent teaching.

8,4 But since we have beaten this sect back once more—like splitting a serpent's head with a cudgel of faith and truth when it is (already lying) on the ground—let us approach the other beast-like sects <that have appeared in the world> for its ruin and because of our promise force ourselves to begin <their refutation>.

28.
Against Cerinthians[1] *or Merinthians, Number eight, but twenty-eight of the series*

1,1 Now Cerinthus in turn, the founder of the so-called Cerinthians, has come from this bestial seed, bringing the world his venom. But almost nothing different from Carpocrates is spouting out into the world, just the same harmful poisons.

1,2[2] For he slanderously gives the same account of Christ as Carpocrates, that he was born of Mary and Joseph's seed, and likewise that the world was made by angels.[3] (3) In the inculcation of his teaching he

[32] ἐν ὑστερήματι. Pourkier: ce n'est plus dans l'Avorton qui'il faudra chercher celui qui a fait Joseph et Marie.

[1] The source of the information in the opening portions of this Sect is Irenaeus, upon whom Hipp. Synt. seems to be dependent. The very short summary notice at PsT 3.2 might be drawn from Hipp. Synt. Filaster may have used Hipp. Synt., Epiph or both. Either by conjecture or from oral tradition, Epiph makes Cerinthus, who he believes taught the necessity of circumcision, the instigator of the controversies about circumcision which the NT records in Acts, 1 Corinthians and Galatians.

[2] With 1,2-7 cf. Iren. I.26.1; Hipp Refut. 7.33; PsT 3.2.

[3] With 28,3 cf. PsT 3.2; Fil. 36.1.

differs from Carpocrates in no way except only in this, that he adhered in part to Judaism. He, however, claims that the Law and prophets have been given by the angels, and the law-giver is one of the angels who have made the world.

1,4 Cerinthus lived in Asia and began his preaching there. (5) I have already said of him that he too preached that the world was not created by the first, supreme power—and that when "Jesus," the offspring of Mary and the seed of Joseph, had grown up, "Christ," meaning the Holy Spirit in the form of a dove, came down to him in the Jordan[4] from the God on high, revealing the unknowable Father to him, and through him to his companions.

1,6 And therefore, because a power had come to him from on high, he performed works of power.[5] And when he suffered, the thing that had come from above flew away from Jesus to the heights.[6] (7) Jesus has suffered and risen again but the Christ who had come to him from above flew away without suffering[7]—that is, the thing which had descended in the form of a dove—and Jesus is not Christ.

2,1 But he too has come to grief, as all you lovers of the truth can see. He claims that the law-giver is not good, but he sees fit to be obedient to his Law—plainly, as to a good one. (2) How can the evil one have given the good Law? If it is good not to commit adultery and good not to murder, how much more must the giver of these commandments be better—if it be granted that the person who does not do these things is good! And how can someone who advises what is good, and gives a good Law, be accused of doing evil? The man who takes this sort of line is crazy!

2,3 Now this man is one of the ones who caused the trouble in the apostles' time,[8] when James wrote the letter to Antioch and said, "We know that certain which went out from us have come unto you and troubled you with words, to whom we gave no such commandment."[9] (4) He is also one of those who opposed St. Peter because he had gone to St. Cornelius when

---

[4] So at PS 2.63 (MacDermot p. 129). The idea is also found at Apoc. Adam 76,28-77,3; 77,16-18; Gr. Seth 51,20-24; Tri. Prot. 50, 12-15; Test. Tr. 30,18-28. At Tri. Trac. 125,5-9 "the Word" descends upon Jesus.

[5] Iren. 26.1: et tunc... virtutes perfecisse. And so at Hipp. Refut. 33.2.

[6] Cf. Apoc. Adam 77,9-18; Tri. Prot. 50,12-15.

[7] Cf. 1 Apoc. Jas. 31,17-22, "I am he who was within me. Never have I suffered in any way, nor have I been distressed, and this people has done me no harm" and cf. Cod. Tch. James 18,6-11. See also Apoc. Adam 77,9-18; G. Seth 55,14-56,14; Apoc. Pet. 81,7-83,8.

[8] Cf. Fil. 36.4-5: Hic sub apostolis beatis quaestionem seditionis commovit, dicens debere circumcidi homines, etc.

[9] Acts 15:24

Cornelius had been vouchsafed a vision of an angel and had sent for Peter. And Peter was dubious and saw the vision of the sheet and the things that were in it, and was told by the Lord to call nothing common or unclean. (5) And so Cerinthus stirred the circumcised multitudes up over Peter on his return to Jerusalem by saying, "He went in to men uncircumcised."[10] (6) Cerinthus did this before preaching his doctrine in Asia and falling into the deeper pit of his destruction. For, because he was circumcised himself he sought an excuse, through circumcision if you please, for his opposition to the uncircumcised believers.[11]

3,1 But because the Lord unfailingly cares for mankind, safeguards the clarity of the truth in the sons of the truth, and has granted the holy apostle Peter to give the refutation of Cerinthus and his party, the stupidity of Cerinthus becomes evident. (2) St. Peter said, "I was in the city of Joppa, and at midday, about the sixth hour, I saw a sheet let down, knit at the four corners, wherein were all manner of four-footed beasts and creeping things. And he said unto me, Slay and eat. And I said, Not so, Lord; for nothing common or unclean hath at any time entered into my mouth. But the voice answered me again from heaven, What God hath cleansed, that call not thou common. And, behold, immediately there were two men already come unto the house, and the Spirit said unto me, Go with them, nothing doubting."[12]

3,3 And then he explained how this had been said to him as a parable and how he had been doubtful at the time, till the Lord showed him plainly the things he was teaching him through the words and images. (4) For the instant he opened his mouth when he had come to Caesarea, the Holy Spirit fell upon Cornelius. And seeing this, Peter said, "Can any man forbid water to these, which have been counted worthy to receive the Holy Ghost as we were at the beginning?" (5) But all this was a mystery and an act of God's lovingkindness, so that St. Peter and everyone else would realize that the salvation of the gentiles is not of man but of God. God had granted the gift of the Holy Spirit, the vision of the angel, and the acceptance of Cornelius' prayer, fasting and alms, beforehand, so that the apostles—St. Peter especially, and the other apostles—would deprive no one truly called by God of that with which they had been entrusted.

[10] Acts 11:4-12

[11] Or, with Klijn and Rinnick: He did everything to propagate circumcision, ostensibly because the believers among the gentiles offered opposition against it, but in reality because he was circumcised himself.

[12] Acts 10:47

4,1 But these doings took place then at the instigation of that false apostle Cerinthus. Another time too, he and his friends caused a discord at Jerusalem itself, when Paul arrived with Titus, and Cerinthus said, "He hath brought in men uncircumcised with him"—speaking now of Titus—"and polluted the holy place."[13] (2) And so Paul says, "But neither Titus, who was with me, being a Greek, was compelled to be circumcised. But because of the false brethren, unawares brought in, who came in privily to spy out our liberty which we have in Christ, to whom we gave place by subjection not even temporarily."[14] And he used to command the uncircumcised, "Be not circumcised. For if ye be circumcised, Christ shall profit you nothing."[15] (3) Circumcision was a temporary expedient until the greater circumcision arrived, that is, the laver of regeneration—as is plain to everyone, and is shown more clearly by the things the apostles said, especially the holy apostle Paul. For he insists, "To them we gave place by subjection, not even temporarily."[16]

4,4 But to anyone who is willing to observe what the apostles went through at that time, it is amazing how the things a spirit of imposture inspired this faction to do betray the character of those who caused the commotion among the apostles with their heresies. (5) For, as I have said, no slight disturbance arose then, after they had rebelled, become false apostles, <and> sent other false apostles—first to Antioch, as I have said already, and to other places—to say, "Except ye be circumcised and keep the Law of Moses, ye cannot be saved."[17] (6) And these are the ones the apostle Paul calls "false apostles, deceitful workers, disguising themselves as apostles of Christ."[18]

5,1 For[19] they use the Gospel according to Matthew—in part and not in its entirety, but they do use it for the sake of the physical genealogy[20]—and they cite the following as a proof-text, arguing from the Gospel, "'It is enough for the disciple that he be as his master.'[21] (2) What does this mean?" they say, "Christ was circumcised; be circumcised yourself![22] Christ lived by

[13] Cf. Acts 21:28.
[14] Gal 2:5
[15] Gal 5:2
[16] Gal. 2:3-5
[17] Acts 15:1
[18] 2Cor ll:13
[19] I.e., their use of Matthew shows that they are masquerading as apostles.
[20] Cf. Fil. 36.3. Iren. 1.26.2 says this of the Ebionites; however, Cerinthus is mentioned in the same passage.
[21] Matt 10:25
[22] Cf. Fil. 36.2: Docet autem circumcidi et sabbatizari.

the Law; you too do the same." And therefore some of them are convinced by those specious arguments as though overcome by deadly drugs, because of the circumcision of Christ. (3) They discount Paul, however, because he did not obey the circumcised.[23] Moreover they reject him for saying, "Whosoever of you are justified by the Law, ye are fallen from grace,"[24] and, "If ye be circumcised, Christ will profit you nothing."[25]

6,1 In turn this Cerinthus, fool and teacher of fools that he is, ventures to maintain that Christ has suffered and been crucified but has not risen yet,[26] but he will rise when the general resurrection of the dead comes. (2) Now this position of theirs is untenable, both the words and the ideas. And so, in astonishment at those who did not believe in the coming resurrection of the dead, the apostle said, "If the dead rise not, then is Christ not raised;[27] "Let us eat and drink, for tomorrow we die"[28] and, "Be not deceived; evil communications corrupt good manners."[29] (3) Again, he likewise gives their refutation to those who say that Christ is not risen yet by saying, "If Christ be not raised, our preaching is vain and our faith is vain. And we also are found false witnesses against God, <because we testified against God> that he raised up Christ, if so be that he raised him not up."[30] <For in Corinth too certain persons arose to say there is no resurrection of the dead>, as though it was apostolic preaching that Christ was not risen <yet> and the dead are not raised (at all).

6,4 For their school reached its height in this country, I mean Asia, and in Galatia as well. And in these countries I also heard of a tradition which said that when some of their people died too soon, without baptism, others would be baptized for them in their names, so that they would not be punished for rising unbaptized at the resurrection and become the subjects of the authority that made the world. (5) And the tradition I heard of says that this is why the same holy apostle said, "If the dead rise not at all, why are they baptized for them?"[31] But others explain the text satisfactorily by saying that, as long as they are catechumens, the dying are allowed baptism before they die because of this hope, showing that the

[23] Iren. 1.26.2
[24] Gal 5:4
[25] Gal 5:2
[26] So at Fil. 36.2
[27] 1 Cor 15:16
[28] 1 Cor 15:32
[29] 1 Cor 15:33
[30] 1 Cor 15:14-15
[31] 1 Cor 15:29

person who has died will also rise, and therefore needs the forgiveness of his sins through baptism.

6,6 Some of these people have preached that Christ is not risen yet, but will rise together with everyone; others, that the dead will not rise at all.[32] (7) Hence the apostle has come forward and given the refutation of both these groups and the rest of the sects at once on <the subject of resurrection>. And in the testimonies that he gave in full he produced the sure proof of the resurrection, salvation and hope of the dead (8) by saying, "This corruptible must put on incorruption, and this mortal must put on immortality,"[33] and again, "Christ is risen, the firstfruits of them that slept."[34] This was to refute both kinds of sects at once and truly impart the unsullied doctrine of his teaching to anyone who wanted to know God's truth and saving doctrine.

7,1 Hence it can be observed at every point that Cerinthus, with his supporters, is pathetically mistaken and has become responsible for the ruin of others, since the sacred scriptures explain it all to us, clearly and in detail. (2) For neither is Christ the product of Joseph's seed—for how could the "product" be a sign and, further, how will be words of Isaiah be upheld, "Behold, the Virgin shall conceive, and bear a son,"[35] and so on? (3) Further, how can the holy Virgin's words to Gabriel, "How shall this be, seeing I know not a man?" be fulfilled—and his answer, "The Holy Ghost shall come upon thee, and the power of the highest shall overshadow thee,"[36] and so on? (4) And once more, how can their stupidity not be exposed when the Gospel plainly says, "Before they came together she was found with child?"[37]

7,5 But that they did not come together at all is plain to see. Heaven preserve us from saying so! Otherwise, he would not have made provision to entrust her to the holy virgin John after the crucifixion, as he says, "Behold thy mother"—and to her, "Behold thy son."[38] (6) He should have entrusted her to her relatives, or to Joseph's sons, if they were his sons by her—I mean James, Joses, Jude and Simon, Joseph's sons by another wife. Joseph had no relations with the Virgin, heaven forbid—after childbearing the Virgin is found inviolate. (7) However, these things have already

---

[32] Cf. Acts of Paul 8.1.12 (H-S II p. 254).
[33] 1 Cor 15:33
[34] 1 Cor 15:20
[35] Isa. 7:14
[36] Luke 1:34-35
[37] Matt 1:18
[38] John 19:26-27

been plainly dealt with in another work of mine, and are going to be dealt with (again).[39] Here I have said something about this subject as though in passing so that, when my intent is to effect the cure of other bites and <prepare> a remedy and preventative for other poisons, I will not divert the reader to different ones. (8) In any case, to a person of understanding their ridiculous teaching will be proved worthless in every way—refuted by the apostles, despised by the wise, and rejected by God and his proclamation of the truth.

8,1 But they are called Merinthians too, I am told. Whether the same Cerinthus was also called Merinthus I have no idea; or whether there was someone else named Merinthus, a colleague of his, God knows! (2) I have already said that not only he himself at Jerusalem often opposed the apostles; but his supporters did it, and in Asia. But it makes no difference whether it was he or whether it was another colleague who supported him, whose views were similar, and who acted with him for the same ends. The whole perversity of their teaching is of this sort and they are called both Cerinthians and Merinthians.

8,3 And having gone through all this about this horrid, snake-like wickedness, we again move on to the next, giving thanks that we have crossed the sea of these evil doctrines unharmed—and praying that when we encounter the rest, as though we were venturing into rough, beast-infested shallows, we will not be harmed but reach the safe haven of the truth, which I shall sketch by contrasting it with the nonsense which is talked about it.

8,4 For to anyone who wishes to examine and describe the forms (of these sects), this one too will truly seem like a snake with two heads because of its dual nomenclature—and like the viper called the "rot viper." Its whole body is covered with long red hair, but it has neither the nature nor the hide of a goat or sheep but those of a snake, and with its bite it does the harm a snake does to those who happen on it. (5) For it ruins its adherents, sometimes by destroying the New Testament's teachings with material from the old religion, and sometimes by circulating their false charges against the apostles who had come from circumcision to faith in Christ, with lying words as though from the New Testament. But having struck and thrashed its rot, poison and fangs with the cudgel of the truth let us hurry on, as I said, by the power of God, to go through the rest.

[39] Ancoratus 60,1; Pan. 78,7f

29.

Against Nazoraeans.[1] *Number nine, but twenty-nine of the series*

1,1 Next after these come the Nazoraeans, at the same time as they or even before them—either together with them or after them, in any case their contemporaries. I cannot say more precisely who succeeded whom. For, as I said, these were contemporary with each other, and had ideas similar to each other's.

1,2 For these people did not give themselves the name of Christ[2] or Jesus' own name, but that of "Nazoraeans." (3) But at that time all Christians alike were called Nazoraeans. They also came to be called "Jessaeans"[3] for a short while, before the disciples began to be called Christians at Antioch. (4) But they were called Jessaeans because of Jesse, I suppose, since David was descended from Jesse and Mary was a lineal descendant of David. This was in fulfillment of sacred scripture, since in the Old Testament the Lord tells David, "Of the fruit of thy belly shall I set upon thy throne."

2,1 I am afraid of <drawing the treatment> of every expression <out too long and so>, though the truth moves me to touch on the considerations for contemplation in every expression, I give this note <in> brief, not to go to great length <in giving the explanation>. (2) Since the Lord said to David, "Of the fruit of thy belly shall I set upon the throne," and, "The Lord sware unto David and will not repent,"[4] it is plain that God's promise is irrevocable. (3) In the first place, what does God have to swear by but "By myself have I sworn, saith the Lord?"[5]—for "God hath no oath by a greater."[6] The divine does not swear, however, but the statement has the function of providing confirmation.

For the Lord swore to David with an oath that he would set the fruit of his belly upon his throne. (4) And the apostles bear witness that Christ had to be born of David's seed, as our Lord and Savior Jesus Christ indeed was. I shall pass over the vast number of testimonies, in order, as I said, not to drag the discussion out to great length.

---

[1] See p. 47 n. 27. This Sect seems to be based on Epiph's personal knowledge, though he has conjectured its history from passages in scripture and Eusebius.

[2] Eusebius, at H. E. 2.17.4 says that the first Christians were not everywhere known as such.

[3] Epiphanius bases this on his memory of the term 'Εσσαῖοι, which Philo uses at Vita Contemplativa 1 for the group Eusebius calls Therapeutae. On the subject see Pourkier p. 113.

[4] Ps 109:4

[5] Gen 22:16

[6] Cf. Heb 6:13.

2,5 But probably someone might say, "Since Christ was physically born of David's seed, that is, of the Holy Virgin Mary, why is he not sitting on David's throne? For the Gospel says, 'They came that they might anoint him king, and when Jesus perceived this he departed...and hid himself in Ephraim, a city of the wilderness.'"[7] (6) But now that I have gotten to this passage and am asked about this text and the reason why the prophecy about sitting on David's throne has not been fulfilled physically in the Savior's case—for some have thought that it has not—I shall still say that it is a fact. No word of God's holy scripture comes to nothing.

3,1 For David's throne and kingly seat is the priesthood in the holy church. The Lord has combined this kingly and high priestly rank and conferred it on his holy church by transferring David's throne to it, never to fail. (2) In time past David's throne continued by succession until Christ himself, since the rulers from Judah did not fail until he came "for whom are the things prepared, and he is the expectation of the nations,"[8] <as> scripture says.

3,3 For the rulers in succession from Judah came to an end with Christ's arrival. Until he came <the> rulers <were anointed priests>,[9] but after his birth in Bethlehem of Judaea the order ended and was altered[10] in the time of Alexander, a ruler of priestly and kingly stock. (4) This position died out with this Alexander from the time of Salina also known as Alexandra, in the time of King Herod and the Roman emperor Augustus. (Though this Alexander was crowned also, as one of the anointed priests and rulers.[11] (5) For when the two tribes, the kingly and priestly, were united—I mean the tribe of Judah with Aaron and the whole tribe of Levi—kings also became priests, for nothing hinted at in holy scripture can be wrong.)[12] (6) But then finally a gentile, King Herod, was crowned, and not David's descendants any more.

3,7 But with the transfer of the royal throne the rank of king passed, in Christ, from the physical house of David and Israel to the church.[13] The

[7] Cf. John 6:15; 11:54.

[8] Gen 49:10

[9] Cf. Jer. Chron. 160,16-17 (Helm).

[10] Cf. Eus. Chron. 61,12-14 (Karst); Jer. Chron. 148,6-8 (Helm). Eusebius' Chronicle might be the source of Epiphanius' explanation.

[11] Another version of this is found at Jer. Chron. 148,11-14 (Helm).

[12] This might have come from Orig. Hom. in Sam. Frgt. 4 (Klostermann, *SC* 3, p. 296) καταγνοὺς οὖν τοῦ Σαοὺλ καὶ βουλόμενος τῷ Δαυὶδ τὰ τῆς ἀρχῆς καὶ τῷ σπέρματι αὐτοῦ φυλᾶξαι τὴν βασιλείαν διὰ τὸν ἐξ αὐτοῦ τεχθησόμενον κατὰ σάρκα βασιλέα τῆς κτίσεως ἁπάσης

[13] The substance of this argument appears at a Justin Apol. 32.1-3; Dial. 11.4; 52.2-4; 120.3-5; 126.1; Iren. 4.10.2; Eus. H. E. 1.6.1-2; 4; 8; Demonstratio 7.

throne is established in God's holy church forever, and has both the kingly and the high-priestly rank for two reasons. (8) It has the kingly rank from our Lord Jesus Christ, in two ways: because he is physically descended from King David, and because he is in fact a greater king from all eternity in virtue of his Godhead. But it has the priestly rank because Christ himself is high priest and the founder of the office[14] of the high priests (9) since James, who was called the Lord's brother and who was his apostle, was immediately[15] made the first bishop.[16] He was Joseph's son by birth, but was ranked as the Lord's brother because of their upbringing together.

4,1 For this James was Joseph's son by Joseph's <first> wife,[17] not by Mary, as I have said in many other places[18] and dealt with more clearly for you. (2) And moreover I find that he was of Davidic descent because of being Joseph's son, <and> that he was born a nazirite—for he was Joseph's first-born, and (thus) consecrated.[19] And I have found further that he also functioned as (high)-priest in the ancient priesthood.[20] (3) Thus he was permitted to enter the Holy of Holies once a year, as scripture says the Law directed the high priests to do. For many before me—Eusebius, Clement and others—have reported this of him. (4) He was allowed to wear the priestly tablet[21] besides, as the trustworthy authors I mentioned have testified in those same historical writings.

4,5 Now our Lord Jesus Christ, as I said, is "priest forever after the order of Melchizedek,"[22] and at the same time hereditary king, so that he may transfer the priesthood along with the lawgiving. (6) And since David's seed, through Mary, is seated on the throne, <his throne endures> forever and of his kingdom there shall be no end. He should now transfer the order of the former kingship; for indeed his kingdom is not earthly, as he said to Pontius Pilate in the Gospel, "My Kingdom is not of this world."[23] (7) For since Christ brings to fulfillment[24] all the things (that have been said) in riddles, the preliminaries have reached a limit.

---

[14] πρύτανις
[15] Eus. H. E. 2.1-2
[16] I.e., thus confirming the fact that Christ was πρύτανις of high priests
[17] Cf. Jer. Vir. Ill. 2. Jerome believes he was the son of "Mary, the sister of the Lord's mother" (Richardson p. 7).
[18] For example at Ancoratus 60,1 ff
[19] Eus. H. E. 2.23.5
[20] Eus. H. E. 2.23
[21] This is said of John at Eus. H. E. 3.31.3.
[22] Heb 5:6
[23] John 18:36
[24] I.e., Heb 3:5

For he who is always king did not come to achieve sovereignty. He granted the crown to those whom he appointed—lest it be thought that he advanced from a lower estate to a higher. (8) For his throne endures, of his kingdom there shall be no end, and he is seated on the throne of David and has transferred David's kingship and granted it, together with the high priesthood, to his own servants, the high priests of the catholic church.

4,9 And there is much to say about this. But in any case, since I have come to the topic of the reason why those who had come to faith in Christ were called Jessaeans before they were called Christians, we said that Jesse was the father of David. And they had been named Jessaeans, either because of this Jesse; or from the name or our Lord Jesus since, being his disciples, they were derived from Jesus; or because of the etymology of the Lord's name. For in Hebrew Jesus means "healer" or "physician,"[25] and "savior." (10) In any case, they had got this name before they were called Christians. But at Antioch, as I have mentioned before and as is the essence of the truth, the disciples and the whole church of God began to be called Christians.

5,1[26] If you enjoy study and have read the passage about them in Philo's historical writings, in his book entitled "Jessaeans," you can find that, in giving his account of their way of life and their hymns and describing their monasteries in the vicinity of the Marean marsh, Philo described none other than Christians.[27] (2) For when he visited the area—the place is called Mareotis—and was entertained by them at their monasteries in the region, he was edified. (3) He arrived there during Passover and observed their customs, and how some of them put off (eating) throughout the holy week of Passover, though others ate every other day and others, indeed, each evening.[28] But all this has been written by Philo on the subject of the Christians' faith and regimen.

5,4 So when they were called Jessaeans then shortly after the Savior's ascension and after Mark had preached in Egypt,[29] in those times certain other persons, supposed followers of the apostles, seceded in their turn. I mean the Nazoraeans, whom I am discussing here. They were Jewish, were attached to the Law, and had circumcision. (5) But it was as though people

---

[25] "Healer" or "physician" might be what Epiph, with his knowledge of Hebrew and Aramaic, makes of θεραπευταί. See below and cf. Eus. H. E. 2.17.3 ἤτοι παρὰ τὸ τὰς ψυχὰς τῶν προσιόντων αὐτοῖς τῶν ἀπὸ κακίας παθῶν ἰατρῶν δίκην…θεραπεύειν.

[26] 5,1-2 is based on Eus. H. E. 2.17.1-24.

[27] Epiph here conflates Eus. H. E. 2.17.16-17 with 2.17.21-22.

[28] Eus. H. E. 2.17.8

[29] See Eus. H. E. 16.1-17.1.

had seen fire under a misapprehension. Not understanding why, or for <what> use, the persons who had kindled this fire were doing it—either to cook their rations with the fire, or burn some dead trees and brush, which are usually destroyed by fire—they kindled fire too, in imitation, and set themselves ablaze.

5,6 For by hearing just Jesus' name, and seeing the miracles performed by the hands of the apostles, they came to faith in Jesus themselves. And since they found that he had been conceived at Nazareth and brought up in Joseph's home, and for this reason is called "Jesus the Nazoraean" in the Gospel—as the apostles say, "Jesus the Nazoraean, a man approved by signs and wonders,"[30] and so on—they adopted this name, so as to be called Nazoreans.

5,7 Not "nazirites"—that means "consecrated persons." Anciently this rank belonged to firstborn sons and men who had been dedicated to God. Samson was one, and others after him, and many before him. Moreover, John the Baptist too was one of these same persons who were consecrated to God, for "He drank neither wine nor strong drink."[31] (This regimen, an appropriate one for their rank, was prescribed for such persons.) (6,1) They did not call themselves Nasaraeans either; the sect of Nasaraeans was before Christ and did not know Christ.

6,2 But besides, as I have indicated, everyone called the Christians Nazoraeans, as they say in accusing Paul the apostle, "We have found this man a pestilent fellow and a perverter of the people, a ring-leader of the sect of the Nazoraeans."[32] (3) And the holy apostle did not disclaim the name—not to profess these people's heresy, but he was glad to own the name his adversaries' malice had applied to him for Christ's sake. (4) For he says in court, "They neither found me in the temple disputing with any man, neither raising up the people, nor have I done any of those things whereof they accuse me. But this I confess unto thee, that after the way which they call heresy, so worship I, believing all things in the Law and the prophets."[33]

6,5 And no wonder the apostle admitted to being a Nazoraean! In those days everyone called Christians this because of the city of Nazareth—there was no other usage of the name at the time. And so people gave the name of <"Nazoraeans"> to believers in Christ, of whom it is written, "because

[30] Acts 2:22
[31] Luke 1:15
[32] Acts 24:5
[33] Acts 24:12-14

he shall be called a Nazoraean."[34] (6) Even today in fact, people call all the sects, I mean Manichaeans, Marcionites, Gnostics and others, by the common name of "Christians," though they are not Christians. However, although each sect has another name, it still allows this one with pleasure, since the name is an ornament to it. For they think they can preen themselves on Christ's name—certainly not on Christ's faith and works!

6,7 Thus Christ's holy disciples too called themselves "disciples of Jesus" then, as indeed they were. But when others called them Nazoraeans they did not reject it, being aware of the intent of those who were calling them that. They were calling them Nazoraeans because of Christ, since our Lord Jesus was called "<the> Nazoraean" himself—as the Gospels and the Acts of the Apostles say—(8) because of his upbringing in the city of Nazareth (now a village) in Joseph's home, after having been born in the flesh at Bethlehem, of the ever-virgin Mary, Joseph's betrothed. For Joseph had settled in Nazareth after leaving Bethlehem and taking up residence in Galilee.

7,1 But these same sectarians whom I am discussing here disregarded the name of Jesus, and neither called themselves Jessaeans, kept the name of Jews, nor termed themselves Christians—but "Nazoraeans" supposedly from the name of the place "Nazareth." But they are Jews in every way and nothing else.

7,2 They use not only the New Testament but the Old Testament as well, as the Jews do. For they do not repudiate the legislation, the prophets, and the books which are called Writings by the Jews and by themselves. They have no different views but confess everything in full accord with the doctrine of the Law and like the Jews, except that they are supposedly believers in Christ. (3) For they acknowledge both the resurrection of the dead and that all things have been created by God,[35] and they declare that God is one, and that his Son is Jesus Christ.

7,4 They are perfectly versed in the Hebrew language, for the entire Law, the prophets, and the so-called Writings—I mean the poetic books, Kings, Chronicles, Esther and all the rest—are read in Hebrew among them, as of course they are among the Jews. (5) They are different from Jews, and different from Christians, only in the following ways. They disagree with Jews because of their belief in Christ; but they are not in accord with Christians because they are still fettered by the Law—circumcision,

---

[34] Matt 2:23

[35] This is said of the Ebionites at Iren. 1.26.2. Cf. Hipp. Refut. 7.34.1; PsT 3.

the Sabbath, and the rest.[36] (6) As to Christ, I cannot say whether they too are misled by the wickedness of Cerinthus and Merinthus, and regard him as a mere man—or whether, as the truth is, they affirm that he was born of Mary by the Holy Spirit.

7,7 This sect of Nazoraeans is to be found in Beroea[37] near Coelesyria, in the Decapolis near Pella, and in Bashanitis at the place called Cocabe[38]—Khokhabe in Hebrew. (8) For that was its place of origin, since all the disciples had settled in Pella after their remove from Jerusalem—Christ having told them to abandon Jerusalem and withdraw from it[39] because of the siege it was about to undergo. And they settled in Peraea for this reason and, as I said, lived their lives there. It was from this that the Nazoraean sect had its origin.

8,1 But they too are wrong to boast of circumcision, and persons like themselves are still "under a curse,"[40] since they cannot fulfill the Law. For how will they be able to fulfil the Law's provision, "Thrice a year thou shalt appear before the Lord thy God, at the feasts of Unleavened Bread, Tabernacles and Pentecost,"[41] on the site of Jerusalem? (2) For since the site is closed off,[42] and the Law's provisions cannot be fulfilled, it must be plain to anyone with sense that Christ came to be the fulfiller of the Law—not to destroy the Law but to fulfill the Law—and to lift the curse that had been pronounced on transgression of the Law. (3) For after Moses had given every commandment he came to the end of the book and "included the whole in a curse"[43] by saying, "Cursed is he that continueth not in all the words that are written in this book to do them."[44]

8,4 Hence Christ came to free what had been fettered with the bonds of the curse by granting us, in place of the lesser commandments which cannot be fulfilled, ones which are greater and which are not inconsistent with the completion of the task as the former ones were. (5) For often in every Sect, when I reached the point, I have explained in connection with the Sabbath, circumcision and the rest, how the Lord has granted us something more perfect.

---

36 Cf. Iren. 1.26.2 (of the Ebionites); Eus. H. E. 3,27.3.
37 Cf. Jer. Vir. Ill.3 (Richardson p. 9).
38 Cf. Eus. H. E. 17.14.
39 Cf. Eus. H. E. 3.5.3.
40 Gal 3:10
41 Cf. Gal 3:22.
42 Cf. Justin Apol. I 47.5-6.
43 Cf. Gal 3:22.
44 Gal 3:10 and Deut 27:26

8,6 But how can people like these be defensible since they have not obeyed the Holy Spirit who said through the apostles to gentile converts, "Assume no burden save the necessary things, that ye abstain from blood, and from things strangled, and fornication, and from meats offered to idols?"[45] (7) And how can they fail to lose the grace of God, when the holy apostle Paul says, "If ye be circumcised, Christ shall profit you nothing... whosoever of you do glory in the Law are fallen from grace?"[46]

9,1 In this Sect too, my brief discussion will be sufficient. People of their kind are refutable at once and easy to detect and, rather (than being heretical Christians), are Jews and nothing else. (2) Yet to the Jews they are very much enemies. Not only do Jewish people bear hatred against them; they even stand up at dawn, at midday, and toward evening, three times a day when they recite their prayers in the synagogues, and curse and anathematize them—saying three times a day, "God curse the Nazoraeans."[47] (3) For they harbor a further grudge against them, if you please, because despite their Jewish origin, they preach that Jesus is <the> Christ—something that is the opposite of those who are still Jews and have not accepted Jesus.

9,4 They have the Gospel according to Matthew in its entirety in Hebrew.[48] For it is clear that they still preserve this as it was originally written, in the Hebrew alphabet. But I do not know whether they have also excised the genealogies from Abraham till Christ.

9,5 But now that we have also detected this sect—like a stinging insect that is small, and yet causes pain with its poison—and have squashed it with the words of the truth, let us go on to the next, beloved, praying for help from God.

---

45 Acts 15:28-29

46 Gal 5:2-4

47 Some variation of the prayer, "For the apostates let there be no hope, and let the rule of wickedness be uprooted swiftly, in our days, and let the *notsrim* (נצרים, Christians) and sectarians (מינים) perish in an instant" etc. is found in the great majority of the liturgical MSS of the Cairo Genizah See Pourkier, and especially Ehrlich and Langer, "Earliest Texts," pp. 63-112. For Christian references to the prayer, see Justin Dial. 16; 47; Jer. In Isa 5:18-19 (Adriaen, *CC* 73 p. 76); Orig. Cels. 2.29.

48 Cf. Eus. H. E. 3.24.6; 39.16; 5.10.3; Theophania 4.12; Jer. Vir. Ill. 3; C. Pelag. 3.2. The Ebionites are said to use the Gospel according to Matthew and none other at Iren. 1.26.2; Eus. H. E. 3.27.4.

30.

Against Ebionites.[1] *Number ten, but thirty of the series*

1,1 Following these and holding views like theirs, Ebion,[2] the founder of the Ebionites, arose in the world in his turn as a monstrosity with many forms, and practically represented in himself the snake-like form of the mythical many-headed hydra. He was of the Nazoraeans' school, but preached and taught other things than they.

1,2 For it was as though someone were to collect a set of jewelry from various precious stones and an outfit of varicolored clothing and tog himself up conspicuously. Ebion, in reverse, took any and every doctrine which was dreadful, lethal, disgusting, ugly and unconvincing, thoroughly contentious, from every sect, and patterned himself after them all. (3) For he has the Samaritans' unpleasantness but the Jews' name, the opinion of the Ossaeans, Nazoraeans and Nasaraeans, the form of the Cerinthians, and the perversity of the Carpocratians. And he wants to have just the Christians' title—most certainly not their behavior, opinion and knowledge, and the consensus as to faith of the Gospels and Apostles!

1,4 But since he is midway between all the sects, as one might say, he amounts to nothing. The words of scripture, "I was almost in all evil, in the midst of the church and synagogue,"[3] are applicable to him. (5) For although he is Samaritan, he rejects the name because of its objectionability. And while professing himself a Jew, he is the opposite of the Jews—though he does agree with them in part as I shall prove later with God's help, through the proofs of it in my rebuttal of them.

2,1 For this Ebion was contemporary with the Jews, and <since he was> with them, he was derived from them. (2) In the first place, he said

[1] Epiphanius draws on Hipp. Synt. which is his source for the name, "Ebion," probably on Irenaeus, and certainly on some version of the Clementina, which he calls the Travels of Peter and which Strecker (*Judenchristentum*) suggests was the Grundschrift of the Clementina. Epiphanius mentions, as a separate document, the Ascents of James, (now Clem. Rec. 1.33-70). He appears to know the Letter of Clement to James, and some other "Epistles of Clement," which might be the ones called the Epistles Concerning Virginity. At 13,2 Epiphanius quotes an extract from an "Ebionite" Gospel according to Matthew; some of his other information is from oral sources.

PsT 3.3 depends upon Hipp. Synt. Tertullian, who speaks of an "Ebion," may also have known this work. Origen, on the other hand, may have had some personal contact with Jewish Christianity. So may Eusebius (H. E. 3.27.4), although he seems to follow Origen.

[2] For the name, Ebion, see Hipp. Refut. 7.34.1; PsT 3.3; Jer. Adv. Lucif. 23; Doctr. Pat. 41; Tert. Carn. Chr. 14; 18; 24; Virg. Vel. 6; Praescr. 10; 33

[3] Prov 5:14

that Christ was conceived by sexual intercourse and the seed of a man, Joseph[4]—I have already said that he agreed with the others in everything, with this one difference, his adherence to Judaism's Law of the Sabbath, circumcision, and all the other Jewish and Samaritan observances. (3) But like the Samaritans he goes still further than the Jews. He added the rule about taking care not to touch a gentile;[5] (4) and that every day, if a man has been with a woman[6] and has left her, he must immerse himself in water—any water he can find, the sea or any other. (5) Moreover, if he should meet anyone while returning from his immersion and bath in the water, he runs back again for another immersion, often even with his clothes on![7]

2,6 This sect now forbids celibacy and continence altogether,[8] as do the other sects which are like it. For at one time they prided themselves on virginity, presumably because of James the Lord's brother,<and so> address their treatises to "elders and virgins."[9]

2,7 Their origin came after the fall of Jerusalem. For since practically all who had come to faith in Christ had settled in Peraea then, in Pella, a town in the "Decapolis"[10] the Gospel mentions, which is near Batanaea and Bashanitis—as they had moved there then and were living there, this provided an opportunity for Ebion. (8) And as far as I know, he first lived in a village called Cocabe in the district of Qarnaim—also called Ashtaroth—in Bashanitis. There he began his evil teaching—the place, if you please, where the Nazoraeans I have spoken of came from. (9) For since Ebion was connected with them and they with him, each party shared its own wickedness with the other. Each also differed from the other to some extent, but they emulated each other in malice. But I have already spoken at length, both in other works and in the other Sects, about the locations of Cocabe and Arabia.

---

[4] Iren. 3.21.1; Eus. H. E. 3.27.2; Origen Cels. 5.61; in Matt 16:12; Tert. Carn. Chr. 14

[5] At Jos. Bell. 2.119 Essenes are said to wash after touching foreigners. Cf. the various regulations forbidding contact with gentiles which are found in the Covenant of Damascus, CD 11,14 (Wise et al. p. 69); 12,6-11 (p. 70). At Clem Hom. 13.4.3 it is said that Christians do not eat at a gentile table.

[6] Cf. Lev 15:18; Clem. Hom. 7.8.2.

[7] At Hipp. Refut. 9.15.4-6 the Book of Elxai is said to prescribe this procedure for a person bitten by a mad dog.

[8] Cf. Ep. Clem. Ad Jac. 7.1-2, and see p. 49, 19,7.

[9] See the First Epistle of the Blessed Clement, the Disciple of Peter the Apostle, 1: "to the blessed brother virgins... to the holy sister virgins..." (Roberts and Donaldson, p. 55).

[10] Cf. Matt 4:25.

3,1 And at first, as I said, Ebion declared that Christ is the offspring of a man, that is, of Joseph. For a while now, however, various of his followers have been giving conflicting accounts of Christ, as though they have decided on something untenable and impossible themselves. (2) But I think it may be since they were joined by Elxai—the false prophet <I mentioned earlier> in the tracts called "Sampsaeans," "Ossenes" and "Elkasaites"—that they tell an imaginary story about Christ and the Holy Spirit as he did.

3,3[11] For some of them even say that Adam is Christ—the man who was formed first and infused with God's breath.[12] (4) But others among them say that he is from above; created before all things, a spirit, both higher than the angels and Lord of all; and that he is called Christ, the heir of the world there.[13] But he comes here when he chooses,[14] as he came in Adam and appeared to the patriarchs clothed with Adam's body. And in the last days the same Christ who had come to Abraham, Isaac and Jacob, came and donned Adam's body, and appeared to men, was crucified, rose and ascended. (6) But again, when they choose to, they say, "No! The Spirit—that is, the Christ—came to him and put on the man called Jesus."[15] And they get all giddy from making different suppositions about him at different times.

3,7 They too accept the Gospel according to Matthew. Like the Cerinthians and Merinthians, they too use it alone. They call it, "According to the Hebrews," and it is true to say that only Matthew expounded and preached the Gospel in the Hebrew language and alphabet[16] in the New Testament.

3,8 But some may already have replied that the Gospel of John too, translated from Greek to Hebrew, is in the Jewish treasuries, I mean the treasuries at Tiberias, and is stored there secretly, as certain Jewish converts have described to me in detail. (9) And not only that, but it is said that the book of the Acts of the Apostles, also translated from Greek to Hebrew, is there in the treasuries, so that the Jews who have read it, the ones who told me about it, have been converted to Christ from this.

4,1 One of them was Josephus—not the ancient Josephus, the author and chronicler, but Josephus of Tiberias, <born> during the old age of

---

[11] With 3,3-5 cf. Hipp. Refut. 9.14.1.

[12] Adam has the Spirit of Christ and is therefore the first appearance in the world of the true prophet: Clem. Hom. 3.20-21; Rec. 1.45.4.

[13] Clem. Hom. 3.20.2.

[14] Loc. cit.

[15] See p. 119 n. 14.

[16] Cf. Iren. 1.26.2; 3.11.7; Eus. H. E. 3.27.4; Jer. C. Pelag 3.2; Vir. Ill. 3 (Richardson p. 8).

the Emperor Constantine of blessed memory. This Josephus was awarded the rank of count by the Emperor himself, and was authorized to build a church for Christ in Tiberias itself, and in Diocaesarea, Capernaum and the other towns. He also suffered a great deal from the Jews themselves before he came to the Emperor's notice.

4,2 For this Josephus was counted as one of their men of rank. There are such persons, <who> rank next after the patriarch and are called "apostles."[17] They attend on the patriarch, and often stay with him day and night without intermission, to give him counsel and refer points of law to him. (3) Now the patriarch at that time was called Ellel. (I think that was how Josephus pronounced his name, unless I am mistaken because of the time). He was descended from the Gamaliel who had been one of their patriarchs. (4) One may suspect, and others have suggested this as well, that these patriarchs were descended from the first Gamaliel, the Savior's contemporary, who gave the godly counsel of refraining from abuse of the apostles.

4,5 When Ellel was dying he asked for the bishop who then lived near Tiberias, and received holy baptism from him *in extremis* for a pretendedly medical reason. (6) For he had sent for him by Josephus, as though he were a doctor, and he had the room cleared and begged the bishop, "Give me the seal in Christ!" (7) The bishop summoned the servants and ordered water prepared, as though intending to give the patriarch, who was very sick, some treatment for his illness with water. They did what they were told, for they did not know. And sending everyone out from pretended modesty the patriarch was vouchsafed the laver and the holy mysteries.

5,1 Josephus told me <this> in conversation. For I heard all this from his own lips and not from anyone else, in his old age when he was about 70 or even more. (2) For I was entertained at his home in Scythopolis; he had moved from Tiberias, and owned a notable estate there in Scythopolis. Eusebius of blessed memory, the bishop of Vercelli in Italy, was Josephus' guest, since he had been banished by Constantius for his orthodox faith. I and the other brethren had come there to visit him, and we were entertained too, along with Eusebius.

5,3 Now when I met Josephus at his home, asked him about himself, and found that he had been a prominent Jew, I also inquired his reason, and why it was that he had come over to Christianity. And I heard all this plainly (from him), not at secondhand from anyone else. (4) And since I

[17] Cf. Eus. In Isa 18:1-2; Jer. In Gal 1:1 (Raspanti p. 11).

think that, because of the Hebrew translations in the treasuries, the things the man went through are worth recording for the edification of the faithful, I deliberately give Josephus' entire reason.

5,5 Josephus was not only privileged to become a faithful Christian, but a great despiser of Arians as well. In that city, I mean Scythopolis, he was the only orthodox Christian—they were all Arians. (6) Had it not been that he was a count, and the rank of count protected him from Arian persecution, he could not even have undertaken to live in the town, especially while Patrophilus was the Arian bishop. Patrophilus was very influential because of his wealth and severity, and his familiar acquaintance with the Emperor Constantius. (7) But there was another, younger man in town too, an orthodox believer of Jewish parentage. He did not even dare <to associate> with me in public, though he used to visit me secretly.

5,8 But Josephus told me something plausible and amusing, though I would think that even <here> he was telling the truth. He claimed that after his wife died, fearing that the Arians might take him by force and make him a cleric—to flatter him into conversion to the sect they would often promise him higher preferments if need be, and to make him a bishop. Well, he claimed that this was why he had married a second wife, to escape their ordinations!

6,1 But I shall go back to telling the story of the patriarch and make Josephus' own story known in all its particulars to those who care to read it, in the words he used to me. (2) "Just as the patriarch was being granted baptism," he told me, "I was peeping in through the cracks in the doors and realized what the bishop was doing to the patriarch—found it out, and kept it to myself. (3) For besides," Josephus said, "the patriarch had a very ample sum of money ready, and he reached out, gave it to the bishop, and said, 'Offer it for me. It is written that things are bound and loosed on earth through the priests of God, and <that> these things will be loosed and bound in heaven.'[18] (4) When this was over," he said, "and the doors were opened, the patriarch's visitors asked him how he was after his treatment, and he replied that he was *very* well For he knew what he was talking about!"

6,5 Then <after> two or three days, with the bishop visiting him often in the guise of a physician, the patriarch fell asleep with a good hope in store. He had entrusted his own son, who was quite young, to Josephus and another very capable <elder>. (6) All business, then, was transacted

[18] Cf. Matt 18:18.

through these two, since the patriarch, being a boy, was still childish, and was being brought up under their supervision.

6,7 During this time Josephus' mind was often troubled over the rites that had been performed in the affair of the baptism, and he was considering what he should do. Now there was a "gazophylacium" there which was sealed—"gaza" means "treasure" in Hebrew. (8) As many had different notions about this treasury because of its seal, Josephus plucked up the courage to open it unobserved—and found no money, but books money could not buy. (9) Browsing through them he found the Gospel of John translated from Greek to Hebrew, as I said, and the Acts of the Apostles—and Matthew's Gospel moreover, which is actually Hebrew. After reading from them he was once more distressed in mind, for he was somehow troubled over the faith of Christ. But now he was prodded for two reasons, his reading of the books and the patriarch's initiation. Still, as often happens, his heart was hardened.

7,1 While all his time was occupied with these things, the boy Ellel had left to be reared as patriarch was growing up. (No one usurps the positions of authority among the Jews, but son succeeds father.) (2) Just as the lad was reaching full vigor some idle youths of his own age with vicious habits unfortunately met him. (I guess he was called Judas, but because of the time I am not quite sure.) (3) His young contemporaries got him into many evil practices, seductions of women and unholy sexual unions. They undertook to help him in his licentious <activities> with certain magic devices—making certain love-philtres and compelling free women with incantations to be brought under duress for his seduction.

7,4 Josephus and his fellow elder, who were obliged to attend the boy, bore this with difficulty and often both charged him and admonished him verbally. But he preferred to listen to the young men, and he hid his indecencies and denied them. And Josephus did not dare to voice his accusations of him openly; instead he admonished him, as though for his education.

7,5 Well, they went to Gadara for the hot baths. There is a gathering there every year. Persons who wish to bathe for a certain number of days arrive from every quarter supposedly to get rid of their ailments, though this is a trick of the devil. For where wonders have been given by God the adversary has already spread his deadly nets—the bathing there is mixed!

7,6 There happened to be a free woman of unusual beauty in the bath. Lured by the habit of his licentiousness the young man rubbed his side against the woman's as he strolled about in the hot-air room. (7) But being Christian, she naturally made the sign of the cross. (There was no need for her to behave improperly and bathe in mixed company. These things happen to simple lay persons, from the laxity of the teachers who do not forewarn them through their instruction.) (8) Still, that God might make his wonders manifest, the youngster, I mean the patriarch, failed in his enterprise. For he sent emissaries to the woman and promised her gifts; but she insulted his messengers and did not yield to the pampered youth's futile efforts.

8,1 Then, when his helpers learned of the boy's pain which he betrayed for the girl, they undertook to prepare more powerful magic for him, as Josephus himself described it to me in full. (2) After sunset they took the unfortunate lad to the neighboring cemetery. (In my country there are places of assembly of this kind, called "caverns," made by hewing them out of cliff sides.) (3) Taking him there the cheats who accompanied him recited certain incantations and spells, and did very impious things to him and in the name of the woman.

8,4 By God's will this came to the attention of the other elder, Josephus' partner, and on realizing what was happening, he told Josephus. And he began by bemoaning his lot, and said, "Brother, we are wretched men and vessels of destruction! What sort of person are we attending?" (5) And when Josephus asked the reason, no sooner were the words out of his mouth than the elder seized his hand and took Josephus to the place where the persons doomed to die, with the youth, were holding their assembly in the cemetery for magic. (6) Standing outside the door they listened to what the others were doing, but withdrew when they came out. (It was not dark yet; it was just about sundown, and one could still see dimly.) (7) After the monsters of impiety had left the tomb Josephus went in and saw certain <vessels> and other implements of jugglery thrown on the ground. They made water on them and covered them with a heap of dust, he said, and left.

8,8 But they knew the sort of woman on whose account they had plotted these wicked things, and he watched to see whether they would win. (9) When the sorcerers had not prevailed—the woman had the aid of the sign and faith of Christ—he learned that the youngster had waited for the girl's arrival on three nights, and later quarreled with the persons who had performed the jugglery because he had not succeeded. (10) This made Josephus' third lesson—where Christ's name was, and the sign of his cross, the power of sorcery did not prevail. But at this point he was by no means convinced that he should become a Christian.

9,1 Then the Lord appeared to him in a dream, and said, "I am Jesus, whom your forefathers crucified; but believe in me." When he was not convinced even by his he fell into grave illness and was given up for lost. But the Lord appeared to him again, and told him to believe and he would be healed. And he promised and recovered, and again persevered in his obstinacy.

9,2 He fell ill a second time in turn, and was given up in the same way. When he was assumed to be dying by his Jewish kin he heard the words from them that they always repeat in secrecy among themselves. (3) An elder, a scholar of the law, came and whispered to him, "Believe <in> Jesus, crucified under Pontius Pilate the governor, Son of God first yet later born of Mary; the Christ of God and risen from the dead. And believe that he will come to judge and quick and the dead." That same Josephus told me this plainly during his story, as I can truthfully say.

9,4 Besides, I have heard this sort of thing from someone else. He was still a Jew from fear of the Jews, but he often spent time in Christian company, and he honored Christians and loved them. He traveled with me in the wilderness of Bethel and Ephraim, when I was going up to the mountains from Jericho and saying something to him about the advent of Christ, and he did not dispute it. (5) I was amazed—he was learned in the Law as well and able to argue—and I asked the reason why he did not dispute, but agreed with me, about Jesus Christ our Lord. I had got no further than this when he too revealed to me that when he himself had been near death they had told him secretly, in a whisper, "Jesus Christ, the crucified Son of God, will judge you." (6) But let this be recorded here, from a genuine report about these persons and about this formula.

10,1 Josephus was still sick. And though, as I said, the presbyter, along with the others, had told him, "Jesus Christ will judge you," he was still hardened. But the Lord in his lovingkindness again said to him in a dream, "Lo, I heal you; but rise and believe!" But though he recovered again, he did not believe. (2) When he was well the Lord appeared to him in a dream once more and scolded him for not believing. And he promised him, "If, for an assurance of your faith, you choose to work any miracle in my name, call upon me and I will do it."

10,3 There was a madman in the city who used to roam the town, I mean Tiberias, naked. If he was dressed he would often tear his clothing apart, as such people will. (4) Now Josephus was overcome with awe and wished to put the vision to the test, although he was still doubtful. So he brought the man inside, shut the door, took water, made the sign of the cross over it, and sprinkled it on the madman with the words, "In the name of Jesus of Nazareth the crucified begone from him, demon, and let him be made whole!"

10,5 Falling down with a loud cry, the man lay motionless for a long time foaming profusely and retching, and Josephus supposed that he had died. (6) But after a while he rubbed his forehead and got up and, once on his feet and seeing his own nakedness, he hid himself and covered his privy parts with his hands, for he could no longer bear to see his own nakedness. (7) Dressed by Josephus himself in one of his own himatia, in proof of his comprehension and sanity, he came and thanked him and God profusely, for he realized that he had been cured through Josephus. He spread word of him in town, and this miracle became known to the Jews there. (8) Much talk ensued in the city from people saying that Josephus had opened the treasuries, found the Name of God in writing and read it, and was working geat miracles. And what they were saying was true, though not in the way they thought.

10,9 Josephus, however, still remained hardened in heart. But the merciful God who is continually arranging good opportunities for those who love him, grants them to those whom he deems worthy of life. (11,1) As things turned out for Josephus himself, after Judas the patriarch, of whom we have spoken, grew up—I guess he was called that—to repay Josephus he granted him the revenue of the apostolate. (2) He was sent to Cilicia with a commission, and on arriving there collected the tithes and firstfruits from the Jews of the province, from every city in Cilicia. (3) At this time he lodged next to the church, I don't know in which city. But he made friends with the bishop there, <went to him> unobserved, borrowed the Gospels and read them.

11,4 Since <he was> very severe as an apostle should be—as I said, this is their name for the rank—and indeed was a reformer, he was always intent on what would make for the establishment of good order and purged and demoted many of the appointed synagogue-heads, priests, elders and "azanites" (meaning their kind of deacons or assistants), many were angry with him. As though in an attempt to pay him back these people took no little trouble to pry into his affairs and find out what he was doing. (5) For this reason a crowd of meddlers burst in upon him at home in his residence, and caught him pouring over the Gospels. They seized the book and grabbed the man, dragged him to the floor with shouts, bore him off to the synagogue with no light mistreatment, and beat him as the Law prescribes. (6) This made his first trial; however, the bishop of the town arrived and got him out. Another time they caught him on a journey, he told me, and threw him into the river Cydnus. <When they saw> him taken by the current they thought he had gone under and drowned, and were glad of it.

11,7 But a little later he was vouchsafed holy baptism—for he was rescued (from the river). He went to court, made friends with the Emperor Constantine, and told him his whole story—how he was of the highest

Jewish rank, and how the divine visions kept appearing to him, since the Lord was summoning him to his holy calling, and the salvation of his faith and knowledge. (8) And the good emperor—a true servant of Christ, and, after David, Hezekiah and Josiah, the king with the most godly zeal—rewarded him with a rank in his realm, as I have said already. (9) He made him a count and told him to ask what he wanted in his turn.

Josephus asked nothing of the emperor but this very great favor—permission by imperial rescript to build Christ's churches in the Jewish towns and villages where no one had ever been able to found churches, since there are no Greeks, Samaritans or Christians among the population. (10) This <rule> of having no gentiles among them is observed especially at Tiberias, Diocaesarea, Sepphoris, Nazareth and Capernaum.

12,1 After receiving the letter and the authorization along with his title, Josephus came to Tiberias. Besides, he had a draft on the imperial treasury, and he himself had been honored with a salary from the emperor.

12,2 And so he began to build in Tiberias. There was a very large temple in the town already, I think they may have called it the Adrianeum. The citizens may have been trying to restore this Adrianeum, which was standing unfinished, for a public bath. (3) When Josephus found this he took the opportunity from it; and as he found that there were already four walls raised to some height, made of stones four feet long, he began the erection of the church from that point.

12,4 But lime was needed, and the other building material. He therefore had a number of ovens, perhaps seven altogether, set up outside the city. (In the language of the country they call these "furnaces.") But the horrid Jews who are always up to trying anything did not spare their usual sorcery. Those grand Jews wasted their time on magic and jugglery to bind the fire, but they did not entirely succeed.

12,5 Well, the fire was smouldering and not doing anything but had practically ceased to be fire.[19] When those whose task it was to feed the fire with fuel—I mean brushwood or scrub—told Josephus what had been done he rushed from the city, stung to the quick and moved with zeal for the Lord. (6) He ordered water fetched in a vessel, (I mean a flask, but the local inhabitants call this a "cacubium,") <and> took this vessel of water in the sight of all—a crowd of Jews had gathered to watch, eager to see how it would turn out and what Josephus would try to do. Tracing the sign of the cross on the vessel with his own finger, and invoking the name of

[19] ἀλλὰ τῆς ἰδίας ὡς εἰπεῖν φύσεως ἐκτὸς ἐγένετο

Jesus, he cried out, (7) "In the name of Jesus of Nazareth, whom my fathers and those of all here present crucified, may there be power in this water to set at naught all sorcery and enchantment these men have wrought, and to work a miracle on the fire that the Lord's house may be finished." (8) With that he wet his hand and sprinkled the water on each furnace. And the spells were broken, and in the presence of all, the fire blazed up. And the crowds of spectators cried, "There is one God, who comes to the aid of the Christians," and went away.

12,9 Though they harmed the man on many occasions, he eventually restored part of the temple at Tiberias and finished a small church. He left then and came to Scythopolis and made his home. However, he completed buildings in Diocaesarea and certain other towns. (10) So much for my account and description of these events, which I recalled here because of the translation of the books, the rendering from Greek to Hebrew of the Gospel of John and the Acts of the Apostles.

13,1 But I shall resume the thread of my argument against Ebion—because of the Gospel according to Matthew the course of the discussion obliged me to insert the whole of the knowledge which I had gained. (2) Now in what they call a Gospel according to Matthew, though it is not the entire Gospel but is corrupt and mutilated—and they call this thing "Hebrew"!—the following passage is found: "There was a certain man named Jesus, and he was about thirty years of age,[20] who chose us. And coming to Capernaum he entered into the house of Simon surnamed Peter, and opened his mouth and said, (3) Passing beside the Sea of Tiberias I chose John and James, the sons of Zebedee,[21] and Simon and Andrew and <Philip and Bartholomew, James the son of Alphaeus and Thomas>, Thaddaeus, Simon the Zealot, and Judas Iscariot.[22] Thee too, Matthew, seated at the receipt of custom, did I call, and thou didst follow me.[23] I will, then, that ye be twelve apostles[24] for a testimony to Israel." (4) And, "John came baptizing, and there went out unto him Pharisees and were baptized, and all Jerusalem. And John had a garment of camel's hair, and a girdle of skin about his loins. And his meat," it says, "was wild honey, whose taste was the taste of manna, as a cake in oil."[25] (5) This, if you

---

[20] Cf. Lk 3:23

[21] Cf. Matt 4:18. What precedes is a combination of the Gospel passages Mark 1:21; 29; Matt 5:2; Matt 4:18.

[22] Cf. Matt 10:2-4; Luke 6:14-16. The list given here, however, is not identical with either.

[23] Cf. Matt 9:9.

[24] Cf. Clem. Rec. 1.40.4; Clem. Alex. Strom. 6.418.2.

[25] Cf. Matt 3:4-5; Num 11:8.

please, to turn the account of the truth into falsehood, and substitute "a cake in honey" for "locusts"!

13,6 But the beginning of their Gospel is, "It came to pass in the days of Herod, king of Judaea, <in the high-priesthood of Caiaphas>, that <a certain> man, John <by name>, came baptizing with the baptism of repentance in the river Jordan, and he was said to be of the lineage of Aaron the priest, the son of Zacharias and Elizabeth, and all went out unto him."[26] (7) And after saying a good deal it adds, "When the people had been baptized Jesus came also and was baptized of John. And as he came up out of the water the heavens were opened, and he saw the Holy Spirit in the form of a dove which descended and entered into him. And (there came) a voice from heaven saying, Thou art my beloved Son, in thee I am well pleased,[27] and again, This day have I begotten thee.[28] And straightway a great light shone round about the place.[29] Seeing this," it says, "John said unto him, Who art thou, Lord?[30] And again (there came) a voice to him from heaven, This is my beloved Son, in whom I am well pleased.[31] (8) And then," it says, "John fell down before him and said, I pray thee, Lord, do thou baptize me. But he forbade him saying, Let it alone, for thus it is meet that all be fulfilled."[32]

14,1 See how their utterly false teaching is all lame, crooked, and not right anywhere! (2) For by supposedly using their same <so-called Gospel according to Matthew> Cerinthus and Carpocrates want to prove from the beginning of Matthew, by the genealogy, that Christ is the product of Joseph's seed and Mary. (3) But these people have something else in mind. They falsify the genealogical tables in Matthew's Gospel and make its opening, as I said, "It came to pass in the days of Herod, king of Judaea, in the high-priesthood of Caiaphas, that a certain man, John by name, came baptizing with the baptism of repentance in the river Jordan" and so on. (4) This is because they maintain that Jesus is really a man, as I said, but that Christ, who descended in the form of a dove, has entered him—as we have found already in other sects—<and> been united with him. Christ himself <is from God on high, but Jesus> is the offspring of a man's seed and a woman.

[26] Cf. Luke 1:5; Mark 1:4-5.
[27] This is closest to Luke 3:21-22.
[28] Heb. 1:5; Ps 2:7; Gospel according to the Hebrews H-S I p. 169 which, however, is a quoted from Epiph. There is no other source for the quotation.
[29] Cf. Justin Dial. 7.
[30] Acts 9:5
[31] Cf. Matt 3:17
[32] Matt 12:47-50

14,5 But again they deny that he is a man, supposedly on the basis of the words the Savior spoke when he was told, "Behold thy mother and thy brethren stand without," "Who are my mother and my brethren? And he stretched forth his hand toward his disciples and said, These are my brethren and mother and sisters, these that do the will of my Father." (6) And so Ebion, as I said, who is crammed with all sorts of trickery, shows himself in many forms—making him a monstrosity, as I indicated above.

15,1 But they use certain other books as well—supposedly the so-called Travels of Peter written by Clement, though they corrupt their contents while leaving a few genuine passages. (2) Clement himself convicts them of this in every way in his general epistles which are read in the holy churches, because his faith and speech are of a different character than their spurious productions in his name in the Travels. He himself teaches celibacy, and they will not accept it. He extols Elijah, David, Samson and all the prophets, whom they abhor.[33]

15,3 In the Travels they have changed everything to suit themselves and slandered Peter in many ways, saying that he was baptized daily[34] for purification as they are. And they say he abstained from flesh and dressed meat as they do, and any other dish made from meat—since both Ebion himself, and Ebionites, entirely abstain from these.[35] (4) When you ask one of them why they do not eat meat, having no explanation they answer foolishly and say, "Since it is a product of the congress and intercourse of bodies, we do not eat it." Thus, according to their own foolish regurgitations, they are wholly abominable themselves, since they are the results of the intercourse of a man and a woman.

16,1 They too receive baptism, apart from their daily baptisms. And they celebrate supposed mysteries from year to year in imitation of the sacred mysteries of the church, using unleavened bread—and the other part of the mystery with water only.

16,2 But as I said, they set side by side two who have been appointed by God, one being Christ, but one the devil. And they say that Christ has been allotted the world to come, but that this world has been entrusted

---

[33] The Clementina are at least suspicious of the prophets. Ep. Pet. Ad Jac. 1.4 warns of being confused by their contradictory utterances. Cf. Clem. Hom. 3.53.2. For a Nag Hammadi attack on the prophets see GT 52.

[34] This seems implied at Clem Hom. 11.1.1-2; Rec. 4.3.1; 8.1.1. See, however, Strecker, *Judenchristentum* p. 208.

[35] Cf. Clem. Hom. 8.15.3-4.

to the devil[36]—supposedly by the decree of the Almighty, at the request of each of them. (3) And they say that this is why Jesus was begotten of the seed of a man and chosen, and thus has been named Son of God by election, after the Christ who came to him from on high in the form of a dove. (4) But they say that he is not begotten of God the Father but created as one of the archangels, and that he is ruler both of angels and of all creatures of <the> Almighty; and that he came and instructed us <to abolish the sacrifices>. (5) As their so-called Gospel says, "I came to abolish the sacrifices, and if ye cease not from sacrifice, wrath will not cease from you."[37] Both these and certain things of the kind are guileful inventions which are current among them.

16,6 They speak of other Acts of Apostles in which there is much thoroughly impious material, and from them arm themselves against the truth in deadly earnest. (7) They lay down certain ascents and instructions in the supposed "Ascents of James," as though he were giving orders against the temple and sacrifices, and the fire on the altar—and much else that is full of nonsense.

16,8 Nor are they ashamed to accuse Paul[38] here with certain fabrications of their false apostles' villainy and imposture. They say that he was Tarsean—which he admits himself and does not deny. And they suppose that he was of Greek parentage, taking the occasion for this from the (same) passage because of his frank statement, "I am a man of Tarsus, a citizen of no mean city."[39] (9) They then claim that he was Greek and the son of a Greek mother and Greek father, but that he had gone up to Jerusalem, stayed there for a while, desired to marry a daughter of the high priest, and had therefore became a proselyte and been circumcised. But since he still could not marry that sort of girl he became angry and wrote against circumcision, and against the Sabbath and the legislation.

17,1 But he is making a completely false accusation, this horrid serpent with his poverty of understanding. For "Ebion," translated from Hebrew to Greek, means "poor." For truly he is poor, in understanding, hope and actuality, since he regards Christ as a mere man, and thus has come to

[36] See Clem. Hom. 3.19.2; 20.2.1-2; Rec. 7.3-4. At Clem. Hom. 8.21.1-2 the "king of the present" (Satan) tempts the "king of the future" (Christ). In Manichean literature see Man. Hom. 41,18-20.

[37] Cf. Clem. Hom. 2.44.2; 3.26.3; 3.45.1-2; 56.4, and Rec. 1.37 1.39.12. Mandaean literature deprecates the sacrifices, e.g. at *Ginza* 9,83; 33,2; 43,8-10.

[38] Cf. Ep. Pet. Ad Jac. 2.5; Clem. Rec. 1.70-71. Ebionite opposition to Paul is mentioned at Iren. 1.26.2; Orig. Cels. 5.65; Hom. 19 in Jer. 18:12 (Klostermann p. 167).

[39] Cf. Acts 21:39.

hope in him with poverty of faith.[40] (2) They themselves, if you please, boastfully claim that they are poor because they sold their possessions in the apostles' time and laid them at the apostles' feet, and went over to a life of poverty and renunciation;[41] and thus, they say, they are called "poor" by everyone. (3) But there is no truth to this claim of theirs either; he was really named Ebion.[42] I suppose the poor wretch was named prophetically by his father and mother.

17,4 And how many other dreadful, false, observances they have, chock full of wickedness! When one of them falls ill or is bitten by a snake, he gets into water and invokes the names in Elxai—of heaven, earth, salt, water, winds, "angels of righteousness" <as> they say, bread and oil[43]—and begins to say, "Come to my aid and rid me of my pain!"

17,5 But I have already indicated, even before this, that Ebion did not know of these things. After a time his followers became associated with Elxai, and they have the circumcision, the Sabbath and the customs of Ebion, but Elxai's delusion. (6) Thus they believe that Christ is a manlike figure invisible to human eyes, ninety-six miles—or twenty-four schoena, if you please!—tall; six schoena, or twenty-four miles wide; and some other measurement through. Opposite him the Holy Spirit stands invisibly as well, in the form of a female, with the same dimensions. (7) "And how did I find the dimensions?" he says. "I saw from the mountains that the heads were level with them, and from observing the height of the mountain, I learned the dimensions of Christ and the Holy Spirit." (8) I have already spoken of this in the Sect, "Against Ossaeans." I have put it down here though, in passing, lest it be thought that I fail from forgetfulness to mention characteristics of any nation and sect which are also found in others.

18,1 Ebion too preached in Asia and Rome, but the roots of these thorny side-growths come mostly from Nabataea and Banias, Moabitis, and Cocabe in Bashanitis beyond Adrai—in Cyprus as well. (2) They compel them to give their children in marriage even when they are too young—with the permission of their teachers, if you please! (Ebionites have elders and heads of synagogues, and they call their church a synagogue, not a church; and they take pride in Christ's name only.) (3) And they do not allow people to contract only one marriage; even if someone should want

[40] Eusebius gives a comparable explanation at H. E. 3.27.1. He knows nothing of an "Ebion."

[41] Cf. Acts 4:34-35.

[42] See p. 133 n. 2.

[43] A shorter version of these "witnesses" is found at Ep. Pet. Ad Jac. 4.1.

to be released from his first marriage and contract another, they permit it—they allow everything without hesitation—down to a second, and a third, and a seventh marriage.

18,4 They acknowledge Abraham, Isaac and Jacob, Moses and Aaron—and Joshua the son of Nun[44] simply as Moses' successor, though he is of no importance. But after these they acknowledge no more of the prophets, but even anathematize David and Solomon and make fun of them. Similarly they disregard Isaiah and Jeremiah, Daniel and Ezekiel, Elijah and Elisha; for they pay them no heed and blaspheme their prophecies,[45] but accept only the Gospel. (5) They say, however, that Christ is the prophet of truth[46] and the Christ; <but> is Son of God by promotion,[47] and by union with the elevation on high which has come to him. They say that the prophets are prophets of <their own> understanding, not of truth. (6) Christ alone, they would have it, is prophet, man, Son of God, and Christ—and as I said before he is a mere man[48] who has come to be called Son of God owing to the virtue of his life.

18,7 Nor do they accept Moses' Pentateuch in its entirety; they reject certain sayings.[49] When you say to them, of eating meat, "Why did Abraham serve the angels the calf and the milk? Why did Noah eat meat, and why was he told to by God, who said, 'Slay and eat?' Why did Isaac and Jacob sacrifice to God—Moses too, in the wilderness?" he will disbelieve those things and will say, "What need for me to read what is in the Law, when the Gospel has come?"

18,8 "Well, how do you know about Moses and Abraham? I know you admit that they exist, and that you put them down as righteous, and your own ancestors."

18,9 Then he will answer, "Christ has revealed this to me," and will blaspheme most of the legislation, and Samson, David, Elijah, Samuel, Elisha and the rest.

---

[44] The Book of Joshua is appended to the Samaritan Pentateuch, perhaps for similar reasons.

[45] Ebionites are said to repudiate the canonical prophets at Method. Conviv. 8.10.

[46] This idea recurs many times in the Clementina. A good specimen is found at Rec. 8.59-62.

[47] Hipp. Refut. 7.34.2: καὶ <γὰρ> τὸν Ἰησοῦν λέγουσι δικαιοῦσθαι ποιήσαντα τὸν νόμον, · διὸ καὶ Χριστὸν αὐτὸν <καὶ υἱὸν> θεοῦ ὠνομᾶσθαι.

[48] Clem. Hom. 16.15.2: "Our Lord neither asserted that there were gods except the Creator of all, not did he proclaim himself to be God." This, however, is a late passage by an Anomoean author.

[49] Clem. Hom. 2.38.1; 45-52; 18.19-20. The Clementina regard any anthropopathic material in the Pentateuch as a corruption of the Law God originally gave to Moses.

19,1 But the tramp is completely exposed by the Savior, who refutes the whole of his deceitful teaching, expressly and as though in summary form with one utterance, when he says, "John came in the way of righteousness, neither eating nor drinking, and they say, He hath a devil. The Son of Man came eating and drinking, <and they say, Behold a man gluttonous and a wine-bibber.">[50] (2) And he certainly does not mean that John never by any chance ate, or that the Savior ate anything and everything—with the suspicion of forbidden foods as well. (3) The passage makes the meaning of the truth plain, since "He is a glutton and a wine-bibber" can mean only the eating of meat and the drinking of wine; and "neither eating nor drinking" means that John did not partake of meat and wine, but only of locusts and honey—water too, obviously.

19,4 But who does not know that the Savior arose from the dead and ate (flesh)? As the holy Gospels of the truth say, "There was given unto him bread, and a piece of broiled fish. And he took it, and did eat, and gave to his disciples."[51] As he also did at the Sea of Tiberias, both eating and giving. (5) And a great deal can be said on this subject. But I must now come to the detailed refutation of their worthless, unsound teachings, and compose the rebuttal of them.

20,1 And first, it must be said of Christ that he is not a mere man. It cannot be that a person conceived <like> a man in every respect will be given to the world for a "sign," as the Holy Spirit foretold of him by saying to Ahaz, "Ask thee a sign"; and since Ahaz would not ask, the prophet then said, "The Lord himself shall give you a sign. Behold the Virgin shall conceive."[52]

20,2 A woman who has been united to a husband and married cannot be called a virgin. But she who has truly had the conception of the Word of God without a husband may properly be called a virgin—(3) as Isaiah himself says in another passage, "A voice of a cry from the city, a voice from the temple, a voice of the Lord of recompense, that rendereth recompense to his enemies. Before she that travailed hath brought forth, before the pain of her travail came, she escaped (it) and was delivered of a man child. Who hath heard of such a thing? Or who hath seen such things? Or hath the earth travailed in one day and brought forth a nation at once? For Zion hath travailed and brought forth her children. And it was I who granted this expectation, and they did not remember, saith the

[50] Matt. 11:18-19
[51] Luke 24:42-43; John 21:12
[52] Isa. 7:11;14

Lord."[53] (4) But which "expectation" and which "children," other than that of a virgin's giving birth (to a child) without labor pains, something that had never happened, and that the child born of Elizabeth by promise for his sake <leaped in the womb before his birth>, even though John was born with labor pains.

20,5 How, then, can these people declare the Savior a mere man, conceived of a man's seed? How will he "not be known," as Jeremiah says of him, "He is a man, and yet who will know him?"[54] (6) For in giving his description the prophet said of him, "Who will know him?" But if he were speaking of a mere man, surely his father would know him and his mother, his relatives and neighbors, the members of his household and his fellow townsmen. (7) But since the human offspring is born of Mary but the divine Word came from above, truly begotten not in time and without beginning, not of a man's seed but of the Father on high, and in the last days consenting to enter a virgin's womb and fashioning flesh from her, patterned after himself—this is why Jeremiah says, "And he is a man, but who will know him?"[55] For as God he came from above, the only-begotten divine Word.

20,8 But the deluded souls are most unfortunate to have abandoned the testimonies of prophets and angels and to be content with those of the deluded Ebion, who wants to do what he likes, and practice the Jewish cusoms even though he is estranged from the Jews. (9) <For> when Gabriel was bringing the tidings to Mary, he pledged his word at once as soon as she said, "How shall this be, seeing I know not a man?" and said, "The Spirit of the Lord shall come upon thee, and the power of the highest shall overshadow thee. Therefore also that which is born of thee shall be called holy, Son of God."[56] (10) By saying, "that which is born," he showed that the flesh <is> from her and the rest of the humanity, but that the power of the highest and the Holy Spirit overshadowed the holy Virgin from above, from the heavens, and the only-begotten Son, the divine Word, has descended from on high—<indicating> both that Christ became man, and that he was born of her in truth. (11) And how much more there is of this sort! But as I promised it is not my custom to range widely, so as not to make my treatise very lengthy.

[53] Isa. 66:6-9
[54] Jerem 17:9
[55] Jerem 17:9
[56] Luke 1:34-35

21,1 But next I shall discuss the other false accusations which they make, against Peter and the other apostles—that every day, before so much as eating bread, Peter had had immersions. (2) Observe the whole of their slander, and the badness hidden under their cheap teaching! Since they are defiled themselves and often indulge themselves sexually on earth, they make lavish use of water for their own reassurance, to deceive themselves if you please, under the impression that they have purification through baptisms. (3) And they are not ashamed to say these offensive things about the apostles, even though the Lord exposes their perversity since, when he came to wash Peter's feet, Peter said, "Thou shalt never wash my feet," and the Savior's answer was, "If I wash not thy feet thou hast no part with me." (4) And when Peter replied, "Not the feet only, but also the head," the Lord returned, "He that is washed once needeth not <to wash> his head, but his feet only; for he is clean every whit."[57]

21,5 He showed, then, that there is no need to make use of immersions, useless customs, and commandments and teachings of men, as he says in the Gospel in agreement with the prophet, "This people honoreth me with their lips, but their heart is far from me. But in vain do they worship me, teaching for doctrines the commandments of men."[58] (6) Why did he fault the Pharisees and Scribes, with their thorough immersions <both> of themselves, and of their platters, cups and the rest? And why does he declare definitively, "To eat with unwashen hands defileth not a man?"[59] Thus not only did he put a stop to the immersion of these things. He even showed that washing one's hands is unnecessary, and that if one would rather <not> wash his hands, it does him no harm.

22,1 And how can their stupidity about the eating of meat not be exposed out of hand? First of all, because the Lord ate the Jewish Passover. Now the Jewish Passover was a sheep and unleavened bread—sheep's flesh roasted with fire and eaten, (2) as his disciples say to him, "Where wilt thou that we prepare for thee that thou mayest eat the Passover?" And the Lord himself says, "Go ye into the city, and ye shall find a man bearing a pitcher of water and ye shall follow whithersoever he goeth, and say ye to the goodman of the house, Where is the guest-chamber, where I shall keep the Passover with my disciples? And he shall show you an upper room furnished; there make ready."[60]

---

[57] John 13:8-10
[58] Matt. 15:8-9
[59] Matt. 15:20
[60] Mark 14:12-15

22,3 And again, the Lord himself says, "With desire I have desired to eat this Passover with you."[61] And he did not simply say "Passover" but "*this* Passover," so that no one could play with it in his own sense. A Passover, as I said, was meat roasted with fire and the rest. (4) But to destroy deliberately the true passage these people have altered its text—which is evident to everyone from the expressions that accompany it[62]—and represented the disciples as saying, "Where wilt thou that we prepare for thee to eat the Passover?" and he supposedly saying, "Did I really desire to eat meat as this Passover with you?"

22,5 But how can their tampering go undetected, when the passage cries out that the "mu" and "eta" are additions? Instead of saying ἐπιθυμίᾳ ἐπεθύμησα they have put in the additional μή. Christ truly said, "With desire I have desired to eat this Passover with you."[63] But they misled themselves by writing in meat and making a false entry, and saying, "Did I really want to eat meat with you as this Passover?" But it is plainly demonstrated that he both kept the Passover, and, as I said, ate meat.

22,6 But they will also be convicted by the vision which was shown St. Peter, through the sheet which contained all sorts of wild beasts, domestic animals, reptiles and birds, and the Lord's voice saying, "Arise, slay and eat!" And when Peter said, "Not so, Lord; nothing common or unclean hath entered into my mouth," the Lord replied, "What God hath cleansed, that call not thou common."[64] (7) For the proof of the truth can be arrived at by two methods. If they say that St. Peter's remark refers inclusively to all foods when he says, "Nothing common or unclean <hath> at any time <entered into my mouth>," so that he would have called cattle, goats, sheep and birds unclean, they will be exposed at once by his previous mode of life. (8) It was after marrying, fathering children[65] and having a mother-in-law that he met the Savior, and he was Jewish. But Jews eat flesh, and among them the eating of meat is not considered abominable or forbidden. (9) Since he had always eaten meat, then—even if we say (he did it only) until he met the Savior—this will prove that he considered nothing unclean which was not declared to be unclean. For in fact he did not attribute commonness or uncleanness to all sorts of meat, but (only) to the ones the Law called common or unclean.

[61] Luke 22:15
[62] I.e., the expression τοῦτο.
[63] Luke 22:15
[64] Acts 11:7-9
[65] The Act of Peter, BG 8502,4, is the legend of Peter's daughter.

22,10 But again—since it is established that he did not hold of all kinds of meat that they were all common, but that he held this of the kinds which are called common and unclean in the Law—to teach him the character of Christ's holy church God told him to consider nothing common. "For all things are pure, when they are received with thanks and praise to God."[66] (11) But even though the riddle referred to the call of the gentiles so that Peter would not regard the uncircumcised as profane or unclean, the expression Peter used did not refer to people but meant the foods the Law prohibits, as anyone can see. And their silly argument has failed from every point of view.

23,1 They pretendedly accept the names of the apostles in order to convince their dupes, and have composed forged books in their names, supposedly by James, Matthew, and other disciples. (2) They list the name of the apostle John among these to make their stupidity detectible in every way. For not only does he refute them in every way by saying, "In the beginning was the Word, and the Word was with God, and the Word was God."[67] (3) <It is clear from his Gospel>, moreover, that he <accepts> the testimonies of the holy prophets. In this Gospel he published their testimonies by giving a good and full account, with the Holy Spirit's help, of the things the Savior said about each oracle (of the prophets) which, as I said, has been fulfilled in Christ. From these prophets the Ebionites have estranged themselves. (4) At the very outset he showed how John himself answered the messengers sent by the Pharisees to John the Baptist with, "I am the voice of one crying in the wilderness, Make straight the way of the Lord, as said the prophet Isaiah."[68] (5) And again, when the Lord overturned the tables of the money-changers and said, "Make not my Father's house an house of merchandise," John himself, taking the testimony from the prophets, I mean from David, said, "They remembered that it was written, The zeal of thine house hath eaten me up."[69] And again, John himself said, "Isaiah saw, being in the Holy Spirit."[70]

24,1 And again, when St. John himself was preaching in Asia, it is reported that he did an extraordinary thing as an example of the truth. Although his way of life was most admirable and appropriate to his apostolic rank and he never bathed, he was compelled to approach the bath by the

---

66 Cf. Rom. 14:20 and 1 Tim. 4:3.
67 John 1:1
68 John 1:23
69 John 2:16-17
70 John 12:41

Holy Spirit who said, "Look what is at the bath!" (2) To his companions' surprise he actually went to the bathing-room, approached the attendant who took the bathers' clothes, and asked who was inside in the bathing-room. (3) And the attendant stationed there to watch the clothes—some people do this for a living in the gymnasia—said to St. John, "Ebion is inside." (4) But John understood at once why the Holy Spirit's guidance had impelled him to approach the bath, as I said—as a memorial to leave us the truth's advice as to who Christ's servants and apostles are, and the sons of that same truth, but what the vessels of the evil one are, and the gates of hell; though these cannot prevail against the rock, and God's holy church which is founded on it. (5) Becoming disturbed at once and crying out John said in an aside audible to all—as a testimony in evidence of undefiled doctrine—"Let's get out of here in a hurry, brothers, or the bath may fall and bury us along with the person who is inside in the bathing-room, Ebion, because of his impiety." (6) And no one need be surprised to hear that Ebion met John. The blessed John had a very long life, and survived till the reign of Trajan.[71] (7) But anyone can see that all the apostles distinguished Ebion's faith (from their own), and considered it foreign to the character of their preaching.

25,1 And how much do I have to say about their blasphemies of St. Paul? First, they say that he was Greek and of gentile parentage, but that he had later become a proselyte. (2) Why does he say "an Hebrew of Hebrews" of himself, then, "of the seed of Abraham, of the tribe of Benjamin, concerning the Law, a Pharisee, being more exceeding zealous of the traditions of my fathers?"[72] (3) And he says elsewhere, "Are they Israelites? So am I. Are they the seed of Abraham? So am I,"[73] and, "Circumcised the eighth day, brought up at the feet of Gamaliel, and an Hebrew of Hebrews."[74]

25,4 What frightful shrieks and snake's hisses of the horrid serpents, and what deadly nonsense! Whose word shall I take? Ebion's and his kind, or St. Peter's, who says, "As my brother, Paul, hath written unto you, which things are deep and hard to be understood, which they who are unlearned and unstable pervert by their own ignorance?"[75] (5) And St. Paul himself testifies in his turn for Peter and says, "James, John and Cephas, who seemed

[71] Cf. Iren. 3.3.4.
[72] Phil. 3:5; Gal. 1:14
[73] 2 Cor. 11:22
[74] Phil.3:5; Acts 22:3
[75] 2 Pet. 3:15-16

to be pillars, gave to me and Barnabas the right hand of fellowship."[76] For even if he said that he was from Tarsus, this is no excuse for the attitude of those who hunt for words <that they have invented> to their own ruin and the ruin of <their> converts. (6) For that matter, scripture also says that Barnabas, whose name was once Joseph but was changed to Barnabas, or "son of consolation," was a Levite from Cyprus. And it is by no means true that, because he was a Cypriote, he was not descended from Levi. Just so, even though St. Paul came from Tarsus, he was not foreign to Israel.

25,7 For since many were dispersed when there was war during the reign of Antiochus Epiphanes and at other times, both by being taken prisoner, and by <fleeing because of> a siege, those who had been taken captive remained in certain places, while everyone who had left for some such reason settled where he could. (8) And so the holy Jeremiah said of Israel because it was so often that they had to flee from their enemies, "And if thou passest over to the Citians, there also shalt thou have no rest."[77] (9) Now anyone can see that Citium means the island of Cyprus, for Cypriotes and Rhodians are Citians. Moreover, the Cypriote and Rhodian stock had settled in Macedonia where Alexander of Macedon came from. And this is why the Book of Maccabees says, "He came out of the land of the Citians";[78] Alexander of Macedon was of Citian descent.

25,10 But to find my place again after giving the information about them because of the chance remark,[79] I am saying that many of the emigrants who had settled in the other countries had Israelite ancestry. (11) For they were called natives of each country besides. Thus Jethro's daughters told their father how Moses had helped them when he drove the shepherds away and watered their sheep. And they went and told their father about it, and when he said, "How is it that ye are come so soon today?" (12) they answered, "An Egyptian delivered us from the shepherds, and also drew water for us and watered our flock." And Jethro answered at once, "Why brought ye him not hither, that he may eat bread?"[80]

25,13 But who does not know that Moses was the son of Amram and Jochabed, Amram was the son of Kohath, Kohath of Levi, Levi of Jacob, Jacob of Isaac, and Isaac of Abraham? And the line of his noble stock and his descent had surely not died out because Moses is called "Egyptian."

[76] Gal. 2:9
[77] Isa. 23:12
[78] 1 Macc. 1:1
[79] I.e., at 25,2
[80] Exod. 2:18-20

(14) But these people whom Ebion has led astray have left the road and set their minds on many crooked ways and an uphill path.

26,1 Again, they are proud of having circumcision,[81] and boast, if you please, that this is the sign and mark of the patriarchs and the righteous men who have lived by the Law; and they think that it makes them their equals. And indeed they want to give the proof of this from Christ himself, as Cerinthus did. (2) Echoing his silly argument they too say, "'It is enough for the disciple that he be as his master.' Christ was circumcised; you be circumcised too!"[82]

26,3[83] ...and that the seeds of the imposture may be discredited in every way. As the sea has a bridle, bars, and gates determined by God; as it has sand for a boundary, and for a commandment, "Hitherto shalt thou come, but no further; in thyself shall thy waves be shattered,"[84] <as> he says—so they will be exhausted within themselves. (4) But there the words about the boundary have been said by God for the ordering of the sea by God's command. Here, however, wickedness, and the imposture that blinds the mind and perverts pious reason, has of itself raised waves against itself beforehand, as it were. It smashes against the harshnesses of its previous pronouncements with other waves of its own opinion, and is constantly being shattered within itself <and> destroying itself.

26,5 Or it is like a horrid serpent which savages itself and becomes its own destruction by bending round from the tail and devouring itself. (6) They say this used to be done by asps which had been sealed up in jars, and when each had destroyed the other the strongest and and fiercest survived. But when it was left alone and got hungry, certain Egyptian naturalists report that it would eat itself up, beginning with its own tail. Hence they also named this appropriately and from the Gorgon's head called this too an "aspidogorgon."[85] (7) So the lame-brained Ebion and his circle have cut themselves up beforehand, and from the outset destroyed the very things of which they are proud. (8) For Christ did not circumcise himself, since he was born as a child. But glory to the merciful God! To avoid admitting the truth Ebion has anticipated himself, so that this even becomes a refutation for him. (9) If he said that Christ had come down from heaven as God and been circumcised by Mary on the eighth day, then—since, as God, he

[81] Cf. Iren. 1.26.2.
[82] Cf. PsT 3.3.
[83] There is a lacuna here.
[84] Job 38:11
[85] The word might originally have referred to the Gorgon's head on Athena's breastplate.

would be allowing this of his own consent—this would provide the tramp with the persuasive argument for circumcision. But since he brings in the idea that Christ, as a mere man, was generated by men, the child cannot be responsible, even though he was circumcised the eighth day. (10) For he did not circumcise himself, but was circumcised by men. Children do not circumcise themselves and are not responsible for their own circumcision; their parents are. They are unknowing, innocent babes, and neither do they know what their parents are doing to them.

27,1 But we say that he both came from heaven as God and remained in the Virgin Mary's womb for the normal period of gestation, so as to take his incarnate humanity entirely from the virgin womb, and provide the dispensation in which he was also circumcised—truly, and not in appearance—on the eighth day. (2) "For he came to perfect the Law and prophets, not to destroy them"[86]—not to declare the Law foreign to himself, but a thing given by himself and continuing as a type until his coming. Thus the deficiencies in the Law would in turn be perfected in him and by him so that the types, come to spiritual perfection, might be preached in truth by him and his apostles—no longer as types but as truth.

27,3 For in this the saying of the Law was fulfilled, one which had stood until his time, and was abolished and yet brought to fulfillment in him—the words of Zipporah, "The blood of the circumcision of my child hath ceased to flow."[87] (4) And she did not say, "I was circumcising my child"—the angel who was sent to her was not instituting circumcision, nor did he leave for fear of the blood of circumcision. But in token of the Child who would stanch the blood of circumcision <he was providing that she would say, "The blood of my child hath ceased to flow">. And on hearing this and having made the provision, he went away. (5) And which child's blood, mark you, but the child's of whom the prophet said, "They shall wish that they were burned with fire. For unto us a child is born, unto us a son is also given,"[88] (6) truly referring to the child who was born to mean his true incarnation; but (saying), "Unto us a son is given," to show that God's Word from above and his Son himself had been given and become man by entering the womb—both human and divine, himself God, himself man; himself a Son given from above, himself a child (humanly) born.

27,7 With this child the blood of circumcision finally ceased to flow, as he says in the Gospel—when Greeks arrived to see him, approached

[86] Cf. Matt. 5:17.
[87] Cf. Exod. 4:25.
[88] Cf. Isa. 9:5-6.

Philip, and told him, "Show us Jesus," and Philip told John (*sic*) and John told Jesus, "Certain Greeks desire to see thee."[89] (8) And the Lord replied at once, "Now hath come the glory of God," to show that physical circumcision, which had served for a while as a type, was passing away, but that uncircumcision in the flesh possesses a greater circumcision in spirit, since it sees Christ and has comprehended him in truth.

28,1 But if these people choose to say, "Then why was Christ circumcised?"—you misguided souls, I have already told you the reason he was circumcised! He was circumcised for many reasons. (2) First, to prove that <he had> really <taken> flesh, because of Manichaeus and those who say he been manifested (only) in appearance. (3) Then, to show that the body was not consubstantial with the Godhead as Apollinarius says, and that he had not brought it down from above as Valentinus says. (4) And to confirm the circumcision which he had given of old and which had served a legitimate purpose until his arrival; and so that the Jews would have no excuse. For if he had not been circumcised they could have said, "We cannot accept an uncircumcised Christ."

28,5 And besides, after commanding Abraham to be circumcised—circumcised as a visible seal but in token of the true and invisible seal that he had been given—Christ needed to confirm this by being circumcised (himself). (6) For the visible circumcision was instituted because of Abraham's doubt, when the holy and righteous man said, as though in doubt, "Shall a son be born unto him that is an hundred years old?" and, "Shall Sarah in her old age bear a son?"[90] And the Lord said at once, "Take me a ram three years old, and a goat, and an heifer,"[91] and so on, and about sundown, when Abraham saw burning torches, an oven and the rest, (7) and after God reprovingly told him, for a safeguard, "Thy seed shall be a stranger in a land that is not theirs, and they shall enslave them for four hundred years,"[92] because of the doubt that had led Abraham to say, "Shall a son be born to him that is an hundred years old?"[93] he imposed physical circumcision on him and his, to keep them from forgetting the God of their fathers after they had been enslaved by idolatrous, unbelieving Egyptians. Thus they would see their circumcision, be reminded and feel abashed, and not deny him.

[89] Cf. John 12:20-22.
[90] Gen. 17:17
[91] Gen. 15:9
[92] Gen. 15:13
[93] Gen. 17:17

28,8 And this remained the case until Christ, and because of it he himself consented to be circumcised, and became true man; though he had come from above from the Father as the divine Word, and did not doff the Godhead but truly wore flesh. (9) He was circumcised in the possession of full humanity, making all his provisions in truth—so that the Jews would have no excuse, as I said, and the Manichaeans and others would be refuted and so that, being circumcised himself, he could with reason abolish circumcision and show that another kind was greater. It was not as though he had no circumcision and was making one up for himself. He had one, but showed that there is no further need of this circumcision, but of the greater one.

29,1 And that he was God as soon as he was born and not a mere man, the magi will plainly show. For after a period of two years—as they told Herod the time the star had risen, "two years ago at the most"[94]—they came to Jerusalem. And on learning by inquiry that Christ must be born in Bethlehem, these same magi left again with the star guiding them, and came from Jerusalem to Bethlehem. (2) And they went in and found him with his mother Mary, and fell down and worshiped him and offered their gifts. (3) Now if he is worshiped at the outset, the child who has been born is not a mere man at birth, but is God and does not become Christ thirty years later, and not after the baptism, but was born as Christ of a virgin, God and man. (4) And thus the angels hymn him at once with, "Glory to God in the highest, and on earth peace, good-will among men,"[95] and give the shepherds tidings, "Unto you is born this day, in the city of David, Christ the Lord."[96]

29,5 And this is not the only proof, you deluded Ebion! Moreover, when he has turned twelve he is found "sitting in the midst of the priests and elders, both questioning them and disputing with them,"[97] and "They were amazed at the gracious discourse which proceeded out of his mouth."[98] (6) And it was not after his thirtieth year that he was doing this, allowing you to say he became Christ when the Spirit had come to him, but right at the age of twelve as I said, as it is written in the Gospel according to Luke.

29,7 But even earlier too when, during his childhood, when Joseph and Mary went up to Jerusalem to worship at the feast and started back,

[94] Matt. 2:16
[95] Luke 2:14
[96] Luke 2:11
[97] Luke 2:48
[98] Luke 4:22

Jesus stayed behind. And they looked for him on the road and among their relatives—Mary had relatives—and could not find him. (8) But she went back and found him, and said, "Son, what hast thou done to us? Behold, thy father and I have sought thee sorrowing." (Joseph was in the position of father to him, for he was not his actual father.) (9) Then the Lord answered her, "Why is it that ye sought me? Wist ye not that I must be in my Father's house?"[99] indicating that the Temple had been built in the name of God, that is, of his own Father. (10) Now if he knew the Temple and his Father from childhood, Jesus was not a mere man when he was born and he was not called Christ and Son (only) after his thirtieth year, after the form of the dove had come to him. Instead he was teaching, even at once and with full assurance, that he had to be in his Father's house.

29,11 And for proof that Joseph was not his father but <was> in the position of father, hear how the same evangelist—the one who quotes Mary as saying, "Thy father and I have sought thee sorrowing"[100]—writes in turn, "And Jesus began to be about thirty years of age, being, *as was supposed*, the son of Joseph."[101] By saying, "as was supposed," he showed that Jesus was not his son, but was supposed to be.

30,1 But the time is going to run short for my discussion in proof of the truth and in refutation of Ebion's weak-mindedness and his phony school of weak-mindedness. (2) What does not make it plain that Joseph was not father to Jesus, but was held to be in the position of father? "Behold," scripture says, "the Virgin shall conceive and bear a son";[102] it didn't say, "Behold, the wife!" (3) And again, it says in another place, "And the heifer shall bear, and they shall say, It hath not borne."[103] Some Manichaeans and Marcionites say that Jesus was not born—hence, "She shall bear, and they shall say, She hath not borne." For Mary has not given birth because of a man's seed, and these people[104] madly tell the lie that she has given birth because of a man's seed. The heifer, then, has in truth borne God, in truth borne man.

30,4 And to show that the Virgin is called "heifer" and that what was left by this heifer was a purification of the defiled, hear the Law saying,

---

[99] Luke 2:48-49
[100] Luke 2:48
[101] Luke 3:23
[102] Isa. 7:14
[103] This quotation is from the Apocryphon of Ezekiel. See Charlesworth I, p. 494, Fragment 3.
[104] I.e., the Ebionites

"Take thee a fiery-red heifer,"[105] indicating the chosen vessel of Mary <by saying, "*Take* thee an heifer." But it says, "fiery-red,"> because of the fieriness of the Savior's Godhead that was contained in the Virgin; for "God," says scripture, "is a consuming fire."[106] (5) And the Law says, "a fiery-red heifer upon whose neck hath never come yoke,"[107] to show that the Virgin, who does not know the yoke of marriage to a husband, is a "heifer."

30,6 But why am I giving most of the arguments? As Isaiah, again, said in the person of the Lord, "Take unto thee a sheet cut from a great, new papyrus-roll"[108]—"sheet" because the Virgin is the product of a man's seed but has been cut off from union with men and separated from natural human behavior. (7) For all human beings are generated by man's seed. But while Christ's generation had its humanity naturally from a woman, the Virgin Mary, it was cut off unnaturally from the human line of descent as Jacob says of him, "Thou didst come up, my son, from a shoot."[109] And he didn't say, "Thou didst come up from a seed." (8) And for this reason the holy Isaiah the prophet says, or rather, the Lord says to him, "Take thee a sheet (cut from) a papyrus-roll,"[110] giving a symbol of sexual intercourse, the way in which men write their entire record. As it also says in the hundred and thirty-eighth psalm, "In thy book shall all be written; they shall be fashioned in a day, and no one is in them,"[111] for it likened the womb to a book.

30,9 This is why David says, "Thine eyes did see my unbaked substance."[112] That is, he said, "You knew me after I was conceived but before I was formed; and even earlier, before my conception." (31,1) But the Hebrew author makes the expression marvelously clear. He called the "unbaked substance" a "golem," which means a grain or granule of flour—something which has not yet come together into a loaf and been kneaded, but is like a particle or fleck detached from a grain of wheat, or the tiny speck that is left by fine flour. (2) Thus he precisely represented a thing of the same shape, the particle that is detached from a man for insemination, and said—giving the expression in Greek translation—"the unbaked substance." In other words, he said, "'Thine eyes did see' the

[105] Numb. 19:2
[106] Deut. 4:24
[107] Numb. 19:2
[108] Isa. 8:1
[109] Cf. Gen. 49:9.
[110] Isa. 8:1
[111] Ps. 138:16.
[112] Ps. 138:16

unformed substance still in the womb, or before the womb"—"God knoweth all things before they be,"[113] as scripture says. But what is meant by "book" and "sheet" is "womb."

31,3 And he did not say, "Take thee a roll," or, "Take thee papyrus," but "a piece"—contrary to people's characteristic custom—because of the likeness of the womb to a place for writing. He said, "new," because of the newness and spotlessness of the Virgin. (4) And <"great">; for great indeed is Mary, the holy Virgin, before God and man! How can we not call her "great," when she contained the Uncontainable, whom heaven and earth cannot contain? Yet he, though uncontainable, was contained by his own choice and consent, willingly and not of necessity. Great, then, is the "sheet of papyrus," and new! Great, because of the marvel; new, because virgin.

31,5 "And write on it," he says, "with a man's pen."[114] And he didn't say, "Someone will write on it with a man's pen"; and he didn't say, "A man will write on it" either, so that Ebion would find no opportunity. If he had said, "A man will write on it," Ebion could say that a man, Joseph, sowed, and that Christ was generated from the seed of a man. (6) But he said, "Write!" to Isaiah about 753 years before the event, so that the truth would be apparent to everyone from the length of the interval—since no one could have sired the child who was to be born, 753 years ahead of time. (7) Then did he say, "Write!" to the prophet for no good reason? No, but to show that the Holy Spirit, who was in the prophet, would himself truly become the agent of the incarnate Christ's conception. For, "The Holy Spirit shall come upon thee, and so on"[115] said the angel Gabriel to Mary. (8) But "with a man's pen" means, "in the image of a man." "For Christ Jesus is man, but he is mediator between God and men,"[116] since he came from on high as divine Word but from Mary as man, though not begotten of man's seed.

31,9 And this is why the prophet says at once, "And he went in unto the prophetess,"[117] to show that Mary is a prophetess—not Ahaz's wife as some mistakenly allege that this was said because of Hezekiah. (10) For Hezekiah had already been born eleven years before. For it was in the third year of

[113] Susannah 42
[114] Isa. 8:1
[115] Luke 1:35
[116] Cf. 1 Tim. 2:5.
[117] Isa. 8:3

his father's reign that the prophecy, "Behold, the Virgin shall conceive,"[118] was delivered. And after the death of Ahaz, who reigned for fourteen years and (then) died, the scripture says at once, "And Hezekiah began to reign; twenty <and five> years old was he when he began to reign."[119] (11) So how could Hezekiah, (who reigned for twenty years after his father), be born during the reign of his father, who reigned for fourteen years, because of the prophecy that Emmanuel would be born of a virgin? Instead, will it not be evident to the wise that Hezekiah had already been born when the prophet delivered the oracle during the reign of Ahaz, Hezekiah's father? (12) Especially since Ahaz's wife was not a prophetess, as anyone can see. This is Mary, who said prophetically, "For from henceforth all generations will call me blessed";[120] Mary, to whom Gabriel came with the tidings that the Spirit who had spoken in Isaiah would come upon her and she would bear a son, our Lord Jesus Christ, through the Holy Spirit—and not by the seed of a man, as these people foolishly and erroneously blaspheme.

32,1 But both the lame-brain's Sabbath observance and circumcision, and the daily baptisms of which he makes use, stand discredited; for Jesus made a point of healing mostly on the Sabbath. And it was not just that he heals, but that he heals in two ways. (2) He directs the persons he has healed to pick their mattresses up and walk. Moreover, on the Sabbath he made clay and anointed the blind man's eyes, but the making of clay is work. (3) Hence, since the apostles had learned from their association with him and from his teaching that the Sabbath had been abolished, they plucked ears of grain on the Sabbath, rubbed them in their hands and ate them. But it was a "second Sabbath after the first" as the Gospel indicates.

32,4 For the Law designated various Sabbaths. The Sabbath proper, which recurs week by week. And the one that is a Sabbath because of the occurrences every month of the new moons and of the successive feasts such as the days of Tabernacles, and of Passover when they sacrifice the lamb and then eat unleavened bread. Further, when they keep the single, annual fast which is called the "Greater Fast," and the other, which they call the "Lesser." (5) For when these days occur, on the second day of the week or the third or the fourth, this too is designated a Sabbath for them.

32,6 Hence, after the Day of Unleavened Bread which had come and been designated a Sabbath, on the Sabbath proper following the Day of

[118] Isa. 7:14
[119] 2 Kms. 18:1-2
[120] Luke 1:48

Unleavened Bread which was considered a Sabbath, the disciples were found going through the standing grain, plucking the ears, and rubbing and eating them. (7) They were proving that the prohibition which is fixed on the Sabbath has been relaxed at the coming of the Great Sabbath—Christ, who gave us rest from our sins, and of whom Noah was a type. On seeing him at birth his father named him Noah by prophecy, and said, "He will give us rest from our sins, or deeds of cruelty."[121]

32,8 But Noah did not give any rest from sins. Lamech made the prophecy of Christ, whose meaning is truly Noah—"Noah" means "rest"—and "Sebeth," which means "rest and Sabbath." (9) In other words, "Christ," in whom the Father and his Holy Spirit have rested, and all holy men have found rest in him by desisting from sins. He is the great, eternal Sabbath, of which the lesser, temporary Sabbath was a type. This served until his coming, had been prescribed by him in the Law, and was abrogated, and fulfilled in him, in the Gospel. For this is what he meant when he said, "The Son of Man is Lord even of the Sabbath day."[122]

32,10 Hence the disciples broke the Sabbath with confidence—since even the priests before them used to break it in the Temple by sacrificing and offering sacrifices to God, to keep the continual sacrifice that was offered every day from coming to an end. And not only did the priests themselves prophesy the Sabbath's abrogation by not remaining idle; besides, circumcision itself broke the Sabbath.

32,11 For when a child was born on the Sabbath as one often was, there was an abrogation of the Sabbath and of circumcision. Thus the dissolution of both was predicted. Obviously, if the ones who were to circumcise the child which had been born on the Sabbath chose to be exact about the eighth day, and they found that it fell on Sabbath and still circumcised the child, they performed a work and broke the Sabbath. (12) But if they put it off so as not to break the Sabbath, they then performed the circumcision on the ninth day, and violated circumcision itself, and its mandatory term of eight days.

33,1 Nor was the first circumcision final. It was given for a sign, as a reminder of things to come, and because of the holy Abraham's doubts when, as I said, he was reproved for them—and as a type of the Greater Circumcision, which fulfills all things equally in those who are held worthy. (2) If the previous circumcision had been for sanctification and the inher-

[121] Cf. Gen. 5:29.
[122] Matt. 12:8

itance of the kingdom of heaven, Sarah would have been deprived of the kingdom—and Rebecca, Leah, Rachel, Jochabed, Miriam the sister of Moses, and all the holy women. They could not have inherited the kingdom of heaven, since they could not have the circumcision of Abraham which, as the Ebionites tell it, God had given him. But if these have not been deprived of the kingdom of heaven though they have no circumcision, the physical circumcision of today is of no force.

33,3 But why does Ebion boast of circumcision, when both the idolaters and the Egyptian priests have it? Moreover the Saracens, also called Ishmaelites, have circumcision, and the Samaritans, Idumaeans and Homerites. Most of these do this, not because of a law, but from some senseless custom.

33,4 And I will simply use a lot of time if I spend it on Ebion's nonsense, because of the way he pointlessly relies on the wording of the Savior's, "It is enough for the disciple that he be as his master,"[123] for his boast that his own circumcision derives from Christ's—which was cut off altogether in him and abolished through him! (5) Still, since the oaf takes this saying of the imitation of Christ, I do not mind showing that it was not said for this reason.

33,6 The Lord explains immediately that he did not say it for this reason but because of persecutions and the way the Jews insulted him, and he says, "If they have persecuted me, they will also persecute you; if they have hated me, they will hate you also."[124] "Call ye not me teacher and Lord? And ye say well, for so I am.[125] If they have called the master of the house Beelzebul, how much more shall they call them of his household?"[126] (7) And, "The servant cannot be above his lord, nor the disciple above his teacher. But let the disciple be perfect in all things, as his teacher"[127]—in other words, ready for persecution, defamation, and whatever may be inflicted on him. (8) Hence St. Paul too said, "Be ye imitators of me, as I also am of Christ."[128] And it was not that he imitated his Master in a wrong way; he did not say, "I am God," or, "I am the Son of God," or, "I am the divine Word." For he says, "I am the least of the apostles," and, "He was seen of me also, as of one born out of due time."[129]

---

[123] Matt 10:25
[124] John 15:21
[125] John 13:13
[126] Matt. 10:25
[127] Matt. 10:24; Luke 6:40
[128] 1 Cor. 1:11
[129] 1 Cor. 15:8-9

34,1 But if you take this text of the imitation of Christ, Ebion, and want to be as your teacher—or rather, as your Lord—in the circumcision you have such silly ideas <about>, stop being like him in circumcision! This will do you no good. The Lord has made it obsolete, as I have shown plainly through many testimonies. (2) For he came and fulfilled it by giving us the perfect circumcision of his mysteries—not of one member only, but by sealing the entire body and cutting it off from sin. And not by saving one portion of the people, males alone, but by truly sealing the entire Christian people, men and women both, and <leading> them ungrudgingly <on> to the inheritance of the kingdom of heaven. And not by providing the seal defectively in weakness, to only one class, males alone; but by revealing the kingdom of heaven to an entire people through his seal, his commandments, and his good teaching.

34,3 But if you want to be like the Lord, Ebion—that is, if you want to be like the teacher—you are very wrong. Stop mimicking him in circumcision. Call Lazarus from the grave, or raise another dead man; cleanse lepers or grant sight to the blind, or heal a paralytic from birth, if you can! But you can't because you are doing the opposite, imprisoned by unbelief, chains of flesh, and insatiable demands of law. (4) Now if you cannot do even these things—which you cannot, because of your wrong belief—I deny <that you are> like Christ. You cannot become like God, for you are a mortal man, and a deluded one. Nor can you call on Christ's name for miracles—and even if you do, you don't succeed. (5) But if you ever did manage to make a paralytic stand, since he had gotten up by the name of Jesus he could get understanding from him too, so as not to tolerate your Sabbath observance but <be able> to learn, from the name of his Healer, "Take up thy bed and go unto thine house on the Sabbath day.[130]

34,6 But I have already said how each of them palms off something different about Christ. Ebion himself did at one time, by saying that he originated as a mere man from sexual intercourse. But at other times the Ebionites who derive from him say that Christ has a heavenly power from God, "the Son," and that the Son puts Adam on and takes him off when convenient. By the power of God I have refuted their various opinions.

34,7 But why should I spend any further time on tidal beaches by the sea, which are flooded here and dry there, and fish are often stranded on some of them and injure people's feet when they cross their high parts because of there being poisonous ones among them—I mean sting-rays,

[130] Mark 2:11; John 3:8-16

sea-snakes, sharks and sea-eels—as I have just now said. (8) I shall leave this spot in its turn, thanking God that I have also put this sect to flight, not half-heartedly but even with a painstaking refutation. (9) But let us address ourselves to others next, beloved, praying for God's help, that he himself may bring our undertakings to fulfillment through me.

31.
Against Valentinians[1]
also called Gnostics. Number eleven, but thirty-one of the series

1,1 After these so-called Ebionites I shall go on to the sect of the Valentinians. For I have made my way through the Ebionites' wickedness, and have promised <to refute> the others that follow by the power of God, although they have the faces of other wild beasts and the poisons, bites and venom of serpents—all the things that are visible, as in a gaping maw; in their teachings—and <the ways> of a fire-breathing dragon, or of a horrid serpent and basilisk. I shall give the best refutation I can of the Valentinians, the people who also title themselves Gnostics. (2) There are ten varieties of Gnostic, each as afflicted as the other with one plague of dreams about their syzygies, ogdoads, and male and female aeons. I shall no longer arrange the treatise by the times of the (sects') succession, but (simply) pass from one to the other.

1,3 For all of these sprouted from the ground at the same time like toadstools and all came to life at once like stunted, smelly shoots and thistly grass and like a den full of scorpions, and, as I said, appeared in an instant like the ugliness of toadstools. This has been said of them already, by the most holy Irenaeus.[2] (4) For they all arose simultaneously but, although it had borrowed its poor excuse (for existing) from the other, each one wanted <to find> even more than the other, and each, for ostentation, had already

[1] Sect 31 is largely dependent upon Irenaeus; 9,1-32,8 are taken verbatim from Iren. Praef.-1.11.1. However, 5,3-56,1 reproduce an otherwise unknown Valentinian source. The details of Valentinus' biography are drawn from oral information.

The earliest mention of Valentinians is found at Justin Dial. 35.6. Tertullian's tractate *Adversus Valentianos* is dependent upon Irenaeus. PsT 4.1-6 is very like Irenaeus but differences in detail suggest that it might represent Hipp. Synt. Fil. 38 seems to combine material from Hipp. Refut. with Hipp. Synt. and may show a knowledge of Epiph. Hipp. Refut. 6,29.21-36 and the NHC *Tripartite Tractate* (I,5) and document XI,2 of NHC are independent of any sources we know. Epiph uses neither, but they have various points of contact with him and Irenaeus.

[2] See Iren. 1.29.1.

devised its own variety of wicked invention. (5) And they all called themselves Gnostics, I mean Valentinus and the Gnostics before him, as well as Basilides, Satornilus and Colorbasus, Ptolemy and Secundus, Carpocrates, and many more.

1,6 But though I have named them all here because the emergence of all of them and their rotten <teaching> came at once, I am still going to discuss the perversity of each one's sowing by itself. For the present I shall go to the heresiarch and tragedian before us, I mean to Valentinus and his teaching, a part of this overall "Gnostic" subject <which is full> of contemptible silliness, as it is found contemptible and ridiculous by the wise.

2,1 Valentinus is the successor of the ones I have placed before him—Basilides and Satornilus, and Ebion, Cerinthus, Merinthus and the others. For all these sprang up evilly in the world at the same time; or rather, Cerinthus, Merinthus and Ebion did a little earlier. For (the Valentinians) grew up along with the ones I have already presented before them.

2,2 Most people do not know Valentinus' homeland or birthplace; to give his birthplace has not been an easy business for any writer. But I have heard a report as though by word of mouth; therefore I shall not overlook it, and though I cannot give his birthplace—to be honest, it is a disputed point—I shall not be be silent about the rumor that has reached me. (3) Some have said he was born a Phrebonite, a native of Paralia in Egypt, and received the Greek education in Alexandria.

2,4 And so, in imitation of Hesiod's Theogony <and> the thirty so-called gods that are mentioned by Hesiod himself, Valentinus, who had memorized the heathen mythological poetry and adopted the notion from those who had lost the truth in his time and before it, wanted to deceive the world with material just like Hesiod's by changing the names into different ones. (5) For he too wants to introduce thirty gods, aeons, and heavens. The first of these is "Depth"—as he himself foolishly said the sort of thing which of course Hesiod, the originator of his idea, had said: "Chaos is the eldest of the gods."[3] But who can fail to see that "chaos" and "depth" mean the same thing?

2,6 But look at the tramp's overblown mythology and his poor teaching! As I said, this man wants to set 30 aeons, whom he also calls gods, side by side, and says that there are 15 males and as many females. (7) He and his school say that each aeon is male and female, and a pair; they say that there

[3] Hesiod Theogony 116. For the comparison of Valentinus' teaching with Hesiod see Iren. 2.14.1f (though Irenaeus says Antiphanes instead of Hesiod). Hipp. Refut. compares it instead with Pythagoras.

are 15 pairs, which they call "syzygies." Altogether there are 30 aeons, and each female brings forth the next aeons with the male as their sire. They are as below, with each male's name placed opposite the female's, side by side: (8) Ampsiou Auraan, Boukoua Thardouou, Ouboukoua Thardeddein, Merexa Atar, Barba Oudouak, Esten Ouananin, Lamertarde Athames, Soumin Allora, Koubiatha Danadaria, Dammo Oren, Lanaphek Oudinphek, Emphiboche Barra, Assiou Ache, Belim Dexiarche, Masemon.

2,9 That is how they are arranged in pairs of male and female. But in consecutive order they go, Ampsiou, Auraan, Boukoua, Thardouou, Ouboukoua, Thardeddein, Merexa, Atar, Barba, Oudouak, Esten, Ouananin, Lamertarde, Athames, Soumin, Allora, Koubiatha, Danadaria, Dammo, Oren, Lanaphek, Oudinphek, Emphiboche, Barra, Assiou, Ache, Belim, Dexiarche, Masemon.[4]

2,10 The translations of these names are,[5] Depth <and> Silence. Mind and Truth. Word and Life. Man and Church. Advocate and Faith. Paternal and Hope. Maternal and Love. Ever-Mindful and Understanding. Desired—also called Light—and Blessedness. Ecclesiasticus and Wisdom. Profound and Mingling. Ageless and Union. Self-Engendered and Blending. Only-Begotten and Unity. Immoveable and Pleasure. (11) Counted in consecutive order from the highest, unnameable being whom they call Father and Depth, to our heaven, the tally of the thirty aeons is, Depth, Silence, Mind, Truth, Word, Life, Man, Church, Advocate, Faith, Paternal, Hope, Maternal, Love, Ever-Mindful, Understanding, Desired—also called Light—Blessedness, Ecclesiasticus, Wisdom, Profound, Mingling, Ageless, Union, Self-Engendered, Blending, Only-Begotten, Unity, Immoveable, Pleasure.

3,1 And this is their mythological romance of the thirty aeons, and their nonsense of a supposed "spiritual Pleroma" in pairs![6] (2) If, by way of comparison, one were to set it beside the one in Hesiod, Stesichorus, and the other Greek poets, he would find that, put parallel, they are precisely the same, and would learn from this that the leaders of these systems are professing to speak in mysteries about nothing that is remarkable. (3) They have done nothing else than to copy the pretended poetic art of the

[4] There are only 29 "names"; either a word has fallen out, or Epiphanius has miscounted. The text of Epiphanius actually gives 33 words, of which Holl eliminated four as duplications. The sense is irrecoverable; Holl suggests sthat the whole may have been a Hebrew or Aramaic prayer or the like, which has been corrupted into unintelligibility.

[5] This list is identical with the one found at Hipp. Refut. 6.29-30.

[6] Iren. 11.13. See n. 9.

Greeks' imposture and heathen mythology, changing nothing except for their altered foreign coinage. (4) For the school of Hesiod too says as follows: First of all comes "Chaos"—(by which they mean "Depth)." Then Night, Erebus, Earth, Aether, Day, Passion, Skill, Destiny, Woe, Lot, Retribution, Reproach, Friendship, Death, Lawlessness, Age, Bane, Desire, Oblivion, Sleep, Combat, Allayer of Care, Arrogance, Kindly, Radiance, Ender of Care, Deceit, Sweet-Singing, Strife.[7]

3,5 And put like this, this consecutive tally of males and females totals thirty. However, if one should wish to see how they artificially unite one to one, he would find the ones that the poets thought appropriate united and coupled as follows. (6) For example, by uniting Depth with Night and Silence, they provided for the birth of Earth. But others say that Heaven, the one they have also called Hyperion—that he was united with Earth and has sired males and females, and the rest, similarly, in succession throughout their whole poem, as the endless, silly nonsense of the myth has it.

3,7 He would find that they are united and coupled like this, and can be put in the following order: Chaos, Night. Erebus, Earth. Aether, Day. Passion, Skill. Destiny, Woe. Lot, Retribution. Reproach, Friendship. Death, Lawlessness. Age, Bane. Desire, Oblivion. Sleep, Combat. Allayer of Care, Arrogance. Kindly, Radiance. Ender of Care, Deceit. Sweet-Singing, Strife. (8) And if one were to study their fabrication, and had a mind to find out how—because they were vainly inspired <to> inappropiate things by the secular Greek poets who left them dazed—<they altered (the poets') error> into labor in vain and trouble for nothing, he would find that they are that much further astray.

4,1 And so they thought that by supposedly searching still higher they could discover a Defect too, through their own demon-possesed thinking. This Defect they call Almighty and Demiurge,[8] and the creator of substances.[9] (2) They say that a latter Ogdoad with seven heavens, patterned

[7] Of the above, only the first eight correspond with the names given at Theogony 116-125.

[8] For "Demiurge" in NHC see Tri. Trac. 104,32-106,5; Ascl. 73,24-26; 75,13-15; Silv. 100,3-14; Val. Exp. 37,32; 38,25; 39,16.

[9] To equate the Demiurge with "Defect" Epiph may here have combined Iren. 1.5.2 with 1.16.3: factorem caeli et terrae...ex altera labe facta emissum...Cf. Tert. Adv. Val. 18.1. ὑστέρημα, "defect," may also be translated "deficiency." However, Defect is not a person in any known Gnostic document. The noun occurs in 16 NHC tractates and in the Cod. Tch. Let. Pet. and Gos. Jud., usually meaning the lack of something, or incompleteness or faultiness. The filling of it is a key idea in Gos. Tr., see 16,31-17,4; 18,31-19,10; 24,55-26,39; cf. Apocry. Jas. 3,34-4,22. A few times the term stands for the entire realm outside the pleroma, e.g. at NHC VIII,2 Let. Pet. 135,15-20: And when she spoke the Arrogant One

after the first Ogdoad, has been created by him in its turn, and he is in the Ogdoad himself, and has made seven heavens after him[10] (3) To this Defect they propose to join an unattached aeon with no female which has come here from the Pleroma in search of the soul which has come from above, from its mother Sophia whose name they like to imagine and represent as Achamoth. Him they <want> to call Savior, Limit, Cross, Limit-Setter, Conductor, and the Jesus[11] who passed through Mary like water through a conduit.[12] (4) He is a light from the Christ on high, and is therefore named Light for his father, after the Light on high; Christ, after the Christ on high; Word, after the Word on high—and is likewise termed Mind <and> Savior. (5) He is constantly ascending above his father the Demiurge, and bringing any who trust in him with him, to the supernal syzygies of the Pleroma[13]

4,6 What foolishness of theirs, and silly talk to match! But as I said, I am also going to show how they combined their drivel with the poetic fabrications of heathen mythology. (7) For after the thirty, <Hesiod and the others also introduce> the one name which stands in the middle and has no female with it; and after it again, the Ogdoad in pairs which is derived from the Demiurge. It too can be set side by side as follows, and these are the names: The first, Exepaphus.[14] Porphyrion, Clotho, Rhyacus, Lachesis, Epiphaon, Atropus, Hyperion, Asterope.

4,8 And this is the stage-piece of these poets. It also contains many other names of what they call gods, male and female, variously named by various of them. They can even make a total of 365,[15] and they are still dreamed of as an occasion for the other sects, which have mounted this tragic piece in their turn. (9) For after the names we have mentioned, Hesiod, Orpheus, Stesichorus and the others say that Uranus and Tartarus have

---

laid hold of (a piece of Sophia), and it became a deficiency (= Cod.Tch. 1 3,24-27). For this meaning cf. Tri. Trac. 81,8-10; 84,5; Or. Wld. 103,25-27; 124,5-7. At the non-Gnostic Silv. 101,31-34 it means the created world.

[10] Cf. Iren. 1.5.2: Et propter hoc Ebdomadum vocant eum, Matrem aut Achamoth Ogodada, servantem numerum primogenitae Pleromatis Ogdoadis. Hebdomad and Ogdoad are also proper names at Hipp. 6.31-37.

[11] Epiph here erroneously makes Jesus a name for Limit, and combines Limit's restoration of Sophia with Savior's restoration of Achamoth at Iren. 1.4.5. With the whole, cf. Hipp. 6.31.5-6; Tert. Adv. Val. 10.3; Exc. Theod. 35.1; 42.1-3; Tri. Trac. 75,10-17; 76, 31-34; 82,10-11. For an almost lyrical presentation of Limit see Val. Exp. 25,22-37. Also note Mand PB 256 (Drowyer p. 213). Limit does not descend to earth in any known Gnostic work.

[12] Iren. 1.7.2; PsT 4.5; Test Tr. 45,14-16

[13] Cf. Gr. Seth 57,7-11.

[14] I.e., Exepaphus is the aeon without a female. Eight names follow, "the ogdoad."

[15] See n. 6 p. 78.

come into being and Cronus and Rhea; Zeus, Hera and Apollo; Poseidon and Pluto, and then any number of what they call <gods>. For a great deal of deceitful error arose from their speculation, and it conceived nonsense and invented many myths to write poems about. (10) And this is the error which appears to be deceiving the minds of these deluded (Valentinians). But everyone with godly enlightenment of mind will find these things ridiculous at first sight.

4,11 But passing over these things, once again <following> the passages from their own books word for word and expression for expression, I am going to give the text of the literature they read, I mean their book. It is as follows:

5,1 "Greeting from <unsearchable>, indestructible Mind to the indestructible among the discerning, the soulish, the fleshly, the worldly, and in the presence of the Majesty![16]

5,2 "I make mention before you of mysteries unnameable, ineffable, and supercelestial, not to be comprehended by principalities, authorities, subordinates or all commingled, but manifest to the Ennoia of the Changeless alone.

5,3 "When, <in> the beginning, the Self-Progenitor[17] himself encompassed all things within himself, though they were within him in ignorance[18]—he whom some call ageless Aeon, ever renewed, both male and female,[19] who encompasses all and is yet unencompassed[20]—(4) then the Ennoia within him (softened the Majesty). Her some have called Ennoia, others, Grace,[21] but properly—since she has furnished treasures of the Majesty to those who are of the Majesty—those who have spoken the truth have termed her Silence,[22] since the Majesty has accomplished all things by reflection without speech.[23] (5) Wishing to break eternal bonds,[24] the

---

[16] μέγεθος or its Coptic equivalent occurs in NHC as a name for the Supreme Being at Apocry. Jas. 15,25-26; Gr. Seth 57,8; Para. Shem 1,6 and *passim*.

[17] See n. 50 p. 100.

[18] Cf. Gos. Tr. 22,27-33; Tri. Trac. 60, 1-34; 72,19-24.

[19] Depth is both male and female at Iren. 1.11.5. Perhaps comparable is Ascl. 20-21 (Festugière pp. 320-323).

[20] Eug. 73,6-9; SJC 96,1-3

[21] Iren. 1.1.1; 1.13.2. For an hypostatized Grace in NHC see Apocry. Jas. 1,5; Apocry. Jn. 4,8; 8,2-8; Gos. Egyp. III,2 52,3-16 and possibly Treat. Res. 45,13.

[22] For Silence in NHC see Apocry. Jn. 40,10-13; Gos. Egyp. III,2 40,18; 41,10 and *passim*; Eug. 88,5-11; SJC 112,7-10; Tri. Prot. 46,13.

[23] Almost the same statement is made at Eug. 88,7-11; SJC 112,9-10; Exc. Theod. 7.1-3. Cf. Such Manichaean passages as Man. Keph. 116,13.

[24] Tri. Trac. 57,26-27: "Yet (the Son) wanted (his fruit) to be known."

imperishable <Ennoia>, as I said, softened[25] the Majesty to a desire for his repose. And by coupling with him she showed forth the Father of Truth whom the perfect have properly termed Man, since he was the antitype of the Ingenerate who was before him.

5,6 "Thereafter Silence, having brought about a natural union of Light with Man[26]—though their coming together was the will for it—showed forth Truth. She was properly named Truth by the perfect, for she was truly like her own mother, Silence—this being the desire of Silence, that the apportionment of the lights of male and female be equal so that the <oneness> which is in them might also be made manifest, through themselves, to the ones which were separated[27] from them as perceptible lights.

5,7 "Thereafter Truth, having manifested a wantonness[28] like her mother's, softened her own Father toward her. They were united in immortal intercourse and ageless union, and showed forth a spiritual tetrad, male and female, a copy of the tetrad already existent, (which was Depth, Silence, Father and Truth).[29] Now this is the tetrad which stems from the Father and Truth: Man, Church, Word, and Life.[30]

5,8 "Then, by the will of the all-encompassing Depth, Man and Church, remembering their father's words, came together and showed forth a dodecad[31] of male and female wantons.[32] The males are Advocate, Paternal, Maternal, Ever-Mindful, Desired—that is, Light—Ecclesiasticus; the females, Faith, Hope, Love, Understanding, Blessed One, Wisdom.

5,9 "Next Word and Life, themselves transforming the gift of union, had congress with each other—though their congress was the will for it—and by coming together showed forth a decad of wantons,[33] they too male and female. The males are Profound, Ageless, Self-Engendered, Only-Begotten, Immoveable. These obtained their names <to> the glory of the All-Encompassing. The females are Copulation, Uniting, Intercourse, Union, and Pleasure. They obtained their names to the glory of Silence.

---

[25] For ἐθήλυνε

[26] Cf. the expression "man of light" which is common in Gnostic and comparable literature; for example at GT 24 and *passim* in PS.

[27] Cf. Exc. Theod. 36.2.

[28] προυνικίαν.

[29] Cf. Iren. 1.1.1; Hipp. Refut. 6.29.5-7.

[30] Cf. Iren. 1.1.1; Hipp. Refut. 6.29.5-7.

[31] The dodecad is mentioned without naming its members.

[32] προυνίκων. Amidon renders: procreative powers.

[33] Cf. Iren. 1.1.2 and Hipp. Refut. 6.30.1-5. At Val. Exp. 30,16-20 the decad and dodecad are προυνίκων.

6,1 "On the completion[34] of the triacad headed by the Father of Truth, which the earthly count without comprehension and go back and count again whenever they encounter it, having yet to find the sum[35]—but it is Depth, Silence, Father, Truth, Man, Church, Word, Life, Advocate, Paternal, Maternal, Ever-Mindful, Desired, Ecclesiasticus, Faith, Hope, Love, Understanding, Blessed One, Wisdom, Profound, Ageless, Self-Engendered, Only-Begotten, Immoveable, Copulation, Uniting, Intercourse, Union, and Pleasure—(2) then he who encompasses all things by unsurpassible understanding, decreeing that another Ogdoad be named in correspondence with the principal Ogdoad which already existed, which was to remain in the Thirty—for it was not the Majesty's intent to be counted—matched with the males (of the first Ogdoad) the males Sole, Third, Fifth and Seventh—and the females Dyad, Tetrad, Hexad and Ogdoad. (3) This Ogdoad, named in correspondence with the prior Ogdoad—Depth, Father, Man, Word, and Silence, Truth, Church and Life—was united with the lights and became a completed Triacad.

6,4[36] "And the prior Ogdoad <was> at rest. But Depth went forth with the support of the Majesty to be united with the multitude of the Triacad. For he consorted with Truth, and the Father of Truth came together with Church, and Maternal had Life to wife, and Advocate had Henad, and Henad was joined with the Father of Truth, and the Father of Truth was with Silence. But the spiritual Word consorted with... by spiritual intercourse and immortal commingling, for the Self-Progenitor was at last rendering his rest indivisible.

6,5 "Thus the Triacad, having completed profound mysteries, having consummated marriage among immortals, showed forth imperishable lights[37] These were termed children of the Intermediate Region[38] and—since they lacked intelligence—were without distinguishing features, reposing uncon-

---

[34] For the completion of the thirty see also Val. Exp. 30,16-20.

[35] Or, with Amidon: and when they reach it, finding no further number go back and count up to it again. For the thought cf. 1 Apoc. Jas 27,1-5: "If you want to give (the 72 heavens) a number now, you will not be able to do so until you cast away from yourself blind thought, this bond of flesh which encircles you." Cf. Cod. Tch. James 13,5-23.

[36] With 6,4 cf. Tri. Trac. 68,26-28: "(the Totalities) were drawn into a mingling and a combination and a unity with one another."

[37] Four great lights are elaborately named at Apocry. Jn. II,1 7,30-8,21; there, they are conscious.

[38] For the common μεσότης see, e.g., Para. Shem 6,13; 13,16-17; PS 2.84 (McDermot p. 188); 2.86 (p. 197). At Gos. Phil. 66,8-16;76,33-36 the "middle" is an undesirable state between "this world" and "the resurrection."

scious without an Ennoia. One who treats of this, unless he understands it in its entirety, is not treating of it.[39]

6,6 "Then, after the emergence of the lights whose vast number one need not count individually but must understand—(for each has been allotted its own name for the knowledge of ineffable mysteries)—(7) Silence, desirous of bringing all things in safety to the election of knowledge, consorted by immortal intercourse but intellectual desire with the second Ogdoad which answers to the first. Now her intellectual desire was the Holy Spirit which is in the midst of the holy churches. By sending this, then, to the second Ogdoad, she persuaded it too to be united with her. (8) Marriage was thus consummated in the regions of the Ogdoad, with Holy Spirit united with Sole, Dyad with Third, Third with Hexad, Ogdoad with Seventh, Seventh with Dyad, and Hexad with Fifth. (9) The whole Ogdoad came together with ageless pleasure and immortal intercourse—for there was no separation from one another and their commingling was with blameless pleasure—and showed forth a Pentad of wantons without females. Their names are, Emancipator, Limit-Setter, Thankworthy, Free-Roaming, Conductor. These were termed sons of the Intermediate Region.

6,10 "I would have you know: Ampsiou, Auraan, Boukoua, Thardouou, Ouboukoua, Thardeddein, Merexa, Atar, Barba, Oudouak, Esten, Ouananin, Lamertarde, Athames, Soumin, Allora, Koubiatha, Danadaria, Dammo, Oren, Lanaphek, Oudinphek, Emphiboche, Barra, Assiou, Ache, Belim, Dexiarche, Masemon." This ends the extract I have made <from> their literature.

7,1 Valentinus also preached in Egypt so that, like the remains of a viper's bones, his seed is still left in Athribitis, Prosopitis, Arsinoitis, Thebais and in Lower Egypt, in Paralia and Alexandria. Moreover, he came to Rome and preached. (2) But on reaching Cyprus—<and> really suffering an actual shipwreck—he abandoned the faith and became perverted in mind. For before this, in those other places, he was thought to have a bit of piety and right faith. But on Cyprus he finally reached the ultimate degree of impiety, and sank himself in this wickedness which is proclaimed by him.

7,3 As I said, both he and his school call our Lord Jesus Christ Savior, Christ, Word, Cross, Conductor, Limit-Setter and Limit. (4) But they say he has brought his body down from above and passed through the Virgin Mary like water through a pipe. He has taken nothing from the virgin

[39] Amidon: For whatever one does, unless one understands it completely, one does not do it.

womb, but has his body from above, as I said.[40] (5) They claim that he is not the original Word; nor the Christ after the Word, who is above among the aeons on high, but that this Christ has been emitted for no other reason than just[41] to come and rescue the spiritual race that is from above.

7,6 They deny the resurrection of the dead, and make some mythological, silly claim that it is not this body which rises, but another which comes out of it, the one they call "spiritual."[42] <There is salvation> only of those "spiritual" persons who are their community and of the others, <the> so-called "soulish," provided that the soulish practice righteousness. But the ones they call "material," "fleshly," and "earthly" perish altogether and cannot be saved at all.[43] (7) Each essence returns to its own origins[44]—the material is abandoned to matter, and the fleshly and earthly to the earth.

7,8 For they believe in three classes[45] of persons: spiritual, soulish and material. They say that they are the spiritual class—as well as "Gnostics"—and have no need of work, but only of knowledge and the incantations of their mysteries. Each of them may do anything with impunity and think nothing of it; they say they will be saved in any case, since their class is spiritual. (9) But the other class of humanity, which they call soulish, cannot be saved of itself unless it saves itself by work and the practice of righteousness. But they say that the material class of humanity can neither contain knowledge, nor receive it even if a person of this class might want to, but must perish body and soul.

7,10 Since their own class is spiritual it is saved with another body, something deep inside them, which they imagine and call a "spiritual body." (11) But the soulish, after working hard and rising above the Demiurge, will be given, on high, to the angels[46] who are with Christ. They recover no part of their bodies; just their souls are given as brides to the angels with Christ, when they are found to possess full knowledge and to have risen above the Demiurge.

8,1 Such is the dramatic piece they offer, and it contains even more than this. I have merely enumerated the things I thought naturally needed to be brought to light as far as I have learned about them—(2) where he came from, when he lived, from whom he took his cue, what his teaching

[40] Cf. Pst 4.5; Fil. 38.6.
[41] Cf. Hipp. Refut. 6.36.3-4.
[42] Iren. 3.4.3; Tert. Praescr. 30; Adv. Val. 4
[43] Cf. Iren. 1.6.1; 7.5; Tri. Trac. 106,6-18.
[44] Cf. Gos. Phil. 53,20-21.
[45] A Manichaean variation on this theme is found at Man. Keph. 269, 17-25.
[46] This is a slip on Epiph's part, since at Iren. 1.7.5 this is said of the spiritual.

is, together with which contemporaries his evil sprouted up in the world. And as I said, I give his teaching in part. Having related these few things thus far, for the rest I shall take the quotation in full from the man I have spoken of, a servant of God, I mean Irenaeus:

From the Writings of St. Irenaeus[47]

9,1 Certain persons have rejected the truth and are introducing novel falsehoods and "endless genealogies which," as the apostle says, "minister questions rather than godly edifying which is in faith."[48] With the specious argument they have villainously hammered together, they are misleading the minds of the simple and take them captive, (2) tampering with the oracles of the Lord and becoming bad expositors of things that have been said well. And they are overthrowing many by leading them away, under the pretense of knowledge, from him who framed and ordered this whole creation, as though they had something higher and greater to display than the God who has made heaven, earth, and everything in them. (3) Persuasively, through the art of rhetoric, they win the innocent to the habit of inquiry,. But they abruptly[49] destroy them by making their opinion of the Creator blasphemous and impious—since they have no ability to distinguish truth from falsehood in anything.

9,4 For error is not shown as it is lest it become detectible when stripped. Villainously decked in a cloak of plausibility, it presents to the simple the appearance of being truer than the truth itself—<an absurd thing even to say!>—by its outward show. (5) As has been said of such persons by a greater man than I, when a piece of glass is artificially made to resemble the stone which is the real precious pearl and of very great value, it will mock some people, if no one there is competent to test it and expose the wicked trick. And when bronze is mixed with silver, what guileless person can readily assay it?

9,6 Now I have read the treatises of the "disciples of Valentinus," as they say themselves, and have met some and understood what they think. To see that—even through no fault of mine—none are snatched away like sheep by wolves since they may not recognize under their outer covering of lambskin the persons the Lord has warned us of, who speak as <we> do but think otherwise, (7) I feel it essential, beloved, that I disclose to you

[47] 9,1-32,1 are quoted directly from Iren. Praef.-1.11.1.
[48] 1 Tim 1:4
[49] ἀπιθανῶς contrasted with πιθανῶς above.

the monstrous, abstruse mysteries which "all cannot receive,"[50] since all have not spat their brains out! Thus when you have learned them too you can make them known to all who are with you, and urge them to beware of the abyss of folly and blasphemy of God.

9,8 And as far as I can I shall also give a brief, clear explanation of the doctrine of those—I mean the Ptolemaeans—who are now repeating the same teaching, a culling from the school of Valentinus, and give <others> the resources for its refutation, by showing, as well as my modest ability allows, that what they say is absurd, untenable, and incompatible with the truth. (9) This though I am neither accustomed to composition nor trained in rhetoric—even while love bids me disclose, to you and to all who are with you, the teachings that have been concealed till now, but by God's grace have now come to light. "For there is nothing covered that shall not be revealed, and hid, that shall not be known."[51]

10,1 As I live among Celts and chiefly occupy myself with a barbarian language, you will not look for rhetoric, which I have not learned, from me—or ability at composition, in which I have no practice, or elegance of style, or persuasiveness, of which I know nothing. (2) Instead you will accept with love what I have written you with love, simply, truly, and in everyday speech, and grow it yourself—as you can, being abler than I—as though you had received seeds and shoots from me. (3) In the breadth of your intellect you will make what I have said in brief bear fruit in abundance and will present powerfully, to those who are with you, the things I have feebly told you. (4) And as I have done my best—since you have been wanting to learn of their doctrine for a long time—not only to make it known to you but also to provide the means of proving its falsity, you too, by the grace the Lord has given you, will do your best to convey it to the rest, so that people may no longer be swept away with their specious argument, which runs as follows:

10,5 They say that, in invisible, heights that cannot be named, there pre-exists a perfect Aeon. Him they call Prior Principle, First Progenitor,[52] and Depth.[53] He is uncontainable and invisible, eternal and ingenerate, and has existed in calm and deep tranquility[54] for boundless ages of time. And with him also is an Ennoia, whom they term both Grace and Silence.[55]

[50] Matt 19:11
[51] Matt 10:26
[52] Eug. 74,21-23: "the Lord of the Universe is not rightly called 'Father,' but προπάτωρ."
[53] At Hipp. Refut. 6.30.7 the Father is ῥίζα καὶ βάθος καὶ βύθος.
[54] Hipp. "Refut. 6.29.5: ἀναπαυόμενος αὐτὸς ἐν ἑαυτῷ
[55] "Silence" is found with no alternative name at Hipp. Refut. 6.29.3.

10,6[56] At some time Depth conceived of emitting a first principle of all things from himself, and like a seed[57] he deposited the emanation he had conceived of emitting <in> his co-existent Silence, as in a womb. (7) Receiving this seed and becoming pregnant, Silence brought forth Mind,[58] the like and equal of the One who had emitted him and alone capable of containing the Father's majesty. This Mind they also call Only-Begotten, and Father and first principle of all things. (8) But with him Truth has been emitted, and this is the first, original Pythagorean tetrad,[59] which they also call the root of all things. For it is Depth and Silence, and then Mind and Truth.

10,9 Realizing why he had been emitted, this Only-Begotten himself emitted Word and Life:[60] the father of all who were to come after him, and the principle and form of the entire Pleroma. But from Word and Life, Man and Church have been emitted as a pair.[61] (10) And this is the original Ogdoad, the root and ground of all things, which they call by four names, Depth, Mind, Word, and Man. (For each is male and female as follows: First Progenitor, to begin with, is united in a pair with his own Ennoia. Only-Begotten, or Mind, is united with Truth, Word with Life, and Man with Church.)

10,11 After these Aeons had been emitted to the glory of the Father, they too desired to glorify him with something of their own,[62] and put forth emanations in pairs. Word and Life emitted ten other Aeons after the emission of Man and Church, and they say their names are as follows: Profound and Copulation, Ageless and Union, Self-Engendered and Pleasure, Immoveable and Intercourse, Only-Begotten and Happiness. These are <the> ten Aeons they claim have been emitted by Word and Life.[63]

10,12 But Man too, with Church, emitted twelve Aeons.[64] They favor these with the names of Advocate and Truth, Paternal and Hope, Maternal and Love, Ever-Mindful and Understanding, Ecclesiasticus and Blessedness, Desired and Wisdom.

---

[56] With 10,6-11 cf. Tert. Praescrip. 33. With 10,6-12 cf. PsT 4.1 and Fil. 38.3-4.

[57] There are 13 occurrences of "seed" in Tri. Trac. Particularly significant examples are found at 60,29-37; 61,1-8.

[58] "Mind" appears in this role at Val. Exp. 22,31-36; 23,31-37; 24, 19-22.

[59] This Tetrad also appears at Val. Exp. 29,26-37.

[60] For Life in a comparable role see Val. Exp. 24,21-22; for Word and Life, Val. Exp. 29,26-37.

[61] Cf. Val. Exp. 29,28; 31,36-37.

[62] With this idea cf. Tri. Trac. 68,3-5.

[63] Cf. Val. Exp. 30,16-17.

[64] Cf. Val. Exp. 30,18-19.

10,13 These are the 30 Aeons of their imposture, which have been kept secret and are not known. This is their invisible, spiritual Pleroma, with its triple division into ogdoad, decad and dodecad. (14) And for this reason they say that the Savior—they prefer not to call him "Lord"—did nothing openly for 30 years, giving indication of the mystery of these Aeons. (15) Moreover, they say, these 30 Aeons are made very plainly known in the parable of the laborers sent into the vineyard,[65] For some are sent about the first hour, some about the third, some about the sixth, some about the ninth, and others about the eleventh. If you add these hours they give a total of 30—one, three, six, nine and eleven are 30—and they hold that the Aeons are made known by the hours. (16) And these are the great, marvelous, ineffable mysteries which they produce—and, of the things the scriptures say in great quantity, these are all that could be matched and compared with their fabrication.

11,1 They say their First Progenitor is known only to Only-Begotten, that is to Mind, who originated from him.[66] To all the rest he is invisible and incomprehensible.[67] Only Mind, they believe, enjoyed the contemplation of the Father and rejoiced in the perception of his immeasurable greatness. (2) And he intended to communicate the greatness of the Father to the remaining Aeons,[68] what he was like and how great he was, and how he was without beginning, uncontainable and impossible to see. But by the Father's will Silence restrained him, because she meant to arouse them all to an intent and yearning to seek after their First Progenitor.[69]

11,3 Similarly the other Aeons also had a sort of silent yearning to see the originator of their seed, and be informed of their root which had no beginning.[70] (4) But the Aeon which was by far the last and the youngest of the twelve emitted by Man and Church—that is, Sophia[71]—sprang forth,

---

[65] Matt 20:1-16. At Apocry. Jas. 8,8-9 it is implied that only the author's community knows the true sense of this parable.

[66] Cf. Apocry. Jn. II,1 4,19-26.

[67] Cf. Tri. Trac. 60,16-29.

[68] A comparable role is played by the Father himself at Tri. Trac. 61,1-9.

[69] The Father himself does this at Tri. Trac. 65,11-17; 71,35-72,10.

[70] The aeons' search for their origin is also mentioned, e.g., at Gos. Tr. 17,4-13; Tri. Trac. 61,24-28; 71,7-11. At U 2.12 (MacDermot p. 229) the "outside worlds" desire to "see" the Father.

[71] Sophia is found as a name nearly 100 times in NHC. Versions of the story of her fall appear at On Res. 46,35-37; Apocry. Jn. III,1 14,9-15,22; Nat. Arc. 94,1-18; Cod. Tch. James 21,12-15; PS 1.31 (McDermot pp. 45-46) and at Zost. 9,16-10,17 though this latter passage is mutilated. Gr. Seth 50,25-51,20 is related, and cf. *Ginza 78,25-28.* Often Sophia is absolved of blame. At 1 Apoc. Jas. not she but Achamoth is at fault. At Gos. Egyp. III,2 56,22-57,13 Sophia appears when Eleleth speaks and Sakla and Nebruel are brought out

and without a union with her consort,[72] Desired, experienced a passion which had begun in Mind and Truth and fallen suddenly upon this errant Aeon—pretendedly a passion of love, but (actually) one of presumption, since she did not have perfect fellowship with the Father as Mind did.

11,5 Then, since she could not (find the Father) because she had set herself an impossible task, and since she had fallen into deep distress[73] at the vastness of the depth, the Father's unsearchability, and her love for him, she stretched farther and farther forward. And she would finally have been engulfed and utterly dissolved by his sweetness[74] if she had not encountered the power which makes all things firm, and keeps watch over them outside of the ineffable majesty. (6) This power they call Limit.[75] Restrained and made fast by Limit,[76] coming to herself with difficulty, and convinced of the Father's incomprehensibility, she abandoned her former Resolve, with the passion inspired by that terror-stricken wonder.

12,1 But some of them speak of Sophia's passion and conversion in terms of the following myth. In her attempt at something impossible and unattainable she gave birth to an essence without form,[77] such a nature as a female could bear.[78] (2) On observing it she was first grieved at the unfinished character of its birth,[79] then afraid that its very existence might come to an end as well—then distraught and at her wits' end, from searching for the cause of what had happened, and how to hide it. (3) But after her submergence in the passions[80] she experienced conversion and tried to return to the Father; and after some time in this venture was exhausted, and became the Father's suppliant.[81] (4) The other Aeons, and especially Mind,

of her. At Or. Wld. 98,11-99,2 the difficulty is caused by her shadow; at Gos. Tr. 16,5-20 by "the Totalities"' ignorance. At Tri. Trac. 74,17-80,11 the protagonist is the Logos, not Sophia, and he is held to be blameless.

72 At Hipp. Refut. 6.30.6-9 Sophia's fault is, not that she desires to attain the Father, but that she desires to emulate him by reproducing without a consort.

73 Cf. Gos. Tr. 17,10-11; Tri. Trac. 77,11-36.

74 For the Father's "sweetness" cf. Tri. Trac. 77,11-27.

75 See Hipp. Refut. 6.32.5-6; Tri. Trac. 75,10-17; 76,31-34; 82,10-11. For an almost lyrical presentation of Limit see Val. Exp. 25,22-37.

76 Cf. PsT 4.2.

77 Material related to this is found at Hipp. Refut. 6.30.9; Gos. Tr. 17,10-36; Tri. Trac. 78,8-17; 95,2-6; Apocry. Jn. 9,25-10,19; Orig. Wld. 99,3-100,28; Zost. 9,16-17; *Ginza* 78,25-28.

78 The female parent contributes only its matter to the offspring, while the male contributes its form; cf. Hipp. Refut. 6.30.8.

79 In Mandaean literature Rucha d'Qudsha, the Mandaean equivalent of Sophia, often laments the imperfection of her offspring, e.g. at *Ginza* 100,31,1-101,5.

80 Cf. Val. Exp. 33,35-37; 34,26-28.

81 Cf. Hipp. Refut. 6.31.1-2; Tri. Trac. 81,8-82,9; Apocry. Jn. 14,1-5. Her prayer of

joined in her supplication.[82] From this, they say, the essence of matter had its first origin: from the ignorance, grief, fear and distraction (of Sophia).

12,5 It was for this reason that the Father emitted Limit in his own image, unpartnered and with no female, through Only-Begotten. (They sometimes conceive of the Father as paired with Silence, but sometimes as above both male and female.)[83] (6) They call this Limit Cross, Redeemer, Emancipator, Limit-Setter, and Conductor.[84] They say that Sophia was purified and made firm by Limit, and restored to her syzygy.[85] (7) For now that her Resolve, with the passion[86] which had arisen later, was separated from her, she remained within the Pleroma. But her Resolve, with the passion, was separated and fenced off by Limit,[87] and once outside him was a spiritual essence <like> a sort of natural germ of an Aeon, but shapeless and without form because it understood nothing. And for this reason they call it a sterile fruit and a female.

13,1 But after its banishment outside the Pleroma of the Aeons, and the restoration to her syzygy of its mother, in order that no Aeon would suffer as she had, by the Father's forethought Only-Begotten emitted yet another pair to fix the Pleroma and make it firm, Christ and Holy Spirit, by whom, <they say>, the Aeons were settled.[88] (2) For Christ taught them the nature of union, (that is), that <only those> who comprehend the ingenerate <are fit for union> with him;[89] and to proclaim among themselves their realization that the Father is uncontainable and incomprehensible and cannot be seen or heard, or that he is known only through Only-Begotten—(3) also that the incomprehensibility of the Father is the cause of the others' eternal endurance, while the cause of their birth and formation is his comprehensibility, that is, his Son. And the newly emitted Christ performed this work among them.

---

repentance is given at Val. Exp. 34,25-31. Gos. Egyp.III,2 hypostatizes a Metanoia which "fills up" the deficiency (59,10-18), resulting in the repentance of "the seed of the archon of this aeon" and others (54,21-60,2).

[82] Cf.Tri. Trac. 86,4-15.

[83] Cf. Hipp. Refut. 6.29.3-4. For Limit in NHC see Tri. Trac. 76,31-34; 82,10-13; Val. Exp. 25,22-24; 26,31-34; 27,30-38.

[84] Cf. Hipp. Refut. 6.30.5-6 and the list of names for the "cross of light" at Acts of John 98 (H-S II p. 185).

[85] Cf PS 2.74 (MacDermot p. 166); Man. Keph. 72,3-6; *Ginza* 311,37-312,9; *Johannesbuch* 36,10-37,4 et al.

[86] For "passion" cf. Tri. Trac. 95,2-6.

[87] The cross plays a comparable role at Test. Tr. 40,25-29.

[88] Hipp. Refut. 6.31.2-3; Gos. Tr. 24,9-20; Tri. Trac. 73,1-8.

[89] Something like this is done by Spirit at Tri. Trac. 71,35-72,19; 73,1-8.

13,4 But after they had all been made equal, Holy Spirit taught them to give thanks and explained the true repose.[90] And thus, they say, the Aeons were made alike in form and sentiment, and all became Minds, all Words, all Men, and all Christs; and similarly the females all became Truths, all Lives, all Spirits and all Churches. (5) But when all things had been fixed in this state, they say, and were perfectly in repose, they hymned the First Progenitor with great joy because they partook of great happiness.

13,6 And in return for this benefit, with one will and purpose each of the whole Pleroma of Aeons, with the consent of Christ and Holy Spirit and with their Father's endorsement, pooled and contributed what was best and brightest in it. Fitly combining these things and becomingly uniting them, (7) they produced an emanation to the honor and glory of Depth,[91] a kind of consummate beauty and star of the Pleroma, its perfect Fruit, Jesus.[92] He is also called Savior; Christ; Word after his father; and All,[93] because he is of all. And angels[94] of the same nature were emitted with him in <his> honor, to be his bodyguard.

14,1 This, then, is the affair they say took place within the Pleroma; and the misfortune of the Aeon who suffered and almost perished when she <experienced> deep <grief> because of her search for the Father; and her solidification after her ordeal by Limit-Cross-Redeemer-Emancipator-Limit-Setter- Conductor; and the production, because of her repentance, of the first Christ and Holy Spirit, later than the Aeons, by their Father; and the joint production, by public subscription, of the second Christ, whom they also term Savior. (2) These things have not been said openly since not everyone can accommodate the knowledge of them, but they have been made known mystically by the Savior in parables to those who can understand them, as follows: (3) The thirty Aeons are made known, as we said, by the thirty years in which they claim the Savior did nothing openly; and by the parable of the laborers in the vineyard. (4) And they say that Paul often names these Aeons very plainly, and further that he has even observed their order by saying, "unto all the generations of the aeons of the aeon."[95]

[90] Cf. The "rest" of the aeons at Tri. Trac. 70,18. More usually in this tractate, "rest" refers to the salvation of an individual. On the subject see Helderman, *Anapausis*.

[91] Cf. Tri. Trac. 86,4-87,17; Corp. Herm. 13.2: ἄλλος ἔσται ὁ γεννώμενος θεοῦ θεὸς παῖς, τὸ πᾶν ἐν πᾶσιν ἐκ πάσων δυνάμεων συνεστώς.

[92] Hipp. Refut. 6.31.1-2.

[93] Cf. Silv. 101,22-26; 102,5; GT 77; Acts of Peter 39 (H-S II p. 316); Corp. Herm. 13. 2.

[94] A more sophisticated version of this is found at Tri. Trac. 87,17-31. Cf. also Apocry. Jn. II,1 8,20-25.

[95] Eph 3:21

(5) Moreover, we too are giving indication of those Aeons when we say, "unto the aeons of the aeons,"[96] at the eucharist. And wherever "aeon" or "aeons" are mentioned, they hold that the reference is to those.

14,6 The emission of the dodecad of Aeons is made known through the Lord's disputation with the doctors of the Law at the age of twelve, and by his choice of the apostles, for there are twelve apostles. (7) And the remaining eighteen Aeons are shown by the fact that, as they say, the Lord spent eighteen months with the disciples after his rising <from> the dead. Moreover, the eighteen Aeons are plainly made known by the first two letters of his name, "iota" and "eta." (8) And they say that the ten Aeons are similarly indicated by the "iota" which begins his name. And this is why the Savior has said, "One iota or one tittle shall not pass away till all things come to pass."[97]

14,9 The passion encountered by the twelfth Aeon is suggested, they say, by the defection of Judas who was the twelfth of the apostles, and because (the Savior) suffered in the twelfth month—they hold that he preached for one year after his baptism. (10) Further, this is shown very clearly in the incident of the woman with the issue of blood. For after suffering for twelve years she was healed by the Savior's arrival, through touching the hem of his garment. And the Savior said, "Who touched me?"[98] for this reason, to teach his disciples of the mystery that had been consummated among the Aeons, and the healing of the Aeon that suffered. (11) For the woman who suffered for twelve years is that power, <which> would have been <completely> dissolved, as they say, by her stretching and the endless running of her essence, if she had not touched the Son's garment—that is, the Truth of the first Tetrad, who is indicated by the hem of the garment. But she stopped this and was rid of the passion. For the power of the Son which issued forth—they hold that this is Limit—healed her, and separated the passion from her.

14,12 And that Savior, the product of all, is the All, is shown, they say, by the words, "All the males[99] that open the womb."[100] For since he is the All, he opened the womb of the suffering Aeon's Resolve, <who> was banished outside the Pleroma, the one they also call a second Ogdoad of whom I shall speak a little later. (13) And they say that, "And he is all,"[101]

---

[96] For the phrase see Tri. Trac. 67,38-68,2.
[97] Matt 5:19
[98] Mark 5:30
[99] That is, πᾶν ἄρρεν
[100] Luke 2:23
[101] Luke 2:23

was obviously said on this account by Paul, and again, "All are for him, and of him are all,"[102] and, "In him dwelleth all the Pleroma of the Godhead."[103] And they interpret, "to gather all in one in Christ, through God,"[104] <in this sense>, and anything else of the kind.

15,1 Then they declare of their Limit, the one they call by a number of names, that he has two activities, the stabilizing and the divisive.[105] Insofar as he stabilizes and makes firm, he is Cross; but insofar as he divides and separates, he is Limit. (2) They say the Savior has made his activities known in the following ways. First the stabilizing, with the words, "He who doth not bear his cross and follow me, cannot be my disciple,"[106] and <again>, "Take up thy cross and follow me."[107] (3) But his divisive activity with the words, "I came not to send peace, but a sword."[108] John too, they say, has made the same thing known by saying, "The fan is in his hand. He will throughly purge his floor, and will gather the wheat into his garner; but the chaff he will burn with fire unquenchable."[109] (4) And with this he has made the Limit's activity known. For they interpret that "fan" as the cross, which consumes everything material as fire consumes chaff, and yet winnows the saved as the fan winnows wheat. (5) But they say the apostle Paul has also mentioned this cross with these words: "For the preaching of Cross is to them that perish foolishness, but unto them that are saved he is a power of God,"[110] and again, "God forbid that I should glory in anything save in the Cross of Christ, through whom the world is crucified unto me, and I unto the world."[111]

15,6 They say this sort of thing about their Pleroma and their fictitious account of all things, and forcibly harmonize things which have been said well with things which they have invented badly. And not only do they try to produce their proofs from the Gospels and apostolic writings, by twisting the meanings and tampering with the interpretations. (Even) more cleverly, and guilefully, they adapt <what they like> from the Law and prophets to their fabrication—(7) since these have numerous parables and allegories

---

[102] Cf. Rom 11:36.
[103] Col 2:9
[104] Eph 1:10
[105] See Val. Exp. 25,22-24; 26,31-34, and especially 27,30-37, where Limit is given four powers rather than two.
[106] Luke 14:27
[107] Cf. Mark 8:34 parr.
[108] Matt 10:34
[109] Matt 10:34
[110] 1 Cor 1:18
[111] Gal 6:14

which can be stretched to mean many things owing to the doubtfulness of their interpretation—and they capture from the truth those who are not keeping careful guard on their faith in one God, the Father almighty, and one Lord Jesus Christ, the Son of God.

16,1 But what they say is outside the Pleroma is something like this. When the Resolve of the heavenly Sophia, whom they also call Achamoth,[112] had been separated, with the passion,[113] from the <supernal> Pleroma, they say that of necessity she was stranded in a shadowy, empty region.[114] For she found herself outside of the light and Pleroma, without shape and form like an untimely birth, because she had understood nothing. (2) But the <higher> Christ, pitying her and reaching out to her through the Cross, gave her form by his own power—only essential form, not the form of knowledge. After doing this he withdrew by contracting his power and left <her>, so that she would realize the passion she had incurred by separation from the Pleroma and would long for the things that are best—[115] since she had a certain savor of immortality, left <her> by Christ and Holy Spirit. (3) Hence she is given both names: Sophia, after her father—for Sophia is said to be her "father"—and Holy Spirit, after the Spirit who is with Christ.

16,4 Formed and become conscious, but immediately emptied of the Word, or Christ, who had been with her invisibly, she started up in search of the light that had left her—and could not overtake it, because of her obstruction by Limit.[116] And here, to prevent her from starting forward, Limit said, "Iao!"[117] This, they claim, is the origin of the name, Iao.

16,5 Unable to pass Limit because of her entanglement with the passion, and left alone outside, she fell victim to every portion of the passion in its many and various forms. She suffered grief because she had not overtaken the light; fear that, as light had left her, so would life; and desperation besides, and she was altogether in ignorance. (6) And unlike her

[112] Achamoth transliterates the Aramaic חכימותא, "Sophia." She appears in NHC and similar literature at 1 Apoc. Jas. 34,3; 35,5-13; 36,5; Cod. Tch. James 21,4;26; 22,7. Gos. Phil. 60,10-15 distinguishes between "Echamoth" and "Echmut."

[113] With this "passion" cf. the "passions" at Tri. Trac. 95,2-6.

[114] Cf. The rehabilitation of ἡ ἔξω Σοφία at Hipp. Refut. 6.32.2-5 and Apocry. Jn. II,1 13,32-14,13. See also Val. Exp. 26,22-26.

[115] At Tri. Trac. 65,1-17 the Father "sows" in the aeons "that [they] might seek after him." Later, at 83,16-27, the Logos "sows" "a pre-disposition to seek and pray to the glorious pre-existent one" in his "defective offspring."

[116] Cf. Val. Exp. 33,25-32.

[117] Cf. PsT 4.2 Jesus cries "Iao" three times at PS 4.136 (MacDermot p. 353). Or. Wld. 101,9-15 explains the name as baby talk addressed to the child of Yaltabaoth.

mother the first Sophia Aeon, she had, not an alternation of the passions but a conflict between them. But another disposition had come upon her as well—that of conversion[118] to the one who had brought her to life.

16,7 They say that she has become the origin and essence of the matter of which this world is composed. The entire soul of the world and the Demiurge has originated from the conversion, while the rest has arisen from the fear and the grief. Everything wet has come from her tears, everything bright from her laughter; and the world's physical components from her grief and terror.[119] (8) For at times, as they say, she would weep and grieve at being left alone in the dark and void, but sometimes she would recall the light that had forsaken her,[120] and she would interrupt her weeping, and laugh.[121] Again, she was sometimes afraid, at other times at her wits' end and distraught.[122]

17,1 But why go on? There would be a lot of dramatics here next and display, with each of them proudly explaining in a different way from which passion the essence of which element has had its origin. (2) Indeed, it makes sense to me that they do not care to teach these things openly to everyone—just to those who can afford to pay even high prices for mysteries of such sublimity![123] (3) For these are no longer like the ones of which our Lord has said, "Freely ye have received, freely give."[124] They are recondite, monstrous, deep mysteries, obtainable with great effort by those who love lies. (4) For who would not spend all he has to learn that seas, springs, rivers, and everything wet has originated from the tears of the suffering Aeon's Resolve, but the light from her laughter, and the world's physical components from her terror and perplexity?

17,5 But I wish to make a contribution of my own to their harvest. Since I see that some water—springs, rivers, rain and the like—is fresh, while sea-water is salt, I presume that not all water has emanated from her tears, for tears are of a salty quality. (6) It is plain, then, that it is this salt water that comes from the tears. But it is likely that, since she fell into great

[118] Cf. the conversion of Sophia at Hipp. Refut. 6.32.2-5, at Val. Exp. 34,10-34, and at Tri. Trac. 81,8-82,9. See also the repentance and prayers of Pistis Sophia at PS 1.32 (MacDermot pp. 46-52) and *passim* in this document.

[119] Cf. Hipp. Refut. 6.32.6-8.

[120] Cf. Tri. Trac. 81,30-82,9.

[121] Cf. Sophia's laughter at Val. Exp. 34,34-39.

[122] Cf. Hipp. Refut. 6.31.2-6; PsT 4.3.

[123] The imparting of teachings or mysteries for payment is forbidden at Apocry. Jn. II,1 31,34-37.

[124] Matt. 10:8

anguish and perplexity, she perspired as well. Therefore, on their hypothesis it must be supposed that springs and rivers, and any other fresh water, has its origin from her <sweat>. (7) For since tears are of one quality, it is not credible that fresh water on the one hand, and salt on the other, issues from them. This is more credible, that the one is from the tears and the other from the sweat. (8) <However>, since certain kinds of water are both hot and bitter, you should understand what she did to emit those, and from which part of her. These are the sorts of conclusion that are in keeping with their premise!

17,9 When their Mother had passed through all the passions and barely surmounted them, they say that she addressed herself to supplication of the light, or Christ, who had left her. As he had gone back to the Pleroma he was probably reluctant to come down a second time himself. But he sent Advocate <to> her—that is, Savior—(10) after the Father had put all power in him and put all under his authority, and the Aeons had done the same, so that "all things might be created in him, visible and invisible, thrones, godheads, dominions."[125]

17,11 So he was sent to her, with his angelic companions.[126] They say that at first, out of respect for him, Achamoth veiled herself in modesty. But then, seeing him with all his bounty, she ran to him, having drawn strength from his appearing. (12) He for his part gave her the form of knowledge[127] and effected the cure of her passions by separating them from her. He did not ignore them—they could not be destroyed like the former Sophia's passions, because they were already habitual and strong.[128] But by the separation of them he set them apart, mixed and solidified them, and from incorporeal passions changed them into incorporeal matter. (13) Then he endowed them with fitness and a nature so that they became compounds and bodies, for the generation of two essences, the inferior one <made from> the passions, and the affective one made from the conversion. For this reason too they say that Savior has done the work of creation with power.[129]

17,14 When Achamoth had got free of the passion and joyfully caught sight of the lights which were with him[130]—that is, of the angels who

[125] Col 1:16

[126] Cf. Hipp. Refut. 6.32.4; Tri. Trac. 87,17-31.

[127] Cf. Tri. Trac. 62,1-3.

[128] From this point through 17,13 cf. Val. Exp. 35,30-37.

[129] Tri. Trac. 96,35-97,5: "thus he beautified the Kingdom…which is filled with the holy spirits and [the] mighty powers which govern them, which the Logos produced and established in power." PsT 4.4 assigns this role to Limit.

[130] Cf. Tri. Trac. 95,35-36: the coming of the Savior and of those who are with him."

were with him—they teach that she conceived fruit in <their> image by yearning for them, a spiritual embryo conceived in the likeness of Savior's bodyguards.

18,1 Since these three things, as they believe, were now in existence—the one which came from the passion, which was matter; the one which came from the conversion, which was the soulish; and the one which she had conceived, the spiritual—her next concern was their formation. (2) But she could not form the spiritual, since it was of her own nature.[131] Instead she addressed herself to the forming of the soulish essence which had arisen from her conversion, and emitted the things she had learned from Savior. (3) And first, they say, from the soulish essence she formed the Father and King of all things[132]—the things of his own nature, the soulish things they call "right"—and of the things which arose from the passion and matter, the things they call "left." (4) For they say that <he> formed everything after him, instigated by the Mother without knowing it. Thus they call him Male-and-Female Progenitor, Without Progenitor, Demiurge, and Father, and say he is father of those on the right, the soulish; demiurge of those on the left, the material; but king of them all. (5) For they say that, because Resolve wanted to create all things in honor of the Aeons, she has made their images—or rather, Savior has made them through her. She herself has preserved <the image> of the invisible Father, since she is not known by the Demiurge. He, however, has preserved the image of the Only-begotten Son; and the archangels and angels he has made, that of the remaining Aeons.

18,6 Thus, as maker of everything soulish and material, they say he has become Father and God of the things outside the Pleroma. For by separating the two commingled essences and making corporeal things from incorporeal, he has created everything heavenly and earthly, and become Demiurge of material and soulish, right and left, heavy and light, upward-tending and downward-tending. (7) For they say that he has constructed seven heavens and is their Demiurge above them. And so they call him Hebdomad; but the Mother, Achamoth, they call Ogdoad[133] so that she preserves the number of the original, first Ogdoad of the Pleroma. (8) But they say the seven heavens are intelligible ones, and suppose that they are angels. The Demiurge himself is an angel, but like a god. And thus they

[131] ὁμοούσιον

[132] At Tri. Trac. 100, 19-30 the Logos appoints a supreme archon who is "Father," "God," "king," "demiurge" etc.

[133] See n. 00 p. 00 [Ogdoad]

also say that since Paradise is above a third heaven it has the significance of a fourth archangel, and that Adam received something from it while he lived in it.

18,9 They claim that the Demiurge thought that he makes these things <entirely> by himself,[134] but that he has made them because Achamoth has emitted them. <For> he has made heaven without knowing heaven, formed man though ignorant of man, and produced earth with no knowledge of earth. (10) And in every case they similarly say that he did not know the forms of the things he was making or the Mother herself, but supposed that he alone was all things. (11) But they claim that the Mother has been the cause of this creative activity of his because she wished to prefer him in this way, though she is the source and origin of her own being and the "lord" of the whole affair. (12) They call her Mother and Ogdoad, and Sophia, Earth, Jerusalem, Holy Spirit and, in the masculine, Lord. She inhabits the Intermediate Region[135] and is above the Demiurge, but is below, or outside, the Pleroma until the consummation.

19,1 Since they say that the material essence is composed of three passions—fear, grief and perplexity—the soulish has originated from the fear and the conversion. (2) They hold that the Demiurge has his origin from the conversion, but everything else that is soulish, such as the souls of brute beasts, wild creatures and men, has theirs from the fear. (3) <And> thus, because he is too weak to know spiritual things, the Demiurge has supposed that he alone is God and has said, through the prophets, "I am God, there is none besides me."[136]

19,4 They teach that wicked spiritual beings[137] have come from the grief. This is the origin of the Devil, whom they also call Ruler of the World,[138] and of demons, angels, and anything spiritual that is wicked. (5) But they say the Demiurge is a soulish son of their Mother, while the Ruler of the World is a creature of the Demiurge. And the Ruler of the World knows what is above him, for he is a wicked spirit; but the Demiurge, being soulish, does not.[139] (6) Their Mother dwells in the place above the

[134] At Hipp. Refut. 6.33.1 she creates through the Demiurge, who is unaware of her work; in NHC see Tri. Trac. 100,36-101,5; 105,29-35; Apocry. Jn. II,1 19,15-33. There is something comparable in Mandaean literature cf. *Ginza* 266,18-24.

[135] For the μεσότης see n. 140.

[136] Hipp. Refut. 6.33.1, and see n. 11 p. 87.

[137] Cf. Eph. 6:12.

[138] Isa 45:21; cf. Hipp. 6.33.1. For the Κοσμοκράτωρ in NHC see Gr. Seth 52,27; 53,28; 55,3; Zost. 1,18.

[139] Cf. Tri. Trac. 79,12-16.

heavens, the Intermediate Region;[140] the Demiurge in the heavenly place, the Hebdomad; <but> the Ruler of the World, in our world.

19,7 As I said, the world's physical components are derived from the consternation and bewilderment, the more distracted (passions)—earth answering to the motionlessness of consternation, water to the movement of fear, air to the fixity of pain. But they teach that fire is inherent in them all as death and decay, just as ignorance lies concealed within the three passions.

19,8 After creating the world the Demiurge also made the man of dust—not by taking him from this dry earth but from the invisible essence, the overflow and runoff of matter. Into him, they declare, he breathed soulishness. (9) And this is the man created "in an image and a likeness";[141] and in an image he is the material man, very like God but not of the same nature. But "in likeness" he is the soulish man; thus his essence is also said to be a "spirit of life" since it originates from a spiritual effluent. (10) Later, they say, the garment of skin was put on him; this they hold to be the man with perceptible flesh.

19,11 But they say the Demiurge is also unknowing of their Mother Achamoth's spiritual embryo which she brought forth at the sight of the angels about Savior, of the same spiritual nature as the Mother. Nor does the Demiurge know that it has been implanted in him surreptitiously, without his knowledge, so as to be sown through him in the soul which stems from him and in this material body, to be incubated <and> grown in these, and become ready for the reception of mature <Reason>.[142] (12) Thus, they say, the Demiurge was unaware of the spiritual man whom Sophia also sowed, with ineffable <power and> providence, through his breath.[143] For as he knew nothing of the Mother, so he knew nothing of her seed[144]—the

---

140 Μεσότης. The term appears to be used in this sense at Gos. Phil. 76,36. It is common in Para. Shem, see 6,13; 13,16-17; 14,19;27; 15,21 etc. but in these cases may mean the material world. The μεσότης of Jesus is found at Gr. Seth 66,7-8.

141 Gen. 1:26

142 τοῦ τελείου <Λόγου>. For the education of "the seeds" see Val. Exp. 37,20-31; of the "members" of the "perfect man" to prepare them for restoration to the Pleroma, see Tri. Trac. 123,3-22. In Mandaean literature cf. *Ginza* 482,22-483,14; *Johannesbuch* 120,5-7 et al.

143 Comparable are the powers breathed into the mixture that becomes the soul at PS 3.131 (MacDermot pp. 336-337). Cf also the "hidden Adam" which is mentioned at *Ginza* 486,14-35.

144 "Seed" in this sense often appears in the Valentinian tractates of NHC, as, e.g., at Gos. Tr. 43,10-14; Tri. Trac. 91,25-32; 95,16-38; 96,19-32; 101,9-14 and Val. Exp. 37,20-35; 40,18-19. Perhaps see also Apocry. Jn. II,1 20,8-24; 30,11-14; Nat. Arc. 96,19-32; 97,5-9;31; Or. Wld. 117,21; Let. Pet. 136,16-18. For the "seed of Seth" see p. 278 n. 2.

seed which they also call Church,[145] a type of the Church on high.[146] (13) They regard this as the man within them,[147] so that they have their soul from the Demiurge, their body of earth and its fleshliness from matter, but their spiritual man from the Mother, Achamoth.[148]

20,1 Since there are three principles,[149] they say that the material, which they also call "left," must perish from its inability to receive any breath of immortality. But the soulish, which they also term "right," being midway[150] between spiritual and material, goes whichever way it is inclined.[151] (2) The spiritual, however, has been sent out to be formed here in conjunction with the soulish,[152] and educated with it in the course of life.[153] And they say that this is the salt,[154] and the light of the world.[155] For the soulish was in need even of perceptible means of instruction; they say that this is why a world has been made. (3) And the Savior has also come for this soulish principle, to save it, since it too has power of self-determination.

20,4 They claim that the Savior has received the first-fruits[156] of the principles he was to rescue. He has received spirituality from Achamoth, has donned the soulish Christ from the Demiurge,[157] and from the dispensation has been clothed with a body the essence of which is soulish but which, by an ineffable art, has been made to become visible, tangible and passible. But they say he has received nothing material at all;[158] matter is not susceptible of salvation.

---

[145] "Church" in this sense is found at Tri. Trac. 93,30-94,22.

[146] The pre-existent, heavenly ἐκκλησία is important in Tri. Trac. and Gr. Seth. It is explained at length at Tri. Trac. 93,20-94,23; see also 58,29-33; 97,5-9 et al and Gr. Seth 50,1-10; 51,14-26 (observe the context); 60,23-25; 65,33-36;8,13-16, and also Eug. 86,18-87,4.

[147] For "inner man" cf. Let. Pet. 137,18-22; Cod. Tch. Let. Pet. 6,1-3.

[148] Comparable accounts of the composition of man are found at the non-Gnostic Silv. 92,10-29; Acts of Thomas 165 (H-S II p. 404).

[149] There are very full accounts of these at Tri. Trac. 103,13-104,3; 106,7-18; 118,14-124,25. At Or. Wld. 117,28-118,2; at 122,7-9 there are three Adams: a material, a soulish and a spiritual.

[150] At Tri. Trac. 103,19-22 the "powers of ambition" are said to be "set in the middle area."

[151] Cf. Tri. Trac. 119,20-24.

[152] The spirit and soul are said to be saved together at Apocry. Jas. 11,39-12,5 and, in Mandaean literature, at *Ginza* 566,18-567,23; 583,2; 587,22 et al.

[153] Cf. Tri. Trac. 123,3-22.

[154] Sophia is called salt at Gos. Phil. 59,30-34. Cf. Matt. 5:13.

[155] Cf. Matt 5:14

[156] Cf. Test. Tr. 32,22-24.

[157] So at Hipp. Refut. 6.35.6, which attributes this doctrine to an "Italian" school of Valentinians. Note also the δημιουργικὴ τέχνη which at 6.35.7 is identified with "the power of the Highest.".

[158] PsT 4.5:...in substantia corporis nostri non fuisse sed spiritale nescio quod corpus de caelo deferentem...

20,5 The consummation will come when everything spiritual has been formed and perfected by knowledge.[159] This means the spiritual persons who have perfect knowledge of God and are initiates of <the>mysteries of Achamoth;[160] they suppose that <they themselves> are these persons. (6) But soulish people, who are established by works and mere faith and do not have the perfect knowledge,[161] have been taught soulish things. We of the church, they say, are these people.[162] (7) And so they declare that good behavior is essential for us—(we cannot be saved otherwise)[163]—but hold that they will surely be saved in any case, not by (any) behavior but because they are spiritual by nature.[164] (8) For as the earthy can have no part in salvation—they say it is not susceptible of it—so the spiritual, in turn, which they claim to be, does not admit of corruption, in whatever deeds they may take part. (9) For as gold buried in mud does not lose its beauty but retains its own nature, since the mud has no power to harm the gold, they too, they say, in whatever material acts they may engage, cannot be harmed or lose their spirituality.[165]

21,1 Hence, the most perfect of them may do without fear all the forbidden things of which the scriptures affirm that those who do them will not inherit the kingdom of God.[166] (2) They casually eat foods which have been sacrificed to idols, and believe they are in no way defiled by them. They are the first to gather for any holiday celebration of the heathen, held in honor of the idols—and some do not even avoid the murderous spectacle, hateful to God and man, of battles with beasts and gladiatorial combat. (3) Some even serve the pleasures of the flesh to excess and say

[159] Cf. the account of the restoration which is given at Tri. Trac. 123,12-124,3.

[160] Cf. Tri. Trac. 118,37-119,7.

[161] Cf. Tri. Trac. 118,27-37; 124,34-131,13.

[162] Cf. Tri. Trac. 122,13-123,3.

[163] Perhaps cf. Tri. Trac. 130,2-27.

[164] Cf. the Valentinian Tri. Trac. 119,16-18. What might be called "salvation by nature" is documented in other types of Gnosticism. See, e.g., Gos. Jud. 43,15-44,4: The souls of every human generation will die. When these people, however, have completed the time of the kingdom and the spirit leaves them their bodies will die, but there souls will be alive and they will be taken up...It is impossible to sow seed on [rock] and harvest its fruit. This also is the way of the [defiled] raced and corruptible Sophia...and cf. Gos. Jud. 37,2-8; 453,16-25; Apoc. Pet. 75,12-76,17 and, less obviously, Gr. Seth 52,10-25; Test. Tr. 67,9-68,11. In Pistis Sophia, souls which have received the higher mysteries are certain of salvation, though with certain qualifications: PS 3.112 (MacDermot pp. 286-291); 3.119 (MacDermot pp. 306-6, 308 et al). None of these sources, however, exempt Gnostics from moral requirements.

[165] See 1 Apoc. Jas. 28,15-20: You have walked in mud, and your garments were not soiled, etc. cf. Cod. Tch. Book of James 15,5-7. The principle is illustrated from a pearl at Gos. Phil. 62,17-26.

[166] Gal. 5:21

they are rendering carnal things to the carnal and spiritual things to the spiritual. (4) And some secretly seduce the women to whom they teach this doctrine, as women have often confessed together with the rest of the imposture, after being deceived by some of them and then returning to God's church. (5) Some, even open in their shamelessness, have enticed any women whom they want away from their husbands, and regarded them as their own wives. (6) Others again, pretending at first to live modestly with them as with sisters, have been exposed in time after the sister has become pregnant by the brother.

21,7 But though they do many other detestable, ungodly things, they cast off on us, who from fear of God guard against sin even in thought and speech,as boors with no understanding. But they exalt themselves above us and call themselves "perfect" and "seed of election." (8) For they say that we receive grace on loan,[167] and so will be deprived of it. But they, as their rightful possession, have the grace come down from above, from the ineffable, unutterable syzygy, and therefore it will be added to them. And thus it is absolutely necessary that they attend at all times to the mystery of the syzygy.

21,9 And they convince the stupid of this by saying in so many words, "Whoever has come into the world and not loved a woman so as to possess her, is not of the truth, and will not depart to the truth. But he who is of the world and has possessed a woman will not depart to the truth because he has possessed a woman in lust."

21,10 And so we, whom they call "soulish" and say are "of the world,"are in need of continence and good behavior so that we may enter the Intermediate Region.[168] But not they, the ones called "spiritual" and "perfect." No deed brings one into the Pleroma, but the seed which is sent from there in its infancy, <and> matures here.

21,11[169] But when all the seed matures, their Mother Achamoth, they say, leaves the Intermediate Region, enters the Pleroma, and receives as her bridegroom Savior, the product of all the Aeons forming a syzygy of Savior and Sophia-Achamoth. And this is the meaning of "bridegroom and bride," and "marriage chamber"[170] means the entire Pleroma. (12) The

[167] Cf. "The names which they received on loan" Tri. Trac. 134,20. At Gos. Judas 53,18-22 non-Gnostics are given "spirits...as a loan."

[168] "The soul" seeks the "place of righteousness" which is "mixed" at PS 3.111 (MacDermot p. 282).

[169] With 21,11-12 cf. Val. Exp. 39,28-35.

[170] Cf. Gr. Seth 57,7-18. At Tri. Trac. 121,15 the elect are the bridal chamber. And see n. 4 p. 232.

spiritual will doff their souls, become intellectual spirits, enter the Pleroma[171] untouched and unseen,[172] and be given as brides to Savior's angels.[173] (13) The Demiurge will move too, to Mother Sophia's place,[174] that is, in the Intermediate Region. And the souls of the righteous will also rest in the Intermediate Region—for nothing soulish can enter the Pleroma. (14) But they teach that after that the fire which is latent in the world will flash forth, catch, consume all matter,[175] be consumed with it,[176] and pass into nothingness. They declare that the Demiurge knew none of this before the Savior's advent.

22,1 But there are those who say that he emitted a Christ too[177]—his own son and <himself> soulish—<and> has spoken of him through the prophets. This is the one who passed through Mary as water goes through a pipe, and to him, at the baptism,[178] that Savior from the Pleroma, the product of all, descended in the form of a dove. The spiritual seed from Achamoth came into him as well. (2) Thus they maintain that our Lord was compounded of these four, preserving the type of the original, first tetrad: the spiritual, which was from Achamoth; the soulish, which was from the Demiurge; the dispensation, which was prepared with ineffable art; and Savior, who was <the> dove that came down to him. (3) And Savior remained impassible; it was not possible that he suffer, since he could not be touched or seen. And so, when Jesus was brought before Pilate, the spirit of Christ that had been implanted in him was taken away.

But the seed from the Mother has not suffered either, they say; it too is impassible, <since it is> spiritual, and invisible even to the Demiurge. (4) In sum, their "soulish Christ" suffered, and the one who was mysteriously prepared by the dispensation so that the Mother could exhibit the type of the higher Christ <through> him—the Christ who was stretched out by Cross and gave Achamoth her essential form. For they say that all these things are types of those others.

22,5 They say that the souls which have Achamoth's seed are better than the rest. Thus they are more loved than the others by the Demiurge,

---

[171] Cf. Tri. Trac. 123,22-23; On Res. 44,13-33.

[172] Cf. Acts of Thomas 148 (H-S II p. 398).

[173] Cf. the account of the soul's final ascent at Corp. Herm. 1.26.

[174] See n. 38 p. 174.

[175] Cf. The final conflagration as it is pictured at Gr. Pow. 45,24-47,7. In the Manichaean Homilies see 39,23-24; 41,5.

[176] The final fire consumes itself at Gr. Pow. 30,15-23; 46,29-32.

[177] Sabaoth creates a Christ at 105,20-29.

[178] See n. 4 p. 119.

though he does not know the reason, and thinks that he is responsible for their quality. (6) And so, they say, he appointed them prophets, priests and kings. And they interpret many passages as having been spoken through the prophets by this seed, since it is of a higher nature. They say that the Mother too has said a great deal about the higher things; however, they <claim> that <many things have been said> both through the Demiurge and through the souls he has created. (7) And to conclude, they cut the prophecies to pieces by holding that this one was uttered by the Mother, that one by the seed and the other one by the Demiurge.[179] (8) Jesus, moreover, has likewise said one thing by Savior's inspiration, another by the Mother's, another by the inspiration of the Demiurge, as I shall show in due course.

22,9 But the Demiurge, not knowing what was above him, was angry at those sayings, despised them and thought that they had various causes: either the prophetic spirit, from some motion of its own; or the man; or the admixture of inferior things. (10) And he remained in this ignorance till the Savior's coming. But when the Savior came, they say, he learned everything from him, and gladly came over to him with his entire host.[180] (11) And he is the centurion of the Gospel, who tells the Savior, "For I also have under my authority soldiers and servants, and whatsoever I command, they do."[181] (12) He will fulfil his function in the world as long as necessary, especially because of his concern for the church and is awareness of the reward in store for him—that he will go to the Mother's place.

23,1 They suppose that there are three kinds of men, spiritual, earthy and soulish, just as there were Cain, Abel and Seth—<to illustrate> the three natures even from these, here not as individuals but as types. (2) The earthy kind departs to corruption. The soulish, if it chooses the better part, rests in the Intermediate Region; if it chooses the worse, it too will depart to the like place.[182] (3) But they hold that when the spiritual (seeds) which Achamoth sows among them—having been trained and nurtured here in righteous souls from then till now, since they are sent as infants—will afterwards be awarded as brides to Savior's angels, once they are deemed

---

[179] See p. 67 n. 36 and contrast Hipp. Refut. 6.35.1, where it is said that all of the Law and the Prophets are from the Demiurge.

[180] At Hipp. Refut. 6.35.1 he learns from Sophia.

[181] Matt. 8:9; Luke 7:8. With the enlightenment of the Demiurge here cf. Nat. Arc. 95,13-25; SJC 120,14-121,3; Para. Shem 22,17-23,8. See also PS 2.86 (MacDermot p. 197) "the archons which have repented"; *Ginza* 88,21-34; 356,31-38; 360,21-370,19.

[182] Cf. Hipp. Refut. 6.31.9 and, in a sense, Corp. Herm.1.19.

mature.[183] But of necessity their souls will have gone to eternal rest in the Intermediate Region with the Demiurge. (4) And in turn they subdivide the souls themselves, and say that some are good by nature, others evil by nature. And it is the good souls that become fit to receive the seed; the souls which are evil by nature would never welcome that seed.[184]

24,1 Since such is their thesis—which the prophets did not proclaim, nor the Lord teach, nor the apostles transmit, (yet) which they take extreme pride in knowing better than the others—they read from uncanonical writings, busily plait what they say into ropes of sand and, not to let their forgery appear unevidenced, (2) try to adapt parables of the Lord, oracles of the prophets, or words of the apostles convincingly to what they have said. They violate the arrangement and sequence of the scriptures, and as far as they are able, dismember the truth. (3) They alter and remodel and, by making one thing out of another, completely fool many with their poorly assembled show of the accommodated oracles of the Lord.

24,4 It is as though a beautiful portrait of a king had been carefully made of fine gems by a wise craftsman, and someone were to destroy the image as it stood, reset those gems and recombine them, and produce a likeness of a dog or fox, and poorly made at that—(5) and then state categorically that this was the beautiful portrait of the king which the wise craftsman had made and, by displaying the gems the former craftsman had fitted becomingly into the king's portrait but the latter had reset badly as a likeness of a dog, defraud with the show of the gems the less experienced who had no idea of the king's appearance, and convince them that this latter poor effigy of the fox was the former beautiful portrait of the king. (6) In precisely the same way these people have cobbled old wives' tales together, and then they extract words, sayings and parables from here and there, and want to adapt the oracles of God to their yarns.

25,1 We have spoken of such things as they match with what is inside their Pleroma. Here are the sorts of thing they try to adapt from scripture to the things outside. (2) They say the Lord has come to the passion in the last days of the world to show the passion that overtook the last of the Aeons,[185] and with this "end"[186] to indicate the end of the affair of the Aeons. (3) They explain the twelve-year-old girl, the ruler of the synagogue's daughter, whom the Lord came and raised from the dead, as a type of

---

[183] Cf. Dia. Sav. 138,16-20.

[184] Different sorts of souls are distinguished at Tri. Trac. 105,29-106,5.

[185] κόσμος = αἴων

[186] τέλος

Achamoth, to whom their Christ gave form when he was extended, and whom he brought to an awareness of the light that had left her.

25,4 They say it was because Savior manifested <himself> to Achamoth when she was outside the Pleroma like an untimely birth[187] that Paul, in the First Epistle to the Corinthians, has said, "Last of all he was seen of me also, as of one born out of due time."[188] (5) In the same epistle he has similarly revealed the coming of Savior to Achamoth with his companions by saying, "The woman ought to have a veil on her head because of the angels."[189] And that Achamoth veiled <her face> in shame when Savior came to her, Moses has made evident by covering his face with a veil.

25,6 And they claim the Lord has indicated the passions she suffered <when she was abandoned by the light>. With his words on the cross, "My God, why hast thou forsaken me?"[190] he has shown that Sophia was abandoned by the light and prevented by Limit from starting forward. With, "My soul is exceeding sorrowful,"[191] he has shown her grief; with, "Father, if it be possible, let this cup pass from me,"[192] her fear. Similarly her bewilderment, with, "and what I should say, I know not."[193]

25,7 They teach that he has shown that there are three kinds of men in the following ways. The material kind by replying, "The Son of Man hath not where to lay his head," to the man who said, "I will follow thee."[194] The soulish, by answering the man who said, "Lord, I will follow thee, but let me first bid farewell to them which dwell in my house," with, "No man having put his hand to the plow and looking back is suitable in the kingdom of heaven."[195] (8) (This man was one of the intermediate kind, they say.) They claim that the man who professed to have performed the greater part of righteousness, and then would not follow but was vanquished by wealth so that he could not become perfect,[196] was similarly soulish. (9) But he showed the spiritual kind, by saying "Let the dead bury their own dead; but go thou and preach the kingdom of God";[197] and by saying of Zacchaeus

---

187 Cf. Nat. Arc. 94,14-15; Or. Wld. 99,9-11; 23-26.
188 1 Cor. 15 8
189 1 Cor. 11:10
190 Matt. 27:46; Mark 15:34
191 Matt. 26:38
192 Matt. 26:39
193 John 12:27
194 Matt. 8:19-20; Luke 9:57-58
195 Luke 9:61-62
196 Cf. Matt. 19:16-22.
197 Matt. 8:22; Luke 9:60

the publican, "Make haste and come down, for today I must abide at thy house."[198] For they assert that these were of the spiritual kind.

25,10 And they say that the parable of the leaven the woman is said to have hidden in three measures of meal[199] shows the three kinds. For they teach that Sophia is called a woman, but that "three measures of meal" are the three sorts of men, spiritual, soulish, earthy. And they teach that "leaven" means the Savior himself.

25,11 Paul too has spoken expressly of earthy, soulish, and spiritual men—where he says, "As is the earthy, such are they also that are earthy";[200] where he says, "The soulish man receiveth not the things of the spirit";[201] and where he says, "A spiritual man examineth all things."[202] And they say that "The soulish man receiveth not the things of the Spirit,"[203] refers to the Demiurge who, being soulish, did not know the Mother who is spiritual, or her seed or the Aeons in the Pleroma.

25,12 Because the Savior received the firstfruits of those he was to save, Paul has said, "If the firstfruits be holy, the lump is also holy."[204] They teach that "firstfruits" means the spiritual[205] but "lump" means ourselves, the soulish church, whose lump they say he received and raised in himself, since he himself was leaven.

26,1 And by saying that he had come for the <sheep> that was lost,[206] they say he made it known that Achamoth strayed outside the Pleroma, and was formed by Christ and sought out by Savior. (2) For they explain that "lost sheep" means their Mother, by whom they hold that the church here has been sown. But "straying" means the time she spent outside the Pleroma, in <all> the passions from which they suppose that matter originated.

26,3 They explain that the woman who swept the house and found the drachma[207] means the Sophia on high, who had lost her Resolve but found her later when all had been purified by Savior's arrival. Therefore, as they believe, she herself was restored to her place within the Pleroma.

---

[198] Luke 19:5

[199] Cf. Matt. 13:33.

[200] 1 Cor. 15:48

[201] 1 Cor. 2:14

[202] 1 Cor. 2:15

[203] 1 Cor. 2:14

[204] Rom. 11:16

[205] Cod. Tch. James 28,14-16: I receive the firstfruits of those who are defiled, so that I may send them up undefiled.

[206] Cf. Matt. 18:2; Luke 15:4.

[207] Cf. Apocry. Jn. 8,9-10.

26,4 They say that Simeon, who took Christ in his arms, thanked God and said, “Lord, now lettest thou thy servant depart in peace according to thy word,”[208] is a type of the Demiurge. When the Savior came he learned of his translation and gave thanks to Depth.

26,5 And they declare that Achamoth is very plainly made known through Anna, whom the Gospel proclaims a prophetess, and who had lived seven years with a husband and always remained a widow after that, till she saw and recognized the Savior and spoke of him to everyone.[209] Achamoth saw Savior briefly <then> with his companions, and always remained in the Intermediate Region afterwards, awaiting the time when he would return and restore her to her syzygy. (6) And her name has been made known by the Savior in saying, “And Sophia is justified by her children,”[210] and by Paul with, “Howbeit we speak of ‘Sophia’ among them that are perfect.” ’[211]

26,7 And they claim that in one instance Paul has spoken specifically of the syzygies within the Pleroma. For of the syzygy which relates to the world he wrote, “This is a great mystery, but I speak concerning Christ and Church.”[212]

27,1 They teach further that John, the disciple of the Lord, has revealed the former Ogdoad. Their exact words are, (2) “John, the disciple of the Lord, desiring to speak of the generation of all by which the Father emitted all things, posits as the first to be generated by God a ‘Beginning,’ which he has called both ‘Son’ and ‘Only-Begotten God.’ In this, in germ, the Father emitted all. (3) And he says that ‘Word’ has been emitted by him, and in Word the entire essence of the Aeons, to which Word himself later imparted form. Since John is speaking of a first act of generation, he rightly begins his teaching with the ‘Beginning,’ that is, the Son and the Word.

27,4 “For he says as follows: ‘In Beginning was Word, and Word was with God, and Word was God. The same was in Beginning with God.”[213] (5) After first distinguishing the three—God, Beginning and Word—he combines again, to show the emission of the two, Son and Word, and their union with each other as well as with the Father. (6) For Beginning is in the Father and of the Father, and Word is in Beginning and of Beginning. He was right, then, in saying, ‘In Beginning was Word,’ for Word was in Son.

208 Luke 2:29
209 Cf. Luke 2:36-38.
210 Luke 7:35
211 1 Cor. 2:6
212 Eph. 5:32
213 John 1:1-2

And in saying, 'And Word was with God', for Beginning <was> indeed <with the Father>. And accordingly, 'Word was God' for what is begotten of God is God. <And by>, 'The same was in Beginning with God,' he indicated their order of emission.

27,7 " 'All things were made by him, and without him was not anything made' "[214] for Word became the cause of the form and the generation for all the Aeons after him. But with 'That which was made in him is Life'[215] he even made reference at this point to a syzygy. He said that all things have been brought into being through Word, but Life in Word. (8)"Thus she who came to be in him is more closely related to him than those who came to be through him, for she is his consort and bears fruit through him. (9) For since adds, 'And Life was the light of men,'[216] by saying 'Man' now he has also made Church known under the same name, to show the partnership of the syzygy through the one name; for Man and Church arise from Word and Life. (10) And he termed Life the 'light of men,' since men are enlightened—that is, formed and made manifest—by her. And Paul says this too, 'Whatsoever is made manifest is light.'[217] Therefore, since Life made Man and Church manifest and brought them into being, she is called their light.

27,11 "With these words, then, John has clearly indicated both the others and the second tetrad: Word and Life, Man and Church. (12) But he has certainly made the first tetrad known as well. For in discussing the Savior and stating that everything outside the Pleroma has been formed by him, he calls him the fruit of the entire Pleroma. (13) For he has called him the 'light' that shines in darkness and was not comprehended by it, because though the Savior bestowed order on all that had resulted from the passion he was not known by them. (14) And John calls him both 'Son' and 'Truth,' and 'Light' and 'Word made flesh, whose glory,' he says, 'we beheld; and his glory was as that of an Only-Begotten, given him of the Father, full of Grace and Truth.'[218] (15) And he says it as follows, 'And Word was made flesh and dwelt among us, and we beheld his glory, the glory as of an Only-Begotten of a Father, full of Grace and Truth.'[219] He made the first tetrad specifically known, then, by saying Father, Grace, Only-Begotten,

[214] John 1:3
[215] John 1:4
[216] John 1:4
[217] Eph. 5:13
[218] John 1:14
[219] John 1:14

and Truth. (16) In this way John has spoken of the first Ogdoad, mother of all the Aeons. For he has said Father, Grace, Only-Begotten, Truth, and Word, Life, Man, and Church."

28,1 You see their method of deceiving themselves, beloved, their abuse of the scriptures to try to prove their fabrication from them. This is the reason I have cited even their actual words, so that from them you may realize the villainy of the craft and the wickedness of the imposture. (2) In the first place, if John intended to reveal the higher Ogdoad, he would have kept to the order of the emanation, and placed the first Tetrad, which they say is the most venerable, among the names that come first. He would then have added the second to show the order of the Ogdoad by the order of the names and not mentioned the first Tetrad after such a long interval, as though he had completely forgotten it and then recalled it at the last minute.

28,3 And then, if he meant to indicate the sygyzies, he would not have left Church's name out. He might have been equally content to name the males in the case of the other syzygies—they too can be understood to go with (their females)—to maintain uniformity throughout. <Or>, if he were listing the consorts of the rest, he would have revealed Man's too, and not left us to get her name by divination.

28,4 <Their> distortion of the exegesis is obvious. Where John proclaims one God almighty, and one Only-begotten, Christ Jesus, through whom he says all things were made, <saying> that he is Son of God, he is only-begotten, he is maker of all, he is the true light that enlightens every man, is creator of the world, is the one who came unto his own, and that he himself became flesh and dwelt among us—(5) these people, speciously perverting the exegesis, hold that there is another Only-Begotten in the series of emanations whom they also call Beginning, and that there was another Savior and another Word, the son of Only-begotten, and another Christ, emitted for the.rectification of the Pleroma (6) They have taken its every statement away from the truth <and> adapted it to their own doctrine by misusing the names so that, to hear them tell it, among so many names John makes no mention of the Lord, Christ Jesus. (7) For though he has said Father, Grace, Only-begotten, Truth, Word, Life, Man, and Church, on their hypothesis he has said it of the first Ogdoad, in which there is no Jesus yet and no Christ, the teacher of John.

28,8 But the apostle himself has made it plain that he has not spoken of their syzygies but of our Lord Jesus Christ, whom he also knows as the Word of God. (9) For in his recapitulation concerning the Word whom he has already said to have been "in the beginning," he adds the explanation, "And the Word was made flesh, and dwelt among us." But on their hypothesis the Word, who never even left the Pleroma, did not become flesh. That was Savior, who was the product of all the Aeons, and of later origin than Word.

29,1 You fools, learn that Jesus himself, who suffered for us, who made his dwelling among us, is the Word of God! If some other Aeon had become flesh for our salvation, the apostle would presumably have spoken of another. But if the Word of the Father, who descended, is <also> the one who ascended—the only-begotten Son of the only God, made flesh for man at the Father's good pleasure—then <John> has not written "Word" of any other, or of an Ogdoad, but of the Lord Jesus Christ.

29,2 Nor, in their view, has the Word become principally flesh. They say that Savior put on a soulish body which had been prepared, by an ineffable providence of the dispensation, to become visible and tangible. (3) But flesh is God's ancient formation from the dust, like Adam, which, John has made clear, God's Word has truly become.

29,4 And their first, original Ogdoad has been demolished. Once it is established that Word, Only-Begotten, Life, Light, Savior and Christ are one and the same and God's Son, and that he himself was made flesh for us, the flimsy structure[220] of <their> Ogdoad is destroyed. And with this wrecked their whole pantomine—which they falsely dream up to disparage the scriptures after fabricating their own hypothesis—has collpased.

29,5 Then they gather expressions and names which lie scattered throughout scripture, move them away, as I said, from their natural setting to an unnatural one, and do the same sort of thing as the persons who set themselves subjects at random and then try to declaim them in lines from Homer, (6) making it seem to the simple that Homer has composed the words on that subject which has been declaimed extemporaneously; and by the artificial sequence of the words, many are rushed into supposing that Homer might have written these things in this way. (7) So with the person who wrote the following in lines from Homer, about the sending of Heracles being by Eurystheus for the dog in Hades. (There is nothing to prevent me from mentioning even these by way of illustration, since <the> enterprise of both parties is one and the same.)

[220] σκηνοπηγία. σκήνη is a flimsy, temporary dwelling.

(8) So spake Eurystheus, son of Sthenelus
Persëides, and sent upon his way
Hard-laboring Heracles, to fetch from Hell
The loathèd Hades' dog. With heavy sighs
He hastened through the town, like to a lion
Bred in the mountains, trusting in its strength.
All they that loved him bare him company,
Young maids, and elders worn with toil and care,
Mourning for him as on his way to death
But lo, gray-eyed Athena, in her heart—
For hers was kin to his—knowing his toil,
Sent Hermes to his aid.

29,9 What innocent person could fail to be swept off his feet by these words, and suppose that Homer had written them in this way, on this subject? But anyone familiar with the works of Homer will recognize <the words but not their subject>, (10) since he knows that some are spoken of Odysseus, some actually of Heracles, but some of Priam and some of Menelaus and Agamemnon. He will take the lines, restore each one to its own <book>, and get rid of the subject <we see here>. (11) So one who holds upright within him the rule of the truth which he has received through baptism will recognize the names, expressions and parables from the scriptures, but not recognize this blasphemous subject. (12) For though he will certify the gems, he will not allow the fox in place of the king's portrait. By restoring each thing that has been said to its own position and fitting it to the naked body of the truth, he will prove their forgery without foundation.

30,1 <But>, since this jerry built structure is beyond redemption, I think it will be well, so that anyone who has perused their farce may apply the argument which demolishes it, to show first how the authors of this story themselves differ from each other, as though inspired by different spirits of error. (2) In this way too we may understand perfectly—even before it is demonstrated—that the truth the church proclaims is sure, and the one they have counterfeited is falsehood.

30,3 For the church, though it is dispersed the whole world over to the ends of the earth, has received from the apostles and their disciples, the faith in one God, the Father Almighty, maker of heaven, earth, the seas, and everything in them. (4) And in one Christ Jesus, the Son of God, who was made flesh for our salvation. (5) And in the Holy Spirit, who through the prophets has proclaimed the dispensations, the advent, the birth from the Virgin, passion, resurrection and bodily assumption into heaven of the beloved <Son>, Christ Jesus our Lord, and his coming from heaven in his Father's glory to gather all things in one and raise the flesh of all mankind; (6) that, by the invisible Father's good pleasure, every knee in heaven, on earth, and under the earth may bow to Christ Jesus, our Lord, God, Savior and King, and every tongue confess him. And that he may pronounce a righteous judgment on all, (7) and consign the spirits of wickedness, the angels who have transgressed and rebelled, and wicked, unrighteous, lawless and blasphemous men, to the eternal fire; (8) but grant life, bestow immortality, and secure eternal glory for the righteous and holy, who have kept his commandments and abode in his love, some from the first, others after repentance.

31,1 Having, as we have said, received this message and this faith the church, though dispersed over all the world, guards them as carefully as though it lived in one house, believes them as with one soul and the same heart, and preaches, teaches and transmits them in unison, as with one mouth. (2) For even if the languages of the world are different, the meaning of the tradition is one and the same. The churches founded in Germany have not believed differently or transmitted the tradition differently—or the ones founded among the Iberians, the Celts, in the east, in Libya, or in the center of the earth. (3) As the sun, a creature of God, is one and the same the world over, so the light <of the mind>, the proclamation of the truth, shines everywhere and illumines all who are willing to come to a knowledge of truth. (4) The ablest speaker of the church's leaders will say nothing different from these things, for no man is above his master[221] nor will the feeble speaker diminish the tradition. For as faith is one and the same, he who has much to say of it cannot enlarge it, and he who has little to say has not diminished it.

31,5 For one to know more or less with understanding means, not changing the actual subject (of our knowledge) and—as though as though not satisfied with him—inventing a new God other than the creator, maker and sustainer of all, or another Christ or Only-Begotten. (6) It means giving further explanation of what has been said in parables, and suiting it to the subject of the faith. It means expounding God's dealings with mankind and his provision for them, and making it plain that God bore with the rebellion of the angels who transgressed, and the disobedience of men. (7) It

[221] Cf. Matt. 10:24.

means proclaiming the reason why one and the same God has made things temporal and eternal, heavenly and earthly, and why, though invisible, God appeared to the prophets, not in one form but present differently to different ones. It means making the reason known why men have been given a number of covenants, and teaching the nature of each; (8) searching out the reason why God confined all in disobedience so as to have mercy upon all; giving thanks for the reason why God's Word became flesh and suffered, and proclaiming the reason why the advent of God's Son appeared in the last times, which is to say that the beginning appeared in the end.

31,9 It means unfolding what scripture says of the end and the things to come; not leaving unsaid the reason why God has made the reprobate gentiles fellow-heirs, of the same body and partakers with the saints; (10) proclaiming how this mortal flesh will put on immortality, this corruptible, incorruption; declaring how God will say, "That which was not my people is my people, and she who was not beloved, is beloved,"[222] and "More are the children of the desolate than the children of the married wife."[223]

31,11 For it was at these things and their like that the apostle cried, "O the depth of the riches both of the Sophia and knowledge of God! How unsearchable are his judgments, and his ways past finding out!"[224] It was not at inventing his Mother up above the Creator and Demiurge, and the Resolve of their erring Aeon, and going on to such a degree of blasphemy. (12) Nor was it <at> teaching still more lies about the Pleroma above her in turn—of thirty Aeons then, <innumerable tribes of them now>—as these teachers say who are truly barren of divine understanding—while all the true church, as we have said, holds one and the same faith the world over.

32,1 Now let us also see their unstable views—how, when there are perhaps two or three of them, they cannot say the same about the same things, but make assertions which contradict each other in thing and name. (2) For Valentinus, the first of the so-called Gnostic sect to adapt its principles to a form characteristic of a school, blurted them out like this, with the declaration that there is <an> unnameable pair, one of which is called Ineffable, and the other Silence. (3) Then a second pair has been emitted from this, one of which he names Father and the other, Truth. Word and Life, and Man and Church, are the fruit of this Tetrad; and this is the first Ogdoad. (4) And he says that ten powers have been emitted from Word and

[222] Hos. 2:25; Rom. 9:25
[223] Isa. 54:1
[224] Rom. 11:33

Life, as we mentioned, and from Man and Church, twelve—one of whom, by rebelling and coming to grief, has caused the rest of the affair.

32,5 And he supposed that there were two Limits, one between Depth and the rest of the Pleroma separating the generate Aeons from the ingenerate Father;[225] the other one separating their Mother from the Pleroma. (6) And Christ has not been emitted from the Aeons in the Pleroma, but together with a certain shadow[226] was produced in memory of better things by the Mother, when she found herself outside. (7) Christ, being male, cut the shadow off and returned to the Pleroma but the Mother, abandoned with the shadow and emptied of spiritual essence, bore another son. And this is the Demiurge, whom he also says is Pantocrator of all who are below him. But like the persons falsely termed Gnostics of whom we shall speak, Valentinus held that a lefthand archon has also been emitted with the Demiurge.

32,8 And he sometimes says that Jesus was emitted by the one whom their Mother inhaled <and> mixed with all things—that is, <by> Desired—but sometimes by the one who returned to the Pleroma, that is, Christ—or sometimes, by Man and Church. (9) And he says that the Holy Spirit was emitted by Truth to examine the Aeons and make them fruitful by entering them invisibly. Through him the Aeons bring forth the fruits of the truth.

This concludes Irenaeus against the Valentinans

33,1 <By giving> both these <explanations> and others like them the elder of whom we have spoken, Irenaeus—fully equipped by the Holy Spirit, sent into the ring by <the> Lord as a champion athlete, and anointed with the heavenly favors of the true faith and knowledge—went over every bit of their nonsense as he wrestled their whole silly story to the ground and defeated it. (2) And he demolished them further, superbly, in his next book, the second, and the others. He seemed to want to drag his opponent after he had already been thrown and beaten, to make a public spectacle of him, and to detect the shameless though feeble challenge of his weak-mindedness that was in him even when he was down. (3) I, however, am content with the few things I have said and the things these writers of the truth have said and compiled, and can see that others have done the work—I mean Clement, Irenaeus, Hippolytus, and many more, who have

[225] Cf. Val. Exp. 27,29-38.

[226] For "shadow" in a comparable sense see Or. Wld. 97,29-98,7; 98,23-99,2.

given the Valentinians' refutation even remarkably well. Being content with these men and in full agreement with them I have no desire at all, as I said, to add to my labor, since from the very contents of the Valentinians' teachings the refutation of them will be <perfectly plain> to any person of understanding.

34,1 In the first place their own ideas vary, and each one sets out to demolish the other's. Secondly, their myths are unprovable since no scripture has said these things—neither the Law of Moses nor any prophet after Moses, neither the Savior nor his evangelists, and certainly not the apostles. (2) If these things were true, the Lord who came to enlighten the world, and the prophets before him, would have told us things of this sort in plain language—and then the apostles too, who confuted idolatry and all sorts of wrongdoing, and were not afraid to write against any unlawful teaching, and opposition. (3) Especially when the Savior himself says, "Unto them that are without, in parables; but to you <the explanation of the parables (is given), for knowledge of the kingdom of heaven.>"[227] (4) Plainly, he explained at once any of his parables in the Gospels. Of course he says who the mustard seed is, who the leaven is, the woman who put the leaven in the three measures, the vineyard, the fig tree, the sower, the best soil.

34,5 Also, these people too are vainly inspired because they are in the power of demons. The most holy apostle Paul says of them, "In the latter times some shall depart from the teaching, giving heed to fables and doctrines of devils."[228] (6) And again, St. James says of this sort of teaching, "This Sophia descendeth not from above, but is earthly, sensual, devilish. But the Sophia that is from above is first of all pure, then peaceable, easy to be intreated, without partiality, full of mercy and good fruits,"[229] and so on. Not one fruit of this Sophia is to be found in these people. (7) With them there is "confusion and every unlawful work,"[230] spawn of devils and serpents' hisses, with each one saying something different at a different time. No mercy or pity is to be found in them, only hair-splittings and disagreements; nowhere purity, nowhere peace, nowhere fairness.

35,1 But again, since the argument demands it, I do want to mention a few of the things they say and refute them, even though I promised to finish. I do not care for the art of rhetoric but for my readers' benefit. (2) Now

[227] Cf. Mark 4:11
[228] 1 Tim. 4:1
[229] Jas. 3:15; 17
[230] Jas 3:10

then, they say that the twelfth Aeon, the one which became defective, dropped out of the twelve entirely, and the number twelve was lost. (3) But they say that this was caused by the defection of Judas, the twelfth apostle, with the consequent disappearance of the number twelve. And similarly of the woman with the issue, and the one who lost the one drachma out of her ten. (4) However it is established that, as the most holy Irenaeus has already said, the twelfth Aeon can neither be represented by Judas[231]—for Judas has perished utterly, but the so-called twelfth Aeon of their fabrication was not emptied; Conductor, or Limit-Setter, stood in front of it and said "Iao" to it, as they say themselves, and this made it firm. (5) Nor can the woman who bled for twelve years be compared with their stage piece. She was healed after the twelve years in which she was afflicted with bleeding. She did not remain unafflicted for eleven years and bleed in the twelfth; instead she bled during the eleven, but was healed in the twelfth.[232] (6) Nor did the woman who had the ten drachmas lose the one for good, allowing for their story of the lost Aeon of matter; she lit her lamp and found the drachma.

36,1 Since all their assertions, then, have been summarily refuted by these two or three arguments, they will be understood by the prudent children of God's holy catholic church as feeble, worthless melodrama. (2) For not to drag my treatise out endlessly by attacking the same people, I shall end my exposition here, set a bound to their wickedness great as it is, and go on to the rest. (3) I call on God to be the guide and help of my weakness, that I may be preserved from this sect and the ones I have mentioned before it—and the ones I plan to exhibit to the studious, who want a precise knowledge of all the foolish assertions there are in the world, and the chains which cannot hold.

36,4 For by sowing his dreaming in many people and calling himself a Gnostic, Valentinus has, as it were, fastened a number of scorpions together in one chain, as in the old and well-known parable. It says that scorpions, one after another, will form a sort of chain to a length of ten or even more, let themselves down from a roof or housetop, and so do their harm to men by guile. (5) Thus both he, and the so-called Gnostics who derive from him, have become authors of imposture and each, taking his cue from him, has been instructed by someone else, added to the imposture after his teacher, and introduced another sect clinging to the one before it. (6) And thus the so-called Gnostics have been divided successively into

---

231 Iren. 2.20.2-5
232 Iren. 2.23.1

different sects themselves; but, as I said, they have taken their cue from Valentinus and his predecessors. (7) Still, since we have trampled on them and on this sect of Valentinus with the teaching of the truth, let us pass them by, but by God's power examine the rest.

32.
Against Secundians[1] *with whom Epiphanes and Isidore are associated. Number twelve, but thirty-two of the series*

1,1 Now that I have passed Valentinus' sect by, worked hard in his sowing of thistles, and <gone through it>, I may say, with a great deal of trouble and hard field labor, I shall go to the remains of his sowing of thistles and snake's carcass, (2) praying to the Lord for the Holy Spirit, that through him I may be able to shield souls from harm by godly teaching and grave speech, and suck the poisons out of those who already have this infection. (3) But of each of the following I shall begin to say, one after another, which teacher was the successor of which of the teachers who were derived from Valentinus and yet teach a sowing other than his.

1,4 Now Secundus, who was one of them and wanted to think of something further, expounded everything in Valentinus' way, but made a louder racket in the ears of the crack-brained. (5) Being like Valentinus as I said, but more conceited than Valentinus, he said that the first Ogdoad is a righthand tetrad and a lefthand tetrad, and therefore taught that the one is called "light," and the other, "darkness." (6) And the power that fell away and came to grief was not one of the thirty aeons, but came after the thirty aeons and was thus one of <their fruits, which> originated lower down, after the other Ogdoad.[2] (7) But as to Christ and the other doctrines he held precisely the same position as Valentinus, his own provider of venom and dispenser of poison.

1,8 Since he does not have many strange doctrines that are distinctive I feel I should rest content with the ones I have mentioned, which are refutable even of themselves. Still, I am going to say a few things about

---

[1] The material concerning Secundus himself, and Epiphanes, is drawn from Iren. 1.11.2-5; at 6,7 Epiph cites Irenaeus by name. To the Irenaean material Epiph adds Clement of Alexandria's comments on Epiphanes and others, quoting verbatim from Strom. 3.2.5.1-2.

The very summary accounts of Secundus at Hipp. 6.38.1-2 and PsT 4.7 represent Hipp. Synt. Tert. Adv. Val. 37-38 depends on Irenaeus. Fil. 40 might be based on Irenaeus, Epiph or both.

[2] Cf. Iren. 1.11.2; Hipp. Refut. 6.38.1; PsT 4.7; Tert. Adv. Val. 38.

him too, lest it appear that I have bypassed the discussion of him because of being at a loss.

1,9 If their tetrads are ranged on the right and the left, it will be found that something is required in between the right and the left. (10) Anything with righthand and lefthand sides stands in between its right and left hands, and there can be no right or left unless the distinction is made because of a body which intervenes between either one. (11) Now then, Secundus you fool and the people who are fooled by you, the center, by which both right and left are determined, (12) must be some one thing, and the right and left which are determined by it cannot be alien to this one thing. And the whole must necessarily be traced back to that which is One, with not one thing above it and nothing below it, except the things it has created. (13) And to those who understand the truth it will be plain that God is one, Father, Son and Holy Spirit. But if God, from whom all things come, is one, there is no "left" in him, or any other defect, or anything inferior except the things he has made. And the things after the Father, Son and Holy Spirit have all been made well, and brought ungrudgingly into being, by himself.

2,1 But even though another snake of his kind comes forward and replies to me that the right and the left are outside of the One, while he himself is the middle, and that the righthand things are embraced by him, and he rejoices in them and names them "right" and "light," but he abhors the lefthand things as strange to him and lying on his left—he had better tell me where he gets this geometry that allows him a to make a neat arrangement of an unalterable right and left. (2) For right or left in us is aptly named from the limbs, which are fixed in the body and never interchangeable. (3) But anything outside us can sometimes be "right" and sometimes "left." The south, or meridial, region, will be called "right" by everyone who is facing east, and the northerly, or arctural region, "left." (4) But on the contrary, when one has turned west the directions will be found to have different names. The southerly and meridial direction which was "right" a minute ago, is transformed into "left" in its turn, and the arctural, or northerly, which has been on one's left, is transformed into his right. (5) Very well, where did the fraud find his divinely ordained geometry? What a lot of nonsense there is of this kind, which mixes everything up!

2,6 But he claims that the Deficiency[3] came into being after the thirty Aeons. All right, Mister, tell me, where did you get the origin of the

---

[3] See p. 170 n. 9.

Deficiency, or the power that fell away! (7) If you found it <grown> from a shoot of the things on high, not a created thing but something generated—created things are not defined as created by you and your master, but the products of successive generations <are supposed> to have grown up, generated and by participation, with each nature receiving from each. (If this is what you mean), on your own terms you are taking up arms against yourself. (8) For if both the later power and the defection have been generated by the things on high, and if it sprouted, let us say, and grew from them, then it partakes of the benefits on high. For the later power communicates with the Pleroma and the Pleroma with the later power, and there can be no difference between the one and the other, or between the other and the one, since they are both in contact at their ends. (9) And on every account, you most wretched of all wretches, you will be caught getting the fodder for your imposture from a devil's second sowing.

3,1 But not to leave out anything that is done and said in any group—even if in each group there are many founders and persons who proudly go beyond their teachers by inventing story after story—I shall go on discussing the ones who are in this sect itself but say something different from the above. (2) I am speaking of Epiphanes[4] the pupil of Isidore, who dragged himself down to a further depth of misery under the cover of hortatory speeches. To tell the truth he took his cue from his own father, Carpocrates; but he was associated with this Secundus' sect, and was a Secundian himself. (3) For there was considerable difference between each of these misguided persons and the other, and a sort of miscellaneous tangle, as we might say, of silly talk.

3,4 This Epiphanes as I said, who was a son of Carpocrates and whose mother's name was Alexandria, is connected with the Secundians. On his father's side he was a Cephallenian. <But> he died early at the age of seventeen[5] as though the Lord, making a better provision for the world, were getting rid of the worthless thorns. (5) After his death, however, those who had gone astray on his account did not get over the plague they had caught from him. (6) At Same he is still honored as a god, even today; the locals have established a sanctuary for him and offer sacrifices and rites every

---

[4] Epiph construes Iren. 1.11.3 as, "Another one, their teacher Epiphanes, says..." and identifies this teacher with the Epiphanes mentioned by name at Clem. Alex. Strom. 3.2.1. Irenaeus' Greek, probably represented by Hipp. Refut. 6.38.2, reads Ἄλλος δέ τις ἐπιφανὴς διδάσκαλος αὐτῶν, οὕτως λέγει... There may in fact be some justification for his identification of Epiphanes; see n. 17 below.

[5] Clem. Alex. Strom. 3.2.5.2

new moon, and have put up altars to him and founded a well-known library in his name, the so-called Library of Epiphanes. (7) The Cephallenians are so far gone in error that they sacrifice and pour libations to him, and have banquets and sing hymns to him in his sanctuary which they have established.[6] (8) But it was because of the excess of his education, both in the arts and in Platonic philosophy[7] that the whole deceit came to them from him, the error about the sect and about the other error, I mean the one that has turned the Samians to idol mania.

3,9 And so Epiphanes was associated with Secundus and his circle. For he copied Secundus' poison, that is, his wordy babble of baneful, reptilian corruption. (4,1) They claim, however, that Isidore[8] in his exhortations was the one responsible for their wickedness. But I cannot find out for certain whether Isidore himself thought the same as they and was originally one of them, or whether he was another hortatory author who had learned from the philosophers. In any case these people are all in the same line of business.

4,2 In the first place Epiphanes himself, together with Carpocrates, who was his father and the leader of his sect, and the people about Carpocrates, ruled that men's wives are to be held in common, taking his cue for this from Plato's Republic and getting what he wanted himself. (3) But he begins by saying that, as the Savior teaches, there are three kinds of eunuch in the Gospel—the eunuch made by men, the eunuch from birth, and the eunuch who becomes one willingly for the kingdom of heaven's sake.[9] (4)[10] "Therefore," he says, "those who are so of necessity do not become eunuchs by reason. But those who make themselves eunuchs for the kingdom of heaven's sake <make this> choice, they say, because of the consequences of matrimony, for fear of the business <of earning> a living. (5) <And by> "It is better to marry than to burn; do not cast thy soul into fire,"[11] he says that the apostle means, "Hold out and fear night and day lest you fall from continence. For a soul that is bent on resistance has a portion of the hope."

4,6 "'Resist a contentious woman,'[12] then'"—as I have already said, (he is) quoting the exhortation—"'says Isidore in so many words in the

[6] Clem. Alex. Strom. 3.2.5.2
[7] Clem. Alex. Strom. 3.2.5.3
[8] Clem. Alex. Strom. 3.1.2.3. The Stromata also mention Isidore at 2.20.113.3 and 6.6.58.2f. In NHC see Test. Tr. 57,6-8.
[9] Matt. 19:12; Clem. Alex. Strom. 3.1.1-2
[10] 4,4-5,3 are quoted directly from Clem. Alex. Strom. 3.1.1.2-3.3.
[11] Cf. 1 Cor. 7:9.
[12] Prov 21:19

Ethics, 'lest you be drawn away from God's grace, and pray with a good conscience once you have ejaculated the fire.[13] But when your thanksgiving descends to petition and for the rest you stand, not upright but on the brink of falling, marry!"'[14]

4,7 Then he says in turn, "'But one who is a youth, or poor, or declining'"—that is, ill—"'and prefers not to marry as reason dictates, let this one not be separated from his brother.'"[15] The wretch is dramatizing and inviting certain shameful suspicions of himself, <for> he says, (8) "'Let him say, Since I have entered the holies I cannot be affected. But if he feels a presentiment let him say, Lay your hand on me, brother, lest I sin; and he will receive aid both intelligible and sensible. Only let him will to achieve the good, and he will attain.'"

4,9 Then again, he says, "'At times we say with our lips, We will not sin, but our minds are bent on sin. Such a man is refraining out of fear from doing the thing he desires, lest he be assessed the penalty. But mankind has certain members which are essential and natural, <and some which are natural> only. Its clothing (with flesh) is natural and essential, but its organ of desire is likewise natural, but <not> essential.'"

5,1 "I have quoted these remarks," the author who wrote against them <says>, "in refutation of those who do not live rightly," and the Basilideans and Carpocratians, and those who are named for Valentinus and Epiphanes, with whom the Secundus whom I placed before him, was associated. (2) For whether the latter passed these horrors on to the fomer or the former to the latter, they bartered for them with each other. And though they differed from each other to some extent they enrolled themselves in the same sect, (3) "and so held that, because of their perfection, they had license even to sin, since they would surely be saved by nature even if they were to sin now—due to their natural election, (I presume), since not even the original authors of these doctrines permit them to do these things."

5,4[16] "As though they were aspiring to something loftier and on a higher plane of knowledge, these too speak of the first tetrad, in this way: "There is a certain principle prior to all of which there can be no preconception, ineffable and unnameable, which I call Unity. With this Unity there coex-

[13] Cf. Thom. Cont. 141,25-31; 143,26-30; 144,14; Man. Keph. 26,15-17.

[14] Holl followed Jülicher's suggested reading, καὶ στῇς εἰς τὸ λοιπὸν, μὴ κατορθώσας, σφαλῆναι, γάμησον.

[15] Perhaps cf. GT 25: "Love your brother like your soul, guard him like the pupil of your eye."

[16] 5,4-7,5 are in part quoted and in part summarized from Iren. 1.11.2-5. See also Hipp. Refut. 6.38.2-4; Tert. Adv. Val. 37.

ists a power which I, likewise, term Oneness. (5) This Unity and Oneness, which are the One, though they had not been emitted themselves, emitted a principle intelligible in all respects, ingenerate and invisible, a principle which reason terms Monad. (6) With this Monad there coexists a power of the same nature as itself, which I term the Unit. These powers, Unity and Oneness, Monad and the Unit,[17] emitted the remaining emanations of the Aeons'"[18]

6,1 Next the authors who had written the truth <about> these people so well refuted <them> in their own treatises–Clement, whom some call Clement of Alexandria, and others, Clement of Athens—(2) and St. Irenaeus besides (who), to poke fun at that tragic drama of theirs, quoted those words and raised <the cry of> (3) "Alas and alack!" over them. "<The> tragic outcry may truly be made for a misfortune as great as that of those who have composed these ridiculous specimens of such a coinage as this—and for so much impudence that he has unblushingly given names to his fabrication. (4) For in saying,' There is a prior principle before all, priorly inconceivable, which I call Unity—and again, 'With this Unity there coexists a power which I, likewise, term Oneness'—he has made the plainest sort of admission that what he has said is his own fabrication, and that he himself has given the fabrication names never given by anyone else. (5) And it is plain that he himself has ventured to coin the names, and if he were not alive the truth would not have had a name. (6) Hence there is nothing to prevent someone else from assigning names of this sort for the same purpose."

6,7 Then in conclusion to this the same blessed Irenaeus—as I said—proposes ridiculous terms himself, saying jokingly that a different nomenclature of his own is worth just as much as their silliness. He makes up family trees of melons, cucumbers and gourds as though for real things, <the aptness of which> must be clear to the studious from what they have read.

7,1 "But others of them in turn have called the first, original Ogdoad by these names: First, Prior Principle; next, Inconceivable; but third, Ineffable, and fourth, Invisible. (2) And from the first, Prior Principle, Beginning has been emitted in the first and fifth <place>.[19] From Inconceivable, in the

---

[17] For these terms see Unger-Dillon.

[18] Clem. Alex. Strom. 3.2.5-3 says of Epiphanes, καθηγήσατο . . . τῆς μοναδικῆς γνώσεως, perhaps linking Epiphanes with the sort of material which is reported at Iren. 1.11.3 and Hipp. 6.38.2.

[19] Cf. ". . . (I) stood upon the first aeon which is the fourth" (Zost. 6,19-20) . . . "I stood upon the second aeon which is the third" (7,6-8) . . . "I stood upon the third aeon which is the second" (7,14-15) . . . "[I stood upon] the fourth aeon which is the first]" (7,20-21).

second and sixth place, Incomprehensible has been emitted; from Ineffable, in the third and seventh place, Unnameable, and from Invisible, Ingenerate. (This is) the Pleroma of the first Ogdoad. (3) They hold that these powers are prior to Depth and Silence, in order to seem more perfect than the perfect and more gnostic than the Gnostics—but one might rightly address these people as, 'You driveling sophists!'

7,4 "Indeed, they have different opinions of Depth himself. Some say he is unattached, neither male nor female, not a thing at all. Others say he is male and female, ascribing hermaphrodism to him. (5) Others again attach Silence to him as bedfellow to form a first syzygy,"[20] and then dramatically produce the rest from him and her. (6) And there is a lot of foolish dreaming in them, lulling their minds into a deep slumber.

7,7 But why spend so much time, since from what has been said the case against them, and their refutation and overthrow, is observable by everyone who wants to keep hold of his life and not be deceived by empty myths. (8) I shall say no more about them. Passing this sect by I shall <go> to the rest to look for a safe way and level path by which to traverse and refute their evils and so bring myself and my hearers to safety by God's power, through the teaching and true contemplation of our Lord. (9) Having trod this viper underfoot with the sandal of the Gospel—like the mousing viper, one which is like many other vipers—let us examine the rest.

33.

Against Ptolemaeans.[1] *Number thirteen, but thirty-three of the series*

1,1 Ptolemy succeeds Secundus, and the man named Epiphanes who got the cue for his own opinion by barter from Isidore. He belongs to the same sect of the so-called Gnostics, and with certain others <is one of> the Valentinians, but he has suppositions which are different from his teachers'. His adherents even pride themselves on his name and are called Ptolemaeans.

1,2[2] This "Ptolemy, with his adherents, has come before us as someone still more expert" than his own teachers and one who invents lots and lots

[20] Iren. 1.11.5. Cf. Hipp. 6.38.3-5.

[1] Sect 33 is drawn from Iren. 1.12.1-3 and the Epistle of Ptolemy to Flora, which it quotes in its entirety. See also Hipp. Refut. 6.38.5-7. Both PsT 4.7, which mentions Ptolemy together with Secundus, and Fil. 49, are from Hipp. Synt. which was plainly quite summary.

[2] 1,2-3,5 is partially quoted and partially paraphrased from Iren. 1.12.1-3. Cf. Hipp. Refut. 6.38.5-7.

of a sort of addition to their teaching. (3) "He invented two consorts for the god they call Depth and bestowed them on him; and these he also called 'dispositions,[3] Conception' (ἔννοια) and Will." (4) Conception had always coexisted with him, continually conceiving of the emission of something, but Will arose in him later. "For he first conceived of emitting <something>," Ptolemy says, "and then he willed to. (5) Thus when Conception and Will, these two dispositions or faculties"—in turn he calls them faculties—"had been mixed together as it were, the emission as a pair of Only-Begotten and Truth took place. (6) These came forth as types and visible images of the Father's two invisible dispositions; Mind of Will, and Truth of Conception. And thus the male became an image of <the later> Will, <but> the female, of the ingenerate Conception. (7) Will, then, was a faculty of Conception. For Conception had always conceived of the emission, but was unable by herself to emit what she had conceived of. But when the faculty of Will supervened, she then emitted that of which she had conceived."

2,1 What nonsense of the lame-brain! No one of sound mind could understand this even of man, let alone of God. (2) Homer strikes me as more sensible than he, with his portrayal of Zeus' worrying, fretting and angry, and lying awake all night over a way to plot against the Achaeans, because Thetis had demanded that the Greek leaders, and the Greeks themselves, be punished for their insult to Achilles. (3) For Ptolemy has thought of nothing more suitable in glorification of what he calls Father of all and Depth, than what Homer has said of Zeus. (4) But rather, he has understood him to be "Zeus, as though he had got the notion from Homer. For" <one> may fairly say that when he was belching out such impudence, <he had> "Homer's apprehension" of Zeus and the Achaeans "rather than <that> of the Lord of all, who simultaneously with the conceiving of it has likewise accomplished that which he willed, and simultaneously with the willing also conceives of that which he willed, for he conceives when he wills, and wills when he conceives. (5) He is all conception, all will, all mind, all light, all eye, all ear, all fount of all that is good," and is subject to no vicissitudes. He is God, and not worried or at a loss like Depth, or Zeus. For in speaking of Depth, Ptolemy mimicked Homer speaking of Zeus.

2,6 But next, in further refutation of the fraud, I am going to subjoin and quote the seductive and dangerous words which were actually written by himself to a woman named Flora—lest anyone think that I am refuting the cheat from hearsay only, without becoming acquainted with his phony

[3] With Depth's "two consorts" cf., in a sense, Val. Exp. 24,19-22: He is [one] who appears [in Silence] and [he is] Mind of the All. [He was] dwelling secondarily with Life.

teaching first. For besides the things I have mentioned, he is not ashamed to blaspheme God's Law given through Moses as well. Here are his words:

Ptolemy's Letter to Flora

3,1 After noting the discrepant opinions about it, my good sister Flora, I think you too will see at once that not many before us have understood the Law given through Moses by accurate knowledge either of the Lawgiver himself or of his commandments. (2) For some say it was given by our God and Father but others, taking the direction opposite to theirs, insist that it was given by our adversary the devil, the author of corruption—as, indeed, they ascribe the creation of the world to him, calling him the father and maker of this universe.

3,3 <But> these parties <have certainly> stuttered in singing their rival songs and, each in their own way, have completely missed the truth of the matter. (4) It is evident, since logical, that the Law has not been made by the perfect God and Father, since it is imperfect and in need of fulfillment by another person, and contains ordinances inappropriate to the nature and intention of such a God. (5) Nor, again, <is it appropriate> to attribute to the iniquity of the adversary a Law which abolishes iniquity—<this must be the opinion of fools>, and persons who cannot draw inferences—in accordance with our Savior's words, "A house or city divided against itself cannot stand."[4]

3,6 And further, depriving the liars beforehand of their unfounded wisdom, the apostle says that the creation of the world is <the Savior's>, that all things were made by him and without him nothing is made,[5] and that creation is the work of a righteous God who hates iniquity, not of a god of corruption. <This latter> is the view of thoughtless persons who take no account of the Creator's providence and are blinded, not only in the eye of the soul, but in the eye of the body as well.

3,7 From the foregoing it will be plain to you that they have completely missed the truth. Each party has got into this predicament in its own way—the one through its ignorance of the God of justice; the other through ignorance of the Father of all, whom none but the only One who knows him has come and made known. (8) But as I have been vouchsafed <knowledge> of both, it is left to me to declare to you and accurately describe both the nature of the Law itself and the person by whom it was

[4] Matt 12:25
[5] Cf. John 1:1;3.

given, the lawgiver. I shall provide the proofs of <the> things I shall say from the words of our Savior, by which alone we are surely guided to the perception of the truth.

4,1 First, it must be understood that the whole of that Law which is contained in the five books of Moses has not been made by one legislator. I mean that it has not been made by God alone, but some of its provisions have been made by men. And the words of the Savior teach us that it is triply divided. (2) It is divided into (the words of) God himself and his legislation, but <it> is also <divided> into (the words of) Moses—not as God legislates through him, but as Moses too made certain provisions of his own notion. And it is divided into (the words of) the elders of the people, for it is plain that <they> too have inserted certain commandments of their own.

4,3 You may now learn how the truth of this can be proved from the words of the Savior. (4) In the Savior's discussion with those who were disputing with him about the bill of divorce—the bill which had been sanctioned by the Law—the Savior told them, "Moses for the hardness of your hearts permitted a man to divorce his wife. For from the beginning it was not so. For God," he said, "hath joined this pair together, and what the Lord hath joined," he said, "let not man put asunder."[6] (5) Here he proves that <the> Law of God, which forbids the separation of a wife from her husband, is one law; but the law of Moses, which permits this couple's separation because of the hardness of their hearts, is another.

4,6 Indeed, in this case Moses is giving a law contrary to God's, for separating is contrary to not <separating>. If, however, we examine Moses' purpose in making this law, we shall find that he made it not of his own choice but of necessity, owing to the frailty of those for whom the laws were made. (7) They could not honor God's intention if forbidden to divorce their wives with whom some were living unwillingly, and so risking being turned further to wickedness and consequent destruction. (8) On his own initiative then, to end this discontent by which they were risking destruction as well, Moses gave them a second law, the law of the bill of divorce, as though exchanging, in a pinch, a lesser evil for a greater. (9) Thus if they could not keep the former law, they would at least keep this, and not be turned to iniquities and evils from which their utter destruction would result. (10) This is Moses' intent in the instances in which he makes laws contrary to God's. Still it is undeniable that Moses' law is here shown to

[6] Matt 19:8;6

be other than God's, even if for the present we have proved it from (only) one example.

4,11 That certain traditions of the elders have been intermingled with the Law the Savior also makes plain. "For God said, Honor thy father and thy mother that it may be well with thee," he says. (12) "But ye," he says, speaking to the elders, "have said, That wherewith thou mightest be profited by me is a gift to God; and ye have nullified the Law of God by the tradition of you elders. (13) And Isaiah cried this out when he said, 'This people honoreth me with their lips, but their heart is far from me. But in vain they do worship me, teaching for doctrines the commandments of men.'"[7] (14) From these passages, then, it is plainly shown that that Law as a whole is divided into three. For in it we have found Moses' own legislation, the legislation of the elders, and the legislation of God himself. And this division of that Law as a whole which I have made here has made clear what in it is true.

5,1 But the one portion, the Law of God himself, is again divided into some three parts. It is divided into the pure legislation with no admixture of evil, which is properly termed the "law" which the Savior came not to destroy but to fulfill. (For that which he fulfilled was not foreign to him <but was in need of fulfillment>, for it was incomplete.) It is also divided into law mixed with inferior matter and injustice, which the Savior abolished as incongruous with his nature. (2) And it is divided also into the typical and allegorical legislation in the image of things that are spiritual and excellent. This the Savior transformed from the perceptible and phenomenal into the spiritual and invisible.

5,3 And the Law of God, the pure Law unmixed with inferior matter, is the Decalogue itself—those ten commandments engraved on the two tablets to prohibit what must be eschewed and enjoin what must be done. These were in need of fulfillment by the Savior, for though they contained the legislation in its pure form they were incomplete.

5,4 The law intemingled with injustice is the law which regards retribution and the requital of those who committed the prior injustice, and enjoins the knocking out of an eye for an eye and a tooth for a tooth, and the retribution of a murder with a murder.[8] For the second offender does no less of an injustice and commits the same act, changing it merely in its order. (5) In any case this commandment was and is just, though owing to

[7] Isa 29:13; Matt 15:4-9
[8] Cf. Lev 24:20.

the frailty of its recipients it was given in violation of the pure law. But it is not in accord with the nature and goodness of the Father of all. (6) It is perhaps appropriate, but is rather a matter of necessity. For in requiring the murderer to be murdered in retaliation, making a second law, and presiding over two murders after forbidding the one, he who opposed even the one murder by saying, "Thou shalt not kill"[9] was an unwitting victim of necessity. (7) Thus the Son who came from him has abolished this portion of the Law, while acknowledging that it too was a law of God—<just as> he has shown agreement with the old school, both in other matters and in his words, "It is God who said, He that curseth father or mother, let him die the death."[10]

5,8 But this is the typical portion of the Law, the part that has been made the image of things which are spiritual and excellent, I mean the laws of sacrifices, circumcision, the Sabbath, fasting, the Passover, the feast of unleavened bread and the like. (9) For all these, being images and allegories, were transformed when the truth appeared. Outwardly and in bodily observance they were abrogated but spiritually they were adopted, with the names remaining the same but the things altered. (10) For the Savior has commanded us to offer sacrifices, not of dumb animals or their odors but by means of spiritual hymns, praises, and thanksgiving, and of charity and acts of kindness to our neighbors. (11) He also desires that we have a circumcision, not of the bodily foreskin but of the spiritual heart—(12) <and> that we keep the Sabbath, for it is his will that we desist from evil works. (13) And that we fast—but it is his will that we keep not the bodily fast but the spiritual, which includes abstinence from all evil.

We do observe outward fasting however, since this can be of some use to the soul as well when done with reason—not in mimicry of someone or by custom, or for the sake of a day, as though a day were set aside <for> it. (14) At the same time it serves as a reminder of the true fast, so that those who are as yet unable to keep that may have a reminder of it through the outward fasting.

5,15 That both the Passover and Feast of Unleavened Bread were likewise images, Paul the apostle makes plain by saying, "As our Passover, Christ has been sacrificed," and, "that ye may be unleavened, not partaking of leaven"—by "leaven" here he means evil—"but that ye may be a new lump.[11]

[9] Exod 20:15
[10] Matt 15:4
[11] 1 Cor 5:7

6,1 Thus even the Law which is acknowledged to be God's is divided into three—into the part which is fulfilled by the Savior (for "Thou shalt not kill," "Thou shalt not commit adultery," and "Thou shalt not bear false witness" are included in his prohibition of anger, lust and oaths). (2) And also into the part that is annulled altogether, for "An eye for an eye and a tooth for a tooth,"[12] which is intermingled with injustice and itself contains an act of injustice, was annulled by the Savior through its opposites. (3) But opposites have the property of canceling each other: "For I say unto you that ye resist not evil by any means, but if a man smite thee, turn to him the other cheek also."[13] (4) There is also the division which has been transformed and altered from the physical to the spiritual—this allegorical legislation in the image of the things that are excellent. (5) For since the images and allegories were indicative of other things, they were rightly performed as long as the truth was not here. But once the truth is here we must do what is proper to the truth, not to the image.

6,6 The Savior's disciples have given proof of these divisions, and so has the apostle Paul. For our sakes he gave proof of the part which consists of images with (his remarks about) the Passover and Feast of Unleavened Bread, as we have said already. And of the part which consists of the law which is mixed with injustice by saying, "The law of commandments contained in ordinances is abolished."[14] And of the part which consists of the law with no admixture of inferior matter by saying, "The Law is holy, and the commandment holy and just and good."[15]

7,1 I think you have been given sufficient proof, so far as this can be done concisely, of the human legislation which has invaded the Law, and of God's Law itself with its triple division. (2) It remains for me to say who this God is who has made the Law. But I feel that this too has been shown you in my earlier remarks, if you have listened attentively. (3) If, as we have explained, the Law was not given by the perfect God himself, and certainly not by the devil—it is not proper even to say this—then this lawgiver is someone other than these. (4) But this is the demiurge and maker of this entire world and everything in it. As he differs from the essences of the other two <and> stands in between them, he may properly be titled "The Intermediate." (5) And if, by his own nature, the perfect God is good—as indeed he is, for our Savior has declared that his Father, whom he made

[12] Matt 5:38
[13] Matt 5:39
[14] Cf. Eph. 2:15.
[15] Rom 7:12

manifest, is the one and only good God—[16] and if a god of the adversary's nature is evil and is marked as wicked by his injustice—then a God who stands between them, and is neither good[17] nor, certainly, evil or unjust, may properly be called "just,"[18] being the arbiter of his sort of justice.

7,6 As he is generate, not ingenerate, this God will naturally be weaker than the perfect God and inferior to his righteousness (there is one Ingenerate, the Father, of whom are all things since all things, each in its own way, have been framed by him. But he will be greater and possessed of more authority than the adversary, and will be of an essence and nature different from the essence of either of these. (7) For the essence of the adversary is corruption and darkness, since he is material and composite. The essence of the unbegotten Father of all is incorruption and self-existent light, simple and uniform. And the essence of this God has shown a sort of dual capacity, but in himself he is the image of the better.

7,8 Do not let this disturb you for now, even though you desire to learn how these natures, that of corruption and that <of> the intermediate, natures which differ in kind, arose from one first principle of all, one which is <simple> and is confessed and believed by us, the unbegotten, imperishable and good—though it is the nature of the good to beget and bring forth its like and its own kind. (9) God willing, you shall learn both their origin and their generation next, since you are adjudged worthy of the apostolic tradition which I have received in my turn, together with the assessment of all its statements by the standard of our Savior's teaching.

7,10 I have not begrudged[19] you these things which have been said in a few words, my sister Flora, and have set forth the brief statement of them, at the same time making the matter sufficiently plain. They will be of the utmost value to you in what follows as well, if, like good soil, hospitable to fertile seeds, you bear the fruit which is their product.

This concludes the letter to Flora

8,1 Who can put up with these words and the idiocy of this charlatan and his supporters—I mean Ptolemy and his circle, who concoct fabrications at such length and baste them together? (2) None of the ancient tragic poets, nor the imitative ones after them—I mean Philistion, and Diogenes who

---

[16] Cf. Matt. 19:17;

[17] This is said of the ὑλικὸς θεός, the καλὸς κόσμος at Corp. Herm. 10.10.

[18] Cf. Cod. Tch. James 18,16-20: But watch out, because the just God is angry, for you have been a servant to him, and that is why you received the name, "James the Just."

[19] Adopting Petavius' conjecture, ἐφθόνησα, for text ἠτόνησα

composed incredible yarns, or all the others who wrote the myths down and recited them, (3) could make up as much falsehood as these people have manufactured horrors for themselves in their impudent attack on their own life, and have smothered their converts' minds with foolish questions and endless genealogies. (4) In fact they themselves did not understand what was under their noses, and yet they professed to survey the heavens with measurements of some sort, and adopted the profession of midwives as though for some heavenly mothers—for non-existent mothers as though they existed. (5) When one hears this from them—if he is a complete fool—he will think that he has learned something sublime from them and easily be swept off his feet by the lie. (Scripture says, "Every bird flocketh with its kind, and a man will cleave to his like.")[20] (6) But if a person of understanding and sound reason should happen on them he will laugh at so much silliness, and from the very subject of the things they say will know the refutation of them. For they are convicted in every way of arming their useless labor's lies against themselves.

8,7 Where did you learn Depth's dimensions, you gentleman and lady Ptolemaeans? And the pregnant mothers' deliveries, and the reasons they got pregnant? (8) You profess to give us the knowledge, as though you had been there and seen the origins of the heavenly beings, as though you were in existence before your so-called Depth himself. (9) But no prophet has ever said this, not Moses himself, not the prophets before him, not the prophets after him, not the evangelists, not the apostles—unless you mean the works of heathen mythology by Orpheus, Hesiod, Hicesius and Stesichorus, in whose writings the generations of men have been turned into names of gods, and human doings made into dramatic poetry. (10) For they too held beliefs of this kind <and>, by making gods of Zeus, Rhea, Hera, Athena, Apollo and Aphrodite and honoring the children of their wickedness, they pushed the world into a delusion of polytheism and idolatry.

8,11 But I won't have much further need for the refutation and rebuttal of you and your kind, Ptolemy, since your forebears have already received the refutation in sufficient measure. Since I have achieved your disgrace through the things I have said, I am going over imposture of the others—calling on God as the aid of my meager ability so that, in every people, I may discover the doctrine they have wickedly invented and make a spectacle of it. And I ask God's grace for my zealous undertaking.

---

[20] Sir 13:16

9,1 However, Ptolemy, not to leave unchallenged the three little literary efforts, the ones you boasted of sending to your girlfriend Flora—(the teachings of serpents always "deceive silly women laden with sins,"[21] as the apostle said).—I have quoted the words themselves here at the right time, and will next give their corresponding refutation—an essential one, or the the root of your tare-like crop might be left.

9,2 You claim that the Law has three divisions, Mister, and that one owes something to God, but one comes from Moses and one from the elders. (3) You can't show <the part> you think was written by the elders; this much is plain. The traditions of the elders are nowhere to be found in the Law. From your ignorance both of the books and of the truth you are imagining these by misrepresenting <and altering> the consequences of every kind of accurate knowledge. (4) The traditions of the elders are called "repetitions"[22] by the Jews, and there are four of them. One is circulated in the name of Moses, a second in that of the person named Rabbi Aqiba, a third of Adda or Judah, and a fourth of the sons of Hasmonaeus. (5) Where, you trouble-maker with your erratic judgment, can you show that the words mentioned by the Savior—"He who shall say to his father Korban, that is, a gift, he shall profit nothing from him"[23]—were said in the five books of the Pentateuch and God's legislation? (6) You can't show it. Your argument has failed then, since the saying is nowhere to be found in the Pentateuch, and you have deceived your dupe Flora for nothing.

9,7 And neither were the laws given by Moses given independently of God. They came from God through Moses, as is shown by the Savior's own verification (of the fact). The very texts you have brought forward, you have assembled against yourself. (8) In the Gospel the Lord says, "Moses wrote for the hardness of your hearts."[24] But what Moses wrote, he did not write independently of God's will; his legislation was inspired by the Holy Spirit.

9,9 For the Lord in the Gospel said, "That which God hath joined together, let not man put asunder." And to let us know how God joined them, he explained it fully <by affixing> the saying, "For this cause shall a man leave his father and his mother and shall cleave to his wife, and they twain shall be one flesh." (10) He then adds, "That which *God* hath joined

[21] 2 Tim 3:6
[22] δευτερώσεις, in Hebrew, mishnahs
[23] Matt 19:6
[24] Matt 19:8

together, let not man put asunder[25]—although the Lord said nothing like this at the time when he formed Adam and Eve, but only, "Let us make him an helpmeet like himself.[26]" (11) Those words were said by Adam when he awoke and said, "This is now bone of my bone and flesh of my flesh. She shall be called wife, for she was taken out of her husband."[27]—And then *he* says, "Therefore shall a man leave his father and his mother, and shall cleave unto his wife, and they twain shall be one flesh."[28]

9,12 Now since God did not say this but Adam did, and yet the Lord in the Gospel testifies that the words spoken through Adam were God's, by his statement itself he proved that in the one case[29] Adam spoke but uttered the words by God's will, while in this one[30] Moses made a law because God had commanded the legislation. (13) And that the making of laws is God's business; this is plain. But God makes laws everywhere, some temporary, some typical, and some to reveal the good things to come, whose fulfillment our Lord Jesus Christ, when he had come, made known in the Gospel.

10,1 But I shall take up your other distinction of gods—again, a triple distinction—and show that this too is slander on your part and simply the work of a charlatan. (2) What sort of third God do we have here—made up of two likenesses although he is neither of the two, having no wickedness or injustice, as you said, and no goodness or luminous essence either, but right in between, "just?" (3) As you are in fact strange to all justice you naturally do not know what justice is, and so you think it is something other than goodness. You'll get good and refuted you tamperer, you stranger to the truth! Justice comes from nowhere but from goodness, and no one can become good other than by being just.

10,4 And so, to praise the legislation and its just men, the Lord said, "Ye garnish the tombs of the prophets, and build the sepulchres of the just, and your fathers killed them."[31] But where have prophets and just men come from, if not from the Father's goodness? (5) And, to prove that the just man belongs in the category of goodness, he said, "Be ye like unto your Father which is in heaven, for he maketh his sun to rise on good and evil, and sendeth rain on just and unjust,"[32] to make it plain that just is good and good is just, and that evil is unjust, and unjust, evil.

---

[25] Matt 19:6
[26] Gen 2:18
[27] Gen 2:23
[28] Gen 2:24
[29] Gen 2:24
[30] Cf. Deut 24:1.
[31] Matt 23:29; Luke 11:47
[32] Matt 5:45

10,6 Nor can you prove the Law's intermixture (with evil) of which you spoke. You have been caught making a false accusation against the Law by your ascription of some intermixture to it because the Law has said, "eye for eye and tooth for tooth,"[33] and because the Law murders the murderer. (7) But it will be shown, from our Lord Jesus Christ's own treatment of the matter, that there was no intermixture, but that the legislation was the same and had the same effect as the commandment given by the Savior, "If a man smite thee on the right cheek, turn to him the other also."[34] (8) For the Law <too> ensured this long ago by saying "an eye for an eye," or in other words, "Turn your other cheek to him." To avoid what would happen to him if he struck a blow, a man would present his cheek to the one who was striking him—knowing that if he put an eye out, he would suffer the same because of the Law.

11,1 A father who wishes to discipline his children progresses with the discipline by suiting it to each age. He surely does not discipline a little baby like a boy, a boy like a youth, or a youth like a grown man. (2) An infant is disciplined with a finger, an older child with the slap of a hand, a boy with a strap, and a youth with a cane. But by law a man is punished with the sword for the more serious offenses. Thus the Lord too, in consequence, made the laws that were suitable for each generation. (3) He chastened the earlier one with fear, as though he were speaking with little children who did not know the power of the Holy Spirit, but he considered full grown adults worthy of full mysteries. (4) For in the Gospel as well, in many places, he <tells> the disciples something like, "Ye know not what I do, but ye shall know hereafter[35]—that is, "when you grow up." And again, "They knew not until he was risen from the dead."[36] (5) And Paul says, "Ye were not able, neither yet are ye able,"[37] to show that commandments become more advanced as time goes on—the same ones, but changed to another form, formulated in one way for the young; in another for the more mature.

11,6 For when the Law enjoined "an eye for an eye,"[38] it did not tell them, "Put one eye out after another," but, "If someone puts an eye out, the eye of the one who put it out will be put out." And to spare his own body, everyone would present his cheek to be struck, and not strike himself. (7) And what is now stated clearly in the Gospel was observed from that

[33] Lev 24:17;20
[34] Matt 5:39
[35] John 13:7
[36] John 2:22
[37] 1 Cor 3:2
[38] Lev 24:20

time on—by compulsion then, as though children were being trained, but now by choice, since adults are being pesuaded.

11,8 But if you claim that this is an involvement—to say "an eye for an eye" and have a murderer put to death—then observe! Even of the day of judgment we see the Savior saying, "His Lord shall come"—but he was saying this of himself, since he is Lord of all—and he says, "and cut the servant himself asunder and appoint his portion with the unbelievers."[39] In other words, by quibbling about words again you are taking up arms even against the Savior; and you would say that he is not good but just—although he is begotten of a good Father, and is good himself—and is different from the Father. (10) So you are capable of separating even him from the nature of the Father, Mister—you who appear before us once more as a dissector and surveyor of the laws, dividing everything into threes!

11,11 And by saying that some things in the Law are written allegorically, as types, you have touched on little bits of the truth, so that with the little bits you can fool people in the other points. (12) "These things" indeed "happened unto them typically, and were written for our admonition on whom the ends of the ages have come"[40] <as> the most holy apostle says, speaking of circumcision, the Sabbath and so on. (13) If only you would tell the truth about everything, and not inflict your nonexistent third, intermediate God on us any more—or rather, not inflict him on yourself any more, and on your dupes!

12,1 But by now, you tramp, I feel that enough has also been said about your remarks. Having refuted them I shall go to the remaining sects, calling as usual on the same God to aid my meager ability in making plain the rebuttal of every distorted heresy. (2) For by what has been said it has been shown that Ptolemy deceived Flora and others with her with a letter as though he had risen out of the sea, summoning sharks and a viper with his own piping. (3) But by entangling him in the net of the truth—the symbolic meaning of which the Lord in the Gospel declared to be the kingdom of heaven—and by exposing him as one of the bad fish by bringing his unsound words to light, we have overcome him with the teaching of the true faith. (4) Having thrashed him by the power of God let us give thanks to God ourselves, and set ourselves, as I said, to go on to the rest as well.

---

[39] Matt 24:50-51

[40] 1 Cor 10:11

ANACEPHALAEOSIS III

Here, also, are the contents of the third Section of the first Volume, which contains thirteen Sects.

34,1 34. Marcosians. A certain Marcus was Colorbasus' fellow student, and he too introduces two first principles. He denies the resurrection of the dead and initiates his female dupes <by creatingc some sort of illusions with chalices <which are turned> dark blue, and purple, by incantation. (2) Like Valentinus, he too holds that everything <is made up> of the twenty-four sounds of the alphabet.

35,1 35. Colorbasus. Colorbasus likewise described the same things but differed somewhat from the other sects, I mean those of Marcus and Valentinus, and taught the emanations and ogdoads differently.

36,1 36. Heracleonites too are carried away with the mythology of the ogdoads, but differently from Marcus, Ptolemy, Valentinus and the others. (2) Moreover, like Marcus they "redeem" their dying members at the end with oil, balsam and water, and pronounce certain Hebrew invocations over the head of the one being supposedly redeemed.

37,1 37. Ophites, the persons who honor the serpent and regard him as Christ, and have an actual snake, the familiar reptile, in a basket of some sort.

38,1 38. Cainites who, together with their predecessors, similarly repudiate the Law and the One who spoke in the Law, deny the resurrection of the flesh and honor Cain, saying that he belongs to the stronger power. (2) But together with him they also deify Judas, together with the company of Korah, Dathan, Abiram, and the Sodomites besides.

39,1 39. Sethians. These in turn honor Seth and claim that he is the child of the Mother on high, who repented of having emitted Cain and then, after the banishment of Cain and the killing of Abel, had congress with the Father on high and, as a pure seed, bore Seth, from whom all humanity was then derived. (2) They too taught about first principles and authorities, and all the doctrines the others taught.

40,1 40. Archontics. These in turn trace the universe to many archons and say that all that has come to be has come from them. And they are also guilty of certain shameful behavior. (2) They reject the resurrection of the flesh and slander the Old Testament. But they use both the Old and the New Testaments, though they handle every saying to suit themselves.

41,1 41. Cerdonians, founded by Cerdo, <who> got his share of the imposture in succession from Heracleon but added to the deceit. He moved from Syria to Rome and preached his doctrine during the episcopate of Hyginus. (2) He declares that two first principles are in opposition to one another, and that Christ is not begotten. He likewise repudiates the resurrection of the dead and the Old Testament.

42,1 42. Marcionites. Marcion of Pontus was the son of a bishop, but he seduced a virgin and went into exile because he was excommunicated by his own father. (2) Arriving at Rome he asked for penance from the <elders> of the time. Since he could not get it he grew angry and taught doctrines contrary to the faith by introducing three first principles, a good, a just and an evil, and saying that the New Testament is foreign to the Old, and to the One who spoke in it.

42,3 He rejects the resurrection of the flesh and administers not just one baptism, but even two and three after lapses into sin. When catechumens die other Marcionites are baptized for them. He unhesitantly allows even women to administer supposed baptism.

43,1 43. Lucianists. An ancient Lucian—not the modern one who was born in Constantine's time—taught doctrines in all respects like Marcion's. But he too, if you please, has further doctrines different from Marcion's.

44,1 44. Apelleans. This Apelles too, like Marcion and Lucian, disparages all of creation and the creator. (2) But unlike them he did not teach three first principles but one first principle and one God, supernal and unnameable, and that he, the one God, has made another. And this God who had been made turned out to be bad, and in his badness made the world.

45,1 45. Severians. A certain Severus in turn, a follower of Apelles, rejects wine and the vine and relates the myth that it was born of the dragon-like Satan and earth, who had had relations with each other. (2) He rejects woman, claiming that she belongs to the left hand power. (3) He introduces certain names of archons as well as certain uncanonical books. Like the other sects he rejects the resurrection of the flesh and the Old Testament.

46,1 46. Tatianists. Tatian flourished in company with the holy martyr Justin who was also a philosopher. But after Justin, the martyr and philosopher, died, Tatian unfortunately became acquainted with Marcion's doctrines, was instructed by him, and both taught the same doctrines as he and added others besides his. He is said to have come from Mesopotamia.

This will summarize the three Sections of Volume One, containing forty-six sects.

34.

Against Marcosians.[1] *Number fourteen, but thirty-four of the series*

1,1[2] A certain Marcus, the founder of the so-called Marcosians, came from the Gnostics and dared to vomit evils into the world that were different from theirs. For he succeeded Secundus, Epiphanes, Ptolemy and Valentinus, but was inspired to gather a further crowd of tramps. (2) For the wretch attracted female and male dupes of his own, and was supposed to be a corrector of the cheats we have mentioned since he was the most adept in magical trickery. (3) But because he deceived all these men and women into regarding him as the most gnostic of all and possessed of the greatest power from the unseen, ineffable realms, he has truly been shown to be the forerunner of the Antichrist. (4) For by combining Anaxilaus' jokes with the villainy of the so-called magicians, and deceiving and bewitching the people who saw and trusted him with these, he drove them to distraction—as his followers still manage to do, even today.

1,5 The people who see the <effects> that have been produced by jugglery suppose that miracles of some sort are being performed by the hands of Marcus and such Marcosians as do these things. (6) For they have lost their minds themselves and, because they do not know how to evaluate it, they do not see that his stunt, as we might call it, has been performed by magic. For they have become completely cracked themselves from being carried away with an wrong opinion.

1,7 It is said that they prepare three chalices of white vinegar mixed with white wine, and during the incantation Marcus gives, his supposed eucharistic prayer, these are suddenly transformed, with one <turning> red as blood, another purple, and another dark blue. (8) But for my part, so as not to commit myself to a second hard task I feel I should be content with the work written against Marcus himself and his successors by the most holy and blessed Irenaeus. I hasten to publish this here word for word, and it runs as follows. For St. Irenaeus himself says the following in his disclosure of the things they did:

---

[1] Sect 34 is entirely dependent upon Iren. 1.13.1-21.4, which it quotes verbatim. Hipp. Refut. 6.39.1ff also reproduces Irenaeus. PsT 5 which mentions Colorbasus in combination with Marcus, and Fil. 42, are based on Hipp. Synt. but give no detalis which are significantly different from Irenaeus.

[2] 1.1-3 is paraphrased from Iren. 1.13.1.

From the writings of St. Irenaeus[3]

2,1 Pretending to consecrate liquids mixed with wine and spinning his invocation out at length, he makes them turn purple and scarlet. It thus seems that Grace, from the realms above the universe, is shedding drops of her blood into his cup at his invocation. And the onlookers are most eager for a taste of that drink, so that the Grace who is being summoned by this magician may shower on them as well.

2,2 Again, he would hand chalices already mixed to women and tell them to consecrate them with him standing by. And when they had, he would bring another chalice out, much larger than the one his dupe had consecrated, empty the smaller one consecrated by the woman into the one he had brought in <and say the eucharistic prayer> adding the words, (3) "May she that is before all, the inconceivable and ineffable Grace, fill thine inner man and increase in thee her knowledge, by sowing the grain of the mustard seed in the good ground." (4) And after he had said things of this sort and had driven the wretched woman to madness it would appear that he was a wonder worker, for the big chalice would be filled from the little one so as even to overflow from it. And by doing other things quite like these he has fooled many people completely and won them to his following.

2,5 He probably has a familiar spirit too, through which he both appears to prophesy himself, and causes such women as he considers worthy of <becoming> participants in his grace to prophesy. (6) (He spends most of his time on women, and the best-dressed, highest-ranking and wealthiest of these.) In the effort to get them in his power he often tells them in flattering terms, "I desire to share my grace with you, for the Father of all continually beholds your angel before his face. But the Majesty's place is in us; we must be restored to the One. (7) First receive Grace from me and through me. Prepare yourself as a bride awaiting her bridegroom, that you may be what I am, and I what you are. Plant the seed of the light in your bridal chamber.[4] Receive the bridegroom from me; contain him and be contained in him. Lo, Grace has descended upon you; open your mouth and prophesy!"

2,8 But if the woman answers, "I have never prophesied and don't know how," he gives another set of invocations to his dupe's consternation,

---

[3] This begins the quotation of Iren. 1.13.1-21.4.

[4] In Gos. Phil. the bridal chamber may mean baptism, the entire Christian initiation rite, or the kingdom of God. At 69,1-70,3 it might mean the eucharist. For other occurrences of the term see 67,23-26; 74,13-24; 82,23-29. On the subject see Schenke, *Philippus-Evangelium*. See also Exeg. Soul 132,12-26.

and tells her, "Open your mouth <and> say any old thing, and you will be prophesying!"

2,9 And made conceited and feather-brained by this, fevered in soul with the expectation that she is going to prophesy, with her heart beating harder than it should, she (10) will pluck up the courage to babble silly things at random—all vainly and impudently, since she has been made feverish by a vain spirit. (As a greater man than I has said of such <prophets>, "An impudent and shameless thing is a soul made feverish by empty air.") (11) And from then on she takes herself for a prophetess and is grateful to Marcus for bestowing his own grace on her, and attempts to repay him not only with the gift of her money—he has amassed considerable wealth in this way—but with bodily union too. For she is eager to be altogether united with him, so as to be restored to the One with him.

2,12 Already—though he took care to cajole them like the rest by telling them to prophesy—some of the more faithful women, who fear God and were not fooled, have spat, cursed, and abandoned such a charlatan as this, <who pretends to breathe something divine (into them)>. (13) They know perfectly well that prophecy is not engendered in men by the sorcerer Marcus. Those to whom God sends his grace from above possess prophecy as a divine gift and speak where and when God wills, not when Marcus says to. (14) A thing that gives an order is greater and more authoritative than a thing that is given an order, since the one takes precedence while the other is subject. Hence if Marcus or anyone else, orders prophecy—and at their dinners they make a regular game of having each other prophesy <by> lot, and divine for them as their passions dictate—then, though he is only a man, the one who orders it is greater than the prophetic spirit and possessed of more authority. But that is not possible. (15) Such spirits as are at their bidding and speak when they choose, are earthy and feeble, although presumptuous and impudent. They are sent by Satan for the deception and ruin of those who fail to maintain in its vigor the faith they received through the church at the outset.

3,1 But that Marcus administers philtres and love-potions to some if not all of the women in order to outrage their bodies as well, they have often confessed on returning to God's church—and to having been corrupted in body by him, and having loved him with great passion. (2) Even one of our deacons in Asia had this misfortune because he welcomed Marcus into his home. His wife was a handsome woman, and she was seduced both in mind and body by this sorcerer, and followed him for a long time. (3) Then, when the brethren had brought her to repentance with great difficulty, she spent the rest of her life in confession, mourning and lamenting her seduction by the magician.

3,4 Certain of his disciples too, who wander about in the same area, have deceived and seduced many women by proclaiming themselves so perfect that no one can equal the greatness of their knowledge—not even Paul or Peter or any other apostle. (5) (They) claim that <they> know more than everyone, that they alone have drunk in the greatness of the knowledge of the ineffable power, and that they are higher than any power. (6) Hence they can do everything freely[5] and have no fear in anything. Because of their redemption they have become untouchable by the judge, and invisible to him. But even if he were to apprehend them they would stand before him with their redemption and say this:[6]

3,7 "O Counselor of God and the primordial mysterious Silence, <through whom> the Majesties, who ever behold the Father's face, draw their forms heavenward with thee as their leader and guide,—the forms that First Progenitor's goodness, that audacious one, imagined,[7]—who then had a dreamlike notion of the things on high and emitted us <in their image>—(8) Lo, the judge is nigh and the herald bids me offer my defense. But do thou, as understanding the case of us both, render an account for <us> both, as one, to the judge!" (9) And the Mother hears them without delay and puts Homer's helmet of invisibility on them, so that they escape the judge unseen,[8] and drawing them up instantly conducts them to the marriage chamber and gives them to their bridegrooms.

3,10 By saying and doing such things they have completely fooled many women in our own area, the Rhone valley, as well. Branded in conscience some of these women even make open confession. Others, who are ashamed to do this but have quietly <withdrawn> themselves somehow, despair of God's life and in some cases have become entirely apostate; while others vacillate, in the proverbial predicament of being neither in nor out—having this fruit from the seed of the children of knowledge!

4,1 This Marcus <then>, says that he and he alone in his uniqueness has become the womb and receptacle of Colorbasus' Silence and brought forth the actual <seed> of Defect,[9] which has somehow been sown in him here. (2) The all-sublime Tetrad has descended to him herself, from the invisible, ineffable realms, in feminine form[10]—because the world

---

[5] Cf. Corp. Herm. 9.4, πάντα γὰρ τῷ τοιούτῳ, κἂν τοῖς ἄλλοις τὰ κακά, ἀγαθά ἐστί.
[6] See p. 104 n. 72.
[7] Cf. "those that had come forth from him in an imaginary way" Tri. Trac. 78,6-7.
[8] Cf. Gos. Phil. 70,5-9; 76,22-29.
[9] This may be the source of Epiph's confusion about "Defect." See p. 170 n. 9.
[10] Tri. Prot. 42,17-18: Now I have come the second time in the likeness of a female and

could not bear her masculine one, he says—disclosed who she was and to him and him alone explained the origin of all things, which she had never revealed to any god or man, speaking as follows:

4,3[11] "When, at the first, the Father <of whom none is the father>, who is inconceivable and without essence, who is neither male nor female, willed that his unutterability become utterable and his invisibility be given form,[12] he opened his mouth and uttered a word[13] like himself. This stood by him and showed him what he was, itself manifest as a form of the invisible.[14] (4) But the pronunciation of the name was as follows: He spoke the first word of his name, which was a "beginning," and its syllable was of four sounds. <And> he subjoined the second syllable, and it too was of four sounds. Next he pronounced the third, and it was a syllable of ten sounds. And he spoke the final one, and it was of twelve sounds. The pronouncing of the entire name, then, became thirty sounds but four syllables.

4,5[15] "Each of the sounds has its own letters, its own impress, and its own pronunciation, forms and representations. There is not one of them that sees the form of that of which it is a sound. Nor can it know it[16] nor, certainly, the pronunciation of its neighbor but, as though it were pronouncing the All, it thinks that what <it> pronounces names the whole. (6) For though each of them is a part of the whole, it makes its own sound as though it had named the All, and does not stop making it until, with its one utterance, it reaches the last letter of the last sound."

4,7 She said that the restoration of all things will come when all have arrived at the one letter, and sound the same exclamation. She supposed that "Amen," when we say it together, is an image of this exclamation. It is the utterances which give form to the Aeon which has no essence and is ingenerate. And they are forms which the Lord has termed "angels" and continually behold the Father's face.[17] (8) She called the common, spoken

---

have spoken with them; Tri. Trac. 64,32-37: if he had formerly revealed himself suddenly to all the exalted ones among the aeons who had come forth from him, they would have perished.

[11] With 4,3-9 cf. Hipp. Refut. 6.42.2-45.1.

[12] Cf. Tri. Trac. 5;7,24-31; 66,13-19; 67,18-19.

[13] The Son is "the word of [the] unutterable" at Tri. Trac. 66,15-16. Perhaps cf. Thunder 14,9-15.

[14] The First Father beholds himself within himself at Eug. 74,21-75,12 = SJC 98,24-99,13.

[15] With what follows perhaps cf. Thunder 20,32-35: I am the name of the sound, and the sound of the name. I am the sign of the letter and the designation of the division.

[16] Cf. the ignorance of the aeons at Tri. Trac. 60,16-26; 72,22-29. But unlike the sounds here, the aeons are said not to speak.

[17] Cf. Matt 18:10.

names of the sounds Aeons, words, roots, seeds, fullnesses and fruits, but said that the individual names peculiar to each one are observably included in the church's name.

4,9 The last letter of the <last> of these sounds sent forth its voice. <The> echo of it came forth in the image of the sounds, and generated sounds of its own. From these, she says, the things here have been reconstituted,[18] and the things before them generated. (10) But the letter itself, she said, whose echo was simultaneous with the echo below, was taken up on high by its own syllable for the completion of the whole.[19] The echo, as though cast outside, has remained below.

4,11 The sound itself, she says, from which the letter, together with its own pronunciation, came below, is of thirty letters. Each of the thirty letters contains other letters, the ones by which the letter's name is said. (12) And the other letters are named with other letters in turn, and the others with others, so that the number of the letters is infinite. But you can understand this better from the following example:

5,1 The sound, delta, contains five letters: delta itself, epsilon, lamda, tau and alpha. These letters, in turn, are written with other letters and the others with others. (2) Now if the entire essence of the delta is infinite, with other letters continually generating others and succeeding each other, how much greater than that sound is the sea of the letters! (3) And if the one letter is infinite in this way, see the depth of the letters of the whole name of which Marcus' Silence held that First Progenitor is made! (4) Hence the Father, who knows that nothing can contain the name, has permitted each of the sounds—which he also calls Aeons—to cry its own pronunciation aloud, since one cannot pronounce the whole.

5,5 After explaining this to him Tetrad said, "Now I wish to show you the Truth herself. I have brought her down from the habitations on high so that you may see her naked and observe her beauty—hear her speak, moreover, and admire her wisdom. (6) See her head, alpha and omega, at the top. Her neck, beta and psi. Her shoulders and arms, gamma and chi. Her breasts, delta and phi. Her diaphragm, epsilon and ypsilon. Her belly, zeta and tau. Her privy parts, eta and sigma. Her thighs, theta and rho. Her knees, iota and pi. Her shins, kappa and omicron. Her ankles, lamda and xi. Her feet, mu and nu." This, according to the sorcerer, is the body

[18] διακεκοσμῆσθαι, the Stoic term for the reconstitution of the universe after its destruction by fire, see Hipp. Refut. Also possible is γεγεννῆσθαι.

[19] Cf. Tri. Trac. 86,4-15: the one who ran on high; Mars. 9,28-10,2: [the] invisible [Spirit] ran up to his place.

of "Truth," this is the form of the sound, this is the impress of the letter. (7) He also calls this sound "Man," and says it is the source of all speech, the origin of every sound, the utterance of everything unutterable, and the mouth of the Silence who cannot be spoken of.

5,8 "And this is her body. But raising <the> thought of your mind aloft, hear from the Truth's own mouth the self-begetting utterance, dispenser of fatherly bounty."

6,1 When Tetrad had said this, Truth looked at him, opened her mouth, and spoke a word. But the word was a name, and the name was the one we know and say, "Christ Jesus." And after naming it she fell silent at once. (2) But while Marcus was waiting for her to say something further, Tetrad came forward again and said, (3) "How trivial you considered the word you heard from the lips of Truth! The one you know, and think you <have> always <had>, is not a name. You have only a sound; you do not know its meaning.[20] (4) 'Jesous' is a notable[21] name of six letters known by all who are called. But the name as known to the Aeons of the Pleroma is complex, and is of a different form and a different impression, known by those brethren whose Majesties are always in its presence.[22]

6,5 "Learn, then, that these twenty-four letters of your alphabet are effluences in the image of the three powers which comprise the sum total of the powers on high. (6)[23] Regard the nine mute consonants as images of the Father and Truth, for they are "mute"—that is, ineffable and unutterable. (7) Regard the voiced consonants, of which there are eight, as images of Word and Life because of their being as it were between the mutes and vowels and receiving the effluence of the ones above them, and the vapor of the ones below. (8) But regard the vowels, of which in turn there are seven, as images of Man and Church; since it was through Man that <the> voice came forth and gave form to the whole. For the echo of the voice provided a form for them.

6,9 <Thus> there are Word and Life with the eight letters, Man and Church with the seven, and Father and Truth with the nine. (10) But the number that had run away in the Father came down upon the sum that lacked (a number). It was sent to the sum from which it had been parted to remedy the situation, so that the equality of the sums, being uniform,

---

[20] At Gos. Phil. 53,23-54,5 all names for holy things as they are "heard in the world" are said to be "deceptive."

[21] ἐπίσημον, the name of the digamma, or six. See below, especially at 7,1.

[22] Cf. Matt 18:10.

[23] A comparable though unrelated discussion of the letters of the alphabet, including a ranking of their importance, is found at Mars. 25,17-34,19.

would yield one value from all in all cases. (11) And thus the sum of seven acquired the value of eight, and the <three> spaces became correspondent with the numbers, since they were ogdoads. Added in three operations they gave the sum of twenty-four."

6,12 But when the three sounds which Marcus himself says are paired with the three values—that is, of (the) six from which the twenty-four sounds flowed out—are multiplied fourfold by the number of the ineffable tetrad, they yield the same total as those (24 sounds) which Marcus says are the number of the unnameable. (13) They (i.e., the three sounds) are worn by the three values in the likeness of the invisible. Our double letters are images of images of these sounds; and when they are included with the twenty-four sounds (of the alphabet) they give <the> sum of the thirty (Aeons), by the value which is proportionate (to the Aeons' value).

7,1 Marcus says that as the fruit of this computation and this dispensation there has appeared, in the likeness of its image, the One who went up the mountain fourth after the six days and became the sixth, and who came down and was held fast on the seventh—a notable (ἐπίσημον) ogdoad and containing in himself the full total of the sounds. (2) When he came for baptism the descent of the dove, which is omega and alpha, made <him> manifest, for its sum is 801.[24]

7,3 Also for this reason Moses has said that man was created on the sixth day. The dispensation <of the passion> also <took place> on the sixth day; for <on the sixth day>, the day of <the> preparation, the last man appeared for the restoration of the first.[25] The sixth hour, at which he was nailed to the tree, is also the beginning and end of this dispensation.[26] (4) For because the perfect Mind, knowing the number six with its power of creation and regeneration, is showing the sons of light its restoration to itself by itself through the appearance of the episemon. This, he says, is why the double letters have the episemon as their total. For combined with the twenty-four sounds, the episemon has completed the thirty-letter name.

7,5 "As its minister this number has employed the quantity of seven,"[27] so says Marcus' Silence, "so that the fruit of its self-willed will may be made manifest. But for the present," she says, "understand this total of six as the one who is formed on the model of the episemon, was as it were divided

[24] Cf. PsT 5.1-2; Fil. 42.2.

[25] I.e., "last man" (= episemon, six) plus "last," plus "first" = ogdoad, eight.

[26] Six plus "beginning" plus "end" = eight.

[27] This is intended to account for the seven heavens or planets, which do not fit Marcus' scheme of sixes and eights. See immediately below.

or cut in two, and remained outside[28]—who, through an emanation from himself, has by his own power and wisdom quickened this world of the seven values[29] which is patterned after the value of the hebdomad, and who has been designated the soul of the visible universe.

7,6 "For his part he does this work as a work performed by his own choice; but since they (i.e., the seven vowel sounds) serve the Mother's Purpose,[30] they are imitations of the inimitable. (7)[31] And the first heaven utters the alpha, the next, the epsilon, the third, <the> eta. The fourth and midmost of the seven, pronounces the value of the iota, the fifth, the omicron, the sixth, the ypsilon. But the seventh, and fourth from the middle, cries out the sound, omega," as Marcus' Silence affirms, who talks all sorts of nonsense but says nothing that is true. (8) "These values," she says, "all ring out together in unison and glorify him by whom they were emitted; and the glory of the sound is sent to First Progenitor. But the echo of this praise drifts earthward," she says, "to become that which forms and generates the things on earth."

7,9 She gives her proof of this from the new-born babes, whose soul, as they issue from the womb, cries out the echo of each of these sounds. Thus, as the seven values glorify the Word, so the soul in infants glorifies him by weeping and wailing <like> Marcus. (10) David, also, has said, "Out of the mouths of babes and sucklings hast thou perfected praise,"[32] on this account, and again, "The heavens declare the glory of God."[33] And thus, when a soul is in trouble and misfortune, to purge itself it cries, "Oh!" as a sign of praise, so that the soul on high will recognize its kinship with it and send it aid.

8,1 And these were the foolish things he said about this whole name which is made of thirty letters, and about Depth, who grew from its letters. And further, about the body of Truth <with> its twelve members <each> composed of two letters, and her voice with which <she conversed without> conversing; and the explanation of the name that was not spoken—and the soul of the world and man, insofar as they have been constituted in an image. (2) But next, beloved, I shall tell you how Tetrad produced an equal numerical value for him from the names (of the Aeons) so that, as

---

[28] The allusion is to the form of the uncial digamma (episemon).
[29] δυνάμεων, "powers."
[30] Ἐνθύμησις.
[31] With the content of 7,7-8 cf. thse vowels of the Name of God as given at Herm. Disc. 61,8-15.
[32] Ps 8:5
[33] Ps 18:2

you have often asked me, you will not be unacquainted with any of his teachings which I happen to know.

8,3 Here, then, is what their all-wise Silence has to say about the origin of the twenty-four sounds. With Soleness there co-exists Oneness. Two emanations from these, Unit and One as we have said, were two times two and made four; for two times two are four. (4) And again, when the two and the four were added they displayed the number six; but these six, multiplied by four, brought forth the twenty-four forms.

8,5 And the names of the first tetrad, which are understood to be holiest of the holy and not utterable, can be known by the Son alone—what they are, the Father knows. But the ones which are pronounced, reverently and with faith, before him, are these: Arretos and Sige, Pater and Aletheia.

8,6 The full total of this tetrad is twenty-four sounds. For the name, Arretos, has seven letters, Seige has five, Pater five, and Aletheia seven. Added together, the twice five and the twice seven, these gave the same number of sounds. (8) And the Savior's spoken name, Jesous, is of six letters, but his unutterable name of twenty-four. "Uios Chreistos" is of twelve letters, but the ineffable name in Christ is of thirty. And she calls him alpha and omega for this reason, to make mention of the dove, since this is "dove's" numerical value.

9,1 But Jesus has the following ineffable origin, she says. From the Mother of all, the first tetrad, the second tetrad[34] came forth in the role of daughter and became an ogdoad, out of which a decad came forth. Now there were a decad and an ogdoad. (2) Joining the ogdoad once more and multiplying it by ten,[35] the decad produced the next number, eighty. Multiplying the eighty by ten again it generated the number 800, so that the sum total of the letters which issue from eight times ten is an eight, an eighty, and an 800, which is "Jesus." (3) For counted by the sum which is found in its letters, the word, "Jesus," is 888. You are now clear as to Jesus' origin beyond the heavens, as they explain it. (4) And this is why the Greek alphabet contains eight units, eight tens, and eight hundreds, giving the figure of 888—in other words, Jesus, who is composed of all the numbers. He is thus called "alpha and omega" to indicate his origin from all.

9,5 And again: When the first tetrad was added to itself cumulatively the number ten was produced; for when one, two, three and four are added they make ten, or iota, and they hold that this is Jesus. (6) But "Chreistos"

[34] For the second tetrad see Val. Exp. 29,25-28; 35-38.

[35] There is a comparable, though not identical multiplication at Val. Exp. 30,30-38.

too, she says, which has eight letters, means the first ogdoad which, in the iota's embrace, brought forth Jesus. (7) He is also called "Uios Chreistos," that is, the dodecad. For the name, Uios, has four letters, while Chreistos has eight; added together these gave the amount of twelve.

9,8 Before the six-letter mark of this name—that is, "Jesus," the Son—appeared, men were in profound ignorance and error. (9) But when the six-letter name was made manifest, which was clothed with flesh to be perceptible to man and contained the six itself and the twenty-four, men learned <it>, ceased from their ignorance and ascended from death to life, for the name became their way to the Father of truth. (10) For the Father of all has willed to dissolve ignorance and abolish death. And the dissolution of ignorance was the recognition of him. Thus the Man was chosen who, by his will, was constituted in the image of the value on high.

10,1 For the Aeons issued from <the second> tetrad. In the tetrad there were Man and Church, Word and Life. Thus powers (= "values") which overflowed from these, he says, brought into being the Jesus who appeared on earth. (2) The angel Gabriel took the part of Word, the Holy Spirit, of Life, and the power of the highest, of Man, while the Virgin played the role of Church. (3) And thus Marcus' "man fashioned by dispensation" was brought into being through Mary; and when he had issued from the womb the Father of all chose him, through Word, to come to the knowledge of him. (4) And when he came to the water, the number which had withdrawn to heaven and become the twelfth descended on him as a dove. In this was the seed of these people, who were sown together with it, and have descended and ascended with it.

10,5 He says that the value itself which descended was the Father's seed, and contained both Father and Son, the ineffable value of Silence which is known through them, and all the Aeons. (6) And this is the Spirit which spoke through Jesus' mouth, which confessed itself Son of Man and made the Father known, <and of course> was united with Jesus in descending upon him. And he says that <Jesus>, the Savior produced by the dispensation, abolished death; but that <Christ> made the Father manifest. (7) He says, then, that <"Jesus"> was the name of the man framed by the dispensation, and that his office was to provide a likeness and form for Man, who was to descend upon him. In containing him Jesus possessed Man himself, Word himself, Father and Ineffable, and Silence and Truth, and Church and Life.

11,1 These things are already beyond "Alas and alack!" and every outcry and lamentation in tragedy. For who can fail to detest the author of such big lies, <badly put together>, when he sees the truth made into an idol by Marcus, and scribbled on with the letters of the alphabet? (2) The Greeks admit that, compared with anything primordial, it was recently—yesterday and the day before, as we say—that they first received sixteen letters from Cadmus. Then later, as time went on, they themselves invented the aspirates at one point and the double consonants at another, and they say that last of all Palamedes added the long vowels to these. (3) Before these things were done among the Greeks then, there was no Truth! For what you call her body, Marcus, is of later origin than Cadmus and his predecessors, later than those who added the rest of the sounds—later even than yourself! For only you have brought down your so-called Truth, <like> an idol.

11,4 But who can put up with your Silence who talks so much nonsense, who names the unnameable, explains the ineffable, searches the unsearchable, and says that he whom you call bodiless and without form has opened his mouth and uttered a Word—like a beast, made up of parts! (5) And his Word, which is like the one who emitted it and which has become a form of the invisible, is composed of thirty sounds, but four syllables. So the Father of all, as you call him, will be composed of thirty sounds but four syllables, in the likeness of Word!

11,6 Or again, who can stand your confinement of the Word of God, the creator, artificer and maker of all, to shapes and numbers—thirty sometimes, sometimes twenty-four, sometimes just six—<and> your dissection of him into four syllables, but thirty sounds? (7) And your reduction of the Lord of all, who established the heavens, to 888, like the alphabet; your subdivision even of the Father himself, who contains all things and yet is uncontained, into a tetrad, an ogdoad, a decad and a dodecad; and your explanation of the ineffability and inconceivability, as you say, of the Father by multiplications like these? (8) You make the essence and subsistence of the One you call incorporeal and without essence out of many letters, with new letters generated by others, though you yourself were the false Daedalus and the bad sculptor of the power before the all-highest! (9) And by subdividing the <essence> you say is indivisible into mutes, vowels and voiced consonants, and falsely attributing their voicelessness to the Father of all and his Ennoia, you have thrust all who trust you into the very height of blasphemy and the greatest impiety.

11,10 Thus it was with justice, and appropriately for such insolence as yours, that the divinely-inspired elder and herald of the truth has cried out at you in verse and said,

11,11 Maker of idols, scanner of portents, Mark,
Skilled in in the arts of astrologue and mage,
Through those confirming lessons taught by error:
To those deceived by thee hast thou shown signs
Which thy sire Satan giveth thee to perform
Through the angelic power of Azazel
For that he deemeth thee the harbinger
Of the villainy of the god opposed to God!

11,12 So far the elder beloved of God. But I shall try to go briefly over the rest of their mysteries, lengthy though they are, and bring to light things which have been concealed for a long time. May this make them easy for everyone to refute!

12,1 By combining the origin of their Aeons with the straying and finding of the sheep, these people who reduce everything to numbers try to give a deeper explanation, and claim that all things are made of a unit and a dyad; (2) and by counting from one to four they generate the decad. For one, two, three and four added together gave birth to the sum of the ten Aeons. But then again the dyad, by proceeding from itself to the episemon—as in "two, four, six"—gave the dodecad. (3) And again, when we count in the same way from two to ten the triacontad is arrived at in which there are an ogdoad, a decad and a dodecad.

12,4 They say that since the dodecad has the episemon in its train the episemon is (its) accident (πάθος which also means "passion"). Thus the sheep ran away and got lost when the error was made about the number twelve—since they claim that the defection was from a dodecad. (5) And they discover by divination that one rebellious value was similarly lost from the <decad>, and this is the woman who lost the drachma, and lit a lamp and found it. (6) After this the numbers that were left—nine in the drachma's case, eleven in the case of the sheep—were also united and gave birth to the number ninety-nine. For nine times eleven are ninety-nine. They say that this is why "Amen" yields this total.

12,7 But I do not mind telling you their explanations in another way, so you will despise their fruit in every respect. They hold that the sound, eta, is an ogdoad if we include the episemon, since it stands eighth after alpha. Then again, by reckoning up the totals of the sounds themselves without the six and adding them cumulatively through eta, they exhibit the triacontad. (8) For if <one> enumerates the sounds from alpha through eta, leaving the episemon out and adding cumulatively, he will arrive at the number thirty. (9) The total from alpha through epsilon is fifteen. Then seven added to this makes twenty-two. But when eta, or eight, is added to this, it has completed the wondrous triacontad. And from this they prove that the Ogdoad is the mother of the thirty Aeons.

12,10 Now since the number thirty is a combination of three numerical values, it was multiplied by three itself and made ninety, for three times thirty are ninety. But the three was also multiplied by itself and generated a nine. And thus, in their view, the Ogdoad gave birth to the ninety-nine. (11) And since the twelfth Aeon (i.e., the letter mu), when it rebelled, deserted the eleven (letters) before it, they say that the form of the (two) letters (found in the letter mu) is parallel to the shape of the lamda—for lamda, or thirty, is the eleventh letter—and that its place in the alphabet reflects the dispensation (mentioned) above.[36] For, omitting the digamma, the sum of the letters themselves from alpha through lamda, added cumulatively with lamda itself included, is ninety-nine.

12,12 But from the very shape of the sound it is plain that lamda, the eleventh letter, came down in search of its like to make up the number of twelve (letters) and was made complete when it found it. (13) For as though it had come in search of its like, and had found it and clasped <it> to itself, lamda filled the place of the twelfth letter—the letter mu is composed of two lamdas. (14) And so they escape the ninety-ninth place by knowledge—that is, they escape Deficiency which is counted on the left hand—and reach the One. When this was added to ninety-nine, it moved them to the right hand.[37]

13,1 As you go through this, beloved, I am well aware that you will roar with laughter <on hearing> the kind of foolishness they think is wise. But people are worthy of mourning when they make this sort of feeble effort to disparage a religion of such dignity, and the amount of the really inexpressible value, and such great dispensations of God, with alpha, beta and numbers. (2) Any, however, who leave the church and put their faith in these old wives' tales, <are> truly self-condemned. These Paul tells us to repudiate after a first and a second admonition. (3) But John, the disciple of the Lord, extended their condemnation further and did not even want them to be greeted by us, "For he that biddeth them godspeed is partaker of their evil deeds."[38] (4) And rightly so, for the Lord says, "It is not lawful to greet the impious."[39] And impious beyond all impiety are these persons

---

[36] I.e., the ogdoad's generation of the ninety-nine.
[37] This interpretation of the Lost Sheep is found at Gos. Tr. 31,35-32,16.
[38] 2 John 11
[39] Isa 48:22

who say that the creator of heaven and earth, the only God almighty above whom there is no other God, has been emitted by a Deficiency, which itself is the product of another Deficiency. As they see it, then, he himself is an emission of a third Deficiency!

13,5 It is truly imperative that we despise and curse this opinion, keep far, <even> very far away from them, and understand that the more they rely on their frauds and delight in them, the more they are animated by the ogdoad of the evil spirits—(6) just as people subject to fits are in worse condition <the> more they laugh, seem to have recovered, and do everything like persons in good health and some things even better. Similarly, the more these people appear to aim high, and exhaust themselves by shooting with a taut string, the more they are of unsound mind.

13,7 When the unclean spirit of folly had gone out, and then found them busy, not with God but with worldly philosophical inquiries, he took with him seven other spirits more wicked than himself. Making their minds conceited—as becomes those who are capable of conceiving of something higher than God—and ready for entire derangement, he inserted the eightfold folly of the evil spirits into them.

14,1 But I want to explain to you besides how they say that the creation itself, which was wrought by the Demiurge in the image of things invisible, was made by the Mother without his knowledge. (2) They say that the four elements, fire, water, earth, and air, were emitted first as an image of the supernal first tetrad and that when their operations are reckoned in with them—that is, heat, cold, dryness and wetness—they are the exact image of the ogdoad.[40]

14,3 <And> next they enumerate ten powers as follows. Seven circular <bodies>, which they also term heavens; then the circle that encloses them, which they also call an eighth heaven; and the sun and moon besides. As these make ten in all, they say they are images of the invisible decad which issued from Word and Life.

14,4 But the dodecad is made known by the so-called circle of the zodiac. For they say that the twelve signs obviously represent the dodecad, the daughter of Man and Church. (5) And since the highest heaven has been counterpoised against the very swift motion of all (the others)—bearing down on their vault itself, and compensating for their speed with its slowness, so that it revolves from sign to sign in thirty years—they say it is an image of Limit, who surrounds their Mother for whom there are

[40] The point seems to be that the Mother is "Ogdoad."

thirty names. (6) And the moon, in turn, which traverses its own heaven in thirty days, portrays the number of the thirty Aeons with the days. (7)[41] The sun too, which makes its revolution in twelve months and follows its circular path back to its starting-point, makes the dodecad visible through the twelve months. But the days also, which are limited to twelve hours, typify the dodecad which <is not> luminous.

14,8 But indeed they say that even the hour, the twelfth part of a day, is composed of thirty parts in the image of the triacontad. (9) And the rim of the zodiacal circle itself is made of 360 parts, for each sign has thirty. And thus they say the image of the union of twelve with thirty is preserved even by the circle. (10) And further, they insist that even the earth is very plainly a type of the dodecad and its children. For they say that it is divided into twelve regions, and in each region, from its position directly below it, it receives <a particular> power from the heavens, and bears offspring in the likeness of the power that is sending its effluent down upon it.

14,11 They say further that when the Demiurge wanted to reproduce the infinity, eternity, boundlessness and timelessness of the Ogdoad on high, he could not portray its stability and eternity because he was a fruit of Deficiency <himself>. So he has sown its eternity in times, seasons, numbers, and long periods of years, with the intention of imitating its endlessness by the great number of the periods of time. (12) And here they say that since Truth deserted him falsehood has followed, and his work will therefore meet with destruction when the times are fulfilled.

15,1 And by saying such things about creation, each of them, so far as he is able, produces <some> further novelty every day. For with them, no one is ripe unless he bears big lies. (2) But I should tell you which prophetic passages they transform, and supply the rebuttal for them.

For they say that when Moses was beginning his work on the creation he displayed the Mother of all at the very outset by saying, "In Beginning God created the heaven and the earth." (3) By naming these four then—God and Beginning, heaven and earth—he portrayed, as they say, their tetrad. And to make its invisibility and hiddenness known he said, "And the earth was invisible and unformed."

15,4 <But> they hold that he has spoken of the second tetrad, the offspring of the first, by naming an abyss, the darkness in themselves, water and the Spirit which was borne above the water. (5) After which, to make

[41] With 14,7-8 cf. the treatment of the divisions of time which is found at Tri. Trac. 73,28-74,2; Eug. 83,20-84,11.

mention of the decad, he said light, day and night; a firmament, evening and what is called early morning; dry land and sea, and further, vegetation; and tenth, trees. And thus he made the ten Aeons known through the ten names.

15,6 And the value of the dodecad is represented in his work as follows. For he says sun and moon; stars and seasons; years and whales and <further>, fish and creeping things, birds and four-legged creatures; wild beasts. And in addition to all these, twelfth, man. They teach that in this way the triacontad has been spoken of by the Spirit through Moses.

15,7 Indeed even the man formed in the image of the value on high has within him the value from the one source—(it is seated in the cranial cavity) from which flow four so-called faculties[42] in the image of the tetrad on high: sight; hearing; the sense of smell, third; fourth, taste. (8) And they say that the ogdoad is made known through the man in the following way. He has two ears, the same number of eyes and further, two nostrils and a dual sense of taste, the taste of bitter and sweet. (9) But they teach that the whole man contains the whole image of the triacontad as follows. He bears the decad on his hands with the fingers, but the dodecad in his entire body, which is divided into twelve members. (They divide it as the body of Truth is divided in their teachings—we have spoken of that.) And the ogdoad then, which is ineffable and invisible, is understood to be concealed in the viscera.

16,1 They claim in turn that the sun, the greater light, was created on the fourth day because of the number of the tetrad. (2) In their teachings the courts of the tabernacle constructed by Moses, which were made of flax, blue, purple, and scarlet, exhibited the same image. (3) They declare that the high priest's robe, which was decorated with four rows of precious stones, indicates the tetrad. And anything <at all> of this sort in the scriptures, which can be reduced to the number four, they say has been put there because of their tetrad.

16,4 But the ogdoad, in turn, is exhibited as follows. They say that man was formed on the eighth day. (For they sometimes hold that he was created on the sixth day and sometimes <on> the eighth, unless they mean that the man of earth was made on the sixth, but the man of flesh on the eighth—for they draw this distinction. (5) And some of them <even> hold that <there was> one man created male and female in God's image

[42] δυνάμεις.

and likeness, and this is the spiritual man; but the man formed from the earth is another one.)

16,6 And they say that the provision of the ark during the flood, in which eight persons were saved, makes the saving ogdoad known very plainly. David too, who was the eighth brother in order of birth, has the same significance. Furthermore even circumcision, which is performed on the eighth day, shows how ogdoad above is cut off from us. (7) And in a word, they say that anything in the scriptures which can be reduced to the number eight is applicable to the mystery of the ogdoad.

16,8 Moreover, they say the decad is indicated by the ten nations God promised to give Abraham for his possession. The provision <concerning> Sarah, that after ten years she gave him her maid Hagar to father children by, has the same meaning. (9) And the servant who was sent by Abraham for Rebecca, and who gave her ten gold bracelets at the well; and her brethren, who kept her for ten days—and further, Rehoboam, who received rule over ten tribes; the ten courts of the tabernacle, and its pillars ten cubits high; Jacob's ten sons, who were sent to Egypt to buy food the first time; and the ten apostles to whom the Lord appeared after the resurrection when Thomas was absent. These, in their opinion, portrayed the invisible decad.

17,1 They also say that the dodecad, on which the mystery of the Deficiency's passion centers—from which passion they hold that the visible things were made—is conspicuously and evidently to be found everywhere in scripture. (2) For example, Jacob's twelve sons, from whom <the> twelve tribes also sprang; the intricate breastplate with its twelve stones; the twelve bells; the twelve stones which were placed at the foot of the mountain by Moses, those too that were set up by Joshua in the river and others on the further bank; the bearers of the ark of the covenant; the stones Elijah set up at the sacrifice of the calf; the number of the apostles.[43] And in a word, they say that everything which preserves the number twelve is a representation of their dodecad.

17,3 It is their contention that they can exhibit the union of all these things, which they call a triacontad, by the thirty-cubit height of Noah's ark; and Samuel, who seated Saul first among his thirty guests; and David, when he was hidden for thirty days in the field, and the thirty who joined him in the cave; and because the length of the holy tabernacle was thirty cubits; and whatever else they find to have the same number as these.

[43] Fil. 42.2-3: columbam...quae descendit...ad dodecim aeonas, id est ad duodecim apostolos.

18,1 <But> to these I feel I must also add the passages they cull from scripture in the attempt to argue for their First Progenitor who was unknown to all before Christ's coming; and to prove that our Lord proclaimed a Father other than the maker of our universe (whom, as I said, they impiously call a fruit of a Deficiency). (2) They reinterpret the prophet Isaiah who indeed said, "Israel doth not know me, and the people doth not understand me,"[44] as having spoken of the ignorance of the invisible Depth. (3) They also force what was said by Hosea, "There is no truth nor knowledge of God in them,"[45] to pertain to the same; and they apply the words, "There is none that understandeth, or seeketh after God; they are all gone out of the way, they are together become unprofitable,"[46] to the ignorance of Depth. (4) They also argue that the words said by Moses, "There shall no man see God and live,"[47] refers to him. They tell the further lie that the creator has been seen by the prophets; but they hold that the <scriptural words>, "There shall no man see God and live," were said of the invisible majesty which is unknown to all. (5) (And that "There shall no man see God" is said of the invisible Father and maker of the universe is plain to us all. However, that this does not refer to their further invention, Depth, but to the Creator, and <that> he himself is the invisible God, will be shown in the course of the treatise.)

18,6 They also say that Daniel meant the same when he asked the angel for the interpretations of the parables, as though he did not know them. Moreover to conceal the great mystery of Depth from him the angel told him, "Go thy way, Daniel, for these words are sealed until the understanding understand, and the white be made white."[48] And they boast that they are the "white" and the "understanding."

18,7 In addition to these they produce an unutterably large number of apocryphal, spurious writings which they have forged themselves, to the consternation of the foolish who do not know the true scriptures. (8)[49] For this purpose they also employ the fraudulent story that when the Lord was a child and learning to read and his teacher, as is customary, told him, "Say Alpha," he answered, "Alpha." (9) And when the teacher in turn told him to say "Beta," the Lord replied, "Tell thou me first what is Alpha, and then will I tell thee what is Beta." And they interpret this to

[44] Isa 1:3
[45] Hos 4:1
[46] Rom 3:11-12
[47] Exod 33:20
[48] Dan 12:9-10
[49] With the story told in 18,8-9 cf. Epistula Apostolorum 4 (James p. 486); Infancy Story of Thomas A 6.3 (H-S I p. 445).

mean that the Lord alone understood the unknowable, and revealed it in the form of the Alpha.

18,10 They also adapt some of the Gospel passages to this type of thing. For example, the Lord's answer to his mother when he was twelve, "Wist ye not that I must be in my Father's house?"[50] they say, proclaimed the Father they did not know to them. And this is why he sent the disciples out to the twelve tribes, preaching the God who was unknown to them. (11) And to the person who addressed him as "Good Master," he confessed the truly good God by saying, "Why callest thou me good? One is good, the Father in the heavens";[51] and they say that "heavens" in this case means "Aeons."

18,12 And they explain that he has shown the Father's ineffability by <not> speaking, because he gave no answer to those who asked him, "By what authority doest thou these things?"[52] and they were baffled by his counter-question instead. (13) Moreover, when he said, "Oft have I desired to hear one of these words, and have found none to say it," they say that the "word" was the word of a person who, by saying "one," would evidence the truly one God whom they had not known. (14) Further, by contemplating Jerusalem, weeping for it, and saying, "If thou hadst known, even thou this day, the things that belong unto peace—but they are hid <from> thee,"[53] with the word, "hid," he has indicated Depth's hiddenness. (15) Again, by saying, "Come unto me, all ye that labor and are heavy laden, and learn of me,"[54] he has proclaimed the Father of Truth. For what they did not know, they say, he promised to teach them .

18,16 <As proof> of all this and a kind of cap to their argument they cite, "I thank thee, Father, Lord of heaven and earth, that thou hast hidden them from the wise and prudent and hast revealed them unto babes. Ah, my Father, for it was good in thy sight. All things are delivered unto me of my Father; and no man knoweth the Father save the Son, and the Son, save the Father, and he to whomsoever the Son shall reveal him."[55] (17) <For> they say that with this the Lord has expressly shown that before his coming no one ever knew their falsely invented Father of truth. And they want to make it out that, since the maker and creator was always

---

[50] Luke 2:9
[51] Mark 10:17-18
[52] Matt 21:23-27 par.
[53] Luke 19:42
[54] Matt 11:28-29
[55] Matt 11:25-27

known by everyone, the Lord has said this too of the the Father whom no one knows, the one they proclaim.

19,1 Their conferral of "redemption"[56] is characteristically invisible and impossible to grasp, stemming as it does from the untouchable, invisible Mother and therefore, because of its instability, cannot be simply summarized—since they each hand it down as they choose. For there are as many "redemptions" as there are mystagogues of this persuasion. (2) When I refute them I shall declare at the proper place that this type of thing has been fobbed off by Satan, as a denial of the baptism of regeneration to God, and for the abolition of all of the faith.

19,3 They say that redemption is a necessity for those who have received the perfect knowledge, so that they may be reborn to the power above all. <It is> impossible to enter the Pleroma otherwise, for in their view this is what transports them to the bottom of Depth. (4) They suppose that the baptism of the visible Jesus <is> for the remission of sins, but the redemption of the Christ who came down into him is for perfection, and that the one is soulish, but the other is spiritual. Baptism has been proclaimed by John for repentance, but redemption has been obtained by Christ for perfection.[57] (5) And it is of this that he says, "And I have another baptism to be baptized with, and am in great haste for it."[58] Moreover, they say that the Lord added this redemption to the sons of Zebedee when their mother asked that they sit in the kingdom with him on his right and left, by saying, "Can ye be baptized with the baptism that I am to be baptized with?"[59] (6) And they claim that Paul has often made express mention of the redemption in Christ Jesus, and that this is the "redemption" which they hand down in complex, inconsistent ways.

20,1 For some of them get a bridal chamber ready,[60] conduct the initiation of their candidates with certain invocations, and claim that the rite they are performing is a spiritual marriage in the likeness of the syzygies on high. (2) But some take them to water, and use the following invocation as they baptize them: "In the name of the unknowable Father of all; of Truth, Mother of all; and of him who descended upon Jesus for union, redemption, and participation in the powers." (3) Others pronounce an

---

[56] At Tri. Trac. 127,25-128,4 baptism is said to be "redemption." See n. 61.

[57] A comparable distinction seems to be implied at On Bapt. A 41,10-38.

[58] Cf. Luke 12:50.

[59] Mark 10:38

[60] See p. 232 n. 4. At Tri. Trac.128,33-35 baptism is referred to as the bridal chamber, and this is often the meaning in Gos. Phil. At Gos. Phil. 69,1-70,3 it might mean the eucharist. On the subject see Schenke, *Das Philippusevangelium*.

invocation with Hebrew names to terrify the candidates the more, as follows: "Basema chamosse baainaoora mistadia rouada, kousta babophor kalachthei." This means something like "More than every power of the Father I call on <thee, who art> termed light, good spirit, and life, for in a body thou didst reign."

20,4 But when others <conduct> the redemption in their turn they pronouce this invocation: "The name hidden from every Godhead, sovereignty and truth, the name which Jesus of Nazareth put on in the girdles of the light of Christ—the Christ who lives by Holy Spirit—for angelic redemption, the name of the restoration: (5) Messia oupharegna mempsai men chal daian mosome daea akhphar nepseu oua Jesou Nazaria." The translation of this is something like, "I do not distinguish the spirit, the heart, and the merciful power above the heavens. May I enjoy the benefit of thy name, O true Savior!" (6) And the officiants themselves pronounce this invocation but the neophyte responds, "I have been stablished and redeemed, and do redeem my soul from this world and all that is of this world in the name of Iao, who redeemed his soul for redemption in the living Christ." (7) Then the congregation add, "Peace be to all on whom this name doth abide!" Then they anoint the candidate with oil[61] of balsam; for they say that this ointment is a type of the sweet savor which is above all.

20,8 Some of them claim that it is unnecessary to bring candidates to the water, but mix oil and water and apply them to the candidates' heads with <certain> invocations like the ones we have given, and hold that this is redemption. But they too anoint with oil of balsam.

20,9 Others reject all this and claim that the mystery of the ineffable, invisible power must not be conducted with visible, perishable creatures, and that of the inconceivable and incorporeal with the perceptible and bodily. (10) The discernment of the ineffable Majesty is perfect redemption in itself.[62] The whole system of ignorance which was brought about by Deficiency's ignorance and passion is dissolved by knowledge, so that knowledge is the redemption of the inner man. (11) And redemption is neither corporeal—for the body is mortal—nor soulish, since the soul too

[61] Together with baptism, chrismation is important in Gos. Phil. See 57,21-28; 67,2-9; 24-30; 69,9-14; 73,16-19 74,12-18. And cf. Acts of Thomas 27 (H-S II p. 456); 121 (p. 507); 157 (p. 526).

[62] At Apoc. Ad. 85,19-31 "hidden knowledge" is said to be holy baptism; at Test. Tr. 69,15-31 baptism is renunciation of the world. Baptism appears to be deprecated at Gos. Jud. 55,21-56,1.

<comes> from Deficiency and is a sort of dwelling-place for the spirit; redemption too, then, must be spiritual. (12) For the inner, spiritual man is redeemed through knowledge, and they are content with the discernment of all things, and this is true redemption.

This concludes the excerpt from Irenaeus

21,1 The blessed elder Irenaeus composed this whole searching inquiry, and gave every detail of all their false teaching in order. Hence, as I have already indicated, I am content with his diligent work and have presented it all word for word, as it stands in his writings. (2) They will be refuted by the very things the holy man has said in opposition to their wickedness. For we believe, as the truth everywhere makes apparent, as sound reasoning indicates and as is in agreement with the standard of piety, the Law and prophets, the ancient patriarchs in succession, in accordance with the Savior's own teaching—(3) for <the Lord> and his apostles plainly teach us to confess one God as Father, the almighty sovereign of all, and our Lord Jesus Christ and his Holy Spirit, one holy Trinity uncreate; while all other things were created out of nothing, subsequent to the Father, Son and Holy Spirit. (4) Now since these things are confessed plainly and believed, by these holy prophets, evangelists, and apostles, no shifty device can withstand the truth's bright beam, as I have often said at length in opposition to every sect. (5) It is thus perfectly plain that, precisely like the other sects, this murderous tramp is tailoring and devising these big things in order to show off and make a nuisance of himself.

22,1 But passing his wickedness by as well, and the wickedness of the people who are called Marcosians after him, let us hurry on to the rest, beloved, and in turn discover their roots and counteract the bitterness of their fruit by making public the refutation of it and all of the facts about them—(2) not for the harm of the readers but for their protection, so that they will not go near any of the sects before or after this one, but read what they have written, become acquainted with their cant and despise it, and flee from its viperous wickedness and, as I said, not go near it.

22,3 The naturalists speak of a viper called the dipsas, which does the following sort of harm. In certain places where there are depressions in the rocks, or little basins hollowed out of rocks as a receptacle, the dipsas finds water, drinks and, after drinking puts its poison into these pools of water. Then any animal that approaches and drinks its fill will feel refreshed because it drank, but it will fall right down and die from the viper's venom, beside the receptacle which has received it. (4) Moreover, if the dipsas strikes someone, his pain from its extremely hot poison will make him thirsty and want a drink, and impel him to keep coming up and drinking. (5) Each time the victim <feels> such deadly pain and <has some water> he will think that it does his injury some good but later, with his stomach filled by that very drink and unable to hold <any> more, he will vomit his life out along with the drink. (6) Thus Marcus too causes the death of his dupes with a drink. But since we have been rescued from this poison by the power of God, let us go on to the rest.

35.
Against Colorbasians.[1] *Number 15, but 35 of the series*

1,1 Colorbasus comes next after these. He drew on Marcus' sorcery, but also grew up like thorns from the root of Ptolemy. In his turn he invented irritants for the world, like goads, other than theirs, by working up a supposedly greater "experience" as though he had come down from heaven. (2) He was originally a partner of Marcus[2] whose ideas were the same as his, their sect being like a two-headed snake. But later, like a head cut off a snake's body and still breathing, he did fatal harm to many by showing them something supposedly greater and more authentic than his contemporaries and predecessors had.

1,3[3] "For he says that the first ogdoad has not been emitted in a descending series, one Aeon by another. As though he had been their midwife himself he maintains that the emanation of the six Aeons has been brought forth, at the same time and once for all, by First Progenitor and his Ennoia. And he and his followers no longer say like the others that Man and Church have been brought forth by Word and Life, but that Word and Life have been brought forth by Man and Church. (4) They also say the following in a different way: When First Progenitor had conceived of emitting something, this was called Father. But since what he emitted was a truth, this was termed Truth. When he willed to show himself, this was

---

[1] Epiph draws his account of the teaching he ascribes to Colorbasus from Iren. 1.12.3-4. PsT 5.1-3 gives what was presumably Hipp. Synt.'s account of Marcus and Colorbasus, treated together. Fil. 42 treats Colorbasus separately, and appears to combine Hipp. Synt. with some garbled Irenaean material, perhaps from Pan. 31,14-6-9.

[2] Knowing from Hipp. Synt. that Colorbasus and Marcus were associates (see PsT 5.1; Hipp. Refut. 6.55.3). Epiph assumes that Colorbasus must be one of the unnamed teachers who, at Iren. 1.12.3, are called qui...putantur prudentiores illorum, and that Marcus' connection with them is confirmed by Iren. 1.13.1.

[3] 1.3-7 is quoted from Iren. 1.12.3-4. Cf. Tert. Adv. Val. 36; 39.

called Man. But the Aeons of which he had previously thought when he emitted them—this was termed Church. Man, also, <sends forth>Word; he is the first-born son. But Life also accompanies Word. And thus a first ogdoad was brought to completion.

1,5[4] "There is also considerable dispute among them about the Savior. Some say he is the product of all and is therefore called 'Well- Pleased," since all of the Pleroma was pleased to glorify the Father through him.[5] Some say he is the product only of the ten Aeons which were emitted by Word and Life <and is called 'Word' and 'Life' accordingly>, preserving the names of his forebears. (6) Others say he is the product of the twelve Aeons produced by Man and Church, and thus, as Man's progeny, confesses <himself> the 'Son of Man.' Others say he originates from Christ and Holy Spirit, <the ones emitted> in order to make the Pleroma firm. He is called "Christ' for this reason, preserving the title of the Father by whom he was emitted. (7) But others, certain bards of theirs as we might call them, say that the First Progenitor of the universe, its First Principle and the First One of whom there can be no conception, is called Man.[6] And this is the great, secret mystery—the power which is above all and encompasses all is called Man! And this is why the Savior says he is Son of Man!"[7]

2,1 Here, too, is Colorbasus' bombastic nonsense—of no use to the world and a figment of his imagination. If one examines it closely he will see from what lies before him that <the cause> of each of these people's opinions is his ambition. (2) From vainglory and their desire to gather a following each of them told any lies that came into his head, not by speaking prophetically—the Holy Spirit did not speak in them—or by taking even one cue from the truth of the prophets and Gospels.

2,3 But the rebuttal of all these people's falsely styled "knowledge" is the same assertion of the truth which has been made against the previous ones. Because they all belong to the school of Valentinus and his

---

[4] With what follows cf. the various names which are given to the Son at Tri. Trac. 87,1-17.

[5] Cf. "The Son in whom the Totalities are pleased," Tri. Trac. 87,1.

[6] The Father of the All is called both "man" and "first man" at Apocry. Jn. CG II,1 14,13-24; at BG 8502,2 47,14-49,9 "the holy perfect Father" is called "man," "first man" and "perfect man." At Gr. Seth 52,30-53,5 the Father of Truth is the "Man of the Greatness." Jeu is "the great Man" at 2 Jeu 50 (MacDermot p. 122) and frequently in Pistis Sophia.

At Eug. 85,9-13, God's first emanation is "man": "The first aeon, then, is that of Immortal Man. The second aeon is that of the Son of Man, who is called 'First Begetter.'" and see SJC 108,1-10; 103,21-105,2. The first emanation is also "man" at Pan. 31,5,5, the Valentinian document. For an extensive discussion of this subject see Schenke, *Der Gott, 'Mensch.'*

[7] Gos. Egyp. III,2 54,1-4: Then came a voice from the height, "the Man exists and the Son of Man!" See also Gos. Egyp. 49,9-10 and 49,16-25.

predecessors and each (simply) interprets his intent differently, they will all incur the same discomfiture.

2,4 For this Colorbasus too has come to bring us a great, absurd deceit. He has made up a name for us, "Man," and given it to the incomprehensible, invisible, holy God, the Father of all. This to combine with his own imposture the saying in which the Savior calls himself Son of Man, and to divert the minds of those who make use of it from Christ's trustworthy and perfectly clear confession about himself to an impossibility, and to the nonsense <of their inquiries about a non-existent ogdoad, as though it existed in the heavens>.

2,5 For suppose we grant that, as this pathetic Colorbasus says, Christ called himself Son of Man because some Father on high of his is named "Man," and not because of the flesh he took from a virgin womb, that is from St. Mary, when he was conceived by the Holy Spirit. (6) What would he say about the thing the same Jesus Christ our Lord said when he told the Jews, "But now ye seek to kill me, a man that has told you the truth, which I heard of my Father?"[8] (7) And here he did not say, "the man, my Father" but, to confess the Father, indicated that he is God of all; but of himself, because he had truly become man, he said that he was man. (8) The apostles too—so that the truth may be established in every way and the origin of the names which are ascribed to the Lord may be known—say, "Jesus, a man approved among you by signs and wonders,"[9] and so on.

2,9 What can you say to this, you most pathetic of all people—since you have come from on high bringing us new names, and you take pride in having dared to attach the name, "Man," to the Lord of all and Father of all himself, as though the Lord is called Son of Man because Man is his Father's name? (10) Find us some other term to fit the Father, <corresponding with> "man approved!" But you never could! Even though "man" also means "male," and we call a male a "man" to distinguish him from a woman, you can still make nothing out of this either. (11) No one can be termed male without certain features and members, hidden and visible. We call a woman "man" too, but not "male"; thus we say both ὁ ἄνθρωπος and ἡ ἄνθρωπος. (12) But when we distinguish sex we call the feminine specifically "woman," but the masculine "male," for this is the distinction between the masculine and feminine sex, the words "male" and "woman." But both the male and the woman are called "man" synonymously.

3,1 Since this is the case, join me, all you servants of God and lovers of the truth, and laugh at the fraud and tramp Colorbasus! Or rather, mourn

---

[8] John 8:40
[9] Acts 2:22

for those who have been deceived, and have destroyed themselves and many others. (2) But let us ourselves thank God that the truth guides its sons in a straight path with short, simple words, and that it disperses, overturns, and gets rid of things that are jarring and loud, though dressed up with much ingenuity. The truth goes softly, as is plain to see from the prophet's oracle. (3) In accusation of those who waste their energy on cleverness, and invent long-winded verbiage to their own deception, the prophet said, "Forasmuch as ye refuse the water of Siloam that goeth softly, the Lord bringeth up upon you the water of the river, the king of the Assyrians."[10] (4) For "water of Siloam" means the "teaching of Him who has been sent." And who can this be but our Lord Jesus Christ, who has been sent from God, his Father? And <he "goes> softly" because <he introduces> no nonsense or fiction, but in truth introduces his holy bride, whom he calls "dove" in the Songs of Solomon because of the dove's harmlessness, gentleness and very great purity.

3,5 And it is surprising that he called the other women, who are not his but have taken his name, "concubines" and "queens" because of the royal name of which each one boasts by having "Christ" inscribed on her. (6) But even though there are eighty concubines—meaning the sects—and then young women without number, he says, "One is my dove, my perfect one"; that is, the holy bride and catholic church herself. "Dove," as I said, because of the dove's gentleness, harmlessness and purity; and "perfect" because she has received perfect grace from God, and perfect knowledge from the Savior himself, through the Holy Spirit.

3,7 The bridegroom himself, then, whose name means "sent," or "Siloam," has water that flows softly—that is, teaching which is quiet and makes no commotion, and is not imaginary and not boastful. (8) And his bride too is a peaceable dove, with no poison, huge teeth or stings—like all these people with their snake-like forms and gush of venom, each doing his best to prepare some poison for the world and do harm to his converts.

3,9 This man is one of them as well. I have hastened to detect him here with divinely-given speech and aid from above, and squash him like the snake with four jaws which is called the malmignatte—or crush him at once like a head cut off from the two-headed viper, the amphisbaena. (10) But I shall pass him by, and once more investigate the rest, and ask in prayer that I may describe them truthfully as I go over them, but harm no one and not be harmed myself.

[10] Isa. 8:6-7

36.

Against Heracleonites.[1] *Number sixteen, but thirty-six of the series*

1,1 One Heracleon, the founder of the so-called Heracleonites, is Colorbasus' successor; he is no less versed in the <foolery> of their nonsense. (2) Whatever they say, he declares too; naturally, since he began as one of them and copied his poison from them. But he wants to surpass them by supposedly devising something further, on his own account, for the sake of gathering his own body of dupes.

1,3 For by forming themselves into the imitation of a body with 100 heads or 100 hands, all these people have mimicked the Cottus or Briareus—also called Aegaeon or Gyes—of the Greek poets' mythology, or the so-called "many-eyed Argus." (4) As the poets told fantastic stories about them in their recitations, saying fabulously that one had 100 hands and sometimes fifty or sometimes 100 heads, and another had 100 eyes—and they say that this is why Hermes is called "Argeïphontes," because he killed Argus with his many eyes—(5) each of these people has named himself a head to establish his own supremacy, slipping in other things besides the wasted effort and insane doctrine of his teachers. But not to go on too long with the composition of the preface, I shall come to the matter in hand.

2,1[2] Heracleon—and the Heracleonites who, as said, derive from him—like Marcus and certain of his predecessors makes allegations about the Ogdoads, I mean the upper and the lower. Then, too, he takes the same view of the syzygies of the thirty Aeons. (2) He too alleges that the Father of all on high, whom he also called "Depth," is a man. He too wants to say that the Father is neither male nor female, but that the Mother of all, whom he calls both Silence and Truth, is derived from him. (3) And derived from her is the second Mother, the one who had the lapse of memory, whom he too calls Achamoth. From her all things were brought into being defectively.

---

[1] For reasons which are unclear, Epiph takes as his source for Sect 36 the last part of Irenaeus' account of the Marcosians, Iren. 1.21.3-5, where the sacramental practices of the Marcosians (Valentinians?) are described.

Heracleon is mentioned at Iren. 2.4.1 and said to be in agreement with Valentinus as to the aeons. PsT 4.8, presumably following Hipp. Synt. says of Heracleon: Introducit enim in primis illud fuisse quod <deum> pronuntiat, et deinde ex illa monada duo, ac deinde reliquos Aeonas. Cf. Fil. 41.

Hipp. Refut. 6.35.6 places Heracleon with Ptolemy in the "Italian school" of Valentinians, who maintain that Jesus' body is ψύχικον. Tert. Adv. Val. 4.2, where there may be some independent information about Valentinians, names Heracleon as an innovator.

[2] 2,1-3 might be Epiph's own conjecture, based on Iren. 2.4.1.

2,4 But he too intends to say more than his predecessors, and it is this. He "redeems" those of their people who are dying and have reached the actual point of death,[3] taking his cue from Marcus, but no longer doing it in Marcus' way—for his part handling it differently by redeeming his dupes at the point of death, if you please. (5) "For sometimes some of them will mix oil with water,[4] and apply it to the head of the dying; others apply the ointment known as balsam, and water." But they have in common the invocation as Marcus before him composed it, with the addition of certain names. And the invocation is this: (6) "Messia oupharegna mempsai men chal daian mosome daea akhphar nepseu oua jesou Nazaria."[5]

2,7 And they do this in order that those who receive these invocations at the point of death, with the water and the oil or ointment mixed with it, will supposedly "become untouchable by the principalities and authorities on high and invisible to them, allowing their inner man to pass them unseen—(8) with their bodies left behind in the created world, while their souls are committed to the Demiurge"[6] on high who originated in Deficiency, and so stay there with him. But as I said their "inner man,"[7] <which is> deeper down inside them than soul and body, ascends beyond him. This, they hold, has descended from the Pleroma on high.

3,1 To the persons of whom they make fools in this way they give the direction,[8] "If you come upon the principalities" and authorities, remember to say this "after your <departure>, (2) 'I am a son of a Father, a Father who was before me;[9] and here and now I am a son. <And> I have come to see all that is mine and all that belongs to others—yet it by no means belongs to others but to Achamoth, who is female and made these things for herself. I derive from the One who was before her and am returning to my own, whence I came.'[10] (3) And so saying he escapes the authorities

---

3 Iren. 1.21.5. Mandaeans also use water in their rite of extreme unction, see Drowyer pp. 64-68.

4 Iren. 1.21.4

5 Irenaeus gives this invocation at 1.21.3 in this account of the Marcosians. F. Gaffin is cited in Rousseau and Doutreleaux, *Sources Chrétiennes* 263, p.270f, as reconstructing a Syriac or Aramaic original whose translation is, "I am anointed and redeemed from myself and from every judgment by the name of Yahweh; redeem me, O Jesus of Nazareth." See Amidon p. 128.

6 This is quoted from Iren. 1.21.5.

7 For "inner man" see Let. Pet. 137,21-22; PS passim, Man. Ps. 173,19-20.

8 This speech, and the one that follows it, is quoted from Iren. 1.21.5. There are longer versions of it at 1 Apoc. Jas. 33,13-34,18 and Cod. Tch. James 19,24-22,23, and a comparable one at Nat. Arc. 92,21-27.

9 Or: the preexisting Father (Amidon).

10 For returning to one's own, or the like, see Apocry. Jas 1,23-24; 14,19-21; Gos. Tr.

but encounters the company of the Demiurge" on high, in the vicinity of the first ogdoad. (They too hold that there is a hebdomad below, after the Demiurge. He is in the seventh <heaven> as an eighth, but defectively and ignorantly.)

3,4[11] "And to the company of the Demiurge" the departed "says, 'I am a vessel more precious than the female who made you. If your Mother is ignorant of her own root, I know myself and realize whence I am,[12] and call upon the imperishable Wisdom who is in the Father, but who is the Mother of your Mother who has no father or even male consort. (5) A female born of a female made you[13] because she did not know even her mother and believed herself to be alone.[14] I, however, call upon her Mother.' (6) On hearing this the company of the Demiurge are most disturbed, and condemn their root and the Mother's stock; but the departed goes to his own casting off his chain[15] and 'angel,' that is, <the> soul," (for they think there is something else in a man, after body and soul). "And this is what I have been able to learn about redemption."

4,1[16] But after listening to the extravagant nonsense of their mime the wise must laugh at the way each one lays down a law different from the other's to suit himself and is not restrained from his own impudence but invents as much as he can. (2) "<And> it is difficult to discover or state all the <doctrines> of the people who" are being spawned and sprouting up among them "even to this day, and every day find something new to say" and delude their converts. So again I shall rest content with what has been said about this sect, for I have given the information I myself have gathered about it.

4,3 Who can fail to see that teaching like theirs is entirely myth and nonsense? Where did you get your body, Mister—you, or your predecessors? Where did you get your soul? Your inmost man? (4) Even if it was from

---

21,11-25; 22,18-20; 34,14-16; Tri. Trac. 117,17-25; 123,4-8; GT 49; 50; Or. Wld. 127,14-15; 1 Apoc. Jas. 35,21-23; Cod. Tch. James 21,15-19; Apoc. Paul 23,9-10; PS 3.112 (MacDermot p. 289).

[11] See p. 104 n. 72.

[12] For this very common Gnostic motif see Apocry. Jas. 12,20-22; Tri. Trac. 60,23-24; GT 3; 111; Gos. Phil. 76,18-22; Thom. Cont. 138,7-20; Dia. Sav. 132,15-16; 134,19-22; Corp. Herm. 1.19.

[13] The reference is to Achamoth, see n. 112 p. 186. Cf. Auth. Teach. 23,22-26, "And yet they are outsiders, without power to inherit from the male, but they will inherit from their mother only." Gos. Phil. 52,21-24 says that "Hebrews" have only a mother, while "Christians" have father and mother.

[14] See n. 11 p. 87.

[15] Cf. The "bondage of the body" at Para. Shem 35,16-17, and see Corp. Herm. I.26.

[16] 4,1-2 is paraphrased from Iren. 1.21.5.

above, from the spirituality on high—as you dramatically say to ensnare your dupes with a promise of hope, so that they may be excited by some goal and thus bewitched by your performance[17]—(even so) tell me, what does the spirituality on high have in common with the material? What does the material have in common with the soulish?

4,5 How could the Demiurge create things that did not belong to him? Why did the <spiritual one> on high hand his spiritual power over to the Demiurge who had not done good work? And why did the Demiurge prefer to mix his own soulish nature with the material and bind his own power fast with matter? (6) But if he does want to mix his own power in with it, matter is not alien to him. And if indeed it is alien, who gave him authority over matter? (7) And first, you fraud, tell me whether he bound the soul with matter because he hated it or because he did not know what would happen. But I know you won't say either!

4,8 For I deny that the body is "matter"—anything but!—or that God's creatures are. However, scripture does know another kind of "matter," in addition to this common matter which is available for their works to every craft and trade. I mean the sordid reflection arising from the reason, and <the> filthy thoughts of sin. (9) For noisome, filthy <thoughts> arise <from an evil heart> like a bad smell and unclean effluent from mud, as the blessed David said when he was persecuted and slandered by wicked men, "I was trapped in matter of an abyss,"[18] and so on.

5,1 But since you suppose that this is called "matter," Heracleon—human bodies and the entire world here—for what purpose did the Demiurge get his own soul mixed up with matter? (2) If it was because he did not know evil—a person who does not know what he intends to make, cannot make it. Neither do we accomplish anything in any craft by making something we do not understand. We both reflect beforehand on the thing we intend to produce, and know what we have chosen to produce before we make it. (3) And though we, surely, are feeble and far inferior to God's power, we know and understand through the understanding he has granted to men. But for you, Heracleon, God-given understanding has resulted in harm, since you do not employ it in a godly way but in an evil pursuit.

5,4 But I shall say it again, why the mixture of the spiritual with the soulish and material? That is, of what you call an inner man, united with the second and third "outer man," I mean with the soul and the body?

[17] The performance of the last rites, which they accept in hope of rising to the highest heaven.

[18] Ps. 68:3

(5) And if it is by the will of the power on high, the Father of all—I mean your "Depth"—then, as I said, the creation around us here, which has been commingled with them, is not incompatible with the things on high. For it is with the consent of the Father on high that the spark, your "spiritual" and inmost man, has been sent down from him from above. (6) And if you say that the Demiurge who is inferior and defective, or the Mother whom you call Achamoth, has received power—that is, spirituality—from above, then the Demiurge cannot be defective and ignorant, or your so-called "Mother" either. How can anyone be in ignorance of the thing he desires? If he desires the better at all, he knows what is right and good. And one who knows the good, and does not detest it but yearns for it, is not strange to the good.

6,1 And not to waste my time by spending in on the tramp's devices, I shall rest content with this. All his nonsense breaks down, since it is plainly acknowledged by everyone that the Lord of all is good, has foreknowledge, and is able to do everything; and that all nature, the creation that is in being, has been well made by him. (2) For nothing can exist without God except only sin, which has no original root and no permanence but appears in us as something imported, and in turn is brought to an end by us. Thus, in composing my heresiology, I have everywhere proved (3) that God, the maker and creator of all, the Father of our Lord Jesus Christ, is one; and that his only-begotten Son, our Lord, Savior and God, is one; and that his Holy Spirit is one (4)—one holy, consubstantial Trinity. By this Trinity all things have been created well—none evil, but good, in keeping with the Goodness which consented to call them in that condition from non-being into being. (5) <To this God>, the Father in the Son, the Son with the Holy Spirit in the Father, be glory, honor and might, forever and ever. Amen.

6,6 But after once more giving a brief rebuttal of this sect I am going on to the rest, and will give my best refutation of each and so complete the overthrow of their pernicious wickedness. (7) For Heracleon may justly be called a lizard. This is not a snake but a hard-skinned beast as they say, something that crawls on four feet, like a gecko. The harm of its bite is negligible, but if a drop of its spittle strikes a food or drink, it causes the immediate death of those who have any. Heracleon's teaching is like that. (8) But as we have detected his poison too, and by God's power have wiped it off the throat or lips of those who would have been harmed, let us go over the rest, as I said, and give the rebuttal of their mischief.

37.

Against Ophites.[1] *Number seventeen, but thirty-seven of the series*

1,1 As I promised by the power of God, with God's help I shall also describe the Ophite sect, which follows next after the last stupidities. In some ways it takes the same course but in others, the customs and gestures of its members, it is different—so that everyone can see from the erratic wandering of the disagreement between them that these sects are guided by error, not truth. The Ophites will now be detected by the treatise, and their sort of stupidity refuted.

1,2 As I said, the Ophites took their cue from the sects of Nicolaus and the Gnostics and the ones before those. But they are called Ophites because of the serpent which they magnify. For they too disgorge strange things as though they were stuffed with the stinking food we mentioned before; and in their error, as I said, they glorify the serpent as a new divinity.

1,3 And see how far the serpent, the deceiver of the Ophites, has gone in mischief! Just as he deceived Eve and Adam at the beginning so even he does now by concealing himself—both now and in the Jewish period up until Christ's coming. (4) Then, even in later times, he seduces greedy humanity further with the food they got through him by disobedience; and he provokes them to further treachery and makes them rebels against the true God. He always promises big things, as he did also at the beginning. Even then he cheated them by saying, "Ye shall be as gods";[2] then, in time, he completed the multiform, monstrous illusion for them. (5) For he had spawned the blasphemous nonsense of idolatry and polytheism long before, by detaching them from the one true God. They were not gods (then), just as they are not (now); <only> God is God. But he was spawning polytheism, the madness for idols, and a deceitful doctrine beforehand.

1,6 But the snake which was visible at that time was not the only cause of this. It was the snake who spoke in the snake—I mean <the> devil—and disturbed the man's hearing through the woman. (7) And the tree was not sin either—God plants nothing evil—but the tree gave them knowledge so that they would know good and evil.

[1] The principal source of this Sect is Hipp. Synt., which is represented by PsT 2.1-4. Epiph uses this rather freely in the course of a homily against the Ophite heresy. He has also drawn on Irenaeus' paraphrase of an Ophitic source at 1.30.1-15. The description of the Ophite eucharist is amplified from oral sources. Epiph's account is not influenced by Hipp. Refut. 5.6.1-11 or by Orig. Cels. 6.24-35, though the latter is related to that of Irenaeus.

[2] Gen 3:5

1,8 And death did not come because of knowledge, but because of disobedience. Indeed the adversary's whole plot at that time was laid, not for the sake of food but to make them disobedient. (9) Hence they disobeyed then, and as an entirely just punishment were expelled from Paradise—not from God's hatred of them but from his care. For the Lord tells them, "Earth thou art, and unto earth shalt thou return."[3] (10) Like a potter the true Craftsman has charge of his own handiwork and vessel, and if this is later rendered defective by disobedience he must not leave it in that condition—when the vessel is still clay, as we might say, and has been rendered unuseable, as though by a crack. (11) Instead he must change the vessel into the original lump, to restore it to its pristine splendor and better still in the regeneration at the resurrection—(12) that is, <renew> the bodies of those who have committed the most grievous sins, and have repented, renounced their errors and been perfected in the knowledge of our Lord Jesus Christ, so that the resurrection of the body from the earth may take place as though the lump, softened by the Craftsman, were being restored to its original form and even better.

2,1 Such was the serpent's scheme against Eve. For the human race is greedy from the first, and always open to seduction by absurd doctrines and empty professions. (2) And in ancient times the serpent remained in hiding and did not disclose the full extent of its poison. But later, after Christ's incarnation, it coughed up and spat out the entire poisonous, wicked invention of its malice, for it proposed itself in the minds of its dupes for glorification and worship as God.

2,3 But the same serpent is recognizable as the author of the deception, both from this school of its followers and from the visible snake. Indeed, sacred scripture calls the devil a serpent; certainly not because he looks like one, but because he appears extremely crooked to men, and because of the treacherous fraud which was at the first perpetrated through a snake.

2,4 In the eyes, then, of those who recognize the truth, this doctrine is a ridiculous thing and so are its adherents who honor the serpent as God. No longer able to deceive the masculine reason which has received the power of the truth from the Lord, the devil turns to the feminine—that is, to men's ignorance—and convinces the ignorant, since he cannot deceive sound reason. (5) He always makes his approach to feminine whims, pleasure and lust—in other words, to the womanish ignorance in men, not to

[3] Gen 3:19

the firm reason which understands everything logically and recognizes God by the law of nature. (6) For their snake says it is Christ. Or rather, it does not—it cannot talk—but the devil does, who has prepared their minds to think in this way.

2,7 Thus, on seeing the snake, who will not recognize the adversary and flee? This is why the Lord assigned enmity against the human race to this particular snake—since, being his pet, it was wholly the devil's instrument, and through it he deceived the man in Paradise—so that, because they had seen the enmity of this visible snake they would flee the plot of its treachery and practically hate even the sight of it.

3,1 These so-called Ophites too ascribe all knowledge to this snake, saying that it became the beginning of men's knowledge,[4] and through mythology they slip the things in that they think are mysteries,[5] though they are mimes, full of absurdity and nonsense.

3,2 For these are certainly myths: They claim that Aeons were emitted from the Aeon on high, and that Ialdabaoth came into being on a lower level.[6] But he was emitted in accordance with the weakness and ignorance of his own mother, that is, the supernal Prunicus.[7] (3) For they say this Prunicus had come down into the waters and become mingled with them, but could not go back up because of being mingled with the weight of matter. For she has been intermingled with the waters and matter, and can no longer withdraw. (4) But she heaved herself up with an effort and stretched herself out, and thus <the> upper heaven was formed. And as she was fixed in place, no longer able either to go up or to come down but fixed and stretched out in the middle, there she remained. (5) For she could not sink down because she had no affinity (with what was below her); but she could not go up because she was heavy from the matter which she had taken on.[8]

---

[4] Cf. PsT 2.1. The snake is "the instructor" at Nat. Arc. 89,31-32; 90,6; Orig. Wld. 118,24-119,18; 119,34-120,6. At Iren. 1.30.15 Sophia herself becomes the snake. For a discussion of this subject see Pagels, *Adam, Eve and the Serpent.*

[5] Epiph is referring to what he believes is the Ophite eucharist; see below at 5,6-8.

[6] PsT 2.2: dicunt enim de illo summo primario Aeoni complures aeones exstitisse inferiores, omnibus tamen istis Aeonem antestare, cuius sit nomen Ialdabaoth.

[7] At Tri. Trac. 105,10-19 the Logos brings forth the Demiurge "[forgetfully], ignorantly and [defectively], and in all the other weak ways." For Prunicus as the mother of Ialdabaoth see Iren. 1.30.4-5. See also p. 00 n. 00.

[8] PsT. 2.2 where, however, this is said of Ialdabaoth. A more elaborate version of all this is found at Iren. 1.30.3.

3,6 But when Ialdabaoth[9] had been emitted in her ignorance he went to the very bottom and begot seven sons,[10] who begot seven heavens.[11] And he closed off the space above him and hid it from view, so that the seven sons he had emitted, being lower down than he, would not know what was above him, but no one at all but him.[12] And he, they say, is the God of the Jews, Ialdabaoth. (7) But this is not so, of course not! God the Almighty will judge them, for he is God both of Jews and Christians, and everyone, and not any Ialdabaoth, as their silly story has it.

4,1[13] Then, they say, when the heights had been closed off by Ialdabaoth's design, these seven sons he had begotten—whether they were aeons, or gods, or angels, they use various terms for them—fashioned the man in the image of their father Ialdabaoth. Not easily or quickly, however, but in the same way in which the earlier sects had made it out in their drivel. For these people too say, "The man was a creeping thing like a worm, not able either to look up or get to his feet.'"[14] (2) But as a scheme against Ialdabaoth the supernal Mother, the one called Prunicus[15]—wishing to empty Ialdabaoth of his power[16] which he had gotten from her by participation[17]—worked in him on the man his sons had formed,[18] intending to drain his power and send a spark[19] from him, the soul supposedly,[20] upon the man. (3) And then, they say, the man stood on his feet, rose in mind above the eight heavens, and recognized and praised the Father on high who is above Ialdabaoth.[21]

4,4 And then, distressed because the things high up above him had been recognized, Ialdabaoth stared bitterly down at the dung of matter and sired a power with a snake-like appearance,[22] which they also call his

---

[9] Cf. PsT 2.2 and Iren. 1.30.3 See also p. 00 n. 00.

[10] Cf. PsT 2.2; Iren. 1.30.3; Nat. Arc. 94,34-95,5; Corp. Herm. I.9.

[11] Cf. Apocry. Jn. II,1 11,4-8.

[12] PsT. 2.3 and Iren. 1.30.6. Cf. Tri. Trac. 79,12-19; 80,24-30; Nat. Arc. 94,4-95,5.

[13] With 4,1-2 cf. Pst 2.3 and Iren. 1.30.6. See also p. 00 n. 00.

[14] PsT 2.3; Iren. 1.30.6. And see p. 00 n. 00.

[15] For Prunicus see p. 85 n. 9.

[16] Iren. 1.30.6: et hoc Sophia operante uti et illius (Ialdabaoth) evacuet ab humectatione luminis etc. See p. 88 n. 16.

[17] Cf. Apocry. Jn. II,110,19-21; 11,8-9; 13,1-5, and the robbery of Pistis Sophia's light-power at PS 1.31 (MacDermot p. 46). See further p. 65 n. 18.

[18] I.e., she is the real agent at Gen 2:7.

[19] Cf PsT 2.4. For the hypostatized "spark" as an emanation in the heavens see Apocry. Jn.6,13-18; Para. Shem 31,22-23; 33,30-34; 46,13-15; *Ginza* 467,30-31. See p. 72 n. 12.

[20] Cf. Tri. Trac. 105,29-106,5.

[21] For the superiority of the first man to his makers see Apocry. Jn II,1 19,32-20,9; 20,28-31; Apoc. Ad. 64,14-19, and in Mandaean literature, *Ginza* 107,14-15; 465,24-27.

[22] Cf. PsT 2.4; Iren. 1.30.5; Acts of Philip 130 (James p. 449).

son. (5) And so, they say, this son was sent on his mission and deceived Eve. And she listened to him, believed him as a son of God,[23] and because of her belief ate from the tree of knowledge.[24]

5,1 Then, whenever they are describing this foolishness and the absurdity of this practice[25]—now that they have composed the tragic piece, as we might say, and this comic opera—they begin to point certain things out to us in support of their false so-called "gods." They say, "Are not our intestines also, by which we live and are nourished, shaped like a serpent?"[26] (2) And in support of their imposture and silly opinion they introduce any number of further points for their dupes. "We glorify the serpent for this reason," they say; "because it has been a cause if their knowledge for the many."[27]

5,3 Ialdabaoth, they say, did not want the Mother on high, or the Father, remembered by men. But the serpent convinced them and brought them knowledge, and taught the man and the woman the whole of the knowledge of the mysteries on high. (4) Hence his father—Ialdabaoth, that is—was angry because of the knowledge he had given men, and threw him down from heaven. (5) And therefore these people who possess the serpent's portion and nothing else, call the serpent a king from heaven. And so, they say, they glorify him for such knowledge and offer him bread.

5,6 For they have a real snake and keep it in a basket of some sort. When it is time for their mysteries they bring it out of the den, spread loaves around on a table, and call the snake to come; and when the den is opened it comes out. And then the snake—which comes up of its own accord and by its villainy—already knowing their foolishness, crawls onto the table and coils up on the loaves. And this they call a perfect sacrifice.

5,7 And so, as I have heard from someone, not only do they break the loaves the snake has coiled on and distribute them to the communicants, but each one kisses the snake on the mouth besides—whether the snake has been charmed into tameness by some sort of sorcery, or coaxed by some

---

[23] PsT. 2.4: cui Eva quasi filio Dei crediderat. Cf. Iren. 1.30.7; Apocry. Jn. II,1 22,3-9 where Christ, not the serpent, gives the command to eat. And see n. 4 above. For a discussion of Gnostic views of Eve see "Gnostic Improvisations on Genesis" in Pagels, *Adam. Eve, and the Serpent* pp. 57-77.

[24] Cf. Iren. 1.30.7.

[25] Their worship of the snake.

[26] Iren. 1.30.15: Sed et propter positionem intestinorum nostrorum, per quae esca infertur, eo quod talem figuram habeant, ostendentem absconditam generatricem Serpentis figurae substantiam in nobis.

[27] Cf. Or. Wld. 118,24-119,18; Nat. Arc. 89,31-90,19.

other act of the devil for their deception. (8) But they worship an animal of that sort and call what has been consecrated by its coiling around it the eucharistic element.[28] And they offer a hymn to the Father on high—again, as they say, through the snake—and so conclude their mysteries.

6,1 But anyone would call <this> foolishness and sheer nonsense. And it will not require refutation by research in sacred scripture; to anyone with godly soundness of mind its absurdity will be self-evident. For all their drivel will at once appear as something silly. (2) If they say hat there is a "Prunicus," as I have already remarked, how can one fail to detect the unsoundness of their notion from the very name? Anything called "seductive" is unseemly. But if it is unseemly it cannot be ranked among things to be preferred. And how can an unseemly thing be praiseworthy?

6,3 And how can it be anything but mythology to say that Prunicus drained Ialdabaoth, and that the spark went down below from him when he was drained; but that once it had lodged in the man, it recognized the person above the person who had been drained? (4) What a very great surprise that the man, with the tiniest of sparks in him, recognizes more than the angels who fashioned him! For the angels, or sons of Ialdabaoth, did not recognize the things above Ialdabaoth; but the man they had made did, by means of the spark!

6,5 Ophites refute themselves with their own doctrines by glorifying the snake at one moment, but at the next making him a deceiver who came to Eve when they say, "he deceived Eve."[29] (6) And they sometimes proclaim him Christ, but sometimes a son of the higher Ialdabaoth, who wronged his sons by shutting off the knowledge of <the> realms on high from them and despised both the Mother and the Father on high, in order to keep the sons he had sired from honoring the Father above him.

6,7 How can the serpent be a heavenly king if he has rebelled against the Father? And if he gives knowledge, why is he denounced as having fooled Eve with a deception? Someone who instills knowledge through deceit is no longer giving knowledge, but ignorance instead of knowledge; and one can truly see that, among them, this is the case. For they have ignorance and think it is knowledge—though when they call their own "knowledge" deceit and ignorance, in this they are telling the truth!

7,1 They cite other texts as well, and say that Moses too lifted the bronze serpent up in the wilderness and exhibited it for the healing of

[28] PsT 2.1: Ipsum (serpentem) introducunt ad benedicenda eucharistia sua.
[29] 2 Cor 11:3

persons who had been bitten by a snake.[30] For they say that that sort of thing serves as the cure for the bite. (2) But once more, they are making these declarations against themselves. For if the bites were snake's bites, and these were harmful, then the serpent is not good. The thing Moses held up in those days effected healing by the sight of it—not because of the nature of the snake but by the good pleasure of God who, by means of the snake, was making a sort of antidote for those who were bitten at that time. (3) It is no surprise if a person is cured through the things by which he was injured. And let no one speak ill of God's creation—as other erring persons do in their turn.

7,4 However, this served the people in the wilderness as a type, for the reason the Lord gives in the Gospel when he comes, "as Moses lifted up the serpent in the wilderness, even so must the Son of Man be lifted up"[31]—which indeed has been done. (5) For dishonoring the Savior like a serpent they were injured by the serpent's scheme, I mean the devil's. And as healing came to those who had been bitten by the lifting up of the serpent, so, at Christ's crucifixion, deliverance has come to our souls from the bites of sin which we have gotten.

7,6 But the same people cite this very text as evidence and say, "Do you not see how the Savior said, 'As Moses lifted up the serpent in the wilderness, even so must the Son of man be lifted up?'[32] And on this account," they say, "he also says in another passage, 'Be ye wise as the serpent and harmless as the dove.' "[33] And what God has rightly ordained for us as symbols of teaching they cite in their own deluded sense.

8,1 For our Lord, the divine Word Jesus Christ, begotten of the Father before all ages without beginning and not in time, is not a serpent—heaven forbid!—but came himself to combat the serpent. (2) If he says, "Be ye wise as the serpent and harmless as the dove,"[34] we must inquire and learn why he introduced these two figures, of the serpent and of the dove, for our instruction. (3) There is nothing wise about a snake except for <the> two following things. When it is being hunted it knows that its whole life is in its head, and it is afraid of the order once given about it by God for the man's sake, "Thou shalt guard against its head, and it shall guard against thy heel."[35] So it coils its whole body over its head and hides its skull, but

[30] Cf. PsT 2.11; Hipp. Refut. 5.16.7-8.
[31] 1 John 3:14
[32] John 3:14
[33] Matt. 10:16
[34] Matt. 10:16
[35] Gen. 3:15

with extreme villainy surrenders the rest of its body. (4) In the same way the only-begotten God, who came forth from the Father, wills that in a time of persecution and a time of temptation we surrender our whole selves to fire and sword, but that we guard our "head"—in other words, that we do not deny Christ, since "The head of every man is Christ, and the head of the woman is the man, and the head of Christ is God,"[36] as the apostle says.

8,5 Again, as the naturalists say of this beast, the snake has another kind of wisdom. When it is thirsty and goes from its den to water to drink, it does not bring its poison with it but leaves it in its den, and then goes and takes its drink from the water. (6) Let us imitate this ourselves so that, when we go to God's holy church for prayer or God's mysteries, we do not bring evil, pleasure, passion, enmity or anything else in our thoughts.

8,7 For that matter, how can we imitate the dove either without keeping clear of evil—though certainly, in many ways doves are not praiseworthy. (8) Doves are insatiable and incessantly promiscuous, lecherous, given to the pleasure of the moment, and weak and small besides. (9) But because of the harmlessness, patience and forbearance of doves—and even more, because of the Holy Spirit's appearance in the form of a dove—the divine Word would have us imitate the will of the Holy Spirit and the harmlessness of the harmless dove and be wise in good but innocent in evil.

And their entire dramatic piece has been demolished. (10) For straight off, by saying, "I fear, lest by any means, as the serpent beguiled Eve through his villainy, so your minds should be corrupted from the sincerity and simplicity of Christ, and from righteousness,"[37] the apostle assigns villainy and treachery to none more than to the devil and the serpent. (11) You see how the apostle pronounced the serpent's dealings with Eve seduction, frightful villainy and deceit, and made it clear that nothing praiseworthy had been done by it.

9,1 Hence their stupidity is discernible and obvious in all respects to anyone who is willing to know the teaching of the truth and the knowledge of the Holy Spirit. (2) But not to waste time, now that I have sailed through this fierce, hazardous storm at sea as well, I shall ready my barque for its other sea voyages, carefully guarding my tongue by God's power and the prayers of saints, (3) so as to espy the tossing of the wild waves as I sail by, and the forms of the poisonous beasts in the seas, but be able to cross and

---

[36] 1 Cor 11:3

[37] 2 Cor 11:3

reach the fair haven of the truth by prayer and supplication, untouched by the poison of sea eel, stingray, dragon, shark and scorpaena. (4) In my case too, the text, "They that go down to the sea shall tell the virtues of the Lord,"[38] will prove applicable. So I shall make my way to another sect after this, for its description.

38.

Against Cainites.[1] *Number eighteen but thirty-eight of the series*

1,1 Certain persons are called Cainites because they have taken the name of their sect from Cain. For these people praise Cain and count him as their father—since they too, in a manner of speaking, are being driven by a different surge of waves without being outside of the same swell and surf; and are peering out of thorny undergrowth, without being outside of the whole heap of thorns even though they differ in name. For there are many kinds of thorn, but the painfulness of being pricked by thorns is in them all.

1,2 Cainites say that Cain is the scion of the stronger power and the authority above; so, moreover, are Esau, Korah and his companions, and the Sodomites.[2] But Abel is the scion of the weaker power. (3) <They acknowledge> all of these as worthy of their praise and kin to themselves. For take pride in their kinship with Cain, the Sodomites,[3] Esau and Korah. And these, they say, represent the perfect knowledge from on high. (4) Therefore, they say, though the maker of this world made it his business to destroy them, he could do them no harm; they were hidden from him and translated to the aeon on high, from which the stronger power comes. For Wisdom allowed them to approach her because they were her own.[4]

1,5 And they say that because of this Judas had found out all about them. For they claim him too as kin and regard him as possessed of superior knowledge, so that they even cite a short work in his name which they call

---

38 Ps 106:23-24

1 The primary sources of Sect 38 are Hipp. Synt. (see PsT 2.5 and Iren. 1.31.1-2).
2 Iren. 1.31.1, cf. PsT 2.5.
3 The Sodomites are witnesses to the truth at Para. Shem 29,12-29. At Gos. Egyp. III,2 56,4-13; 60,9-18, Sodom and Gomorrah are the source of the heavenly seed of Seth. In the passages Apoc. Adam 71,8-72,14 and 74,26-76,7 they are (75,1-3) "the great men who have not been defiled."
4 Iren. 1.1.31. See p. 291 n. 24.

a Gospel of Judas.[5] (6) And they likewise forge certain other works against "Womb." They call this "Womb" the maker of this entire vault of heaven and earth and say, as Carpocrates does, that no one will be saved unless they progress through all (possible) acts.[6]

2,1 For while each of them is doing some unspeakable thing supposedly with this excuse, performing obscenities and committing every sin there is, he invokes the name of each angel—both real angels, and the ones they fictitiously call angels. And he attributes some wicked commission of every sin on earth to each of them, by offering his own action in the name of whichever angel he wishes. (2) And whenever they do these things they say, "This or that angel, I am performing thy work. This or that authority, I am doing thy deed."[7] (3) And this is what they call perfect "knowledge," since, if you please, they have taken their cue for venturing without fear on wicked obscenities from the mothers and fathers of sects whom we have already mentioned—I mean the Gnostics and Nicolaus, and their allies Valentinus and Carpocrates.

2,4 Further, I have now learned of a book in which they have forged certain assertions which are full of wickedness, containing such things as "This is the angel who blinded Moses. These are the angels who hid the companions of Korah, Dathan and Abiram, and removed them elsewhere."

2,5 But again, others forge another brief work in the name of the apostle Paul, full of unspeakable abominations, which the so-called Gnostics also use, (and) which they call an Ascension of Paul—taking their cue from the apostle's statement that he has ascended to the third heaven and heard ineffable words, which man may not speak. And these, they say, are the ineffable words.[8]

2,6 But they teach these things and others of the sort for the sake of honoring the wicked and repudiating the good. For <they claim>, as I said, that Cain is the offspring of the stronger power and Abel of the weaker. These powers had intercourse with Eve[9] and sired Cain and Abel; and Cain

[5] Iren. 1.31.1: Judae Evangelium illud vocantes. It is generally agreed that this is the Gospel of Judas of the Codex Tchacos.

[6] Iren. 1.31.2: Hysteran autem factorem caeli et terrae vocant. At Apocry. II,1 Jn. 5,4-5 Barbelo is First Thought, or the womb, of everything, cf. Pr. Thank. 64,21-30. For Womb see also Para. Shem 4,30; 6,7 and *passim.*

[7] For the whole of this see Iren. 1.31.2.

[8] The Apocalypse of Paul, NHC V,2, says nothing of the "unutterable words" although at 22,29-23,5 it gives a speech Paul makes in order to pass above the Ancient of Days.

[9] Cf. Apocry. Jn. II,1 23,35-24,25 and the archons' attempt to abuse Eve at Nat. Arc. 89,17-30; 116,33; Orig. Wld. 116,12-117,14. At Iren. 1.30.7 the archons sire angels.

was the son of the one, Abel of the other. (7) And <both> Adam and Eve were the offspring of powers or angels like these. And the children the powers had begotten, I mean Cain and Abel, quarreled, and the scion of the stronger power murdered the scion of the lesser and weaker.

3,1 But they too interweave the same mythology with their gift of ignorance about these same deadly poisons by advising their followers that everyone must choose the stronger power, and separate from the lesser, feeble one—that is, from the one which made heaven, the flesh and the world—and rise above it to the uttermost heights through the crucifixion of Christ. (2) For this is why he came from above, they say, so that the stronger power might act in him by triumphing over the weaker and betraying the body. (3) And some of them say this; others, other things. For some say that Christ was betrayed by Judas because Christ was wicked, and wanted to pervert the provisions of the Law. For they commend Cain and Judas, as I said, and they say, "This is why he has betrayed him; he intended to abolish things that had been properly taught."

3,4 But others say, "No, he betrayed him even though he was good, in accordance with the heavenly knowledge. For the archons knew," they say, "that if Christ were surrendered to the cross the weaker power would be drained. (5) And when Judas found this out," they say, "he eagerly did everything he could to betray him, performing a good work for our salvation. And we must commend him and give him the credit, since the salvation of the cross was effected for us through him, and for that reason the revelation of the things on high."[10]

3,6 But they are deceived in every way in not honoring or praising anyone who is good. It is obvious that these things, I mean their ignorance and deceit, have been sown in them by the devil. (7) The scriptural words, "Woe unto them that call good evil and evil good, that put darkness for light and light for darkness; that call sweet bitter and bitter sweet,"[11] are applicable to them. (8) Old and New Testaments speak out in every way in denunciation of Cain's impiety. These on the contrary, lovers <of> darkness that they are and imitators of evildoers, hate Abel but love Cain and give their praise to Judas. (9) And they counterfeit a pernicious "knowledge" by setting up two powers, a weaker and stronger, which quarrel with each

[10] PsT 2.6 also gives two versions of Judas' motive, though they are not the same as those given here. At Gos. Jud. 56,19-20 Jesus says to Judas, "You will sacrifice the man who bears me," i.e., apparently, You will free me from my body of flesh. The text of Gos. Jud. 57,1-11 though very defective, seems to suggest that the consummation will result from Jesus' crucifixion. And see Fil. 34.1-2 and Iren 1.31.11.

[11] Isa. 5:20

other and see to it that there can be no changing of one's mind in the world, but of those who are born here, some are by nature derived from evil, others from goodness. They say that no one is good or bad by choice, but by nature.

4,1 And first, let us see how the Old Testament says of Cain, "Thou art cursed from the earth, which hath opened her mouth to receive thy brother's blood at thy hand," and again, "Thou art cursed in thy works, and shalt go sighing and trembling upon the earth."[12] (2) And the Lord in the Gospel spoke of him in agreement with the Old Testament, when Jews told him, "We have God as our father."[13] But the Lord said to them, "Ye are sons of your father the devil, for he is a liar because his father was a liar. He was a murderer, and abode not in the truth. When he speaketh a lie he speaketh of his own, for his father was a liar also."[14]

4,3 And so, from hearing this said, the other sects allege that the devil is the father of the Jews, and that he has another father, and that his father in turn has a father. (4) But they are speaking impudently and blinding their own reason. They are tracing the devil's ancestry to the Lord of all, the God of the Jews, the Christians and all men, by saying that he is the father of the devil's father—the God who gave the Law through Moses and has done so many wonders!

4,5 But this is not so, beloved. To begin with, the Lord himself, who cares for us in all things, <meant> Judas when he said that their father was the devil—to keep us from deviating from the plain sense with one quibble and supposition after another. (6) He has called Judas both "Satan" and "devil" in saying to his disciples, "Have I not chosen you twelve, and one of you is a devil?"[15] meaning, not devil by nature but devil in intent. (7) Again, in another passage he says, "Father, Lord of heaven and earth, keep those whom thou hast given me. While I was with them I kept them, and none of them is lost but the son of perdition."[16] (8) Once more, he says elsewhere, "The Son of Man must be betrayed as it is written of him, but woe unto him by whom he shall be betrayed. It were better for him if he had not been born,"[17] and so on.

[12] Gen. 4:11-12
[13] John 8:41
[14] John 8:44
[15] John 6:70
[16] John 17:11-12
[17] Matt. 26:24

4,9 Hence we know from every source that he was speaking to the Jews about Judas. "For of whom a man is overcome, of the same he is brought in bondage";[18] and the person one trusts, him he has as his father and the author of his belief. (10) The Lord, then, says, "Ye are sons of your father, the devil,"[19] because they trusted Judas instead of Christ, just as Eve at the beginning turned away from God and trusted the serpent. (11) Then, he says it because Judas was not merely a liar but a thief as well, as the Gospel says. That was why he entrusted him with the bag—so that he would be without excuse when, from greed, he delivered his master into the hands of men.

4,12 Who is Judas' father then, the "liar before him," but Cain, whose imitator Judas was? Lying to his brother as though in affection, Cain deceived and cajoled him with the lie, and took him out to the plain, raised his hand and killed him. (13) Thus Judas too says, "What will ye give me, and I will deliver him unto you?"[20] and, "Whomsoever I kiss, that same is he; hold him fast."[21] And the betrayer said, "Hail, Master," when he came, honoring him with his lips, but with his heart far removed from God.

5,1 Hence this Judas, who became their father in denial of God and betrayal, a Satan and devil not by nature but in intent, has himself become a son by imitation of the murderer and liar, Cain. For Cain's "father" before him was a liar too—not Adam, but the devil—(2) whose imitator Cain became in fratricide, hatred and falsehood, and contradicting God by saying, "Am I my brother's keeper? I know not where he is."[22] (In the same way the devil says, "Doth Job fear God for nought?"[23] to the Lord.) (3) For since the devil himself deceived Adam and Eve with the lie, "Ye shall be as gods and shall not die,"[24] telling an untruth and showing pretended friendship, Cain, in imitation of him, deceived his brother with a pretense of affection by saying, "Let us go out to the plain."[25]

5,4 This is why St. John too said, "He that hateth his brother, the same is not made perfect in love, but is of Cain, who slew his brother. And wherefore slew he him? Because his works were evil and he envied

---

[18] 2 Pet. 2:19
[19] John 8:44
[20] Matt 26:48-49
[21] Matt 25:48
[22] Gen 4:9
[23] Job 1:9
[24] Gen. 3:4;5
[25] Gen 4:8

his brother's, for they were good."[26] (5) So these people who prefer to envy Abel with his good works but honor Cain—how can they not be convicted when the Savior expressly pronounces the severe sentence against them by saying , "Of this generation all righteous blood shall be required, from the blood of righteous Abel which was shed at the beginning unto Zacharias the prophet, whom ye slew between the temple and the altar,"[27] and so on.

6,1 Hence Judas did not betray the Savior because of knowledge as these people say; nor are the Jews to be rewarded for crucifying the Lord, though we indeed have salvation through the cross. (2) Judas did not betray him so that it would bring about our salvation, but from the ignorance, envy and greed of the denial of God. (3) Even if scripture can say that Christ was to be surrendered to a cross—or even if the sacred scripture predicts the offenses that will be committed by ourselves in the last days—none of us, who commit the transgressions, can find any defense by alleging the testimony of the scripture that foretells the commission of them. (4) We do not do these things because scripture <fore>told them, but scripture foretold them because we would do them—from God's foreknowledge and to remove any suspicion that God, who is good and yet inflicts his wrath upon sinners, can be ruled by emotion. (5) For God's anger at every sinner does not stem from emotion. The Godhead is impassible and visits its wrath on men, not because it has been seized with irritation or mastered and overcome by anger. God shows his impassibility by telling us beforehand of the judgment to come and the just penalty to be exacted, to indicate the impassibility of the Godhead.

6,6 Hence scripture foretold these things, forewarning and teaching us in accordance with its foreknowledge, so that we need not encounter the implacable wrath of God—a wrath not determined by emotion and not the result of mastery by it, but which has been prepared beforehand, with entire justice, for men who commit sin and do not truly repent.

7,1 So also with the cross. It was not because sacred scripture said they would that the Jews crucified the Savior and Judas betrayed him; but because Judas would betray, and the Jews crucify him, sacred scripture foretold this in the Old Testament and the Lord in the Gospel. (2) Hence Judas did not betray the Lord—as the Cainites say he did—in awareness of the benefit that would come to the world. He betrayed him knowing that he was his master, but not knowing that he would be the world's salvation. (3) How could he be the one who saw to men's salvation, the man who heard "son

[26] 1 John 3:15; 4:18; 3:12
[27] Matt 23:35

of perdition"[28] from the Savior himself; "Better for that man if he had not been born";[29] "Friend, do that for which thou art come";[30] "One of you shall betray me";[31] "He that eateth bread with me hath lifted up his heel against me";[32] (here the Gospel quotes an earlier text from the Psalter); and, "Woe unto him by whom the Son of Man is betrayed?"[33]

7,4 For Judas himself made the whole truth about himself apparent; and even <of> himself, though unwillingly, he exposed the stupidity of those who praise him, by repenting later after getting the thirty pieces of silver as his price, and returning the money as though he had done something bad—bad for himself, and bad for the executioners as well. (5) But to do good of himself, for us and for the world, the Lord has surrendered himself to become our salvation.

7,6 Hence we do not thank the betrayer, Judas, but the merciful Savior who laid down his life for us—for his own sheep, as he himself said. (7) If Judas thought he had done a good thing, why did he later say, "I repent that I have betrayed innocent blood,"[34] and return the money? As it was written of him in the prophets, "And he returned the thirty pieces of silver, the price of him that was valued of the children of Israel."[35] And again, in another prophet, "If ye deem proper, give me my price, or forbear." (8) And again, in another prophet, "And they gave the silver, the price of him that was valued, and he said, Cast it into the refiner's furnace, and see whether it be proved, as I was proved of the children of Israel."[36]

8,1 And how many points can be gathered from the sacred scripture about the prophecies which have been fulfilled in our Lord—not concerning Judas' work for good, but concerning the delivery for us, not of necessity but of his free choice, of our Savior and Lord Jesus Christ the Son of God, and the provision of the cross for our salvation! (2) But I know I am stringing the texts out too long—as one more prophet says, "Let his habitation be desolate, and his bishopric let another take,"[37] <meaning that Judas[38] died badly>. (4) Thus the apostles made Matthias one of them in his stead,

---

[28] John 17:12
[29] Matt 26:24
[30] Matt. 26:30
[31] Matt. 26:30
[32] John 13:18; Ps. 40:10
[33] Matt 26:24
[34] Matt 27:4
[35] Cf. Zech. 11:12
[36] Zech. 11:12-13; Matt 27:9
[37] Acts 1:20; Ps. 68:6; 108:8
[38] Acts 1:18; Matt. 27:5

saying "from which Judas by transgression fell, that he might go to his own place."[39] (5) And which "place" but the one the Savior had designated for him by saying that he was a "son of perdition?" For this "place of perdition" was reserved for him where he obtained a portion instead of a portion and, instead of apostolic office, the place of perdition.

8,6 But I think enough has been said about this, beloved. Let us go on again to another to expose once more the obscure, savage, poisonous teachings of the members of the remaining sects who, to the world's harm, have gotten cracked by the bogus inspiration of the devil. (7) After exposing the opinion of such people who yearn for the worst—an opinion that resembles poisonous dung beetles—and crushing it by God's power because of its harmfulness, let us call on God for aid, sons of Christ, as we set our minds to the investigation of the others.

39.

Against Sethians.[1] *Number nineteen, but thirty-nine of the series*

1,1 "Sethians" is yet another Sect, of that name. It is not to be found everywhere, nor is the one before it, the so-called sect of "Cainites"; most of these too have probably been uprooted from the world by now. For that which is not of God will not stand; it flourishes for a while, but has no permanence at all.

1,2 I think I may have met with this sect in Egypt too—I do not precisely recall the country in which I met them. And I found out some things about it by inquiry in an actual encounter, but have learned other things from treatises.

1,3 For these Sethians proudly trace their ancestry to Seth the son of Adam,[2] glorify him, and attribute to him whatever <is held> to be virtuous—the marks of virtue and righteousness, and anything of the kind.

---

[39] Acts 1:25

[1] The source of this Sect is primarily literary (cf. what Epiph says at 1,2) and seems to be Hipp. Synt., which is represented by PsT 2,7-9. Some of Epiph's information, however, was obtained at first hand. The "Sethians" of Hipp. Refut. 5.19-22 are not relevant here. On the subject of the Sethians see Schenke, Turner, Wisse.

[2] In several NHC tractates Gnostics are represented as the "seed" (σπέρμα) or "race" (γένος) of Seth, distinct from other peoples. See Apocry. Jn. II,1 9,14-16; 25,9-16; Gos. Egyp. III,2 59,9-17; 60,2-18; 61,23-62,19; 64,22-24; Apoc. Adam 65,3-9; 66,1-6; 71,8-72,14; 85,19-22; Gr. Seth 63,8-9; Zost. 130,14-17; Stel. Seth 119,2; 120,1-16. At Apocry. Jn. II,1 25,1-2; Gos. Egyp. III,2 56,13-22 this seed or race is said to be preexistent; it comes to earth later. It is usually called σπορά rather than σπέρμα by Epiph.

What is more, they even call him Christ[3] and maintain that he is Jesus. (4) And they give their teaching in the following form: all things, they say, are the work of angels[4] and not of the power on high.

2,1 For in this regard they agree with the previous sect, the sect of the Cainites: Two men were born at the very beginning, and Cain and Abel were the sons of the two. And in quarreling about them the angels went to <war with> each other, and so brought it about that Abel was killed by Cain. (2) For the angels' quarrel was a struggle over the human stocks,[5] since these two men, the one who had sired Cain and the one who had sired Abel, <were at odds with each other>. (3) But the power on high has won, the one they call Mother and Female.[6] For they have the idea that there are both mothers on high, and females and males, and they all but say "kindreds and patriarchies" too.

2,4[7] Since the so-called Mother and Female had won, finding that they had killed Abel, they say, she reflected, caused the generation of Seth, and put her power in him—planting. in him a seed of the power from above, and the spark that was sent from above for a first planting and origin of the seed. (5) And this is the origin of righteousness, and the election of a seed and stock, so that the powers of the angels who made the world and the two primordial men would be purged by *this origin and this seed. (6) For this reason the stock of Seth is derived separately from this origin, since it is elect and distinct from the other stock.

2,7 For as time went on, they say, and the two stocks, Cain's and Abel's, were together, <and> had come together because of great wickedness and had intercourse, the Mother of all, who had kept watch, wanted to make the seed of men pure, as I said, since Abel had been killed. And she chose this Seth and made him pure,[8] and planted the seed of her power and purity in him alone.

---

[3] Cf. PsT 2.9 and see Gos. Jud. 52,4-6: The first is [S]eth, who is called 'the Christ.' Van der Vliet, however, considers this a textual error: see his "Judas and the Stars" pp. 146-151. Seth is clearly identified with Jesus at Gos. Egyp. CG IV,2, 62,24-64,9; 65,16-18 and perhaps at Apoc. Adam 76,8-77,18; Gr. Seth 51,20-52,10, though in this latter tractate the name Seth is found only in the title. See n. 13 below.

[4] Cf. PsT 4.7.

[5] PsT 2.7. Val. Exp. 38,24-33: And Cain [killed] Abel his brother, for [the Demiurge] breathed into [them] his spirit. And there [took place] the struggle with the apostasy of the angels and mankind, those of the right with those of the left, and those in heaven with those on earth, the spirits with the carnal, and the Devil against God. See also Tri. Trac. 83,34-84,36.

[6] The Holy Spirit is Prima Femina et Mater viventium at Iren. 1.30.1-2. PsT 2.7 says only "Mater." See p. 00.00.

[7] With 2,7 cf. PsT 2.7.

[8] καθαρὸν ἔδειξεν. Or: showed him to be pure.

3,1 But once more, seeing a great deal of intercourse and unruly appetition on the part of angels and men since the two breeds had come together for intercourse, and seeing that their unruliness had caused certain origins of (new) breeds, Mother and Female returned and brought the flood, and destroyed the entire human race <and> all of the opposing stock—in order that, supposedly, only the pure stock that derived from Seth and was righteous would remain in the world, for the origin of the stock from on high and the spark of righteousness.[9]

3,2 But without her knowledge the angels in their turn slipped Ham, who, was of their seed,[10] into the ark. For they say that of the eight persons who were saved in Noah's then ark, seven were of the pure stock but one was Ham, who belonged to the other power and got in unknown to the Mother[11] on high.[12] (3) A plan of this sort, of the angels' contrivance, was thus carried out. For, they say, since the angels had learned that all their seed would be wiped out in the flood, they smuggled Ham in by some knavery to preserve the wicked stock they had created.

3,4 And for this reason forgetfulness and error have overtaken men, and the inordinate impulses of sins and a conglomeration of evil have arisen in the world. And thus the world reverted to its ancient state of disorder, and was as filled with evils as it had been at the beginning, before the flood. (5) But from Seth by descent and lineage came Christ, Jesus himself, not by generation but by appearing miraculously in the world. He is Seth himself, who visited men then and now[13] because he was sent from above by the Mother.

4,1 This is the way they say all this came about. But doctrines like these are foolish, weak and full of nonsense, as everyone can plainly see. (2) Two men were not formed (at the beginning) but one man, Adam, and from Adam came Cain, Abel and Seth. And <the human stocks>

---

[9] PsT 2.8. At Gos. Egyp. III,2 61,1-5 and Apoc. Adam 69,2-18 the Flood is sent to wipe out the seed of Seth.

[10] The seed of Ham and Japheth mingle with the seed of Seth at Apoc. Adam 73,13-29.

[11] "The Mother" is found in a Sethian hymn at Gos. Egyp. III,2 67,4-6.

[12] PsT 2.9

[13] At Gos. Egyp. III,2. 51,5-22 the heavenly Seth is the son of Adamas and the father of "the immoveable race." At 55,17-56,21 he receives his seed through Plesithea (the equivalent of Eve?) and places it in the "fourth aeon." At 59,9-60,18 he comes to earth bringing his seed, which he places in Sodom. At 62,24-64,8 he is "sent," as Jesus, "to save her (the race) that went astray." See also 65,16-18 and 63,4-8.

In the simpler version of Apocry. Jn. II,1 Seth is the son of Pigera-Adamas and is placed over the "second aeon" (8,29-9,14). At 24,35-25,2 Adam begets the earthly Seth in the likeness of the (heavenly) "son of man." At Gos. Judas 52,4-6, strangely, "Seth, who is called Christ" is one of the five angels who rule over the underworld. But see n. 3 above.

up until the flood cannot derive from two men but must derive from one, since all the stocks have their own origins in the world <from> Adam. (3) And in turn, every human breed since the flood derives from Noah, the one man not derive—not from different men but from one, Noah, Seth's lineal descendant; and it is not divided into two, but is one stock. (4) And so Noah's wife, his sons Shem, Ham and Japheth, and the three wives of his sons, are all trace their ancestry to Seth, not to the two men of the Sethians' mythology, who never existed.

5,1 They compose certain books in the names of great men and say that there are seven books in Seth's name,[14] and give the name, "Strangers," to other, different books.[15] And they compose another in the name of Abraham which they call an "apocalypse" and is full of wickedness, and others in the name of Moses., and others in others' names.

5,2 Lowering their own minds to great absurdity they say that Seth's wife is a certain Horaia. Take a look at their stupidity, beloved, so that your will despise their melodrama, mythological nonsense and fictitious claptrap in every way. (3) There are certain other sects which say there is a power to whom they give the name "Horaia." Now these people say that the one whom others regard as a power and call Horaia, is Seth's wife!

5,4 Thus we can show—as you know, beloved—both that Seth was a real man and that he got no unusual endowment from above, but was the blood brother of Cain and Abel, from one father and one mother. (5) For scripture says, "Adam knew Eve his wife, and she conceived and bare Cain"; and she named him Cain, meaning "acquisition," saying, "I have acquired a son through the Lord God."[16] (6) Again, in the case <of> Abel, "Adam knew Eve his wife and she conceived and bare a son and called his name Abel."[17] (7) And much farther on, after the death of Abel, "And Adam knew Eve, his wife, and she conceived and bare a son, and called his name Seth," meaning "recompense." "For," she said, "God hath raised up for me a seed instead of Abel, whom Cain slew."[18] (8) But the expression, "I have acquired *through God*," and " *God* hath raised up for me," show that

---

[14] Books of Seth in NHC are VII,2 *The Second Treatise of the Great Seth* and VII,5 *The Three Steles of Seth*. Gos. Egyp. III,2 68,10-12 attributes this book to Seth, and the same may be true of Allog. 68,25-28.

[15] For books termed Allogenes, "Stranger," see NHC XI,3 and Tractate 4 of the Codex Tchacos. Porphyry mentions an Apocalypse of Allogenes at Vita Plotini 16.

[16] Gen 4:1

[17] Cf. Gen 4:1-2.

[18] Gen 4:25

the one God, the maker of all is also the giver of these offspring. (9) And that Cain and Seth, at least, took wives is plain—for Abel was killed in his early youth, not yet married.

6,1 But as we find in Jubilees which is also called "The Little Genesis," the book even contains the names of both Cain's and Seth's wives,[19] so that the persons who recite myths to the world may be put to shame in every way. (2) For after Adam had sired sons and daughters it became necessary at that time that the boys marry their own sisters. Such a thing was not unlawful, as there was no other human stock. (3) Indeed, in a manner of speaking Adam himself practically married his own daughter who was fashioned from his body and bones and had been formed by God in conjunction with him, and it was not unlawful. (4) And his sons were married, Cain to the older sister, whose name was Saue; and a third son, Seth, who was born after Abel, to his sister named Azura.[20]

6,5 And Adam had other sons too as the Little Genesis says, nine after these three,[21] so that he had two daughters but twelve sons, one of whom was killed but eleven survived. (6) You have the reflection of them too in the Genesis of the World, the first Book of Moses, which says, "And Adam lived 930 years, and begat sons and daughters, and died."[22]

7,1 But when humanity had expanded and Adam's line was growing longer, the strict practice of lawful wedlock was gradually extended. (2) And then, since Adam had had children and children's children, and daughters were born to them in direct descent, they no longer took their own sisters in marriage. Even before the written Law given by Moses the rule of lawful wedlock was reduced to order, and they took their wives from among their cousins. (3) And now, while humanity was expanding in this way, the two stocks were commingled—Cain's with Seth's and Seth's with the other, and so were the other stocks of Adam's sons.

7,4 Then finally, when the flood had destroyed all of mankind at once, Noah alone, who found favor with God, was preserved, because he had been found righteous in that generation. (5) And as I said before, he prepared his ark by God's decree, as the true scriptures tell us. The same book of the truth states that he was preserved in it, and with him the seven souls I have mentioned—I mean his own wife and three sons, and their wives, likewise three.[23] (6) And the truth affirms that for this reason remnants of

---

[19] Jub. 4.9; 11
[20] Jub. 4.9-11
[21] Jub. 4.10
[22] Cf. Gen 15:3-5.
[23] Cf. Gen 7:7; 1 Pet 3:20.

the generation of men were again left in the world. And so, as time went on from generation to generation and with son succeeding father, the world had come to span five generations.

8,1 And the foundation of Babylon in Assyria took place at that time, and the tower that they built then. (2) And, as I have already explained in the foregoing Sects with regard to the series of generations I dealt with earlier, all humanity then consisted of 72 men, who were princes and patricians—32 of Ham's stock, 15 of Japheth's, and 25 of Shem's. And so the tower and Babylon were built.

8,3 After this tribes and languages were dispersed over the entire earth. And since the 72 <who> were then building the tower were scattered by the languages—because they had been confused, and <divorced> from the one language that they knew—each one, by God's will, was infused with a different language and acquired it. (4) The existence of the (various) languages from then until now began with them, so that <anyone who> cares to, can discover the originator of each language. For example Iovan, for whom the Ionians who possess the Greeks' ancient speech are named, acquired Greek.[24] Theras[25] acquired Thracian; Mosoch,[26] Mossynoecian; Thobel,[27] Thessalian; Lud,[28] Lydian; Gephar,[29] Gasphenian; Mistrem[30] Egyptian; Psous,[31] Axomitian; and Armot,[32] Arabian. And not to mention them individually, each of the rest was infused with his own tongue. And thus the continuation of every language in the world was extended.

9,1 Why is it, then, that these people have told their lies, interpolating their own mythology, imagining and dreaming of unreal things as though they were real, and banishing what is real from their own minds? But the whole thing is an idea of the devil which he has engendered in human souls. (2) It is amazing to see how he deceived man into many offenses and dragged him down to transgression, to fornication, adultery and incontinence, to the madness of idols, to sorcery and bloodshed, to rapine and insatiate greed, to trickery and gluttony, and any number of such things—but never before Christ's coming ventured to say a blasphemous word against his own Master or meditate open rebellion. (3) For he was awaiting

[24] Hipp. Chron. 60 (Bauer-Helm p. 12,4)
[25] Hipp. Chron. 63 (op. cit. p. 12,6-7)
[26] Hipp. Chron. 169 (op. cit. p. 26,9)
[27] Hipp. Chron. 61 (op. cit. p. 12,5)
[28] Hipp. Chron. 111 (op. cit. p. 18,13)
[29] Hipp. Chron. 168 (op. cit. p. 26,8)
[30] Hipp. Chron. 95 (op. cit. p. 17,2)
[31] Hipp. Chron. 96 (op cit. 17,8)
[32] Hipp. Chron. 178 (op. cit. p. 27,17)

Christ's coming as he says, "It is written of thee that he shall give his angels charge concerning thee, and in their hands they shall bear thee up."[33] (4) He had always heard the prophets proclaim the coming of Christ <and> that there would be a redemption of those who had sinned and yet repented through Christ, and he thought that he would obtain some mercy. (5) But when the wretch saw that Christ had not accepted his turnabout for salvation's sake he opened his mouth against his own Master and spewed the blasphemy out, implanting in men the suggestion that they deny their real Master and seek the one who was not real.

9,6 Now the Sethians too will be exposed in every way as victims of deception, by the following argument: Seth has died, and the years of his life are recorded. He went the way of all flesh after living for 912 years, having fathered sons and daughters as sacred scripture says. (7) And next his son, his name was Enosh, also lived for 905 years, and departed this life after fathering sons and daughters, as the same book of the truth says.

10,1 Therefore if Seth died then, and his sons in succession also lived and departed this life, how will it be found that he is the Lord who was conceived of the ever-virgin Mary after consenting to human life—who was begotten at no point in time, who is always with the Father as the divine Word subsistent; (2) but who came in the last days, fashioned flesh in his own image from a virgin womb and, having taken the human soul, thus became perfect man? (3) The Lord who proclaimed the mysteries of life to us, appointed his disciples as workers of righteousness, and instructed the human race in his teaching, himself and through them—not by revealing the teachings of the Sethians or calling himself Seth as they, foolishly and overcome by a sort of drunkenness, have lost the truth.

10,4 But now, though the <rebuttal of the> sect is brief, I do not need to extend its refutation, and am content with just what is here. Their stupidity is easy to puncture and is self-refuting and self-exposing, not only with regard to their kidnaping of Christ and their falsely alleged belief and affirmation that he is Seth, but because of the two men as well. (5) For if the powers had their origin from above, nothing which was done by the two powers was made and done without the one power—whom, indeed, they call the Mother of *all*. For the one power is plainly the cause of the two powers, and nothing that has been done, has been done without it. (6) And once the beginning is shown to be one, they will return to the confession that the Master of all, and the Creator and Maker of the whole, is one.

---

[33] Matt 4:6; Luke 4:11

10,7 But since we have said these things about this sect as well, beloved, and have exposed the poison of their reptilian brood of the asp family, let us once more go to another, in the same order of the treatise.

40.
Against Archontics.[1] *Number 20, but forty of the series*

1,1 A sect of Archontics comes after these although it is to be found in few places, or only in the province of Palestine. But by now they may also have brought their poison to Greater Armenia. (2) Moreover, this tare has already been sown in Lesser Armenia by a man who came from Armenia to live in Palestine during the reign of Constantius at about the time of his death. His name was Eutactus though he was "disorderly" rather (than "orderly"), and after learning this wicked doctrine he returned to his homeland and taught it.

1,3 As I said he got it—like getting poison from an asp—in Palestine from an old man unworthily named Peter, who used to live in the district of Eleutheropolis <and> Jerusalem, three mile-stones beyond Hebron; they call the village Kephar Baricha.

1,4 To begin with, this old man had an extraordinary garment, stuffed with hypocrisy. For he actually wore a sheep's fleece on the outside, and it was not realized that on the inside he was a ravening wolf. He appeared to be a hermit because he lived in a certain cave, gathered many, supposedly for the ascetic life, and he was called "father," if you please, because of his age and his dress. He had distributed his possessions to the poor, and he gave alms daily.

1,5 He had belonged to many sects in his early youth but during Aetius' episcopate he was accused and convicted of being a Gnostic, and was then deposed from the presbyterate—at some time he had been made a presbyter. After his conviction he was banished by Aetius and went to live in Arabia at Cocabe where the roots of the Ebionites and Nazoraeans were—as I have indicated of Cocabe in many Sects.

1,6 He returned later, however, as though having come to his senses with the approach of old age. But he was secretly carrying this poison within him and went unrecognized by everyone until finally, from things he had whispered to certain persons, he was exposed for what he was

[1] This Sect is based upon Epiph's experience and upon Gnostic sources, particularly on a work he calls *The Harmony*.

and anathematized and refuted by my poor self. (7) And after that he took up residence in the cave, abhorred by all and isolated from the brotherhood and from most who cared for their salvation.

1,8 This Eutactus—if, indeed, he was "orderly"—was entertained by this old man on his way home from Egypt, imbibed the old man's wicked doctrine and, receiving this poison as choice merchandise, brought it back to his own country. For as I said, he came from Lesser Armenia, near Satale. (9) On his return to his homeland, then, he polluted many there, in Lesser Armenia. For he had unfortunately become acquainted with certain rich men, with a woman of senatorial rank, and with other persons of distinction, and through these prominent people he ruined many of his countrymen. The Lord quickly removed him from the world, only he had sown his tare.

2,1 These people too have forged some apocrypha of their own, and these are their names. They call one book a "Lesser Harmony," if you please, and another a "Greater Harmony." They heap up certain other books, moreover, <and add these> to any they may light on, to give the appearance of confirming their own error through many sources. (2) And by now they also have the ones called the "Strangers"—there are books with this title.[2] And they take cues from the Ascension of Isaiah, and from still other apocrypha.

2,3 But everything <about their sect can be seen> from the book called the Harmony in which they say there is an ogdoad of heavens and a hebdomad, and that there are archons for each heaven. And certain belong to the seven heavens, one archon to one heaven, and there are bands (of angels) for each archon, and the shining Mother[3] is at the very top in the eighth heaven—like the other sects.

2,4 Some of them are defiled in body by licentiousness; but others make a show of pretended fasting, if you please, and deceive the simple by taking pride in some kind of ascetic discipline in the guise of hermits.[4] (5) And as I mentioned, they say that there is a principality and authority for every heaven and certain angelic servitors, since each archon has sired

---

[2] See p. 281 n. 14.

[3] See p. 100 n. 14.

[4] A comparable accusation might be implied by Gos. Jud. 40,7-16: After him another man will stand up from the [fornicators], and another [will] stand up from the slayers of children, and another from those who sleep with men and those who abstain (ⲛⲉⲧⲛⲏⲥⲧⲉⲩⲉ)...and those who say, "We are like angels".

and created his own retinue.[5] But there is no resurrection of the flesh, only of the soul.[6]

2,6 They execrate baptism, though there may be some who have previously been taken and baptized.[7] And they make light of participation in the mysteries, and of their goodness, as something that is foreign to them and has been instituted in the name of Sabaoth.[8] (Like certain other sects they hold that he is in the eighth heaven, ruling as an autocrat and lording it over the others.) (7) They say that the soul is the food of the principalities and authorities, and that they cannot live without it, since it is some of the ichor on high and affords them power.[9] (8) But if it has come into knowledge and avoided the baptism of the church and the name of Sabaoth the lawgiver it ascends heaven by heaven and offers its defense to each authority, and thus rises above them to the supernal Mother and the Father of all, the very place from which it descended into this world.

2,9 I have already said that they execrate baptism as "deadly flies, causing the preparation of the oil of sweetness to stink"[10]—as the parable is given by the Preacher, with reference to them and people of their kind. For they are truly flies which are deadly and death-dealing, and which spoil the aromatic oil of sweetness—God's holy mysteries which are granted us in baptism for the remission of sins.

3,1 But one might be surprised to find some things of great usefulness even in the naturalists if he emulates the bee in wisdom, which settles on every plant and gathers what is useful to it. (2) For the wise man never loses anywhere but profits by everything; but the unwise will incur loss as the holy prophet says, "Who is wise, and he shall understand these things? And

---

[5] Cf. Eug. 88,17-89,2.

[6] Note Treat. Res. 47,1-12: Therefore never doubt concerning resurrection... For if you were not existing in the flesh, you received flesh when you entered this world. Why will you not receive flesh when you ascend into the Aeon? That which is better than flesh, which is for it the cause of life, that which came into being on your account, is it not yours? Other passages which could be interpreted as teaching a "resurrection of the soul" are Test. Tr. 34,25-38,27; 44,3-7; Gos. Jud. 43,12-44,7; 53,16-26.

[7] Baptism is bitterly condemned at Para. Shem 37,19-38,27; Test. Tr. 69,7-22, and probably at Gos. Judas 55,21f though this text is fragmentary. See also the Marcosian objections to baptism which are mentioned at 34,20,9-12, p. 252. At the Mandaean *Ginza* 255,5-10 Christian baptism is called the "sign of (the fallen) Ruha."

[8] Gos. Jud. 34,6-11 states the same kind of objection to the eucharist. See also Gos. Jud. 56,11-13.

[9] Cf. Dia. Sav. 122,19; PS 1.26 (McDermot pp. 36-37); 1.27 (p. 39) et al.

[10] Eccles 10:1

who hath the word of the Lord, and he shall know them. For the ways of the Lord are straight, but the transgressors shall fail in them."[11]

3,3 For I find even in the so-called naturalists—or rather, I see for myself—that it is the nature of dung-beetles, which some call bylari, to roll in foulness and dung, and this is food and work for them. But to other insects this same filthy food of theirs <is plainly> offensive and evil-smelling. (4) For bees too, this dung and foul odor is death, while to dung-beetles it is work, nourishment, and an occupation. For bees, in contrast, fragrance, blossoms and perfumes serve as refreshment, an acquisition and food, and as work and an occupation. But such things are the reverse for the dung-beetles, or bylari.

3,5 Anyone who desires to test them, as the naturalists say, can cause the death of dung-beetles by taking a bit of perfume, I mean balsam or nard, and applying it to them. They die instantly because they cannot stand the sweet odor. (6) Thus these people too, with their desire for copulation, fornication and wickedness, set their hope on evil things, but if they come near the holy font and its sweet fragrance, they die blaspheming God and despising his sovereignty.

4,1 But I shall demolish them with one or two texts. Even though there are things called principalities and authorities, they have not been established apart from God, especially not in the heavens. (2) For scripture does know of "angels and archangels," not as ranged in opposition but as "ministering spirits, sent forth to minister for them who shall be heirs of salvation."[12]

4,3 Even on earth indeed there are many "authorities" in each kingdom, but under one king. "The powers that be are ordained of God," as the apostle says: "Whosoever, therefore, resisteth the power resisteth the ordinance of God, (4) since the rulers are not against the good, but for the good, and not against the truth, but for the truth. Wilt thou not be afraid of the power?" he says. "Do that which is good, and thou shalt have praise of the same. For he beareth not the sword in vain. For he is a minister ordained of God for this very thing, for him that doeth evil."[13] (5) And you see how this worldly authority has been appointed by God and has received the right of the sword, not from any other source but from God, for retribution. And we cannot say that because there are principalities

[11] Hos 3:2
[12] Heb 1:14
[13] Rom 13:1-4; 2 Cor 13:8

and authorities in the world, their king is not a king. The principalities and authorities exist, and so does their king.

4,6 We see on earth—it is plainly evident—that the principalities are not opposed to the king but set under him, for the administration of the whole kingdom and the good ordering of earth, where there are murders and wars, mistakes and instructions, instances of order and disorder. And authorities exist for this reason, the good ordering and disposition of all God's creatures in an orderly system for the governance of the whole world. (7) And so in heaven—but most especially there, where there is no envy, jealousy, disorder, contention, discord, conspiracy, robbery or anything else of this nature—authorities have been appointed for another task. (8) Which task do I mean but the repetition of the hymn, the unalloyed praise on high? On its account our bountiful God and king has willed to grant each of his creatures its proper glory, that the splendor, incomprehensibility and awesomeness of his kingdom may always be glorified. Plainly, then, those Archontics have gone wrong from not knowing the grace of God.

5,1 As I have mentioned already, they say the devil is the son of the seventh authority, that is, of Sabaoth. Sabaoth is God of the Jews and the devil is his wicked son, but is on earth to oppose his own father. (2) And his father is neither like him—nor, again, is he the incomprehensible God whom they call "Father," but he belongs to the left-hand authority.

5,3 People of their sort tell yet another myth, that the devil came to Eve, lay with her as a man with a women, and sired Cain and Abel by her. (4) That was why the one attacked the other—from their jealousy of each other and not, as the truth is, because Abel had somehow pleased God. Instead they concoct another story and <say>, "Because they were both in love with their own sister, Cain attacked Abel and killed him for this reason." For as I mentioned they say that they were actually of the devil's seed.

5,5 Whenever they want to fool someone they cite texts from the sacred books—I have mentioned this in another Sect as well—<to the effect that> the Savior said, "Ye are of Satan," to the Jews and, "Whensoever he speaketh a lie he speaketh of his own, for his father was a liar also."[14] (6) This allows them to say, if you please, that Cain was the <son> of the devil because the Savior said that the devil was a murderer from the beginning; and to say that the devil was <a liar because his father was a liar>, (7) to prove that Cain's father was the devil, and that the devil's

[14] John 8:44

father was the lying archon. The fools say, in blasphemy against their own head, that this is Sabaoth himself, (8) since they suppose that Sabaoth is a name for some god.

Already in the previous Sects I have dealt at length with the translation of Sabaoth and other names—Eli and Elohim, El and Shaddai, Elyon, Rabboni, Jah, Adonai and Jahveh—(9) since they are all to be translated as terms of praise, and are not as it were given names for the Godhead. Here too I hasten to give them in translation. (10) "El" means "God"; "Elohim," "God forever"; "Eli," "my God"; "Shaddai," "the Sufficient"; "Rabboni," "the Lord"; "Jah," "Lord"; "Adonai," "He who is existent Lord." "Jahveh" means, "He who was and is, He who forever is," as he translates for Moses, "'He who is' hath sent me, shalt thou say unto them."[15] "Elyon" is "highest." And "Sabaoth" means, "of hosts"; hence "Lord Sabaoth," means, "Lord of Hosts." (11) For wherever scripture uses the expression, "Sabaoth," <"Lord"> is put next to it. <Scripture> does not merely cry, "Sabaoth said to me," or, "Sabaoth spoke," but says immediately, "Lord Sabaoth." For the Hebrew says, "Adonai Sabaoth," which means "Lord of hosts."[16]

6,1 And it is in vain that they and people like themselves quibble, in the blindness of their minds, at things which have been rightly said. (2) There is nothing said about the devil in what the Savior said to the Jews, as is obvious to any follower of the truth; he said what he did to them on Judas' account. (3) They were no children of the Abraham who entertained him beneath the oak of Mamre before his incarnation. They condemned themselves to becoming sons of the treason of Judas who is called Satan and devil by the Lord, as he says, "Have I not chosen you twelve, and one of you is a devil?"[17] (4) And because of this, to show his evil nature, the Lord said, "Whensoever he speaketh a lie he speaketh of his own."[18] And the Gospel also says, in another passage, "He was a thief, and himself bare the bag."[19]

6,5 As his father, then, Judas, who was called "devil," had Cain, who deceived his brother Abel with a lie and killed him and also falsely said,"I know not,"[20] when he was asked by the Lord, "Where is Abel thy brother? (6) Suitably, then, he too, since he had mimicked the actual devil's behav-

[15] Exod 3:14
[16] Cf. Gos. Egyp. III,2 48,14-15: Adonaios who is called Sabaoth.
[17] John 6:70
[18] John 8:44
[19] John 12:6
[20] Gen 4:9

ior, was rightly designated his son by the Savior. For "Of whom a man is overcome, of the same is he also brought in bondage."[21] And each of us, whatever he does, will get as fathers the ones who have done it before him, by his imitation of them. (7) It has been clearly explained, then, that the Savior's saying, "Ye are children of the devil"—and again, "Whensoever he speaketh a lie he speaketh of his own, for his father was a liar"[22]—was a reference to Judas and Cain. (8) Accordingly, "For his father was a liar," referred to the devil himself, because of the deeds like his which were done by each of them. For in breathing into the serpent's mouth the devil has spoken all lies, and this is how he deceived Eve then.

6,9 And their erring mythology about these passages is discredited even though scripture says, "As Cain slew his brother, for he was of the devil."[23] It has been fully demonstrated that he was called the devil's son not, as they suppose, because of Eve's conceiving from the devil's seed as in conjugal intercourse and physical union and bearing Cain and Abel, but because of his similar character and his imitation of the devil's wickedness.

7,1 But again, the same people say that Adam had intercourse with his own wife, Eve, and sired Seth as his own actual son. And then, they say, the power on high came down with the ministering angels of the good God, (2) snatched Seth himself, whom they also call "Stranger," bore him aloft somewhere and nurtured him for some time so that he would not be killed.[24] And long afterwards it brought him back down to this world and made him spiritual, and yet physical <in appearance>, so that the <Demiurge>, and the other authorities and principalities of the god who made the world, would not prevail against him. (3) And they say he no longer worshiped the creator and demiurge, but recognized the ineffable power and the good God on high,[25] <and> that he worshiped him, and made many revelations about the maker of the world and its principalities and authorities.

7,4 <And so> they have also composed certain books in the name of Seth himself, saying that they have been given by him, and others in the

[21] 2 Pet 2:19

[22] John 8:44

[23] 1 John 3:12

[24] Cf. Irenaeus 1.31.11. Something comparable is said of Sabaoth at Nat. Arc.95,19-22; Orig. Wld. 104,17-22. In the Mandaean *Ginza* this is said of Shitil at 443,9-11, and of John the Baptist at *Johannesbuch* 116,13-19. Cf. also the disappearance of Judas into a shining cloud at Gos. Jud. 57,16-23.

[25] Sabaoth recognizes Pistis in this way and worships her at Or. Wld. 103,32-104,6. Adam recognizes "the likeness of his own foreknowledge and hence begets Seth at Apocry. Jn. II,1 23,35-25,2.

name of him[26] and his seven sons. (5) For they say he sired seven <sons> called "Strangers,"[27] as I have also said in other Sects, I mean The Gnostics and The Sethians.)

7,6 They say that there are other prophets too, a Martiades and a Marsianus, who were snatched up into the heavens and came down three days later.[28] (7) And there are many things which they make up and write down falsely, fabricating blasphemies against the true God the Almighty, the Father of our Lord Jesus Christ, as though he were an archon and an originator of evil—a thing of which they are convicted by their own words.

7,8 For if an originator of evils is also an evildoer how can it not be found at once that God is good, as I have said in the other Sects, since he legislated against fornication, adultery, rapine and covetousness? For they too say he is God of the Jews—but he gave the Jews the Law, in which he forbade all these things of which they call him the originator! And how can he be called Satan's father, when he has given so many warnings against Satan?

7,9 And suppose he is foreign to the God they call high, and is not God the Almighty himself—our King and Lord, <proclaimed> in Law, Prophets, Gospels and Apostles, himself God the[29] Lord, and Father of our Lord Jesus Christ. Why does the Lord himself plainly teach (that he is) in the Gospel, and say, "I thank thee, Father, *Lord of heaven and earth*" to show that his Father is God of all?

8,1 And again, to hint that there will be a resurrection of the dead, the Son of this God says, "Destroy this temple, and in three days I will raise it up."[30] But by "temple" he meant his own body, which would be "destroyed" by the hands of men—that is, killed. (2) But something which was not a body but an apparition—as these people in their turn say[31]—could

---

[26] See p. 98 n. 34.

[27] Cf. Three Stel. 120-11-13: they are from other races, they are not similar. And see p. 281 n. 15.

[28] Cf. U 7 (MacDermot p. 235): The powers of all the great aeons have given homage to the power which is in Marsanes. They said, "Who is this who has been these things before his face, that he has thus revealed concerning him?" NHC X,l is entitled *Marsanes*. Marsanes is also mentioned at Eus. H. E. 6.12.

[29] Matt 11:25

[30] John 2:19

[31] For NHC examples of at least quasi-docetism, see 2 Apoc. Jas. 57,10-19; Gr. Seth 53,23-26; 55,16-56,19; 27-30; Apoc. Pet. 81,3-83,15; Melch. 5,2-11, however, polemicizes against docetism. See also Man. Ps. 191,4-8; 196,22-26 as well as the Acts of John 87-99 (H-S II pp. 179-180); 101-102 (pp. 185-186); Acts of Paul VII.1.14 (H-S II p. 254).

not have fallen into someone's hands and been raised the third day, as he promised. (3) By such a provision it is plainly proved that the resurrection of the dead is undeniable, and <that> the soul does not need a speech of defense to give before each authority—this too is a fabrication of theirs, as we have said—but needs the Lord's deed of lovingkindness, sustained by works and faith. (4) So says the most holy Paul, writing to Timothy with these words: "That thou mayest know how thou oughtest to behave thyself in the house of the Lord, which is the church of the living God, the pillar and ground of the truth,[32] which the many having deserted have turned unto fables and words of folly,[33] understanding neither what they say nor whereof they affirm,[34] of whom are Phygelus and Hermogenes."[35] (5) In his second epistle, moreover, he says that Hymenaeus and Philetus have gone wrong about the truth.[36] They were followers of this sect themselves, proclaiming another God and endless genealogies, (6) implanting fresh error in men by saying that the world was not made by God but by principalities and authorities, and that the resurrection has already come in the children who are begotten by each of their parents, but that there will be no resurrection of the dead. And see the character of the truth, brothers, and the refutation of their disorder!

8,7 But I suppose that enough has been said about these people too. I shall pass this sect by and make my way to the rest, saying only that, with the variety of its names for archons, this sect seems very like the tangled malignity of serpents. (8) For in a way the poisonous emission of their imposture has been taken at random from many snakes. It has the dragon's arrogance, for example, the treachery of the toad that inflates itself, the pull in the opposite direction of the gudgeon's breath, the pride of the quick-darting serpent, and calamine's uselessness. (9) But now that we have crushed the heads of all these with the statement of the truth, beloved, let us go on to the rest, and try by God's inspiration to disclose the error of each.

[32] 1 Tim 3:15
[33] 2 Tim 4:4
[34] 1 Tim 1:7
[35] 2 Tim 1:15
[36] Cf. 2 Tim 2:17

41.

Against Cerdonians.[1] *Number twenty-one, but forty-one of the series*

1,1 One Cerdo succeeds these and Heracleon—a member of the same school, who took his cue from Simon and Satornilus. He was an immigrant from Syria who came to Rome[2] and appeared there, utter wretch that he was, as his own scourge and the scourge of his followers.

1,2 For the human race is wretched when it leaves God's way and strays, and has perished by separating itself from God's calling. (3) The proverb of the dog attending to the reflection of <the food> it had in its mouth applies to people like these. Looking into a pond, and thinking that the reflection in the water was larger than the food in its mouth, it opened its mouth and lost the food it had. (4) So these people, who had found the way and yet wanted to get hold of the reflection which had been formed in their imaginations, not only lost the nourishment which God had, as it were, graciously placed in their mouths, but drew destruction upon themselves as well.

1,5 Cerdo, then, lived in the time of bishop Hyginus, the ninth in succession from the apostles James, Peter and Paul.[3] Since his doctrine partakes of the other heresiarchs' foolishness it appears to be the same, but with him it is different and takes the following form:

1,6 He too has proclaimed two first principles to the world, and two supposed gods, one good, and unknown to all, whom Cerdo has called the Father of Jesus—and one the demiurge, who is evil and knowable,[4] and has spoken in the Law and appeared to the prophets[5] and often become visible. (7) Christ is not born of Mary and has not appeared in flesh, but since he exists in appearance he has also been manifest in appearance, and done everything in appearance.[6] And Cerdo too rejects the resurrec-

---

[1] The sources of this Sect are Irenaeus (1.27.1) and Hipp. Synt. (PsT 6.1). Eus. H. E. 4.11.1-2 depends upon Irenaeus, as does Hipp. Refut. 10.19.1-4. Fil. 44 uses Hipp. Synt. Hipp. Refut. 10.19.1-4 treats of Cerdo and Marcion together and appears to have a different source.

[2] Eus. H. E. 4.11.1 and Fil. 46 mention Cerdo's Syrian origin.

[3] This date, and the notice of the succession, are found at Iren. 1.27.1; Eus. H. E. 4.11.1.

[4] This paragraph comes chiefly from Hipp. Synt.; see PsT 6.1: initia duo, id est duos deos etc. Iren. 1.27.1 furnishes hunc enim cognosci illum autem ignorari. PsT calls the creator saevum; Epiph, probably reflecting the original, πονηρόν; Fil 4.1, malum. Iren. and Hipp. Refut. 7.37.1 say δίκαιον/justum.

[5] PsT 6.1: Hic prophetias et legem repudiat.

[6] Cf. PsT. 6.1; Fil. 44.2.

tion of the flesh, and repudiates the Old Testament which was given by Moses and the prophets, as something foreign to God. (8) But Christ has come from on high, from the unknown Father, to put an end to the rule and tyranny of the world-creator and demiurge here, as many of the sects have declared of course. (9) After a short time in Rome he imparted his venom to Marcion, and Marcion thus became his successor.

2,1 Since this sect is just as detectible (as the last), my remarks about it will be brief. And once again, I shall begin the refutation of Cerdo from the very things he says. (2) For that there cannot be two first principles at once is obvious. Either the two principles are derived from some one; or the one is a second principle, while the other is the cause and principle of the second. So we shall need either to find a cause for the two or find which of them, being the principle of the other, <is its cause>, as I said. (3) And thus our minds must be led back by every route to the one, the principle which is found to be the first, the source either of the second or of both, as I have shown.

2,4 But the two first principles cannot possibly exist at once, nor can the one possibly differ from the other. For if they differ there are two of them; but by adding up to two they have become more than one. But since the one, first number is required, "two" are subordinate to the number which is "one" and prior, the cause of "two." (5) For the "two," which come after the number "one," or single, first principle, cannot be their own cause since the unit, which comes first of all, is always required.

2,6 For if it is apparent that the two are of one accord and mutually complaisant and harmonious, with one of them consenting to the permanence of the other and the other rejoicing in its partnership with the first, what conflict is there between the two of them? (7) But if they are in conflict, and each is equally as strong as the other, then, although Christ came to do away with the one, he cannot be capable of destroying its tyranny. It will stand its ground and have the ability to struggle with the invisible, unnameable power on high and hold out, and can never be destroyed.

3,1 The fool says that both the Law and the prophets belong to the inferior, contrary principle, but that Christ belongs to the good one. (2) Then why did the prophets make prophecies which typified Christ, unless the power that spoke in the Law, the prophets, and the Gospels was one and the same? As he says, "Lo, here am I that speak in the prophets," and so on. (3) And why did the Lord also, in the Gospel, <cry out>, "Had ye believed Moses, ye would have believed me also, for he wrote of me?"[7]

---

[7] Luke 1:8

3,4 And I could say a great deal about proof-texts, just as Cerdo did to gather his own school when he sprouted up in the world at an evil juncture and led his dupes astray. (5) But I shall pass it by as well since I have destroyed it like a bembix or wasp—flying insects with stings, that suddenly take wing and dart at us—with God's self-evident faith, (6) with the saving teaching of our Lord Jesus Christ, who said, "See ye be not deceived, for many false prophets shall come in my name"; and with the teaching of the apostle, who spoke of these false Christs, false teachers and false brethren, and warned us against them. <And> proceeding to the rest in our series, I shall give the description of the others.

42.

Against Marcionites.[1] *Number twenty-two, but forty-two of the series*

1,1 Marcion, the founder of the Marcionites, taking his cue from Cerdo, appeared in the world as a great serpent himself and became the head of a school by deceiving a throng of people in many ways, even to this day. (2) The sect is still to be found even now, in Rome and Italy, Egypt and Palestine, Arabia and Syria, Cyprus and the Thebaid—in Persia too moreover, and in other places. For the evil one in him has lent a great deal of strength to the deceit.

1,3 He was a native of Pontus[2]—I mean of Helenopontus and the city of Sinope, as is commonly said of him. (4) In early life he supposedly practiced celibacy, for he was a hermit and the son of a bishop of our holy catholic church.[3] But in time he unfortunately became acquainted with a virgin, cheated the virgin of her hope and degraded both her and himself,[4] and for seducing her was excommunicated by his own father. (5) For because of his extreme piety his father was one of those illustrious

[1] This Sect follows the outline of Hipp. Synt., which is represented by PsT 6.2-3 and Fil. 45; it inserts data from Irenaeus. (Fil. may have used Epiph as well.) Epiph has also read Eusebius (H. E. 4.11.1; 5.13.1-4) and his data about Marcion's "gods" may be based on a faulty memory of this author. Reproduced is Epiph's own treatise on Marcion's canon, from which he gives a number of quotations. Epiph takes reports of Marcion's and Cerdo's teachings as interchangeable, since he regards the latter as Marcion's master.

The earliest mention of Marcion is found at Justin Apol. 1.26.5. Tertulllian's long treatise *Adversus Marcionem* utilizes, among its other sources, some of Marcion's own writings. The source of Hipp. Refut. 7.27.1;30 is not obvious.

[2] Cf. Justin. Apol. 26.5; Iren. 1.27.2; Hipp. Refut. 7.29.1; 10.19.1 Pst 6.2; Fil. 45.1; Eus. H. E. 5.13.4 (where Marcion is called ὁ λύκος Πόντικος); Tert. Adv. Marc. 1.1.4; 3.6.3.

[3] PsT 6.2

[4] PsT 6.2. The same sort of thing is said of Apelles at Tert. Praescr. 30.

men who take great care of the church, and was exemplary in the exercise of his episcopal office. (6) Though Marcion begged and pleaded many times, if you please, for penance, he could not obtain it from his own father. For the distinguished old bishop was distressed not only because Marcion had fallen, but because he was bringing the disgrace on him as well.

1,7 As Marcion could not get what he wanted from him by fawning, unable to bear the scorn of the populace he fled his city and arrived at Rome itself after the death of Hyginus, the bishop of Rome. (Hyginus was ninth in succession from the apostles Peter and Paul). Meeting the elders[5] who were still alive and had been taught by the disciples of the apostles, he asked for admission to communion, and no one would grant it to him. (8) Finally, seized with jealousy since he could not obtain high rank besides entry into the church, he reflected and took refuge in the sect of that fraud, Cerdo.

2,1 And he began—at the very beginning, as it were, and as though at the starting-point of the questions at issue—to put this question to the elders of that time: "Tell me, what is the meaning of, 'Men do not put new wine into old bottles, or a patch of new cloth unto an old garment; else it both taketh away the fullness, and agreeth not with the old. For a greater rent will be made'"?[6]

2,2 On hearing this the good and most sacred elders and teachers of God's holy church gave him the appropriate and fitting answer, and equably explained, (3) "Child, 'old bottles' means the hearts of the Pharisees and scribes, which had grown old in sins and not received the proclamation of the gospel. (4) And 'the old garment' received a 'worse rent' just as Judas received a further rent through his own fault and no one else's because,al though he had been associated with the eleven apostles and called by the Lord himself, he had grown old in greed and had not received the new, holy, heavenly mystery's message of hope. (5) For his mind was not in tune with the high hope and heavenly call of the good things to come, in place of worldly wealth and vanity, and the love of passing hope and pleasure."

2,6 "No," Marcion retorted, "there are other explanations besides these." <And> since they were unwilling to receive him, he asked them plainly, "Why will you not receive me?"

[5] Fil. 45.1: Urbem Roman devenit, ibique degens sceleratam heresin seminabat, atque interrogans presbyteros sanctae catholicae ecclesiae…

[6] Matt. 9:16-17; Luke 5:36. PsT 6.2 makes Marcion cite Matt. 7:17. Fil. 45.2 gives both citations, opening the possibility that this author knew Epiph as well as Hipp. Synt. Matt. 7:17 is referred to at Hipp. Refut. 10.19.3 and at Tert. Adv. Marc. 3.15.5; 4.11.10.

2,7 "We cannot without your worthy father's permission," was their answer. There is one faith and one concord, and we cannot oppose our excellent colleague, your father.

2,8 Becoming jealous then and roused to great anger and arrogance Marcion made the rent, founding his own sect and saying, "I am going to tear your church, and make a rent in it forever." He did indeed make a rent of no small proportions, not by rending the church but by rending himself and his converts.

3,1 But he took his cue from that charlatan and swindler, Cerdo.[7] For he too preaches two first principles. But adding something to him, I mean to Cerdo, he exhibits something different in his turn by saying that there are three principles.[8] One is the unnameable, invisible one on high which he likes to call a "good God,"[9] but which has made none of the things in the world.[10] (2) Another is a visible God, a creator and demiurge.[11] But the devil is as it were a third god and in between these two, the visible and the invisible.[12] The creator, demiurge and visible God is the God of the Jews, and he is a judge.[13]

3,3 Celibacy[14] too is preached by Marcion himself, and he preaches fasting on the Sabbath. Marcionite supposed mysteries are celebrated in front of the catechumens.[15] He uses water in the mysteries.

3,4 He claims that we should fast on the Sabbath for the following reason: "Since it is the rest of the God of the Jews who made the world

---

[7] Fil. 45.3: Deque hoc accipiens interpretationem a sanctis presbyteris non acquiescebat veritati sed magis Cerdonis sui doctoris firmabat mendacium. Cf. Eus. H. E. 4.11.2.

[8] From Eus. H. E. 5.13.4: ἄλλοι...οὐ μόνον δύο ἀλλὰ καὶ τρεῖς ὑποτίθεντα φύσει, ὧν ἔστιν ἀρχηγὸς καὶ προστάτης Σύνερως. Epiph has forgotten the attribution to Syneros. PsT 6.1-2 and Iren 1.27.2 attribute the doctrine of two Gods to Cerdo as does Tert. Adv. Marc. *passim*. Hipp. Refut. 7.31.1-2 ascribes the doctrine of two Gods to Marcion, and of three to the Marcionite teacher Prepon. See also Adam 1.2.

[9] At Hipp. Refut. 10.19.1-2 the "principles "are ἀγαθόν, δίκαιον, ὕλην or ἀγαθόν, δίκαιον, πονηρόν, ὕλην. PsT 6.1, as of Cerdo, says unum bonum, alterum saevum. Fil. 46, also as of Cerdo, gives: unum bonum et unum malum annuntians.

[10] Cf. Iren. 1.27.2; PsT 6.1; Hipp. Refut. 10.19.1.

[11] Iren. 1.27.2: quem et Cosmocratorem dicit; Hipp. Refut. 30.3.4: δημιουργόν.

[12] None of Epiph's sources speak of the devil as god. Epiph may be extrapolating from the πονηρός/saevus of Hipp. Refut. 10.19.1/PsT 6.1. For a god intermediate (μέσον) between the two others see Hipp. Refut. 7.31.2, where the idea is ascribed to one Prepon, and Ptolemy's Epistle to Flora at Pan. 42,7,4.

[13] That is, "just." Iren. 1.27.1; Eus. H. E. 4.17.2; Hipp. Refut. 7.31.2, and see Pan. 42.7.4.

[14] Hipp. Refut. 7.30.3-4; 10.19.4; Clem. Strom. 3.3.12.1-2; 4.25.1-2; Tert. Adv. Marc. 1.29.1. Epiph, however, contradicts this at 43,1,5.

[15] Tert. Praescr. 41.1-2, although Tertullian does not specify Marcionites.

and rested the seventh day, let us fast on this day, so as to do nothing congenial to the God of the Jews,"[16] (5) He denies the resurrection of the flesh like many of the sects; he says that resurrection, life and salvation are of the soul only.[17]

3,6 Marcionite baptism is not administered just once; in Marcionite congregations it is allowable to give up to three baptisms and more to anyone who wishes, as I have heard from many. (7) But he got into this way of allowing the giving of three baptisms and even more because of the scorn he suffered from his disciples who had known him, for his transgression and the seduction of the virgin. (8) Since he was in a state of grievous sin after seducing the virgin in his own city and fleeing, the tramp invented a second baptism for himself. He said that it is permissible for as many as three baths, that is baptisms, to be given for the remission of sins, so that if one were to fall away the first time he might repent and, on repentance, receive a second baptism—and a third likewise, if he transgresses after the second.

3,9 But to make his ridicule certain he mendaciously cites a text as supposedly persuasive, to show that he was cleansed again after his transgression and thereafter counts as innocent—a text that can be deceptive, but does not mean what he says it does: (10) after the Lord had been baptized by John he told his disciples, "I have a baptism to be baptized with, and why do I wish it if I have already accomplished it?"[18] And again, "I have a cup to drink, and why do I wish to if I am going to fill it?"[19] And so he held that several baptisms may be administered.

4,1 But this is not all. He rejects both the Law and all the prophets,[20] and says that the prophets have prophesied by the inspiration of the archon who made the world. (2) And he says that Christ has descended from on high, from the invisible Father who cannot be named, for the salvation of souls and the confusion of the God of the Jews, the Law, the prophets, and anything of the kind. (3) The Lord has gone down even to Hades to save Cain, Korah, Dathan, Abiram, Esau, and all the gentiles who had not known the God of the Jews. (4) But he has left Abel, Enoch, Noah, Abraham, Isaac, Jacob, Moses, David, and Solomon there because, as he

[16] Cf. Tertullian's discussion at Adv. Marc. 4.12.

[17] Iren. 1.27.3; PsT 6.1; Tert. Adv. Marc. 5.10.15; Res. Mort. 2; Adam. 7; Gos. Phil. 56,26-57,22; Treat. Res. 47,30-48.2 and see p. 00 n. 00.

[18] Luke 12:50

[19] Iren. 1.27.1; Eus. H. E. 4.11.2; PsT 6.1; Tert. Adv. Marc. 1.19.4; 4.34.15

[20] Tert. Adv. Marc. 1.19; 4.34

says, they recognized the God of the Jews, the maker and creator, and have done what is congenial to him, and did not devote themselves to the invisible God.[21]

4,5 They even permit women to administer baptism! For, given that they even venture to celebrate the mysteries in front of catechumens, everything they do is simply ridiculous.[22] (6) As I indicated, Marcion says resurrection is not of bodies but of souls, and he assigns salvation to these and not to bodies. And he similarly claims that there are reincarnations of souls, and transmigrations from body to body.

5,1 But his futile nonsense fails in every respect, as I have already argued in other Sects. How can the soul, which has not fallen, rise? How can we speak of its resurrection, the resurrection of the soul which has not fallen? Whatever falls needs an arising (2) but a soul does not fall, a body does. Hence common usage is correct in calling the body a "carcass" and so is the Lord himself, who said, "Wheresoever the carcass is, there will the eagles be gathered together."[23]

5,3 For we do not shut souls up in tombs. We deposit bodies in the ground and cover them up, and as a hope their resurrection is preached, like the resurrection of a grain of wheat. (4) The holy apostle has borne his witness as to the grain of wheat and other seeds and so has the Lord himself in the Gospel, "Except a corn of wheat fall and die, it abideth alone."[24] (5) But the holy apostle says, "Thou fool!" (For he is calling "fool" the unbeliever who is completely in doubt and asks, "How can the resurrection be, with what body do they come?" And to such he says immediately, "Thou fool, that which thou sowest is not quickened except it die.")[25] (6) And the scripture has shown at every point that there is a resurrection of the grain which has fallen, that is of the body which is buried, and not of the soul. (7) And how can the soul come by itself? How can it reign by itself, when it did good or evil together with a body? The judgment will not be just, but the reverse!

6,1[26] And how can Marcion's own tally of three principles be substantiated? How can <the one which> does work—either the work of salvation, or the other kinds—in the bad god's territory be considered "good"? (2) For

---

[21] Iren. 1.27.3
[22] Tert. Praescr. 41.5
[23] Matt. 24:28
[24] John 12:24
[25] 1 Cor 15:35-36
[26] The argument developed from here through 7,9 is based in part on Iren. 2.1.2-5.

suppose the world does not belong to him, and yet he sent his Only-begotten into the world to take things from someone else's world, which he neither begot nor made—it will be found, either that he is invading someone else's domain or that, being poor and having nothing of his own, he is advancing against another person's territory to procure things which he does not already have.

6,3 And how can the demiurge act as judge between both parties? Whom can he judge, then? If he presides as judge over the articles which have been taken from the God on high, he is more powerful than the God on high—seeing that he hales the possessions of the God on high into his court, or so Marcion thought.

6,4 And if he is a judge at all, he is just. But from the word, "just," I shall show that goodness and justice are the same thing. Anything that is just is also good. (5) It is because of his being good that, with impartial justice, God grants what is good to one who has done good. And he cannot be opposed to the good God in point of goodness, since he provides the good with good on the principle of justice, and the bad with the penalty of retribution.

6,6 Nor, again, can he be good if he gives the good reward to the unrepentantly evil at the end, even though for now he makes his sun rise on good and evil men and provides them with his rain, because of their freedom of choice at this present. (7) The nature of a God who provides the evil with the reward of salvation in the world to come, and does not rather hate what is wicked and evil, cannot be good and just.

6,8 But as to Marcion's third, evil god. If he has the power to do evil things and master either the denizens of the world who belong to the God on high or the ones who belong to the intermediate, just God—then this god must be stronger than the two whom Marcion calls Gods, since he has the power to seize what is not his. (9) And then the two will be adjudged weaker than the one evil god, since they are powerless to resist and rescue their possessions from the one who is seizing them and turning them into evil.

7,1 And to realize what a joke the tramp's nonsense is, let us observe it again in another light. If the evil god is at all evil, and yet he seizes the good men from the good God and the just ones from the just God and does not seize only his own, then the evil god will turn out not to be evil—desiring the good and claiming them at law, because they are better. (2) And if, besides, he judges his own and exacts a penalty from wrongdoers, this judge of evil men cannot be evil after all. And Marcion's thesis will turn out to be self-refuting in every way.

7,3 But again, tell me, how did the three principles come to be? And who was it that set a boundary for them? If each is enclosed in its own space, then these three, which are enclosed in certain places that contain them, cannot be considered perfect. The thing that contains each one must be greater than the thing that is contained. And the thing that is contained can no longer be called "God" but rather, the boundary which contains it must (be so called).[27]

7,4 But even if, when they met, each one was allotted its own place by concession and, being in its own place, no principle crowds or encroaches on another, the principles cannot be opposed to each other, and none of them can be considered evil. They mind their own business in a just, calm and tranquil fashion, and do not try to overstep.[28]

7,5 But if the evil god is overpowered, coerced and oppressed by the God on high although he has received his allotment and is in his own place, and no part of this place belongs to the God on high nor has anything here, I mean in the evil god's territory, been created by him—the God on high will turn out to be the more tyrannical, certainly not "good," since he sent his own Son, or Christ, to take what belonged to someone else.

7,6 And where is the boundary which, according to the tramp's statement of his thesis, separates the three first principles? We shall need a fourth of some kind, abler and wiser than the three and an expert surveyor, who assigned its limits to each and made peace between the three, so that they would not quarrel or send anyone into each other's realms.[29] (7) And this person who convinced the three principles will be found to be a fourth—both wiser and abler than the others. And he too, once more, must be sought in his own place, from which he came to intervene between the three and wisely assign its portion to each, so that they would not wrong each other.

7,8 But if the two principles are resident in the realm of the one, that is, the realm of the demiurge, with the evil one <always active> in his territories and the good God's Christ a visitor there, then the judge will turn out not be only a demiurge and a judge, but good as well, since he permits the two to do what they please in his domain. Or else we shall find that he is feeble and unable to stop the alien robbers of his possessions.

7,9 But if he is even inferior in power, then his creation cannot exist, but would have given out long ago—carried off every day to his own realm

---

[27] See Iren. 2.1.2-3.

[28] See Iren. 2.1.5.

[29] Irenaeus says this of a "third" at 2.1.3.

by the evil god, and to the realms on high by the good one. And how can the creation still stand? (10) But if you say that it will come to an end eventually, and that it is possible for it to come to a complete end through the attentions of the good God, then will not the good God be responsible for the damage? Yet he never created that which he later saw fit to perfect, and he was certainly not its original maker, before most men were wronged, found themselves detained by the judge, and (so) have remained below.

8,1 But again, he cites sacred scripture without understanding it properly, and deceives the innocent by perverting the letter of the apostle's, "Christ hath redeemed us from the curse of the Law, being made a curse for us."[30] He says, "If we were his, he would not 'buy' what was his own. (2) He entered someone else's world as a 'buyer' to redeem us, since we were not his. For we were someone else's creation, and he therefore 'bought' us at the price of his own life."

8,3 The fool has no notion that Christ has not become a curse either—perish the thought!—but has lifted the curse our sin had brought upon us by crucifying himself and becoming himself the death of death and a curse on the curse. Thus Christ is not a curse but a lifting of the curse, and a blessing to all who truly believe in him.

8,4 And "redeemed" <must> also <be understood> in this sense. Paul did not say "bought", and Christ did not enter foreign territory to plunder or buy. If he had bought he would have bought because he did not own and, like a beggar, would have acquired what he did not have. (5) And if our owner had sold us, he would have sold in desperation, and thus been under pressure from some moneylender. But this is not the case; for Paul did not say "bought," but "redeemed."

8,6 This same holy apostle says something similar to this, "redeeming the time, because the days are evil."[31] And we do not buy days, or pay for days; he said this meaning the <constancy which is attained through patient endurance>, and the patience of longsuffering. (7) Thus the word "redeemed" suggested the reason for his acceptance of an incarnation in the world, an incarnation where<by>, though the impassible God, he undertook to suffer for us, remaining in the impassibility which is proper to his Godhead and yet <reckoning as his own> the very thing that he had undertaken to suffer for us—not buying us from foreigners but accepting the affair of the cross for our sakes, by choice and not of necessity. (8) Hence

---

[30] Gal 3:13
[31] Eph. 5:16

Marcion's assertions stand refuted at every point. And there are many arguments in rebuttal of his stage-machinery and melodrama, which, contrary to him, are drawn from pious reason and creditable exposition.

9,1 But I shall come to his writings, or rather, to his tamperings. This man has only Luke as a Gospel, mutilated at the beginning because of the Savior's conception and his incarnation.[32] (2) But this person who harmed himself <rather> than the Gospel did not cut just the beginning off. He also cut off many words of the truth both at the end and in the middle, and he has added other things besides, beyond what had been written. And he uses only this (Gospel) canon, the Gospel according to Luke.

9,3 He also possesses ten Epistles of the holy apostle, the only ones he uses, but not all that is written in them. He deletes some parts of them, and has altered certain sections. He uses these two volumes (of the Bible) but has composed other treatises himself for the persons he has deceived.

9,4 Here are what he calls Epistles: 1. Galatians. 2. Corinthians. 3. Second Corinthians. 4. Romans. 5. Thessalonians. 6. Second Thessalonians. 7. Ephesians. 8. Colossians. 9. Philemon. 10. Philippians. He also has parts of the so-called Epistle to the Laodiceans.

9,5 From the very canon that he retains, of the Gospel and the Pauline Epistles, I can show with God's help that Marcion is a fraud and in error, and can refute him very effectively. (6) For he will be refuted from the very works which he acknowledges without dispute.[33] From the very remnants of the Gospel and Epistles which he still has, it will be demonstrated to the wise that Christ is not foreign to the Old Testament, and hence that the prophets are not foreign to the Lord's advent—(7) <and> that the apostle preaches the resurrection of the flesh and terms the prophets righteous, and Abraham, Isaac and Jacob among the recipients of salvation—and that all the teachings of God's holy church are saving, holy, and firmly founded by God on faith, knowledge, hope and doctrine.

10,1 I am also going to append the treatise which I had written against him before, a your instance, brothers, hastening to compose this one. (2) Some years ago, to find what falsehood this Marcion had invented and what his silly teaching was, I took up his very books which he had <mutilated>, his so-called Gospel and Apostolic Canon. From these two books I made a series of <extracts> and selections of the material which would serve to refute him, and I wrote a sort of outline for a treatise, arranging the

[32] Iren. 1.27.2; PsT 6.2; Fil. 45.5; Adam. 2.3; 19

[33] Iren. promises to do the same at 1.27.4 though his treatise, if he wrote it, does not survive. See also Book 4 of Tert. Adv. Marc.

points in order, and numbering each saying one, two, three (and so on). (3) And in this way I went through all of the passages in which it is apparent that, foolishly, he still retains against himself these leftover sayings of the Savior and the apostle.

10,4 For some of them had been falsely entered by himself, in an altered form and unlike the authentic copy of the Gospel and the meaning of the apostolic canon. (5) But others were exactly like both the Gospel and Apostle, unchanged by Marcion but capable of completely demolishing him. By these it is shown that <the> Old Testament is in agreement with the New, and the New with the Old. (6) In turn, other sayings from the same books give intimation that Christ has come in the flesh and been made perfect man among us. (7) Others in turn, moreover, confess the resurrection of the dead, and that God is one almighty Lord of all, himself the maker of heaven and earth, and of everything on earth. They do not counterfeit the call of the Gospel nor, certainly, do they deny the maker and artificer of all, but make manifest the One who is plainly confessed by the Apostolic Canon and the Proclamation of the Gospel. (8) And here, below, is my treatise, as follows:

Preface to the Publication concerning Marcion's Bible and the Refutation of It

11,1 Whoever cares to understand the phony inventions of the deceiver Marcion thoroughly and perceive the false contrivances of this victim (of the devil), should not hesitate to read this compilation. (2) I hasten to present the material from his own Gospel which is contradictory to his villainous tampering, so that those who are willing to read the work may have this as a training-ground in acuity, for the refutation of the strange doctrines of his invention.

11,3 For the (Marcionite) canon of Luke is revelatory of <their form of the Gospel>: mutilated as it is, without beginning, middle or end, it looks like a cloak full of moth holes.

11,4 At the very beginning he excised everything Luke had originally composed—his "inasmuch as many have taken in hand," and so forth, and the material about Elizabeth and the angel's announcement to Mary the Virgin; about John and Zacharias and the birth at Bethlehem; the genealogy and the story of the baptism. (5). All this he cut out and turned his back on, and made this the beginning of the Gospel, "In the fifteenth year of Tiberius Caesar," and so on.

11,6 He starts from there then and yet, again, does not go on in order. He falsifies some things, as I said, he adds others helter-skelter, not going straight on but disingenuously wandering all over the material. Thus:

1. "Go shew thyself unto the priest, and offer for thy cleansing, according as Moses commanded—that this may be a testimony unto you,"[34] instead of the Savior's "for a testimony unto them."

2. "But that ye may know that the Son of Man hath power to forgive sins upon earth."[35]

3. "The Son of Man is lord also of the Sabbath."[36]

4. "Judas Iscariot, which was a betrayer." Instead of, "He came down with them," he has, "He came down among them."[37]

5. "And the whole multitude sought to touch him. And he lifted up his eyes,"[38] and so forth.

6. "In the like manner did your fathers unto the prophets."[39]

7. "I say unto you, I have not found so great faith, no, not in Israel."[40]

8. "Blessed is he who shall not be offended in me,"[41] is altered. For he had it as though it refers to John.

9. "He it is of whom it is written, Behold, I send my messenger before thy face."[42]

10. "And entering into the Pharisee's house he reclined at table. And the woman which was a sinner, standing at his feet behind him, washed his feet with her tears, and wiped and kissed them."[43]

11. And again, "She hath washed my feet with her tears, and wiped and kissed them."[44]

12. He did not have, "His mother and his brethren," but only, "Thy mother and thy brethren."[45]

13. "As they sailed he fell asleep. Then he arose and rebuked the wind and the sea."[46]

14. "And it came to pass as they went the people thronged him, and a woman touched him, and was healed of her blood. And the Lord said,

[34] Luke 5:14. Cf. Tert. Adv. Marc. 4.9.9-10.
[35] Luke 5:24
[36] Luke 6:5
[37] Luke 6:16-17
[38] Luke 6:19-20
[39] Luke 6:23
[40] Luke 7:9. Cf. Tert. Adv. Marc. 4.18.1.
[41] Luke 7:23
[42] Luke 7:27. Cf. Adam. 2.18; Tert. Adv. Marc. 4.18.7
[43] Luke 7:36-38
[44] Luke 7:44-45
[45] Luke 8:19-20
[46] Luke 8:23-24

Who touched me?" And again, "Someone hath touched me; for I perceive that virtue hath gone out of me."[47]

15. "Looking up to heaven he pronounced a blessing upon them."[48]

16. "Saying, The Son of Man must suffer many things, and be slain, and be raised after three days."[49]

17. "And, behold, there were talking with him two men, Elijah and Moses in glory."[50]

18. "Out of the cloud, a voice, This is my beloved Son."[51]

19. "I besought thy disciples." But in addition to, "And they could not cast it out," he had, "And he said to them, O faithless generation, how long shall I suffer you?"[52]

20. "For the Son of Man shall be delivered into the hands of men."[53]

21. "Have ye not read so much as this, what David did: he went into the house of God."[54]

22. "I thank thee, Lord of heaven."[55] But he did not have, "and earth," nor did he have, "Father." He is shown up, however; for further down he had, "Even so, Father."

23. He said to the lawyer, "What is written in the Law?" And after the lawyer's answer he replied, "Thou hast answered right; this do, and thou shalt live."[56]

24. And he said, "Which of you shall have a friend, and shall go unto him at midnight, asking three loaves?" And then, "Ask, and it shall be given. If a son shall ask a fish any of you that is a father, will he for a fish give him a serpent, or a scorpion for an *egg*? If, then, ye evil men know of good gifts, how much more the Father?"[57]

25. The saying about Jonah the prophet has been gutted; Marcion had, "This generation, no sign shall be given it." But he did not have anything about Nineveh, the queen of the south, and Solomon.[58]

---

[47] Luke 8:42-46. Cf. Tert. Adv. Marc. 4.20.7-8.
[48] Luke 9:16
[49] Luke 9:22. Cf. Tert. Adv. Marc. 4.21.7.
[50] Luke 9:30-31. Cf. Tert. Adv. Marc. 4.22.1;16.
[51] Luke 9:35. Cf. Tert. Adv. Marc. 4.22.1.
[52] Luke 9:40-41. Cf. Tert. Adv. Marc. 4.23.1.
[53] Luke 9:44
[54] Luke 6:3-4. Cf. Tert. Adv. Marc. 4.12.5.
[55] Luke 10:21. Cf. Tert. Adv. Marc. 4.25.1.
[56] Luke 10:26-28.
[57] Luke 11:5; 9-13. Cf. Tert. Adv. Marc. 4.26.28.
[58] Luke 11:29-32

26. Instead of, "Ye pass over the judgment of God,"[59] he had, "Ye pass over the calling of God."

27. "Woe unto you, for ye build the sepulchres of the prophets, and your fathers killed them."[60]

28. He did not have, "Therefore said the wisdom of God, I send unto them prophets," and the statement that the blood of Zacharias, Abel and the prophets will be required of this generation.[61]

29. "I say unto my friends, Be not afraid of them that kill the body. Fear him which, after he hath killed, hath authority to cast into hell." But he did not have, "Are not five sparrows sold for two farthings, and not one of them is forgotten before God?"

30. Instead of, "He shall confess before the angels of God,"[62] Marcion says, "before God."

31. He does not have, "God doth clothe the grass."[63]

32. "And your Father knoweth ye have need of these things,"[64] physical things, of course.

33. "But seek ye the kingdom of God, and all these things shall be added unto you."[65]

34. Instead of, "Your Father," Marcion had, "Father."[66]

35. Instead of, "In the second or third watch," he had, "in the evening watch."[67]

36. "The Lord of that servant will come and will cut him in sunder, and will appoint his portion with the unbelievers."[68]

37. "Lest he hale thee to the judge and the judge deliver thee to the officer."[69]

38. There is a falsification from "There came some that told him of the Galilaeans whose blood Pilate had mingled with their sacrifices" down to the place where he speaks of the eighteen who died in the tower at Siloam; and of "Except ye repent" <and the rest> until the parable of the fig tree

---

59 Luke 11:42. Cf. Tert. Adv. Marc. 4.27.4.
60 Luke 11:47. Cf. Tert. Adv. Marc. 4.27.8.
61 Luke 11:49-51
62 Luke 12:8. Cf. Tert. Adv. Marc. 4.28.4.
63 Luke 12:28.
64 Luke 12:30. Cf. Tert. Adv. Marc. 4.29.3.
65 Luke 12:31. Cf. Tert. Adv. Marc. 4.29.5
66 Luke 12:32
67 Luke 12:38
68 Luke 12:46. Cf. Tert. Adv. Marc. 4.29.9.
69 Luke 12:58. Cf. Tert. Adv. Marc. 4.29.16.

of which the cultivator said, "I am digging about it and dunging it, and if it bear no fruit, cut it down."[70]

39. "This daughter of Abraham, whom Satan hath bound."[71]

40. Again, he falsified, "Then ye shall see Abraham, and Isaac, and Jacob, and all the prophets, in the kingdom of God." In place of this he put, "When ye see all the righteous in the kingdom of God and yourselves thrust"—but he put, "kept"—"out." "There shall be weeping and gnashing of teeth."[72]

41. Again, he falsified, "They shall come from the east and from the west, and shall sit down in the kingdom," "The last shall be first," and "The Pharisees came saying, Get thee out and depart, for Herod will kill thee"; also, "He said, Go ye, and tell that fox," until the words, "It cannot be that a prophet perish out of Jerusalem," and, "Jerusalem, Jerusalem, which killest the prophets and stonest them that are sent, Often would I have gathered, as a hen, thy children," "Your house is left unto you desolate," and, "Ye shall not see me until ye shall say, Blessed."[73]

42. Again, he falsified the entire parable of the two sons, the one who took his share of the property and spent it in dissipation, and the other.[74]

43. "The Law and the prophets were until John, and every man presseth into it."[75]

44. The story of the rich man, and that Lazarus the beggar was carried by the angels into Abraham's bosom.[76]

45. "But now he is comforted,"[77] again meaning this same Lazarus.

46. Abraham said, "They have Moses and the prophets; let them hear them, since neither will they hear him that is risen from the dead."[78]

47. He falsified, "Say, We are unprofitable servants: we have done that which was our duty to do."[79]

48. When the ten lepers met him. Marcion excised a great deal and wrote, "He sent them away, saying, Show yourselves unto the priests"; and he substituted different words for others and said, "Many lepers were in

---

[70] Luke 13:1-9
[71] Luke 13:16
[72] Luke 13:28. Cf. Tert. Adv. Marc. 4.30.5.
[73] Luke 13:29-35
[74] Luke 15:11-32
[75] Luke 16:16. Cf. Tert. Adv. Marc. 4.33.7.
[76] Luke 16:22. Tert. Adv. Marc. 4.34.10; cf. Adam. 2.10.
[77] Luke 16:25. Cf. Adam. 2.10.
[78] Luke 16:29; 31. Tert. Adv. Marc. 4.34.10; cf. Adam. 2.10.
[79] Luke 17:10

the day of Elisha the prophet, and none was cleansed, saving Naaman the Syrian."[80]

49. "The days will come when ye shall desire to see one of the days of the Son of Man."[81]

50. "One said unto him, Good master, what shall I do to inherit eternal life? He replied, Call not thou me good. One is good, God." Marcion added, "the Father," and instead of, "Thou knowest the commandments," says, "I know the commandments."[82]

51. "And it came to pass that as he was come nigh unto Jericho, a blind man cried, Jesus, thou Son of David, have mercy on me. And when he was healed, he said, Thy faith hath saved thee."[83]

52. Marcion falsified, "He took unto him the twelve, and said, Behold, we go up to Jerusalem, and all things that are written in the prophets concerning the Son of Man shall be accomplished. For he shall be delivered and killed, and the third day he shall rise again"[84] He falsified the whole of this.

53. He falsified the passage about the ass and Bethphage, and the one about the city and the temple, because of the scripture, "My house shall be called an house of prayer, but ye make it a den of thieves."[85]

54. "And they sought to lay hands on him and they were afraid."[86]

55. Again, he excised the material about the vineyard which was let out to husbandmen, and the verse, "What is this, then, The stone which the builders rejected?"[87]

56. He excised, "Now that the dead are raised, even Moses showed at the bush, in calling the Lord the God of Abraham and Isaac and Jacob. But he is a God of the living, not of the dead."[88]

57. He did not have the following: "Now that the dead are raised, even Moses showed, saying that the God of Abraham, the God of Isaac, and the God of Jacob is God of the living."[89]

---

[80] Luke 17:12; 14; 4:27. Cf. Tert. Adv. Marc. 4.35.4; 6.

[81] Luke 17:22

[82] Luke 18:18-20. Cf. Hipp. Refut. 7.31.6; Adam. 2.17; Orig. De Princ. 2.5.1; 5.4; Tert. Adv. Marc. 4.36.4.

[83] Luke 18:35; 38; 42. Cf. Adam. 4.14; Tert. Adv. Marc. 4.36.9-10.

[84] Luke 18:31-33

[85] Luke 19:29-46

[86] Luke 20:19

[87] Luke 20:9-17

[88] Luke 20:37-38

[89] Luke 20:37-38

58. Again he falsified, "There shall not an hair of your head perish."[90]

59. Again, he falsified the following: "Then let them which are in Judaea flee to the mountains," and so on, because of the words subjoined in the text, "until all things that are written be fulfilled."[91]

60. "He communed with the captains how he might deliver him unto them."[92]

61. "And he said unto Peter and the rest, Go and prepare that we may eat the passover."[93]

62. "And he sat down, and the twelve apostles with him, and he said, With desire I have desired to eat this passover with you before I suffer."[94]

63. He falsified, "I will not any more eat thereof until it be fulfilled in the kingdom of God."[95]

64. He falsified "When I sent you, lacked ye anything," and so on, because of the words, "This also that is written must be accomplished, And he was numbered among the transgressors."[96]

65. "He was withdrawn from them about a stone's cast, and kneeled down, and prayed."[97]

66. "And Judas drew near to kiss him, and said..."[98]

67. He falsified what Peter did when he struck the servant of the high priest and cut off his ear.[99]

68. "They that held him mocked him, smiting and striking him and saying, Prophesy, who is it that smote thee?"[100]

69. After, "We found this fellow perverting the nation," Marcion added, "and destroying the Law and the prophets."[101]

70. The addition after "forbidding to give tribute" is "and turning away the wives and children."[102]

71. "And when they were come unto a place called Place of a Skull they crucified him and parted his garments, and the sun was darkened."[103]

---

[90] Luke 21:18
[91] Luke 21:21-22
[92] Luke 22:4
[93] Luke 22:8
[94] Luke 22:14-15. Cf. Tert. Adv. Marc. 4.40.1.
[95] Luke 22:16
[96] Luke 22:35; 37
[97] Luke 22:41
[98] Luke 22:47-48
[99] Luke 22:50
[100] Luke 22:63-64
[101] Luke 23:2
[102] Luke 22:47-48
[103] Luke 23:33; 34; 44. Cf. Matt 24:29; Mark 13:24; Tert. Adv. Marc. 4.42.4-5.

72. Marcion falsified the words, "Today thou shalt be with me in paradise."[104]

73. "And when he had cried with a loud voice he gave up the ghost."[105]

74. "And, lo, a man named Joseph took the body down, wrapped it in linen and laid it in a sepulchre that was hewn out of the rock."[106]

75. "And the women returned and rested the sabbath day according to the Law."[107]

76. "The men in shining garments said, Why seek ye the living among the dead? He is risen; remember all that he spake when he was yet with you, that the Son of Man must suffer and be delivered."[108]

77. He falsified what Christ said to Cleopas and the other when he met them, "O fools, and slow to believe all that the prophets have spoken: Ought not he to have suffered these things?" And instead of, "what the prophets have spoken," he put, "what I said unto you." But he is shown up since, "When he broke the bread their eyes were opened and they knew him."[109]

78. "Why are ye troubled? Behold my hands and my feet, for a spirit hath not bones, as ye see me have."[110]

11,7 And in further opposition to this heresiarch I also attach, to this arrangement (of texts) which has been laboriously accumulated against him by myself, such other texts as I find in his works, as in an arbitrary version of the apostle Paul's epistles; not all of them but some of them—(I have listed their names in the order of his Apostolic Canon at the end of the complete work)—and these mutilated as usual by his rascality. (8) <(They are) remains of the truth which he preserves> as, to be honest, <there are> remains of the true Gospel in his Gospel in name which I have given above. All the same, he has adulterated everything with fearful ingenuity.

From the Epistle to the Romans, number four in Marcion's canon but number one in the Apostolic Canon.

1(28). "As many as have sinned without law shall also perish without law, and as many as have sinned in the Law shall be judged by the Law.

[104] Luke 23:43
[105] Luke 23:46. Cf. Tert. Adv. Marc. 4.42.6.
[106] Luke 23:50; 53. Cf. Tert. Adv. Marc. 4.42.7.
[107] Luke 23:56
[108] Luke 24:5-7. Cf. Tert. Adv. Marc. 4.43.5.
[109] Luke 24:25-26; 30-31. Cf. Adam. 4.12; Tert. Adv. Marc. 4.43.4.
[110] Luke 24:38-39. Cf. Adam. 5.12; Tert. Adv. Marc. 4.43.6.

For not the hearers of the Law are just before God, but the doers of the Law shall be justified."[111]

2(29). "Circumcision verily profiteth if thou keep the Law; but if thou be a breaker of the Law, thy circumcision is made uncircumcision."[112]

3(30). "Which hast the form of knowledge and of the truth in the Law."[113]

4(31). "For when we were yet without strength, in due time Christ died for the ungodly."[114]

5(32). "Wherefore the Law is holy, and the commandment holy and just and good."[115]

6(33). "That the requirement of the Law might be fulfilled in us."[116]

7(34). "For Christ is the fulfillment of the Law for righteousness to everyone that believeth."[117]

8(35). "He that loveth his neighbor hath fulfilled the Law."[118]

The First Epistle to the Thessalonians, <number five in Marcion's canon>, but number eight in ours.

The Second Epistle to the Thessalonians, <number six in Marcion's canon>, but number nine in ours.

From the Epistle to Ephesians, number seven <in Marcion's canon>, but number five in ours.

1(36) "Remember that ye, being in time past gentiles, who are called uncircumcision by that which is called the circumcision in the flesh made by hands; that at that time ye were without Christ, being aliens from the commonwealth of Israel, and strangers from the covenants of promise, having no hope, and without God in the world. But now in Christ Jesus ye who sometimes were far off are made nigh by his blood. For he is our peace, who hath made both one,"[119] and so on.

2(37). "Wherefore he saith, Awake thou that sleepest, and arise from the dead, <and> Christ shall give thee light."[120]

---

111 Rom 2:13
112 Rom 2:25
113 Rom 2:20
114 Rom 5:6
115 Rom 7:12. Cf. Adam. 2.20; Tert. Adv. Marc. 5.13.14.
116 Rom 8:4
117 Rom 10:4. Cf. Tert. Adv. Marc. 5.14.6.
118 Rom 13:8.
119 Eph 2:11-14. Cf. Adam. 2.18; Tert. Adv. Marc. 5.17.12; 14.
120 Eph 5:14

3(38). "For this cause shall a man leave his father and mother, <and> shall be joined unto his wife, and they two shall be one flesh,"[121] minus the phrase, "unto his wife."

<From the Epistle> to the Colossians, number eight <in Marcion's canon>, but number seven in ours.

1(39). "Let no man therefore judge you in meat, or in drink, or in respect of an holyday, or of the new moon and sabbath days, which are a shadow of things to come."[122]

The Epistle to Philemon, number nine <in Marcion's canon>, but number thirteen, or even fourteen, in ours.

The Epistle to the Philippians, number ten <in Marcion's canon>, but number six in ours.

<From the Epistle> to the Laodiceans, number eleven <in Marcion's canon>.

1(<40>). "(There is) one Lord, one faith, one baptism, one God and Father of all, who is above all, and through all, and in all."[123]

From the Epistle to the Galatians, number one <in Marcion's canon>, but number four in ours.

1. "Learn that the just shall live by faith. For as many as are under the Law are under a curse; but, The man that doeth them shall live by them."[124]

2. "Cursed is everyone that hangeth upon a tree; but he that is of promise is by the freewoman."[125]

3. "I testify again that a man that is circumcised is a debtor to do the whole Law."[126]

<4.> In place of, "A little leaven leaveneth the whole lump," he put, "corrupteth the whole lump."[127]

<5.> "For all the Law is fulfilled by you; thou shalt love thy neighbor as thyself."[128]

6. "Now the works of the flesh are manifest which are these: Adultery, fornication, uncleanness, lasciviousness, idolatry, witchcraft,hatred, variance, emulations, wrath, strife, seditions, factions, envyings, drunkenness, revellings—of the which I tell you before, as I have also told you in time past, that they which do such things shall not inherit the kingdom of God."[129]

[121] Eph 5:31. Cf. Tert. Adv. Marc. 5.18.9.
[122] Col. 2:16-17. Cf. Tert. Adv. Marc. 5.19.9.
[123] Cf. Eph. 4:5-6; Adam. 2.19.
[124] Gal 3:11b; 10a; 12b
[125] Gal. 3:13; 4:23; Cf. Tert. Adv. Marc. 5.3.10; 4.8.
[126] Gal 5:3
[127] Gal 5:9
[128] Gal 5:14. Cf. Tert. Adv. Marc. 5.4.12.
[129] Gal 5:19-21

7. "They that are Christ's have crucified the flesh with the affections and lusts."[130]

8. "For neither do they themselves who are circumcised (now) keep the Law."[131]

<From the> First <Epistle> to the Corinthians, number two in Marcion's own canon and in ours.

1(9). "For it is written, I will destroy the wisdom of the wise, and will bring to naught the understanding of the prudent."[132]

2(10). "That, according as it is written, He that glorieth, let him glory in the Lord."[133]

3(11). "Of the first beings of this world that come to naught."[134]

4(12). "For it is written, He taketh the wise in their own craftiness." And again, "The Lord knoweth the thoughts of men, that they are vain."[135]

5(13). "For even Christ our passover is sacrificed."[136]

6(14). "Know ye not that he which is joined to an harlot is one body? For two, saith he, shall be one flesh."[137]

7(15). Given in an altered form. In place of, "in the Law," he says "in the Law of Moses." But before this he says, "Or saith not the Law the same also?"[138]

8(16). "Doth God take care for oxen?"[139]

9(17). "Moreover, brethren, I would not that ye should be ignorant how that our fathers were under the cloud, and all passed through the sea, and did all eat the same spiritual meat, and did all drink the same spiritual drink. For they drank of a spiritual rock that followed them, and that rock was Christ. But with many of them God was not well pleased. Now these things were our examples, to the intent we should not lust after evil things, as they also lusted. Neither be ye idolaters as were some of them; as it is written, The people sat down to eat and drink, and rose up to play. Neither let us tempt Christ," until the words, "These things happened unto them for examples, and they were written for us,"[140] and so on.

[130] Gal 5:24

[131] Gal 6:13

[132] 1 Cor 1:19. Cf. Tert. Adv. Marc. 5.5.5.

[133] 1 Cor 1:31. Cf. Tert. Adv. Marc. 5.5.10.

[134] 1 Cor 2:6

[135] 1 Cor 3:19-20. Cf. Tert. Adv. Marc. 5.6.12.

[136] 1 Cor 5:7. Cf. Adam. 2.18; Tert. Adv. Marc. 5.7.3.

[137] 1 Cor 6:16

[138] 1 Cor 9:9; 8. "Of Moses" is also in the "ecclesiastical text." Adam. 1.22 witnesses to its presence in Marcion's canon.

[139] 1 Cor 9:9. Cf. Tert. Adv. Marc. 5.7.10.

[140] 1 Cor 10:1-9; 11. Cf. Adam. 2.18; Tert. Adv. Marc. 5.7.12-14.

10(18). "What say I then? That sacrificial meat is anything, or that that which is offered in sacrifice to idols is anything? But the things which they sacrifice, they sacrifice to devils and not to God."[141] But Marcion added, "Sacrificial meat."

11(19). "A man ought not to have long hair, forasmuch as he is the image and glory of God."[142]

12(20). "But God hath composed the body."[143]

13(21). Marcion has erroneously added the words, "on the Law's account," <after>, "Yet in the church I had rather speak five words with my understanding."[144]

14(22). "In the Law it is written, With men of other tongues and other lips will I speak unto this people."[145]

15(23). "Let your women keep silence in the church; For it is not permitted unto them to speak; but they are commanded to be under obedience, as also saith the Law."[146]

16(24). On resurrection of the dead: "Brethren, I make known unto you the gospel which I preached unto you."[147] Also, "If Christ be not raised, it is in vain,"[148] and so on. "So we preach, and so ye believed..."[149] that Christ died, and was buried, and rose again the third day...When this mortal shall have put on immortality, then shall be brought to pass the saying that is written, Death is swallowed up in victory."[150]

From the Second Epistle to the Corinthians, number three in Marcion's canon and ours

1(25). "For all the promises of God have their Yea in him; therefore through him we utter Amen to God."[151]

2(26). "For we preach not ourselves, but Christ Jesus the Lord; and ourselves your servants through Jesus. For God who commanded the light to shine out of darkness..."[152]

---

141 1 Cor 10:19
142 1 Cor 11:7. Cf. Adam. 5.23; Tert. Adv. Marc. 5.8.1.
143 1 Cor 12:24
144 1 Cor 14:19
145 1 Cor 14:21. Cf. Tert. Adv. Marc. 5.18.10.
146 1 Cor 14:34. Cf. Adam. 2.18; Tert. Adv. Marc. 5.8.11.
147 1 Cor 15:1
148 1 Cor 15:17
149 1 Cor 15:11
150 1 Cor 15:3-4
151 2 Cor 1:20. Cf. Adam. 2.18.
152 2 Cor 4:5-6. Cf. Adam 2.19; Tert. Adv. Marc. 5.11.11.

3(27). "We having the same Spirit of faith also believe and therefore speak." But he excised, "according as it is written."[153]

11,9 This is Marcion's corrupt compilation, containing a version and form of the Gospel according to Luke, and an incomplete one of the apostle Paul—not of all his epistles (10) but simply of Romans, Ephesians, Colossians, Laodiceans, Galatians, First and Second Corinthians, First and Second Thessalonians, Philemon and Philippians. (11) (There is no version) of First and Second Timothy, Titus, and Hebrews <in his scripture at all, and> even the epistles that are there <have been mutilated>, since they are not all there but are counterfeits. (12) And <I found> that this compilation had been tampered with throughout, and had supplemental material added in certain passages—not for any use, but for inferior, harmful strange sayings against the sound faith, <fictitious> creatures of Marcion's cracked brain.

11,13 I have made this laborious, searching compilation from the scripture he has chosen, Paul and the Gospel according to Luke, <so that> all who are attempting to contradict his imposture may understand that the altered sayings have been fraudulently inserted, (14) and that any not in their proper places have been stolen from them by his audacity. For the oaf thought that only these run counter to his false notion.

11,15 But there is a third <work> of my scholarship: the compilation of whatever material he and we have in common, and whose meaning is the Savior's incarnation and his testimony to the agreement of the New Testament with the Old—and the acknowledgment in the Gospel, by the Son of God, that God is the maker of heaven and earth and the same God who spoke in the Law and the prophets, and that this God is his own Father. (16) And here is the brief arrangement of that work of mine, transcribed word for word by myself from copies of Marcion in the form of scholia with exegetical comments, to serve as an outline. (17) But so that the difficult things in it will not be obscure to some and fail to be understood, I shall in turn explain of the several entries in order—I mean the first entry, the second, the third (and so on)—the reason why each saying was selected and transferred here.[154] I begin as follows.

[153] 2 Cor 4:13

[154] I.e., in what follows the quotations from Marcion with Epiph's occasional comments on the text, were the "scholia and notes." These were collected for the benefit of anyone who wanted to write a full dress refutation of Marcion. The elenchi which accompany them are being written by Epiph now, as part of his *Panarion*.

Scholion <One>, from Marcion's Own Version of the Gospel "Go, show thyself unto the priest, and offer for thy cleansing, according as Moses commanded—that this may be a testimony unto you" instead of the Savior's "for a testimony unto them."

(a) Elenchus 1. How could the Lord whose teachings—as you say—were always against the Law, say to the persons he had healed, I mean to the leper, "Go, show thyself unto the priest?" Since he says, "to the priest," he does not reject the priesthood of the Law.

(b) "And offer for thy cleansing." Even if you excise "the gift," it will be evident, from the word, "offer," that he is speaking of a gift.

(c) "For thy cleansing, according as Moses commanded." If he advises obedience to Moses' commandment, he is not rejecting or insulting the God of the Law, but acknowledging that both he and God, his Father, have given the Law to Moses.

(d) You have twisted the wording, Marcion, by saying "testimony unto you" instead of "testimony unto them." In this too you have plainly lied against your own head. If he were saying, "testimony unto you," he would be calling himself to witness that "I came not to destroy the Law or the prophets, but to fulfil."[155]

Scholion 2. "But that ye may know that the Son of Man hath power to forgive sins upon earth."

Elenchus 2. If he calls himself "Son of Man," the Only-begotten does not deny his humanity, and there is no use in your yapping about his being manifest in appearance. And if he has authority on earth, the earth is not foreign to his creations and his Father's.

Scholion 3. "The Son of Man is lord also of the Sabbath."

Elenchus 3. The Savior is acknowledging two things at once in teaching that he is both Son of Man and Lord of the Sabbath, so that the Sabbath will not be thought foreign to this creation, <and he himself will not be thought foreign to the Father's Godhead>—even if, in the last analysis, he is called Son of Man because of the incarnation.

Scholion 4. "Judas Iscariot, which was a betrayer." Instead of, "He came down with them," he has, "He came down among them."

(a) Elenchus 4. Judas Iscariot, "which was a betrayer." Betrayer of whom, pray? Surely of the One who was arrested—yes indeed, and who has been crucified and has suffered many things. (b) But how can he be

[155] Matt 5:17

arrested and crucified if, as you claim, Marcion, he is not tangible? You say he is an apparition! (c) But your opinion will be refuted because the text calls Judas a "betrayer," for he betrayed his own master and delivered him into the hands of men. (d) And it does you no good to say, "He came down among them," instead of, "with them." You cannot declare someone a phantom when you later show, even though unintentionally, that he is tangible.

Scholion 5. "And the whole multitude sought to touch him. And he lifted up his eyes," and so forth.

Elenchus 5. Again, how could the multitude have touched him if he was intangible? And what sort of eyes did he raise to heaven, if he was not composed of flesh? But he did this to show that the mediator between God and man is a man, Christ Jesus, and that he has both—his flesh from men, but his invisible essence from God the Father.

Scholion 6. "In the like manner did your fathers unto the prophets."

Elenchus 6. If he has mentioned prophets he does not deny prophets. If he avenges the murder of the prophets and blames their murderers and persecutors, he is not foreign to prophets. Rather, he is their god, who establishes their authenticity.

Scholion 7. "I say unto you, I have not found so great faith, no, not in Israel."

Elenchus 7. If "*even* in Israel" he did not find "such faith" as he did in the gentile centurion, then he is not finding fault with Israel's faith. For if it were faith in a strange God and not faith in his Father himself, he would not speak in praise of it.

Scholion 8. "Blessed is he who shall not be offended in me," is altered. For he had it as though with reference to John.

(a) Whether this refers to John or to the Savior himself, he still says "blessed" of those who do not stumble, whether at him or at John, so that they will not make things up which they do not learn from him.

(b) But there is a more important consideration here, the real reason why the Savior spoke. Lest it be thought that John, whom he had ranked as the greatest of those born of woman, was greater even than the Savior himself—since he too was born of woman—he says as a safeguard, "And blessed is whoso shall not be offended in me."

(c) Hence he says, "He that is less in the kingdom is greater than he." Chronologically, counting from his birth in the flesh, he was six months "less" than John; but as John's God he was plainly "greater" in the kingdom. (d) For the Only-begotten did not come to say anything in secret, or to tell any lie about his own message. He says, "I have not spoken in secret, but openly."[156] For he is truth, as he says, "I am the way and the truth."[157] The way, then, contains no error; nor does the truth lie by concealing itself.

Scholion 9. "He it is of whom it is written, Behold, I send my messenger before thy face."

(a) Elenchus 9. If God's only-begotten Son recognizes John and foreknows him, and because he foreknows him tells those who are willing to know the truth that this is the one of whom it is written, "I send my messenger before thy face"—(b) then the one who said in writing, "I send my messenger before thy face," God the eternal who has spoken in the prophets and Law, was not foreign to his own Son, Jesus Christ. (c) For he sends his messenger before his face—before the face of a Son honored by a Father. He was not sending his messenger to serve a foreigner of whom, as you say, Marcion, he was even the opposite.

Scholion 10. "And entering into the Pharisee's house he reclined at table. And the woman which was a sinner, standing at his feet behind him, washed his feet with her tears, and wiped and kissed them."

Elenchus 10. "Entering" is indicative of a body, for it indicates a house and the dimensions of a body. And "reclining" can be said only of a person <with> a solid body, which is lying down. And as to the woman's washing his feet with her tears, she did not wash the feet of an apparition or phantom; she wiped, washed and kissed them because she felt the touch of the body.

Scholion 11. And again, "She hath washed my feet with her tears, and wiped and kissed them."

Elenchus 11. Lest you think, Marcion, that the sinful woman's washing, anointing and kissing of the Savior's feet was merely people's supposition, the Savior himself confirms it and teaches that it did not take place in appearance but in reality—confidently affirming, for the Pharisee's refutation and your own, Marcion, and the refutation of people like yourself, "She hath washed my feet and kissed them." But which feet, other than feet made of flesh, bones and the rest?

Scholion 12. He did not have, "His mother and his brethren," but simply "Thy mother and thy brethren."

(a) Elenchus 12. Even though you falsify the Gospel's wording earlier, Marcion, to keep the evangelist from agreeing with the words which some

[156] Cf. John 18:20.
[157] John 14:6

had said, "thy mother and thy brethren," you cannot get round the truth. (b) Why did he not call many women mothers? Why did he not speak of many countries? How many persons say any number of things of Homer? Some claim he was Egyptian—others, that he was from Chios; others, from Colophon; others, a Phrygian. Others, Meletus and Critheidus, say that he came from Smyrna. Aristarchus declared him an Athenian, others a Lydian from Maeon, others, a Cypriote from the district of Propodias in the environs of Salamis—though Homer was a man, surely! But because of his having been in many countries, he has caused many to (give) a different description (of him).

(c) But here, when they were speaking of God and Christ, they did not suppose that he had many mothers—just the one who had actually borne him. Or many brothers—only Joseph's sons by his actual other wife. And you cannot take up arms against the truth.

(d) And do not let the thing the Lord said, "Who are my mother and brethren?" mislead you. He did not say this to deny his mother, but to reproach the untimely speech of the person who spoke when there was such a large crowd surrounding him, when his saving teaching was pouring forth and he himself was busy with healings and preaching. For the speaker to cut him off by saying, "Behold thy mother and thy brethren," was an obvious interruption. (e) And if it was not because he received the message with joy—not that he did not know they had come before he heard it, but because he foreknew that they were standing outside—then he would have said this to counter the speaker's untimely utterance with a rebuke, as he once told Peter, "Away from me, Satan, for thou intendest not the things that be of God, but the things that be of man."[158]

Scholion 13. "As they sailed he fell asleep. Then he arose and rebuked the wind and the sea."

(a) Elenchus 13. Who fell asleep, pray? You won't dare to say this of the Godhead—or even if you should you will be blaspheming against your own head, you madman. But anyone can see that the truly incarnate Christ, needing sleep, fell asleep because of his bodily nature. (b) For those who woke him did not see an apparition, but One truly incarnate. Of course they are bearing witness that they roused him by shaking and calling him! (c) For when it says he "arose"—the God in flesh who had fallen asleep, the One who had come from heaven and donned flesh for us "arose" as man, but as God "rebuked" the sea and caused <a calm>.

---

[158] Mark 8:33

Scholion 14. "And it came to pass as they went the people thronged him, and a woman touched him, and was healed of her blood. And the Lord said, Who touched me?" And again, "Somebody hath touched me; for I perceive that virtue hath gone out of me."

(a) Elenchus 14. "As they went." It did not say, "as he went," so as not to represent him as "going" other than as wayfarers usually do. But as to, "The people thronged him," the crowds could not throng a spirit. And a woman who touched him and was healed touched, not air but human tangibility. (b) For to show that the woman's touch of his body was not merely apparent, he teaches (the contrary) by saying, "Who touched me? For I perceive that virtue hath gone out of me."

Scholion 15. "Looking up to heaven he pronounced a blessing upon them."

Elenchus 15. If he looked up to heaven and pronounced a blessing upon them, he did not have the forms of eyes and the other members in (mere) appearance.

Scholion 16. "Saying, The Son of Man must suffer many things, and be slain, and be raised after three days."

(a) Elenchus 16. If the only-begotten Son of God acknowledged that he was the Son of Man, and <would> suffer and be put to death, this is an axe pointed at you, Marcion, grubbing up your whole root—you scion of thorns, you waterless cloud, you barren tree with dead leaves! (b) For he says in turn, "and be raised again after three days." But what was it that was raised, except the very thing that had suffered and been buried in the sepulchre? There could be no funeral and interment of a phantom, a wind, a spirit, or an illusion, and no resurrection of them.

Scholion 17. "And behold, there talked with him two men, Elijah and Moses in glory."

(a) Elenchus 17. Marcion, I can well believe that the holy Zechariah's pruninghook (raised) against you is typified by these words—cutting away all the falsehood against the Law and the prophets that you have invented. (b) For because you would deny the Law and the prophets and call them foreign to the Savior and his glory and inspired teaching, he brought both men with him in his own glory, and showed them to his disciples. And the disciples showed them to us and the world—that is to everyone who desires life—to chop your roots with the first as with an axe, and with the second, trim your branches off as with the pruninghook of the utterance of the truth—the branches which secrete the hemlock and deadly poison for men, the oily sap of blasphemy! (c) For if Moses, to whom Christ entrusted the Law long ago, were a stranger to him, and if the prophets were strangers, he would not reveal them with him in his own glory.

(d) For see the wonder! He did not show them to us in the tomb, or beside the cross. But when he revealed the portion of his glory to us as though for a pledge, then he brought the saints, I mean Moses and Elijah, with him, to show that these were fellow-heirs of his kingdom.

Scholion 18. "Out of the cloud a voice, This is my beloved Son."

(a) Elenchus 18. Anyone can see that the cloud is not in the remote heights or above the heavens, but is in the creation around us from which the voice came to the Savior. (b) Hence, even though the Father spoke from a cloud to indicate the Son to the disciples, the demiurge is not a different person but the same One who bore witness to his own Son out of a cloud, and is not, as Marcion claims, master only of the realms above heaven.

Scholion 19. "I besought thy disciples." But in addition to, "And they could not cast it out," he had, "And he said to them, O faithless generation, how long shall I suffer you?"

Elenchus 19. "How long" is an indication of a time span in Christ's incarnate life; "O faithless generation," indicates that the prophets worked miracles in his name and believed as we find Elijah doing, and Elisha and the others.

Scholion 20. "For the Son of Man shall be delivered into the hands of men."

Elenchus 20. The appearance of a "Son of Man," and of one who will be "delivered into the hands of men," is not the appearance of an apparition or phantom, but the sight of a body and limbs.

Scholion 21. "Have ye not read so much as this, what David did: he went into the house of God."

Elenchus 21. If he calls the house of the tabernacle which Moses erected a "house of God," he does not deny the Law, or the God who spoke in the Law. For he says that the person who is his father is "God," <and the Father spoke in the Law through the Son and the Holy Spirit>, or the Only-begotten spoke in it himself. For a Trinity, Father, Son and Holy Spirit, is regularly at work in the Law, the prophets, the Gospels and the Apostles.

Scholion 22. "I thank thee, Lord of heaven." But he did not have "and earth" or "Father." He is shown up, however; for further on he had, "Even so, Father."

(a) Elenchus 22. He gives thanks to the "Lord of heaven," Marcion, even if you take away "<and> earth"—<and> even if you remove "Father" so as not to show that Christ is calling the demiurge his father. For the limbs of the truth remain alive. (b) Just as you forgetfully retained "Even so, Father," Marcion, as a leftover, <so the heaven whose Lord you admit the Father is, is the heaven of the created world around us>. Hence it is proven by every means that Christ is giving thanks to his own Father and calling him "Lord of heaven." And your madness is severe, since it does not see where the truth is going.

Scholion 23. "He said to the lawyer, What is written in the Law?" And after the lawyer's answer he replied, "Thou hast answered right. This do, and thou shalt live."

(a) Elenchus 23. Since he is truth, the Son of God deceived no one who inquired about life, for he had come for man's life. Since life is his concern and since he indicates to the man who is keeping the Law that the Law is life—and since he told the person who answered in terms of the Law that he had spoken rightly and "This do and thou shalt live"—(b) who could be cracked enough to believe Marcion when he blasphemes against the God who has granted men both the Law and the grace of the Gospel and be carried away with one who has received none of his teaching either from the Law or from the Holy Spiritt?

Scholion 24. And he said, "Which of you shall have a friend, and shall go unto him at midnight, asking three loaves?" And then, "Ask, and it shall be given. If a son shall ask a fish of any of you that is a father, will he for a fish give him a serpent, or a scorpion for an egg? If ye then, being evil, know of good gifts, how much more the Father?"

(a) Elenchus 24. The wilfulness of the swindler's way of life is exposed by this text. The way of life he practices is not for continence' sake, or for the good reward and hope of the contest, but for impiety and the badness of a wrong opinion. (b) For he teaches that one must not eat meat, and claims that those who eat flesh are liable to the judgment, as they would be for eating souls.

(c) But this is altogether foolish. The flesh is not the soul; the soul is in the flesh. And we do not say that the soul in animals is as valuable as men's, but is simply a soul to make the animal alive. But this pitiable wretch, together with those who share this opinion, supposes that the same soul is in men and in animals.

(d) This is the futile supposition of many misguided sects. For Valentinus and Colorbasus, and all Gnostics and Manichaeans, claim that there is a reincarnation of souls as well as transmigrations of the souls of ignorant persons—as they say themselves on the basis of some myth. They say that the soul returns and is reembodied in each of the animals until it comes to awareness, and so, cleansed and set free, departs to the heavens.

(e) And in the first place, the whole worthless contrivance of the myth itself stands exposed. No one else can know the exact truth of these things better than our Lord Jesus Christ, who came for "the sheep that was lost"—that is, for the souls of men. (f) Because he was in charge of them he healed them in body and soul, <as> the Lord of body and soul and giver of the life here and the life to come. And he did not raise those who had died—I mean Lazarus, the ruler's son, and the daughter of the ruler of the synagogue—in order to do them harm, as in the sects' doctrine that the body is a prison. He raised them to do them good, and in the knowledge that both our sojourn here in the flesh, and the coming resurrection of flesh and soul, are by his decree.

(g) And if, again, he knew that the soul in animals and human beings is one soul and he came to secure its salvation, then, after he had cleansed one demoniac—I mean the one who came out of the tombs—he should not have told the demons to go and kill two thousand swine. Not if the souls of the men and the swine were just alike! Why would he cause the destruction of two thousand in order to care for one?

(h) But if, again, Marcion twists round like a serpent by craftily replying that Christ freed the swine's souls from their bodies in order to allow their ascent—then he should not have returned Lazarus to his body, since he had been set free from it! Instead, he should have freed the demoniac himself from the chain of the body as well! But he did not; rather, he provided for the body as he did, knowing what was to its advantage.

(i) Your argument about the soul has crumpled, Marcion, and your followers' argument, and the other sectarians'. And yet I am going to speak once more of your bogus way of life, since you say that eating meat is wicked and unlawful. (j) But the Savior refutes you, knowing more than you and giving the better teaching with such a saying as this: he says, "Which of you, whose son shall ask for a fish, will give him a serpent, or, for an egg, a scorpion?" And further on, "If ye then, being evil, know how to give good gifts unto your children, how much more shall your heavenly Father?"[159] (k) Thus, if he called a fish and an egg "good gifts," nothing God has granted is evil if it is eaten with thanksgiving; and your malice stands refuted in every respect.

Scholion 25. The saying about Jonah the prophet has been falsified; Marcion had, "This generation, no sign shall be given it." But he did not have the passages about Nineveh, the queen of the south, and Solomon.

(a) Elenchus 25. Even in the very places you see fit to falsify, Marcion, you cannot avoid the truth. Even if you remove the <part> about the prophet Jonah—which signifies the Savior's dispensation[160]—and take out

[159] Luke 11:11-13
[160] οἰκονομία, in this case, his death and resurrection.

the part about the queen of the south and Solomon, and the story of Nineveh's salvation and the preaching of Jonah, the very saying of the Savior that precedes these will expose <you>. (b) For he says, "*This* generation asketh a sign, and there shall no sign be given it,"[161] implying that those who preceded this generation were vouchsafed signs from heaven by God. (c) Thus Elijah worked a miracle with the fire which came down from heaven and took his sacrifice. Moses divided the sea, pierced the rock and water flowed forth, brought manna from heaven. Joshua the son of Nun stopped the sun and moon. And in any case, even if the swindler conceals what is written in scripture, he will do the truth no harm but will estrange himself from the truth.

Scholion 26. Instead of, "Ye pass over the judgment of God" he had, "Ye pass over the calling of God."

(a) Elenchus 26. Where is there not refutation for you? Where can one <not> get evidence against you? The earlier sources agree with the later ones when your tampering is being exposed. (b) For if he says, "Ye hold the traditions of your elders and pass over the mercy and judgment of God," find out for how long he accuses them of doing this, and when the tradition of the elders arose! (c) You will find that the tradition of Adda arose after the return from Babylon, but that the tradition of Aqiba had come into being even before the Babylonian captivities, and that of the sons of Hasmonaeus at the time of Alexander and Antiochus, 190 years before Christ's incarnation. (d) As early as that, then, judgment was by the Law and mercy was by the prophets, and your trashy argument is a failure from every standpoint.

Scholion 27. "Woe unto you, for ye build the sepulchres of the prophets, and your fathers killed them."

(a) Elenchus 27. If he expresses his concern for the prophets by reproaching the people who killed them, the prophets were not strange to him. They were his servants, and sent before him by himself, the Father and the Holy Spirit, as messengers to prepare for his coming in the flesh.

They witnessed to the New Testament as well. (b) Moses, by saying, "The Lord God will raise up unto you a prophet of your brethren, like unto me."[162] Jacob before him, by saying, "Thou hast come up, my son Judah, from a young plant; falling down thou didst sleep. There shall not fail a ruler from Judah"[163]—and shortly after that, "till he come for whom

[161] Luke 11:29
[162] Deut 18:15
[163] Gen 49:9-10

are the things prepared, and he is the expectation of the gentiles, and in him shall the gentiles hope."[164]

(c) Isaiah: "Behold, the Virgin shall conceive";[165] Jeremiah: "And he is a man, and who shall know him?"[166] Micah: "And thou, Bethlehem," some other material, and, "out of thee shall come for me a governor,"[167] and so on. Malachi: "The Lord shall suddenly come to the temple";[168] David: "The Lord said unto my Lord, sit thou on my right hand,"[169] and so on. And there is a great deal to say, with the Savior himself, also, saying, "Had ye believed Moses ye would have believed me also, for he wrote of me."[170]

Scholion 28. He did not have, "Therefore said the wisdom of God, I send unto them prophets," and the statement that the blood of Zacharias, Abel and the prophets will be required of this generation.

Elenchus 28. Here too there is a great embarrassment for you, Marcion, since the standard of the truth is preserved, and your removal of the texts you have stolen can be discovered from the authentic copy of Luke's Gospel with the passages which are still there, and your excisions exposed.

Scholion 29. "I say unto my friends, Be not afraid of them that kill the body. Fear him which, after he hath killed, hath authority to cast into hell." But he did not have, "Are not five sparrows sold for two farthings, and not one of them is forgotten before God."

(a) Elenchus 29. Marcion, the lines, "I say unto my friends, be not afraid of them that kill the body; fear him which, after he hath killed the body, hath authority to cast the soul into hell," compel you to acknowledge the sequel of the parable as well. For no event occurs without God, even if you take out the part about the sparrows.

(b) Defend yourself then, Marcion, about the words you have left in the text, and tell us your opinion of the person who has "authority." For if you should say that he is Christ's Father, your so-called "good God"—then, even though you make a wrong distinction, still, since he has "authority," you have granted that he is a judge and awards everyone what they deserve.

(c) If, however, you say that not he, but the demiurge you keep yapping about is really a judge, tell me who has given him the authority! If he has it of himself, he is supreme and is possessed of authority—but if he has

---

164 Gen 49:10
165 Isa 7:14
166 Jerem 17:9
167 Micah 5:2
168 Mal 3:1
169 Ps 109:1
170 John 5:45

the authority to judge, he also has the authority to save! For he who is able to judge, is also able to pardon.

(d) And from another standpoint: If, when the judge casts the souls into hell, the good God does not rescue them even though he is in full charge of these very souls, how can he be "good"? It must be that the judge is stronger than he, and he cannot deliver them from his power—or that he can and does not want to and then, where is his goodness?

(e) But if, since the judge created the souls himself he also has the right to judge them, why does your mythical God on high do things part way and save (only) certain ones? For if he saves them by taking them from someone else's domain, he is covetous, since he has a desire for someone else's souls. But if you deny that this is covetousness, since what he does is good and for salvation, you are making him a respecter of persons who does not do good equally to all, but (only) in part.

Scholion 30. Instead of, "He shall confess before the angels of God," Marcion says, "before God."

Elenchus 30. If he alters the truth even in its least important expression it he is convicted of deviating from God's way in every respect. For a person who dares to alter any part of the scriptures is not in the way of the truth to begin with.

Scholion 31. He does not have, "God doth clothe the grass."

Elenchus 31. Even though you do not leave the written phrases as they were when they were spoken by the Savior, still the passages are preserved in the Gospel of the holy church—even if you deny the God who has created all and cares for all things, even the grass, by his word, and who is confessed by the Savior.

Scholion 32. "And your Father knoweth that ye have need of these things," meaning material things.

Elenchus 32. The Father knows that the disciples need material things, and provides for such. But he provides, not in another world but here, making the provision for his own servants, not in someone else's territory but in the one he has created.

Scholion 33. "But seek ye the kingdom of God, and all these things shall be added unto you."

(a) Elenchus 33. If we draw our sustenance from the creatures of one God, while another one is the God of the kingdom of heaven, how can the saying be self-consistent? Either what is here is his and the kingdom is his, and he accordingly "adds" everything here—which is his—because of the burden of our longing for his kingdom. (b) Or the kingdom and the world there are his, while what is here belongs to the demiurge, and the demiurge consents to the kingdom of the God on high by rendering aid to those who seek the righteousness and kingdom of the God on high. (c) But since consent is one and is not at variance, there cannot be two first principles, or three. For God, in fact, is one, the one who made all things, but made them well, not the opposite. Sin and error, however, belong to us, by virtue of our willing them and not willing them.

Scholion 34. Instead of, "Your Father," Marcion had, "Father."

Elenchus 34. Even here you will do us no harm, but lend further confirmation to us. For you have admitted that the Savior said his Father provides for the things that are here.

Scholion 35. Instead, "in the second or third watch," he had, "in the evening watch."

Elenchus 35. The oaf stands convicted of stupidly distorting the sacred words in accordance with his own opinion. Watches are not kept in the daytime but at night, and extend successively from evening until the first hour—not from dawn till evening, as he is caught tampering with them.

Scholion 36. "The Lord of that servant will come and will cut him in sunder, and will appoint him his portion with the unbelievers."

(a) Elenchus 36. Who is it that cuts the servant in two, pray? If it is the demiurge and judge whom you call God who will do this, then the believers belong to him. For to punish the servant who is not doing well, he assigns his portion with the unbelievers.

(b) But if it is Christ's Father, or Christ himself, who will do this, then you are plainly preserving the testimony against yourself in your own teaching. For in admitting that either Christ or his Father will do this, you have unambiguously acknowledged that the judge and the good God are the same, and that <he> who provides for those who are here, and for those who are there, is one.

Scholion 37. "Lest he hale thee to the judge, and the judge deliver thee to the officer."

(a) Elenchus 37. You say that the demiurge is a judge and that each of his angels is an officer, and that they will call the sinners to account for their deeds. But which deeds other than the errors and sins which Jesus also detests, and you say that you too forbid? (b) Now if the demiurge and judge detests the same deeds that the good God detests, by the fact and by the common consent he is shown to be one and the same (as he).

Scholion 38. There was falsification of "There came some that told him of the Galilaeans whose blood Pilate had mingled with their sacrifices" until the mention of the eighteen who died in the tower at Siloam, and of "Except ye repent" <and so forth>, until the parable of the fig tree of which the cultivator said, "I am digging about it and dunging it, and if it bear no fruit, cut it down."

(a) Elenchus 38. The bandit caused the removal of all this to conceal the truth from himself, because of the Lord's agreement with Pilate who had rightly condemned such persons, and because the men at Siloam died rightly, since they were sinners and God punished them in this way. (b) But when people tamper with imperial decrees, the copies with certified texts are produced from the archives to rebut the fools. Thus too, when the Gospel is brought forth from the king's palace, that is, God's holy church, it exposes the flies that spot the king's fine robes.

Scholion 39. "This woman, being a daughter of Abraham, whom Satan hath bound."

Elenchus 39. If, when he has come, the Lord takes care of Abraham's daughter, Abraham is no stranger to him. For he acknowledges his approval of him by showing pity for his daughter.

Scholion 40. Again, he falsified, "Then shall ye see Abraham, and Isaac, and Jacob and all the prophets in the kingdom of God." In place of this he put, "When ye see all the righteous in the kingdom of God, and yourselves thrust"—but he put "kept"—"out." There shall be weeping and gnashing of teeth.'"

(a) Elenchus 40. How plain the traces of the truth are! No one can hide a road. He can lead men off it, and hide it from those who do not know it, but from those who are familiar with it it is impossible to hide it. (b) For he cannot make the ground invisible where the road used to be. And even if he makes it hard to see, since the road's location surely remains the person who tampered with the road is exposed by those who know it.

(c) Now then, observe the traces of the route. To whom did he say this but to the Jews? And if he said it to the Jews, he proved by the same token that they were within the kingdom, and were being cast out by the righteous. (d) Now who could <these> be but the forefathers of the Jews, Abraham, Isaac, Jacob, and the prophets? For he did not say, "Ye shall see the righteous entering and yourselves not entering," but, "Ye shall see the righteous *in* the kingdom and yourselves cast out." (e) And he gave an anticipatory ruling regarding "the ones cast out"; but he showed that those who were already righteous were not unrelated to them by birth or calling, but had been called with them, and justified already before his incarnation. (f) And though <he meant that the Jews> remain outside, <he surely did not mean all of them>, since the patriarchs are within.

And how can there be gnashing of teeth at the judgment, you fool, if there is no resurrection of bodies?

Scholion 41. Again, he falsified, "They shall come from the east and from the west, and shall sit down in the kingdom," "The last shall be first," "The Pharisees came saying, Get thee out and depart, for Herod will kill thee." Also, "He said, Go ye and tell that fox," till the words, "It cannot be that a prophet perish out of Jerusalem" and, "Jerusalem, Jerusalem, which killest the prophets and stonest them that are sent," "Often would I have gathered, as a hen, thy children," "Your house is left unto you desolate," and, "Ye shall not see me until ye shall say, Blessed."

Elenchus 41. See the extent of his presumption! How much of the Gospel will he amputate? It is as though someone were to take an animal, chop half of its body off, and try to convince the ignorant with the (remaining) half, by saying that the animal looked like that, and nothing had been removed from it.

Scholion 42. Again, he falsified the entire parable of the two sons, the one who took his share of the property and spent it on dissipation, and the other.

Elenchus 42. The results of his tampering (here) will be no different from his previous presumptions. He is inflicting the loss on himself, while the truth remains as God has taught it.

Scholion 43. "The Law and the prophets were until John, and every man presseth into it."

Elenchus 43. If he prescribes a Law and names prophets, and does not declare the Law lawlessness or accuse the prophets of being false prophets, it is plainly acknowledged that the Savior has testified to the prophets; and it is proved that they prophesied of him.

Scholion 44. The material about the rich man, and Lazarus the beggar's being carried by the angels into Abraham's bosom.

(a) Elenchus 44. Observe! Abraham was included by the Lord among those who live and are blessed, and are in the inheritance of repose, and Lazarus was vouchsafed a place in his bosom! (b) Do not insult Abraham any more, Marcion, who recognized his own Master and said "Lord, the judge of all the earth"[170] to him. For see, it was testified by the Lord himself that Abraham is righteous, and no stranger to the life which is praised by the Savior.

Scholion 45. "But now he is comforted," again meaning Lazarus.

Elenchus 45. If Lazarus is comforted in the bosom of Abraham, Abraham is not excluded from the comfort of life.

Scholion 46. Abraham said, "They have Moses and the prophets, let them hear them, for neither will they hear him who is risen from the dead."

(a) Elenchus 46. It is not as though Abraham were still in the world and were testifying to the Law of Moses and the prophets under some misapprehension, or that he does not know what comes of these; it is after he has experienced the repose there. (b) For it is testified by the Savior in the parable that Abraham obtained salvation after death by the teachings of Law and prophets—and by practicing them before there was a Law! (c) And likewise, that those too who kept the Law after that, and obeyed the prophets, are in his bosom and depart to life with him. Of these Lazarus was one, who was vouchsafed the blessedness of Abraham's life-giving bosom through the Law and the prophets.

Scholion 47. He falsified, "Say, we are unprofitable servants; we have done that which was our duty to do."

Elenchus 47. He does not accept even the safeguard of the Lord's teaching! As a safeguard for his own disciples, lest they lose the reward of their labor through arrogance, he would counsel humility. But Marcion does not accept this; in everything he was inspired by pride, not truth.

Scholion 48. When the ten lepers met him. Marcion cut a great deal out and wrote, "He sent them away, saying, Show yourselves unto the priests," and yet he made a substitution and said, "Many lepers were in the days of Elisha the prophet, and none was cleansed, saving Naaman the Syrian."

Elenchus 48. Here too the Lord calls Elisha a prophet, and says that he himself is accomplishing the things which, equally, had been done before him by Elisha—in refutation of Marcion and all who make light of God's prophets.

Scholion 49. "The days will come when ye shall desire to see one of the days of the Son of Man."

Elenchus 49. If he counts days, designates a time, and calls himself Son of Man, he indicated both a limit to his life, and a term of the days of his preaching. Thus the Word is not without flesh, but a body is his choice.

Scholion 50. "One said unto him, Good master, what shall I do to inherit eternal life? He replied, "Call not thou me good. One is good, God." Marcion added, "the Father," and instead of, "Thou knowest the commandments" says, "I know the commandments."

Elenchus 50. To keep from showing that the commandments have already been written, he says, "I know the commandments." But the whole point is plain from what follows. And if he says that a "Father" is "good" and terms him God, he is rightly teaching the man who wants to inherit eternal life out of his Father's Law, and is not belittling or rejecting him. Instead he is bearing witness that those who lived under the Law, both Moses and the other prophets, have inherited eternal life.

Scholion 51. "And it came to pass that as he was come nigh unto Jericho, a blind man cried, Jesus, thou Son of David, have mercy on me. And when he was healed, he said, Thy faith hath saved thee."

Elenchus 51. There can be no lie in faith; if there is a lie, it is not faith. Now he says, "Son of David," and the man who confessed the name is commended and granted his request. He has not been reproved as a liar, but congratulated as a believer. (b) Therefore the One who granted sight to the blind for his calling upon the name was not without flesh. His being was real and not apparent, physically born of David's seed, of the holy Virgin Mary and through the Holy Spirit.

Scholion 52. Marcion falsified, "He took unto him the twelve and said, Behold, we go up to Jerusalem, and all things that are written in the prophets concerning the Son of Man shall be accomplished. For he shall be delivered and killed, and the third day he shall rise again." He falsified this in its entirety.

Elenchus 52. To make sure that he would not be upright in anything and, not being upright, would be convicted of tampering in every way. For he concealed the lines to deny what is said of the passion, if you please. But since he later admits that Christ has been crucified, his labor of tampering (with the text) will be labor in vain for him.

Scholion 53. He falsified the section about the ass and Bethphage—and the one about the city and temple, because of the scripture, "My house shall be called an house of prayer, but ye make it a den of thieves."

(a) Elenchus 53. Wickedness does not see its own refutation, for it is blind. Marcion thinks he can conceal the road of the truth, but this is not possible. (b) For he jumped right over it, completely bypassing the sections we have mentioned because of their testimony that the temple site was Christ's and built in his name, and leaving out the entire passage about the journey from Jericho and how he got to Bethphage. For there actually was an ancient highway to Jerusalem by way of the Mount of Olives, and it was not unknown to those who also describe the temple site.

(d) But for his refutation out of his own mouth Marcion says, "It came to pass on one of those days, as he taught *in the temple*, they sought to lay hands on him and were afraid,"[171] as we read in next paragraph, 54. (e) How he got from Jericho to the temple will be learned from the journey itself and the length of the road. But this should make it plain that the crook concealed what happened on the road, and what the Savior himself

[171] Cf. Luke 20:19

said in the temple before this saying,[172] I mean (that he said), "My house shall be called an house of prayer"[173] and so on, as the prophecy runs.

Scholion 54. "And they sought to lay hands on him and they were afraid."

Elenchus 54. This was considered and expounded in the last elenchus, with the appropriately brief explanation.

Scholion 55. Again, he excised the material about the vineyard which was let out to husbandmen, and the verse, "What is this, then, The stone which the builders rejected?"

Elenchus 55. This will do us no harm. Even if he cut it out he did not cut if off from us, but caused a loss to himself and his followers. For there is ample refutation of him by a greater number of texts.

Scholion 56. He excised, "Now that the dead are raised, even Moses showed at the bush, in calling the Lord the God of Abraham and Isaac and Jacob. But he is a God of the living, not of the dead."

(a) Elenchus 56. One can be amazed at the lame-brain's stupidity in not seeing that this testimony is equivalent to Lazarus the beggar's, and to the parable of those who are not allowed to enter the kingdom. He left the remains of these parables (in place) and did not falsify them; indeed, to his own embarrassment he has left "There shall be weeping and gnashing of teeth."[174] (b) But if a finger is dipped in water after departure fom this life and a tongue is cooled with water—as the rich man said to Abraham on Lazarus' account—and there is gnashing of teeth and wailing, this is a sign of a resurrection of bodies, even if the oaf falsifies the Lord's true sayings about the resurrection of the dead.

Scholion 57. He did not have the following: "Now that the dead are raised, even Moses showed, saying that the God of Abraham, the God of Isaac, and the God of Jacob is God of the living."

Elenchus 57. Since the Savior repeated the parable I have inserted it twice, so that I will not be like the tramp, Marcion, and leave any of the scriptures out. <But> the rejoinder to his tampering has been given already, in the elenchus just above.

Scholion 58. Again, he falsified, "There shall not an hair of your head perish"...(Elenchus 58 is missing.)

---

[172] I.e., "as he taught in the Temple." Marcion omits "My house shall be called a house of prayer."

[173] Matt 21:13

[174] Luke 13:28

Scholion 59. Again, he falsified the following: "Then let them which are in Judaea flee to the mountains" and so on, because of the words subjoined in the text, "until all things that are written be fulfilled."

(a) Elenchus 59. Because of his own forgetfulness he thinks that everyone is as stupid as he, and fails to realize that even if he leaves an unimportant text in place it serves for the exposure of the texts he has falsified, even though there are many of them. Thus nothing will keep anyone who wants to from comparing the things he acknowledges with these witnesses which he has falsified. (b) For it will be shown that <the words he left in place> in which, after his death, Abraham said, "They have Moses and the prophets; let them hear them,"[175] agree with these words that he has removed. What the prophets and Moses said came from God the Father, from the Lord himself the Son of God, and the Holy Spirit; and once written they had to be fulfilled.

Scholion 60. "He communed with the captains how he might deliver him unto them."

(a) Elenchus 60. What lunacy of Marcion's! Who "communed" but Judas? And to do what, but to "deliver" the Savior? And if the Savior is "delivered," the one who is "delivered" cannot be appearance, but is truth. If he was only a spirit, he was not delivered to men of flesh. As man, however, he had become tangible, <and> since he had put on flesh, willingly delivered himself into human hands.

(b) But they contradict themselves from stupidity. Indeed, I was arguing once with some of his disciples, some Marcionite or other, and remarking how it says in the Gospel that the Spirit took Jesus into the wilderness to be tempted by the devil. And he asked me, "How could Satan tempt the true God, who is both greater than he and, as you say, his Lord, Jesus his Master?"

(c) With God's help I received a flash of insight and answered him, "Don't you believe that Christ was crucified?"

"Yes," he said, and did not deny it.

"Who crucified him, then?"

"Men," he said.

(d) Then I said to him, "Who is more powerful—men, or the devil?" "The devil," he said.

But when he said this, I replied, "If the devil is more powerful than men, but men, who are weaker, crucified Christ, it's no wonder he was tempted

---

175 Luke 16:29

by the devil too! (e) With entire willingness and under no necessity Christ has given himself for us, truly suffering, not from weakness but by choice, to set us an example, and <pay> the devil's claim for our salvation by his suffering of the cross, for the condemnation of sin and the abolition of death."

Scholion 61. "And he said unto Peter and the rest, Go and prepare that we may eat the Passover."

Elenchus 61. Marcion, the text contains a cloud of arrows aimed at you, all in one testimony. If he gives orders to prepare for him to eat the Passover, and the Passover was kept before Christ's suffering, it was surely because it was instituted by the Law. (b) But since Christ was living by the Law, it was plain that he did not come to destroy the Law, but to fulfill it. And if a king does not destroy a law, the commandment in the Law is neither profane nor abhorrent to the king. (c) But if, when the Law is sacred and the commandment in it is acknowledged to be such, a king should add something to the commandment as a greater gift, the splendor of the addition appears by his authority. Now since the legislation and the additional gift are those of one and the same king, it is clear to everyone, and plain, that the king who has made the addition is not opposed to the Law.

(d) Thus it has been proved that the Old Testament is in no way contrary to the Gospel or the succession of the prophets. But you have brought your refutation on yourself in many ways, Marcion—or rather, you have been compelled to by the truth itself. (e) The ancient Passover was nothing but the slaughter of a lamb and the eating of meat, the partaking of flesh meat with unleavened bread. And who but the truth itself—as I said—has kept you from suppressing your refutation altogether? For the Lord Jesus, with his disciples, has eaten these meat-dishes that you abhor, keeping the Passover as prescribed in the Law.

(f) And don't tell me that he was naming beforehand the mystery he was about to celebrate when he said, "I desire to eat the Passover with you."[176] To shame you in every way the truth does not place the mystery at the beginning, or you might deny it. It says, "*After supper* he took certain things and said, This is such and such,"[177] and left no room for tampering. For it made it plain that he went on to the mystery after eating the Jewish Passover, that is, "after supper."

Scholion 62. "And he sat down, and the twelve apostles with him, and he said, With desire I have desired to eat the Passover with you before I suffer."

---

[176] Luke 22:15

[177] Cf. Luke 22:20.

Elenchus 62. The Savior sat down, Marcion, and the twelve apostles sat down with him. If he "sat down" and they "sat down" with him, one expression cannot have two different meanings, even if it can be differentiated in its dignity and manner. For you must either admit that the twelve apostles have also sat down in appearance, or that he has really sat down because he really has flesh.

(b) And (he said), "With desire I have desired to eat this Passover with you before I suffer," to show that a Passover is already portrayed in the Law before his passion, both becoming the guarantee of his passion and calling forth something more perfect—showing too <that>, as the holy apostle also said, "The Law was our guardian until Christ." But if the Law is a guardian until Christ, the Law is not unrelated to Christ.

Scholion 63. He falsified, "I say unto you, I will not any more eat thereof until it be fulfilled in the kingdom of God."

Elenchus 63. Marcion took this out and tampered with it, to avoid putting food or drink in the Kingdom of God, if you please. He was unaware, oaf that he is, that spiritual, heavenly things can correspond with the earthly, partaken of in ways that we do not know. (b) For the Savior testifies in turn, "Ye shall sit at my table, eating and drinking in the kingdom of heaven."

(c) Or again, he falsified these things to show, if you please, that the legislation in the Law has no place in the kingdom of heaven. Then why did Elijah and Moses appear with him on the mount in glory? But no one can accomplish anything against the truth.

Scholion 64. He falsified, "When I sent you, lacked ye anything?" and so on, because of the words, "This also that is written must be accomplished, And he was numbered among the transgressors."

Elenchus 64. Even if you falsify the words, the places they belong are evident from the fact, since the Law precedes them, the prophets foretell them, and the Lord fulfills them.

Scholion 65. "He was withdrawn from them about a stone's cast, and kneeled down and prayed/"

(a) Elenchus 65. When he knelt down he knelt visibly, and did it perceptibly. But if he did it perceptibly, then he performed the act of kneeling in the <human> manner. Therefore the Only-begotten did not sojourn among us without flesh. (b) For to him "every knee shall bow, of things in heaven, and things on earth, and things under the earth"[178]—the knees of heavenly beings supernaturally, of earthly beings perceptibly, of those under the earth in their own fashion. But here he did everything in truth so as to be seen and touched by his disciples, and not to deceive.

---

[178] Phil 2:10

Scholion 66. "And Judas drew near to kiss him, and said..."

Elenchus 66. He drew near to a corporeal Master and a God who had taken a body, to kiss real lips, not apparent, pretended ones.

Scholion 67. He falsified what Peter did when he struck the servant of the high priest and cut off his ear.

(a) Elenchus 67. The cheat concealed what had actually happened, meaning to hide it out of deference to Peter, but (in fact) removing something that was said to the Savior's glorification. (b) But it will do no good; even though you excise them; we know the miracles of God. After the cutting off of the ear the Lord took it again and healed it, in proof that he is God and did God's work.

Scholion 68. "They that held him mocked him, smiting and striking him and saying, Prophesy, who is it that smote thee?"

Elenchus 68. That "they that held," "mocked," "smite," "strike," and "Prophesy, who is it that smote thee," was not appearance, but indicative of tangibility and physical reality, is plain to everyone, Marcion, even if you have gone blind and will not acknowledge God's plain truth.

Scholion 69. After "We found this fellow perverting the nation," Marcion added, "and destroying the Law and the prophets."

(a) Elenchus 69. How will you not be detected? How will you not be exposed as perverting the way of the Lord? For when, in order to slander yourself—I won't say, "the Lord"—you add something here that is not in the text <and> say, "We found this fellow destroying the Law and the prophets," the opposite of this will refute you, you expender of wasted effort, since the Savior himself says, "I came not to destroy the Law and the prophets, but to fulfill."[179] (b) Now the same person <who> says, "I came not to destroy," cannot be accused of destroying. For the text did not say this, but, "We found him perverting the nation, saying that he himself is Christ, a king."

Scholion 70. An addition after, "forbidding to give tribute," is, "and turning away their wives and children."

(a) Elenchus 70. Who will get himself out onto a cliff, in fulfillment of scripture's, "He that is evil to himself, to whom will he be good?" For falsifying something that is written, but adding something that is not, is an example of the utmost rashness, wickedness, and unsafe travel—especially in the Gospel, which is forever indestructible.

[179] Matt 5:17

(b) And the additions themselves have no place in the Gospel and contain no hidden meaning. Jesus did not turn wives or children away; he himself said, "Honor thy father and mother," and, "What God hath joined together, let no man put asunder."

(c) But even though he did say, "Except a man leave father, and mother, and brethren, and wife, and children and the rest, he is not my disciple," this was not to make us hate our parents. It was to prevent our being led <to follow the teaching> of another faith at our fathers' and mothers' command, or to behavior contrary to the Savior's teaching.

Scholion 71. "And when they were come unto a place called Place of a Skull, they crucified him and parted his raiment, and the sun was darkened."

(a) Elenchus 71. Glory to the merciful God, who fastened your chariots together, Marcion, you Pharaoh, and though you hoped to escape, sank them in the sea! Though you make all possible excuses you will have none here. If a man has no flesh, neither can he be crucified.

(b) Why did you not evade this great text? Why did you not try to conceal this great event, which undoes all your evil which you have devised from the beginning? (c) If he was really crucified, why can you not see that the Crucified is tangible, and his hands and feet are fastened with nails? This could not be an apparition or phantom, as you say, but was truly a body which the Lord had taken from Mary—our actual flesh, bones, and the rest. For even in your teaching it is admitted that the Lord was nailed to a cross!

Scholion 72. Marcion removed the words, "Today thou shalt be with me in paradise."

(a) Elenchus 72. You removed this rightly and suitably, Marcion, for you have removed own entry into paradise. You will neither enter yourself nor allow your companions to enter. For by their very nature both deceivers and deceived hate what is good.

Scholion 73. "And when he had cried with a loud voice he gave up the ghost."

Elenchus 73. If he expired and gave a loud cry, Marcion, why did he expire, or what was it that was expired? But it is obvious, even if you deny it—his soul which, with his divine nature, had left the body, while the body remained lifeless, as the truth is.

Scholion 74. "And, lo, a man named Joseph took the body down, wrapped it in linen and laid it in a sepulchre that was hewn in stone."

Elenchus 74. If the removal, the wrapping, and the deposit in a rock-hewn tomb do not convince you, Marcion, who is a bigger fool than you?

What else that was plainer could scripture show when, to make the entire truth manifest, it exhibited the tomb, its location, what kind it was, the putting of the body there for three days, and the wrapper of the shroud?

Scholion 75. "And the women returned and rested the sabbath day according to the Law."

(a) Elenchus 75. Why did the women return? And why does the scripture say that they rested, Marcion, if not to give their witness which exposes your stupidity? (b) See here, women testify, apostles, Jews, angels—and Joseph, who took a real, tangible body down and wrapped it up! As scripture says, if a man has perverted himself to his own condemnation, who can put him to rights?[185]

Scholion 76. "The men in shining garments said, Why seek ye the living among the dead? He is risen; remember all that he spake when he was yet with you, that the Son of Man must suffer and be delivered."

(a) Elenchus 76. Not even these holy angels convince you, Marcion, though they confess that Christ has spent three days among the dead, and after that is alive, and dead no longer. (In his divine nature he is always alive, and was not put to death at all; but physically he had been put to death for the three days, and was alive again.) (b) For they tell the women, "He is risen; he is not here." And what does "He is risen" mean but that he also fell asleep? For they make it clearer: "Remember that while he was yet with you he told you these things, that the Son of Man must suffer."

Scholion 77. He falsified what Christ said to Cleopas and the other disciples when he met them, "O fools, and slow to believe all that the prophets have spoken. Ought not he to have suffered these things?" And instead of "what the prophets have spoken," he put, "what I have said unto you." But he is exposed, since "When he broke the bread their eyes were opened and they knew him."

Elenchus 77. Tell me, Marcion, how was the breaking of the bread done? In appearance, or with a solid body actually at work? For when he arose from the dead he truly arose in his sacred body itself; <therefore he truly broke the bread>.

(b) But you have replaced, "Is not this what the prophets have spoken?" Marcion, with, "Is this not what I said unto you?" (c) If he had told them, "*I* said unto you," they would surely have recognized him from the phrase, "I said." Why, then, is it at the breaking of the bread that scripture says, "Their eyes were opened and they knew him and he vanished?"

(d) For it was fitting for him, since he was God and was transforming his body into a spiritual one, to show that it was a true body but that it vanished when he chose, since all things are possible to him. (e) Even Elisha, in fact, who was a prophet and had received the grace from God, prayed God that his pursuers be smitten with blindness, and they were smitten and could not see him as he was. (f) Moreover, in Sodom the angels concealed Lot's door, and the Sodomites could not see it. Was Lot's door an apparition too, Marcion? But you are left with no reply. For he plainly broke the bread and distributed it to his disciples.

Scholion 78. "Why are ye troubled? Behold my hands and my feet, for a spirit hath not bones as ye see me have."

(a) Elenchus 78. Who can fail to laugh at the driveler who has foolishly dragged himself and the souls of others down to hell? If he had not acknowledged these words his imposture would be plausible, and his dupes would be pardonable. (b) But now, since he acknowledged these texts and did not take them out, and his followers read them too, his sin and theirs remains and the fire is inescapable for him and them, since they have no excuse. For the Savior has clearly taught that <even after> his resurrection he has bones and flesh, as he testified himself with the words, "as ye see me have."

12,1 This is the publication of the treatise against Marcion based on the remains of the Gospel he preserves, which I have composed on his account and which, in my opinion, is adequate to expose his deceit. (2) But I shall also go on to the next part, the texts from the Apostle which he still preserves, and which I have, again, selected in the same way. I have put <the> ones from the Epistle to the Galatians first, and keep that order throughout, for in Marcion's canon Galatians stands first. (3) At the time I did not make my selection <in> his <order> but in the order of the Apostolic Canon, and put Romans first. But here I cite in accordance with Marcion's canon.

<From the Epistle to the Galatians>

Scholion 1. Learn that the just shall live by faith. For as many as are under the Law are under a curse; but, The man that doeth them shall live by them."

(a) Elenchus 1. The saying, "Learn that the just shall live by faith," as the apostle gives it is reference to an ancient scripture. Such things <have been taken over> by the apostle for our salvation, as statements from the Law and prophets (which are) about a new covenant and are conjoined with our hope. (b) And he says, "They are under a curse," because there was a threat in the Law against Adam's disobedience, until the One who had come from above arrived, clothed himself with a body made of Adam's clay, and changed the curse into a blessing.

Scholion 2. "Cursed is everyone that hangeth upon a tree; but he that is of the promise is by the freewoman."

Elenchus 2. Again, by showing that the provision of the incarnation and cross was made for the purpose of lifting the curse, and that it had been written in the Law first, and prophesied, and then fulfilled in the Savior, the holy apostle gave plain indication that the Law is not alien to the Savior. For it prophesied and witnessed to the things that were to be done by him.

Scholion 3. "I testify that a man that is circumcised is a debtor to do the whole Law."

Elenchus 3. He does not say "he is debtor" with regard to something that is forbidden, but with regard to a heavier burden which can be lightened. For there is one Master who is able both to burden and, of his free choice, to lighten the burden of those who have not refused to accept salvation through his grace at his coming in the flesh.

Scholion 4. In place of, "A little leaven leaveneth the whole lump," he put, "corrupteth the whole lump."

Elenchus 4. So that there would be nothing true in his canon he has almost nowhere dealt with the scriptures without tampering with them. But the explanation of the saying comes from the analogy itself. Leaven, by its nature, is a product of a lump and leavening comes from the lump; and a person drawing the analogy of the symbol intelligently would not do away with the nature in the original terms.

Scholion 5. "For all the Law is fulfilled by you; thou shalt love thy neighbor as thyself."

Elenchus 5. What use would the holy apostle have for practicing the Law if the New Testament had been separated from the ancient legislation? But to show that the two Testaments are testaments of the one God, and that their agreement <as to> the possibility of fulfilling the Law by the love of neighbor, which does perfect good, is made equally known in the two Testaments, he said that love is the fulfillment of the Law.

Scholion 6. "Now the works of the flesh are manifest, which are these: Adultery, fornication, uncleanness, lasciviousness, idolatry, witchcraft, hatred, variance, emulations, wrath, strife, seditions, factions, envyings, drunkenness, revelings—of the which I tell you before, as I have also told you in time past, that they which do such things shall not inherit the kingdom of God."

(a) Elenchus 6. What marvelous mysteries the precepts of God's <apostle> are—the opposite of <the tramp's imposture>! For Marcion attributed everything dreadful to the flesh. But flesh was not always in existence; the flesh <came into being> on the sixth day of creation, with the fashioning of Adam. It had its origin from that time, I mean the time of Adam's fashioning, to confound those who say that evil is everlasting and primordial.

(b) Nor, in fact, did the flesh sin from the time of its fashioning, or its Fashioner might be held responsible for sin, because he had fashioned the flesh as a sinful thing. Neither did evil pre-exist the thing God had fashioned. Adam fell into disobedience later on, and <as> a free agent deliberately committed the sin against himself by his own choice, I mean (the sin of) breaking faith with his Master through disobedience. (c) Where, then, was evil before there was flesh? And why did the flesh not do evil as soon as it was fashioned, but later on? And that disposes of what is said about the origin of evil! Evil cannot be primordial, since whether it is done or not is up to the flesh, whose origin came later. Nor, in turn, is the flesh without an inheritance in the heavens.

(d) And let no one seize hold of the holy apostle's words, "Flesh and blood shall not inherit the kingdom of God";[180] he is not censuring all flesh. How can the flesh be accused which has not done these things? (e) But let me make the point with other proofs as well. For Paul says, "Who shall lay anything to the charge of God's elect?"[181] How can the holy Mary not inherit the kingdom of heaven, flesh and all, when she did not commit fornication or uncleanness or adultery or do any of the intolerable deeds of the flesh, but remained undefiled? (f) Therefore Paul does not mean that flesh cannot inherit the kingdom of heaven, but means carnal men who do evil with the flesh—fornication, idolatry and the like. (g) And your villainy has been exposed by every method, you misguided Marcion, since the truth has anticipated you everywhere, and safeguards the trustworthiness of the message of life.

Scholion 7. "They that are Christ's have crucified the flesh with the affections and lusts."

(a) Elenchus 7. If they that are Christ's have crucified the flesh too, Marcion, it is plainly in imitation of Christ that Christ's servants have made the flesh, with its affections and lusts, clean—showing that he himself has crucified flesh. Therefore they too have crucified the flesh, with the same intent as their Master. (b) And if they have crucified the flesh, it is inconceivable that flesh which has suffered for Christ does not reign with Christ, as the holy apostle indicates elsewhere, "As ye are partakers of the sufferings of Christ, so shall ye be also of the glory."

---

[180] 1 Cor 15:50

[181] Rom 8:33

Scholion 8. "For neither do they themselves who are circumcised (now) keep the Law."

(a) Elenchus 8. Thus the former circumcision had not been forbidden in its own day, if it kept the Law. But the Law announced that Christ would come to provide a law of liberty, and in Christ's time physical circumcision would no longer serve. For the true circumcision through Christ, of which it was a type, has come.

(b) And even if they who are still marked by the earlier circumcision keep the whole Law, this will no longer count for them as observance of the Law. For the Law said of Christ that "The Lord God will raise up unto you a prophet, of my brethren, like unto me; unto him ye shall hearken."[182] But since they have not hearkened to Christ "Circumcision is made uncircumcision unto them" and their observance of the Law is no longer observance.

(c) The Law is good, then, and circumcision is good, since from the Law and circumcision we have come to know Christ, his more perfect Law, and his more perfect circumcision.

From the <First> Epistle to the Corinthians, for this is their second Epistle and ours.

Scholion 1 and 9. "For it is written, I will destroy the wisdom of the wise, and will bring to naught the understanding of the prudent."

Elenchus 1 and 9. If the apostle culls evidence in proof of truth and good doctrine from the things that are written in the prophets, the prophets are not foreign to the truth, the good God, and his good doctrine.

Scholion 2 and 10. "That, according as it is written, He that glorieth, let him glory in the Lord."

(a) Elenchus 2 and 10. If a person who glories in the Lord is praiseworthy in the prophet's writings but knows the God of the Law as Lord—the God you call judge, Marcion, and demiurge, and just—then this God is none other than the Father of Christ, whose disciple Paul is. (b) For from the prophet's teaching, Paul, who was appointed by Christ as teacher of the gentiles, drew pure water, as it were, from teachings like these and from these very teachings, and watered the church which was entrusted to him.

Scholion 3 and 11. "of the first beings of this world, that come to naught."

(a) Elenchus 3 and 11. If there are many "first beings" (ἄρχοντες) of this world, Marcion, and if such beings are going to come to naught, you

[182] Deut 18:15

will be forced to give up your search for the roots of three first principles (ἀρχαί) but to hunt for another myth of many principles, many roots and much melodrama. (b) And when you make one up by quibbling—for you can't find one (ready-made)—the words, "that come to naught," will confront you. And your imaginary root of the first principles, which has no first principle of its own, will be demolished by the words of the author who said, "that come to naught."

For whatever comes to an end is not eternal; if it had a beginning, it will have to have an end as well. (c) It is impossible for anything that has a beginning to be everlasting unless the Existent should will it—the Cause of that which once did not exist, but had a beginning of existence. Now "the Existent" is Father, Son and Holy Spirit; the non-existent are all created things, which have had a beginning of existence. Among these is that which is called, and is, evil, which began with men, who came into existence but at one time did not exist. But since evil began at the same time that man <began>, who once did not exist, <there will also be a time> when evil will no longer exist. (d) It will undoubtedly be eliminated, since the Existent does not consent to a thing that had a beginning and then placed itself among evil things. For it will be brought to an end after the resurrection. And not only then. It has been brought to an end since the proclamation of the Law—and even before the Law by many who have lived by the law of nature, and still more, surely, since Christ's incarnation.

(e) But it will be ended entirely after the resurrection of the dead, since "They are sown in corruption, they are raised in incorruption,"[183] doing evil no longer, dying no longer. (f) And that it will be ended the same saying of the apostle, "The first beings of this world *that come to naught*," will testify. And the case you have made has been demolished in every way, Marcion, since it is imaginary, false, shaky and irrational.

Scholion 4 and 12. "For it is written, He taketh the wise in their own craftiness." And again, "The Lord knoweth the thoughts of men, that they are vain."

Elenchus 4 and 12. "It is written," which introduces a citation, and the corresponding "The Lord knoweth," are not strange to the person who selected the words of the saying—I mean the holy apostle, in whose writings the citation is found. And from this citation it will be evident that the character of the apostle's preaching is not different from that of the Old Testament from which he got his text.

---

[183] 1 Cor 15:42

Scholion 5 and 13. "For even Christ our Passover is sacrificed."

(a) Elenchus 5 and 13. If the apostle acknowledges a Passover and does not deny that Christ was sacrificed, the Passover is not foreign to Christ, who truly, not in appearance, sacrifices a lamb for a Passover, as the Law prescribes. Of this lamb Christ, who was not sacrificed (only) in appearance and did not suffer without flesh, is a type. (b) For how could a spirit be sacrificed? It is plain <that>that it could not.

But since he could not have been sacrificed without flesh, and yet—as is acknowledged by the apostle's undoubted testimony—he was truly sacrificed, <it is plain that he had clothed himself with flesh>. (c) Therefore it is plainly proven on all counts that the Law was not foreign to him. The Law was temporarily in force as a type until the coming of Christ, the more perfect and manifest Lamb, who was sacrificed in truth—the Lamb which the actual lamb which was sacrificed in ancient times anticipated. But as "our Passover, Christ was sacrificed."

Scholion 6 and 14. "Know ye not that he which is joined to an harlot is one body? For two, saith he, shall be one flesh."

Elenchus 6 and 14. If the Law is not true, why do truthful persons take the testimonies from the Law? One of them is God's holy apostle Paul, who took this text, together with many others, in manifest proof of truth, and of the proclamation of the good God.

Scholion 7 and 15. Given in an altered form. In place of, "in the Law," he says, "in the Law of Moses." But before this he says, "Or saith not the Law the same also?"

(a) Elenchus 7 and 15. Even if you change the form in the second expression, Marcion, and think that by your having written, "in the Law of Moses," you have separated the Law from God by means of that "Moses," the union (of the two texts) just before this refutes your foolishness—(that is, the union of) "Or saith not the Law the same also?" (with) "For it is written in the Law, Thou shalt not muzzle the mouth of the ox that treadeth out the corn."[184] (b) No matter if you added Moses' name you have done us no harm, but have helped us by tying the evidence against yourself together at every point and unwittingly admitting, through the phrases, "in the Law of Moses," and, "the Law saith," that the Law of Moses is God's Law.

(c) For the apostle goes on in agreement with this by saying in the next sentence, "Doth God take care for oxen? Or saith he it altogether for our sakes?" But if the Law has spoken for the apostles' sakes then, likewise,

[184] 1 Cor 9:8-9, ἣ καὶ ὁ νόμος ταῦτα οὐ λέγει; ἐν γὰρ τῷ Μωϋσέως νόμῳ γέγραπται· οὐ κημώσεις βοῦν ἀλοῶντα.

the God who spoke in the Law is looking after Christ's apostles by ordering that they not be "muzzled"—either so that they may teach the doctrine of Christ himself, or so that they may receive their daily bread from the people without fear. He therefore does not know the apostles to be foreign to his own Godhead; nor do the apostles regard him as a foreign God.

(d) By this Godhead's inspiration the holy apostle has given the testimony of all creatures through saying, "Doth God take care for oxen? But for the apostles' sakes hath he spoken." And if God has spoken for the apostles' sakes, and yet he is the creator of men and beasts, including oxen and sparrows, reptiles and insects, fish and the rest—then he is concerned for all, each in its own proportion.

(e) And he is taking care for all when he says, "Thou, Lord, shalt save both man and beast";[185] "Who provideth for the raven his food?"[186] "The young of the ravens cry to the Lord, seeking their meat";[187] and, "Thou shalt give to all their meat in due season."[188] But he did not forbid the muzzling of a threshing ox while the oxen are in the act of threshing, since this would show that God cannot feed his creature otherwise than with the fodder men provide for their cattle. (f) The holy apostle showed that it was not for lack of fodder that God provided for oxen through the thresher by forbidding him to muzzle his oxen, but by the figurative language about the apostles indicated their relation (to this).

(g) For truly, God manifestly makes provision for all and is concerned for all alike. For the holy apostle was not writing in contradiction of the Savior, to give the rabble an excuse of that sort. (h) Sparrows are less important than oxen, and of them the Savior said, "Five sparrows are sold for two farthings,"[189] and again, "Are not two sparrows sold for one farthing?"[190] Therefore, if two sparrows are sold for one farthing, and one will not fall into a snare without your heavenly Father, God provides for all alike, but cares for his more important creatures by the more important mode, that of spiritual reasoning. (i) Hence there is entire agreement that the same God is Maker, Demiurge, and Law-giver in Old and New Testaments, a good God and a just, and Lord of all.

185 Ps 35:7
186 Job 38:41
187 Job 38:41
188 Ps 194:15
189 Luke 12:6
190 Matt 10:29

Scholion 8 and 16. I have already dealt fully with this, and expounded it at length, in the preceding paragraph. Hence I consider it superfluous to speak of it again, and am content with what has been said.

Scholion 9 and 17. "Moreover, brethren, I would not that ye should be ignorant how that all our fathers were under the cloud and all passed through the sea, and did all eat the same spiritual meat, and did all drink the same spiritual drink. For they drank of a spiritual rock that followed them, and that rock was Christ. But with many of them God was not well pleased. Now these things were our examples, to the intent we should not lust after evil things, as they also lusted. Neither be ye idolaters as were some of them; as it is written, The people sat down to eat and drink, and rose up to play. Neither let us tempt Christ," until the words, "These things happened unto them for examples, and they were written for us," and so on.

(a) Elenchus 9 and 17. Such madness! When the sun is rising, what person who has eyes will wander away from the light? If the holy apostle says that the men of those days were his fathers and were under a cloud and passed through the sea, that there is both a spiritual meat and a spiritual drink, and that they have eaten and drunk from a spiritual rock that followed them, but the rock was Christ—(b) (if that is what he says), who will believe the stupidity of Marcion who befogs his own mind and the minds of his followers by claiming that Christ is unrelated to the events in the Law, which the apostle admits took place in reality and not in appearance.

(c) But the apostle says that Christ was not pleased with most of them, surely because of their unlawful behavior. But if he was not pleased with people who did things which were unlawful in terms of the Law, then he was angry with such people in his capacity as Giver of the Law, and he is teaching that the Law is his, that it was given for a time, and that it served a legitimate purpose until his incarnation. For it is proper for a householder to give his staff, at each particular time, the orders that are appropriate for it.

(d) But he adds at once, "These things were our examples, that we might not lust after evil things as they also lusted. Neither be ye idolaters, as were *some* of them"—not extending the sentence to them all. (e) And how do you know this, Paul? He replies by saying, "As it is written, The people sat down to eat and drink and rose up to play." So, then, the written scripture from which the apostle also takes his verdict against the lawbreakers, is true.

(f) Then again, "Neither let us tempt the Lord." But Marcion put "Christ" in place of "Lord." "Lord" and "Christ" are the same even if Marcion doesn't think so, since Christ's name has already been set down where it is said, "The rock was Christ, yet with many of them he was not well pleased."

(g) Again, when he is expounding the whole purpose of the passage the holy apostle says, "These things happened unto them for examples, and were written for our admonition." Now if the things that happened to them as examples were written for our admonition, the One who wrote for our admonition about the events that took place then, was looking after us whose admonition he was composing, so that we would not become desirous of evils. (h) But if he does not want us to be desirous of evils, then he is good, not evil. For he urges us to be in the same state as he, this same good God, who is likewise just—God of those who were written about earlier and of those who are admonished later, Creator of all, Demiurge, Lawgiver, Giver of the Gospels and Guide of the Apostles.

Scholion 10 and 18. "What say I, then? That sacred meat is anything, or that meat offered in sacrifice to idols is anything? But the things which they sacrifice, they sacrifice to demons and not to God." But Marcion added, "sacred meat."

(a) Elenchus 10 and 18. "What say I, then? Is meat offered in sacrifice to idols anything? But the things which they sacrifice, they sacrifice to demons and not to God." In saying that those who sacrifice to idols sacrifice to demons, not God, the apostle did not disown the ancient time of the fathers which extended till his time, while Jerusalem stood. (b) Therefore he was not condemning those who sacrificed to God while there was a need for sacrifices. But he does condemn those who sacrifice to idols—not for sacrificing, but for sacrificing to idols instead of God. (Nor do they sacrifice to prepare for eating the food God has granted them. They are sacrificing to demons and <rendering service> to nonsense.)

(c) But you added "sacred meat" (ἱερόθυτον), Marcion, thinking that, by confusing the two terms, "sacred" (ἱερός) and "idol", you could make the nature of the two (types of sacrifice) into one. And this is not the case. (d) If sacrifice was being offered specifically to Christ after the coming of the new covenant, and animals were being sacrificed in his name, then your sophistical falsehood would have proved persuasive, on the grounds that those who sacrifice to God now were sacrificing to Christ, whereas those who sacrificed then in the temple at Jerusalem, and those who sacrifice to idols, were lumped together and would be sacrificing to demons, not God. But as no one has sacrificed animals to Christ since the advent of Christ and the new covenant, the addition in your text is obvious.

(e) But even if the language about "sacred meat" and "meat offered to idols" actually stood in the Apostle, they would be taken as one and the same by persons of sound reason. The expression would be used carelessly by the apostle because of the habit of people who always called the idol "sacred."

(f) And your false notion has collapsed in every way, since the truth has been established that those who sacrifice to idols—whether what they did or do <is called> "sacred meat" as they say, <or "sacrifice to idols">—are <still> acting a lie and sacrificing to demons, not God. But (this is) not (true of) those who once sacrificed with perfect propriety in accordance with the Law.

(g) But now that this is no longer done[191]—by his will, as he said even from the first through the prophet Jeremiah, "To what purpose dost thou bring to me incense from Sheba and sweet cane from a far country?" and again, "Thy sacrifices are not sweet unto me";[192] and elsewhere, "Take away thy sacrifices, O Israel, and eat flesh. For I gave your fathers no commandment concerning sacrifices in the day that I took them by the hand to bring them out of the land of Egypt, but this thing I commanded them, that every man deal justly with his neighbor."[193]

(h) But when the same God who said, "I gave no such commandment," also said to Moses, in the Law, "If any man of the children of Israel shall offer a sacrifice of the beeves or of the sheep, let him offer a male without blemish"[194]—and again, "If any sin and be overcome by a transgression, let him offer a sheep"; and again, "If the people sin, let them offer a calf"—[195] he showed that he willingly accepted the sacrifices which once were offered for the people's salvation, not because he needed or wanted them, but in deference to their weakness and people's preconception, to divert men's minds from polytheism to the knowledge of the one God. (i) For since their minds had been firmly set on the sacrifice which, as though in piety, they were offering to idols for their own atonements and salvation, he willed that, lest they feel any distress because of their habituation, they transfer their customary practices to himself—to wean them away from them <by allowing> them to do this in his name for a while, rather than in the names of an imaginary pantheon. Then finally, when they had learned to know the One and come to believe firmly in the One, he would tell them, "Do I eat bulls' flesh or drink the blood of goats?"[196] and, "Did ye offer unto

[191] μηκέτι τούτου γενομένου. In the long series of quotations which make up this passage, Epiph loses sight of his main verb.

[192] Jerem 6:20

[193] Jerem 7:21-23

[194] Cf. Lev 22:18-19.

[195] Cf. Lev 5:17-18 and 4:13-14.

[196] Ps 49:3

me sacrifice in the wilderness forty years, O house of Israel?"[197]—though many sacrifices were offered then, surely—(k) to show that they were not offering to him, though he accepted this and they were offering in his name. (He accepted it) because of their inherited custom in such matters, until he could undermine it by drawing them away from their customary worship of many gods to the One, and from the One they could finally learn that he had not needed and did not need sacrifices; (l) and at last he would remove the entire reason for the sacrifices through the incarnation of Christ himself. For the one sacrifice has put an end to all the previous ones—the sacrifice of Christ, that is, for, as the scripture says, "As our Passover, Christ is sacrificed."[198] Of this Sacrifice, Passover and teaching the Law became a guardian; for because of the type, it led and brought them back to the more perfect teaching.

Scholion 11 and 19. "A man ought not to have long hair, forasmuch as he is the image and glory of God."

Elenchus 11 and 19. The apostle not only declares man to be God's image, but to be God's glory as well. And by representing the hair as physical—for it grows specifically on the body, not the soul—he declares, through his acknowledgment of things from the Old Testament which are applied in the New, that this created thing is therefore not unrelated to the good God.

Scholion 12 and 20. "But God hath compounded the body."

Elenchus 12 and 20. If "God" (ὁ θεός) has compounded the body, the apostle is preaching no other God than the true God. And if he confesses that "God" has compounded the body by means of its members, he knows no other "God" than the Demiurge himself, he who is good, creator and just, the maker of all. Of all these works of his one is man, well compounded by him by means of his members.

Scholion 13 and 21. Marcion has erroneously added the words, "on the Law's account," <after> "Yet in the church I had rather speak five words with my understanding."

(a) Elenchus 13 and 21. Thus the languages too are by the gift of the Spirit. But what sort of languages does the apostle mean? <He says, "languages in the church,"> to show <those who> preened themselves on the sounds of Hebrew, which are well and wisely diversified in every expression, in various complex ways—on the pretentious kind of Greek,

[197] Amos 5:25
[198] 1 Cor 5:7

moreover, the speaking of Attic, Aeolic and Doric—<that God does not permit just one language in church, as some of the people <supposed> who had stirred up the alarms and factions among the Corinthians, to whom the Epistle was being sent.

(b) And yet Paul agreed that both using the Hebrew expressions and teaching the Law is <a gift> of the Spirit. Moreover, to condemn the other, pretentious forms of Greek, he said he spoke with "tongues" rather (than those) because he was an Hebrew of Hebrews and had been brought up at the feet of Gamaliel; and he sets great store by the scriptures of these Hebrews , and <makes it clear> that they are gifts of the Spirit. Thus, in writing to Timothy about the same scriptures, he said, "For from thy youth thou hast learned the sacred scriptures."[199]

(c) And further, he said the same sort of thing <to> the people who had been trained by the Greek poets and orators, and added in the same way, "I speak with tongues more than ye all,"[200] to show that he was more fully versed in the Greek education as well. (d) Even his style shows that he was educated, since Epicureans and Stoics could not withstand him <when he preached the Gospel with wisdom at Athens>, but were defeated by the inscription on the altar, "To the unknown God," which he read learnedly—which was read literally by him, and immediately paraphrased as "Whom ye ignorantly worship, him declare I unto you."[201] (e) And (they were defeated) again when he said, "A prophet of their own hath said, Cretans are always liars, evil beasts, slow bellies,"[202] meaning Epimenides, who was an ancient philosopher and erected the idol in Crete. Callimachus the Libyan also extended his testimony to himself by quoting Callimachus and saying falsely of Zeus:

> The men of Crete are liars alway, Lord;
> 'Twas men of Crete that built thy tomb, though thou
> Hast never died; thy being is eternal

(f) And yet you see how the holy apostle explains of languages, "Yet in church I had rather utter five words with my understanding," that is, "in translation." As a prophet benefits his hearers with prophecy in the Holy Spirit by bringing things to light which have already been furnished to

---

[199] 2 Tim 3:15
[200] 1 Cor 14:18
[201] Acts 17:23
[202] Tit 1:12

his understanding, I too, says Paul, <want> to speak so that the church may hear and be edified—not edify myself with the boast of Greek and Hebrew which I know, instead of edifying the church with the language which it understands.

(g) But you have added, "on the Law's account," Marcion, as though the apostle meant, "I want <to speak> (no more than) five words in church on the Law's account." Shame on you, you second Babylon and new rabble of Sodom! How long are you going to confuse the tongues? How long will you venture against beings you cannot harm? For you are attempting to violate angelic powers by expelling the words of the truth from the church and telling the holy Lot, "Bring the men out!"[203]

(h) And yet your attempt is an attempt on yourself. You will not expel the words of the truth, but you will strike yourself blind and pass your life in utter darkness—fumbling for the door and not finding it, till the sun rises and you see the day of judgment, on which the fire will confront your falsehood also. For this is waiting for you, when you see. (i) "On the Law's account" is not in the apostle, and you have made it up yourself. But even if the apostle were to say, "on the Law's account," he would be saying it, in harmony with his own Lord, not in order to destroy the Law but to fulfil it.

Scholion 14 and 22. "In the Law it is written, With men of other tongues and other lips will I speak unto this people."

(a) Elenchus 14 and 22. "If the Lord did not fulfill the things that had previously been said in the Law, why would the apostle need to mention things from the Law which are fulfilled in the New Testament? Thus the Savior showed that it was he himself who had spoken in the Law even then, and threateningly declared to them, "Therefore was I grieved with this generation and said, They do always err in their hearts, and I sware that they shall not enter into my rest."[204] For the same reason he promised to speak to them through men of other tongues—as indeed he did, and they did not enter. (b) For we find him saying this to his disciples: "Unto you are given the mysteries of the kingdom, but unto them in parables, that seeing they may not see,"[205] and so on. Hence (if) the Old Testament sayings (are) fulfilled everywhere in the New, it is plain to everyone that the two Testaments are not Testaments of two different Gods, but of the same God.

---

[203] Gen 19:5
[204] Ps 94:10-11
[205] Mark 4:11-12

Scholion 15 and 23. "Let your women keep silence in the church; For it is not permitted unto them to speak, but they are commanded to be under obedience, as also saith the Law."

(a) Elenchus 15 and 23. If God's holy apostle enjoins good order on God's holy church on the Law's authority, then the Law from which he took the good order is not disorderly; nor is it the law of a foreign God because it subjected wife to husband. For this was satisfactory to the apostle too in his legislation for the church—as he says, "as also saith the Law."

(b) And where did the Law say so, but when God said at once to Eve, "Thy resort shall be to thy husband, and he shall rule over thee?" For even though it is also found in other passages the original statement of it is here. (c) Now if the wife was declared subject to the husband from then on by God's ordinance—and if the apostle subjects her accordingly, and not in disagreement with the God who made husband and wife, then the apostle too, by commanding it, shows decisively that he is a lawgiver for the same God to whom both the Law and the whole Old Testament belong, and that the New Testament is the same God's as well—that is, the two Testaments, which then and now subjected wife to husband for the sake of an equivalent godly order.

Scholion 16 and 24. On resurrection of the dead: "Brethren, I make known unto you the Gospel ye believed... that Christ died, and was buried, and rose again on the third day... When this mortal shall have put on immortality, then shall be brought to pass the saying that is written, Death is swallowed up in victory."

(a) Elenchus 16 and 24. "Brethren, I make known unto you the Gospel which I preached unto you." If he has preached it and is making it known again, it is not a different Gospel or a different knowledge, subsequent to the one knowledge and the one Gospel which is one throughout the four Gospels and the Apostles—to the shame of Marcion who arrived so many years later, after the time of Hyginus, the ninth bishop of Rome in succession after the perfecting of the apostles Peter and Paul.[206] (b) And so, since he knew by the Holy Spirit that Marcion and his kind would twist the road whose foundation had been properly laid, the same holy apostle secured it by saying, "Though we, or an angel, preach any other Gospel unto you than that which ye have received, let him be accursed."[207] (c) This is why he no longer said, "I am preaching the Gospel to you," but, "I am

[206] Cf. Iren. 3.4.2-3.
[207] Gal 1:8

making the Gospel known to you"—not a different one, but the one I have preached to you already, of which I am now reminding you. "I am making it known to you for the same reason that I preached it to you, if you hold fast to it, unless you have believed in vain. For unless you hold it fast as I preached it to you, you have believed in vain apart from it."

(d) "For I preached to you that Christ died for our sins according to the scriptures." Not in accordance with a a myth, or in accordance with the teaching of those who, of their own motion, are going to say things that are not in scripture. For the Jews, of their own motion say that he has not risen; and Marcion and the rest, that he has suffered and been buried in appearance. But I am giving you assurance in accordance with the scriptures.

(e) For he adds immediately, "So we preached, and so ye believed, that Christ died, and was buried, and rose the third day"; and in the same breath, "If the dead rise not, then is not Christ raised. And if Christ be not risen, then is our preaching vain." (f) And after all this, "For this mortal must put on immortality, and this corruptible must put on incorruption."[208] And he did not say that this mortal contains immortality, or that this corruptible contains incorruption, but that the mortal and corruptible puts on immortality and incorruption. (g) And what is "mortal" but the body, which does not merely contain immortality in itself but is fit for immortality and is to put in on—not with the body discarded and immortality put on by the soul which cannot die, but with the mortal putting on immortality and the corruptible—that is, the body—putting on incorruption?

For there is both a death and a temporary decay of the body because of the dissolution which was brought upon it by Adam's disobedience. (h) But because he is speaking of the benefits which will be brought to fulfillment in it, Paul, through his promise, indicates their coming fulfillment by saying, "Then shall be brought to pass the saying that is written, Death is swallowed up in victory," meaning the resurrection of the dead which will take place at that time. For death was swallowed up in part by the resurrection of Christ and those who arose with him—"For many bodies of the saints arose and went into the holy city,"[209] as the Gospel says. But then it will be swallowed up in victory, when it disappears altogether from everyone.

From the Second Epistle to the Corinthians. This stands third in Marcion but in an altered way, since in his canon Galatians is placed first.

---

[208] 1 Cor 15:53

[209] Matt 27:52-53

Scholion 1 and 25. "For all the promises of God have their Yea in him; therefore through him we utter the Amen to God."

(a) Elenchus 1 and 25. Open your eyes, Marcion, and be saved! But if you no longer can—for you have died—let your dupes open their eyes and escape from you, as from a dreadful serpent which injures any who come near it. (b) For if "All the promises of God have their Yea in him," but the apostle knows God's promises through the Law and the prophets, then the Yea of the promises' fulfillment was surely confirmed in Christ. (c) Hence Christ is not alien to the ancient Law and the prophets, or to the God who spoke in the Law and has fulfilled his promises in Christ!

Nor is Christ opposed to the God who has given the Law and the prophets. (d) For the reason. Paul says, why the Amen is also uttered to God through Christ, is that the promises which were made become Yea through him. For it is God the Father who promised but Christ who confirms, and the Amen proper is secured through him in those who are confirmed by his promise, and who have recognized his Father as the God who spoke in the Law and has given deliverance, in the Gospel, to those who believe. It is they who say, through Christ who himself is saying it, "Yea, Father, for so it seemed good in thy sight."[210]

Scholion 2 and 26. "For we preach not ourselves, but Christ Jesus the Lord and ourselves your servants through Jesus. For it is God who said, Out of darkness shall light shine."

(a) Elenchus 2 and 26. The apostles do not preach themselves, but Christ Jesus, as Lord. Therefore there can be no sect or church named for the apostles. We have never heard of Petrists, Paulians, Bartholomaeans, or Thaddaeans; from the first we have heard one message, the message of all the apostles, (b) which proclaims not themselves but Christ Jesus as Lord. This is why they all gave one name for the church—not their own name but the name of their Lord Jesus Christ, since they were first called Christians at Antioch. This is the only catholic church, having no <name> but that of Christ. It is a church of Christians—not of Christs but of Christians, since Christ is one, and they are named Christians after the one Christ. (c) But all <the sects sprouted up> after this church and its messengers—no longer of the same character <but>, from their given names of, Manichaeans, Simonians, Valentinians, Ebionites—plainly <foreign to it>. You too are one of those, Marcion, and your dupes have been given your name because you preached yourself, not Christ.

---

210 Matt 11:26

(d) He says next, "For God who said, Out of darkness light shall shine." But which "God" if not the one God who brought light out of darkness in the prophet? That is, in place of human unbelief and ignorance he caused light and knowledge to shine, in Christ, in the hearts of us who were once idolatrous gentiles, but <have> now <come to know> the God who promised then in the prophet that his light would shine in the world—and who thus is not foreign to the Old and New Testaments. I have kept trying to convince you of this, Marcion, from the written remains of the Gospel which you have in your possession, and not be taken in by you.

Scholion 3 and 27. "We, having the same Spirit of faith, also believe and therefore speak." But he excised "according as it is written."

(a) Elenchus 3 and 27. Whatever ventures you may make you will not be given an opening. Even if you excise "according as it is written," the consequences of the words that used to be written are plain. (b) After, "I believed, and therefore have I spoken," the apostle immediately added the exact equivalent and said, "We, having the same Spirit of faith, likewise believe and therefore speak." (c) But it is plain to everyone that the line beginning, "I believed <and therefore have I spoken>" is written in the Hundred Fifteenth Psalm, one which has the Alleluia superscription and is part of David's roll and a prophecy of his own. (d) So the apostle took the text and likewise, speaking as one of the apostles, said, "Therefore we also believe and speak." (He said, not "Therefore *I* believed and spoke," but, "*We* believe, therefore we speak," to link himself with the other apostles.)

(e) And he says, "having the same Spirit" to show that the Spirit which spoke in David is the same Spirit which is in the apostles. The Spirit by whose inspiration David believed when he prophesied is the Spirit in which they too believe and speak.

(f) But the injustice and, one might say, the greed of <the tramp's> sick ideas is great. For since Paul maintains that the Spirit is one and the same, how can Marcion's stupidity, which admits that the holy apostle has said this, dare to say that there was one Spirit then, and another which was in the apostles?

From the Epistle to the Romans, Epistle Four, for this is where it stands in Marcion, thus making certain that he can get nothing right.

Scholion 1 and 28. "As many as have sinned without law shall also perish without law; and as many as have sinned in the Law shall be judged by the Law. For not the hearers of the Law are just before God, but the doers of the Law shall be justified."

(a) Elenchus 1 and 28. If as many as sinned without law will also perish without law, then the Law, when kept, is conducive of salvation and does not permit those who keep it to perish. And if those who sinned by the Law will be judged by the Law, then the Law is judge of their transgressions; though it is not a Law of destruction but of righteous judgment, judging the transgressors in holiness.

(b) "For not the hearers of the Law are just before God, but the doers of the Law shall be justified." If the Law, when kept, justifies the person who keeps it, then the Law on account of which those who keep the Law are constituted righteous, is not unrighteous or bad. (c) But from the Law is derived its prophetically proclaimed faith in Christ, without whom no one can be justified and again, by believing in whom no one can be justified if he believes differently than the testimony which is prophetically given by the Law. For Christ is the fulfillment of the Law as is said in the Apostle: "Christ is the fulfillment of the Law for justification,"[211] to show that there can be no righteousness without the Law and Christ. (d) For neither will the Jews, who have not received Christ, be justified without Christ; nor will you be justified, Marcion, since you deny the Law.

Scholion 2 and 29. "Circumcision verily profiteth, if thou keep the Law; but if thou be a breaker of the Law, thy circumcision is made uncircumcision."

Elenchus 2 and 29. If the holy apostle declares that circumcision will be beneficial, who can cast aspersions on things that are beneficial unless he is going to behave like the serpent? For you are like the serpent, Marcion; it too, turning what God had said around, misled Eve by saying, "Ye shall certainly not die!"[212]

(b) For Paul linked Law with circumcision, showed that circumcision was appropriate to the Law, and declared it to be the ordinance of the same God who had once given circumcision and the Law for our assistance. And when Christ is believed on the Law's authority, he enables the believers to say and do what is perfect.

Scholion 3 and 30. "Which hast the form of knowledge and of the truth in the Law."

Elenchus 3 and 30. If knowledge has a form, and the nature of a thing is apparent from its form, but the apostles and their disciples, who have the knowledge and the truth, have acquired the nature, that is, the knowledge and the truth, from the form of the Law, then the Law is not foreign to the

[211] Cf. Rom 10:4
[212] Gen 3:4

knowledge and the truth. For through the form in the Law the messengers of the truth came to know the knowledge and truth.

Scholion 4 and 31. "For when we were yet without strength, in due time Christ died for the ungodly."

(a) Elenchus 4 and 31. The words "yet" and "died" are not indicative of appearance but of reality. If Christ was an appearance what need was there for "yet" to be said—when Christ could have been manifest in appearance at any time, then and now, without any need to say, "while we were yet without strength." (b) For his death *then* <is evident> from the word "yet", (the death) <by which he paid in full what was owed for us> and justified us by that death, so that he has no further need to die. For he died once for sinners, and need not die any more on his own account.

Scholion 5 and 32. "Wherefore the Law is holy, and the commandment holy, and just, and good."

Elenchus 5 and 32. Paul assents to the holiness of the Law and of the commandment which was given in it, and by calling this commandment holy, just and good, has certified it with three witnesses—to refute you, Marcion, and teach us that it is the Law of the holy One whose commandment is also holy, and that he is himself the holy and good (God). (b) Therefore, as the commandment of a good God, it is called good; as the commandment of a holy God, it is called holy; as the commandment of a just God, it is called just. For he who <proclaims it> then and now—he who is holy, just and good—is one. Therefore his commandment then and now, in the Law and in the New Testament, is also holy, just and good.

Scholion 6 and 33. "That the requirement of the Law might be fulfilled in us."

Elenchus 6 and 33. If the requirement of the Law is fulfilled in the apostles and in us, Marcion, how dare you call the Law foreign to God's apostles, who are justified in accordance with their fulfilment of the Law?

Scholion 7 and 34. "For Christ is the fulfillment of the Law for righteousness to everyone that believeth."

(a) Elenchus 7 and 34. If Christ has come for righteousness for all who believe, while the Law cannot be fulfilled unless Christ fulfills it by his coming, you will not be perfected, you Jews, by remaining in the Law, unless you believe and accept the Christ who has come. (b) But neither can you be saved in Christ, Marcion, since you reject the first principle and root of the proclamation, which is the Law from which Christ is known and which perfects one who does not despise the Law as alien to Christ

Scholion 8 and 35. "He that loveth his neighbor hath fulfilled the Law."

Elenchus 8 and 35. If the Law is fulfilled by the love of neighbor, then the Law, which commands the love of neighbor is not foreign to Christ, and to God the Father of our Lord and God Jesus Christ. For God is love, and everything he proclaims is always proclaimed alike, both then and now, in the Old Testament and the New.

Since Marcion has a distorted version of everything from the <First> Epistle to the Thessalonians, the fifth Epistle—so it stands in Marcion's canon but it is the eighth in the Apostle—I cite nothing from it.

Since Second Thessalonians, the sixth Epistle in Marcion but the ninth in The Apostle, has likewise been distorted by Marcion himself, again I cite nothing from it.

Of Ephesians, the seventh Epistle in Marcion, but the fifth in The Apostle, (I cite) the following:

Scholion 1 and 36. "Remember that ye, being in time past gentiles, who are called uncircumcision by that which is called the circumcision in the flesh made by hands; that at that time ye were without Christ, being aliens from the commonwealth of Israel, and strangers from the covenants of promise, having no hope, and without God in the world. But now in Christ Jesus, ye who sometimes were far off are made nigh by the blood of him. For he is our peace, who hath made of both one," and so on.

(a) Elenchus 1 and 36. "Remembering," by its nature, means the remembrance of a time. "They who are called by that which is called" means the types of the (real) things, (and Paul says) "in the flesh" to show that the type in the flesh was awaiting the time of the Spirit, in order to manifest the more perfect things instead of the type. (b) For without Christ the uncircumcised had been alienated from the commonwealth of Israel, and were strangers to covenant and promise. Such people had no hope but were without God in the world, as is shown by the words of the apostle.

(c) But you can neither see nor hear, Marcion, or you would realize how many good things there were to which the holy apostle says the Law was conducive for those who had lived by the Law in those days. "For in Christ Jesus ye who were once afar off <have> now <been made> nigh through his blood. For he is our peace, who hath made of both one." (d) But if he made both one, and if he did not destroy the one but bring the other into being, then that which came first is not foreign to him and he did not separate the second from the first. He gathered them both into one, not anyhow or in appearance, but truthfully by his blood, as the apostle's sound teaching makes clear.

Scholion 2 and 37. "Wherefore he saith, Awake thou that sleepest, and arise from the dead, and Christ shall give thee light."

(a) Elenchus 2 and 37. Where did the apostle get "Wherefore he saith" but, plainly, from the Old Testament? This is in[213] Elijah. But what was Elijah's background? Surely, he was one of the prophets who lived by the Law, and he can be found in the Law and the Prophets. (b) Now if it was of Christ that he prophesied, "Awake thou that sleepest and arise from the dead, and Christ shall give thee light" then the type of this had been brought to fulfillment through Lazarus and the others, though they themselves were dubious of it. Martha and Mary said, "Already he stinketh, for he hath been dead four days,"[214] and the friends of the ruler of the synagogue said, "Trouble not the master any further,"[215] and the Master himself said, "Fear not; she is not dead, but sleepeth."[216]

(c) For clearly, from then on the Gospel proclaimed that there would be resurrection through Christ, and to show Christ's capability (of this), showed the masterful ease (with which he raised the dead). For as it is easy for a man to raise, not a dead person but a sleeper, with a call, so it was the easiest thing in the world for Christ to say, "Lazarus, come forth!"[217] or "Qumi, qumi, talitha," "Get up, child!"[218] (d) Through these <plain> and manifest demonstrations the Gospel pointed to the call of ourselves, who were then asleep, from our dead works and heavy slumber; <and> to Christ, raising us and giving us light by his call. This is its second relation (to the prophecy). (e) But the final, universal (fulfillment) is expected when the same Christ who says, "I am the resurrection,"[219] calls everyone, raises them body and soul, and gives them light by his coming arrival.

Scholion 3 and 38. "For this cause shall a man leave his father and mother, and shall be joined unto his wife, and they two shall be one flesh," minus the phrase, "unto his wife."

Elenchus 3 and 38. Even if you falsify the phrase "<unto his> wife," Marcion, it has been shown many times that the contents of the Law are not foreign to the teachings of the apostle. For the whole of your tampering will be evident from the words, "They shall be one flesh."

From the Epistle to the Colossians, the eighth Epistle in Marcion but the seventh in the Apostle.

[213] Holl suggests emending to Isaiah, see Holl-Dummer, *Epiphanius II* p. 180.
[214] John11:39
[215] Luke 8:49
[216] Luke 8:52
[217] John 11:43
[218] Mark 5:41
[219] John 11:25

Scholion 1 and 39. "Let no man therefore judge you in meat, or in drink, or in respect of an holyday, or of the new moon and sabbath days, which are a shadow of things to come."

(a) Elenchus 1 and 39. A shadow, Marcion, is not cast in any way but by a body, and there cannot be a body if a shadow is not cast by it. (b) Therefore, by the remains of the truth of the sacred scriptures which you still preserve, your dupes should be convinced that the ordinances of those times were not foreign to the good things to be revealed. They were temporary provisions about food and drink, and concerning festivals, new moons and sabbaths. (c) These were the shadows of those good things. And by these shadows we have apprehended the body of the good things now present, which were foreshadowed in the Law and fulfilled in Christ.

The Epistle to Philemon, number nine,

(a) for this is its position in Marcion; but in the Apostle it stands last. In some copies, however, it is placed thirteenth before Hebrews, which is fourteenth, but other copies have the Epistle to the Hebrews tenth, before the two Epistles to Timothy, the Epistle to Titus, and the Epistle to Philemon. (b) However all sound, accurate copies have Romans first, Marcion, and do not place Galatians first as you do. In any case I cite nothing from this Epistle, Philemon, since Marcion has it in a completely distorted form.

The Epistle to the Philippians, number ten,

for this is its position in Marcion, tenth and last, but in the Apostle it stands sixth. Likewise I make no selections from it either, since in Marcion it is distorted.

This concludes Marcion's arrangement <of the> remains of the words and their subject which he preserves from Luke's Gospel and The Apostle. From it I have selected the parts of the material he retains which are against him, and have placed the refutations next to them. But in his own Apostolic Canon, as he called it, he also added, of the so-called Epistle to the Laodiceans:

Scholion 1 and 40 "(There is) one Lord, one faith, one baptism, one God and Father of all, who is above all, and through all, and in all."

(a) Elenchus 1 and 40. In agreement with the Epistle to the Ephesians, Marcion, you have also gathered these testimonies against yourself from the so-called Epistle to the Laodiceans. Thus, at the end of the work, we may find what you have to say by reading it and, by finding what your teachings are, see through[220] your heretical inventions, the three first principles with

[220] Epiph here plays on ἀναγνόντες, γνόντες and καταγνῶσιν.

no first principles of their own which are different from each other. (b) For the holy apostle's thesis and his authentic preaching are nothing like this, but are different from your fabrication. (c) He plainly meant, "(There is) one Lord, one faith, one baptism, one God, the same Father of all, the same above all, the same through all and in all"—through the Law and the prophets, and in all the apostles and the rest.

13,1 This is my <treatise>, prefaced in the foregoing selections from the scripture which is still preserved in Marcion's own canon. Anyone who examines its collection (of texts) must be struck with awe at the dispensations of <the> bountiful God. (2) If every matter is attested and established by three witnesses, how has God granted me, by a dispensation, to put together here, as I said, a sheer total of 78 testimonies from the Gospel, and 40 from the Apostle? (3) And these are preserved in Marcion to this day and <not> disputed, so that there are 118 altogether, and all contradicting Marcion's own opinion—as though in the person of the Lord's name through eighteen, and in the name of the blessing on its right through the hundred.[221] (4) And in addition to these <he is refuted> in another, further testimony, <the one> outside of the Gospel and The Apostle. For the utter wretch Marcion did not see fit to quote this testimony from Ephesians but from Laodiceans, which is not in the Apostle. (5) Since, among his many failures, the oaf foolishly does not read these testimonies, he pathetically does not see the refutation that awaits him, although it is on record every day.

13,6 And no one need be surprised at this. Since he professed to have some of the Gospel and Apostle, how could he help preserving at least a few words of the scripture? (7) Since sacred scripture's whole body, as it were, is alive, what dead limb could he find agreeing with his opinion, in order to drag in a falsehood against the truth? (8) Instead he amputated many of the limbs, as we might say, and mutilated and falsified them, but retained some few. But the very limbs he retained are still alive and cannot be killed, but have the lifegiving property of their meaning, even if, in his canon, they have been cut off in innumerable small chunks.

14,1 But after all this I recall further that some of these same Marcionites who, blundering into an abyss of blasphemy and completely cracked from their own devilish teaching, are not ashamed to give a bad name to the heavenly generation of the Lord whom they barely saw fit to mention even by name—and that in rejecting his divinity in some other insolent

[221] ιη, or 18 = Jesus, plus ἀμήν, or 99. To make 100 texts from the Epistles, the additional text from Laodicaeans must be added to the 99.

way. (2) For some of them have dared, as I said, shamelessly to call the Lord himself the son of the evil one. Others disagree, but call him the son of the judge and demiurge. (3) <But> since he is the more compassionate and good, he has abandoned his own father below—the demiurge, say some, others say the evil one—and has taken refuge on high with the good God in realms ineffable, and come over to his side. (4) And Christ has been sent into the world by him and come in opposition to his own father, to annul all the legislation of his real father—either of the God who spoke in the Law or of the God of evil whom they rank as the third principle. (For they explain him variously, as I said, one calling him the demiurge, another the evil one.)

15,1 But to anyone with sense it is plain that these things are the thought and teaching of an unclean spirit. There should be no need to defend ourselves on this subject or supply a counter-argument against Marcion, who has become completely forgetful of his own salvation. (2) All intelligent people can detect his blasphemous nonsense and shameless work of destruction. (3) But since it is my policy not to leave room for thorns but to hew them out with God's sword—which scripture calls "<sharper> than any two-edged sword, piercing even to the dividing asunder of soul and spirit, of joints and marrow"[222]—I do not mind saying a few things even to this.

16,1 In the first place, if a good person is the scion of an evil one, the account of the first principles will not hold up. If Christ's father is evil—perish the thought, he is good!—but if he is evil, he is capable of having a change of heart, just as his offspring has been changed.

16,2 But otherwise. If the Only-begotten really came to save mankind, take a thief to Paradise, call a publican from a tax office to repentance, cure a whore of fornication when she anoints his feet, and do still <other> good things because he is good, kind and merciful, (3) far more should he have taken his pity on his own father and made him well first—to show his perfect goodness perfectly by converting his father first, from pity for his father. As scripture says, "to do good first unto them who are of the household of faith"[223]—how much more, have mercy on our own fathers!

16,4 But to the explanation and the rebuttal of Marcion I have added this further point. If Christ is the son of the one God and yet took refuge with the other, the other will not accept him as trustworthy. (5) If he did not keep faith with his own Father, from his previous behavior he will not be believed by the other either.

[222] Heb 4:12
[223] Gal 6:10

16,6 Again, moreover, from another standpoint: Are you, Marcion, <going to> accuse the good God of being unable to save those whom he intended to save, and who had received mercy from him through Christ, because he lacked an envoy? (7) For if Christ had not taken refuge with the God on high, to hear Marcion tell it, the good God would have had no one to send—if Christ's father had not come into conflict with his own son, as Marcion says.

16,8 But besides, otherwise. If Christ is the son of the demiurge, but is opposed to the creation and his father's work, as the opponent of his father's arrangement he could have destroyed mankind as soon as he came into the world, to eliminate his actual father's work. (9) Or again, once he had received the power to cure, heal and save, he should have shown the work of mercy on his own father before all, and begun by persuading his father to become like him. Thus, after he had been good to himself and his father both, one and the same goodness would become <the cause> of men's salvation.

16,10 But the truth is not as Marcion's worthless piece of fiction <has it>. There are no three first principles and no other father of Christ, nor is Christ an offspring of wickedness—perish the thought! (11) He says, "I am in the Father, and the Father in me."[224] And if he is saying falsely that he has a father, his falsely alleged father cannot be in him, or he in the father. (12) He, however, who truthfully teaches that his real Father is always good, always God and the creator of all, and that he is in him and with him, spells the threat against Marcion out with his words, "He that honoreth not the Son as he honoreth the Father, the wrath of God abideth on him."[225] (13) But by now I have shown, with many testimonies, that the God who is one , the Father of our Lord Jesus Christ, is good and the begetter of good, love and the begetter of love, fount of life and the begetter of a fount of life—"With thee is the well of life,"[226] says the scripture. He is truth and the begetter of truth, light and the begetter of light, life and the Person who begets life without beginning, eternally, and not in time. And Marcion's imposture has been refuted in every respect.

16,14 Since this is the case, and since by God's inspiration I have accomplished the cheat's downfall though much authentic proof, let us go once more to the rest—now that this present sect has been trodden underfoot like a great asp, by the unimpeachable word of the Savior who said,

[224] John 14:10
[225] Cf. John 5:23; 3:36.
[226] Ps 35:10

"I have given you power to tread on serpents and scorpions, and over all the power of the adversary."[227] And let us set ourselves to investigate the futilities of the others and refute them completely, calling on God for aid in all things.

43.
Against Lucianists.[1] *Number twenty-three, but forty-three of the series*

1,1 Lucian is one of the ancients, not the modern one who was born during the old age of Constatine and whom the Arians, if you please, count as a martyr. This Lucian, the recent one I mean, was an adherent of the sect of the Arians. I shall speak of him later, in the refutation of them; now, however, the discussion pertains to the ancient Lucian. (2) For he was a companion of Marcion's,[2] formed a society himself by detaching it from Marcion, and founded his own sect. The Lucianists, as the ancient ones were called, derived from him.

1,3 His doctrines are like Marcion's in every way; but I have been told, and my impression of him is, <that he has only the New Testament. I do not know, however, whether he tampers with the Gospel like Marcion.> For to tell the truth, as these people were ancient and were snuffed out in short order, it has been difficult for me to track them down. The partial knowledge of his doctrines that I have is this:

1,4 After supposedly establishing that the demiurge, judge and just God is one God, but that the good God, likewise, is another and the evil God is someone else, Lucian, like Marcion, also likes to cite certain texts from the scripture of the prophets in support of his opinion. The ones I mean are, "Vain is he that serveth the Lord,"[3] and, "They withstood God and were delivered."[4]

1,5 Over and beyond the teaching[5] of his master he rejects marriage entirely and teaches celibacy not for celibacy's sake, but to refuse assent

---

[227] Luke 10:19

[1] Epiph has used Hipp. Synt. as his source, but this says no more than that Lucian was Marcion's disciple and agreed with him. Epiph reconstructs Lucian's teachings on this basis, but adds some information which he has obtained orally (1,3-5).

[2] Cf. Hipp. Refut. 7.37.2; PsT 6.3; Fil. 46; Orig. Cels. 2.27.

[3] Mal 3:14

[4] Mal 3:15

[5] Marcion taught celibacy; see p. 298 n. 14. Epiph might be referring to the reason Lucian gives for his requirements of celibacy.

to the works of the demiurge. He teaches that people should refrain from marriage in opposition to the prospering of the demiurge through procreation in the world—"From this matrimony," he says, "prosperity accrues to the demiurge through procreation in the world."[6]

1,6 But he will be detected for what he is, and refuted by the opposition which I have already offered his master, since I have given his rebuttal and refutation with many arguments: in what kinds of passages, and how many of them, the Gospel agrees with the Old Testament; (7) how our Lord himself acknowledges both that the making of the world is his very own and that the creation is his Father's—above all, to sum up, with a crowning argument found in St. John, "In the beginning was the Word, and the Word was with God, and the Word was God. All things were made by him, and without him was not anything made that was made,"[7] and the rest.

2,1 But he himself can certainly be refuted at once. For though he may like to say that the bond of matrimony is refused for the sake of opposing the things the demiurge has made and refusing assent to them so as not to cooperate with the demiurge—thus keeping entirely away from the work of the demiurge—how can his opinion be anything but irrational, easy to detect, and refutable at once? (2) For observe, the tramp and charlatan solicits the loan both of food and clothing, both drinkables and edibles, from creation and the handiwork of the demiurge, and there is no way he can avoid these things and make no use of them.

2,3 For God the Lord and Demiurge, in caring for all, makes his sun rise on evil and good, sends his rain on those who blaspheme and those who glorify him, and nourishes all. (4) (This is) not by some senseless, unfeeling decree but, because of the vengeance he has ordained at the coming judgment, he is patient and, in keeping with his aid to all, orders all things by his own decrees and wisdom, so that the repentant may receive his pardon and obtain salvation. (5) But if they should persist in their blasphemous opinions and the vain beliefs which God never gave them, then, after their departure when they have no more free agency, <he will punish them justly>—not, however, passing the sentence that will be theirs from wrath or inflicting their coming punishments as in anger; (6) he has given forewarning of all this because of his Godhead which is not subject to passions. (It will be) because of the <wickedness> with which each of the unrighteous, by doing something to his own harm, has become accessory

---

[6] See the polemic against matrimony at Test. Tr. 29,26-30.

[7] John 1:1;3

to his own <condemnation>. God is not to blame for our defection and our condemnation because of it.

2,7 And so this man too can be detected as in every way part and parcel of the sects before and after him, and one of the sons of perdition—as the truth shows us, and the light of the Gospel which brightly illumines the whole world, and truly saves the sons of the true faith. (8) Therefore, as though we had killed a snake quickly with a short cudgel <when it peeped> from its hole[8] and had left it dead, let us go on to the rest as promised, availing ourselves of God's help for the establishment of his truth.

44.
Against Apelleans.[1] *Number 24, but forty-four of the series*

1,1 The successor of this Lucian is Apelles—not the saint who is commended by the holy apostle[2] but another person, the founder of the Apelleans. He too was the fellow-student of Lucian himself, and Marcion's disciple[3]—like a thick growth of offshoots from a single root of many thorns!

1,2 Apelles likes to teach his doctrines differently than from the others and, arming himself against his own teacher and against the truth, propounds doctrines like the following for the sake of gathering his own school of misguided people. (3) This is not the way it was, he claims, but Marcion is wrong—to make it evident that stupidity refutes itself in every way, and that wickedness is crushed to bits within itself by raising up its refutation against itself—while the truth is always steadfast and in need of no assistance, but self-authenticating and always commended in the sight of the God who is <truly> God.

1,4 Now this Apelles and his school claim that there are neither three first principles, nor two, as Lucian and Marcion thought, but, he says,

---

[8] Holl ἐκ τῆς ὀπῆς; Text σκόπου.

[1] With this Sect cf. Hipp. Refut. 7.38; 10.20; PsT 6.4-6; Fil. 47; Eus. H. E. 5.13.1-8; Tert. De Anima 23.3; 36.3; Carn. Chr. 1.6-8; Adv. Marc. 3.11; 4.17; Praescr. 30; 33; 34; Res. Carn. 2.5. There are noticeable resemblances to Hipp. Refut. 7.38.2-3 and PsT 6.5, see nn. 8 and 13. However the source of this Sect, which omits striking details found in Epiph's usual sources, is not obvious.

[2] Rom 16:10

[3] Hipp. Refut. 7.38.1; 10.20.1; PsT 6.4; Fil. 47; Tert. Adv. Marc. 3.11; 4.17

there is one good God,[4] one first principle, and one power that cannot be named. Nothing here in this world is of any concern to this one God—or first principle, if you prefer. (5) However, this same holy and good God on high made one other God.[5] And the God who was created as another God created all things—heaven, earth, and everything in the world. (6) But he proved not to be good, and his creatures not to be well made. Because of his inferior intelligence, his <creatures> have been badly created.[6]

1,7 Who can put up with assertions like these and not laugh instead at this sort of wasted effort? It will be made evident in two ways that, in holding such an opinion, he is in the wrong. (8) And so I shall address him as though he were here: "Tell me, Mister! You will either admit, Apelles, that God had no knowledge of the future when he created a God who, you claim, has made his creations badly—or else he foreknew that the God he was creating would turn out like that, and he made him for this reason, so as not to be responsible for his bad creations. (9) From every standpoint the God on high must himself be the demiurge, since he made the one God who has made everything. The God who has made the creatures cannot be responsible for them; this must be the God on high, who made the creator even though he himself is the demiurge of all things.

2,1 But he says that Christ, the son of the good God on high, has come in the last time, as has his Holy Spirit, for the salvation of those who come to the knowledge of him. (2) And at his coming he has not appeared (merely) in semblance, but has really taken flesh. Not from Mary the Virgin, but he has real flesh and a body—<though> neither from a man's seed nor from a virgin woman. (3) He did get real flesh, <but> in the following way. On his way from heaven[7] he came to earth, says Apelles, and assembled his own body from the four elements.[8]

---

[4] PsT 6.4: Hic introducit unum deum <in> infinitis superioribus partibus; Fil. 47.2: ego unum principium praedico quem Deum conosco; and cf. Eus. H. E. 5.13.1-2; 5-7. In contrast

[5] PsT 6.4: Hic introducit unum Deum. Hunc... fecisse... et alium Virtutem quam dominum dicit sed angelum ponit; Fil. 47.2: Deus... fecit etiam alteram Virtutem quem Deum scio esse sescundum. Hipp. Refut. 7.38.1-2; 20.1 makes Apelles predicate four Gods, though he calls all but the first "angels."

[6] Fil. 47.3: Hic autem deus qui fecit mundum non est, inquit, bonus. This might have come from Epiph; contrast PsT 6.4:... cui mundo permiscuisse paenitentiam quia non illum tam perfecte fuissset quam ille superior mundus institutus fuisset.

[7] PsT 6.5: Christum... in eo, quo de superioribus partibus descenderit, ipso descensu sideream sibi carnem et aëream contexuisse.

[8] 2,1-3 Cf. Hipp. Refut. 7.38.3; 10.2. For Christ's assumption of flesh from the elements see also Tert. Adv. Marc. 3.11. At NHC's Gr. Seth 51, 4-7 Sophia builds "houses" from

2,4 And why is this man too not pressed, so that his wickedness may be detected in its following of the ancient Greek poets' beliefs about this nonsense? For he too claims, like them and even more foolishly, that the Savior gave substance to his own body. (5) <He took> the dry part of it from the dry element, the warm part from the warm element, the wet part from the wet and the cool from the cool,[9] and so fashioning his own body he has appeared in the world in reality and taught us the knowledge on high, (6) and to despise the demiurge and disown his works. And he showed us which sayings are actually his and in which scripture, and which come from the demiurge.[10] "Thus," Apelles tells us, "he said in the Gospel, Be ye able money-changers.[11] For from all of scripture I select what is helpful and make use of it."

2,7 Then, says Apelles, Christ allowed himself to suffer in that very body, was truly crucified and truly buried and truly arose, and showed that very flesh to his own disciples.[12] (8) And he dissolved that very humanity of his, reapportioned its own property to each element and gave it back, warm to warm, cool to cool, dry to dry, wet to wet. And so, after again separating the body of flesh from himself, he soared away to the heaven[13] from which he had come.[14]

3,1 What a lot of theater on the part of people who say such things—a clown act, as anyone can see, rather than a promise of life or the character of wisdom! (2) If Christ really destroyed the very body he had taken, why would he prepare it for himself in the first place? (3) But if he prepared it for some use but had finished using it, he should have left it in the ground—especially as, in your view, the sight of our hope, the resurrection of the flesh, need not be brought to pass. (4) But to give himself more

---

the "elements below," though not for himself but for the "fellow workers" of the "sons of light."

[9] Hipp. Refut. 7.38.3: ἀλλ' ἐκ τῆς τοῦ παντὸς οὐσίας μερῶν σῶμα πεποιηκέναι τουτέστι θερμοῦ καὶ ψυχροῦ, καὶ ὑγροῦ και ξηροῦ.

[10] Cf. Eus. H. E. 5.13.2. At Orig. Cels. 5.54 Apelles is said to disparage the miracle narratives in the Jewish scriptures. See also Orig. in Gen. Hom. 2.2 (Baehrens 27,17-30,3).

[11] A version of this saying appears at PS 3.134 (MacDermot, p. 348).

[12] Hipp. Refut. 7.38.4: Αὖθις δὲ ὑπὸ Ιουδαίων ἀνασκοπολισθέντα θανεῖν, καὶ μετὰ τρεῖς ἡμέρας ἐγερθέντα φανῆναι τοῖς μαθηταῖς…

[13] Hipp. Refut. 7.38.5: σάρκα…δείξας ἀπέδωκε γῇ…ἑκάστοις τὰ ἴδια ἀπέδωκε, λύσας πάλιν τὸν δεσμὸν τοῦ σώματος τουτέστιν θερμῷ τὸ θερμόν, ψυχρῷ τὸ ψυχρόν, ὑγρῷ τὸ ὑγρόν, ξηρῷ τὸ ξηρόν, καὶ οὕτως ἐπορεύθην πρὸς τὸν ἀγαθὸν πατέρα; PsT 7.5: Hunc in resurrectionem singulis quibusdam elementis quae in descensu suo mutuatus fuisset is ascensu reddidisse, et sic dispersus quibusque partibus corporis sui partibus in caelum spiritum tantum reddidisse, and the similar Fil. 47.6.

[14] Cf. Apocry. Jas. 2.23-25.

trouble for nothing he raised it again—preparing it and yet laying it in a tomb, dissolving it and, like a conscientious debtor, distributing to each element the part he had taken from it.

3,5 And if he was really giving <its own> back to each element—that is, giving the cool part to the cool, the warm part to the warm—these things could not have been seen by his disciples.[15] But this is not true of the body, which is dry! (6) For "the dry" is surely a body, flesh and bones, and "the wet" is surely the humors, and flesh dissolving into wetness. He surely indicated these things very plainly to the apostles when he was discarding them—(7) as, first of all, when his body was being buried Joseph of Arimathaea was privileged to wrap it in a shroud and lay it in a tomb. (8) And the women too, at the same time, could see where the remains had been left, so that they could honor them with perfumes and fragrant oils, as (he had been honored) at the first. (9) But this falsehood of yours is not revealed anywhere, you Apelleans, by any of the holy apostles, for it is not so. They were able to see the two invisible men, and saw himself ascending to heaven and received by a shining cloud, but they did not see his remains left anywhere—there was no need for that, and it was not possible. And Apelles, and his school of Apelleans, are lying.

4,1 About the other flesh and the rest he taught things similar to his master Marcion, claiming that there is no resurrection of the dead, and he saw fit likewise to hold all the other doctrines that <Marcion used to teach in disparagement of> earthly <creatures>.[16]

4,2 But his reasoning will be demolished as a silly thing and wrong in every way. For darkness will not prevail where the light is glimpsed, nor will falsehood remain once the truth is <visible>. (3) If you use the scriptures at all, Apelles and your Apellean namesakes, you will find yourselves refuted from these very scriptures.

4,4 In the first place, God made man in the image of God ; and the Maker of man said, "Let *us* make man in our image and after our likeness."[17]—as though one were to return from your erring sect to the truth as though escaping darkness and arising from night, and find the light of the knowledge of God dawning on him like the sun and brighter. (5) For to anyone in his right mind it will be evident that the Person who said, "Let us make man," is God the Father of all. But to join him he is inviting

---

[15] I.e., these things are invisible. The dry and the wet parts, Epiph will go on to say, were visible and seen by the disciples when Jesus was buried, thus disproving Apelles' thesis.

[16] Cf. Hipp. Refut. 10.20.2; PsT 6.6; Tert. De Anima 32.3; Carn. Chr. 8.

[17] Gen 1:26

the divine Word, the only-begotten Son who is ever with him, begotten of him without beginning and not in time—and at one and the same time his Holy Spirit, who is not foreign to him or to his own Son. (6) For if the God who fashioned man—that is, who also created the world—were different from the good God on high from whom Christ descended, Christ would not have taken a body for himself and fashioned it, thus patterning himself after the demiurge.[18] (7) But it is plain that he himself, to whom the Father said, "Let us make man in our image and after our likeness," is the demiurge of man and the world. (8) And from the one work he will be plainly proved to be the workman, since this is he who fashioned man's body from earth then, and made it a living soul.

4,9 Thus St. John testified in the holy Gospel, "In the beginning was the Word, and the Word was with God, and the Word was God. The same was in the beginning with God. All things were made in him, and were made by him, and apart from him was not anything made,"[19] and the rest. (10) But if all things <were made> in him, and made by him, he himself formed Adam then. And in turn, he himself formed the body once more, from the Virgin Mary, patterned after himself, and perfectly united his entire humanity, which was formed by him then and which was now united with himself.[20]

4,11 But suppose he took another person's work, one belonging to the God who had fashioned the first man badly and who, according to your teaching, is bad. And suppose that he made any use of the bad products which the bad maker, as you say, had produced. Then, by his use of them, by his doing them good, and by his own image, he was involved in the badness of their maker. But this is unacceptable. (12) For if he became incarnate, he has taken not only flesh but a soul as well. This must be plain. Otherwise, why did he say, "I have power to take my soul and power to lay it down"?[21] (13) Thus, in assuming the whole business, the thing the Demiurge called his "image," the Word assumed humanity in its entirety and came with body and soul, and everything that makes a man. (14) Now since these things were accomplished in this way, your poison has altogether lost its strength and your edifice without foundation has toppled, lacking the firmness of the support of the truth.

[18] I.e., like any human body, Christ's was made in the image of God.
[19] John 1:1-3
[20] That is, united it with his Godhead after his ascension. See De Inc. 2,8-3,1, p. 57.
[21] John 10:18

5,1 But if, besides, you take what you choose from sacred scripture and leave what you choose, you have set up as a judge—not as an interpreter of the laws, but as a culler out of things which were not written to suit you—things that are true, but but which in your teaching have been falsely altered to suit your deceit and the deceit of your dupes.

5,2 But if a bad maker really produced the things here, I mean the world, why did the emissary of the good Father come to such a world? And if it was to save human beings, then he was in charge of his own, and their demiurge can have been no one else. (3) And if he was not providing for his own, but wants to encroach on the domain of others and save what does not belong to him, then he is a parasite hovering around someone else's possessions. Or he is an egotist, out to get things that are not his, in order to appear better than their creator in the other person's possessions which he is trying to save. And thus he cannot be trustworthy. (4) Or, you tramp, from what you say he is a person of no consequence and, lacking his own creation, he covets the possessions of others and tries to hijack them by helping himself, from someone else's stock, to souls which do not belong to him and his Father.

5,5 If the souls are his, however, and it is evident that they have come from above, then they were sent from your good God on high into a good world, not into something which was poorly made. (6) But if they were sent to serve some purpose, of which you probably give a mythological account, and were diverted to another one on their arrival—if, in other words, they were sent to do something right but accomplished something wrong—it will be evident that the God who sent them had no foreknowledge. For he sent them for one purpose, and it turned out that they did something else. (7) Or again, if you say that they have not come by his will, but by the tyranny of the God who seizes them, then the inferior demiurge, the creation of the good God, is more powerful than the good God—since he snatched the good God's propertiy from him and put it to his own use.

5,8 How can you escape refutation when the Savior himself says, "I have power to lay my soul down and to take it"[22]—meaning that he himself has taken a soul, laid it down and taken it again, so that the soul is not foreign to him and the work of another creator? (9) And again, he will plainly have a good body. No one good can be induced to make use of evil work. Otherwise he will be contaminated himself from partaking of the evil, by the ill effect of the intermixture.

[22] John 10:18

5,10 And tell me, what was the point of his abandoning his body again after its resurrection, even though he had raised it, and of apportioning to the four elements, warm to warm, cool to cool, dry to dry, wet to wet? (11) If he raised it in order to destroy it again, this must surely be stage business, not reality. But our Lord Jesus Christ raised the very thing which he had fashioned in his own image and took it with him, body with soul and all the manhood in its entirety. (12) For God gave him his seat as, in the words of the apostle, "God raised him and made him sit with him in heavenly places"[23]—as the two testify who appeared to the apostles in shining garments, "Ye men of Galilee, why stand ye gazing up into heaven? This same Jesus, which is taken up from you into heaven, will some come *in like manner* as ye have seen him being taken up."[24]

6,2 And long after our Savior's ascension—to deprive you of another excuse for mischief against the truth—when God's holy martyr Stephen was being stoned by the Jews he answered and said, "Behold, I see heaven opened, and the Son of Man standing at the right hand of the Father."[25] This was to display the body itself, truly risen to the spiritual realm with the Godhead of the Only-begotten, wholly united with the spiritual and one with Godhead. (3) The sacred body itself is on high with the Godhead—altogether God, one Son, the Holy One of God seated at the Father's right hand. As the Gospels of Mark and the other evangelists put it, "And he ascended up to heaven and sat on the right hand of the Father."[26] And your and your dupes' trashy yarn will be a complete failure from every standpoint.

6,4 And of the resurrection of the dead, hear the apostle saying, "this corruptible must put on incorruption, and this mortal must put on immortality."[27] (5) For unless the mortal (body) were to put on immortality and the corruptible (body) incorruption, the Immortal would not have come to die, so as to suffer, sleep the three days and rise in the mortal body, and thus take it up in himself, united with his Godhead and glory, allowing us, because of his good sojourn among us, truly to obtain all that we had hoped for—showing himself a pattern and a pledge for us, for the hope of the full realization of life.

7,1 Since these things are so and have been said,[28] why should I waste more time, for refutation or anything else, on this wasp which, although

[23] Eph 2:6
[24] Acts 1:11
[25] Acts 7:56
[26] Mark 16:19
[27] 1 Cor 15:33
[28] An unusual locution. Lipsius suggests that Epiph means "said in my source."

it is inconsiderable, has a sting that smarts? It has destroyed its own sting, and the counterfeit doctrine of its error has been proved untenable and trashy.

7,2 For they say that the wasp with the painful sting which some have called the "smarting wasp" has a short poisoned sting that cannot cause great pain, but is as poisonous as it is possible for it to be. (3) And whenever someone goes through (the weeds) and destroys its den or house—it makes hives and something like a honeycomb in bushy weeds, and in these hives deposits its seed and begets its offspring. But if someone going through breaks into the honeycomb with a staff or club and knocks it down, as I said, the formidable but feeble wasp itself comes out in a rage. (4) And if it finds a rock nearby, or a tree, from the rage that has filled it it sets on it buzzing, darts at it and stings it. And yet it can do no harm to the rock or the tree, and certainly not to the man even if it bites him, except to the extent of a little pain. (5) And least of all can it hurt the rock; it breaks its sting and dies, but the rock cannot be harmed by the likes of it. (6) Thus, like the smarting wasp, this wasp-like creature which can cause a little pain will be demolished by colliding with the rock, that is, wilth the truth, and breaking its sting.

7,7 But now that I have finished with this sect I am going to the others in turn, trusting, as my hope is in God, that by God's inspiration my task will be accomplished.

45.

Against Severians.[1] *Number twenty-five, but forty-five of the series*

1,1 After these there follows <Severus>, who was either their contemporary or <born> about <their> time. I cannot speak of his time for certain, but they were quite close to each other. At all events, I shall give what information I have.

1,2 One Severus the founder of the so-called Severians arose, following next after Apelles. His fairy stories are the ones I am now about to relate. (3) He too attributes the creation around us to principalities and authorities and holds that, in some unnameable and very high heaven and world, there is a good God. (4) But he claims that the devil is the son of the chief

[1] Eusebius at H. E. 4.29.4-5 makes Severus a follower of Tatian, who teaches about "invisible aeons" and who further uses the Law and the Prophets while rejecting Paul. There is no obvious connection between this and the account Epiph gives here.

archon[2] in the authorities' retinue, whom he sometimes terms Ialdabaoth[3] and sometimes Sabaoth.[4] This son whom he has begotten is a serpent. (5) But he was cast to earth by the power on high, and after descending in the form of a serpent he became aroused and lay with the earth as with a woman and, since he ejaculated the seed of its generation, the vine was sired by him.[5]

1,6 And when he is telling stories for proof of their nonsens, <he wants> the snakelike roundness of the vine to be a representation[6] (of it), and says that the vine's twisty shape itself is like a snake. (7) And the grapes of the vine, also, are like drops or flecks of poison because the rounded form of each grape is either globular, or (first) tapering and (then) fat. (8) And for this reason it is wine that confuses people's minds and sometimes makes them amorous[7] and sometimes rouses them to frenzy or, again, renders them angry, since the body becomes dim-witted from the power of the wine and the poison of this dragon. Persons of this persuasion accordingly abstain from wine altogether.

2,1 They also claim, as the Archontics have, that woman is the work of Satan. Hence they say that those who have conjugal intercourse are doing Satan's work. (2) And moreover, half of man is God's but half is the devil's. (2) He says that from the navel up man is the work of the power of God, but from the navel down he is the work of the evil authority. And this, he says, is why anything involving pleasure, frenzy and lust happens below the navel. But other sects too have made this claim.[8]

3,1 And so Severus too is exposed, in every way, as the follower of the other tramps who have prepared these poisons for the world. For he will be refuted easily; the rebuttal in his case will require no very great effort. (2) For the body as a whole is pervaded by the things which God has rightly placed in it. I mean desires, which God has placed there, not for a anything irregular but for good use and the orderliness of essential need. (I am speaking the desire for sleep, food, drink, clothing, and all the others which arise in us at our own pleasure and God's). (3) Thus I can prove too that even sexual desire itself is nothing wrong. (4) It has been

---

[2] Apocry. Jn. II,1 10,19-21: "the first archon."

[3] See p. 85 n. 9.

[4] See p. 85 n. 10.

[5] Cf. Orig. Wld. 109,26-29; Plutarch De Iside et Osiride 6,353B.

[6] ἐκτυποῦν. Cf. Pan. 65,6,8.

[7] Cf. Orig. Wld. 109,26-29.

[8] See the polemics against sexual intercourse found *passim* in Thom. Cont., and at Test. Tr. 29,22-30,17; 65,1-8.

given for seemly procreation, as seeds have been given to the earth for an abundant yield of the good produce God has created, I mean <pasturage> and fruit trees. Thus sexual desire was given to the human race to fulfill the commandment, "Increase and multiply and fill the earth."[9]

4,1 Severians use certain apocrypha as I have heard, but also the canonical books in part, hunting out only those texts which they can reinterpret by combining them to suit themselves.[10] (2) For that the vine was neither engendered by the devil nor sired by a snake is plain to everyone. How could this be, when the Lord himself gives his testimony and says, "I shall not drink of the fruit of the vine until I drink it new with you in the kingdom of heaven."[11] (3) And since, shining its rays in accordance with God's foreknowledge from first to last, the truth has framed its words beforehand against the evils that threaten us, the sacred scripture foretold the rout of those who would rise up against the truth. (4) For example, in refutation of the pathetic, deluded Severus, the Lord himself somewhere expressly calls himself the vine and says, "I am the true vine."[12] If the vine's name were at all blameworthy, he would not make a comparison of the name with himself.

4,5 Moreover the apostles as well, in the work called the Constitution, say, "The catholic church is God's plantation and vineyard."[13] Again, moreover, in giving the parable of the vineyard in the Gospel, the Lord himself says, "A certain man that was an householder, having a vineyard, let it out to husbandmen and sent seeking fruit, and they would not give it."[14] And again, moreover, "A man that was an householder, having a vineyard, went out seeking laborers for his vineyard, both about the third hour, and the sixth, and the ninth, and the eleventh."[15] In conclusion, then, the fraud too which has been fabricated by this cheat has been damaged beyond repair by a word of the truth. For even if the darkness appears when the light is not there, its disappearance will be caused by a tiny spark of refutation.

4,9 But I have dealt summarily with this sect since, as I have already stated, its cure is easy, and not much effort is required to establish the truth against it. But above all, I am pretty sure that it has no more adherents except a very few in the far north. (10) Now that I have crushed it all at

[9] Gen 1:28
[10] Eus. H. E. 4.29.5
[11] Matt 26:29
[12] John 15:1
[13] Didascalia 1.1
[14] Matt 21:33-35
[15] Matt 20:1-6

once like a horrid scorpion, let me move on from this sect and investigate the rest—calling God's power to my aid that I may speak the truth and escape harm myself, particularly as I shall be touching on a such dreadful, baneful doctrinal malice.

46.
Against Tatianists.[1] *Number twenty-six, but fotry-six of the series*

1,1 One Tatian, who lived either at the same time as they or after them, arose as their successor and presented the teaching of his own nonsense. (2) And at first, due to his Greek background and education,[2] he flourished[3] together with Justin[4] the philosopher, a holy man and dear to God who had been converted from Samaritanism to faith in Christ. (3) This Justin was Samaritan, <but> after coming to believe in Christ, practicing a rigorous asceticism and exhibiting a life of virtue, he finally suffered martyrdom for Christ and was granted the perfect crown at Rome, during the prefecture of Rusticus[5] and the reign of Hadrian.

1,4 Since Tatian flourished with Justin he bore himself well at first and was sound in the faith, as long as he was with St. Justin Martyr. (5) But when St. Justin died[6] it was as though a blind man <who> needed a guide had been deserted by his escort and, once deserted, had got out onto a precipice because of his blindness and fell off with nothing to stop him, until he plunged to his death. It was like this with Tatian.

1,6 The information which has come my way says that he was Syrian.[7] However he first founded his school in Mesopotamia about the twelfth year of Antoninus, the Caesar who was surnamed Pius.[8] (7) For after the

[1] The primary source of this Sect may well be Hipp. Synt., which is represented by PsT 7.1 and Fil. 48; see Pourkier pp. 343-361. However, Epiph has filled out this meager report from other sources. Iren. 1.28.1 gives much the same information as Epiph; he is followed by Hipp. Refut. 8.16.1 and Eus. H. E. 4.29.3. Epiph appears to have used Eusebius' Chronicle, Clement's Stromata, and perhaps the Martyrdom of Justin and Origen's Serial Comments on Matthew. See nn. 4,6.

[2] Cf. Tatian Oratio 42.

[3] Pourkier: il fu à son sommet

[4] Iren. 1.28.1

[5] Martyrdom of Justin, sec. 1

[6] PsT 7.1; Fil. 48; Iren. 1.2;8.1; Eus. H. E. 4.29.3

[7] Clem. Strom. 3.12.81.1

[8] The source of this information is Eus. p. 206,13. Chron. Epiph has confused Antoninus Pius with Marcus Aurelius, whom Eusebius elsewhere calls Marcus Antoninus qui et Verus. See Pourkier p. 350 n. 33.

perfecting of St. Justin he moved from Rome to the east and lived there and, falling into an evil way of thinking, he too introduced certain aeons in the style of Valentinus' mythology,[9] and certain principles and emanations. (8) He established his teaching mostly between Antioch by Daphne and Cilicia but even more in Pisidia, for the so-called Encratites[10] have gotten their share of his poison from him, in succession. (9) It is said that the Diatessaron,[11] which some call "According to the Hebrews," was written by him.

2,1 He too teaches the same doctrines as the ancient sects. And in the first place, he claims that Adam cannot be saved.[12] And he preaches continence, regards matrimony as fornication and seduction, and claims that marriage is no different from fornication but the same thing.[13] Thus he adopted his deceitful style of life in the guise of continence and continent behavior, like a ravening wolf putting a sheep's fleece on and deceiving his dupes with the temporary disguise. (10) He celebrates mysteries too in imitation of the holy church, but uses only water in these mysteries.[14]

2,4 He too will collapse in every way with his inconsistent teaching. I believe that both he and his school have been snuffed out already and come to an end. For where are there not arguments to refute someone like this? (5) First, <it must be said to him too>—as I have explained already, and <said to> the sects which make such claims—that there cannot be many first principles which are generative of a succession of generated principles. (6) The many principles will turn out to be one, <as> the effects of the one real cause of them all. And there cannot be many first principles other than the one which has been the cause of these, and all things must be traced to the one sole monarchy. And this man's attempt to persuade has fallen flat, since it is falsehood, not truth, and can have no persuasiveness. For the whole of his teaching is foolish.

2,7 And if Adam, the lump, cannot be saved, neither can any <product of> the lump be saved. For if the one who was formed first and made

[9] PsT 7.1; Fil. 48; Iren. 1.28.1; Hipp. Refut. 8.16.1; Eus H. E. 4.29.3

[10] Iren. 1.28.1 and Eus. H. E. 4.29.1; Chron. 206,13 make Tatian the founder of the Encratites. See Pan. 47.1.7.

[11] Eusebius attributes the Diatessaron to Tatian at H. E. 4.29.6.

[12] PsT 7.1; Iren. 1.28.1; 3.23.8; Hipp. Refut. 8.16.1; Eus. H. E. 4.29.3

[13] Iren. 1.28.1; Hip. Refut. 8.16.1; Eus. H. E. 4.29.6; Jer. Adv. Jov. 1.3; 2.16; Clem. Strom. 3.12.81.1-3

[14] Epiph assumes that this was Tatian's practice because Encratites were reputed to follow it. For Gnostic or encratite parallels see Acts of Peter 1.2 (H-S 2 p. 188); Acts of Thomas 121 (H-S II p. 288); Acts of Paul 7 (H-S II p. 253). For the practice in catholic circles see Cyprian of Carthage Ep. 63.11.1; 14.1.

from virgin soil will have no part in salvation, how will things begotten of him obtain salvation?

3,1 For Tatian will prove to be contradicting himself in two ways. He claims that matrimony is not from God, but is fornication and uncleanness—and yet he thinks that he, the child of matrimony, born of a woman and the seed of a man, can be saved! (2) In turn, then, he has demolished his own blasphemy against matrimony. If he, the result of a marriage, will obtain salvation, then marriage is not fornication whatever he may choose to say, since it produces the ones who have a part in salvation.

3,3 But if his assertion that marriage is unlawful can be proved, then all the more will Adam be saved. Adam was no product of marriage; he was fashioned by the hand of Father, Son and Holy Spirit, as was said to the Son by the holy Father himself, "Let us make man in our image and after our likeness."[15] (4) And why can Adam, of whom you despair, not be saved when, on coming into the world, our Lord Jesus Christ himself raised the dead in their actual bodies after their deaths—like Lazarus, and the widow's son, and the daughter of the ruler of the synagogue? (5) And if it was not he himself who fashioned Adam from earth at the beginning, why did he spit on the ground, make clay, anoint the eyes of the man born blind, and make him see—(6) to show that he himself, with the Father and the Holy Spirit, was his fashioner and by applying the clay was adding the missing part to the defective place in the man born blind? He has plainly done this to repair the defective part.

3,7 But again, Tatian, if it is the Lord who both fashioned Adam and then destroys the man he fashioned first but saves the others, how stupid of you! (8) To the best of your ability you are attributing inability to the Lord , if he was unable to save his first-fashioned—who had been expelled from Paradise for one transgression, had been subjected to no light discipline, had spent his life in sweat and toil and lived opposite Paradise to remind him of his good life there—if he was unable to save him through his repentance <at the end>.

3,9 <Or else you are attributing cruelty to the Lord>, if he was able to save Adam but showed no mercy. Why did Christ descend even to the underworld? Why did he take his three day sleep before he arose? Where is the application of "that he might be Lord both of the dead and of the living?"[16] Lord of which "living and dead," if not of those who stand in

[15] Gen 1:26
[16] Rom 14:9

need of his aid on earth and under it? (10) And how can that which comes from the lump not be holy if the lump itself is not holy, as we find in the holy apostle? For this same holy apostle says of Eve too, "She shall be saved through childbearing, if they continue in faith and righteousness."[17]

4,1 And much can be said about this—just as, to everyone with sense, the obvious blasphemy and clouded thinking of Tatian and his Tatianist namesakes will be plain. (2) As for them, I have gone briefly over the kind of bites they inflict—harmful ones, like mosquito bites—and have healed them with the Lord's truth and power, applying a salve of the Lord's teaching to people who have been bitten by Tatian's assertions. For the Lord himself says, "I am not come but for the lost sheep of the house of Israel."[18] (3) And thus he said in parables that a man went down from Jerusalem to Jericho, the man he also said fell among thieves, to show that the sheep is also the person who went down from Jerusalem—the one who fell from the greater glory to diminution, and the one who was drawn away from the one commandment of his true shepherd, and went astray. (4) We thus believe that the holy Adam, <our> father, is among the living. For his sake and the sake of us all, his descendants, Christ came to grant amnesty to whose who had always known him and not strayed from his divinity, but were detained in Hades for their lapses—an amnesty through repentance for those who were still in the world, one through mercy and deliverance to those who were in Hades.

5,1 And so we must be surprised at someone (like Tatian) who knows—as I too have found in the literature—that our Lord Jesus Christ was crucified on Golgotha, nowhere else than where Adam's body lay buried.[19] (2) For after leaving Paradise, living opposite it for a long time and growing old, Adam later came and died in this place, I mean Jerusalem, and was buried there, on the site of Golgotha. (3) This is probably the way the place, which means "Place of a Skull," got its name, since the contour of the site bears no resemblance to a skull. (4) Neither is it on some peak so that this can be interpreted as a skull, as we say of <the> head's position on a body. Nor is it on a height. (5) And indeed, it is no higher than the other "places" either. Opposite it is the Mount of Olives, which is higher; and Gibeon, eight milestones off, is the highest (of the three). Even the

[17] 1 Tim 2:15

[18] Matt 15:24

[19] The earliest mention of this tradition, and the probable source of Epiph,'s information, is Orig. Com. Ser. in Matt 126 on Matt 27:33 (Klostermann, p. 265). Cf. Tert. Adv. Marc. 46.3.2.

height which was once in Zion but has now been leveled was itself taller than Golgotha.

5,6 Why the name "Of the Skull" then, unless because the skull of the first-formed man had there and his remains were laid to rest there, and so it had been named "Of the Skull"? (7) By being crucified above them our Lord Jesus Christ mystically showed our salvation, through the water and blood that flowed from him through his pierced side—at the beginning of the lump beginning to sprinkle our forefather's remains, (8) to show us too the sprinkling of his blood for the cleansing of our defilement and that of any repentant soul; and to show, as an example of the leavening and cleansing of the filth our sins have left, the water which was poured out on the one who lay buried beneath him, for his hope and the hope of us his descendants.

5,9 Thus the prophecy, "Awake thou that sleepest and arise from the dead, and Christ shall give thee light,"[20] was fulfilled here. For even though it is speaking of us, who are dead in our works and asleep with a deep sleep of ignorance, this <was> the start of the mystery. <For indeed>, it includes the manner <of the resurrection>. (10) And not without reason or idly; it says, "Many bodies of the saints arose"—as the Gospel puts it—"and went with him into the holy city."[21] And it did not say "souls of the saints" arose; the actual bodies of the saints arose and went into the holy city with him, and so on.

5,11 And now that we have brushed this mosquito's bites off by every means with the oil of God's lovingkindness, our Lord's incarnation, and the light of the Gospel of truth, let us again press on to the rest as usual, by the power of God.

[20] Eph 5:14
[21] Matt 27:52-53

CORRECTED PASSAGES

34,16,3 Holl στοιχείοις: Klostermann στίχοις

36,1,3 Holl Γύγης: Weymann Γύης

37,5,3 Holl ὄφις: Klostermann οὗτος

38,6,4 Holl εἶπεν: Klostermann <προ>εἶπεν

39,2,5 Holl τῆς τοι<αύ>της: Klostermann ταύτης τῆς

42,11,7 Holl <παρ'>ἡμῶν: Klostermann ἡμῖν

42,11,15 elenchus 12b Holl Προποδιάδος: or, Welcker προπεδιάδος: or, Dummer Προποιτίδος

42,11,15 elenchus 40b Holl δέ: Klostermann γε

42,11,15 elenchus 77a Holl πόθεν: Riedinger πῶς

Holl ἀπὸ φαντασίας: Riedinger κατὰ φαντασίαν

Riedinger <διὸ καὶ τὸν ἄρτον ἔκλασεν ἐν ἀληθείᾳ>

42,12,3 elenchus 3 and 27 Klostermann <διὸ ἐλάλησα>

43,2,2 Holl ἄλλως: Klostermann ἁπλῶς

46,2,6 Holl αἱ γὰρ οὖσαι πολλαὶ καὶ μία, <ἅτε> ἐκ τῆς μίας ὑπαρχοῦσαι οὔσης αἰτίας τῶν πάσων, εὑρεθήσονται: Klostermann αἱ γὰρ οὖσαι πολλαὶ κατὰ μίαν ἐκ τῆς μιᾶς ὑπαρχοῦσαι (ἐκ τῆς οὔσης πρώτης αἰτίας τῶν πάσων) εὑρεθήσονται

INDEX OF REFERENCES

Nag Hammadi Codices

Other Gnostic Sources

Patristic Sources

SUBJECT INDEX

[1] The idea is most commonly represented by some form of the verb ἐνανθρωπέω. See Collatz, *Epiphanius IV.*

NAG HAMMADI AND MANICHAEAN STUDIES

23. Attridge, H.W. (ed.). *Nag Hammadi Codex I* (The Jung Codex). II. Notes. 1985. ISBN 90 04 07678 6
24. Stroumsa, G.A.G. *Another seed. Studies in Gnostic mythology*. 1984. ISBN 90 04 07419 8
25. Scopello, M. *L'exégèse de l'âme*. Nag Hammadi Codex II, 6. Introduction, traduction et commentaire. 1985. ISBN 90 04 07469 4
26. Emmel, S. (ed.). *Nag Hammadi Codex III, 5*. The Dialogue of the Savior. 1984. ISBN 90 04 07558 5
27. Parrott, D.M. (ed.) *Nag Hammadi Codices III, 3-4 and V, 1 with Papyrus Berolinensis 8502,3 and Oxyrhynchus Papyrus 1081*. Eugnostos and the Sophia of Jesus Christ. 1991. ISBN 90 04 08366 9
28. Hedrick, C.W. (ed.). *Nag Hammadi Codices XI, XII, XIII*. 1990. ISBN 90 04 07825 8
29. Williams, M.A. *The immovable race*. A gnostic designation and the theme of stability in Late Antiquity. 1985. ISBN 90 04 07597 6
30. Pearson, B.A. (ed.). *Nag Hammadi Codex VII*. 1996. ISBN 90 04 10451 8
31. Sieber, J.H. (ed.). *Nag Hammadi Codex VIII*. 1991. ISBN 90 04 09477 6
32. Scholer, D.M. *Nag Hammadi Bibliography 1970-1994*. 1997. ISBN 90 04 09473 3
33. Wisse, FFF. & M. Waldstein, (eds.). *The Apocryphon of John*. Synopsis of Nag Hammadi Codices II,1; III,1; and IV,1 with BG 8502,2. 1995. ISBN 90 04 10395 3
34. Lelyveld, M. *Les logia de la vie dans l'Evangile selon Thomas*. A la recherche d'une tradition et d'une rédaction. 1988. ISBN 90 04 07610 7
35. Williams, F. (Tr.). *The Panarion of Epiphanius of Salamis*. Book I (Sects 1-46). 1987. Reprint 1997. ISBN 90 04 07926 2
36. Williams, F. (Tr.). *The Panarion of Epiphanius of Salamis*. Books II and III (Sects 47-80, De Fide). 1994. ISBN 90 04 09898 4
37. Gardner, I. *The Kephalaia of the Teacher*. The Edited Coptic Manichaean Texts in Translation with Commentary. 1995. ISBN 90 04 10248 5
38. Turner, M.L. *The Gospel according to Philip*. The Sources and Coherence of an Early Christian Collection. 1996. ISBN 90 04 10443 7
39. van den Broek, R. *Studies in Gnosticism and Alexandrian Christianity*. 1996. ISBN 90 04 10654 5
40. Marjanen, A. *The Woman Jesus Loved*. Mary Magdalene in the Nag Hammadi Library and Related Documents. 1996. ISBN 90 04 10658 8
41. Reeves, J.C. *Heralds of that Good Realm*. Syro-Mesopotamian Gnosis and Jewish Traditions. 1996. ISBN 90 04 10459 3
42. Rudolph, K. *Gnosis & spätantike Religionsgeschichte*. Gesammelte Aufsätze. 1996. ISBN 90 04 10625 1
43. Mirecki, P. & J. BeDuhn, (eds.). *Emerging from Darkness*. Studies in the Recovery of Manichaean Sources. 1997. ISBN 90 04 10760 6
44. Turner, J.D. & A. McGuire, (eds.). *The Nag Hammadi Library after Fifty Years*. Proceedings of the 1995 Society of Biblical Literature Commemoration. 1997. ISBN 90 04 10824 6

45. Lieu, S.N.C. *Manichaeism in Central Asia and China.* 1998. ISBN 90 04 10405 4
46. Heuser, M & H.-J. Klimkeit. *Studies in Manichaean Literature and Art.* 1998. ISBN 90 04 10716 9
47. Zöckler, T. *Jesu Lehren im Thomasevangelium.* 1999. ISBN 90 04 11445 9
48. Petersen, S. *"Zerstört die Werke der Weiblichkeit!"*. Maria Magdalena, Salome und andere Jüngerinnen Jesu in christlich-gnostischen Schriften. 1999. ISBN 90 04 11449 1
49. Van Oort, J. , O. Wermelinger & G. Wurst (eds.). *Augustine and Manichaeism in the Latin West.* Proceedings of the Fribourg-Utrecht International Symposium of the IAMS. 2001. ISBN 90 04 11423 8
50. Mirecki, P. & J. BeDuhn (eds.). *The Light and the Darkness.* Studies in Manichaeism and its World. 2001. ISBN 90 04 11673 7
51. Williams, F.E. *Mental Perception.* A Commentary on NHC, VI,4: The Concept of Our Great Power. 2001. ISBN 90 04 11692 3
52. Pleše, Z. *Poetics of the Gnostic Universe.* Narrative and Cosmology in the *Apocryphon of John.* 2006. ISBN 90 04 11674 5
53. Scopello, M. *Femme, Gnose et manichéisme.* De l'espace mythique au territoire du réel. 2005. ISBN 90 04 11452 1
54. Bethge, H., S. Emmel, K.L. King, & I. Schletterer (eds.). *For the Children, Perfect Instruction.* Studies in Honor of Hans-Martin Schenke on the Occasion of the Berliner Arbeitskreis für koptisch-gnostische Schriften's Thirtieth Year. 2002. ISBN 90 04 12672 4
55. Quispel, G. *Gnostica, Judaica, Catholica* (in preparation) ISBN 90 04 13945 1
56. Pedersen, N., *Demonstrative Proof in Defence of God.* A Study of Titus of Bostra's *Contra Manichaeos* – The Work's Sources, Aims and Relation to its Contemporary Theology. 2004. ISBN 90 04 13883 8
57. Gulácsi, Z. *Mediaeval Manichaean Book Art.* A Codicological Study of Iranian and Turkic Illuminated Book Fragments from 8th-11th Century East Central Asia. 2005. ISBN 90 04 13994 X
58. Luttikhuizen, G.P. *Gnostic Revisions of Genesis Stories and Early Jesus Traditions.* 2005. ISBN 90 04 14510 9
59. Asgeirsson, J.M., A.D. DeConick & R. Uro (eds.). *Thomasine Traditions in Antiquity.* The Social and Cultural World of the Gospel of Thomas. 2006. ISBN 90 04 14779 9
60. Thomassen, E., *The Spiritual Seed – The Church of the 'Valentinians'.* 2006. ISBN 90 04 14802 7
61. BeDuhn, J. & P. Mirecki (eds.). *Frontiers of Faith.* The Christian Encounter with Manichaeism in the Acts of Archelaus. 2007. ISBN 978 90 04 16180 1
62. Scopello, M. (ed.). *The Gospel of Judas in Context.* Proceedings of the First International Conference on the Gospel of Judas *Paris, Sorbonne, October 27th-28th, 2006.* 2008. ISBN 978 90 04 16721 6
63. Williams, F. (tr.). *The* Panarion *of Epiphanius of Salamis: Book I.* (Sects 1-46) Second Edition, Revised and Expanded. 2009. ISBN 978 90 04 17017 9
64. BeDuhn, J.D. (ed.). *New Light on Manichaeism.* Papers from the Sixth International Congress on Manichaeism. 2009. ISBN 978 90 04 17285 2
65. Scholer, D.M. *Nag Hammadi Bibliography 1995-2006.* 2009. ISBN 978 90 04 17240 1